FILM ART
An Introduction

SEVENTH EDITION

David Bordwell
Kristin Thompson
University of Wisconsin

McGraw
Hill

Boston   Burr Ridge, IL   Dubuque, IA   Madison, WI   New York
San Francisco   St. Louis   Bangkok   Bogotá   Caracas   Kuala Lumpur
Lisbon   London   Madrid   Mexico City   Milan   Montreal   New Delhi
Santiago   Seoul   Singapore   Sydney   Taipei   Toronto

Higher Education

Film Art: An Introduction

Published by McGraw-Hill, a business unit of The McGraw-Hill Companies, Inc., 1221
Avenue of the Americas, New York, NY, 10020. Copyright © 2004, 2001, 1997, 1993, 1990,
1986, 1979 by the McGraw-Hill Companies, Inc. All rights reserved. No part of this
publication may be reproduced or distributed in any form or by any means, or stored
in a database or retrieval system, without the prior written consent of The McGraw-
Hill Companies, Inc., including, but not limited to, in any network or other electronic
storage or transmission, or broadcast for distance learning.
Some ancillaries, including electronic and print components, may not be available to
customers outside the United States.

This book is printed on acid-free paper.

4 5 6 7 8 9 0 VNH VNH 0 9 8 7 6 5

ISBN 0-07-248455-1

Publisher: *Chris Freitag*
Senior sponsoring editor: *Melody Marcus*
Marketing manager: *Lisa Berry*
Production editor: *David Sutton*
Senior production supervisor: *Richard DeVitto*
Lead designer: *Jean Mailander*
Cover designer: *Susan Breitbard*
Cover photo: *Film Still from* Chungking Express *by the Courtesy of Block 2 Pictures, Inc.*
Compositor: *Thompson Type*
Typeface: *Times*
Printer: *Von Hoffman Press*

Library of Congress Cataloging-in-Publication Data

Bordwell, David.
     Film art : an introduction / David Bordwell, Kristin Thompson.—7th ed.
        p.   cm.
     Includes bibliographical references and index.
     ISBN 0-07-248455-1 (alk. paper)
     1. Motion pictures—Aesthetics.   I. Thompson, Kristin, 1950–   II. Title.

PN1995.B617 2003
791.43'01–dc21   2003045907

www.mhhe.com

To our parents
Marjorie and Jay Bordwell
and Jean and Roger Thompson

About the Authors

David Bordwell is Jacques Ledoux Professor of Film Studies at the University of Wisconsin–Madison. He holds a master's degree and a doctorate in film from the University of Iowa. His books include *The Films of Carl-Theodor Dreyer* (University of California Press, 1981), *Narration in the Fiction Film* (University of Wisconsin Press, 1985), *Ozu and the Poetics of Cinema* (British Film Institute/ Princeton University Press, 1988), *Making Meaning: Inference and Rhetoric in the Interpretation of Cinema* (Harvard University Press, 1989), *The Cinema of Eisenstein* (Harvard University Press, 1993), *On the History of Film Style* (Harvard University Press, 1997), and *Planet Hong Kong: Popular Cinema and the Art of Entertainment* (Harvard University Press, 2000). He has won a University Distinguished Teaching Award.

Kristin Thompson is an Honorary Fellow at the University of Wisconsin–Madison. She holds a master's degree in film from the University of Iowa and a doctorate in film from the University of Wisconsin–Madison. She has published Eisenstein's *Ivan the Terrible* (Princeton University Press, 1981), *Exporting Entertainment: America in the World Film Market 1907–1934* (British Film Institute, 1985), *Breaking the Glass Armor: Neoformalist Film Analysis* (Princeton University Press, 1988), *Wooster Proposes, Jeeves Disposes, or, Le Mot Juste* (James H. Heineman, 1992), *Storytelling in the New Hollywood: Understanding Classical Narrative Technique* (Harvard University Press, 1999), and *Storytelling in Film and Television* (Harvard University Press, 2003). In her spare time she studies Egyptology.

The authors have also collaborated on *Film History: An Introduction* (McGraw-Hill, 2nd. ed., 2003) and, with Janet Staiger, on *The Classical Hollywood Cinema: Film Style and Mode of Production to 1960* (Columbia University Press, 1985).

Brief Contents

Preface   xv

PART ONE | **Film Production, Distribution, and Exhibition**
CHAPTER ONE   Film Production, Distribution, and Exhibition   1

PART TWO | **Film Form**
CHAPTER TWO   The Significance of Film Form   47
CHAPTER THREE   Narrative as a Formal System   68

PART THREE | **Types of Films**
CHAPTER FOUR   Film Genres   107
CHAPTER FIVE   Documentary, Experimental, and Animated Films   128

PART FOUR | **Film Style**
CHAPTER SIX   The Shot: Mise-en-Scene   175
CHAPTER SEVEN   The Shot: Cinematography   229
CHAPTER EIGHT   The Relation of Shot to Shot: Editing   294
CHAPTER NINE   Sound in the Cinema   347
CHAPTER TEN   Style as a Formal System   389

PART FIVE | **Critical Analysis of Films**
CHAPTER ELEVEN   Film Criticism: Sample Analyses   413

PART SIX | **Film History**
CHAPTER TWELVE   Film Form and Film History   463

Glossary   501
Credits   507
Index   509

Contents

Preface   xv

PART ONE

Film Production, Distribution, and Exhibition

CHAPTER ONE   Film Production, Distribution, and Exhibition   2

Mechanics of the Movies   2
Bringing the Film to the Spectator   8
Box: Independent Production and Mainstream Hollywood:
    The Case of Good Machine   16
Making the Movie: Film Production   20
Modes of Production   33
Notes and Queries   41

PART TWO

Film Form

CHAPTER TWO   The Significance of Film Form   48

The Concept of Form in Film   48
Principles of Film Form   59
Summary   66
Notes and Queries   66

CHAPTER THREE   Narrative as a Formal System   68

Principles of Narrative Construction   68
Box: Playing Games with Story Time   77
Narration: The Flow of Story Information   82
The Classical Hollywood Cinema   89
Narrative Form in *Citizen Kane*   91
Summary   103
Notes and Queries   103

PART THREE

Types of Films

CHAPTER FOUR   Film Genres   108

Understanding Genre   109
Box: A Contemporary Genre: The Crime Thriller   112
Three Genres   118
Summary   126
Notes and Queries   127

CHAPTER FIVE   Documentary, Experimental, and Animated Films   128

Documentary   128
Experimental Film   146
The Animated Film   162
Summary   171
Notes and Queries   171

PART FOUR

Film Style

CHAPTER SIX   The Shot: Mise-en-Scene   176

What Is Mise-en-Scene?   176
Realism   177
The Power of Mise-en-Scene   177
Aspects of Mise-en-Scene   179
Box: The Film Actor's Tool Kit   201
Putting It All Together: Mise-en-Scene in Space and Time   207
Narrative Functions of Mise-en-Scene: *Our Hospitality*   220
Summary   225
Notes and Queries   225

CHAPTER SEVEN   The Shot: Cinematography   229

The Photographic Image   229
Box: From Monsters to the Mundane: Computer-Generated Imagery in *The Lord of the Rings*   249
Framing   252
Duration of the Image: The Long Take   284
Summary   290
Notes and Queries   290

CHAPTER EIGHT   The Relation of Shot to Shot: Editing   294

What Editing Is   294
Dimensions of Film Editing   296
Continuity Editing   310
Box: Intensified Continuity: *L.A. Confidential* and
Contemporary Editing   327
Alternatives to Continuity Editing   333
Summary   343
Notes and Queries   344

CHAPTER NINE   Sound in the Cinema   347

The Powers of Sound   348
Fundamentals of Film Sound   350
Dimensions of Film Sound   359
Box: Rhythm on Two Tracks: A Dance of Death in
The Last of the Mohicans   361
Functions of Film Sound: *A Man Escaped*   377
Summary   385
Notes and Queries   385

CHAPTER TEN   Style as a Formal System   389

The Concept of Style   389
Analyzing Film Style   391
Style in *Citizen Kane*   394
Style in *Gap-Toothed Women*   401
Style in *The River*   404
Style in *Ballet Mécanique*   407
Style in *A Movie*   409
Notes and Queries   412

PART FIVE

Critical Analysis of Films

CHAPTER ELEVEN   Film Criticism: Sample Analyses   414

The Classical Narrative Cinema   415
Narrative Alternatives to Classical Filmmaking   428
Documentary Form and Style   443
Form, Style, and Ideology   452
Notes and Queries   462

PART SIX

Film History

CHAPTER TWELVE   Film Form and Film History   464
Early Cinema (1893–1903)   465
The Development of the Classical Hollywood
    Cinema (1908–1927)   468
German Expressionism (1919–1926)   472
French Impressionism and Surrealism (1918–1930)   474
Soviet Montage (1924–1930)   478
The Classical Hollywood Cinema after the Coming of Sound   481
Italian Neorealism (1942–1951)   485
The French New Wave (1959–1964)   486
The New Hollywood and Independent Filmmaking   489
Contemporary Hong Kong Cinema   493
Notes and Queries   496

Glossary   501
Credits   507
Index   509

Preface

When we undertook the writing of *Film Art: An Introduction* in 1977, film had only recently become a regular subject of study in universities. There were a few introductory film textbooks available at the time, but they seemed to us oversimplified and lacking a clear organization in their description of the basic techniques that make up a film.

Our goal was to provide a text that would describe those techniques—mise-en-scene, cinematography, editing, and sound—in a systematic, clear, but thorough way. Beyond that, we wanted to deal with something that was ignored in earlier books—the overall form (or shape or structure) of a film that resulted from the filmmakers' choices and combination of specific techniques. We wanted to discuss whole films, not simply isolated scenes.

Although *Film Art* has undergone several revisions since that first edition, our goal has remained the same: to introduce the reader to the fundamental aspects of cinema as an art form. By stressing film as art, we seek to isolate those basic features of film that can constitute it as such. *Film Art* explores how the film medium gives us experiences akin to those offered by painting, sculpture, music, literature, theater, architecture, or dance.

As we wrote this book, we envisioned readers of three sorts. First is the interested general reader who frequently goes to the movies and would like to know more about them. Second is the student in an introductory film course, for whom *Film Art* functions as a textbook. Third is the more advanced student of film, who may find here a convenient outline of the principal issues and concepts in cinema studies and a set of suggestions for more specialized work.

Film Art first appeared more than two decades ago, and during that time a number of other introductory film texts have surfaced. We believe, however, that *Film Art* still offers the single most comprehensive and systematic description of the filmic art that has been written. It is gratifying to us that scholarly works on cinema often cite *Film Art* as an authoritative source on matters of film style and form.

ORGANIZATION OF THE TEXT

Analyzing the Whole Film

Organizationally, *Film Art* offers a distinct approach to studying its topic. It might be possible to randomly survey all contemporary approaches to film studies, but we judged this to be too eclectic for an introductory text. Instead, we present an approach that leads the reader in logical steps through the techniques and structures that make up the *whole film.* Audiences experience whole films, not snippets or abstract themes. If the particular film is the center of our inquiry, we need an approach that will help us understand it through analysis. The approach we have chosen emphasizes the film as an artifact—made in particular ways, having a unity and a set of concrete techniques, existing in history. We can outline our approach in a series of questions.

How does a film get from the planning stages to the screen?   To understand film as an art, we must first understand how people create the artifact and disseminate it to audiences. This question leads to a study of film production, distribution, and exhibition (**Part One**).

How does an entire film function?   We assume that, like all artworks, a film may be understood as a *formal* construct. That is, it is made up of parts that relate to one another in specific and deliberate ways in order to have an effect on an audience. In **Part Two,** we examine what film form is and how it affects us. We also introduce the most familiar type of film form—the narrative.

How do we classify films?   We seldom go to the movies without having some idea of the kind of film we will be seeing. **Part Three** looks at two ways of classifying films. One way is by *genre,* such as when we label a film as a Western, a musical, or a horror film. Another way is by our assumptions concerning the filmmaker's intentions and the way in which the film was made. In addition to live-action narrative films, we recognize documentaries, experimental films, and animated films.

How do film techniques contribute to film form?   Film is a specific medium, and every film contains a distinctive combination of many stylistic techniques that combine to create a whole. In **Part Four,** we examine the artistic possibilities of the four primary film techniques: mise-en-scene, cinematography, editing, and sound. In each case we also analyze how these techniques contribute to a film's overall form.

How may we analyze a film critically?   Armed with both a conception of film form and a knowledge of film technique, we can go on to analyze *specific films* as artworks. We analyze several important films of various kinds as examples in **Part Five.**

How does film art change through history?   Although a thorough history of cinema would require many volumes, here we can suggest how the formal aspects of film work within historical contexts. We survey the most noteworthy *periods and movements in film history* to show how understanding form helps us define films' larger context (**Part Six**).

This approach to the entire film resulted from several years of teaching introductory film courses. As teachers, we wanted students to see and hear more in the films we studied, but it was evident that simply providing the lecturer's view would not teach students how to analyze films on their own. Ideally, we decided, students should master a repertory of *principles* that would help them examine films more closely. We became convinced that the best way to understand cinema is to use general principles of film form to help analyze specific films. Our success with this approach led us to decide that this book should be skills-centered. By learning basic concepts of film form and technique, the reader can sharpen his or her perception of any particular film.

The stress on skills has another consequence. Although we refer to a great many films, we assume that very few readers will have seen all of the titles we mention, and certainly no teacher could possibly show every title during a course. Because *Film Art* stresses the acquisition of conceptual skills, the reader need not see all of the films we mention in order to grasp the general principles. Many other films could be used to make the same points. For example, the possibilities of camera movement can be as easily illustrated with *La Ronde* as with *Grand Illusion*. To exemplify classical Hollywood filmmaking, *My Darling Clementine* will serve as well as *North by Northwest*. Indeed, although a course syllabus could adhere closely to the series of major examples used in *Film Art*, teachers might decide to use a wholly different set of films with equal effect. Our book rests not on titles but on concepts.

Frame Enlargements and Captions

Film Art: An Introduction has several unique features. A book on film must be heavily illustrated, and most are. Many film books, however, use production stills—photographs taken during filming. These are taken with a still camera, almost never placed in the same position as the motion-picture camera. The result is a picture that does not correspond to any image in the finished film. All of our images from films are frame enlargements—magnified photographs taken from images on the actual strip of film. In recent years, some books have been illustrated with frames scanned from video copies of films. We have taken most of our frame enlargements directly from 35mm and 16mm distribution copies of films. (For more on frame enlargements, see the Notes and Queries for Chapter 1.)

Notes and Queries Sections

Another unique feature of this book is the Notes and Queries sections at the end of most chapters. In these sections we attempt to raise issues, provoke discussion, and suggest further reading and research. As chapter supplements, the Notes and Queries sections constitute a resource for the advanced undergraduate, the graduate student, and the interested general reader.

Bibliography, Glossary, and Internet Sites

Although the Notes and Queries sections act as bibliographic sources for specific issues in most chapters, the final chapter, on film history, demanded its own bibliography. We have provided a list of the most basic and current introductions to the main periods and movements in film history discussed in Chapter 12.

Film is an art form based on elaborate technical components like camerawork and editing. To clarify the terminology involved, we offer a glossary of terms at the end of the book. In addition, we include a list of many of the best Internet sites related to cinema.

NEW TO THE SEVENTH EDITION

When we set out to write an introduction to film in 1977, we could not have anticipated that it would meet with a welcome warm enough to carry it through seven editions. This version of *Film Art: An Introduction* seeks to enrich the ideas set forth in preceding editions. We have again tried to make the book more comprehensive, flexible, and up to date.

Improved Design and Illustrations

The seventh edition represents the most dramatic changes ever in the overall look of *Film Art.* By going to four-color printing throughout the book, we have been able to expand the number of color frame enlargements used as illustrations. When *Film Art* first appeared, it had one modest color-insert page with sixteen frame enlargements. That insert grew gradually over the years to 63 color plates in the sixth edition. Now we are pleased to be able to use hundreds of color frames, often from films that were previously illustrated only in black and white. We have also taken advantage of new printing technology to improve the clarity of the black-and-white frames. This change allows us to offer an even greater range of illustrations from world cinema. As our title states, we treat film as an art, and this edition comes much closer to the kinds of design used in books about painting and the other visual arts.

New "Cut-in" Boxes

The use of boxes to highlight selected important topics in our other textbook, *Film History: An Introduction,* has proven so popular with users that we have adopted a similar feature here. Seven chapters include Cut-ins, boxes that take a closer look at issues of importance in contemporary cinema. In Chapter 1, we discuss the production, distribution, and exhibition of films. Since the early 1990s, independent cinema has become increasingly visible and has in some cases moved into the mainstream; we examine the successful independent firm Good Machine and its absorption into the larger firm Vivendi Universal.

In Chapter 3, we deal with the ways in which recent films, like *Memento, Sliding Doors,* and *Groundhog Day,* play with the order of story events—a vivid way of demonstrating the story–plot distinction central to our discussion of narrative form. Chapter 4, on genre, highlights a particularly important contemporary genre, the crime thriller. In Chapter 6, on mise-en-scene, we go into greater detail concerning one important area, acting—especially the modern tendency to center on the face—and how control of the features and the use of makeup (for men as well as women) are used to create performances.

Chapter 7's Cut-in deals with the important expansion of computer-generated imagery (CGI) in filmmaking. Using a state-of-the-art special-effects film, *The Lord of the Rings,* we explain how CGI is used for obvious purposes like the creation of monsters but also for more mundane purposes at every stage of planning, production, and postproduction. In Chapter 8, we examine a pervasive but little-noticed aspect of modern film style, the exaggeration of classical filmmaking principles and the emergence of intensified continuity, looking shot by shot at a scene from *L.A. Confidential.* Finally, Chapter 9 also narrows in on part of the climactic scene of Michael Mann's *The Last of the Mohicans,* showing how closely timed musical and visual tracks can heighten the effect of cinematic action.

A New Sample Analysis: *Chungking Express*

With each edition, we try to find films that seem particularly suited to the classroom and that we can add to our chapter of short model analytical essays. Wong Kar-wai's *Chungking Express* seems to us such a film—one that students find

SUPPORT FOR INSTRUCTORS

Revised Instructor's Manual

The instructor's manual has been revised to reflect the extensive changes in Chapter 1, "Film Production, Distribution, and Exhibition" as well as the boxes added to Chapters 1, 3, 4, 6, 7, 8, and 9. An updated list of useful addresses is offered.

Online Support

The Website and Online Learning Center (www.mhhe.com/filmart) is an Internet-based resource for students and faculty alike. Instructors will find the password-protected Instructor's Manual and a wide array of options for testing and research.

The online content of *Film Art* is supported by WebCT, eCollege.com, and Blackboard. To find out more, contact your local McGraw-Hill representative or visit www.mhhe.com/solutions.

As an adopter, you may also be eligible to use our PageOut service to get you and your course up and running online in a matter of hours—at no cost to you and without knowing HTML. To find out more, contact your local McGraw-Hill representative or visit www.pageout.net.

SUPPORT FOR STUDENTS

Updated Filmviewer's Guide

The *Filmviewer's Guide,* included with *Film Art: An Introduction,* suggests how readers can get more out of the moviegoing experience and how they can improve their ability to write about the films they see. It offers practical advice on what to look for in watching films, both in theaters and on video, suggests ways to take notes, and indicates some strategies for writing argumentative papers and journalistic film reviews.

New Online Learning Center www.mhhe.com/filmart

McGraw-Hill offers extensive Web resources for students with Internet access. Students will find the Online Learning Center of particular use with *Film Art* because, for each chapter, it offers objectives, discussion questions, and online testing. In addition to text-specific exercises, the site hosts links to assist with researching topics in film on the World Wide Web.

intriguing, enjoyable, and challenging in its unconventional presentation of two stories. Its narrative form moves outside the classical tradition, and we offer *Chungking Express* as a further example of how filmmakers devise original alternatives to that tradition.

A New Historical Section on Hong Kong Cinema

Chungking Express exemplifies a modern national cinema that has only recently come to wide international attention. Hong Kong has fostered an important national cinema that thrived for decades in the face of Hollywood competition and without any government subsidies. We offer a brief overview of how this situation came about and what distinctive formal and stylistic traits characterize modern Hong Kong cinema.

ACKNOWLEDGMENTS

Over the past 26 years, many people have aided us greatly in the writing and revision of this book. We are grateful to David Allen, Rick Altman, Tino Balio, John Belton, Joe Beres, Ralph Berets, Les Blank, Vince Bohlinger, Eileen Bowser, Edward Branigan, Martin Bresnick, Ben Brewster, Michael Budd, Peter Bukalski, Elaine Burrows of the British Film Institute, Richard B. Byrne, Mary Carbine, Jerome Carolfi, Corbin Carnell, Jerry Carlson, Kent Carroll, Noël Carroll, Paolo Cherchi Usai of George Eastman House, Jeffrey Chown, Gabrielle Claes and the staff of the Cinémathèque Royale de Belgique, Bruce Conner, Kelley Conway, Mary Corliss of the Museum of Modern Art Film Stills Department, Susan Dalton of the American Film Institute, Robert E. Davis, Ethan De Seife, Dorothy Desmond, Marshall Deutelbaum, Kathleen Domenig, Susan Felleman, Maxine Fleckner-Ducey of the Wisconsin Center for Film and Theater Research, Don Fredericksen, Jon Gartenberg, Ernie Gehr, Kathe Geist, Douglas Gomery, Claudia Gorbman, Ron Gottesman, Eric Gunneson, Debbie Hanson, Howard Harper, Denise Hartsough, Kevin Heffernan, Paul Helford, Linda Henzl, Richard Hincha, Jan-Christopher Horak of the Munich Film Museum, Lea Jacobs, Bruce Jenkins, Kathryn Kalinak, Charlie Keil, Vance Kepley, Laura Kipnis, Barbara Klinger, Jim Kreul, Don Larsson, Jenny Lau, Thomas M. Leitch, Gary London, José Lopez of New Yorker Films, Patrick Loughney of the Library of Congress Motion Picture Division, Moya Luckett, Mike Maggiore of the Walker Art Center, Charles Maland, Mark McClelland of Films Inc., Roger L. Mayer of MGM Inc., Norman McLaren, Jackie Morris of the National Film Archive, Charles Musser, Kazuto Ohira of Toho Films, David Popowski, Badia Rahman, Paul Rayton, Leo Salzman, Rob Silberman, Charles Silver of the Museum of Modern Art Film Study Center, Ben Singer, Joseph Evans Slate, Harry W. Smith, Jeff Smith, Michael Snow, John C. Stubbs, Dan Talbot of New Yorker Films, Richard Terrill, Jim Udden, Edyth von Slyck, Beth Wintour, Chuck Wolfe, and Andrew Yonda.

In preparing this edition, we are grateful to several of the above, as well as to Lucius Barre, Rodney Hill and Suzanne Fedak of Wellspring Media; James Shamus and Peter Kujawski of Focus Features; Ben Shao and Carol Li of the Taipei Economic and Cultural Office in Chicago; John Simons; Katerina Soukup of Igloolik Isuma Productions; and Beth Wintour, Texas Tech University.

As always, we thank our team at McGraw-Hill—Allison McNamara, Melody Marcus, Lisa Berry, David Sutton, Nadia Bidwell, Jean Mailander, and Shannon Gattens.

David Bordwell
Kristin Thompson

Film Production, Distribution, and Exhibition

Chapter 1

Film Production, Distribution, and Exhibition

Motion pictures are so much a part of our lives that it's hard to imagine a world without them. Our appetite for film sustains an immense industry. Today every film that makes its way into a theater is part of a process involving a sophisticated technology and thousands of workers.

MECHANICS OF THE MOVIES

You are entering a theater with some friends. You pay for your ticket, scan the posters announcing upcoming releases, buy popcorn and soda at the concession stand, and meander toward the auditorium screening the film you've selected. Once inside, you settle into your seat and prepare to be amused, moved, provoked, or just entertained. The lights dim, leaving only the Exit signs glowing. As sound fills the theater from all sides, the screen becomes a bright rectangle filled with a moving picture.

Already something fairly mysterious is happening. You have the *impression* of seeing a moving image, but this is an illusion. The smoothly moving picture you see consists of thousands of slightly different still images called **frames** projected in rapid succession. Each frame flashing by is accompanied by bursts of blackness. Although you aren't aware of it, the screen is completely dark for nearly half the time you're watching! Our eyes ignore the gaps and see continuous light. Just as important, our minds somehow create a continuous action out of a string of still pictures.

What makes a movie move? No one knows the full answer. Many people have speculated that the effect results from "persistence of vision," the tendency of an image to linger briefly on our retina. Yet if this were the real cause, we'd see a bewildering blur of superimposed stills instead of smooth action. At present, researchers believe that two psychological processes are involved in cinematic motion: critical flicker fusion and apparent motion.

If you flash a light faster and faster, at a certain point (around 50 flashes per second) you will see not a pulsating light but a continuous beam. A film is usually shot and projected at 24 still frames per second. The projector shutter breaks the light beam once as a new image is slid into place and once while it is held in place. Thus each frame is actually projected on the screen twice. This raises the number of flashes to the threshold of what is called *critical flicker fusion.* Early silent films were shot at a lower rate (often 16 or 20 images per second), and projectors broke the beam only once per image. The picture had a pronounced flicker—hence an early slang term for movies, "flickers," which survives today when people call a film a "flick."

Apparent motion is a second factor in creating cinema's illusion. If a visual display is changed rapidly enough, our eye can be fooled into seeing movement. Neon advertising signs often seem to show a thrusting arrow, but that illusion is created simply by static lights flashing on and off at a particular rate. It seems likely that certain cells in our eye or brain are devoted to analyzing motion, and any stimulus resembling movement tricks those cells into sending the message that motion is present.

Apparent motion, like critical flicker fusion, is a quirk within our visual system. To take advantage of these quirks and create the illusion of movement, inventors had to devise certain machines. Some of these go back before the invention of film **(1.1, 1.2).** Film as we know it began when the images were imprinted on a strip of flexible celluloid.

After your movie is over, imagine that a friendly manager lets you into the projection room at the rear of the theater. There you'll find the movie mounted on the *projector* as a ribbon of celluloid. It is very long: The movie that lasted two hours takes up over two miles of film. There is so much footage because a sound movie runs through the projector at 90 feet per minute.

Like a reel-to-reel tape recorder, the projector unwinds the film from one reel, passes it through the lens mechanism, and winds it up on another reel. The projection booth you're visiting has put the entire film on one big platter, with another platter below it to take it up. This arrangement allows the operator to use only one projector for showing the whole movie. Other theaters use a "changeover" system alternating between two projectors, each one using a reel holding about 25 minutes of film.

Interestingly, the projector is very much like two other machines involved in creating the movie we see. In each one, a mechanism controls how light is admitted to the film, advances the strip of film a frame at a time, and exposes it to light for the proper interval. At the heart of cinema are machines that, in essence, pull a strip of sensitive plastic past a light.

First, there is the *camera* **(1.3).** In a light-tight chamber, a drive mechanism feeds the unexposed motion-picture film from a reel (a) past a lens (b) and aperture (c) to a take-up reel (d). The lens focuses light reflected from a scene onto each frame of film (e). The mechanism moves the film intermittently, with a brief pause while each frame is held in the aperture. A shutter (f) admits light through the lens only when each frame is unmoving and ready for exposure. The standard shooting rate for sound film is 24 frames per second (fps).

1.1 The Mutoscope, a 19th-century entertainment, displayed images by flipping a row of cards in front of a peephole.

1.2 The Zoetrope, an earlier device, printed its images on a strip of paper that was rotated in a drum.

1.3 The camera.

1.4   The contact printer.

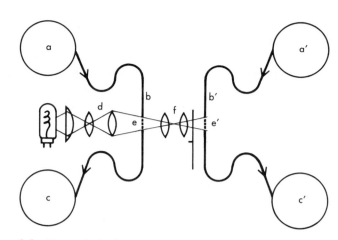

1.5   The optical printer.

After a film has been processed, it runs through a machine similar to the camera, the *printer* (**1.4, 1.5**). Printers exist in various designs, but all consist of light-tight chambers that drive a negative or positive roll of film from a reel (a) past an aperture (b) to a take-up reel (c). At the same time, a roll of unexposed film (a´, c´) moves through the aperture (b or b´), either intermittently or continuously. By means of a lens (d), light beamed through the aperture prints the image (e) on the unexposed film (e´). The two rolls of film may pass through the aperture simultaneously. A printer of this sort, called a *contact* printer, is diagrammed in 1.4. Contact printers are used for making workprints and release prints, as well as for various special effects. In another sort of printer, the *optical* printer, light coming through the original may be beamed to the unexposed roll through lenses, mirrors, or prisms. This is shown in (f) in 1.5. Optical printers are used for rephotographing camera images, for making prints of different gauges, and for certain special effects, such as freeze-frames.

The printer is something of a combined camera and projector. Like a projector, it controls the passage of light through exposed film (the original negative or positive). Like a camera, it focuses light to form an image (on the unexposed roll of film).

Now we can see that the projector is basically an inverted camera, with the light source inside the machine rather than in the world outside (**1.6**). A drive mechanism feeds the film from a reel (a) past a lens (b) and aperture (c) to a take-up reel (d). Light is beamed through the images (e) and magnified by the lens for projection on a screen. Again, a mechanism moves the film intermittently past the aperture, while a shutter (f) admits light only when each frame is pausing. As we've seen, the standard projection rate for sound film is 24 frames per second, and the shutter blocks and reveals each frame twice in order to reduce the flicker effect on the screen.

Although the filmmaker can create *non*photographic images on the film strip by drawing, cutting, or punching holes, etching, or painting, most filmmakers have relied on the camera, the printer, and other photographic technology. The images that we see in movement are usually created photographically.

In the projection booth, the projectionist hands you a scrap of film. Turning it over, you notice that one side is much shinier than the other. Like film used in still photography, motion-picture film consists of a transparent acetate *base* (the shiny side), which supports an *emulsion,* layers of gelatin containing light-sensitive

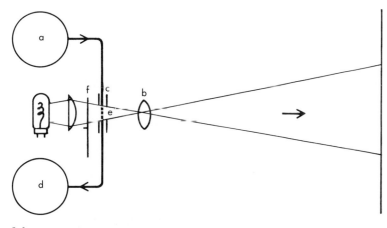

1.6   The projector.

materials. On a black-and-white film strip the emulsion contains grains of silver halide. When light reflecting from a scene strikes them, it triggers a chemical reaction that makes the crystals cluster into tiny specks. Billions of these specks are formed on each frame of exposed film. Taken together, these specks form a latent image which corresponds to the areas of light and dark in the scene filmed. Chemical processing makes the latent image visible as a configuration of black grains on a white ground. The resulting image is either a negative one, from which positive prints can be struck, or a positive one (called a *reversal* image).

Color film emulsion has more layers. Three of these contain chemical dyes, each one sensitive to a primary color (red, yellow, or blue). Extra layers filter out light of other colors. During exposure and development, the silver halide crystals create an image by reacting with the dyes and other organic chemicals in the emulsion layers. With color negative film, the developing process yields an image that is opposite, or complementary, to the original color values: For example, blue shows up on the negative as yellow. Most professional filmmaking uses negative emulsion so as to allow better control of print quality and larger numbers of positive prints to be made. Sometimes, however, amateur filmmakers use color reversal film, which yields a positive image with colors conforming to the original scene.

Looking at the scrap of film in your hands, you can see what enables it to run through a camera, a printer, and a projector. The strip is perforated along both edges, so that small teeth (called sprockets) in the machines can seize the perforations (sprocket holes) and pull the film at a uniform rate and smoothness. You also notice that the strip reserves space for a sound track.

The size and placement of the perforations and the area occupied by the sound track have been standardized around the world. So too has the width of the film strip, which is called the **gauge** and is measured in millimeters. The strip you are holding is a piece of 35mm film, which is the normal commercial gauge, but other gauges also have been standardized internationally: Super 8mm, 16mm, and 70mm **(1.7–1.11).**

Usually image quality increases with the width of the film because the greater picture area gives the images better definition and detail. All other things being equal, 35mm provides significantly better picture quality than does 16mm, and 70mm is superior to both. The finest image quality currently available for public screenings is that offered by the Imax system **(1.12).**

The print we see of a film, however, may not be in the gauge of the original. Most films shown in cinema courses on 16mm were originally shot on 35mm. During the 1950s and 1960s, several films were produced and shown on 70mm, but few venues are equipped to show them in that gauge today, so revivals are shown in 35mm. Often, quality deteriorates when a film shot on one gauge is transferred to another one. A 35mm print of Keaton's *The General* will almost certainly be

1.8   16mm film is used for both amateur and professional film work. A variable-area optical sound track runs down the right side.

1.7   Super 8mm has been a popular gauge for amateurs and experimental filmmakers. *The Year of the Horse,* a concert film featuring Neil Young, was shot entirely on Super 8.

1.9   35mm is the standard theatrical film gauge. The sound track, a variable-area one, runs down the left alongside the images.

1.10   In this 35mm strip from *Jurassic Park,* note the optical stereophonic sound track, encoded as two parallel squiggles. The stripe along the left edge, the Morse code–like dots between the stereophonic track and the picture area, and the speckled areas around the sprocket holds indicate that the print can also be run on various digital sound systems.

1.11 70mm film, another theatrical gauge, has often been used for historical spectacles and epic action films. In this strip from *The Hunt for Red October*, a stereophonic magnetic sound track runs along both edges of the film strip.

1.12 The Imax image is printed on 70mm film but runs horizontally along the strip, allowing each image to be 10 times larger than 35mm and triple the size of 70mm. The Imax film can be projected on a very large screen with no loss of detail.

photographically superior to a 16mm print, whereas a film shot on Super 8 will look fuzzy and grainy if printed and projected in 35mm. Independent filmmakers who work in 16mm face the problem that blowing up their negative to 35mm will decrease photographic quality. It was largely to solve this problem that a higher-fidelity 16mm format, called Super 16, was developed.

You've already noticed the sound track running down the film strip you're examining. The sound track may be either *magnetic* or *optical.* In the magnetic type (1.11), one or more strips of magnetic recording tape run along the film's edges. During projection, the film's track is "read" by a sound head similar to that on a tape recorder. Magnetic tracks are rather rare in theaters today.

Your film strip has an optical sound track, which encodes sonic information in the form of patches of light and dark running down along the frames. During production, electrical impulses from a microphone are translated into pulsations of light which are photographically inscribed on the moving film strip. When the film is projected, the optical track produces varying intensities of light that are translated back into electrical impulses and then into sound waves. The optical sound track of 16mm film is on the right side (1.8), while 35mm puts an optical track on the left (1.9, 1.10). In each the sound is encoded as *variable-area,* a wavy contour of black and white along the picture strip.

A film's sound track may be *monophonic* or *stereophonic.* The 16mm film strip (1.8) and the first 35mm film strip (1.9) have monophonic optical tracks. Stereophonic optical sound is registered as a pair of squiggles running down the left side (1.10). For digital sound, a string of dots and dashes running along the film's perforations, between the perforations, or close to the very left edge of the frames provides the sound-track information (1.10). The projector scans these marks as if reading a bar code.

Your trip behind the scenes reminds us that movies, with all their appeals to our emotions and imagination, depend upon some very tangible materials and machines. The dynamic images and sounds we experience are conjured up from a strip of perforated celluloid carrying certain kinds of information. Important as technology is, though, it is only part of the story. To get a fuller sense of how films reach an audience, we must return to the theater lobby.

BRINGING THE FILM TO THE SPECTATOR

When you went into the movie theater, you were not thinking of critical fusion frequency or film gauges. You were a customer, participating in a business transaction. Like most businesses, filmmaking involves creating the product, distributing it, and retailing it. In this business, the three phases are known as production, distribution, and exhibition.

Theatrical and Nontheatrical Exhibition

We are most familiar with the **exhibition** phase, the moment when we pay for a movie ticket or rent a videocassette or watch a film on television. Commercial movie houses showing current films constitute *theatrical* exhibition sites, while all other presentations, such as home video or screenings in schools, libraries, and hospitals, are considered *nontheatrical.* While some films, chiefly experimental and documentary films, are made for nontheatrical showing, the most visible sector of movie exhibition remains the first-run theater. Most commercial theaters show mass-entertainment movies, while others specialize in foreign or independent films.

GUS VAN SANT: Your films have dominated the museum circuit in America—Minneapolis, Columbus . . .

DEREK JARMAN: Yes, Minneapolis in particular. That's where the films have actually had their life. They've crept into the student curriculum—which is a life. And now they go on through video. I never really feel shut out.

— Gus Van Sant, director, interviewing Derek Jarman, independent filmmaker

Far more people will see a Hollywood film on video than in its initial release. Only a small part of the population visits theaters regularly. In the United States, habitual moviegoers—who make up less than 20 percent of the audience—account for 66 percent of total ticket sales. You probably watch more films on video than in theaters. Studios earn much more from home video than from theatrical release. So why is the movie theater still important? The theatrical screening focuses public interest: Critics review the film, television programs publicize it, and people tell others about it. The theatrical run is the film's launching pad, determining how successful it will be in other markets. Theatrical hits may account for as much as 80 percent of a video store's rentals.

The most heavily patronized theaters belong to chains or circuits, and these are in turn controlled by relatively few companies. To be efficient businesses, theater chains have tried to standardize exhibition and minimize costs. The multiscreen cinemas of today testify to both these aims. By offering a variety of programs, multiplexes can lure more people than a single-screen cinema, and they can cut costs through centralized projection and concession sales. Multiplexes have also raised the standard of film presentation, offering stadium seating and multichannel sound. Some multiplexes have become entertainment centers, boasting videogame arcades and snacks adjusted to local tastes—popcorn and candy around the world, but also beer (in Europe) and dried squid (in Hong Kong). There are also theaters, often with only a single screen, which specialize in foreign or independent movies.

Theatrical exhibition is seasonally driven. In Europe, autumn has traditionally been the heavy moviegoing period, while in North America, people flock to theaters during June, July, and August. As we would expect, the summer audience is dominated by teenagers looking for light entertainment. Blockbuster action films, horror movies, science-fiction tales, and raunchy comedies are the "tentpole" or "locomotive" films that distributors hope will pay for the less successful ones. American distributors tend to save their most prestigious adult-oriented films for the period from Thanksgiving to New Year's, because that is when the film industry is considering candidates for its spring Academy Awards.

Distribution: The Center of Power

Exhibitors rent films from **distribution** companies, and these form the core of economic power in the film industry. Distributors link filmmakers to audiences and supply exhibitors with a reliable stream of material to show. In the United States, exhibitors bid for each film a distributor releases, and in most states they must be allowed to see the film before bidding. Elsewhere in the world, distributors may practice *blind booking* (forcing exhibitors to rent a film without seeing it) or even *block booking* (forcing exhibitors to rent a package of films in order to get a few desirable items).

The major film distributors—Warner Bros., Paramount, Disney/Buena Vista, Columbia, Twentieth Century Fox, and Universal—provide mainstream entertainment to theater chains around the world. The distributors sponsor trade shows where exhibitors are treated to screenings of forthcoming releases, usually accompanied by splashy parties and chances to meet stars. The films released by the majors attract 95 percent of ticket sales in the United States and Canada and more than half of the international market. These giant distributors all belong to multinational corporations devoted to leisure activities. (See Box, pp. 14–15.)

The major distributors have won such power because large companies can best endure the high risks of theatrical moviemaking. Filmmaking is costly, and most

Film and video are both moving-image media. Although our concern is primarily with film, video is converging with cinema in several ways.

There is a fundamental difference of materials and technology. Cinema is a photographic medium. Light reflected from the scene creates an image by triggering chemical changes on the film emulsion. Video, in contrast, translates light waves into electrical pulses and records those on magnetic tape, disk, or hard drive. In analog video, phosphors in the camera's tube pick up light from a scene. Digital video (DV), the dominant production technology and coming to be the preferred consumer format, captures light reflected from the scene on a computer chip behind the camera lens. As in a music CD, the information is encoded as a string of ones and zeros.

The highest standard of digital video is the high-definition (HD) format, which offers many more lines of resolution than conventional U.S. or European video. It replaces interlaced arrays (as on a typical television monitor) with progressive-scan arrays (as on a computer monitor), which yields a cleaner image. Sony has recently developed a 24p HD camera, which provides 24-frame video compatible with the rate of motion-picture film. It could also be adjusted to the frame rates suitable for North American or European television broadcast, DVDs, or Internet transmission. As of 2002, the Sony system was digital video's closest approximation to cinema.

Yet even a high-definition video image carries significantly less information than motion-picture film. A broadcast-quality video frame can display about 350,000 pixels (picture elements), while Sony's 24p video frames currently have around 2 million pixels. A frame of 35mm motion-picture film can contain the equivalent of over 12 million pixels. The widest range of color possible in video is about 17 million hues, a staggering number until we realize that film can display over 800 million. Digital storage also requires that picture information be compressed, and this often yields blocky breakup during movement and "aliasing"—jagged edges where straight lines should be. Image artifacts are particularly apparent in long shots of landscapes or densely packed architecture. Finally, from an archival point of view, preserving moving images on film is preferable to digital tape or disk, which deteriorates much more rapidly.

No pictures can capture the vast range of light intensities that our eyes can detect, but cinema comes closer than video. Film stock can convey fine details of light, color, and texture because of its robust *contrast* ratio, the

1.13 For *The Buena Vista Social Club,* Wim Wenders used mini-DV cameras to follow Cuban musicians around Havana. The high contrast and blown-out light areas (note the top of the hat) are characteristic of video. For more on the film's production, see www.buenavistasocialclub.de.

relation between the brightest and the darkest areas of the image. The Sony 24p DV camera can produce a contrast ratio of up to 150:1, while 35mm film negative can reach 1000:1. This means that film more faithfully renders extremes of bright and dark, pure black and pure white, as well as smooth gradations from one color or light level to another. Video steps up contrasts; pale colors look brighter, while saturated colors look even more saturated. Because video accentuates contrast, when a film is transferred to video, its colors are likely to look warmer. A video image shot in mixed lighting conditions—say, a scene including both sunlight and deep shade—will lose more textures than a film image will **(1.13)**. High-definition digital video is less contrasty and can preserve details in dark areas, but bright areas still tend to burn out or blow out into pure white patches.

Despite the differences between the two media, there are many areas of convergence. Low-budget filmmakers have been attracted by the comparatively low costs of digital video cameras and tape. DV cameras are easy to set up, and takes can be reviewed immediately for errors, so shooting moves more quickly than in a film-based project. If lit by an experienced cinematographer, even consumer-format video can look very attractive, as in Spike Lee's *Bamboozled,* filmed by Ellen Kuras. Perhaps most important, audiences do not notice shortcomings in image quality if the story is engrossing. Strong plots and performances helped carry *Chuck and Buck, The Anniversary Party, Atanarjuat:*

1.14 In *julien donkey-boy,* transferring low-fidelity video to film creates hallucinatory images.

The Fast Runner, and other independent films shot on digital video.

Sometimes the video format ideally suits the subject the filmmaker wants to present. *Series 7: The Contenders* poses as a reality-TV program in which contestants compete in a murder game, trailed by camera crews recording the killings on video. Other directors seek to explore the distinctive look of video imagery. Lars von Trier's *Dancer in the Dark* uses highly saturated DV imagery to suggest the fantasy world of a young mother going blind. Harmony Korine shot *julien donkey-boy* with mini-DV consumer video cameras and then blew up the footage several times to film. In the final result, pixels and grain create a unique texture, and the high contrast exaggerates pure colors and shapes **(1.14).**

Bigger-budget filmmakers have taken advantage of the economies offered by digital video. A string of animated feature films, launched by *Toy Story* (5.80), bypassed the time-consuming process of cel animation (see p. 163) and created cartoon characters directly on computer. George Lucas filmed *Star Wars: Episode II—Attack of the Clones* entirely with Sony's 24p HD cameras, saving millions of dollars. The same system was used for *Spy Kids 2,* which director Robert Rodriguez claimed cost far less than if it had been made on film. The digital format allowed him to edit, mix sound, and create special effects in his garage in Austin, Texas.

Lucas also embraces digital cinema for the control it offers. In *Attack of the Clones,* computer-generated imagery (CGI) made it possible to create vast futuristic landscapes full of dynamic movement **(1.15).** Lucas claimed that if an actor blinked at the wrong time, he would digitally erase the blink. He is convinced that the lower cost and greater flexibility of digital video will make it the format of choice for most filmmakers. Rodriguez agrees: "I've abandoned film forever. You can't go back. It's like trying to go back to vinyl after you've got recordable DVD."

Most digital features shown commercially have been screened from film transfers, but some distributors have been pressing exhibitors to install video projectors. If movies could be sent to theaters on hard drives or via satellite links, studios would save hundreds of millions of dollars in laboratory costs. Lucas intended *Attack of the Clones* to be screened widely in a digital format, although only a few theaters screened it electronically. Most exhibitors have resisted converting, but not just because the quality of projection still leaves much to be desired. Electronic projectors can cost as much as $200,000 (compared with $30,000 for a film projector), and any model is likely to become obsolete quickly. The chief incentive for

1.15 The chase through the airways of Coruscant in *Attack of the Clones,* with backgrounds and motion created through CGI.

1.16 Extreme tonal contrast, washed-out colors, and an overbright sky evoke video reports of the Persian Gulf War in the 35mm feature *Three Kings*.

going digital, many exhibitors believe, is that the public might pay higher prices to see films in that format.

Digital technology has made its widest impact on post-production. Finishing a film now depends heavily on software for editing, sound, and special effects.

Those who shoot on video sometimes try to match the "film look," but at the same time some filmmakers work-ing in 35mm have given their footage a rawer quality. Both Steven Soderberg's *Traffic* and David O. Russell's *Three Kings* manipulate film stock and printing to suggest the harsh contrasts and blown-out skies that digital video can yield **(1.16).** Experiments with achieving a "video look" on film point up another way in which the two media are converging.

films do not make profits in theatrical release. Worldwide, the top 10 percent of all films released garner 50 percent of all box-office receipts. The most popular 30 percent of films account for 80 percent of receipts. Typically, a film breaks even or shows a profit only after it has been released on cable, satellite, or home video.

So great is the distributor's bargaining power that the movie theater gets a surprisingly small percentage of total box-office receipts (known as the *gross* or *grosses*). One standard contract guarantees the distributor a minimum of 90 percent of the first week's gross, dropping gradually to 30 percent after several weeks. This arrangement isn't favorable to the exhibitor. A failure that closes quickly will yield almost nothing to the theatre, and even a successful film will make most of its money in the first two or three weeks of release, when the exhibitor gets less of the revenue. Averaged out, a long-running success will yield no more than 50 percent of the gross to the theater. To make up for this drawback, the distributor allows the exhibitor to deduct from the gross the expenses of running the theater (a negotiated figure called the *house nut*). In addition, the exhibitor gets all the cash from the concession stand, which may deliver up to 70 percent of the theater's profits. Without high-priced snacks, movie houses couldn't survive.

Once the grosses are split with the exhibitor, the share returning to the distribution company (the *rentals*) is further divided. A major U.S. distributor typically takes 35 percent of the rentals as its distribution fee. If the distributor helped fund the film, it takes another percentage off the top. In addition, the cost of prints and advertising (currently around $30 million for a high-end film) are deducted as well. What remains comes back to the filmmakers. Out of the proceeds the producer must pay all *profit participants*—the directors, actors, executives, and investors who have negotiated a share of the rental returns.

For most films, the amount returned to the production company is relatively small. Once the salaried workers have been paid, the producer and other major players must wait, perhaps years, to receive their share from video and other ancillary markets. Because of this delay, and the suspicion that the major distributors practice misleading accounting, the most powerful actors and directors have demanded "first-dollar" participation, meaning their share will derive from the earliest money the picture returns to the distributor.

Independent and overseas filmmakers usually don't have access to direct funding from major distribution companies, so they try to presell distribution rights to finance production. Alternatively, they try to attract distributors' attention by showcasing their film at festivals. Michael Moore's documentary on gun control, *Bowling for Columbine,* sold to several European distributors after winning a prize at the 2002 Cannes festival, while at that year's Toronto International Film Festival, major U.S. distributors bought rights to the French *Jet Lag* and the Chinese *Together.*

Specialized distributors, such as the New York firms Kino and Milestone, rent foreign and independent films to art cinemas, colleges, and museums. As audiences for these films grew in the 1990s, major distributors acquired specialized distribution companies. The independent Miramax generated enough low-budget hits (*My Left Foot, The Crying Game*) to be purchased by the Disney corporation. With the benefit of Disney's funding and wider distribution reach, Miramax movies like *Pulp Fiction, Scream,* and *Shakespeare in Love* earned even bigger box-office receipts. Other major companies, such as Sony, have subsidiaries to handle films aimed at the art-house market. Sony Classics' release, *Crouching Tiger, Hidden Dragon* was successful enough to break out of art-house screens and win large grosses at multiplexes. (See Box, pp. 16–18.)

"Selling food is my job. I just happen to work in a theater."

— A theater manager in upstate New York

By belonging to powerful multinational conglomerates, film distributors gain access to bank financing, stock issues, and other media markets. Just as important, multimedia distributors can build *synergy*—the coordination of sectors within the company around a single piece of content, usually one that is "branded." *The X-Files*, a film released in 1998, grew out of a brand launched on television five years earlier. News Corp.'s Twentieth Century Fox Television subsidiary produced the series and broadcast it on Fox's U.S. cable channel. When the first season was released on video in Japan and Europe, it became a huge success, and the series was soon programmed on News Corp.'s international satellite platform BSkyB. The series spawned video games (from Fox Interactive), books (from HarperCollins, owned by News Corp.), music CDs (from Fox Music), and clothing, notebooks, and other merchandise (via Fox Licensing and Merchandising). The theatrical film was only one more link in synergy's "value chain."

Synergy and branding work together. Every product promotes the others, and each part of the parent corporation gets a bit of the business. Although synergy sometimes proves unsuccessful, multimedia giants are in the best posi-

1.17 *Lethal Weapon:* As Murtagh and Riggs leave a hot-dog stand, they pass in front of a movie theater advertising *The Lost Boys,* another Warner Bros. film (released four months after *Lethal Weapon*). The prominence of Pepsi-Cola in this shot is an example of *product placement*—featuring well-known brands in a film in exchange for payment or cross-promotional services.

tion to take advantage of it. One film can even advertise another within its story **(1.17)**.

Six Major Media Companies and Some of Their Holdings

	AOL Time Warner	Disney	Viacom	Sony	News Corp.	Vivendi Universal
Film production and distribution	Warner Bros., CastleRock, New Line, Fine Line	Buena Vista, Hollywood Pictures, Touchstone, Walt Disney Pictures, Miramax	Paramount Pictures	Columbia Pictures, TriStar, Mandalay, Sony Pictures Classics	Twentieth Century Fox, Fox Searchlight	Universal, Working Title, Universal Focus

American films have long been the world's most popular, and many earn more abroad than at home. The Hollywood studios have planted distribution subsidiaries in most major countries. These branch offices arrange for prints to be made in the local language (either dubbing in the dialogue or adding subtitling) and schedule the film's release. Local circumstances dictate when a Hollywood film opens. A film may be released in Europe many months after the U.S. opening, but it is likely to be released in Asia much sooner, largely because the region's widespread video piracy tends to erode the audience. With strong marketing units in every region, the majors can distribute non-U.S. films as well as Hollywood products. For example, Kazuo Miyazaki's popular animated films (*My Neighbor Totoro, Spirited Away*) are now distributed on video by Disney's Buena Vista arm—even in Japan itself.

Six Major Media Companies (continued)

	AOL Time Warner	Disney	Viacom	Sony	News Corp.	Vivendi Universal
Movie theaters	Cinamerica (50% with Viacom)		Famous Players, Cinamerica (50% with AOL Time Warner)	Loews Cineplex Entertainment		
Broadcast, cable, and satellite TV	CNN, HBO, WB TV, Turner Network Television, Turner Classic Movies, Cartoon Network	ABC network, A & E, Disney Channel, Lifetime, ESPN, local TV stations	CBS, MTV, VH1, Nickelodeon, UPN, Showtime, Comedy Central	Sony Pictures Television	Twentieth Century Fox TV, Fox Broadcasting Company, Sky TV, Star TV	Universal Television, USA Network (partial ownership)
Publishing	Little, Brown; Warner Books, *Time, Life, Sports Illustrated, People,* DC Comics	Capital City newspapers, magazines, Hyperion Books	Simon & Schuster, Prentice-Hall, Free Press, Webster's Dictionary		Newspapers, *TV Guide,* HarperCollins, Westview Press	Penguin, Putnam
Music	Warner Music, Atlantic, Elektra, America Online Internet service	Disney Music		Columbia, Epic, Sony Classical		Music Corporation of America, PolyGram
Other	Six Flags theme parks, Atlanta Braves, Atlanta Hawks	Merchandising, Disney theme parks and resorts, the Mighty Ducks	Blockbuster video stores, Great America and Kings Dominion theme parks	Video games, consumer electronics (Walkman, Trinitron, etc.), professional electronics (high-definition video, etc.)	Sheep farming, airlines	Beverages, Universal theme parks, real estate, Universal Interactive

Selling The Film   Distributors make prints, schedule release dates, and launch advertising campaigns. For big companies, distribution can be efficient because the costs can be spread out over many units. A poster design can be used in various markets, and a distributor who orders a hundred prints from a laboratory will pay less per print than the filmmaker who orders one. Still, distribution costs have risen dramatically in recent years, largely because of greater film output and increased competition. Today, when the average Hollywood film is estimated to cost around $50 million to make, it costs an additional $30 million to distribute.

The distributor provides not only the movie but also a publicity campaign, the costs of which are shared by the exhibitor. The theater will be supplied with "trailers," the previews of coming attractions. There may be a music video to build

Independent Production and Mainstream Hollywood: The Case of Good Machine

During the 1990s, independent film production and distribution companies achieved more prominence. With the major Hollywood firms increasingly concentrating on wide-release blockbusters, smaller firms could target films toward more specific audiences. Niche audiences, however, could be fairly large, and during the decade many independent films became substantial hits. These films seldom made as much as the summer "tent-pole" films, but they attracted the attention of big producers because they were relatively cheap to make or acquire and hence could be profitable with minimal risk. In 1993, Disney started a trend by buying the prestigious independent firm Miramax, which had successfully distributed such films as *sex, lies, and videotape* (1989) and *Reservoir Dogs* (1992); as a subsidiary, Miramax continued to operate as a largely autonomous firm.

One company that exemplifies the rise of the independents is Good Machine, which was founded in New York in 1991 by Columbia University film professor James Schamus and producer Ted Hope. The pair sought to match a project's potential income to a reasonable budget. Good Machine's partners quickly assumed a high profile. Schamus produced prominent Chilean émigré director Raoul Ruiz's *The Golden Boat* and executive-produced Todd Haynes's *Poison* (winner of the Grand Prize at Sundance, the premiere film festival for independents. Hope produced Hal Hartley's *Trust* (winner of the Sundance screenplay award). The latter two were to remain among the most respected American independent films of the decade.

Hartley continued working with Ted Hope for *Simple Men* (1992) and *Amateur* (1994), while Good Machine executive-produced Haynes's *Safe* (1995). The firm also produced two films directed by actor Edward Burns, *The Brothers McMullen* (1995) and *She's the One* (1996).

The filmmaker most closely linked to Good Machine was Ang Lee, whose first feature, *Pushing Hands* (1992), was pro-duced on a budget of $400,000. Schamus collaborated on the screenplay, and he continued to play this dual role as producer and scriptwriter on other Lee films, including *The Wedding Banquet* (1993), *Eat Drink Man Woman* (1994), and *The Ice Storm* (1997). *Variety* claimed that, given its small budget, *The Wedding Banquet* was proportionately the most profitable film of 1993—exactly what made independent films attractive to the big studios. *The Ice Storm* won Schamus the prize for best screenplay at Cannes.

By 1993, Good Machine's consistent success attracted increasing attention within the mainstream industry. Aside from Schamus's screenplay award, Schamus and Hope took four films to the Sundance festival. Paramount expressed interest in making Good Machine its "classics" division, but the negotiations came to nothing. Good Machine was expanding its foreign interests and in August formed Good Machine International. Its president, David Linde, had formerly run Miramax's foreign sales and had marketed *Pulp Fiction* (1994) abroad. GMI began to import films, including Joan Chen's *Xiu Xiu the Sent-Down Girl* (1999) and Lars von Trier's *Dancer in the Dark* (2000).

In 2000, Good Machine gained even greater prominence with an unexpected foreign-language hit. With Schamus again co-scripting and producing and Lee directing, the pair participated in an American–Hong Kong–Taiwanese co-production, *Crouching Tiger, Hidden Dragon*. The film, made on a modest budget of about $15 million, was successfully marketed to a broad spectrum of niche audiences beyond the usual action-film fans, including teenage girls, women, and audiences interested in Asian culture **(1.18)**. Its strong plot and balletic swordplay scenes, staged by veteran Hong Kong fights choreographer Yuen Wo-ping, gave the martial-arts genre a new respectability among mature audiences. Viewers unaccustomed to foreign-language films found themselves willingly reading subtitles. *Crouching Tiger, Hidden*

1.18 The prominence of two female characters in both the swordplay and romance storylines of *Crouching Tiger, Hidden Dragon* made the film appealing to women as well as to male action fans.

Dragon ultimately grossed over $200 million and won four Oscars. Also in 2000, Good Machine made a hit of a modest romantic comedy by Jenniphr Goodman, *The Tao of Steve*. The film's cinematography, editing, and acting belied its low budget, and it became a date movie for the art-house set.

During 2001, its last year as a small independent firm, Good Machine distributed Todd Field's first feature, *In the Bedroom*. It also planned a larger, popularly oriented production for Lee: *The Hulk*.

While Good Machine prospered, a series of events occurred that resulted in the small company's being absorbed into one of the world's largest media conglomerates, Vivendi Universal:

September 1997: Good Machine International becomes the exclusive foreign sales company for another successful American independent firm, October Films.

October 1997: Universal, which already owns a share of the Sundance Channel, buys a majority stake in October Films.

1999: Universal sells October to Barry Diller, who renames it USA Films.

2000: Universal forms a subsidiary, Universal Focus, to distribute independent films such as *Billy Elliot*.

2001: Universal buys USA Films back from Diller.

May 2002: Vivendi Universal buys Good Machine and merges it into USA Films and Universal Focus, creating a new company, Focus Features. USA Films becomes a production wing within Focus.

For Vivendi Universal, the roughly $10 million paid to acquire Good Machine brought it both prestige and the potential for profitable films made on modest budgets. It also brought in Ang Lee, a director who could move between independent films and popcorn movies, as he did with *The Hulk*. Other talented directors could be attracted to a company with a successful track record.

Good Machine followed a major trend of the 1990s independents by becoming the "art" or "niche" wing of a much larger company. It was bolstered by the combination with USA Films, which had recently released several major independent films, most notably Steven Soderbergh's *Traffic* (2000), Joel and Ethan Coen's *The Man Who Wasn't There* (2001), and Robert Altman's *Gosford Park* (2001). Focus continued distributing Mira Nair's *Monsoon Wedding* (2002), which had been picked up by USA Films.

Schamus and Linde stayed on to head Focus, maintaining a considerable amount of control. They also now had a ready source of funding, rather than needing to find support for each individual project. Hope struck out on his own as an independent producer, though he enjoyed a "first look" deal with

1.19   The suburban couple in *Far from Heaven,* already starting to fracture.

Focus. Focus's first acquisition for distribution was Roman Polanksi's *The Pianist,* winner of the 2002 Palme d'Or at the Cannes Film Festival. Later that year the company returned to its Good Machine roots by taking over the American distribution of Todd Haynes's award-winning *Far from Heaven* **(1.19),** which premiered at the Venice Film Festival.

In May, industry trade journal *Variety* remarked, "this freshly minted indie with deep studio pockets stands as the hottest go-to shingle for a top-flight indie project." The comment points up how loose the term "independent" had become by this point, since, strictly speaking, Good Machine was now wholly owned by a conglomerate. Yet Schamus and Linde had declared their intentions to continue supporting the small, often prestigious, films that had made Good Machine attractive to Vivendi Universal, and that kind of film had come to be thought of as "independent"—whatever its source.

interest in the movie and its soundtrack album, "infotainment" TV programs will build audience awareness, and a cable channel may run a "Making of . . ." program. For print journalists the distributor will provide press kits, complete with photos and background information. Local TV outlets will get "electronic press kits" containing star sound bites and clips of splashy scenes. Even a modestly budgeted production like *Waiting to Exhale* had heavy promotion: five separate music videos, star visits to the Oprah Winfrey show, and promotions in thousands of bookstores and beauty salons. *My Big Fat Greek Wedding* cost $5 million to produce, but the distributor spent over $10 million publicizing it.

Distributors have also learned the power of the Internet. Webpages entice potential viewers with plot information, star biographies, games, screensavers, and links to merchandising. The Net proved crucial in marketing *The Blair Witch Project* to its target audience of young summer filmgoers. While cutting their $35,000 movie, directors Daniel Myrick and Eduardo Sanchez filled a website with fake documents about the legend of the Blair Witch and the mysterious fate of the students who had disappeared while investigating her. Fan sites sprang up before the film had been screened. The small distribution firm Artisan Entertainment committed $15 million to promoting it, updating the webpage and leaking the trailer to other movie-related sites. *The Blair Witch Project* became one of the most profitable films ever made, earning over $130 million in North America alone.

Merchandising is one form of promotion that pays back its investment directly. Manufacturing companies buy the rights to use the film's characters, title, or im-

"This was a Web site that was an entertainment experience in itself. The movie was an extension of the Web site."

— A studio marketing executive on *The Blair Witch Project*

ages on products. Children's films are released accompanied by toys, games, clothing, lunchboxes, schoolbags, and tie-ins with fast-food outlets. Such spin-offs can be immensely profitable. By 1992, *Star Wars* merchandise had racked up sales of $2.6 billion—more than the films themselves had earned.

Nearly all major motion pictures rely on merchandising, if only of a novelization or a sound track CD, to lower production and distribution costs and to provide new profit centers. A common practice is "cross-promotion," which allows both a film and a product line to be advertised at once. MGM arranged for the stars of the James Bond film *Tomorrow Never Dies* to appear in advertisements for Heineken, Smirnoff, BMW, Visa, and Ericsson. The five companies spent nearly $100 million on the campaign, which publicized the film around the world. As payback, the film included scenes prominently featuring the products. *Austin Powers: The Spy Who Shagged Me* had advertising partnerships with Mitsubishi, Heineken, Visa, Virgin Atlantic, Philips Electronics, Starbucks, and the American Academy of Periodontology ("Don't Forget to Floss, Baby!"). Even less mainstream fare has relied on cross-promotion: The documentary *Hoop Dreams* was publicized by Nike and the National Basketball Association.

The marketing of the film does not end when it starts playing theaters. Distribution executives track the box-office receipts of a film's opening weekend and report them to their superiors, the production company, and the press. Distribution companies also undertake exit polling to gauge whether filmgoers will recommend the picture to their friends. Most films achieve their largest audience on the opening weekend, but a few build an audience more slowly as viewers tell their friends about them. Across the spring and summer of 2002, the $5 million romantic comedy *My Big Fat Greek Wedding* rose in box-office ranking largely on the strength of word of mouth. It eventually surpassed $210 million in North American ticket sales.

Ancillary Markets   When a film leaves theatrical exhibition, its life is far from over. Since the late 1970s, video has created a vast array of ancillary markets, and these typically return more money than the original release. (Since 1988, U.S. home video has generated more than twice the income of domestic theatrical box office.) Distribution companies carefully plan their video "windows" to widen the film's availability gradually. A release appears first over hotel television systems and airline flights, then on pay-per-view television, then on cable television and DVD or videocassette, and eventually on network broadcast and cable reruns. Video has proved a boon to smaller distributors as well: Foreign and independent films usually yield slim theatrical returns, but video markets can make these items profitable.

The ultimate extension of video distribution may be cyberspace. Major film companies are experimenting with websites that deliver movies on demand. Already digital versions of some independent films are available on the Internet, and hundreds of sites offer bootlegged versions of studio releases. In 2002, buccaneering fans uploaded pirated video copies of *Signs* and *Star Wars: Episode II—Attack of the Clones*. Thanks to the enormous number of video distribution channels and exhibition sites, movies permeate world culture as never before. Yet films now appear in so many guises that it is hard to recapture a sense of the way the original looked. (See Box, pp. 21–23.)

A film can continue its life in other media. *Star Wars* spawned bestselling paperback novels; *Buffy the Vampire Slayer* was spun off as a comic book and TV series; Universal's theme park offers a ride based on *Back to the Future; Grease* and *The Lion King* were adapted as Broadway shows; *Die Hard* and *A Bug's Life* became video games; *Beetlejuice* turned into a TV cartoon. Because distribution

"Our underlying philosophy is that all media are one."

— Rupert Murdoch, owner of News Corp. and Twentieth Century Fox companies belong to multinational conglomerates, films often serve as "content" fed to the company's other media outlets.

Beyond Hollywood: International Distribution and Exhibition

The major production and distribution companies are identified with America, but many belong to international companies. The Japanese electronics firm Sony owns Columbia Pictures, Australia's News Corp. owns Twentieth Century Fox, and a French firm, Vivendi, owns Universal. In addition, many of the world's top media companies are European and Asian. Asahi Broadcasting of Japan invests in film studios, as does the newspaper chain Nippon Herald. Sylvio Berlusconi, currently prime minister of Italy, runs a conglomerate consisting of film production and distribution companies, book and magazine publishers, and the country's top commercial TV broadcaster. Many regional and national distributors acquire films from each other.

Worldwide, theatrical grosses were $17.5 billion dollars in 2001. The sources of income are distributed very unevenly. The United States is by far the most lucrative market, contributing over 40 percent of the total. By nation, Japan comes in second; its ticket prices are the highest in the world (averaging $10 in 2001). Western European and Asian–Pacific countries follow. Providing about 25 percent of global box office, Western Europe (including the United Kingdom and the Nordic countries) emerges as the most important regional market outside North America.

The less significant market regions are Latin America, Eastern Europe, mainland China, India, the Middle East, and Africa. The underdeveloped economies of these regions cannot sustain high admission prices; in Latin America, a movie ticket averages $3. China and India have huge populations, but because of low ticket prices (an average of $0.13), together they contributed only about $700 million to the 2001 global total—less than Germany did. For all these reasons, filmmakers around the world aim for distribution in the United States, Western Europe, and Japan.

MAKING THE MOVIE: FILM PRODUCTION

The movie that is distributed and exhibited to us must first be produced. The process of film **production** involves not only technology and funding but also people working together. Most films go through three phases of production.

1. *Preparation.* The idea for the film is developed and committed to paper in some form. The filmmaker also begins to acquire funds to support the film.

2. *Shooting.* Here the filmmaker creates images in the form of **shots.** A shot is a series of frames produced by the camera in an uninterrupted operation. The filmmaker also records sounds, consisting of dialogue, noises, or music.

3. *Assembly.* At this stage, which may overlap with the shooting phase, the images and sounds are combined in their final form. This involves cutting picture and sound, executing special effects, adding music or extra dialogue, and adding titles.

Every phase changes what went before. The idea for the film may be radically modified when the script is hammered out; the script's presentation of the action may be drastically changed in shooting; and the material that is shot takes on new significance in the process of assembly. As the French director Robert Bresson puts it, "A film is

Film and Video: Where Did the Picture Go?

Filmmakers often complain that video versions don't look like their original films. Sometimes it's a matter of technical differences between the two media. (See Box, pp. 10–12.) But films are also deliberately altered for video exhibition. Versions for airline video projection and for broadcast television trim sex and violence and eliminate potentially offensive dialogue from sound tracks. Sometimes TV versions are created during production: The broadcast version of *The Silence of the Lambs* contains different footage than the theatrical release. Broadcasters also use "time compression," a device that speeds up the film slightly so more commercials can be squeezed in. Even "premium" cable channels snip out nudity and use redubbed lines of dialogue.

What about a rental video? Doesn't that conform to the original theatrical release? Often not. Directors occasionally revise films for video release, as Sam Raimi did with *The Evil Dead* by eliminating a crudely animated shot of lightning striking a tree (and depriving many fans of their favorite shot). Songs are often replaced in video release, largely because the rights could not be negotiated. Some video rental chains force distribution companies to prepare softer versions of R-rated films. And, as in broadcast and cable exhibition, video rental copies alter the image to fit the TV screen.

The most apparent difference between a rental video and the original film involves the shape of the screen. Since the mid-1950s virtually all films have been designed to be shown on wide theater screens, not squarish TV monitors. High-definition televisions (HDTV) with wider screens are slowly gaining a share of the market, but these are still not as wide as many theatrical films made since the 1950s.

One solution has been to release some video copies of films with *letterboxing,* dark horizontal bands at the top and bottom of the TV screen that approximate the film's original shape on theater screens. This practice became widespread on home video in 1985, when Woody Allen, who controlled the video release of his film *Manhattan* (1979), insisted that the film be released letterboxed. In 1986, the Criterion company started a series of letterboxed laser discs, and this type of video formatting has grown in popularity. Many viewers, however, find letterboxing distracting, especially if their television screens are relatively small; they often opt for the *full-frame* video versions of films, where the image has no black masking. Such versions often begin with the enigmatic warning, "This film has been modified from its original version. It has been formatted to fit your television."

Today many films are released in letterboxed video versions, though the practice remains more common with DVDs than with VHS cassettes. Some DVDs contain both the letterboxed and full-frame versions of the same film. Because *A Bug's Life* was made in digital animation, the filmmakers recomposed the original widescreen shots to fit household TV monitors, thus providing both letterboxed and full-frame versions where the entire original image is visible.

DVDs are rapidly gaining on VHS in popularity, with some films selling more copies on DVD than on VHS. In 2002, a record 70 percent of the video sales of *The Lord of the Rings: The Fellowship of the Ring* were DVDs, and slightly more letterboxed than full-frame DVDs were purchased. Compare this with the sales of the two best-selling video titles of 2000: *Tarzan,* 7 percent on DVD, and *Toy Story 2,* 12 percent on DVD. DVDs offer the additional attractions of better visual quality and, in many cases, extra features like voiceover commentaries by filmmakers and documentaries on the making of the film.

No video version of a film wholly replicates the film image as it appeared on the theater screen. Even letterboxed images do not necessarily show absolutely the entire image, since very wide films are often cropped slightly at the sides. The changes in the pictures in full-frame versions, however, are more dramatic. There have been a number of approaches to creating full-frame images. One older method is called "pan and scan," where as much as 50 percent of the image can disappear.

In preparing the video version, a "controller" watches the film and decides what portions of the widescreen image to eliminate. If the controller decides that important action is taking place at opposite ends of the frame, a computer-controlled scanner moves across the image—hence the name for the process, panning and scanning. Sometimes the controller decides to make separate shots out of what was originally a single shot **(1.20–1.22)**. Whatever choice is made, the original film is altered, often drastically.

As a result, nearly all videocassette copies of films made in the past 40 years alter the compositions intended by the filmmakers. Accepting the inevitable, some directors "shoot for the box" and try to keep all the important action in an area that will survive the transfer to video **(1.23, 1.24)**. They may hope that letterboxed versions on DVD and some cassettes will be faithful to their original images. James Cameron shot *Titanic* with an eye to successful video sales, using Super 35mm film stock. In this process, additional image area is exposed above and below the widescreen composition. Those

1.20 In Otto Preminger's *Advise and Consent*, a single shot in the original . . .

1.21 . . . becomes a pair of shots and . . .

1.23 Many widescreen compositions try for only one center of interest . . .

1.22 . . . loses the sense of actors simultaneously reacting to each other.

1.24 . . . so that the video version can concentrate on it. Note, however, the loss of compositional balance and the change of scale; the actor dominates the frame in a way she does not in the original (from *Aliens*).

parts of the image are not included in the theatrical versions, but they are put into full-frame videos to give a TV-shaped picture. Often, however, the upper and lower areas tend not to include much of interest, while important parts of the horizontal composition may be lost **(1.25, 1.26).**

As a final example, consider a shot from Paul Thomas Anderson's widescreen film *Magnolia* **(1.27–1.29).** Here two characters have been balanced at opposite sides of the frame, and one nearly vanishes in the full-frame video.

1.25 As Rose, the heroine of *Titanic*, feels the exhilaration of "flying" on the ship's prow, the strongly horizontal composition emphasizes her outstretched arms as "wings" against a wide horizon.

1.26 Nearly all sense of the horizontal composition has disappeared in the video version, as more of the sky is visible, and one of Rose's arms is largely outside the frame.

1.27 This framing from *Magnolia* keeps both the patient and nurse visible through much of their conversation and also balances the light bedclothes and the darkness around the nurse.

1.29 In the full-frame VHS copy, the framing selects the nurse and holds the framing on him, while only the patient's covered legs and feebly moving hands are visible.

1.28 The letterboxed DVD image largely preserves this balance, though the very edges of the wide frame have been cropped out.

born in my head and I kill it on paper. It is brought back to life by the actors and then killed in the camera. It is then resurrected into a third and final life in the editing room where the dismembered pieces are assembled into their finished form."

These three phases include many particular jobs. Most films that we see in theaters culminate from dozens of specialized tasks carried out by hundreds of experts. This fine-grained division of labor has proved to be a reliable way to prepare, shoot, and assemble large-budget movies.

The Preproduction Phase

In professional filmmaking, the preparation phase is known as *preproduction.* At this point, two roles are central: that of producer and that of screenwriter.

The tasks of the *producer* are chiefly financial and organizational. She or he may be an "independent" producer, unearthing film projects and trying to convince production companies or distributors to finance the film. Or the producer may work for a distribution company and generate ideas for films. A studio may also hire a producer to put together a particular package.

The producer nurses the project through the script process, obtains financial support, and arranges to hire the personnel who will work on the film. During shooting and assembly, the producer usually acts as the liaison between the writer or director and the company that is financing the film. After the film is completed, the producer will often have the task of arranging the distribution, promotion, and marketing of the film and of monitoring the paying back of the money invested in the production.

A single producer may take on all these tasks, but in the contemporary American film industry the producer's work is further subdivided. The *executive producer* is often the person who arranged the financing for the project or obtained the literary property (although many filmmakers complain that the credit of executive producer is sometimes given to people who did little work). Once the production is under way, the *line producer* oversees the day-to-day activities of director, cast, and crew. The line producer is assigned by an *associate producer,* who acts as a liaison with laboratories or technical personnel.

The chief task of the *screenwriter* is to prepare the *screenplay* (or script). Sometimes the writer will send a screenplay to an agent, who submits it to a production company. Or an experienced screenwriter meets with a producer in a "pitch session," where the writer can propose ideas for scripts. The first scene of Robert Altman's *The Player* satirizes pitch sessions by showing celebrity screenwriters proposing strained ideas like "*Pretty Woman* meets *Out of Africa.*" Alternatively, sometimes the producer has an idea for a film and hires a screenwriter to develop it. This course of action is common if the producer has bought the rights to a novel or play and wants it adapted into a film.

The screenplay will go through several stages. These stages include a *treatment,* a synopsis of the action; then one or more full-length scripts; and a final version, the *shooting script.* Extensive rewriting is common, and writers have resigned themselves to seeing their work recast over and over. Often the director or star will want changes in the script. For example, in the original screenplay of *Witness* the protagonist was Rachel, the Amish widow with whom John Book falls in love. The romance, and Rachel's confused feelings about Book, formed the central plot line. But the director, Peter Weir, wanted to emphasize the clash between pacifism and violence. So William Kelley and Earl Wallace revised their screenplay to emphasize the mystery plot line and to center the action on Book, who brings urban crime into the peaceful Amish community. Shooting scripts are constantly altered too. Some directors allow actors to modify the dialogue, and problems on location or in

1.30   A publicity still for Alfred Hitchcock's *Notorious,* showing a scene that was eliminated from the final film. The actress sitting next to Cary Grant, apparently given a prominent part in this sequence, can be glimpsed in only one other scene.

a set may necessitate changes in the scene. In the assembly stage, script scenes that have been shot are often condensed, rearranged, or dropped entirely **(1.30).**

If the producer or director finds one writer's screenplay unsatisfactory, other writers may be hired to revise it. Most Hollywood screenwriters earn their living by rewriting other writers' scripts. As you may imagine, this often leads to conflicts about which writer or writers deserve onscreen credit for the film. In the American film industry, these disputes are adjudicated by the Screen Writers' Guild.

As the screenplay is being written or rewritten, the producer is planning the film's finances. He or she has sought out a director and stars to make the package seem a promising investment. The producer must prepare a budget spelling out *above-the-line costs* (the costs of literary property, scriptwriter, director, and major cast) and *below-the-line costs* (the expenses allotted to the crew, secondary cast, the shooting and assembly phases, insurance, and publicity). The sum of above- and below-the-line costs is called the *negative cost* (that is, the total cost of producing the film's master negative). In 2001, the average Hollywood negative cost ran about $50 million.

The producer must also prepare a daily schedule for shooting the film. This will be done with an eye on the budget. The producer assumes that the separate shots will be made out of continuity—that is, in the most convenient order for production—and put in proper order in the editing room. Since transporting equipment and personnel to a location is a major expense, producers usually prefer to shoot all the scenes taking place in one location at one time. For *Jurassic Park,* the main characters' arrival on the island and their departure at the end of the film were both shot at the start of production, during the three weeks of location in Hawaii. A producer must also plan to shoot around actors who can't be on the set every day. Many producers try to schedule the most difficult scenes early, before cast and crew begin to tire. For *Raging Bull* the

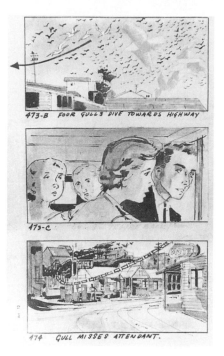

1.31 A page from the storyboard for Hitchcock's *The Birds.*

complex prizefight sequences were filmed first, with the dialogue scenes shot later. Keeping all such contingencies in mind, the producer comes up with a schedule that juggles cast, crew, locations, and even seasons and geography most efficiently.

The Production Phase

Although *production* is the term for the entire process of making a film, Hollywood filmmakers also use it to refer to the shooting phase (as in, "Now that we've got a finished script, we go into production next week"). Production is also known as *principal photography.*

The *director* is often involved at various stages of preproduction, but he or she is primarily responsible for overseeing the shooting and assembly phases. Within most film industries, the director is considered the single person most responsible for the look and sound of the finished film.

Because of the specialized division of labor in large-scale production, the director orchestrates the contributions of several units.

1. During the preparation phase, the director has already begun to work with the *set* unit, or *production design* unit, headed by a *production designer.* The production designer is in charge of visualizing the film's settings. This unit creates drawings and plans that determine the architecture and the color schemes of the sets. Under the production designer's supervision, an *art director* supervises the construction and painting of the sets. The *set decorator,* often someone with experience in interior decoration, modifies the sets for specific filming purposes, supervising a staff who find props and a *set dresser* who arranges things on the set during shooting. The *costume designer* is in charge of planning and executing the wardrobe for the production.

   Working with the production designer, a graphic artist may be assigned to produce a **storyboard,** a series of comic-strip-like sketches of the shots in each scene, including notations about costume, lighting, camerawork, and other matters **(1.31).** Most directors do not demand a storyboard for every scene, but action sequences and shots using special effects or complicated camerawork tend to be storyboarded in detail. The storyboard gives the cinematography unit and the special-effects unit a preliminary sense of what the finished shots should look like.

2. During the shooting, the director will rely on what is called the *director's crew.* This includes

   a. The *script supervisor,* known in the classic studio era as a "script girl." (Today one-fifth of Hollywood script supervisors are male.) The script supervisor is in charge of all details of **continuity** from shot to shot, such as details of performers' appearances (in the last scene, was the carnation in the left or right buttonhole?), props, lighting, movement, camera position, and the running time of each shot.

   b. The *first assistant director,* a jack-of-all-trades who, with the director, plans out each day's shooting schedule and sets up each shot for the director's approval, while keeping track of the actors, monitoring safety conditions, and keeping the energy level high.

   c. The *second assistant director,* who is the liaison among the first assistant director, the camera crew, and the electricians' crew.

   d. The *third assistant director,* who serves as messenger for director and staff.

   e. The *dialogue coach,* who feeds performers their lines and speaks the lines of offscreen characters during shots of other performers.

f. The *second unit director,* who films stunts, location footage, action scenes, and the like, at a distance from where principal shooting is taking place.

3. The most visible group of workers is the *cast.* The cast may include *stars,* well-known players assigned to major roles and likely to attract audiences. The cast also includes *supporting players,* or performers in secondary roles; *minor players;* and *extras,* those anonymous persons who pass by in the street, come together for crowd scenes, and fill distant desks in large office sets. One of the director's major jobs is to shape the performances of the cast. Most directors will spend a good deal of time explaining how a line or gesture should be rendered, reminding the actor of the place of this scene in the overall film, and helping the actor create a coherent performance. The first assistant director usually works with the extras and takes charge of arranging crowd scenes.

On some productions, there are still more specialized roles. *Stunt persons* will be supervised by a *stunt coordinator;* professional dancers will work with a *choreographer.* If animals join the cast, they will be handled by a *wrangler.* There have been pig wranglers (*Mad Max beyond Thunder Dome*), snake wranglers (*Raiders of the Lost Ark*), and spider wranglers (*Arachnophobia*).

4. Another unit of specialized labor is the *photography unit.* This leader is the *cinematographer,* also known as the *director of photography,* or *DP.* The cinematographer is an expert on photographic processes, lighting, and camera technique. The cinematographer consults with the director on how each scene will be lit and filmed (**1.32**). The cinematographer supervises

a. The *camera operator,* who runs the machine and who may also have assistants to load the camera, adjust and follow focus, push a dolly, and so on.

1.32   On the set of *Citizen Kane,* Orson Welles directs from his wheelchair on the far right, cinematographer Gregg Toland crouches below the camera, and actress Dorothy Comingore kneels at the left. The female script supervisor can be seen in the background left.

b. The *key grip,* the person who supervises the *grips.* These workers carry and arrange equipment, props, and elements of the setting and lighting.

c. The *gaffer,* the head electrician who supervises the placement and rigging of the lights. In Hollywood production the gaffer's assistant is called the *best boy.*

5. Parallel to the photography unit is the *sound unit.* This is headed by the *production recordist* (also called the *sound mixer*). The recordist's principal responsibility is to record dialogue during shooting. Typically the recordist will use a portable tape recorder, several sorts of microphones, and a console to balance and combine the inputs. The recordist will also attempt to tape some ambient sound when no actors are speaking. These bits of room tone will later be inserted to fill pauses in the dialogue. The recordist's staff includes

a. The *boom operator,* who manipulates the boom microphone and conceals radio microphones on the actors.

b. The *third man,* who places other microphones, lays sound cables, and is in charge of controlling ambient sound.

Some productions also have a *sound designer,* who enters the process during the preparation phase and who, like the production designer, plans a sonic style appropriate for the entire film.

6. A *special-effects unit* is charged with preparing and executing process shots, miniatures, matte work, computer-generated graphics, and other technical shots **(1.33).** During the planning phase, the director and the production designer will have determined what effects will be needed, and the special-effects unit consults with the director and the cinematographer on an ongoing basis. On a contemporary production, the special-effects unit can number hundreds of workers, from puppet- and model-makers to specialists in digital compositing.

7. A miscellaneous unit includes a *makeup staff,* a *costume staff, hairdressers,* and *drivers* (who transport cast and crew).

1.33   Sculpting a model dinosaur for *Jurassic Park: The Lost World.* The model was scanned into a computer for digital manipulation.

8. During shooting, the producer is represented by a unit often called the *producer's crew.* This consists of the *production manager,* also known as the *production coordinator* or the *associate producer.* This person will manage daily organizational business, such as arranging for meals and accommodations. A *production accountant* (or *production auditor*) monitors expenditures, a *production secretary* coordinates telephone communications among units and with the producer, and *production assistants* (or *PAs*) run errands. Newcomers to the film industry often start out working as production assistants.

All this coordinated effort, involving perhaps hundreds of workers, results in many thousands of feet of exposed film and recorded sound-on-tape. For every shot called for in the script or storyboard, the director usually makes several **takes,** or varying versions, of that shot. For instance, if the finished film requires one shot of an actor saying a line, the director may make several takes of that speech, each time asking the actor to vary the delivery. Not all takes are printed, and only one of those becomes the shot included in the finished film. Extra footage can be used in coming-attractions trailers and electronic press kits.

Because shooting usually proceeds out of continuity, the director and crew must have some way of labeling each take. As soon as the camera starts, one of the cinematographer's staff holds up a *slate* before the lens. On the slate is written the production, scene, shot, and take. A hinged arm at the top, the clapboard, makes a sharp smack that allows the recordist to synchronize the sound track with the footage in the assembly phase **(1.34).** Thus every take is identified for future reference. There are also electronic slates which keep track of each take automatically and provide digital readouts.

1.34 A slate shown at the beginning of a shot in Jean-Luc Godard's *La Chinoise.*

In filming a scene, most directors and technicians follow an organized procedure. While crews set up the lighting and test the sound recording, the director rehearses the actors and instructs the cinematographer. The director then supervises the filming of a *master shot.* The master shot typically records the entire action and dialogue of the scene. There may be several takes of the master shot. Then portions of the scene are restaged and shot in closer views or from different angles. These shots are called *coverage,* and each one may require many takes. Today most directors shoot a great deal of coverage, often by using two or more cameras filming at the same time. The script supervisor checks to ensure that continuity details are consistent within all these shots.

For most of film history, scenes were filmed with a single camera, which was moved to different points for different setups. More recently, with pressures to finish principal photography as fast as possible, the director and the camera unit will use two or more cameras. Action scenes are often shot from several angles simultaneously because chases, crashes, and explosions are difficult to repeat for retakes. The battles in *Gladiator* were filmed by 7 cameras, while 13 cameras were used for stunts in *XXX.* For dialogue scenes, a common tactic is to film with an A camera and a B camera, an arrangement that can capture two actors in alternating shots. The lower cost of digital video cameras has allowed some directors to experiment with shooting conversations from many angles at once, hoping to capture unexpected spontaneity in the performance. Scenes in Spike Lee's *Bamboozled* were filmed with as many as 11 mini-DV cameras. According to director Lars von Trier, some scenes in *Dancer in the Dark* employed 100 digital cameras.

When special effects are to be included, the shooting phase must carefully plan for them. In many cases, actors will be filmed against neutral blue or green backgrounds so

1.35 For the climax of *Jurassic Park,* the actors were shot in the set of the visitor's center, but the velociraptors and the *Tyrannosaurus rex* were computer-generated images added later.

that their figures may be inserted into computer-created settings. Or the director will film performers with the understanding that other material will be composited into the frame **(1.35).**

The Postproduction Phase

Filmmakers call the assembly phase *postproduction.* (If something goes wrong, someone may promise to "fix it in post.") Yet this phase does not begin simply after the shooting is finished. Postproduction staff members work behind the scenes throughout shooting.

Before the shooting has begun, the director or producer has probably hired an *editor* (also known as the *supervising editor*). This person catalogues and assembles the takes produced during shooting. The editor also works with the director to make creative decisions about how the footage can best be cut together.

Because each shot usually exists in several takes, because the film is shot out of continuity, and because the master-shot/coverage approach yields so much footage, the editor's job can be a vast one. A 100-minute feature, which amounts to about 9000 feet of 35mm film, may have been carved out of 500,000 feet of film. For this reason, postproduction on major Hollywood pictures often takes five to seven months. Sometimes several editors and assistants will be brought in.

Typically, the editor receives the processed footage from the laboratory as quickly as possible. This footage is known as the *dailies,* or the *rushes.* The editor inspects the dailies, leaving it to the *assistant editor* to synchronize image and sound and to sort the takes by scene. The editor will meet with the director to examine the dailies, or if the production is filming far away, the editor will call to inform the director of how the footage looks. Since retaking shots is costly and troublesome, constant checking of the dailies is important for spotting any problems with focus, exposure, framing, or other visual factors. From the dailies the director selects the best takes and the editor records the choices. To save money, dailies are often shown to the producer and director on video, but since video can conceal defects in the original footage, editors will check the original shots before cutting the film.

As the footage accumulates, the editor assembles it into a *rough cut*—the shots loosely strung in sequence, without sound effects or music. Rough cuts tend to run long; that of *Apocalypse Now* ran seven and a half hours. From the rough cut the editor, in consultation with the director, builds toward a *fine cut* or *final cut.* The unused shots constitute the *outtakes.* While the final cut is being prepared, a *second unit* may be shooting *inserts,* footage to fill in at certain places. These are typically

Some Terms and Roles in Film Production

The rise of packaged productions, pressures from unionized workers, and other factors have led producers to credit everyone who worked on a film. Meanwhile, the specialization of large-scale filmmaking has created its own jargon. Some of the most colorful terms (gaffer, best boy) are explained in the text. Here are some other terms that you may see in a film's credits.

ACE: After the name of the editor; abbreviation for the American Cinema Editors, a professional association.

ASC: After the name of the director of photography; abbreviation for the American Society of Cinematographers, a professional association. The British equivalent is the BSC.

Additional photography: A crew shooting footage apart from the *principal photography* supervised by the director of photography.

Casting director: Searches for and auditions performers for the film. Will suggest actors for *leading roles* (principal characters) as well as *character parts* (fairly standardized or stereotyped roles).

Clapper boy: Crew member who operates the clapboard that identifies each take.

Dialogue editor: Sound editor specializing in making sure recorded speech is audible.

Dolly grip: Crew member who pushes the dolly that carries the camera, either from one setup to another or during a take for moving camera shots.

Foley artist: A sound-effects specialist who creates sounds of body movement by walking or by moving materials across large trays of different substances (sand, earth, glass, and so on). Named for Jack Foley, a pioneer in postproduction sound.

Greenery man: Crew member who chooses and maintains trees, shrubs, and grass in settings.

Lead man: Member of set crew responsible for tracking down various props and items of decor for the set.

Loader: Member of photography unit who loads and unloads camera magazines, as well as logging the shots taken and sending the film to the laboratory.

Matte artist: Member of special-effects unit who paints backdrops that are then photographically incorporated into a shot in order to suggest a particular setting.

Model-maker: (1) Member of production design unit who prepares architectural models for sets to be built. (2) Member of the special-effects unit who fabricates scale models of locales, vehicles, or characters to be filmed as substitutes for full-size ones.

Optical effects: Laboratory workers responsible for such effects as fades and dissolves.

Property master: Member of set crew who supervises the use of all *props,* or movable objects in the film.

Publicist, Unit publicist: Member of producer's crew who creates and distributes promotional material regarding the production. The publicist may arrange for press and television interviews with the director and stars and for coverage of the production in the mass media.

Scenic artist: Member of set crew responsible for painting surfaces of set.

Still photographer: Member of crew who takes photographs of scenes and behind-the-scenes shots of cast members and others. These photographs may be used to check lighting or set design or color, and many will be used in promoting and publicizing the film.

Timer, Color timer: Laboratory worker who inspects the negative film and who adjusts the printer light to achieve consistency of color across the finished product.

Video assist: The use of a video camera mounted alongside the motion-picture camera to check lighting, framing, or performances. In this way, the director and the cinematographer can try out a shot or scene on tape before committing it to film.

long shots of cities or airports or close-ups of objects. At this point titles will be prepared and further laboratory work or special-effects work may be done.

Until the mid-1980s, editors cut and spliced the *work print,* footage printed from the camera negative. In trying out their options, editors were obliged to rearrange the shots physically. Now virtually all commercial films are edited electronically. The dailies are transferred to videotape, then to a hard drive. The editor enters notes on each take directly into a computer database. Such electronic editing systems, usually known as *nonlinear* systems, permit random access to the entire store of footage. The editor can call up any shot, paste it alongside any other shots, trim it, or junk it. Some systems allow special effects and music to be tried out as well. Although nonlinear systems have greatly speeded up the process of cutting, the editor usually asks for a work print of key scenes in order to check for color, details, and pacing.

Once the shots are arranged in something approaching final form, the *sound editor* takes charge of building up the sound track. The director, the composer, the picture editor, and the sound editor view the film and agree on where music and effects will be placed, a process known as *spotting.* The sound editor may have a staff whose members specialize in mixing dialogue, music, or sound effects.

Surprisingly little of the sound recorded during filming winds up in the finished movie. Often half or more of the dialogue is rerecorded in postproduction, using a process known as *automated dialogue replacement* (ADR, for short). ADR usually yields better quality than location sound. With the on-set recording serving as a *guide track,* the sound editor records actors in the studio speaking their lines (called **dubbing** or *looping*). Nonsynchronized dialogue such as the babble of a crowd (known in Hollywood as "walla") will be added by ADR as well.

Similarly, very few of the noises we hear in a film were recorded during filming. A sound editor adds sound effects, drawing on the library of stock sounds or creating particular effects for this film. Sound editors routinely manufacture footsteps, cars crashing, pistol shots, a fist thudding into flesh (often produced by whacking a watermelon with an axe). In *Terminator 2* the sound of the T-1000 cyborg passing through cell bars is that of dog food sliding slowly out of a can. Sound-effects technicians have sensitive hearing. One veteran notes the differences among doors: "The bathroom door has a little air as opposed to the closet door. The front door has to sound solid; you have to hear the latch sound. . . . Don't just put in any door, make sure it's right."

Like picture editing, sound editing relies on computer technology. The editor can store recorded sounds in a database, classifying and rearranging them in any way desired. A sound's qualities can be modified digitally—clipping off high or low frequencies, changing pitch, reverberation, equalization, or speed. The boom and throb of underwater action in *The Hunt for Red October* were slowed down and reprocessed from such mundane sources as a diver plunging into a swimming pool, water bubbling from a garden hose, and the hum of Disneyland's air-conditioning plant. One technician on the film calls digital sound editing "sound sculpting."

During the spotting of the sound track the film's *composer* has entered the assembly phase as well. The composer compiles cue sheets that list exactly where the music will go and how long it should run. The composer writes the score, although she or he will probably not orchestrate it personally. While the composer is working, the rough cut will be synchronized with a *temp dub,* accompaniment pulled from recorded songs or classical pieces. Musicians record the score with the aid of a *click track,* a taped series of metronome beats synchronized with the final cut.

"[ADR for *Apocalypse Now*] was tremendously wearing on the actors because the entire film is looped, and of course all of the sound for everything had to be redone. So the actors were locked in a room for days and days on end shouting. Either they're shouting over the noise of the helicopter, or they're shouting over the noise of the boat."

— Walter Murch, sound designer

Dialogue, effects, and music are recorded on different magnetic tapes, and each bit of sound may occupy a separate track. At a final mixing session, the director, editor, and sound editor put dozens of such separate tracks together into a single master track. The sound specialist who performs the task is the *rerecording mixer.* Often the dialogue track is organized first, then sound effects are balanced with that, and finally music is added to create the final mix. Often there will need to be equalization, filtering, and other adjustments to the track. Once fully mixed, the master track is transferred onto sound recording film, which encodes the magnetic sound as optical or digital information on 35mm film.

The film's *camera negative,* which was used to make the dailies and the work print, is normally too precious to serve as the source for final prints. Instead, from the negative footage the laboratory draws an *interpositive,* which in turn furnishes an *internegative.* This internegative is assembled in accordance with the final cut, and it will be the primary source for future prints. Then the master sound track is synchronized with it. The first positive print, complete with picture and sound, is called the *answer print.* After the director, producer, and cinematographer have approved an answer print, *release prints* are made for distribution. These are the copies shown in theaters.

The work of production does not end when the final theatrical version has been assembled. In consultation with the producer and director, the postproduction staffs prepare airline and broadcast television versions. In some cases, different versions may be prepared for different countries. Scenes in Sergio Leone's *Once upon a Time in America* were completely rearranged for its American release. European prints of Stanley Kubrick's *Eyes Wide Shut* featured more nudity than American ones, in which some naked couples were blocked by digital figures added to the foreground. Once the various versions are decided upon, each is copied to a master videotape, the source of future versions. This video transfer process often demands new judgments about color quality and sound balance.

Many fictional films have been made about the process of film production. Federico Fellini's *8½* concerns itself with the preproduction stage of a film that is abandoned before shooting starts. François Truffaut's *Day for Night* takes place during the shooting phase of a project interrupted by the death of a cast member. The action of Brian De Palma's *Blow Out* occurs while a low-budget thriller is in sound editing. *Singin' in the Rain* follows a single film through the entire process, with a gigantic publicity billboard filling the final shot.

MODES OF PRODUCTION

Large-Scale Production

The fine-grained division of labor we've been describing is characteristic of *studio* filmmaking. A studio is a company in the business of manufacturing films. The most famous studios flourished in Hollywood between the 1920s and the 1960s—Paramount, Warner Bros., Columbia, and so on. These companies owned equipment and extensive physical plants, and they retained most of their workers on long-term contracts (**1.38,** p. 36). Each studio's central management planned all projects, then delegated authority to individual supervisors, who in turn assembled casts and crews from the studio's pool of workers. Organized as efficient businesses, the studios created a tradition of carefully tracking the entire process through paper records. At the start there were versions of the script; during shooting, reports were

Over the past 20 years, all phases of film production have been changed by computer technology. There is software to help draft screenplays, prepare budgets and schedules, draw storyboards, prepare set designs, test makeup, and diagram camera placement. Composers can prepare first drafts of scores directly on digital synthesizers and send the results to the director for fast synchronization with edited sequences. Cinematographers can previsualize complicated camera movements in "virtual sets." Filmmakers speak of the "digital backlot," software programs that can put performers into artificially composed settings that automatically change the angle of sunlight or the texture of rain or fog. For the final storm in *The Truman Show,* shots of the hero's sailboat in a studio tank were blended with a vast seascape created digitally.

The arrival of digital, or nonlinear, editing has drastically changed the assembly process. Databases enable editors to keep track of every take and bit of sound. In the days when editors cut directly on film, they had to splice and resplice the footage if they wanted to try out different arrangements. Now, with all takes stored on the hard drive, shots can be rearranged in seconds. Neil Travis, editor of *Patriot Games,* prepared the sequence in which Jack Ryan watches in horror as a satellite transmits infrared images of a commando raid on a terrorist camp. With the aid of digital editing, Travis began trimming two frames off every shot, again and again, until he pared the shots down to mere flashes. To do all this by hand would have been discouragingly slow, because Travis would have had to order many reprints of the shots and to keep track of dozens of bits of film. Now that fast cutting is easy, the pace of movie editing has picked up. In *Armageddon,* which has nearly 4000 shots, the average shot lasts only 2.3 seconds.

Other phases of postproduction have been transformed by **computer-generated imagery (CGI).** By transferring photographed film to a digital format, it is now easy to delete distracting background elements, to clone a character (as in *Multiplicity*), or to build crowds out of only a few spectators (in several scenes of *Forrest Gump*). Flying characters are filmed suspended from cables, which are then digitally erased. Digital compositing can construct virtual characters like Jar Jar Binks in *The Phantom Menace* and create wounded soldiers, as in *Saving Private Ryan*'s Omaha beach assault.

The natural home for CGI is fantasy and science fiction. For *The Matrix,* still photographs were digitized to create

1.36 For *The Matrix* a ring of still cameras captured all aspects of figures in flight . . .

virtual sets seen in smoothly changing three-dimensional perspectives, as if filmed by a moving camera. Software added lens distortions, color shifts, light flare, and even film grain. Directors Larry and Andy Wachowski wanted midair combats in which the camera could glide rapidly around gunmen who are frozen in place or floating in slow motion. The effect was achieved through surrounding the wire-suspended actors with 120 still cameras and feeding the sep-

arate images to a high-speed computer's motion-capture system. The filmmakers had already previsualized the fighters' movements on computer and were able to provide the system with information about every twist and leap. The software then created synthetic in-between images based on the frames on either side, so that the shot could vary the speed of the action at will. The result was larger-than-life movement in a virtual world (**1.36, 1.37**).

1.37　. . . permitting the final shot to move around characters hovering in space.

1.38 In a World War II–era publicity photo, MGM studio head Louis B. Mayer, front row center, shows off his stable of contract stars.

written about camera footage, sound recording, special-effects work, and laboratory results; in the assembly phase there were logs of shots catalogued in editing and a variety of cue sheets for music, mixing, looping, and title layout. This sort of record keeping has remained a part of large-scale filmmaking, though now it is done for the most part on computer.

Although studio production might seem to resemble a factory's assembly line, it was always more creative, collaborative, and chaotic than turning out cars or TV sets. Each film is a unique product, not a replica of a basic design. In studio filmmaking, skilled specialists collaborated to create such a product while still adhering to a blueprint prepared by management.

The centralized studio production system has virtually disappeared. The giants of Hollywood's golden age have become distribution companies, although they often initiate, fund, and oversee the making of the films they distribute. The old studios had stars and staff under long-term contracts, so the same group of people might work together on film after film. Now each film is planned as a distinct package, with director, actors, staff, and technicians brought together for this project alone. The studio may provide its own soundstages, sets, and offices for the project, but in most cases the producer arranges with outside firms to supply cameras, catering, locations, special effects, and everything else required.

Still, the detailed production stages remain similar to what they were in the heyday of studio production. In fact, filmmaking has become vastly more complicated in recent years, largely because of the expansion of production budgets and the growth of computer-based special effects. *Titanic* listed over 1,400 names in its final credits.

No division of labor can prevent all problems. Every large-scale production is plagued by compromises, accidents, and foul-ups. Weather may throw the shooting off schedule. Disagreements may result in the firing of a producer or a cinematographer. Last-minute script changes or poor reactions in a test screening may require that some scenes be reshot. Weary filmmakers admit that at any moment the whole enterprise could run out of control. Every major film that is released, good or bad, is remarkable to the extent that it got finished at all, and the precise division of labor created by the studio tradition is largely responsible.

Exploitation and Independent Production

Not all films using the division of labor we have outlined are big-budget projects financed by major companies. There are also low-budget *exploitation* products tailored to a particular market—in earlier decades, fringe theatres and drive-ins; now, videocassette rentals. Troma Films, maker of *The Toxic Avenger,* is probably the most famous exploitation company, turning out horror movies and teen sex comedies for $100,000 or even less. Nonetheless, exploitation filmmakers usually divide the labor along studio lines. There is the producer's role, the director's role, and so on, and the production tasks are parceled out in ways which roughly conform to mass-production practices. True, in such circumstances people often double up on jobs: The director might produce the film and write the script; the picture editor might cut sound as well.

To take an extreme example, Robert Rodriguez made *El Mariachi* as an exploitation film for the Spanish-language video market. The 21-year-old director also functioned as producer, scriptwriter, cinematographer, camera operator, still photographer, and sound recordist and mixer. Rodriguez's friend Carlos Gallardo starred, coproduced, and coscripted; he also served as unit production manager and grip. Gallardo's mother fed the cast and crew. *El Mariachi* wound up costing only about $7000.

Unlike *El Mariachi,* most exploitation films don't enter the theatrical market, but other low-budget productions, loosely known as "independent" films, do. Independent films are made for the theatrical market but without major distributor financing. Sometimes the independent filmmaker is a well-known director, such as Jane Campion, David Cronenberg, or Alan Rudolph, who prefers to work with budgets significantly below the industry norm. The lower scale of investment allows the filmmaker more freedom in choosing stories and performers. The director usually initiates the project and partners with a producer to get it realized. Financing often comes from European television firms, with major U.S. distributors buying the rights if the project seems to have good prospects. For example, David Lynch's low-budget *The Straight Story* was financed by French and British television before it was bought for distribution by Disney.

As we would expect, these industry-based independents organize production in ways very close to the full-fledged studio mode. Nonetheless, because these projects require less financing, the directors can demand more control over the production process. Woody Allen, for instance, is allowed by his contract to rewrite and reshoot extensive portions of his film after he has assembled an initial rough cut.

The category of independent production is a roomy one, and it also includes more modest projects by less well known filmmakers. Examples would be Edward Burns's *The Brothers McMullen* and Victor Nuñez's *Ulee's Gold.* Even though their budgets are much smaller than for most commercial films, independent productions face many obstacles (**1.39**). Filmmakers may have to finance the project

"Deep down inside, everybody in the United States has a desperate need to believe that some day, if the breaks fall their way, they can quit their jobs as claims adjusters, legal secretaries, certified public accountants, or mobsters, and go out and make their own low-budget movie. Otherwise, the future is just too bleak."

— Joe Queenan, critic and independent filmmaker

1.39 In making *Just Another Girl on the IRT,* independent director Leslie Harris used locations and available lighting in order to shoot quickly; she finished filming in just 17 days.

1.40 In *The Riddle of Lumen,* Brakhage turns shadows and everyday objects into vivid distant patterns.

1.41 *Meshes of the Afternoon:* Multiple versions of the protagonist played by the filmmaker, Maya Deren.

themselves, with the help of relatives and friendly investors; they must also find a distributor specializing in independent and low-budget films. But many filmmakers believe the advantages of independence outweigh the drawbacks. Independent production can treat subjects that large-scale studio production ignores. No film studios would have supported Jim Jarmusch's *Stranger than Paradise* or Kevin Smith's *Clerks.* Because the independent film does not need as large an audience to repay its costs, it can be more personal and controversial. And the production process, no matter how low-budget, still relies on the basic roles and phases established in the studio tradition.

Small-Scale Production

In large-scale and independent production, many people work on the film, each one a specialist in a particular task. But it is also possible for one person to do everything: plan the film, finance it, perform in it, run the camera, record the sound, and put it all together. Such films are seldom seen in commercial theatres, but they are central to experimental and documentary traditions.

Consider Stan Brakhage, whose films are among the most directly personal ever made. Some, like *Window Water Baby Moving,* are lyrical studies of his home and family **(1.40).** Others, such as *Dog Star Man,* are mythic treatments of nature; still others, such as *23rd Psalm Branch,* are quasi-documentary studies of war and death. Funded by grants and his personal finances, Brakhage prepares, shoots, and edits his films virtually unaided. While he was working in a film laboratory, he also developed and printed his footage. With over 150 films to his credit, Brakhage has proved that the individual filmmaker can become an artisan, executing all the basic production tasks.

The 16mm and digital video formats are customary for small-scale production. Financial backing often comes from the filmmaker, from grants, and perhaps obliging friends and relatives. There is very little division of labor: The filmmaker oversees every production task and will perform many of them. Although technicians or performers may help out, the creative decisions rest with the filmmaker. Experimentalist Maya Deren's *Meshes of the Afternoon,* was shot by her husband, Alexander Hammid, but she scripted, directed, and edited it and performed in the central role **(1.41).**

Such small-scale production is also common in documentary filmmaking. Jean Rouch, a French anthropologist, has made several films alone or with a small crew in his efforts to record the lives of marginal people living in alien cultures. Rouch wrote, directed, and photographed *Les Maîtres fous* (1955), his first widely seen film. Here he examined the ceremonies of a Ghanaian cult whose members lived a double life: Most of the time they worked as low-paid laborers, but in their rituals they passed into a frenzied trance and assumed the identities of their colonial rulers.

Similarly, Barbara Koppel devoted four years to making *Harlan County, U.S.A.,* a record of Kentucky coal miners' struggles for union representation. After eventually obtaining funding from foundations, she and a very small crew spent thirteen months living with miners during the workers' strike. During filming Koppel acted as sound recordist, working with cameraman Hart Perry and sometimes also a lighting person. A large crew was ruled out not only by Koppel's budget but also by the need to fit naturally into the community. Like the miners, the filmmakers were constantly threatened with violence from strikebreakers **(1.42).**

Sometimes small-scale production becomes *collective* production. Here instead of a single filmmaker shaping the project, several film workers participate equally. The group shares common goals and makes production decisions demo-cratically. Roles may also be rotated: The sound recordist one day may serve as cinematographer on the next.

1.42 *Harlan County, U.S.A.:* The driver of a passing truck fires at the crew.

Not surprisingly, the political movements of the late 1960s fostered many ef-forts toward collective film production. In the United States, the Newsreel group was founded in 1967 as an effort to document the student protest movement. News-reel attempted to create not only a collective production situation, with a central coordinating committee answerable to the complete membership, but also a com-munity distribution network that would make Newsreel films available for local ac-tivists around the country. During the late 1960s and early 1970s, the collective produced dozens of works, including *Finally Got the News* and *The Woman's Film.* After the mid-1970s, Newsreel moved somewhat away from purely collective pro-duction, but it retained certain policies characteristic of the collective mode, such as equal pay for all participants in a film. Members of Newsreel such as Robert Kramer, Barbara Koppel, and Christine Choy have gone on to work independently.

A more recent instance of collective production is the Canadian film *Atanarjuat: The Fast Runner.* Three Inuits (Zacharias Kunuk, Paul Apak Angilirq, Paul Qulitalik) and one New Yorker (Norman Cohn) formed Igloolik Isuma Productions in 1990. After making several video shorts and a television series, the group composed a screenplay based on an oral tale about love, murder, and revenge. With funding from television and the National Film Board, cast and crew spent six months shooting in the Arctic, camping in tents and eating seal meat. "We don't have a hierarchy," Cohn explained. "There's no director, second, third or fourth assistant director. We have a team of people trying to figure out how to make this work." Because of the communal nature of Inuit life, the Igloolik team expanded the collective effort by bringing local people into the project. Some had to relearn traditional skills for making tools and clothes from bone, stone, and animal skins. "The Inuit process is very horizontal. We made our film in an Inuit way, through consensus and collaboration." Showcasing the strengths of professional digital Beta video **(1.43),** *Atanarjuat: The Fast Runner* won the prize for best first film at the 2002 Cannes Film Festival. That, said Cohn, con-vinced people "that a bunch of Eskimos from the end of the world could be sophisti-cated enough to make a movie."

Small-scale production allows the filmmakers to retain tight control of the project. Now that video, particularly the digital format, is easily transferred to film, small-scale production will probably become more visible. *The Cruise, The Blair Witch Project, The War Room, Startup.com, Tape, The Gleaners and I,* and other

1.43 The hero of *Atanarjuat: The Fast Runner* pauses in his flight across the ice.

recent releases indicate that the theatrical market has room for works made by single filmmakers or tiny production units.

Implications of Different Modes of Production

We often categorize films on the basis of how they were made. For example, we often distinguish a *documentary* film from a *fiction* film on the basis of production phases. Usually the documentary filmmaker controls only certain variables of preparation, shooting, and assembly. Some variables (such as script, rehearsal) may be omitted, whereas others (such as setting, lighting, behavior of the figures) are present but often uncontrolled. In interviewing an eyewitness to an event, the filmmaker typically controls camera work and editing, but does not tell the witness what to say or how to act. For example, there was no script for the documentary *Manufacturing Consent: Noam Chomsky and the Media;* filmmakers Mark Achbar and Peter Wintonick instead shot long interviews in which Chomsky explained his ideas. The fiction film, on the other hand, is characterized by much more control over script and other aspects of the preparation and shooting phases.

Similarly, a *compilation* film assembles images and sounds that provide historical evidence on a topic. The compilation filmmaker may skip the shooting stage and create a story from archive footage, as in the television series *The World at War* and *Biography.* David Wolper's biography of John Lennon, *Imagine,* was one of the rare compilation films to be released theatrically.

One more kind of film is distinguished by the way it's produced: the **animated** film, which is created frame by frame. Either images are drawn on the film strip itself, or, more often, the camera photographs a series of drawings or three-dimensional models. In either case animation is characterized by unusual production work at the shooting stage.

Production and Authorship
There is another implication of the way movies get made. Who, it is often asked, is the "author," the person responsible for the film? In individual production the author must be the solitary filmmaker—Stan Brakhage, Louis Lumière, yourself. Collective film production creates collective authorship: The author is the entire group. The question of authorship becomes difficult to answer only when asked about large-scale production, particularly in the studio mode.

Studio film production assigns tasks to so many individuals that it is often difficult to determine who controls or decides what. Is the producer the author? In the prime years of the Hollywood system, the producer might have had nothing to do with shooting. The writer? The writer's script might be completely transformed in shooting and editing. So is this situation like collective production, with group authorship? No, because there is a hierarchy in which a few main players make the key decisions.

Moreover, if we consider not only control and decision making but also individual style, it seems certain that some studio workers leave recognizable and unique traces on the films they make. Cinematographers such as Gregg Toland, set designers such as Hermann Warm, costumers such as Edith Head, choreographers such as Gene Kelly—the contributions of these people stand out within the films they made. So where does the studio-produced film leave the idea of authorship?

Most people who study cinema regard the director as the film's "author." Although the writer prepares a screenplay, later phases of production can modify it beyond recognition. And although the producer monitors the entire process, he or she seldom controls moment-by-moment activity on the set. It is the director who makes the crucial decisions about performance, staging, lighting, framing, cutting, and sound. On the whole, the director usually has most control over how a movie looks and sounds.

This doesn't mean that the director is an expert at every job or dictates every detail. The director can delegate tasks to trusted personnel, and directors often work habitually with certain actors, cinematographers, composers, and editors. In the days of studio moviemaking, directors learned how to blend the distinctive talents of cast and crew into the overall movie. Humphrey Bogart's unique talents were used very differently by Michael Curtiz in *Casablanca,* John Huston in *The Maltese Falcon,* and Howard Hawks in *The Big Sleep.* Gregg Toland's cinematography was pushed in different directions by Orson Welles (*Citizen Kane*) and William Wyler (*The Best Years of Our Lives*).

Today, well-established directors can control large-scale production to a remarkable degree. Steven Spielberg and Ethan and Joel Coen can insist on editing manually, not digitally. Both Robert Altman and Martin Scorsese dislike ADR and use much of the on-set dialogue in the finished film. In the days of Hollywood's studio system, some directors exercised power more indirectly. Most studios did not permit the director to supervise editing, but John Ford would often make only one take of each shot. Precutting the film "in his head," Ford virtually forced the editor to put the shots together as he had planned.

Around the world, the director is generally recognized as the key player. In Europe, Asia, and South America, directors frequently initiate the film and work closely with scriptwriters. In Hollywood, directors usually operate on a freelance basis, and the top ones select their own projects. If a production runs into trouble, the production company will seldom fire the director; more often, the producer will get the blame. For the most part, it is the director who shapes the film's unique form and style, and these two components are central to cinema as an art.

NOTES AND QUERIES

The Illusion of Movement

A useful introduction to visual perception is Donald D. Hoffman, *Visual Intelligence: How We Create What We See* (New York: Norton, 1998). A technical treatment of the illusion of movement in film is offered in Julian E. Hochberg, "Representation of Motion and Space in Video and Cinematic Displays," in Kenneth R. Boff, Lloyd Kaufman, and James P. Thomas, eds., *Handbook of Perception and Human Performance,* vol. 1, "Sensory Processes and Perception" (New York: Wiley, 1986), chap. 22. Stuart Liebman uses the perceptual mechanisms of illusion to analyze an experimental film in "Apparent Motion and Film Structure: Paul Sharit's *Shutter Interface,*" *Millennium Film Journal* **1,** 2 (Spring–Summer 1978): 101–109.

The Technical Basis of Cinema

André Bazin suggests that humankind dreamed of cinema long before it actually appeared: "The concept men had of it existed so to speak fully armed in their minds, as if in some platonic heaven" [*What Is Cinema?* vol. 1 (Berkeley: University of California Press, 1967), p. 17]. Still, whatever its antecedents in Greece and the Renaissance, the cinema became technically feasible only in the 19th century.

Motion pictures depended on many discoveries in various scientific and industrial fields: optics and lens making, the control of light (especially by means of arc lamps), chemistry (involving particularly the production of cellulose), steel production, precision machining, and other areas. The cinema machine is closely related to other machines of the period. For example, engineers in the 19th century designed machines that could intermittently unwind, advance, perforate, advance again, and wind up a strip of material at a constant rate. The drive apparatus on cameras and projectors is a late development of a technology that had already made feasible the sewing machine, the telegraph tape, and the machine gun. The 19-century origins of film, based on mechanical and chemical processes, are particularly evident today, since we've become accustomed to electronic and digital media.

On the history of film technology, see Barry Salt's *Film Style and Technology: History and Analysis* (London:

Starword, 1983); David Bordwell, Janet Staiger, and Kristin Thompson's *The Classical Hollywood Cinema: Film Style and Mode of Production to 1960* (New York: Columbia University Press, 1985), parts 4 and 6; many essays in Elisabeth Weis and John Belton, eds., *Film Sound: Theory and Practice* (New York: Columbia University Press, 1985); and Michael Allen's "From *Bwana Devil* to *Batman Forever:* Technology in Contemporary Hollywood Cinema," in Steve Neale and Murray Smith, eds., *Contemporary Hollywood Cinema* (London: Routledge, 1998), pp. 109–129. Primary sources of technological information are included in Raymond Fielding, ed., *A Technological History of Motion Pictures and Television* (Berkeley: University of California Press, 1967). Douglas Gomery has pioneered the economic history of film technology: For a survey, see Robert C. Allen and Douglas Gomery, *Film History: Theory and Practice* (New York: Knopf, 1985). The most comprehensive reference book on the subject is Ira Konigsberg, *The Complete Film Dictionary* (New York: Penguin, 1997). An entertaining appreciation of film technology is Nicholson Baker's "The Projector," in his *The Size of Thoughts* (New York: Vintage, 1994), pp. 36–50.

Film Distribution and Exhibition

For comprehensive surveys of the major "content providers" today, see Benjamin M. Compaine and Douglas Gomery, *Who Owns the Media? Competition and Concentration in the Mass Media Industry* (Mahwah, N.J.: Erlbaum, 2000); Barry R. Litman, *The Motion Picture Mega-Industry* (Boston: Allyn & Bacon, 1998); and Edward S. Herman and Robert W. McChesney, *The Global Media: The New Missionaries of Global Capitalism* (London: Cassell, 1997). Tiiu Lukk examines how *Pulp Fiction, Hoop Dreams, Welcome to the Dollhouse,* and other films were distributed in *Movie Marketing: Opening the Picture and Giving It Legs* (Beverly Hills, Calif.: Silman-James, 1997). Douglas Gomery's *The Hollywood Studio System* (London: Macmillan, 1985) traces the history of today's major distribution companies, showing their roots in vertically integrated studios, which controlled both production and exhibition.

On moviegoing see Bruce A. Austin's *Immediate Seating: A Look at Movie Audiences* (Belmont, Calif.: Wadsworth, 1988). Douglas Gomery's *Shared Pleasures: A History of Moviegoing in America* (Madison: University of Wisconsin Press, 1992) offers a history of U.S. exhibition.

Stages of Film Production

Several how-to-do-it books discuss basic stages and roles of film production. Especially good are Kris Malkiewicz,

Cinematography, 2d ed. (New York: Prentice-Hall, 1989); Steven Ascher and Edward Pincus, *The Filmmaker's Handbook* (New York: Plume, 1999); and Ken Dancyger, *The World of Film and Video Production: Aesthetics and Practices* (New York: Harcourt College, 1999).

There are many informative discussions of the studio mode of production in the United States. See Alexander Brouwer and Thomas Lee Wright, *Working in Hollywood: 64 Film Professionals Talk about Moviemaking* (New York: Crown, 1990); Eric Taub, *Gaffers, Grips, and Best Boys* (New York: St. Martin's, 1987); Paul N. Lazarus III, *Working in Film: The Marketplace in the '90s* (New York: St. Martin's, 1993); and John Morgan Wilson, *Inside Hollywood: A Writer's Guide to Researching the World of Movies and TV* (Cincinnati: Writer's Digest, 1998). More detailed accounts can be found in Jason E. Squire's *The Movie Business Book,* 2d ed. (New York: Simon & Schuster, 1992). A useful reference work is Harvey Rachlin's *TV and Movie Business: An Encyclopedia of Careers, Technologies and Practices* (New York: Crown, 1991).

Entire books are devoted to particular jobs and phases of production. The Focal Press publishes manuals for various specialties, including Pat P. Miller, *Script Supervising and Film Continuity* (1986); Marvin M. Kerner, *The Art of the Sound Effects Editor* (1989); and Dominic Case, *Motion Picture Film Processing* (1985). For the producer, see Paul N. Lazarus III, *The Film Producer* (New York: St. Martin's, 1991) and Lynda Obst's acerbic memoir, *Hello, He Lied* (New York: Broadway, 1996). Art Linson, producer of *The Untouchables* and *Fight Club,* has written two entertaining books about his role: *A Pound of Flesh: Perilous Tales of How to Produce Movies in Hollywood* (New York: Grove, 1993) and *What Just Happened? Bitter Hollywood Tales from the Front Line* (New York: Bloomsbury, 2002). The details of organizing preparation and shooting are explained in Alain Silver and Elizabeth Ward's *The Film Director's Team: A Practical Guide for Production Managers, Assistant Directors, and All Filmmakers* (Los Angeles: Silman-James, 1992). Many "making-of" books include examples of storyboards; see also Steven D. Katz, *Film Directing Shot by Shot* (Studio City, Calif.: Wiese, 1991), John Hart, *The Art of the Storyboard* (Boston: Focal Press, 1999) and Mark Simon *Storyboards: Motion in Art* (Boston: Focal Press, 2000). On setting and production design, see Ward Preston, *What an Art Director Does* (Los Angeles: Silman-James, 1994). Norman Hollyn's *The Film Editing Room Handbook* (Los Angeles: Lone Eagle, 1999) offers a detailed account of image and sound editing procedures. Newer video- and computer-based methods are discussed in Steven E. Browne, *Nonlinear Editing Basics: Electronic Film and Video Editing* (Boston: Focal Press, 1998). The techniques of special effects receive detailed discussion in a richly designed magazine, *Cinefex.*

Several books explain how independent films are financed, produced, and sold. The most wide-ranging are David Rosen and Peter Hamilton, *Off-Hollywood: The Making and Marketing of Independent Films* (New York: Grove Weidenfeld, 1990) and Gregory Goodell, *Independent Feature Film Production: A Complete Guide from Concept through Distribution,* 2d ed. (New York: St. Martin's, 1998). Billy Frolick's *What I Really Want to Do Is Direct* (New York: Plume, 1997) follows seven film-school graduates trying to make low-budget features. Christine Vachon, producer of *Boys Don't Cry* and *Far from Heaven,* shares her insights in *Shooting to Kill* (New York: Avon, 1998).

In *How I Made a Hundred Movies in Hollywood and Never Lost a Dime* (New York: Random House, 1990), Roger Corman reviews his career in exploitation cinema. A sample passage: "In the first half of 1957 I capitalized on the sensational headlines following the Russians' launch of their Sputnik satellite. . . . I shot *War of the Satellites* in a little under ten days. No one even knew what the satellite was supposed to look like. It was whatever I said it should look like" (pp. 44–45). Corman also supplies the introduction to Lloyd Kaufman's *All I Needed to Know about Filmmaking I Learned from the Toxic Avenger: The Shocking True Story of Troma Studios* (New York: Berkley, 1998), which details the making of such Troma classics as *The Class of Nuke 'Em High* and *Chopper Chicks in Zombietown.* See as well the interviews collected in Philip Gaines and David J. Rhodes, *Micro-Budget Hollywood: Budgeting (and Making) Feature Films for $50,000 to $500,000* (Los Angeles: Silman-James, 1995).

John Pierson, a producer, distributor, and festival scout, traces how *Clerks; She's Gotta Have It; sex, lies, and videotape;* and other low-budget films found success in *Spike, Mike, Slackers, and Dykes* (New York: Hyperion, 1995). Emanuel Levy's *Cinema of Outsiders: The Rise of American Independent Film* (New York: New York University Press, 1999) provides a historical survey. The early history of an important distributor of independent films, Miramax, is examined in Alissa Perren, "sex, lies and marketing: Miramax and the Development of the Quality Indie Blockbuster," *Film Quarterly* **55** 2 (Winter 2001–2002): 30–39.

We can learn a great deal about production from careful case studies. See Rudy Behlmer, *America's Favorite Movies: Behind the Scenes* (New York: Ungar, 1982); Aljean Harmetz, *The Making of "The Wizard of Oz"* (New York: Limelight, 1984); John Sayles, *Thinking in Pictures: The Making of the Movie "Matewan"* (Boston: Houghton Mifflin, 1987); Ronald Haver, *"A Star Is Born": The Making of the 1954 Movie and Its 1985 Restoration* (New York: Knopf, 1988); Stephen Rebello, *Alfred Hitchcock and the Making of "Psycho"* (New York: Dembuer, 1990); Paul M. Sammon, *Future Noir: The Making of "Blade Runner"* (New York: HarperPrism, 1996); and Dan Auiler, *"Vertigo": The Making of a Hitchcock Classic* (New York: St. Martin's, 1998). John Gregory Dunne's *Monster: Living Off the Big Screen* (New York: Vintage, 1997) is a memoir of eight years spent rewriting the script that became *Up Close and Personal.* Many of Spike Lee's productions have been documented with published journals and production notes; see, for example, *"Do The Right Thing": A Spike Lee Joint* (New York: Simon & Schuster, 1989). For the independent scene, Vachon's *Shooting to Kill,* mentioned above, documents the making of Todd Haynes's *Velvet Goldmine.*

Directors Speak

Collections of interviews with filmmakers have become common in recent decades. We will mention interviews with designers, cinematographers, editors, sound technicians, and others in the chapters on individual film techniques. The director, however, supervises the entire process of filmmaking, so we list here some of the best interview books: Peter Bogdanovich, *Who the Devil Made It* (New York: Knopf, 1997); Mike Goodrich, *Directing* (Crans-Prés-Céligny, 2002); Jeremy Kagan, *Directors Close Up* (Boston: Focal Press, 2000); Andrew Sarris, ed., *Interviews with Film Directors* (Indianapolis: Bobbs-Merrill, 1967); Eric Sherman, *Directing the Film: Film Directors on Their Art* (Boston: Little, Brown, 1976); Laurent Tirard, *Moviemakers' Master Class: Private Lessons from the World's Foremost Directors* (New York: Faber and Faber, 2002). Since 1992, Faber and Faber (London) has published an annual collection of interviews called *Projections.* Two important Hollywood directors have written books on their craft: Edward Dmytryk's *On Screen Directing* (Boston: Focal Press, 1984) and Sidney Lumet's *Making Movies* (New York: Knopf, 1995).

Screenwriting and Rules

In mass-production filmmaking the screenwriter is expected to follow traditional storytelling patterns. For several decades, Hollywood has called for scripts about strong central characters who struggle to achieve well-defined goals. According to most experts, a script ought to have a three-act structure, with the first-act climax coming about a quarter of the way into the film, the second-act climax appearing about three-quarters of the way through, and the climax of the final act resolving the protagonist's problem.

Writers will also be expected to include *plot points,* twists that turn the action in new directions.

These formulas are discussed in Syd Field, *Screenplay: The Foundations of Screenwriting* (New York: Delta, 1979); Linda Seger, *Making a Good Script Great* (New York: Dodd, Mead, 1987); and Michael Hauge, *Writing Screenplays That Sell* (New York: HarperCollins, 1988). Kristin Thompson has argued that many finished films have not three but four major parts, depending on how the protagonist defines and changes important goals. See her *Storytelling in the New Hollywood: Understanding Classical Narrative Technique* (Cambridge, Mass.: Harvard University Press, 1999). Older but still useful books on screenwriting are Eugene Vale, *The Technique of Screenplay Writing* (New York: Grosset & Dunlap, 1972) and Lewis Herman, *A Practical Manual of Screen Playwriting for Theater and Television Films* (New York: New American Library, 1974). Pat McGilligan has collected reminiscences of screenwriters in a series of interview books called *Backstory,* from the University of California Press. A historical overview is Tom Stempel, *FrameWork: A History of Screenwriting in the American Film* (New York: Continuum, 1988).

Small-Scale Production

There are few studies of artisanal and collective film production, but here are some informative works. On Jean Rouch, see Mick Eaton, ed., *Anthropology—Reality—Cinema: The Films of Jean Rouch* (London: British Film Institute, 1979). The makers of *Harlan County, U.S.A.* and other independent documentaries discuss their production methods in Alan Rosenthal, *The Documentary Conscience: A Casebook in Film Making* (Berkeley: University of California Press, 1980). Maya Deren's work is analyzed in P. Adams Sitney, *Visionary Film: The American Avant-Garde, 1943–1978,* 2d ed. (New York: Oxford University Press, 1979). Stan Brakhage ruminates on his approach to filmmaking in *Brakhage Scrapbook: Collected Writings* (New Paltz, N.Y.: Documentext, 1982). For information on other experimentalists, see Scott MacDonald, *A Critical Cinema: Interviews with Independent Filmmakers* (Berkeley: University of California Press, 1988) and David E. James, *Allegories of Cinema: American Film in the Sixties* (Princeton, N.J.: Princeton University Press, 1989).

Collective film production is the subject of Bill Nichols, *Newsreel: Documentary Filmmaking on the American Left* (New York: Arno, 1980) and Michael Renov, "Newsreel: Old and New—Towards an Historical Profile," *Film Quarterly* **41** 1 (Fall 1987): 20–33. Collective production in film and other media is discussed in John Downing, *Radical Media: The Political Experience of Alternative Communication* (Boston: South End Press, 1984).

Production Stills versus Frame Enlargements

A film may live in our memory as much through photographs as through our experiences of the movie. The photograph may be a copy of a single frame taken from the finished film; this is usually called a *frame enlargement.* Most movie photographs we see in books and magazines, however, are *production stills,* images shot by a still photographer on the set.

Production stills are usually photographically clearer than frame enlargements, and they can be useful for studying details of setting or costume. But they differ from the image on the film strip. Usually the still photographer rearranges and relights the actors and takes the shot from an angle and distance not comparable to that shown in the finished film. Frame enlargements therefore offer a much more faithful record of the finished film.

For example, both **1.44** and **1.45** have been used to illustrate discussion of Jean Renoir's *Rules of the Game.* In 1.44, a production still, the actors have been posed for the most balanced composition and the clearest view of all three. It is not, however, faithful to the finished film. The

1.44   A production still from Renoir's *The Rules of the Game.*

1.45   A frame from *The Rules of the Game.*

actual shot from the film is shown in 1.45. The frame enlargement shows that the composition is looser than that of the production still. The frame enlargement also reveals that Renoir uses the central doorway to suggest action taking place in depth. Here, as often happens, a production still does not capture important features of the director's visual style.

Virtually all of the photographs in this book are frame enlargements.

Film and Video

Detailed comparisons of film and digital video as media can be found in Scott Billups, *Digital Moviemaking: The Filmmaker's Guide to the 21st Century* (Studio City, Calif.: Wiese, 2000); Maxie D. Collier, *The ifilm Digital Video Filmmaker's Handbook,* ed. Scott Smith (Hollywood: Lone Eagle, 2001); Ben Long and Sonja Schenk, *The Digital Filmmaking Handbook,* 2nd ed. (Hingham, Mass.: Charles River Media, 2002); and Drew Campbell, *Technical Film and TV for Nontechnical People* (New York: Allworth, 2002). Three contemporary filmmakers discuss the relation of cinema to video in Roger Ebert and Gene Siskel, *The Future of the Movies: Interviews with Martin Scorsese, Steven Spielberg, and George Lucas* (Kansas City, Mo.: Andrews and McMeel, 1991).

On using video to help plan shots during production, the Polish director Andrzej Wajda remarks, "For a director who has grown up with and been formed by film, video is a technique that offers no resistance. The lighting is always sufficient, the camera movement incredibly light and facile—too facile—and what is more, if you don't like what you just did you can simply erase it and start again from scratch. . . . This means you work without tension, without the familiar atmosphere of being on the edge, constantly at risk. The problem, of course, is that that tension, that sense of risk, is precisely what characterizes the work in a good film" [Wajda, *Double Vision: My Life in Film,* trans. Rose Medina (New York: Holt, 1989), pp. 43–44].

The boundaries between cinema and video have long been blurred. Steven Spielberg began his career directing for television and returned years later with *Amazing Stories.* David Lynch made the series *Twin Peaks* for network television, while Spike Lee, Martin Scorsese, and John Woo direct commercials and MTV clips. David Fincher (*Se7en*), Michael Bay (*Pearl Harbor*), and Spike Jonze (*Being John Malkovich*) began in music video. On the relation between the U.S. film industry and television, see Tino Balio, ed., *Hollywood in the Age of Television* (Boston: Unwin Hyman, 1990).

PART TWO

Film Form

Chapter 1 outlined some ways in which people, working with technology, make films. Now we can get a little more abstract and ask other questions. By what principles is a film put together? How do the various parts relate to one another to create a whole? Answering these questions will help us understand how we respond to individual movies and how cinema works as an artistic medium.

In the next two chapters we will start to answer such aesthetic questions. We assume that a film is not a random collection of elements. If it were, viewers would not care if they missed the beginnings or endings of films or if films were projected out of sequence. But viewers do care. When you describe a book as "hard to put down" or a piece of music as

"absorbing," you are implying that a pattern exists there, that an internal system governs the relations among parts and engages your interest. This system of relationships among parts we shall call *form.* Chapter 2 examines form in film to see what makes that concept so important to the understanding of cinema as an art.

Although there are several ways of organizing films into unified formal wholes, the one that we most commonly encounter in commercial feature films involves telling a story. Chapter 3 examines how *narrative form* can arouse our interest and coax us to follow a series of events from start to finish. Narrative form holds out the expectation that these events are headed toward dramatic changes and a satisfying outcome.

Chapter 2

The Significance of Film Form

If you are listening closely to a song on a CD and the music is abruptly switched off, you are likely to feel a little frustrated. If you start reading a novel, become engrossed in it, and then misplace the book, you will probably feel the same way.

Such feelings arise because our experience of artworks is patterned and structured. The human mind craves form. For this reason, form is of central importance in any artwork, regardless of its medium. The entire study of the nature of artistic form is the province of the aesthetician, and it is too large a question for us to deal with extensively here. (See the first part of the Notes and Queries to this chapter for pertinent readings.) But some ideas about aesthetic form are indispensable in analyzing films.

Form as System

Artistic form is best thought of in relation to a perceiver, the human being who watches the play, reads the novel, listens to the piece of music, or views the film. Perception in all phases of life is an *activity*. As you walk down the street, you scan your surroundings for salient aspects—a friend's face, a familiar landmark, a sign of rain. The mind is never at rest. It is constantly seeking order and significance, testing the world for breaks in the habitual pattern.

Artworks rely on this dynamic, unifying quality of the human mind. They provide organized occasions in which we exercise and develop our ability to pay attention, to anticipate upcoming events, to draw conclusions, and to construct a whole out of parts. Every novel leaves something to the imagination; every song asks us to expect certain developments in the melody; every film coaxes us to connect sequences into a larger whole. But how does this process work? How does an inert object, the poem on a piece of paper or the sculpture in the park, draw us into such activities?

Some answers to this question are clearly inadequate. Our activity cannot be *in* the artwork itself. A poem is only words on paper; a song, just acoustic vibrations; a film, merely patterns of light and dark on a screen. Objects do nothing. Evidently, then, the artwork and the person experiencing it depend on one another.

The best answer to our question would seem to be that the artwork *cues* us to perform a specific activity. Without the artwork's prompting, we could not start the process or keep it going. Without our playing along and picking up the cues, the artwork remains only an artifact. A painting uses color, line, and other techniques to invite us to imagine the space portrayed, to compare color and texture, to run our eye over the composition in a certain direction. A poem's words may guide us to imagine a scene, to notice a break in rhythm, or to expect a rhyme. A sculpture's shape, volume, and materials prompt us to move around it, noticing how its mass fills the space it occupies. In general, any work of art presents cues that can elicit a particular activity from the perceiver.

We can go further in describing how an artwork cues us to perform activities. These cues are not simply random; they are organized into *systems*. Let us take a system as any set of elements that depend on and affect one another. The human body is one such system; if one compartment, the heart, ceases to function, all of the other parts will be in danger. Within the body there are individual, smaller, systems, such as the nervous system or the optical system. A single small malfunction in a car's workings may bring the whole machine to a standstill; the other parts may not need repair, but the whole system depends on the operation of each part. More abstract sets of relationships also constitute systems, such as a body of laws governing a country or the ecological balance of the wildlife in a lake.

As with each of these instances, a film is not simply a random batch of elements. Like all artworks, a film has **form.** By film form, in its broadest sense, we mean the overall system of relations that we can perceive among the elements in the whole film. In this part of the book and in Part Four (on film style), we shall be surveying the sorts of elements a film may possess. Since the viewer makes sense of the film by recognizing these elements and reacting to them in various ways, we shall also be considering how form and style participate in the spectator's experience.

This description of form is still very abstract, so let us draw some examples from one film that many people have seen. In *The Wizard of Oz* the perceiver can notice many particular elements. There is, most obviously, a set of *narrative* elements. These constitute the film's story. Dorothy dreams that a tornado blows her to Oz, where she encounters certain characters. The narrative continues to the point where Dorothy awakens from her dream to find herself home in Kansas. We can also pick out a set of *stylistic* elements: the way the camera moves, the patterns of color in the frame, the use of music, and other devices. Stylistic elements depend on the various film techniques we will be considering in later chapters.

Because *The Wizard of Oz* is a system and not just a hodgepodge, the perceiver actively relates the elements within each set to one another. We link and compare narrative elements. We see the tornado as causing Dorothy's trip to Oz; we identify the characters in Oz as similar to characters in Dorothy's Kansas life. Various stylistic elements can also be connected. For instance, we recognize the "We're Off to See the Wizard" tune whenever Dorothy picks up a new companion. We attribute unity to the film by positing two subsystems—a narrative one and a stylistic one—within the larger system of the total film.

Moreover, our minds seek to tie these subsystems to one another. In *The Wizard of Oz,* the narrative subsystem can be linked to the stylistic subsystem. Film colors identify prominent landmarks, such as Kansas (in black and white) and the Yellow Brick Road. Movements of the camera call our attention to story action. And the music serves to describe certain characters and actions. It is the overall pattern of relationships among the various elements that makes up the form of *The Wizard of Oz.*

"SCREENPLAYS ARE STRUCTURE."

— William Goldman (scriptwriter, *Butch Cassidy and the Sundance Kid*)

"Because of my character, I have always been interested in the *engineering* of direction. I loved hearing about how [director] Mark Sandrich would draw charts of Fred Astaire's musicals to work out where to put the dance numbers. What do you want the audience to understand? How do you make things clear? How do you structure sequences within a film? Afterwards—what have you got away with?"

— Stephen Frears, director

"Form versus Content"

Very often people assume that "form" as a concept is the opposite of something called "content." This assumption implies that a poem or a musical piece or a film is like a jug. An external shape, the jug, *contains* something that could just as easily be held in a cup or a pail. Under this assumption, form becomes less important than whatever it is presumed to contain.

We do not accept this assumption. If form is the total system which the viewer attributes to the film, there is no inside or outside. Every component *functions as part of the overall pattern* that is perceived. Thus we shall treat as formal elements many things that some people consider content. From our standpoint, subject matter and abstract ideas all enter into the total system of the artwork. They may cue us to frame certain expectations or draw certain inferences. The perceiver relates such elements to one another dynamically. Consequently, subject matter and ideas become somewhat different from what they might be outside the work.

For example, consider a historical subject, such as the United States Civil War. The real Civil War may be studied, its causes and consequences disputed. But in a film such as D. W. Griffith's *The Birth of a Nation,* the Civil War is not neutral content. It enters into relationships with other elements: a story about two families, political ideas about Reconstruction, and the epic film style of the battle scenes. Griffith's film depicts the Civil War in a way that is coordinated with other elements in the film. A different film by another filmmaker might draw on the same subject matter, the Civil War, but there the subject would play a different role in a different formal system. In *Gone with the Wind* the Civil War functions as a backdrop for the heroine's romance, but in *The Good, the Bad, and the Ugly* the war aids three cynical men in their search for gold. Thus subject matter is shaped by the film's formal context and our perceptions of it.

Formal Expectations

We are now in a better position to see how film form guides the audience's activity. Why does an interrupted song or an uncompleted story frustrate us? Because of our urge for form. We realize that the system of relationships within the work has not yet been completed. Something more is needed to make the form whole and satisfying. We have been caught up in the interrelations among elements, and in the absence of cues we cannot develop and complete the patterns.

One way in which form affects our experience, then, is to create the sense that "everything is there." Why is it satisfying when a character glimpsed early in a film reappears an hour later or when a shape in the frame is balanced by another shape? Because such relations among parts suggest that the film has its own organizing laws or rules—its own system.

Moreover, an artwork's form creates a special sort of involvement on the part of the spectator. In everyday life, we perceive things around us in a practical way. But in a film the things that happen on the screen serve no such practical end for us. We can see them differently. In life if someone fell down on the street, we would probably hurry to help the person up. But in a film when Buster Keaton or Charlie Chaplin falls, we laugh. We shall see in Chapter 7 how even as basic an act of filmmaking as framing a shot creates a particular way of seeing. We watch a pattern that is no longer just "out there" in the everyday world but that has become a calculated part within a self-contained whole. Film form can even make us perceive things anew, shaking us out of our accustomed habits and suggesting fresh ways of hearing, seeing, feeling, and thinking.

To get a sense of the ways in which purely formal features can involve the audience, try the following experiment. Assume that "A" is the first letter of a series. What follows?

AB

"A" was a cue, and on this basis you made a formal hypothesis, probably that the letters would run in alphabetical order. Your expectation was confirmed. What follows AB? Most people say "C." But form does not always follow our initial expectation.

ABA

Here form takes us by surprise, puzzles us. If we are puzzled by a formal development, we readjust our expectations and try again. What follows ABA?

ABAC

Here the possibilities were chiefly two: ABAB or ABAC. (Note that your expectations *limit* possibilities as well as select them.) If you expected ABAC, your expectation was gratified and you can confidently predict the next letter. If you expected ABAB, you still should be able to make a strong hypothesis about the next letter.

ABACA

Simple as this game is, it illustrates the involving power of form. You as a viewer or listener don't simply let the parts parade past you. You enter into an active participation with them, creating and readjusting expectations as the pattern develops.

Now consider a story in a film. *The Wizard of Oz* begins with Dorothy clutching a dog and running down a road **(2.1).** Immediately we form expectations. Perhaps she will meet another character or arrive at her destination. Even such a simple action asks that the audience participate actively in the ongoing process by making certain hypotheses about "what will happen next" and readjusting expectations accordingly. Eventually we come to expect that Dorothy will get her wish to return to Kansas. Indeed, the settings of the film give *The Wizard of Oz* a large-scale ABA form: Kansas-Oz-Kansas.

2.1 Dorothy pauses while fleeing with Toto at the beginning of *The Wizard of Oz.*

Expectation pervades our experience of art. In reading a mystery story, we expect that a solution will be offered at some point, usually the end. In listening to a piece of music, we expect repetition of a melody or a motif. (Many songs that alternate verses and refrain follow the ABACA pattern we have just outlined.) In looking at a painting, we search for what we expect to be the most significant features, then scan the less prominent portions. From beginning to end, our involvement with a work of art depends largely on expectations.

This does not mean that the expectations must be immediately satisfied. The satisfaction of our expectations may be delayed. In our alphabet exercise, instead of presenting ABA we might have presented this:

AB . . .

The ellipsis the revelation of the next letter, and you must wait to find it out. What we normally call *suspense* involves a delay in fulfilling an established expectation. As the term implies, suspense leaves something suspended—not only the next element in a pattern but also our urge for completion.

Expectations may also be cheated, as when we expect ABC but get ABA. In general, *surprise* is a result of an expectation that is revealed to be incorrect. We do not expect that a gangster in 1930s Chicago will find a rocket ship in his garage; if he does, our reaction may require us to readjust our assumptions about what can happen in this story. (This example suggests that comedy often depends on cheating expectations.)

One more pattern of our expectations needs tracing. Sometimes an artwork will cue us to hazard guesses about what has come *before* this point in the work. When Dorothy runs down the road at the beginning of *The Wizard of Oz,* we wonder not only where she is going but where she has been and what she is fleeing from. Similarly, a painting or photograph may depict a scene that asks the viewer to speculate on some earlier event. Let us call this ability of the spectator to frame hypotheses about prior events *curiosity.* As Chapter 3 will show, curiosity is an important factor in narrative form.

Already we have several possible ways in which the artwork can actively engage us. Artistic form may cue us to make expectations and then gratify them, either quickly or eventually. Or form may work to disturb our expectations. We often associate art with peace and serenity, but many artworks offer us conflict, tension, and shock. An artwork's form may even strike us as unpleasant because of its imbalances or contradictions. Many people find atonal music, abstract or surrealist painting, and experimental writing highly disturbing. Similarly, experimental films may jar rather than soothe us. Viewers frequently feel puzzled or shocked by *Eat, Scorpio Rising,* and other avant-garde works (pp. 146–147). And we shall encounter similar problems when we examine the editing of Eisenstein's *October* (Chapter 8) and the style of Godard's *Breathless* (Chapter 11).

Yet even in disturbing us, such films still arouse and shape formal expectations. For example, on the basis of our experience of most movie stories, we expect that the main characters introduced in the first half of a film will be present in the second half. Yet this does not happen in Wong Kar-wai's *Chungking Express.* When our expectations are thwarted, we may feel disoriented for a time, but then we adjust them to look for other, more appropriate, ways of understanding the film's form.

If we can adjust our expectations to a disorienting work, it may involve us deeply. Our uneasiness may lessen as we get accustomed to a work's unusual formal system. Hollis Frampton's *Zorns Lemma,* for example, slowly trains the viewer to associate a series of images with the letters of the alphabet. Viewers often become quite absorbed in watching the series take shape as a cinematic picture puzzle.

As *Chungking Express* and *Zorns Lemma* also suggest, a disturbing work can reveal to us our normal expectations about form. Such films are valuable because they coax us to reflect on our taken-for-granted assumptions about how a movie must behave.

There is no limit to the number of ways in which a film can be organized. Some films will ask us to recast our expectations in drastic ways. Still, our enjoyment of the cinema can increase if we welcome the unfamiliar experiences offered by formally challenging films.

Conventions and Experience

Our ABAC example illustrates still another point. One guide to your hunches was *prior experience.* Your knowledge of the English alphabet makes ABA an unlikely sequence. This fact suggests that aesthetic form is not a pure activity isolated from other experiences.

Precisely because artworks are human artifacts and because the artist lives in history and society, he or she cannot avoid relating the work, in some way, to other works and to aspects of the world in general. A tradition, a dominant style, a popular form—some such elements will be common to several different artworks. These common traits are usually called *conventions. Genres,* as we shall see in Chapter 4, depend heavily on conventions. It is a convention of the musical film that characters sing and dance, as in *The Wizard of Oz.* It is one convention of narrative form that the conclusion solves the problems that the characters confront, and *Wizard* likewise accepts this convention by letting Dorothy return to Kansas. Bodies of conventions constitute *norms* of what is appropriate or expected in a particular tradition. Through obeying or violating norms, artists relate their works to other works.

From the spectator's standpoint, the perception of artistic form will arise from cues within the work and from prior experiences—experiences derived from everyday life and from other artworks. You were able to play the ABAC game because you had learned the alphabet. You may have learned it in everyday life (in a classroom, from your parents) or from an artwork (as some children now learn the alphabet from television cartoons). Similarly, we are able to recognize the "journey" pattern in *The Wizard of Oz* because we have taken trips and because we have seen other films organized around this pattern (such as *Stagecoach* or *North by Northwest*) and because the pattern is to be found in other artworks, such as Homer's *Odyssey* or J. R. R. Tolkien's *The Lord of the Rings*. Our ability to spot cues, to see them as forming systems, and to create expectations is guided by our real-life experiences and our knowledge of formal conventions.

In recognizing film form, then, the audience must be prepared to understand formal cues through knowledge of life and of other artworks. But what if the two principles come into conflict? In ordinary life people don't simply start to sing and dance, as they do in *The Wizard of Oz*. Very often conventions demarcate art from life, saying implicitly, "In artworks of this sort the laws of everyday reality don't operate. By the rules of *this* game, something 'unreal' *can* happen." All stylized art, from opera, ballet, and pantomime to slapstick comedy, depends on the audience's willingness to suspend the laws of ordinary experience and to accept particular conventions. It is simply beside the point to insist that such conventions are unreal or to ask why Tristan sings to Isolde or why Buster Keaton doesn't smile. Very often the most relevant prior experience for perceiving form is not everyday experience but previous encounters with works having similar conventions.

Further, artworks can create new conventions. A highly innovative work can at first seem odd because it refuses to conform to the norms we expect. Cubist painting, twelve-tone music, and the French "New Novel" of the 1950s seemed bizarre initially because of their refusal to adhere to conventions. But a closer look may show that an unusual artwork has its own rules, creating an unorthodox formal system that we can learn to recognize and respond to. Eventually, the new systems offered by such unusual works may themselves furnish conventions and thus create new expectations.

Form and Feeling

Certainly emotion plays a large role in our experience of form. To understand this role, let us distinguish between *emotions represented in* the artwork and an *emotional response felt by* the spectator. If an actor grimaces in agony, the emotion of pain is represented within the film. If, on the other hand, the viewer who sees the painful expression laughs (as the viewer of a comedy might), the emotion of amusement is felt by the spectator. Both types of emotion have formal implications.

Emotions represented within the film interact as parts of the film's total system. For example, that grimace of pain might be consistent with the character's response to bad news. A character's sly expression may prepare us for the later revelation of his or her villainous side. Or a cheerful scene might stand in contrast to a mournful one. A tragic event might be undercut by light-hearted music. All emotions present in a film may be seen as systematically related to one another through that film's form.

"To a story-teller a journey is a marvelous device. It provides a strong thread on which a multitude of things that he has in mind may be strung to make a new thing, various, unpredictable, and yet coherent. My chief reason for using this form was technical."

— J. R. R. Tolkien

"If my film makes one more person feel miserable, I'll feel I've done my job."

— Woody Allen

The spectator's emotional response to the film is related to form as well. We have just seen how cues in the artwork interact with our prior experience, especially our experience of artistic conventions. Often form in artworks appeals to ready-made reactions to certain images (for example, involving sexuality, race, social class). But form can create new responses instead of harping on old ones. Just as formal conventions often lead us to suspend our normal sense of real-life experience, so form may lead us to override our everyday emotional responses. People whom we would despise in life may become spellbinding as characters in a film. We can be enthralled by a film about a subject that normally bores us. One cause of these experiences lies in the systematic way we become involved in form. In *The Wizard of Oz* we might, for example, find the land of Oz far more attractive than Kansas. But because the film's form leads us to sympathize with Dorothy in her desire to go home, we feel great satisfaction when she finally returns to Kansas.

It is first and foremost the dynamic aspect of form that engages our feelings. Expectation, for instance, spurs emotion. To have an expectation about "what happens next" is to invest some emotion in the situation. Delayed fulfillment of an expectation—suspense—may produce anxiety or sympathy. (Will the detective find the criminal? Will boy get girl? Will the melody return?) Gratified expectations may produce a feeling of satisfaction or relief. (The detective solves the mystery, boy does get girl, the melody returns one more time.) Cheated expectations and curiosity about past material may produce puzzlement or keener interest. (So he isn't the detective? This isn't a romance story? Has a second melody replaced the first one?)

Note that all of these possibilities *may* occur. There is no general recipe by which a novel or film can be concocted to produce the "correct" emotional response. It is all a matter of context—that is, of the particular system that is each artwork's overall form. All we can say for certain is that the emotion felt by the spectator will emerge from the totality of formal relationships she or he perceives in the work. This is one reason why we should try to notice as many formal relations as possible in a film; the richer our perception, the deeper and more complex our response may become.

Taken in context, the relations between the feelings represented in the film and those felt by the spectator can be quite complicated. Let us take an example. Many people believe that no more sorrowful event can occur than the death of a child. In most films this event would be represented so as to summon up the sadness we would also feel in life. But the power of artistic form can alter the emotional tenor of even this event. In Jean Renoir's *The Crime of M. Lange* the cynical publisher Batala rapes and abandons Estelle, a young laundress. After Batala disappears, Estelle becomes integrated into the courtyard community and returns to her former fiancé. But Estelle is pregnant by Batala and bears his child. The scene when Estelle's employer, Valentine, announces that the child was born dead is one of the most emotionally complex in cinema. The first reactions represented are solemnity and sorrow; the characters display grief. Suddenly Batala's cousin remarks, "Too bad. It was a relative." In the film's context this is taken as a joke, and the other characters break out in smiles and laughter. The shift in the emotion represented in the film catches us off guard. Since these characters are not heartless, we must readjust our reaction to the death and respond as they do—with relief. Estelle's survival is far more important than the death of Batala's child. The film's formal development has rendered appropriate a reaction that might be perverse in ordinary life. This is a daring, extreme example, but it dramatically illustrates how both emotions onscreen and our responses depend on the context created by form.

Form and Meaning

Like emotion, **meaning** is important to our experience of artworks. As an active perceiver, the spectator is constantly testing the work for larger significance, for what it says or suggests. The sorts of meanings that the spectator attributes to the work may vary considerably. Let us look at four things we might say about the meaning of *The Wizard of Oz.*

1. *Referential meaning. In the Depression, a tornado takes a girl from her family's Kansas farm to the mythical land of Oz. After a series of adventures, she returns home.*

This is very concrete, close to a bare-bones plot summary. Here the meaning depends on the spectator's ability to identify specific items: the American Depression of the 1930s, the state of Kansas, features of Midwestern climate. A viewer unacquainted with such information would miss some of the meanings cued by the film. We can call such tangible meanings *referential,* since the film refers to things or places already invested with significance.

A film's subject matter—in *The Wizard of Oz,* American farm life in the 1930s—is often established through referential meaning. And, as one would expect, referential meaning functions within the film's overall form, in the way that we have argued that the subject of the Civil War functions within *The Birth of a Nation.* Suppose that instead of having Dorothy live in flat, spare, rural Kansas, the film made Dorothy a child living in Beverly Hills. When she got to Oz (transported there, perhaps, by a hillside flash flood), the contrast between the crowded opulence of Oz and her home would not be nearly as sharp. Here the referential meanings of Kansas play a definite role in the overall contrast of settings that the film's form creates.

2. *Explicit meaning. A girl dreams of leaving home to escape her troubles. Only after she leaves does she realize how much she loves her family and friends.*

This assertion is still fairly concrete in the meaning it attributes to the film. If someone were to ask you the point of the film—what it seems to be trying to get across—you might answer with something like this. Perhaps you would also mention Dorothy's closing line, "There's no place like home," as a summary of what she learns. Let us call this sort of openly asserted meaning an *explicit meaning.*

Like referential meanings, explicit meanings function within the film's overall form. They are defined by context. For instance, we might want to take "There's no place like home" as a statement of the meaning of the entire film. But, first, *why* do we feel that as a strongly meaningful line? In ordinary conversation it is a cliché. In context, however, the line is uttered in close-up, it comes at the end of the film (a formally privileged moment), and it refers back to all of Dorothy's desires and ordeals, recalling the film's narrative development toward the achievement of her goal. It is the *form* of the film that gives the homily an unfamiliar weight.

This example suggests that we must examine how explicit meanings in a film interact with other elements of the overall system. If "There's no place like home" adequately and exhaustively summarizes the meaning of *The Wizard of Oz,* no one need ever see the film; the summary would suffice. But like feelings, meanings are formal entities. They play a part along with other elements to make up the total system.

Usually we cannot isolate a particularly significant moment and declare it to be *the* meaning of the whole film. Even Dorothy's "There's no place like home," however strong as a summary of *one* meaningful element in *The Wizard of Oz,* must be placed in the context of the film's entire beguiling Oz fantasy. If "There's no place like home" were the whole point of the film, why is there so much that is pleasant in Oz? The explicit meanings of a film arise from the *whole* film and are set in dynamic formal relation to one another.

In trying to see the meaningful moments of a film as parts of a larger whole, it is useful to set individually significant moments against one another. Thus Dorothy's final line could be juxtaposed to the scene of the characters getting spruced up after their arrival at the Emerald City. We can try to see the film as not about one or the other but rather about the relation of the two—the risk and delight of a fantasy world versus the comfort and stability of home. Thus the film's total system will be larger than any one explicit meaning we can find in it. Instead of asking, "What is this film's meaning?" we can ask, "How do *all* the film's meanings interrelate formally?"

3. ***Implicit meaning.*** *An adolescent who must soon face the adult world yearns for a return to the simple world of childhood, but she eventually accepts the demands of growing up.*

This is considerably more abstract than the first two statements. It assumes something that goes beyond what is explicitly stated in the film: that *The Wizard of Oz* is in some sense about the passage from childhood to adulthood. In this view, the film suggests or implies that, in adolescence, people may desire to return to the apparently uncomplicated world of childhood. Dorothy's frustration with her aunt and uncle and her urge to flee to a place "over the rainbow" become examples of a general conception of adolescence. Let us call this suggestion an *implicit meaning.* When perceivers ascribe implicit meanings to an artwork, they are usually said to be *interpreting* it.

Clearly, **interpretations** vary. One viewer might propose that *The Wizard of Oz* is really about adolescence. Another might suggest that it is really about courage and persistence or that it is a satire on the adult world. One of the appeals of artworks is that they seem to ask us to interpret them, often in several ways at once. Again, the artwork cues the spectator to perform certain activities—here, building up implicit meanings. But once again the artwork's overall form shapes the viewer's sense of implicit meanings.

Some viewers approach a film expecting to learn lessons about life. They may admire a film because it conveys a profound or relevant message. Important as meaning is, though, this attitude often errs by splitting the film into the content portion (the meaning) and the form (the vehicle for the content). The abstract quality of implicit meanings can lead to very broad concepts often called *themes.* A film may have as its theme courage or the power of faithful love. Such descriptions have some value, but they are very general; hundreds of films fit them. To summarize *The Wizard of Oz* as being simply about the problems of adolescence does not do justice to the specific qualities of the film as an experience. We suggest that the search for implicit meanings should not leave behind the *particular* and *concrete* features of a film.

This is not to say that we should not interpret films. But we should strive to make our interpretations precise by seeing how each film's thematic meanings are suggested by the film's total system. In a film, both explicit and implicit meanings depend closely on the relations between narrative and style. In *The Wizard of Oz,* the Yellow Brick Road has no meaning in and of itself. But if we examine the function it fulfills in relation to the narrative, the music, the colors, and so on, we can argue that the Yellow Brick Road does indeed function meaningfully. Dorothy's strong desire to go home makes the Road represent that desire. We want Dorothy to be successful in getting to the end of the Road, as well as in getting back to Kansas; thus the Road participates in the theme of the desirability of home.

Interpretation need not be an end in itself. It also helps in understanding the overall form of the film. Nor does interpretation exhaust the possibilities of a device. We can say many things about the Yellow Brick Road other than how its meaning relates to the film's thematic material. We could analyze how the Road becomes the stage for dances and songs along the way. We could see how it is narratively important because an indecision at a crossroads allows Dorothy to meet the Scarecrow. We could work out a color scheme for the film, contrasting the yellow road, the red slippers, the green Emerald City, and so forth. From this standpoint, interpretation may be seen as one kind of formal analysis, one that seeks to reveal a film's implicit meanings. Those meanings should be constantly tested by placing them within the concrete texture of the whole film.

4. ***Symptomatic meaning.*** *In a society where human worth is measured by money, the home and the family may seem to be the last refuge of human values. This belief is especially strong in times of economic crisis, such as that in the United States in the 1930s.*

Like the third statement, this is abstract and general. It situates the film within a trend of thought that is assumed to be characteristic of American society during the 1930s. The claim could apply equally well to many other films, as well as to many novels, plays, poems, paintings, advertisements, radio shows, political speeches, and a host of cultural products of the period.

But there is something else worth noticing about the statement. It treats an explicit meaning in *The Wizard of Oz* ("There's no place like home") as a manifestation of a wider set of values characteristic of a whole society. We could treat implicit meanings the same way. If we say the film implies something about adolescence as a crucial time of transition, we could suggest that emphasis on adolescence as a special period of life is also a recurrent concern of American society. So, it is possible to understand a film's explicit or implicit meanings as bearing traces of a particular set of social values. We can call this *symptomatic meaning,* and the set of values that get revealed can be considered a social **ideology.**

The possibility of noticing symptomatic meanings reminds us that meaning, whether referential, explicit, or implicit, is largely a social phenomenon. Many meanings of films are ultimately ideological; that is, they spring from systems of culturally specific beliefs about the world. Religious beliefs, political opinions, conceptions of race or sex or social class, even our most deeply seated notions of life—all these constitute our ideological frame of reference. Although we may live as if our beliefs were the only true and real explanations of how the world is, we need only compare our own ideology with that of another group or culture or era to see how historically and socially shaped many of those views are: In other times or places, *home* and *adolescence* do not carry the meanings they carry in 21st-century America.

Films, like other artworks, can be examined for their symptomatic meanings. Again, however, the abstract and general quality of such meanings can lead us away from the concrete form of the film. As when analyzing the implicit meanings, the viewer should strive to ground symptomatic meanings in the film's specific aspects. A film *enacts* ideological meanings through its particular and unique formal system. We shall see in Chapter 11 how the narrative and stylistic system of *Meet Me in St. Louis* can be analyzed for ideological implications.

In short, films have meaning because we attribute meanings to them. We cannot therefore regard meaning as a simple product to be extracted from the film. Our minds will probe an artwork for significance at several levels, seeking referential meanings, explicit meanings, implicit meanings, and symptomatic meanings. The more abstract and general our attributions of meaning, the more we risk loosening our grasp on the film's specific formal system. As analysts, we must balance our concern for that concrete system with our urge to assign it wider significance.

Evaluation

In talking about an artwork, people often *evaluate* it; that is, they make claims about its goodness or badness. Reviews in popular magazines exist almost solely to tell us whether a film is worth seeing; our friends often urge us to go to their latest favorite. But all too often we discover that the film that someone else esteemed appears only mediocre to us. At that point we may complain that most people evaluate films only on the basis of their own, highly personal, tastes.

How, then, are we to evaluate films with any degree of objectivity? We can start by realizing that there is a difference between *personal taste* and *evaluative judgment.* To say, "I liked this film" or "I hated it," is not equal to saying, "It's a good film," or "It's wretched." Very few people in the world limit their enjoyment only to the greatest works. Most people can enjoy a film they know is not particularly good. This is perfectly reasonable—unless they start trying to convince people that these pleasant films actually rank among the undying masterpieces. At that point others will probably stop listening to their judgments at all.

We may set aside, therefore, personal preference as the sole basis for judging a film's quality. Instead, the critic who wishes to make a relatively objective evaluation will use specific *criteria.* A criterion is a standard which can be applied in the judgment of many works. By using a criterion, the critic gains a basis for comparing films for relative quality.

There are many different criteria. Some people evaluate films on "realistic" criteria, judging a film good if it conforms to their view of reality. Aficionados of military history might judge a film entirely on whether the battle scenes use historically accurate weaponry; the narrative, editing, characterization, sound, and visual style might be of little interest to them.

Other people condemn films because they don't find the action plausible. They will dismiss a scene by saying, "Who'd really believe that X would meet Y just at the right moment?" We have already seen, though, that artworks often violate laws of reality and operate by their own conventions and internal rules.

Viewers can also use moral criteria to evaluate films. Most narrowly, aspects of the film can be judged outside their context in the film's formal system. Some viewers might feel any film with nudity or profanity is bad, while other viewers might find just these aspects praiseworthy. More broadly, viewers and critics may employ moral criteria to evaluate a film's overall significance, and here the film's complete formal system becomes pertinent. A film might be judged good because of its overall view of life, its willingness to show opposed points of view, or its emotional range.

While "realistic" and moral criteria are well-suited to particular purposes, this book will suggest criteria that assess films as artistic wholes. Such criteria should allow us to take each film's form into account as much as possible. *Coherence* is one such criterion. This quality, often conceived as unity, has traditionally been held to be a positive feature of artworks. So too has *intensity of effect.* If an artwork is vivid, striking, and emotionally engaging, it may be considered more valuable.

Another criterion is *complexity.* We can argue that, all other things being equal, complex films are good. A complex film engages our interest on many levels, creates a multiplicity of relations among many separate formal elements, and tends to create interesting formal patterns.

Yet another formal criterion is *originality.* Originality for its own sake is pointless, of course. Just because something is different does not mean that it is good. But if an artist takes a familiar convention and uses it in a way that makes it fresh again or creates a new set of formal possibilities, then (all other things being equal) the resulting work may be considered good from an aesthetic standpoint.

Note that all these criteria are matters of degree. One film may be more complex than another, but the second film may be more complex than a third one. Moreover, there is often a give-and-take among the criteria. A film might be very complex but lack coherence or intensity. Ninety minutes of a black screen would make for an original film but not a very complex one. A slasher movie may create great intensity in certain scenes but be wholly unoriginal, as well as disorganized and simplistic. In applying the criteria, the analyst must often weigh one against another.

Evaluation can serve many useful ends. It can call attention to neglected artworks to make us rethink our attitudes toward accepted classics. But just as the discovery of meanings is not the only purpose of formal analysis, we suggest that evaluation is most fruitful when it is backed up by a close examination of the film. General statements ("*The Wizard of Oz* is a masterpiece") seldom enlighten us very much. Usually an evaluation is helpful insofar as it points to aspects of the film and shows us relations and qualities we have missed: "*The Wizard of Oz* skillfully compares characters in Kansas and Oz, as when Miss Gulch's written order to take Toto is echoed by the Wicked Witch's fiery skywriting to the citizens of the Emerald City, 'Surrender Dorothy.'" Like interpretation, evaluation is most useful when it drives us back to the film itself as a formal system, helping us to understand that system better.

In reading this book, you will find that we have generally minimized evaluation. We think that most of the films and sequences we analyze are more or less good on the formal criteria we mentioned, but the purpose of this book is not to persuade you to accept a list of masterpieces. Rather, we believe that if we show in detail how films may be understood as artistic systems, you will have an informed basis for whatever evaluations you wish to make.

PRINCIPLES OF FILM FORM

Because film form is a system—that is, a unified set of related, interdependent elements—there must be some principles that help create the relationships among the parts. In disciplines other than the arts, principles may be sets of rules or laws. In the sciences principles may take the form of physical laws or mathematical propositions. In practical work, such principles provide firm guidelines about what is possible. For example, engineers designing an airplane must obey fundamental laws of aerodynamics.

In the arts, however, there are no absolute principles of form that all artists must follow. Artworks are products of culture. Thus many of the principles of artistic form are matters of convention. In Chapter 4, we shall examine how various genres can have very different conventions. A Western is not in error if it does not follow the conventions of, say, a horror film. The artist obeys (or disobeys) norms— bodies of conventions, not laws.

But within these social conventions, each artwork tends to set up its own specific formal principles. The forms of different films can vary enormously. We can distinguish, however, five general principles that the spectator perceives in a film's formal system: function, similarity and repetition, difference and variation, development, and unity/disunity.

Function

If form in cinema is the overall interrelation among various systems of elements, we can assume that every element in this totality has one or more **functions.** That is, every element will be seen as fulfilling one or more roles within the whole system.

Of any element within a film we can ask, What are its functions? In our example of *The Wizard of Oz,* every element in the film fulfills one or more roles. For instance, Miss Gulch, the woman who wants to take Toto from Dorothy, reappears in the Oz section as the Wicked Witch. In the opening portion of the film Miss Gulch frightens Dorothy into running away from home. In Oz the Witch prevents Dorothy from returning home by keeping her away from the Emerald City and by trying to seize the ruby slippers.

Even an element as apparently minor as the dog Toto serves many functions. The dispute over Toto causes Dorothy to run away from home and to get back too late to take shelter from the tornado. Later, Toto's pursuit of a cat makes Dorothy jump out of the ascending balloon and miss her chance to go back to Kansas. Toto's gray color, set off against the brightness of Oz, creates a link to the black and white of the Kansas episodes at the film's beginning. Functions, then, are almost always multiple. Both narrative and stylistic elements have functions.

One useful way to grasp the function of an element is to ask what other elements demand that it be present. For instance, the narrative requires that Dorothy run away from home, so Toto functions to motivate this action. Or, to take another example, Dorothy must seem completely different from the Wicked Witch, so costume, age, voice, and other characteristics function to contrast the two. Additionally, the switch from black-and-white to color film functions to signal the arrival in the bright fantasy land of Oz.

Note that the concept of function does not always depend on the filmmaker's intention. Often discussions of films get bogged down in the question of whether the filmmaker really knew what he or she was doing in including a certain element. In asking about function, we do not ask for a production history. From the standpoint of intention, Dorothy may sing "Over the Rainbow" because MGM wanted Judy Garland to launch a hit song. From the standpoint of function, however, we can say that Dorothy's singing that song fulfills certain narrative and stylistic functions. It establishes her desire to leave home, its reference to the rainbow foreshadows her trip through the air to the color Oz sequences, and so forth. In asking about formal function, therefore, we ask not, "How did this element get there?" but rather, "What is this element *doing* there?" and "How does it cue us to respond?"

One way to notice the functions of an element is to consider the element's **motivation.** Because films are human constructs, we can expect that any one element in a film will have some justification for being there. This justification is the motivation for that element. For example, when Miss Gulch appears as the Witch in Oz, we justify her new incarnation by appealing to the fact that early scenes in Kansas have established her as a threat to Dorothy. When Toto jumps from the balloon to chase a cat, we motivate his action by appealing to notions of how dogs are likely to act when cats are around.

Sometimes people use the word "motivation" to apply only to reasons for characters' actions, as when a murderer acts from certain motives. Here, however, we will use "motivation" to apply to any element in the film that the viewer justifies on some grounds. A costume, for example, needs motivation. If we see a man in beggar's clothes in the middle of an elegant society ball, we will ask why he is dressed in this way. He could be the victim of practical jokers who have deluded him into believing that this is a masquerade. He could be an eccentric millionaire out to shock his friends. Such a scene does occur in *My Man Godfrey*. The motivation for the beggar's presence at the ball is a scavenger hunt; the young society people have been assigned to bring back, among other things, a beggar. An event, the hunt, *motivates* the presence of an inappropriately dressed character.

Motivation is so common in films that spectators tend to take it for granted. Shadowy, flickering light on a character may be motivated by the presence of a candle in the room. (We may be aware that in production the light is provided by offscreen lamps, but the candle purports to be the source and thus motivates the pattern of light.) A character wandering across a room may motivate the moving of the camera to follow the action and keep the character within the frame. When we study principles of narrative form (Chapter 3) and various types of films (Chapters 4 and 5), we will look more closely at how motivation works to give elements specific functions.

Similarity and Repetition

In our example of the ABACA pattern, we saw how we were able to predict the next steps in the series. One reason for this was a regular pattern of repeated elements. Like beats in music or meter in poetry, the repetition of the A's in our pattern established and satisfied formal expectations. Similarity and repetition, then, constitute an important principle of film form.

Repetition is basic to our understanding any film. For instance, we must be able to recall and identify characters and settings each time they reappear. More subtly, throughout any film we can observe repetitions of everything from lines of dialogue and bits of music to camera positions, characters' behavior, and story action.

It is useful to have a term to help describe formal repetitions, and the most common term is **motif.** We shall call *any significant repeated element in a film* a motif. A motif may be an object, a color, a place, a person, a sound, or even a character trait. We may call a pattern of lighting or camera position a motif if it is repeated through the course of a film. The form of *The Wizard of Oz* uses all these kinds of motifs. Even in such a relatively simple film, we can see the pervasive presence of similarity and repetition as formal principles.

Film form uses general similarities as well as exact duplication. To understand *The Wizard of Oz*, we must see the similarities between the three Kansas farmhands and the Scarecrow, Tin Man, and Cowardly Lion. We must notice additional echoes between characters in the frame story and in the fantasy (**2.2–2.5**). The duplication is not perfect, but the similarity is very strong. Such similarities are called *parallelism,* the process whereby the film cues the spectator to compare two or more distinct elements by highlighting some similarity. For example, at one point Dorothy says she feels that she has known the Scarecrow, Tin Man, and Cowardly Lion before. At another point, the staging of a shot reinforces this familiarity (**2.6, 2.7**)

Motifs can assist in creating parallelism. The viewer will notice, and even come to expect, that every time Dorothy meets a character in Oz, the scene will end with the song "We're Off to See the Wizard." Our recognition of parallelism provides part of our pleasure in watching a film, much as the echo of rhymes contributes to the power of poetry.

"You can take a movie, for example, like *Angels with Dirty Faces,* where James Cagney is a child and says to his pal Pat O'Brien, 'What do you hear, what do you say?'—cocky kid—and then as a young rough on the way up when things are going great for him he says, 'What do you hear, what do you say?' Then when he is about to be executed in the electric chair and Pat O'Brien is there to hear his confession, he says, 'What do you hear, what do you say?' and the simple repetition of the last line of dialogue in three different places with the same characters brings home the dramatically changed circumstances much more than any extensive diatribe would."

— Robert Towne, screenwriter, *Chinatown*

2.2   The itinerant Kansas fortune-teller, Professor Marvell, bears a striking resemblance to . . .

2.3   . . . the old charlatan known as the Wizard of Oz.

2.4   Miss Gulch's bicycle in the opening section becomes . . .

2.5   . . . the Witch's broom in Oz.

2.6   As the Lion describes his timidity, the characters are lined up to form a mirror reversal of . . .

2.7   . . . the earlier scene where the others taunted Zeke for being afraid of the pigs.

Difference and Variation

The form of a film could hardly be composed only of repetitions. AAAAAA is pretty boring. There must also be some changes, or **variations,** however small. Thus difference is another fundamental principle of film form.

We can readily understand the need for variety, contrast, and change in films. Characters must be distinguished, environments must be delineated, different times or activities must be established. Even within the image, we must distinguish differences in tonality, texture, direction and speed of movement, and so on. Form needs its stable background of similarity and repetition, but it also demands that differences be created.

This means that although motifs (scenes, settings, actions, objects, stylistic devices) may be repeated, those motifs will seldom be repeated *exactly*. Variation will appear. In *The Wizard of Oz,* the three Kansas hired hands are not exactly the same as their "twins" in Oz. Parallelism thus requires a degree of difference as well as striking similarity. When Professor Marvel pretends to read Dorothy's future in a small crystal ball, we see no images in it (2.2). Dorothy's dream transforms the crystal into a large globe in the Witch's castle, where it displays frightening scenes **(2.8).** Similarly, the repeated motif of Toto's disruption of a situation changes function. In Kansas it disturbs Miss Gulch and induces Dorothy to take Toto away from home, but in Oz his disruption prevents Dorothy from returning home.

Differences among the elements may often sharpen into downright opposition among them. We are most familiar with formal oppositions as clashes among characters. In *The Wizard of Oz* Dorothy's desires are opposed, at various points, by the differing desires of Aunt Em, Miss Gulch, the Wicked Witch, and the Wizard, so that the film's formal system derives many dynamics from characters in conflict. But character conflict is not the only way the formal principle of difference may manifest itself. Settings, actions, and other elements may be opposed. *The Wizard of Oz* also presents color oppositions: black-and-white Kansas versus colorful Oz, Dorothy in red, white, and blue versus the Witch in black, and so on. Settings are opposed as well—not only Oz versus Kansas but also the various locales within Oz **(2.9, 2.10).** Voice quality, musical tunes, and a host of other elements play off against one another, demonstrating that any motif may be opposed by any other motif.

2.8   Through her crystal ball, the Wicked Witch mocks Dorothy.

Not all differences are simple oppositions, of course. Dorothy's three Oz friends—the Scarecrow, the Tin Woodman, and the Lion—are distinguished not only by external features but also by means of a three-term comparison of what they lack (a brain, a heart, courage). Other films may rely on less sharp differences, suggesting a scale of gradations among the characters, as in Jean Renoir's *The Rules of the Game*. At the extreme, an abstract film may create minimal variations among its parts, such as in the slight changes that accompany each return of the same footage in J. J. Murphy's *Print Generation*.

Repetition and variation are two sides of the same coin. To notice one is to notice the other. In analyzing films, we ought to look for similarities *and* differences. Shuttling between the two, we can point out motifs and contrast the changes they undergo, recognize parallelisms as repetition, and still spot crucial variations.

2.9   Centered in the upper half of the frame, the Emerald City creates a striking contrast to . . .

Development

One way to keep ourselves aware of how similarity and difference operate in film form is to look for principles of development from part to part. Development will constitute some patterning of similar and differing elements. Our pattern ABACA is based not only on repetition (the recurring motif of A) and difference (the varied insertion of B and C) but also on a principle of *progression* that we could state as a rule: Alternate A with successive letters in alphabetical order. Though simple, this is a principle of *development,* governing the form of the whole series.

Think of formal development as *a progression moving from beginning through middle to end.* For example, the story of *The Wizard of Oz* shows development in many ways. It is, for one thing, a *journey:* from Kansas through Oz to Kansas. The good witch Glinda emphasizes this formal pattern by telling Dorothy that "It's always best to start at the beginning" **(2.11).** Many films possess such a journey plot. *The Wizard of Oz* is also a *search,* beginning with an initial separation from home, tracing a series of efforts to find a way home, and ending with home being found. Within the film there is also a pattern of *mystery,* which usually has the same beginning-middle-end pattern. We begin with a question (Who is the Wizard of Oz?), pass through attempts to answer it, and conclude with the question answered (The Wizard is a fraud.). Most feature-length films are composed of several developmental patterns.

2.10   . . . the similar composition showing the castle of the Wicked Witch of the West.

In order to analyze a film's pattern of development, it is usually a good idea to make a **segmentation.** A segmentation is simply a written outline of the film that breaks it into its major and minor parts, with the parts marked by consecutive numbers or letters. If a narrative film has ten **scenes,** then we can label each scene with

2.11 Dorothy puts her feet on the literal beginning of the Yellow Brick Road, as it widens out from a thin line.

a number running from one to ten. It may be useful to divide some parts further (for example, scenes 6a and 6b). Segmenting a film enables us not only to notice similarities and differences among parts but also to plot the overall progression of the form. Following is a segmentation for *The Wizard of Oz.*

THE WIZARD OF OZ: PLOT SEGMENTATION

C. Credits
1. Kansas
    a. Dorothy at home, worried about Miss Gulch's threat to Toto
    b. Running away, Dorothy meets Professor Marvel, who induces her to return home
    c. A tornado lifts the house, with Dorothy and Toto, into the sky
2. Munchkin City
    a. Dorothy meets Glinda, and the Munchkins celebrate the death of the Wicked Witch of the East
    b. The Wicked Witch of the West threatens Dorothy over the Ruby Slippers
    c. Glinda sends Dorothy to seek the Wizard's help
3. The Yellow Brick Road
    a. Meeting the Scarecrow
    b. Meeting the Tin Man
    c. Meeting the Cowardly Lion
4. The Emerald City
    a. The Witch creates a poppy field near the City, but Glinda rescues the travelers
    b. The group is welcomed by the City's citizens
    c. As they wait to see the Wizard, the Lion sings of being king
    d. The terrifying Wizard agrees to help the group if they obtain the Wicked Witch's broomstick
5. The Witch's Castle and Nearby Woods
    a. In the woods, flying monkeys carry off Dorothy and Toto
    b. The Witch realizes that she must kill Dorothy to get the ruby slippers
    c. The Scarecrow, Tin Man, and Lion sneak into the Castle; in the ensuing chase Dorothy kills the Witch
6. The Emerald City
    a. Although revealed as a humbug, the Wizard grants the wishes of the Scarecrow, Tin Man, and Lion
    b. Dorothy fails to leave with the Wizard's hot-air balloon but is transported home by the ruby slippers
7. Kansas—Dorothy describes Oz to her family and friends
E. End credits

In Chapters 3 and 5 we will consider how to segment various types of films.

    Another way to size up how a film develops formally is to *compare the beginning with the ending.* By looking at the similarities and differences between the beginning and ending, we can start to understand the overall pattern of the film. We can test this advice on *The Wizard of Oz.* A comparison of the beginning and ending reveals that Dorothy's journey ends with her return home; the journey has been a search for an ideal place "over the rainbow" and has turned into a search for a way back to Kansas. The final scene repeats and develops the narrative elements of the opening. Stylistically, the beginning and ending are the only parts that use black-and-white film stock. This repetition supports the contrast the narrative creates between the dreamland of Oz and the bleak landscape of Kansas.

At the film's end Professor Marvel comes to visit Dorothy (**2.12**), reversing the situation of her visit to him when she had tried to run away. At the beginning he had convinced her to return home; then, as the Wizard in the Oz section, he had also represented her hopes of returning home. Finally, when she recognizes Professor Marvel and the farmhands as the basis of the characters in her dream, she remembers how much she had wanted to come home from Oz.

Earlier, we suggested that film form engages our emotions and expectations in a dynamic way. Now we are in a better position to see why. The constant interplay between similarity and difference, repetition and variation, leads the viewer to an active, developing awareness of the film's formal system. It may be handy to visualize the film's development in static terms by segmenting it, but we ought not to forget that formal development is a *process*.

2.12 The visits of the final scene.

Unity/Disunity

All of the relationships among elements in a film create the total filmic system. Even if an element seems utterly out of place in relation to the rest of the film, we cannot really say that it isn't part of the film. At most, the unrelated element is enigmatic or incoherent. It may be a flaw in the otherwise integrated system of the film—but it does affect the whole film.

When all the relationships we perceive within a film are clear and economically interwoven, we say that the film has **unity.** We call a unified film tight, because there seem to be no gaps in the formal relationships. Every element present has a specific set of functions, similarities and differences are determinable, the form develops logically, and no element is superfluous.

Unity is, however, a matter of degree. Almost no film is so tight as to leave no end dangling. For example, at one point in *The Wizard of Oz,* the Witch refers to her having attacked Dorothy and her friends with insects, yet we have never seen them, and the mention becomes puzzling. In fact, a sequence of a bee attack was originally shot but then cut from the finished film. The Witch's line about the insect attack now lacks motivation. More striking is a dangling element at the film's end. We never find out what happens to Miss Gulch; presumably she still has her legal order to take Toto away, but no one refers to this in the last scene. The viewer may be inclined to overlook this disunity, however, because Miss Gulch's parallel character, the Witch, has been killed off in the Oz fantasy and we do not expect to see her alive again. Since perfect unity is scarcely ever achieved, we ought to expect that even a unified film may still contain a few unintegrated elements or unanswered questions.

If we look at unity as a criterion of evaluation, we may judge a film containing several unmotivated elements as a failure. But unity and disunity may be looked at nonevaluatively as well, as the results of particular formal conventions. For example, *Pulp Fiction* lacks a bit of closure in that it never reveals what is inside a briefcase that is at the center of the gangster plot. The contents, however, give off a golden glow, suggesting that they are of very great value (as well as evoking the "whatsit" in *Kiss Me Deadly,* a classical film noir). By not specifying the goods, the film invites us to compare characters' reactions to them—most notably, in the last scene in the diner, when Pumpkin gazes at it lustfully and the newly spiritual hitman Jules calmly insists that he will deliver it to his boss. In such ways, momentary disunities contribute to broader patterns and thematic meanings.

SUMMARY

If one issue has governed our treatment of aesthetic form, it might be said to be *concreteness*. Form is a specific system of patterned relationships that we perceive in an artwork. Such a concept helps us understand how even elements of what is normally considered content—subject matter, or abstract ideas—take on particular functions within any work.

Our experience of an artwork is also a concrete one. Picking up cues in the work, we frame specific expectations that are aroused, guided, delayed, cheated, satisfied, or disturbed. We undergo curiosity, suspense, and surprise. We compare the particular aspects of the artwork with general conventions that we know from life and from art. The concrete context of the artwork expresses and stimulates emotions and enables us to construct many types of meanings. And even when we apply general criteria in evaluating artworks, we ought to use those criteria to help us discriminate more, to penetrate more deeply into the particular aspects of the artwork. The rest of this book is devoted to studying these properties of aesthetic form in cinema.

We can summarize the principles of film form as a set of questions that you can ask about any film.

1. Of any element in the film, you can ask, What are its functions in the overall form? How is it motivated?

2. Are elements or patterns repeated throughout the film? If so, how and at what points? Are motifs and parallelisms asking us to compare elements?

3. How are elements contrasted and differentiated from one another? How are different elements opposed to one another?

4. What principles of progression or development are at work throughout the form of the film? More specifically, how does a comparison of the beginning and ending reveal the overall form of a film?

5. What degree of unity is present in the film's overall form? Is disunity subordinate to the overall unity, or does disunity dominate?

In this chapter we have examined some major ways in which films as artworks can engage us as spectators. We have also reviewed some broad principles of film form. Armed with these general principles, we can press on to distinguish more specific *types* of form that are central to understanding film art.

NOTES AND QUERIES

Form in Film and the Other Arts

Many of the ideas in this chapter are based on ideas of form to be found in other arts. All of the following constitute helpful further reading: Monroe Beardsley, *Aesthetics* (New York: Harcourt Brace and World, 1958), especially chaps. 4 and 5; Rudolf Arnheim, *Art and Visual Perception* (Berkeley: University of California Press, 1974), especially chaps. 2, 3, and 9; Leonard Meyer, *Emotion and Meaning in Music* (Chicago: University of Chicago Press, 1956); E. H. Gombrich, *Art and Illusion* (Princeton, N.J.: Princeton University Press, 1961).

On the relation of form to the audience, see the book by Meyer mentioned above. The ABACA example is borrowed from Barbara Herrnstein Smith's excellent study of literary form, *Poetic Closure* (Chicago: University of Chicago Press, 1968). Compare Kenneth's Burke's claim: "Form is the creation of an appetite in the mind of the auditor and the adequate satisfying of that appetite." [See Kenneth Burke, "Psychology and Form," in *Counter-Statement* (Chicago: University of Chicago Press, 1957), pp. 29–44.]

This chapter presupposes that any filmmaker uses basic formal principles. But is the filmmaker fully aware of doing so? Many filmmakers use formal principles intuitively, but others apply them quite deliberately. Spike Lee's cinematographer Ernest Dickerson remarks, "A motif we used throughout [*School Daze*] was two people in profile, 'up in each other's face.' That was a conscious decision" [*Uplift the Race: The Construction of "School Daze"* (New York: Simon & Schuster, 1988), p. 110].

Form, Meaning, and Feeling

Some psychoanalytical theories of the spectator characterize the emotional appeal of cinema as involving "pleasure" and "unpleasure." An example is Laura Mulvey, "Visual Pleasure and Narrative Cinema," *Screen* **16,** 3 (Autumn 1975): 6–18. A somewhat different line of argument is pursued in Charles Affron, *Cinema and Sentiment* (Chicago: University of Chicago Press, 1982), which concentrates on how narrative structures create identification with the characters or their situations.

Many critics concentrate upon ascribing implicit and symptomatic meanings to films—that is, interpreting them. A survey of interpretive approaches is offered in R. Barton Palmer, *The Cinematic Text: Methods and Approaches* (New York: AMS Press, 1989). David Bordwell's *Making Meaning: Inference and Rhetoric in the Interpretation of Cinema* (Cambridge, Mass.: Harvard University Press, 1989) reviews trends in film interpretation.

Linear Segmentation and Diagramming

Dividing a film into sequences in order to analyze its form is usually called *segmentation*. It is usually not difficult to do, though most often we do it intuitively. Film theory has devoted some consideration to the principles by which we segment a film. See Raymond Bellour, "To Analyze, to Segment," *Quarterly Review of Film Studies* **1,** 3 (August 1976): 331–354.

The most influential explanation of how to segment a narrative film has been Christian Metz's famous "Grand Syntagmatic of the Image Track." Metz suggests that there are eight basic sorts of sequences (with some subdivisions and expectations). See Christian Metz, *Film Language,* translated by M. Taylor (New York: Oxford University Press, 1974) and Stephen Heath, "Film/Cinetext/Text," *Screen* **14,** 1–2 (Spring–Summer 1973): 102–127.

Usually a feature-length film will have no more than 40 sequences and no fewer than 5, so if you find yourself dividing the film into tiny bits or huge chunks, you may want to shift to a different level of generality. Of course, sequences and scenes can also be further subdivided into subsegments. In segmenting any film, an outline format or a linear diagram may help you visualize formal relations (beginnings and endings, parallels, patterns of development). We employ an outline format in discussing modes of filmmaking in Chapter 5 and in discussing *Citizen Kane.*

Chapter 3

Narrative as a Formal System

Stories surround us. In childhood we learn fairy tales and myths. As we grow up, we read short stories, novels, history, and biography. Religion, philosophy, and science often present their doctrines through parables and tales: The Judeo-Christian tradition's Bible and Torah are huge collections of stories. Plays tell stories, as do films, television shows, comic books, paintings, dance, and many other cultural phenomena. Much of our conversation is taken up with telling tales—recalling an event from the past or telling a joke. Even newspaper articles are called stories, and when we ask for an explanation of something, we may say, "What's the story?" We cannot escape even by going to sleep, since we often experience our dreams as little narratives, and we recall and retell the dreams in the shape of stories. Narrative is a fundamental way that humans make sense of the world.

The prevalence of stories in our lives is one reason that we need to take a close look at how films may embody **narrative form.** When we speak of "going to the movies," we almost always mean that we are going to see a narrative film—a film that tells a story.

Narrative form is most common in fictional films, but it can appear in all other basic types. For instance, documentaries often employ narrative form. *Primary* tells the story of how Hubert Humphrey and John F. Kennedy campaigned in the Wisconsin presidential primary of 1960. Many animated films, such as Disney features and Warner Bros. short cartoons, also tell stories. Some experimental and avant-garde films use narrative form, although the story or the way it is told may be quite unusual, as we shall see in Chapter 5.

Because stories are all around us, spectators approach a narrative film with definite expectations. We may know a great deal about the particular story the film will tell. Perhaps we have read the book on which a film is based, or we have seen the film to which this is a sequel. More generally, though, we have anticipations that are characteristic of narrative form itself. We assume that there will be characters and some action that will involve them with one another. We expect a series of incidents that will be connected in some way. We also probably expect that the problems or conflicts arising in the course of the action will achieve some final state—either they will be resolved or, at least, a new light will be cast on them. A spectator comes prepared to make sense of a narrative film.

As the viewer watches the film, she or he picks up cues, recalls information, anticipates what will follow, and generally participates in the creation of the film's form. The film shapes particular expectations by summoning up curiosity, suspense, and surprise. The ending has the task of satisfying or cheating the expectations prompted by the film as a whole. The ending may also activate memory by cueing the spectator to review earlier events, possibly considering them in a new light. When *The Sixth Sense* was released in 1999, many moviegoers were so intrigued by the surprise twist at the end that they returned to see the film again and trace how their expectations had been manipulated. As we examine narrative form, we will consider at various points how it engages the viewer in a dynamic activity.

What Is Narrative?

We can consider a narrative to be *a chain of events in cause-effect relationship occurring in time and space.* A narrative is thus what we usually mean by the term *story,* although we shall be using story in a slightly different way later. Typically, a narrative begins with one situation; a series of changes occurs according to a pattern of cause and effect; finally, a new situation arises that brings about the end of the narrative.

All the components of our definition—causality, time, and space—are important to narratives in most media, but causality and time are central. A random string of events is hard to perceive as a story. Consider the following actions: "A man tosses and turns, unable to sleep. A mirror breaks. A telephone rings." We have trouble grasping this as a narrative because we are unable to determine the causal or temporal relations among the events.

Consider a new description of these same events: "A man has a fight with his boss; he tosses and turns that night, unable to sleep. In the morning, he is still so angry that he smashes the mirror while shaving. Then his telephone rings; his boss has called to apologize."

We now have a narrative. We can connect the events spatially: The man is in the office, then in his bed; the mirror is in the bathroom; the phone is somewhere else in his home. More important, we can understand that the three events are part of a series of causes and effects. The argument with the boss causes the sleeplessness and the broken mirror. A phone call from the boss resolves the conflict; the narrative ends. In this example, time is also important. The sleepless night occurs before the breaking of the mirror, which in turn occurs before the phone call; all of the action runs from one day to the following morning. The narrative develops from an initial situation of conflict between employee and boss, through a series of events caused by the conflict, to the resolution of the conflict. Simple and minimal as our example is, it shows how important causality, space, and time are to narrative form.

The fact that a narrative relies on causality, time, and space does not mean that other formal principles cannot govern the film. For instance, a narrative may make use of parallelism. As Chapter 2 points out (p. 61), parallelism posits a similarity among different elements. Our example was the way that *The Wizard of Oz* made the three Kansas farmhands parallel to Dorothy's three Oz companions. A narrative may cue us to draw parallels among characters, settings, situations, times of day, or any other elements. In Veřá Chytilová's *Something Different,* scenes from the life of a housewife and from the career of a gymnast are presented in alternation. Since the two women never meet and lead entirely separate lives, there is no way that we

"Narrative is one of the ways in which knowledge is organized. I have always thought it was the most important way to transmit and receive knowledge. I am less certain of that now—but the craving for narrative has never lessened, and the hunger for it is as keen as it was on Mt. Sinai or Calvary or the middle of the fens."

— Toni Morrison

"I had actually trapped myself in a story that was very convoluted, and I would have been able to cut more later if I'd simplified it at the script stage, but I'd reached a point where I was up against a wall of story logic. If I had cut too much at that stage, the audience would have felt lost."

— James Cameron, director, on *Aliens*

can connect the two stories causally. Instead, we compare and contrast the two women's actions and situations—that is, we draw parallels.

Another documentary, *Hoop Dreams,* makes even stronger use of parallels. Two high school students from Chicago's black ghetto dream of becoming professional basketball players, and the film follows as each one pursues his athletic career. The film's form invites us to compare and contrast their personalities, the obstacles they face, and the choices they make. In addition, the film creates parallels between their high schools, their coaches, their parents, and older male relatives who vicariously live their own dreams of athletic glory. Parallelism allows the film to become richer and more complex than it might have been had it concentrated on only one protagonist.

Yet *Hoop Dreams,* like *Something Different,* is still a narrative film. Each of the two lines of action is organized by time, space, and causality. The film suggests some broad causal forces as well. Both young men have grown up in urban poverty, and because sports is the most visible sign of success for them, they turn their hopes in that direction.

Plot and Story

We make sense of a narrative, then, by identifying its events and linking them by cause and effect, time, and space. As viewers, we do other things as well. We often infer events that are not explicitly presented, and we recognize the presence of material that is extraneous to the story world. In order to describe how we perform such activities, we can draw a distinction between *story* and *plot* (sometimes called *story* and *discourse*). Since this distinction is basic to understanding narrative form, we need to examine it in a little more detail.

We often make assumptions and inferences about events in a narrative. For instance, at the start of Alfred Hitchcock's *North by Northwest* we know we are in Manhattan at rush hour. The cues stand out clearly: skyscrapers, bustling pedestrians, congested traffic **(3.1).** Then we watch Roger Thornhill as he leaves an elevator with his secretary, Maggie, and strides through the lobby, dictating memos **(3.2).** On the basis of these cues, we start to draw some conclusions. Thornhill is an executive who leads a busy life. We assume that before we saw Thornhill and Maggie, he was also dictating to her; we have come in on the middle of a string of events in time. We also assume that the dictating began in the office, before they got on the elevator. In other words, we infer causes, a temporal sequence, and another locale even though none of this information has been directly presented. We are probably not aware of having made these inferences, but they are no less firm for going unnoticed.

The set of *all* the events in a narrative, both the ones explicitly presented and those the viewer infers, constitutes the **story.** In our example the story would consist of at least two depicted events and two inferred ones. We can list them, putting the inferred events in parentheses:

(Roger Thornhill has a busy day at his office.)

Rush hour hits Manhattan.

(While dictating to his secretary, Maggie, Roger leaves the office and they take the elevator.)

Still dictating, Roger gets off the elevator with Maggie and they stride through the lobby.

The total world of the story action is sometimes called the film's *diegesis* (the Greek word for "recounted story"). In the opening of *North by Northwest,* the traffic,

3.1 Hurrying Manhattan pedestrians in *North by Northwest.*

3.2 Maggie takes dictation from Roger Thornhill.

streets, skyscrapers, and people we see, as well as the traffic, streets, skyscrapers, and people we assume to be offscreen, are all diegetic because they are assumed to exist in the world that the film depicts.

The term **plot** is used to describe everything visibly and audibly present in the film before us. The plot includes, first, all the story events that are directly depicted. In our *North by Northwest* example, only two story events are explicitly presented in the plot: rush hour and Roger Thornhill's dictating to Maggie as they leave the elevator.

Second, the film's plot may contain material that is extraneous to the story world. For example, while the opening of *North by Northwest* is portraying rush hour in Manhattan, we also see the film's credits and hear orchestral music. Neither of these elements is diegetic, since they are brought in from *outside* the story world. (The characters cannot read the credits or hear the music.) Credits and such extraneous music are thus *nondiegetic* elements. In Chapters 8 and 9 we will consider how editing and sound can function nondiegetically. At this point, we need only notice that the film's plot—the totality of the film—can bring in nondiegetic material.

3.3   A hopeful investor in the play enters the theater . . .

Nondiegetic material may occur elsewhere than in credit sequences. In *The Band Wagon,* we see the premiere of a hopelessly pretentious musical play. Eager patrons file into the theater **(3.3),** and the camera moves closer to a poster above the door **(3.4).** There then appear three black-and-white images **(3.5–3.7)** accompanied by a brooding chorus. These images and sounds are clearly nondiegetic, inserted from outside the story world in order to signal that the production was catastrophic and "laid an egg." The plot has added material to the story for comic effect.

In sum, story and plot overlap in one respect and diverge in others. The plot explicitly presents certain story events, so these events are common to both domains. The story goes beyond the plot in suggesting some diegetic events which we never witness. The plot goes beyond the story world by presenting nondiegetic images and sounds that may affect our understanding of the story. A diagram of the situation would look like this:

3.4   . . . and the camera moves in on a poster predicting success for the musical . . .

Story

Presumed and inferred events	Explicitly presented events	Added nondiegetic material

Plot

We can think about these differences between story and plot from two perspectives. From the standpoint of the storyteller, the filmmaker, the story is the sum total of all the events in the narrative. The storyteller can present some of these events directly (that is, make them part of the plot), can hint at events that are not presented, and can simply ignore other events. For instance, though we learn later in *North by Northwest* that Roger's mother is still close to him, we never learn what happened to his father. The filmmaker can also add nondiegetic material, as in the example from *The Band Wagon.* In a sense, then, the filmmaker makes a story into a plot.

3.5   . . . but three comic nondiegetic images reveal it to be a flop: ghostly figures on a boat . . .

From the perceiver's standpoint, things look somewhat different. All we have before us is the plot—the arrangement of material in the film as it stands. We create the story in our minds on the basis of cues in the plot. We also recognize when the plot presents nondiegetic material.

The story–plot distinction suggests that if you want to give someone a synopsis of a narrative film, you can proceed in two ways. You can summarize the story, starting from the very earliest incident that the plot cues you to assume or infer and

3.6   . . . a skull in a desert . . .

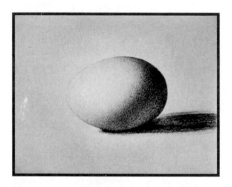

3.7   . . . and an egg.

running straight through to the end. Or you can tell the plot, starting with the first incident you encountered in watching the film.

Our initial definition and the distinction between plot and story constitute a set of tools for analyzing how narrative works. We shall see that the story–plot distinction affects all three aspects of narrative: causality, time, and space.

Cause and Effect

If narrative depends so heavily on cause and effect, what kinds of things can function as causes in a narrative? Usually the agents of cause and effect are *characters.* By triggering and reacting to events, characters play roles within the film's formal system.

Most often, characters are persons, or at least entities like persons—Bugs Bunny or E. T. the extraterrestrial or even the singing teapot in *Beauty and the Beast.* For our purposes here Michael Moore is a character in *Roger and Me* no less than Roger Thornhill is in *North by Northwest,* even though Moore is a real person and Thornhill is fictional. In any narrative film, either fictional or documentary, characters create causes and register effects. Within the film's formal system, they make things happen and react to the twists and turns of events.

In film narrative, characters have several properties. They usually have a body (though sometimes a character is only a ghostly voice, as when the dead Obi-Wan Kenobi urges the Jedi master Yoda to train Luke Skywalker in *The Empire Strikes Back*). Characters also often possess character *traits.* When we say that a character in a film was "complex" or "well developed," we really mean that the character was a collection of several varying traits. A minor character may have only one or two traits. A memorable character such as Sherlock Holmes is a mass of traits, some bearing on his habits (his love of music, his addiction to cocaine) and others reflecting his basic nature (his penetrating intelligence, his disdain for stupidity, his professional pride, his occasional gallantry).

In general, a character's traits are designed to play a causal role in the narrative. The second scene of Alfred Hitchcock's *The Man Who Knew Too Much* (1934) shows that the heroine, Jill, is an excellent shot with a rifle. For much of the film, this trait seems irrelevant to the action, but in the last scene Jill is able to shoot one of the villains when a police marksman cannot do it. This skill with a rifle is not a natural part of a person named Jill; it is a trait that helps make up a character named Jill, and it serves a particular narrative function. Character traits can involve attitudes, skills, preferences, psychological drives, details of dress and appearance, and any other specific quality the film creates for a character.

Not all causes and effects in narratives originate with characters. In the so-called disaster movies, an earthquake or tidal wave may precipitate a series of actions on the parts of the characters. The same principle holds when the shark in *Jaws* terrorizes a community. (The film may personify these natural causes by assigning them human traits like malevolence. In *Jaws,* the shark is seen as vengeful and cunning.) Still, once these natural occurrences set the situation up, human desires and goals usually enter the action to develop the narrative. A man escaping from a flood may be placed in the situation of having to decide whether to rescue his worst enemy. In *Jaws,* the townspeople pursue a variety of strategies to deal with the shark, propelling the plot as they do so.

In general, the spectator actively seeks to connect events by means of cause and effect. Given an incident, we tend to hypothesize what might have caused it or what it might in turn cause. That is, we look for causal motivation. We have mentioned an instance of this in Chapter 2: In the scene from *My Man Godfrey,* a scavenger hunt serves as a cause that justifies the presence of a beggar at a society ball (see p. 61). Causal motivation often involves the planting of information in advance of a scene. In *L.A. Confidential,* the idealistic detective Exley confides in his cynical colleague Vincennes about how the murder of his father had driven him to enter law enforcement. He had privately named the unknown killer "Rollo Tomasi," a name that he has turned into an emblem of all unpunished evil. This conversation initially seems like a simple bit of psychological insight. Yet later, when the corrupt police chief Smith shoots Vincennes, the latter mutters "Rollo Tomasi" with his last breath. When the puzzled Smith asks Exley who Rollo Tomasi is, Exley's earlier conversation with Vincennes motivates his shocked realization that the dead Vincennes has given him a clue identifying his killer. Near the end, when Exley is about to shoot Smith, he says that the chief is Rollo Tomasi. Thus an apparently minor detail returns as a major causal and thematic motif. And perhaps the unusual name, Rollo Tomasi, functions to help the audience remember this important motif across several scenes.

Most of what we have said about causality pertains to the plot's direct presentation of causes and effects. In *The Man Who Knew Too Much,* Jill is shown to be a good shot, and because of this she can save her daughter. The townsfolk in *Jaws* respond to the shark attack that is shown at the start of the film. But the plot can also lead us to *infer* causes and effects and thus build up a total story. The detective film furnishes the best example of how this active construction of the story may work.

A murder has been committed. That is, we know an effect but not the causes—the killer, the motive, perhaps also the method. The mystery tale thus depends strongly on curiosity, our desire to know events that have occurred before the plot action begins. It is the detective's job to disclose, at the end, the missing causes—to name the killer, explain the motive, and reveal the method. That is, in the detective film the climax of the plot (the action that we see) is a revelation of prior incidents in the story (events which we did not see). We can diagram this.

a. **Crime conceived**
b. **Crime planned**
c. **Crime committed**
d. **Crime discovered**
e. **Detective investigates**
f. **Detective reveals a, b, and c**

Although this pattern is most common in detective narratives, any film's plot can withhold causes and thus arouse our curiosity. Horror and science-fiction films often leave us temporarily in the dark about what forces lurk behind certain events. Not until three-quarters of the way through *Alien* do we learn that the science officer Ash is a robot conspiring against the rest of the crew to protect the alien. We shall see that the plot of *Citizen Kane* delays revealing what causes the hero to say "Rosebud" on his deathbed. In general, whenever any film creates a mystery, it does so by suppressing certain story causes and by presenting only effects in the plot.

The plot may also present causes but withhold story effects, prompting suspense and uncertainty in the viewer. After Hannibal Lecter's attack on his guards in the Tennessee prison in *The Silence of the Lambs,* the police search of the building raises the possibility that a body lying on top of an elevator is the wounded Lecter. After an extended suspense scene, we learn that he has switched clothes with a dead guard and escaped.

A plot's withholding of effects is perhaps most disruptive at the end of a film. A famous example occurs in the final moments of François Truffaut's *The 400*

3.8   The final image of *The 400 Blows* fails to provide closure.

Blows. The boy Antoine Doinel has escaped from a reformatory and runs along the seashore. The camera zooms in on his face and the frame freezes **(3.8).** The plot does not reveal whether he is captured and brought back, leaving us to speculate on what might happen next.

Time

Causes and their effects are basic to narrative, but they take place in time. Here again our story–plot distinction is of some help in clarifying how time shapes our understanding of narrative action.

As we watch a film, we construct story time on the basis of what the plot presents. For example, the plot may present events out of chronological order. In *Citizen Kane,* we see a man's death before we see his youth, and we must build up a chronological version of his life. Even if events are in chronological order, most plots do not show every detail from beginning to end. We assume that the characters spend uneventful time sleeping, traveling from place to place, eating, and the like, but the story duration containing irrelevant action has simply been skipped over. Another possibility is to have the plot present the same story event more than once, as when a character recalls a traumatic incident. In *House of Games,* the heroine accidently fires a gun and apparently kills a policemen; in a later scene, a quick shot of the gun firing by the man's stomach shows us her sudden memory of the moment. Similarly, in John Woo's *The Killer,* an accident in the opening scene blinds a singer, and later we see the same event again and again as the protagonist regretfully thinks back to it.

Such options mean that in constructing the film's story out of its plot, the viewer tries to put events in chronological *order* and to assign them some *duration* and *frequency.* We can look at each of these temporal factors separately.

Temporal Order   We are quite accustomed to films that present events out of story **order.** A flashback is simply a portion of a story that the plot presents out of chronological order. In *Edward Scissorhands,* we first see the Winona Ryder character as an old woman telling her granddaughter a bedtime story. Most of the film then consists of a lengthy depiction of events that occurred when she was a high school girl. Such reordering does not confuse us because we mentally rearrange the events into the order in which they would logically have to occur: Childhood comes before adulthood. From the plot order, we infer the story order. If story events can be thought of as ABCD, then the plot that uses a flashback presents something like BACD. Similarly, a flashforward—that is, moving from present to future then back to the present—would also be an instance of how plot can shuffle story order. A flashforward could be represented as ABDC.

Our example of the detective film is also pertinent here. A detective film not only manipulates story causality by holding back key events, but the film also juggles story order. The plot presents events surrounding the crime only when the detective reveals them at the climax.

One common pattern for reordering story events is an alternation of past and present in the plot. In the first half of Terence Davies' *Distant Voices, Still Lives* we see scenes set in the present during a young woman's wedding day. These alternate with flashbacks to a time when her family lived under the sway of an abusive, mentally disturbed father. Interestingly, the flashback scenes are arranged out of chronological story order: Childhood episodes are mixed with scenes of adolescence.

Sometimes a fairly simple reordering of scenes can create complicated effects. The plot of Quentin Tarantino's *Pulp Fiction* begins with a couple deciding to rob the diner in which they are eating breakfast. This scene takes place somewhat late in the story, but the viewer doesn't learn this until near the end of the film, when the robbery interrupts a dialogue involving other, more central, characters eating breakfast in the same diner. Just by pulling a scene out of order and placing it at the start, Tarantino creates a surprise. Later in *Pulp Fiction* a hired killer is shot to death. But he reappears alive in subsequent scenes, which show him and his partner trying to dispose of a dead body. Tarantino has shifted a block of scenes from the middle of the story (before the man was killed) to the end of the plot. By coming at the film's conclusion these portions receive an emphasis they would not have if they had remained in their chronological story order.

Temporal Duration   The plot of *North by Northwest* presents four crowded days and nights in the life of Roger Thornhill. But the story stretches back far before that, since information about the past is revealed in the course of the plot. The story events include Roger's past marriages, the U.S. Intelligence Agency's plot to create a false agent named George Kaplan, and Van Damm's series of smuggling activities.

In general, a film's plot selects certain stretches of story **duration.** This could involve concentrating on a short, relatively cohesive time span, as *North by Northwest* does, or by highlighting significant stretches of time from a period of many years, as *Citizen Kane* does when it shows us the protagonist in his youth, skips over some time to show him as a young man, skips over more time to show him middle-aged, and so forth. The sum of all these slices of story duration yields an overall plot duration.

But we need one more distinction. Watching a movie takes time—20 minutes or two hours or eight hours (for example, Hans Jürgen Syberberg's *Our Hitler: A Film from Germany*). There is thus a third duration involved in a narrative film, which we can call screen duration. The relationships among story duration, plot duration, and screen duration are complex (see Notes and Queries for further discussion), but for our purposes we can say that the filmmaker can manipulate screen duration independently of the overall story duration and plot duration. For example, *North by Northwest* has an overall story duration of several years (including all relevant prior events), an overall plot duration of four days and nights, and a screen duration of about 136 minutes.

Just as plot duration selects from story duration, so screen duration selects from overall plot duration. In *North by Northwest,* only portions of the film's four days and nights are shown to us. An interesting counterexample is *Twelve Angry*

Men, the story of a jury deliberating a murder case. The 95 minutes of the movie approximate the same stretch of time in its characters' lives.

At a more specific level, the plot can use screen duration to override story time. For example, screen duration can *expand* story duration. A famous instance is that of the raising of the bridges in Sergei Eisenstein's *October.* Here an event that takes only a few moments in the story is stretched out to several minutes of screen time by means of the technique of film editing. As a result, this action gains a tremendous emphasis. The plot can also use screen duration to compress story time, as when a lengthy process is condensed into a rapid series of shots. These examples suggest that film techniques play a central role in creating screen duration. We shall consider this in more detail in Chapters 7 and 8.

Temporal Frequency   Most commonly, a story event is presented only once in the plot. Occasionally, however, a single story event may appear twice or even more in the plot treatment. If we see an event early in a film and then there is a flashback to that event later on, we see that same event twice. Some films use multiple narrators, each of whom describes the same event; again, we see it occur several times. This increased **frequency** may allow us to see the same action in several ways. The plot may also provide us with more information, so that we understand the event in a new context when it reappears. This occurs in *Pulp Fiction,* when the robbery of the diner, shown at the start of the film, takes on its full significance only when it is repeated at the climax. In *Run Lola Run,* a single event is repeated many times after it first occurs: Lola's boyfriend reports by phone that he has lost a bag (*Tasche*) full of drug money, and we hear him and Lola shouting "Tasche" several times, even though we realize that they really only say it once or twice each. The repetition of their shouts underlines their terror in a way characteristic of this hyperkinetic movie. In our examination of *Citizen Kane* we shall see another example of how repetition can recontextualize old information.

The various ways that a film's plot may manipulate story order, duration, and frequency illustrate how the spectator must actively participate in making sense of the narrative film. The plot supplies cues about chronological sequence, the time span of the actions, and the number of times an event occurs, and it is up to the spectator to make assumptions and inferences and to form expectations. In some cases, understanding of temporal relations can get quite complicated. In *The Usual Suspects,* a seemingly petty criminal spins an elaborate tale of his gang's activities to an FBI agent. His recounting unfolds in many flashbacks, some of which repeat events we witnessed in the opening scene. Yet a surprise final twist reveals that some of the flashbacks must have contained lies, and we must piece together both the chronology of events and the story's real cause–effect chain. Such play with time scrambling has become more common in recent decades. (See Box.)

Often we must motivate manipulations of time by the all-important principle of cause and effect. For instance, a flashback will often be justified as caused by some incident that triggers a character's recalling some event in the past. The plot may skip over years of story duration if they contain nothing important to the chains of cause and effect. The repetition of actions may also be motivated by the plot's need to communicate certain key causes very clearly to the spectator.

Space

In some media, a narrative might emphasize only causality and time. Many anecdotes do not specify where the action takes place. In film narrative, however, **space**

Playing Games with Story Time

For a spectator, reconstructing story order from the plot might be seen as a sort of game. Most Hollywood films make this game fairly simple. Still, just as we enjoy learning the rules of new games rather than playing the same one over and over, in unusual films we can enjoy the challenge of unpredictable presentations of story events.

Since the 1980s, occasional films have exploited that enjoyment by using techniques other than straightforward flashbacks and flashforwards to tell their stories. Such techniques include placing the story events out of order in novel ways. *Pulp Fiction* (1994) begins and ends with stages of a restaurant hold-up—seemingly a conventional frame story. Yet in fact the final event to occur in the story—the Bruce Willis character and his girlfriend fleeing Los Angeles—happens well before the last scene. The reordering of events is startling and confusing at first, but it is dramatically effective in the way the conclusion forces us to rethink events we have seen earlier. The success of *Pulp Fiction* made such a play with story order more acceptable in American filmmaking. *GO* (Doug Liman, 1999) presents the actions of a single night three times, each time from a different character's point of view. We cannot fully figure out what happened until the end, since various events are withheld from the first version and shown in the second and third. In 2001, Christopher Nolan presented all the scenes of *Memento* in reverse order. This tactic reflected the hero's selective memory loss, but it also posed a challenge to the viewer. Again audiences were intrigued and tried to piece together the story—though even the most determined reconstruction of events revealed that Nolan had left ambiguities and thus had avoided complete closure.

Pulp Fiction, GO, and *Memento* were independent films, but more mainstream Hollywood movies have also played with the temporal relations of story and plot. Steven Soderbergh's *Out of Sight* (1998) begins with the story of an inept bank robber who falls in love with an FBI agent who pursues him despite her obvious attraction to him. As their oddball romance proceeds, there are a series of flashbacks not motivated by any character's memory. These seem to involve a quite separate plotline, and their purpose is puzzling until the film's second half, when the final flashback, perhaps a character's recollection, loops back to the action that had begun the film and thus helps explain the main plot events.

Mainstream films tend to play with story time in a less daring way. They typically use science-fiction or fantasy premises to present alternative futures, or what we might call "what if?" narratives. Such films typically present a situation at the beginning, then show how it might proceed along different cause–effect chains if one factor were to be changed. *Sliding Doors* (Peter Howitt, 1998), for example, shows the heroine, Helen, fired from her job and heading home to her apartment, where her boyfriend is in bed with another woman. We see Helen entering the subway and catching her train, but then the action runs backwards and she enters again, this time bumping into a child on the stairs and missing the train. The rest of the film's plot moves between two alternative futures for Helen. By catching the train Helen arrives in time to discover the affair and moves out, while by missing the train she arrives after the other woman has left and hence she stays with her faithless boyfriend. The plot moves back and forth between these mutually exclusive cause–effect chains before neatly dovetailing them at the end.

Groundhog Day (Harold Ramis, 1993) helped to popularize "what if?" plots. On February 1, an obnoxious weatherman, Phil, travels to Punxsutawney to cover the famous Groundhog Day ceremonies. He then finds himself trapped in February 2, which repeats over and over, with variants depending on how Phil acts each day, sometimes frivolously, sometimes breaking

3.9 During one repetition of February 2 in *Groundhog Day*, Phil tests whether he can get away with crimes, getting himself tossed in jail in the evening . . .

3.10 . . . only to find himself waking up, as on other Groundhog Days, back in bed at the bed-and-breakfast inn.

laws (**3.9** and **3.10**), and later trying to improve his life. Only after many such days does he become an admirable character, and the repetitions mysteriously stop.

Neither *Sliding Doors* nor *Groundhog Day* provides any explanation for the forking of its protagonist's life into various paths. We simply must assume that some higher power has intervened in order to improve his or her situation. Other films may provide some justification for the changes, such as a time machine. The three *Back to the Future* films (Robert Zemekis, 1985, 1989, 1990) posit that Marty's friend Doc has invented such a machine, and in the first film it accidentally transports Marty back to 1955, a time just before his parents fell in love. By accidentally changing the cir-

cumstances that caused their romance, Marty endangers his own existence in 1985. Despite being comedies aimed primarily at teenagers and despite providing the time-machine motivation for the changes, the three films, and particularly Parts I and II, created complex crisscrossings of cause and effect. Although Marty induces his parents to fall in love and returns safely to 1985 (where his life has been improved as a result of his first time trip), events that take place in his life in 2015 again have effects in 1955, as the villain Biff uses the time machine to travel back and change what happened then in yet another way— one that ends with terrible consequences for Doc and for Marty's whole family. Marty must again travel back to 1955 to prevent Biff's change of events, and by the end of Part II, he becomes trapped there, while Doc is accidentally sent back to 1885. Marty joins him there in Part III for another set of threatened changes to the future. If all this sounds complicated, it is. Although the narrative maintains a remarkably unified series of cause–effect chains, it becomes so convoluted that at one point Doc diagrams events for Marty (and us) on a blackboard!

Not surprisingly, such narrative games were influenced by a similar trend in European art films. In 1981, Polish director Krzysztof Kieslowski made *Blind Chance*, which showed three sets of consequences depending on whether the protagonist caught a train at the beginning or not. Unlike *Sliding Doors*, however, *Blind Chance* presents these alternative futures as self-contained stories, one after the other. The same approach appears in *Run Lola Run* (Tom Tykwer, 1998, Germany), where the heroine's desperate attempts to replace a large sum that her inept boyfriend owes to drug dealers are shown as three stories that end very differently after small changes of action on Lola's part. (Alternative versions of events based on characters' conflicting recollections had already been used, most famously in Akira Kurosawa's *Rashomon* [1950] and Alain Resnais's *Last Year at*

3.11 In one storyline of *Sliding Doors,* Helen helpfully gets her hair cut short so that we can distinguish her from . . .

3.12 . . . the Helen of the other storyline, who keeps her hair long. (A bandage on her forehead was a crucial clue before the haircut, when the two Helens were otherwise identical.)

Marienbad [1961]. We shall see a similar tactic at work in *Citizen Kane.*)

Although temporal scrambling and "what if?" premises make it more difficult for us to piece story events together, filmmakers usually give us enough clues along the way to keep us from frustration. Usually the film does not provide a huge number of alternative futures—perhaps only two or three. Within these futures, the cause–effect chain remains linear, so that we can piece it together. The characters and settings tend to remain quite consistent for all the alternative storylines—though often small differences of appearance are introduced to help us keep track of events (**3.11** and **3.12**). The individual storylines tend to parallel each other. In all three presentations of events in *Run Lola Run* the goal is the same, even though the progression and outcomes are different. The final presentation of events tends to give us the impression of being the real, final one, and so "what if?" films tend to achieve a sense of closure. Characters even tend to talk about the events that have changed their lives, as we saw with Doc's blackboard explanation in *Back to the Future II.* In *Sliding Doors,* Helen remarks, "If only I had just caught that bloody train, it'd never have happened."

These films often appeal to the way we think in ordinary life. We are apt at times to speculate about how our lives would be different if a single significant event had been different. Thus we easily understand the sort of game that these films present, and we are willing to play it.

is usually an important factor. Events tend to occur in particular locales, such as Kansas or Oz; the Flint, Michigan, of *Roger and Me;* or the Manhattan of *North by Northwest.* We shall consider setting in more detail when we examine mise-en-scene in Chapter 6, but we ought briefly to note how plot and story can manipulate space.

Normally, the place of the story action is also that of the plot, but sometimes the plot leads us to infer other locales as part of the story. We never see Roger Thornhill's office or the colleges that kicked Kane out. Thus the narrative may ask us to imagine spaces and actions that are never shown. In Otto Preminger's *Exodus,* one scene is devoted to Dov Landau's interrogation by a terrorist organization he wants to join. Dov reluctantly tells his questioners of life in a Nazi concentration camp. Although the film never shows this locale through a flashback, much of the scene's emotional power depends on our using our imagination to fill in Dov's sketchy description of the camp.

Further, we can introduce an idea akin to the concept of screen duration. Besides story space and plot space, cinema employs screen space: the visible space within the frame. We shall consider screen space and offscreen space in detail in Chapter 7, when we analyze framing as a cinematographic technique. For now, it is enough to say that just as screen duration selects certain plot spans for presentation, so screen space selects portions of plot space.

Openings, Closings, and Patterns of Development

In Chapter 2 our discussion of formal development within the film suggested that it is often useful to compare beginnings and endings. This holds true for narrative form as well, since a narrative's use of causality, time, and space usually involves a change from an initial situation to a final situation.

A film does not just start, it *begins.* The opening provides a basis for what is to come and initiates us into the narrative. In some cases, the plot will seek to arouse curiosity by bringing us into a series of actions that has already started. (This is called opening *in medias res,* a Latin phrase meaning "in the middle of things.") The viewer speculates on possible causes of the events presented. *The Usual Suspects* begins with a mysterious man named Keyser Söze killing one of the main characters and setting fire to a ship. Much of the rest of the film will deal with how these events came to pass. In other cases, the film begins by telling us about the characters and their situations before any major actions occur. Either way, some of the actions that took place before the plot started will be stated or suggested so that we can start to connect up the whole story. The portion of the plot that lays out story events and character traits important in the opening situation is called the *exposition.* In general, the opening raises our expectations by setting up a specific range of possible causes for and effects of what we see. (Indeed, the first quarter or so of a film's plot is often referred to as the *setup.*)

No film can explore all the possibilities hovering in our mind at the start. As the plot proceeds, the causes and effects will define narrower patterns of development. There is no exhaustive list of possible plot patterns, but several kinds crop up frequently enough to be worth mentioning.

Most patterns of plot development depend heavily upon the ways that causes and effects create a change in a character's situation. The most common general pattern is a *change in knowledge.* Very often, a character learns something in the course of the action, with the most crucial knowledge coming at the final turning point of the plot. In *Witness,* when John Book, hiding out on an Amish farm, learns that his partner has been killed, his rage soon leads to a climactic shoot-out.

A very common pattern of development is the *goal-oriented* plot, in which a character takes steps to achieve a desired object or state of affairs. Plots based on *searches* would be instances of the goal plot. In *Raiders of the Lost Ark,* the protagonists try to find the Ark of the Covenant; in *Le Million,* characters search for a missing lottery ticket; in *North by Northwest,* Roger Thornhill looks for George Kaplan. A variation on the goal-oriented plot pattern is the *investigation,* so typical of detective films, in which the protagonist's goal is not an object, but information, usually about mysterious causes. In more strongly psychological films, such as Fellini's *8½,* the search and the investigation become internalized when the protagonist, a noted film director, attempts to discover the source of his creative problems.

Time or space may also provide plot patterns. A framing situation in the present may initiate a series of flashbacks showing how events led up to the present situation, as in *The Usual Suspects'* flashbacks. *Hoop Dreams* is organized around the two main characters' high school careers, with each part of the film devoted to a year of their lives. The plot may also create a specific duration for the action, a deadline. In *Back to the Future,* the hero must synchronize his time machine with a bolt of lightning at a specific moment in order to return to the present. This creates a goal toward which he must struggle. Or the plot may create patterns of repeated action via cycles of events: the familiar "here we go again" pattern. Such a pattern occurs in Woody Allen's *Zelig,* in which the chameleonlike hero repeatedly loses his own identity by imitating the people around him.

Space can also become the basis for a plot pattern. This usually happens when the action is confined to a single locale, such as a train (Anthony Mann's *The Tall Target*) or a home (Sidney Lumet's *Long Day's Journey into Night*).

A given plot can, of course, combine these patterns. Many films built around a journey, such as *The Wizard of Oz* or *North by Northwest,* involve deadlines. Jacques Tati's *Mr. Hulot's Holiday* uses both spatial and temporal patterns to structure its comic plot. The plot confines itself to a beachside resort and its neighboring areas, and it consumes one week of a summer vacation. Each day certain routines recur: morning exercise, lunch, afternoon outings, dinner, evening entertainment. Much of the film's humor relies on the way that Mr. Hulot alienates the other guests and the townspeople by disrupting their conventional habits **(3.13).** Although cause and effect still operate in *Mr. Hulot's Holiday,* time and space are central to the plot's formal patterning.

For any pattern of development, the spectator will create specific expectations. As the film trains the viewer in its particular form, these expectations become more and more precise. Once we comprehend Dorothy's desire to go home, we see her

3.13 In *Mr. Hulot's Holiday,* Hulot's aged, noisy car has a flat tire that breaks up a funeral.

every action as furthering or delaying her progress toward her goal. Thus her trip through Oz is hardly a sightseeing tour. Each step of her journey (to the Emerald City, to the Witch's castle, to the Emerald City again) is governed by the same principle—her desire to go home.

In any film, the pattern of development in the middle portion may delay an expected outcome. When Dorothy at last reaches the Wizard, he sets up a new obstacle for her by demanding the Witch's broom. Similarly, in *North by Northwest,* Hitchcock's journey plot constantly postpones Roger Thornhill's discovery of the Kaplan hoax, and this, too, creates suspense. The pattern of development may also create surprise, the cheating of an expectation, as when Dorothy discovers that the Wizard is a fraud or when Thornhill sees the minion Leonard fire point-blank at his boss Van Damm. Patterns of development encourage the spectator to form long-term expectations that can be delayed, cheated, or gratified.

A film does not simply stop; it *ends.* The narrative will typically resolve its causal issues by bringing the development to a high point, or *climax.* In the climax, the action is presented as having a narrow range of possible outcomes. At the climax of *North by Northwest,* Roger and Eve are dangling off Mount Rushmore, and there are only two possibilities: They will fall, or they will be saved.

Because the climax focuses possible outcomes so narrowly, it typically serves to settle the causal issues that have run through the film. In the documentary *Primary,* climax takes place on election night; both Kennedy and Humphrey await the voters' verdict and finally learn the winner. In *Jaws* several battles with the shark climax in the collapse of the boat, the death of Captain Quint, the apparent death of Hooper, and Brody's final victory. In such films the ending resolves, or closes off, the chains of cause and effect.

Emotionally, the climax aims to lift the viewer to a high degree of tension or suspense. Since the viewer knows that there are relatively few ways the action can develop, she or he can hope for a fairly specific outcome. In the climax of many films, formal resolution coincides with an emotional satisfaction.

A few narratives, however, are deliberately anticlimactic. Having created expectations about how the cause–effect chain will be resolved, the film scotches them by refusing to settle things definitely. One famous example is the last shot of *The 400 Blows* (p. 74). In Michelangelo Antonioni's *L'Eclisse* ("The Eclipse"), the two lovers vow to meet for a final reconciliation but never do.

In such films, the ending remains relatively open. That is, the plot leaves us uncertain about the final consequences of the story events. Our response becomes less firm than it does when a film has a clear-cut climax and resolution. The form may encourage us to imagine what might happen next or to reflect on other ways in which our expectations might have been fulfilled.

NARRATION: THE FLOW OF STORY INFORMATION

A plot presents or implies story information. The opening of *North by Northwest* shows Manhattan at rush hour and introduces Roger Thornhill as an advertising executive; it also suggests that he has been busily dictating before we see him. Filmmakers have long realized that the spectator's interest can be aroused and manipulated by carefully divulging story information at various points. In general, when we go to a film, we know relatively little about the story; by the end we know a lot more, usually the whole story. What happens in between?

   The plot may arrange cues in ways that withhold information for the sake of curiosity or surprise. Or the plot may supply information in such a way as to create expectations or increase suspense. All these processes constitute **narration,** the plot's way of distributing story information in order to achieve specific effects. Narration is the moment-by-moment process that guides us in building the story out of the plot. Many factors enter into narration (see Notes and Queries), but the most important ones for our purposes involve the *range* and the *depth* of story information that the plot presents.

Range of Story Information

The plot of D. W. Griffith's *The Birth of a Nation* begins by recounting how slaves were brought to America and how people debated the need to free them. The plot then shows two families, the northern Stoneman family and the southern Camerons. The plot also dwells on political matters, including Lincoln's hope of averting civil war. From the start, then, our range of knowledge is very broad. The plot takes us across historical periods, regions of the country, and various groups of characters. This breadth of story information continues throughout the film. When Ben Cameron founds the Ku Klux Klan, we know about it at the moment the idea strikes him, long before the other characters learn of it. At the climax, we know that the Klan is riding to rescue several characters besieged in a cabin, but the besieged people do not know this. On the whole, in *The Birth of a Nation* the narration is very *unrestricted:* We know more, we see and hear more, than any of the characters can. Such extremely knowledgeable narration is often called *omniscient narration.*

   Now consider the plot of Howard Hawks's *The Big Sleep.* The film begins with the detective Philip Marlowe visiting General Sternwood, who wants to hire him. We learn about the case as he does. Throughout the rest of the film, Marlowe is present in every scene. With hardly any exceptions, we don't see or hear anything that he cannot see and hear. The narration is thus *restricted* to what Marlowe knows.

   Each alternative offers certain advantages. *The Birth of a Nation* seeks to present a panoramic vision of a period in American history (seen through peculiarly racist spectacles). Omniscient narration is thus essential to creating the sense of many destinies intertwined with the fate of the country. Had Griffith restricted narration the way *The Big Sleep* does, we would have learned story information solely through one character—say, Ben Cameron. We could not witness the prologue scene or the scenes in Lincoln's office or most of the battle episodes or the scene of Lincoln's assassination, since Ben is present at none of these events. The plot would now concentrate on one man's experience of the Civil War and Reconstruction.

   Similarly, *The Big Sleep* derives functional advantages from its restricted narration. By limiting us to Marlowe's range of knowledge, the film can create curiosity and surprise. Restricted narration is important to mystery films, since the films engage our interest by hiding certain important causes. Confining the plot to an investigator's range of knowledge plausibly motivates concealing other story information. *The Big Sleep* could have been less restricted by, say, alternating scenes of Marlowe's investigation with scenes that show the gambling boss, Eddie Mars, planning his crimes, but this would have given away some of the mystery. In each of the two films, the narration's range of knowledge functions to elicit certain reactions from the viewer.

   Unrestricted and restricted narration are not watertight categories but rather two ends of a continuum. Range is a matter of degree. A film may present a broader range of knowledge than does *The Big Sleep* and still not attain the omniscience of *The Birth of a Nation.* In *North by Northwest,* for instance, the early scenes confine us pretty much to what Roger Thornhill sees and knows. After he flees from the United Nations building, however, the plot moves to Washington, where the members of the United States Intelligence Agency discuss the situation. Here the viewer learns something that Roger Thornhill will not learn for some time: The man he seeks, George Kaplan, does not exist. Thereafter, we have a greater range of knowledge than Roger does. In at least one important respect we also know more than the Agency's staff: We know exactly how the mix-up took place. But we still do not know many other things that the narration could have divulged in the scene in Washington. For instance, the Intelligence Agency's staff do not identify the agent they do have working under Van Damm's nose. In this way, any film may oscillate between restricted and unrestricted presentation of story information. (For more on narration in *North by Northwest,* see pp. 418–423.)

In fact, across a whole film, narration is never completely unrestricted. There is always something we are not told, even if it is only how the film will end. Usually, therefore, we think of a typical unrestricted narration as operating in the way that it does in *The Birth of a Nation:* The plot shifts constantly from character to character to change our source of information. Similarly, a completely restricted narration is not common. Even if the plot is built around a single character, the narration usually includes a few scenes that the character is not present to witness. Though *Tootsie*'s narration remains almost entirely attached to actor Michael Dorsey, a few shots show his acquaintances shopping or watching him on television.

The plot's range of story information creates a *hierarchy of knowledge,* and this may vary somewhat depending on the film. At any given moment, we can ask if the viewer knows more than, less than, or as much as the characters do. For instance, here is how hierarchies would look for the three films we have been discussing. The higher someone is on the scale, the greater his or her range of knowledge:

The Birth of a Nation (unrestricted narration)	*The Big Sleep* (restricted)	*North by Northwest* (mixed and fluctuating)
viewer	viewer—Marlowe	the Agency
all characters		viewer
		Thornhill

An easy way to analyze the range of narration is to ask, "Who knows what when?" The spectator must be included among the "whos," not only because we may get more knowledge than any one character but also because we may get knowledge that *no* character possesses. We shall see this happen at the end of *Citizen Kane.*

Our examples suggest the powerful effects that narration can achieve by manipulating the range of story information. Restricted narration tends to create greater curiosity and surprise for the viewer. For instance, if a character is exploring a sinister house and we see and hear no more than the character does, a sudden revelation of a hand thrusting out from a doorway will startle us. In contrast, as Alfred Hitchcock pointed out, a degree of unrestricted narration helps build suspense. He explained it this way to François Truffaut:

> We are now having a very innocent little chat. Let us suppose that there is a bomb underneath this table between us. Nothing happens, and then all of a sudden, "Boom!" There is an explosion. The public is surprised, but prior to this surprise, it has seen an

"In the first section [of *Reservoir Dogs*], up until Mr. Orange shoots Mr. Blonde, the characters have far more information about what's going on than you have—and they have conflicting information. Then the Mr. Orange sequence happens and that's a great leveller. You start getting caught up with exactly what's going on, and in the third part, when you go back into the warehouse for the climax you are totally ahead of everybody—you know far more than any one of the characters."

— Quentin Tarantino

absolutely ordinary scene, of no special consequence. Now, let us take a suspense situation. The bomb is underneath the table and the public knows it, probably because they have seen the anarchist place it there. The public is aware that the bomb is going to explode at one o'clock and there is a clock in the decor. The public can see that it is a quarter to one. In these conditions this innocuous conversation becomes fascinating because the public is participating in the scene. The audience is longing to warn the characters on the screen: "You shouldn't be talking about such trivial matters. There's a bomb beneath you and it's about to explode!"

In the first case we have given the public fifteen seconds of surprise at the moment of the explosion. In the second case we have provided them with fifteen minutes of suspense. The conclusion is that whenever possible the public must be informed. [François Truffaut, *Hitchcock* (New York: Simon & Schuster, 1967), p. 52.]

Hitchcock put his theory into practice. In *Psycho,* Lila Crane explores the Bates mansion in much the same way as our hypothetical character is doing above. There are isolated moments of surprise as she discovers odd information about Norman and his mother. But the overall effect of the sequence is built on suspense because we know, as Lila does not, that Mrs. Bates is in the house, possibly in the fruit cellar, or possibly stalking Lila. (Actually, as in *North by Northwest,* our knowledge is not completely accurate, but during Lila's investigation we believe it to be.) As in Hitchcock's anecdote, our superior range of knowledge creates suspense because we can anticipate events that the character cannot.

Depth of Story Information

A film's narration not only manipulates degrees of knowledge but also manipulates the depth of our knowledge. Here we are referring to how deeply the plot plunges into a character's psychological states. Just as there is a spectrum between restricted and unrestricted narration, there is a continuum between objectivity and subjectivity.

A plot might confine us wholly to information about what characters say and do: their external behavior. Here the narration is relatively *objective.* Or a film's plot may give us access to what characters see and hear. We might see shots taken from a character's optical standpoint, the **point-of-view shot,** or hear sounds as the character would hear them what sound recordists call *sound perspective.* This would offer a greater degree of subjectivity, one we might call *perceptual subjectivity.*

There is the possibility of still greater depth if the plot plunges into the character's mind. We might hear an internal voice reporting the character's thoughts, or we might see the character's inner images, representing memory, fantasy, dreams, or hallucinations. This can be termed *mental subjectivity.* In such ways, narrative films can present story information at various depths of the character's psychological life.

Does a restricted range of knowledge create a greater subjective depth? Not necessarily. *The Big Sleep* is quite restricted in its range of knowledge, but we very seldom see or hear things from Marlowe's perceptual vantage point, and we never get direct access to his mind. *The Big Sleep* uses almost completely objective narration. The omniscient narration of *The Birth of a Nation,* however, plunges to considerable depth with optical point-of-view shots, flashbacks, and the hero's final fantasy vision of a world without war. Hitchcock delights in giving us greater knowledge than his characters have, but then at certain moments he confines us to their perceptual subjectivity (for instance, through point-of-view shots). Range and depth of knowledge are independent variables.

Incidentally, this is one reason why the term point of view is ambiguous. It can refer to range of knowledge (as when a critic speaks of an "omniscient point of

3.14   In *North by Northwest,* Roger Thornhill looks in Van Damm's window (objective narration).

3.15   A shot from Roger's point of view follows (perceptual subjectivity).

3.16   This is followed by another shot of Roger looking (objectivity again).

view") or to depth (as when speaking of "subjective point of view"). In this book, we will use point of view only to refer to perceptual subjectivity, as in the phrase "optical point-of-view shot."

Manipulating the depth of knowledge can have many functions and effects. Plunging to the depths of mental subjectivity can increase our identification with a character and can cue stable expectations about what the characters will later say or do. The memory sequences in Alain Resnais's *Hiroshima mon amour* and the fantasy sequences in Fellini's *8½* yield information about the protagonists' traits and possible future actions that would be less vivid if presented objectively. A subjectively motivated flashback can create parallels among characters, as does the flashback shared by mother and son in Kenji Mizoguchi's *Sansho the Bailiff.* A plot can create curiosity about a character's motives and then use some degree of subjectivity—for example, inner commentary or subjective flashback—to explain the cause of the behavior. In *The Sixth Sense,* the child psychologist's odd estrangement from his wife begins to make sense when we hear his inner recollection of something his young patient had told him much earlier.

On the other hand, objectivity can be an effective way of withholding information. One reason that *The Big Sleep* does not treat Marlowe subjectively is that the detective genre demands that the detective's reasoning be concealed from the viewer. The mystery is more mysterious if we do not know his hunches and conclusions before he reveals them at the end. At any moment in a film we can ask "How deeply do I know the characters' perceptions, feelings, and thoughts?" The answer will point directly to how the narration is presenting or withholding story information in order to achieve a formal function or a specific effect on the viewer.

One final point about the depth of knowledge that the narration presents: Most films insert subjective moments into an overall framework of objectivity. For instance, in *North by Northwest,* point-of-view editing is used as we see Roger Thornhill crawl up to Van Damm's window (**3.14–3.16**). Similarly, a dream sequence will often be bracketed by shots of the sleeper in bed.

Flashbacks offer a fascinating instance of the overarching power of objective narration. They are usually motivated as mental subjectivity, since the events we see are triggered by a character's recalling the past. Yet, once we are inside the flashback, events will typically be presented from a wholly objective standpoint. They will usually be presented in an unrestricted fashion, too, and may even include action that the remembering character could have no way of knowing.

In other words, most films take objective narration as a baseline from which we may depart in search of subjective depth but to which we will return. There are, however, other films that refuse this convention and that mix objectivity and subjectivity in ambiguous ways. Fellini's *8½,* Buñuel's *Belle du jour* and *That Obscure Object of Desire,* and Resnais's *Last Year at Marienbad* are good examples. Here, as elsewhere, the manipulation of story information is not just a matter of what action takes place in the film. Any choice about range or depth has concrete effects on how the spectator thinks and feels about the film as it progresses.

The Narrator

Narration, then, is the process by which the plot presents story information to the spectator. This process may shift between restricted and unrestricted ranges of knowledge and varying degrees of objectivity and subjectivity. Narration may also use a *narrator,* some specific agent who purports to be telling us the story. The narrator may be a *character* in the story. We are familiar with this convention from literature, as when Huck Finn or Jane Eyre recounts a novel's action. In Edward Dmytryk's film *Murder, My Sweet,* the detective tells his story in flashbacks, addressing the information to inquiring policemen. In the documentary *Roger and Me,* Michael Moore frankly acknowledges his role as a character narrator. He starts the film with his reminiscences of growing up in Flint, Michigan, and he appears on camera in interviews with workers and in confrontations with General Motors security staff.

A film can also use a *noncharacter narrator.* Noncharacter narrators are common in documentary. We never learn who belongs to the anonymous "voice of God" we hear in *The River, Primary,* or *Hoop Dreams.* A fictional film may employ this device as well. *Jules and Jim* uses a dry, matter-of-fact, commentator to lend a flavor of objectivity, while other films might call on this device to lend a sense of realism, as in the urgent voice-over we hear during *The Naked City.*

A film may play on the character/noncharacter distinction by making the source of a narrating voice uncertain. In *Film about a Woman Who . . . ,* we might assume that a character is the narrator, but we cannot be sure because we cannot tell which character the voice belongs to. In fact, it may be coming from an external commentator.

Note that either sort of narrator may present various sorts of narration. A character narrator is not necessarily restricted and may tell of events that she or he did not witness, as the relatively minor figure of the village priest does in John Ford's *The Quiet Man.* A noncharacter narrator need not be omniscient and could confine the commentary to what a single character knows. A character narrator might be highly subjective, telling us details of his or her inner life, or might be objective, confining his or her recounting strictly to externals. A noncharacter narrator might give us access to subjective depths, as in *Jules and Jim,* or might stick simply to surface events, as does the impersonal voice-over commentator in *The Killing.* In any case, the viewer's process of picking up cues, erecting expectations, and constructing an ongoing story out of the plot will be partially shaped by what the narrator tells or does not tell.

Summing Up Narration

We can summarize the shaping power of narration by considering George Miller's *The Road Warrior* (also known as *Mad Max II*). The film's plot opens with a voice-over commentary by an elderly male narrator who recalls "the warrior Max." After presenting an exposition telling of the worldwide wars that led society to degenerate into gangs of scavengers, the narrator falls silent. The question of his identity is left open.

The rest of the plot is organized around Max's encounter with a group of peaceful desert people. They want to flee to the coast with the gasoline they have refined, but they are under siege by a gang of vicious marauders. The cause–effect chain involves Max's agreement to work for the settlers in exchange for gasoline. Later, after a brush with the gang leaves him wounded, his dog dead, and his car demolished, Max commits himself to helping the people escape their compound. The struggle against the encircling gangs comes to its climax in an attempt to escape with a tanker truck, with Max at the wheel.

Max is at the center of the plot's causal chain. Moreover, after the anonymous narrator's prologue, most of the film is restricted to his range of knowledge. Like Philip Marlowe in *The Big Sleep,* Max is present in every scene, and almost everything we learn gets funneled through him. The depth of story information is also consistent. The narration provides optical point-of-view shots as Max drives his car

3.17   A point-of-view shot as Max drives up to an apparently abandoned gyro in *The Road Warrior.*

3.18   The injured Max's dizzy view of his rescuer uses double exposure.

(3.17) or watches a skirmish through a telescope. When he is rescued after his car crash, his delirium is rendered as mental subjectivity, using the conventional cues of slow-motion, superimposed imagery, and slowed-down sound **(3.18).** All of these narrational devices encourage us to sympathize with Max.

At certain points, however, the narration becomes more unrestricted. This occurs principally during chases and battle scenes, where we witness events Max probably does not know about. In such scenes, unrestricted narration functions to build up suspense by showing both pursuers and pursued or different aspects of the battle. At the climax, Max's truck successfully draws the gang away from the desert people, who escape to the south. But when his truck overturns, Max—and we—learn that the truck holds only sand. It has been a decoy. Thus our restriction to Max's range of knowledge creates a surprise.

There is still more to learn, however. At the very end, the elderly narrator's voice returns to tell us that he was the feral boy whom Max had befriended. The desert people drive off, and Max is left alone in the middle of the highway. The film's final image—a shot of the solitary Max receding into the distance as we pull back **(3.19)**—suggests both a perceptual subjectivity (the boy's point of view as he rides away from Max) and a mental subjectivity (the memory of Max dimming for the narrator).

3.19   As the camera tracks away from Max, we hear the narrator's voice: "And the Road Warrior? That was the last we ever saw of him. He lives now only in my memories."

In *The Road Warrior,* then, the plot's form is achieved not only by causality, time, and space but also by a coherent use of narration. The middle portion of the film channels our expectations through an identification with Max, alternating with more unrestricted portions. And this middle section is framed by the mysterious narrator who puts all the events into the distant past. The narrator's presence at the opening leads us to expect him to return at the end, perhaps explaining who he is. Thus both the cause–effect organization and the narrational patterning help the film achieve coherence and closure.

THE CLASSICAL HOLLYWOOD CINEMA

The number of possible narratives is unlimited. Historically, however, fictional cinema has tended to be dominated by a single mode of narrative form. We shall refer to this dominant mode as the "classical Hollywood cinema." This mode is "classical" because of its lengthy, stable, and influential history, "Hollywood" because the mode assumed its most elaborate shape in American studio films. The same mode, however, governs many narrative films made in other countries. For example, *The Road Warrior,* though an Australian film, is constructed along classical Hollywood lines. And many documentaries, such as *Primary,* rely upon conventions derived from Hollywood's fictional narratives.

This conception of narrative depends on the assumption that the action will spring primarily from *individual characters as causal agents.* Natural causes (floods, earthquakes) or societal causes (institutions, wars, economic depressions) may serve as catalysts or preconditions for the action, but the narrative invariably centers on personal psychological causes: decisions, choices, and traits of character.

Often an important trait that functions to get the narrative moving is a *desire.* The character wants something. The desire sets up a goal, and the course of the narrative's development will most likely involve the process of achieving that goal. In *The Wizard of Oz* Dorothy has a series of goals, as we have seen: first to save Toto from Miss Gulch, then to get home from Oz. The latter goal creates short-term goals along the way: getting to the Emerald City and then killing the Witch.

If this desire to reach a goal were the only element present, there would be nothing to stop the character from moving quickly to achieve it. But there is a counterforce in the classical narrative: an opposition that creates conflict. The protagonist comes up against a character whose traits and goals are opposed to his or hers. As a result, the protagonist must seek to change the situation so that he or she can achieve the goal. Dorothy's desire to return to Kansas is opposed by the Wicked Witch, whose goal is to obtain the ruby slippers. Dorothy must eventually eliminate the Witch before she is able to use the slippers to go home. We shall see in *His Girl Friday* how the two main characters' goals conflict until the final resolution (pp. 415–418).

Cause and effect imply *change*. If the characters did not desire something to be different from the way it is at the beginning of the narrative, change would not occur. Therefore characters and their traits, particularly desire, are a strong source of causes and effects.

But don't all narratives have protagonists of this sort? Actually, no. In 1920s Soviet films, such as Sergei Eisenstein's *Potemkin, October,* and *Strike,* no *individual* serves as protagonist. More recently, Jacques Rivette's *L'Amour Fou* and Robert Altman's *Nashville* experiment with eliminating protagonists. In films like those of Eisenstein and Yasujiro Ozu, many events are seen as caused not by characters but by larger forces (social dynamics in the former, an overarching Nature in the latter). In narrative films such as Michelangelo Antonioni's *L'Avventura,* the protagonist is not active but passive. So the active, goal-oriented protagonist, though common, does not appear in every narrative film.

In the classical Hollywood narrative the chain of actions that results from predominantly psychological causes tends to motivate most other narrative events. Time is subordinated to the cause–effect chain in a host of ways. The plot will omit significant durations in order to show only events of causal importance. (The hours Dorothy and her entourage spend walking on the Road are omitted, but the moments during which she meets a new character are presented.) The plot will order story chronology so as to present the cause–effect chain most strikingly. For instance, in one scene of *Hannah and Her Sisters,* Mickey (played by Woody Allen) is in a suicidal depression. When we next see him several scenes later, he is bubbly and cheerful. Our curiosity about this abrupt change enhances his comic explanation to a friend, via a flashback, that he achieved a serene attitude toward life while watching an anarchic Marx Brothers film.

Specific devices make plot time depend on the story's cause–effect chain: the *appointment* (which motivates characters' encountering each other at a specific moment) and the *deadline* (which makes plot duration dependent on the cause–effect chain). Motivation in the classical narrative film will strive to be as clear and complete as possible—even in the fanciful genre of the musical, in which song-and-dance numbers become motivated as either expressions of the characters' emotions or stage shows mounted by the characters.

Narration in the classical Hollywood cinema exploits a variety of options, but there is a strong tendency for it to be objective in the way discussed on pp. 85–86. That is, there is a basically objective story reality, against which various degrees of perceptual or mental subjectivity can be measured. Classical cinema also tends toward fairly unrestricted narration. Even if we follow a single character, there are portions of the film giving us access to things the character does not see, hear, or know. (*North by Northwest* and *The Road Warrior* remain good examples of this tendency.) This weighting is overridden only in genres that depend heavily on mystery, such as the detective film, with its reliance on the sort of restrictiveness we saw at work in *The Big Sleep.*

Finally, most classical narrative films display a strong degree of **closure** at the end. Leaving few loose ends unresolved, these films seek to complete their causal chains with a final effect. We usually learn the fate of each character, the answer to each mystery, and the outcome of each conflict.

Again, none of these features is necessary to narrative form in general. There is nothing to prevent a filmmaker from presenting the dead time, or narratively unmotivated intervals between more significant events. (François Truffaut, Jean-Luc Godard, Carl Dreyer, and Andy Warhol do this frequently, in different ways.) The filmmaker's plot can also reorder story chronology to make the causal chain *more* perplexing. For example, Jean-Marie Straub and Danièle Huillet's *Not Reconciled* moves back and forth among three widely different time periods without clearly signaling the shifts. Dušan Makavejev's *Love Affair, or the Case of the Missing Switchboard Operator* uses flashforwards interspersed with the main plot action; only gradually do we come to understand the causal relations of these flashforwards to the present-time events.

The filmmaker can also include material that is unmotivated by narrative cause and effect, such as the chance meetings in Truffaut's films, the political monologues and interviews in Godard's films, the intellectual montage sequences in Eisenstein's films, the transitional shots in Ozu's work, and so on. Narration may be completely subjective, as in *The Cabinet of Dr. Caligari,* or it may hover ambiguously between objectivity and subjectivity as in *Last Year at Marienbad.* Finally, the filmmaker need not resolve all of the action at the close; films made outside the classical tradition sometimes have quite open endings.

We shall see in Chapter 8 how the classical Hollywood mode also makes cinematic space serve causality by means of continuity editing. For now we can simply note how the classical mode tends to treat narrative elements and narrational processes in specific and distinctive ways. The classical Hollywood mode is, however, only one system among many that have been and could be used for constructing films

NARRATIVE FORM IN *CITIZEN KANE*

With its unusual form and varied style, *Citizen Kane* invites us to analyze how principles of narrative function across an entire film. *Kane*'s investigation plot carries us toward analyzing how causality and goal-oriented characters may operate in narratives. The film's manipulations of our knowledge shed light on the story–plot distinction. *Kane* also shows how ambiguity may arise when certain elements are not clearly motivated. Furthermore, the comparison of *Kane*'s beginning with its ending indicates how a film may deviate from the patterns of classical Hollywood narrative construction. Finally, *Kane* clearly shows how our experience can be shaped by the way that narration governs the flow of story information.

Overall Narrative Expectations

We have seen in Chapter 2 that our experience of a film depends heavily on the expectations we bring to it and the extent to which the film confirms them. Before you saw *Citizen Kane,* you may have known only that it is regarded as a film classic. Such an evaluation would not give us a very specific set of expectations. A 1941 audience would have had a keener sense of anticipation. For one thing, the film was rumored to be a disguised version of the life of the newspaper publisher William Randolph Hearst. Spectators would thus be looking for events and references keyed to Hearst's life.

Several minutes into the film itself, the viewer can form more specific expectations about pertinent genre conventions. The early "News on the March" sequence suggests that this film may be a fictional biography, and this hint is confirmed once the reporter, Thompson, begins his inquiry into Kane's life. The film does indeed follow the conventional outline of the fictional biography, which typically covers an individual's whole life and dramatizes certain episodes in the period. Examples of this genre would be *Anthony Adverse* (1936) and *The Power and the Glory* (1933). (The latter film is often cited as an influence on *Citizen Kane* because of its complex use of flashbacks.)

The viewer can also quickly identify the film's use of conventions of the newspaper-reporter genre. Thompson's colleagues resemble the wisecracking reporters in *Five Star Final* (1931), *Picture Snatcher* (1933), and *His Girl Friday* (1940). In this genre, the action usually depends on a reporter's dogged pursuit of a story against great odds. We are therefore prepared to expect not only Thompson's investigation but also his triumphant discovery of the truth. In the scenes devoted to Susan, there are also some conventions typical of the musical film: frantic rehearsals, backstage preparations, and, most specifically, the montage of her opera career, which parodies the conventional montage of singing success in films like *Maytime* (1937). More broadly, the film evidently owes something to the detective genre, since Thompson is aiming to solve a mystery (What is Rosebud?) and his interviews resemble those of a detective questioning suspects in search of clues.

Note, however, that *Kane*'s use of genre conventions is somewhat equivocal. Unlike many biographical films, *Kane* is more concerned with psychological states and relationships than with the hero's public deeds or adventures. As a newspaper film, *Kane* is unusual in that the reporter fails to get his story. And *Kane* is not exactly a standard mystery, since it answers some questions but leaves others unanswered. *Citizen Kane* is a good example of a film that relies on genre conventions but often thwarts the expectations they arouse.

The same sort of equivocal qualities can be found in *Kane*'s relation to the classical Hollywood cinema. Even without specific prior knowledge about this film, we expect that, as an American studio product of 1941, it will obey norms and rules of that tradition. In most ways it does. We shall see that desire propels the narrative, causality is defined around traits and goals, conflicts lead to consequences, time is motivated by plot necessity, and narration is objective, mixing restricted and unrestricted passages. We shall also see some ways in which *Citizen Kane* is more ambiguous than most films in this tradition. Desires, traits, and goals are not always spelled out; the conflicts sometimes have an uncertain outcome; at the end, the narration's omniscience is emphasized to a rare degree. The ending in particular does not provide the degree of closure that one would expect in a classical film. Our analysis will show how *Citizen Kane* draws on Hollywood narrative conventions but also violates some of the expectations that we bring to a Hollywood film.

Plot and Story in *Citizen Kane*

In analyzing a film, it is often helpful to begin by segmenting it into sequences. Sequences are often demarcated by cinematic devices (fades, dissolves, cuts, black screen, and so on) and form meaningful units. In a narrative film, the sequences constitute the parts of the plot.

Most sequences in a narrative film are called *scenes*. The term is used in its theatrical sense, to refer to distinct phases of the action occurring within a relatively unified space and time. Our segmentation of *Citizen Kane* appears below. (In segmenting films, we will label the opening credits with a "C," the end title with an "E," and all other segments with numbers.) In this outline, numerals refer to major parts, some of which are only one scene long. In most cases, however, the major parts consist of several scenes, and each of these is identified by a lower-case letter. Many of these segments could be further divided, but this segmentation suits our immediate purposes.

Our segmentation lets us see at a glance the major divisions of the plot and how scenes are organized within them. The outline also helps us notice how the plot organizes story causality and story time. Let us look at these factors more closely.

CITIZEN KANE: PLOT SEGMENTATION

C. Credit title
1. Xanadu: Kane dies
2. Projection room:
  a. "News on the March"
  b. Reporters discuss "Rosebud"
3. El Rancho nightclub: Thompson tries to interview Susan
4. Thatcher library:
  a. Thompson enters and reads Thatcher's manuscript

First flashback
  b. Kane's mother sends the boy off with Thatcher
  c. Kane grows up and buys the *Inquirer*
  d. Kane launches the *Inquirer*'s attack on big business
  e. The Depression: Kane sells Thatcher his newspaper chain

  f. Thompson leaves library

5. Bernstein's office:
  a. Thompson visits Bernstein

Second flashback
  b. Kane takes over the *Inquirer*
  c. Montage: the *Inquirer*'s growth
  d. Party: the *Inquirer* celebrates getting the *Chronicle* staff
  e. Leland and Bernstein discuss Kane's trip abroad
  f. Kane returns with his fiancée Emily

  g. Bernstein concludes his reminiscence

6. Nursing home:
  a. Thompson talks with Leland

Third flashback
  b. Breakfast table montage: Kane's marriage deteriorates

  c. Leland continues his recollections

Third flashback (cont.)
  d. Kane meets Susan and goes to her room
  e. Kane's political campaign culminates in his speech
  f. Kane confronts Gettys, Emily, and Susan
  g. Kane loses election and Leland asks to be transferred
  h. Kane marries Susan
  i. Susan's opera premiere
  j. Because Leland is drunk, Kane finishes Leland's review

  k. Leland concludes his reminiscence

7. El Rancho nightclub:

    a. Thompson talks with Susan

Fourth flashback

    b. Susan rehearses her singing

    c. Susan's opera premiere

    d. Kane insists that Susan go on singing

    e. Montage: Susan's opera career

    f. Susan attempts suicide and Kane promises she can quit singing

    g. Xanadu: Susan bored

    h. Montage: Susan plays with jigsaw puzzles

    i. Xanadu: Kane proposes a picnic

    j. Picnic: Kane slaps Susan

    k. Xanadu: Susan leaves Kane

    l. Susan concludes her reminiscence

8. Xanadu:

    a. Thompson talks with Raymond

Fifth flashback

    b. Kane destroys Susan's room and picks up paperweight, murmuring "Rosebud"

    c. Raymond concludes his reminiscence; Thompson talks with the other reporters; all leave

    d. Survey of Kane's possessions leads to a revelation of Rosebud; exterior of gate and of castle; the end

E. End credits

Citizen Kane's Causality

In *Citizen Kane,* two distinct sets of characters cause events to happen. On the one hand, a group of reporters seeks information about Kane. On the other hand, Kane and the characters who know him provide the subject of the reporters' investigations.

The initial causal connection between the two groups is Kane's death, which leads the reporters to make a newsreel summing up his career. But the newsreel is already finished when the plot introduces the reporters. The boss, Rawlston, supplies the cause that initiates the investigation of Kane's life. Thompson's newsreel fails to satisfy him. Rawlston's desire for an angle for the newsreel gets the search for Rosebud under way. Thompson thus gains a goal, which sets him delving into Kane's past. His investigation constitutes one main line of the plot.

Another line of action, Kane's life, has already taken place in the past. There too a group of characters has caused actions to occur. Many years before, a poverty-stricken boarder at Kane's mother's boardinghouse has paid her with a deed to a gold mine. The wealth provided by this mine causes Mrs. Kane to appoint Thatcher as young Charles's guardian. Thatcher's guardianship results (in somewhat unspecified ways) in Kane's growing up into a spoiled, rebellious young man.

Citizen Kane is an unusual film in that the object of the investigator's search is not an object but a set of character traits. Thompson seeks to know what aspects of Kane's personality led him to say "Rosebud" on his deathbed. This mystery motivates Thompson's detective-like investigation. Kane, a very complex character, has many traits that influence the other characters' actions. As we shall see, however, *Citizen Kane*'s narrative does not ultimately define all of Kane's character traits.

Kane himself has a goal; he too seems to be searching for something related to Rosebud. At several points characters speculate that Rosebud was something that Kane lost or was never able to get. Again, the fact that Kane's goal remains so vague makes this an unusual narrative.

Other characters in Kane's life provide causal material for the narrative. The presence of several characters who knew Kane well makes Thompson's investigation possible, even though Kane himself has died. Significantly, the characters provide a range of information that spans Kane's entire life. This is important if we are to be able to reconstruct the progression of story events in the film. Thatcher knew Kane as a child; Bernstein, his manager, knew his business dealings; his best friend, Leland, knew of his personal life (his first marriage in particular); Susan Alexander, his second wife, knew him in middle age; and the butler, Raymond, managed Kane's affairs during his last years. Each of these characters has a causal role in Kane's life, as well as in Thompson's investigation. Note that Kane's wife Emily does not tell a story, since Emily's story would largely duplicate Leland's and would contribute no additional information to the present-day part of the narrative, the investigation. Hence the plot simply eliminates her (via a car accident).

Time

The order, duration, and frequency of events in the story differ greatly from the way the plot of *Citizen Kane* presents those events. Much of the film's power arises from the complex ways in which the plot cues us to construct the story.

To understand this story in its chronological order and assumed duration and frequency, the spectator must follow an intricate tapestry of plot events. For example, in the first flashback, Thatcher's diary tells of a scene in which Kane loses control of his newspapers during the Depression (4e). By this time Kane is a middle-aged man. Yet in the second flashback Bernstein describes Kane's youthful arrival at the *Inquirer* and his engagement to Emily (5b, 5f). We mentally sort these plot events into a correct chronological story order, then continue to rearrange other events as we learn of them.

Similarly, the earliest *story* event about which we learn is Mrs. Kane's acquisition of a deed to a valuable mine. We get this information during the newsreel, in the second sequence. But the first event in the *plot* is Kane's death. Just to illustrate the maneuvers we must execute to construct the film's story, let us assume that Kane's life consists of these phases:

Boyhood

Youthful newspaper editing

Life as a newlywed

Middle age

Old age

Significantly, the early portions of the plot tend to roam over many phases of Kane's life, while later portions tend to concentrate more on particular periods. The "News on the March" sequence (2a) gives us glimpses of all periods, and Thatcher's manuscript (4) shows us Kane in boyhood, youth, and middle age. Then the flashbacks become primarily chronological. Bernstein's recounting (5) concentrates on episodes showing Kane as newspaper editor and fiancé of Emily. Leland's recollections (6) run from newlywed life to middle age. Susan (7) tells of Kane as a middle-aged and an old man. Raymond's perfunctory anecdote (8b) concentrates on Kane in old age.

The plot becomes more linear in its ordering as it goes along, and this aids the viewer's effort to understand the story. If every character's flashback skipped around Kane's life as much as the newsreel or Thatcher's account does, the story would be much harder to reconstruct. As it is, the early portions of the plot show us the results of events we have not seen, while the later portions confirm or modify the expectations that we formed earlier.

By arranging story events out of order, the plot cues us to form specific anticipations. In the beginning, with Kane's death and the newsreel version of his life, the plot creates strong curiosity about two issues. What does "Rosebud" mean? And what could have happened to make so powerful a man so solitary at the end of his life?

There is also a degree of suspense. When the plot goes back to the past, we already have quite firm knowledge. We know that neither of Kane's marriages will last, that his friends will drift away, and so on. The plot encourages us to focus our interest on *how and when* a particular thing will happen. Thus many scenes function to delay an outcome that we already know is certain. For example, we know that Susan will abandon Kane at some point, so we are constantly expecting her to do so each time he bullies her. For several scenes (7b–7j) she comes close to leaving him, though after her suicide attempt he mollifies her. The plot could have shown her walking out (7k) much earlier, but then the ups and downs of their relations would have been less vivid, and there would have been no suspense.

This process of mentally rearranging plot events into story order might be quite difficult in *Citizen Kane* were it not for the presence of the "News on the March" newsreel. The first sequence in Xanadu disorients us, for it shows the death of a character about whom we so far know almost nothing. But the newsreel gives us a great deal of information quickly. Moreover, the newsreel's own structure uses parallels with the main film to supply a miniature introduction to the film's overall plot:

A. Shots of Xanadu

B. Funeral; headlines announcing Kane's death

C. Growth of financial empire

D. Silver mine and Mrs. Kane's boardinghouse

E. Thatcher testimony at congressional committee

F. Political career

G. Private life; weddings, divorces

H. Opera house and Xanadu

I. Political campaign

J. Depression

K. 1935: Kane's old age

L. Isolation of Xanadu

M. Death announced

A comparison of this outline with the one for the whole film shows some striking similarities. "News on the March" begins by emphasizing Kane as "Xanadu's Landlord"; a short segment (A) presents shots of the house, its grounds, and its contents. This is a variation on the opening of the whole film (1), which consisted of a series of shots of the grounds, moving progressively closer to the house. That opening sequence had ended with Kane's death; now the newsreel follows the shots of the house with Kane's funeral (B). Next comes a series of newspaper headlines announcing Kane's death. In a comparison with the plot diagram of *Citizen Kane,* these headlines occupy the approximate formal position of the whole newsreel itself (2a). Even the title card that follows the headlines ("To forty-four million

U.S. news buyers, more newsworthy than the names in his own headlines was Kane himself. . . .") is a brief parallel to the scene in the projection room, in which the reporters decide that Thompson should continue to investigate Kane's "newsworthy" life.

The order of the newsreel's presentation of Kane's life roughly parallels the order of scenes in the flashbacks related to Thompson. "News on the March" moves from Kane's death to summarize the building of Kane's newspaper empire (C), with a description of the boardinghouse deed and the gold mine (including an old photograph of Charles with his mother, as well as the first mention of the sled). Similarly, the first flashback (4) tells how Thatcher took over the young Kane's guardianship from his mother and how Kane first attempted to run the *Inquirer.* The rough parallels continue: The newsreel tells of Kane's political ambitions (F), his marriages (G), his building of the opera house (H), his political campaign (I), and so on. In the main plot Thatcher's flashback describes his own clashes with Kane on political matters. Leland's flashback (6) covers the first marriage, the affair with Susan, the political campaign, and the premiere of *Salammbo.*

These are not all of the similarities between the newsreel and the overall film. You can tease out many more by comparing the two closely.

The crucial point is that the newsreel provides us with a map for the investigation of Kane's life. As we see the various scenes of the flashbacks, we already expect certain events and have a rough chronological basis for fitting them into our story reconstruction.

The extensive use of flashbacks in *Kane* allows us to see many past events directly, and hence story and plot duration are close to the same. We know that Kane is 75 years old at his death, and the earliest scene shows him at perhaps 10. Thus the plot covers roughly 65 years of his life, plus the week of Thompson's investigation. The single earlier story event of which we only hear is Mrs. Kane's acquisition of the mine deed, which we can infer took place a few years before she turned her son over to Thatcher; the story runs a bit longer than the plot—perhaps closer to 70 years. This time span is presented in a screen duration of almost 120 minutes.

Like most films, *Citizen Kane* uses ellipses. The plot skips over years of story time, as well as many hours of Thompson's week of investigations. But plot duration also compresses time through montage sequences, such as those showing the *Inquirer*'s campaign against big business (4d), the growth of the paper's circulation (5c), Susan's opera career (7e), and Susan's bored playing with jigsaw puzzles (7h). Here long passages of story time are condensed into brief summaries quite different from ordinary narrative scenes. We will discuss montage sequences in more detail in Chapter 10, but we can already see the value of such segments in condensing story duration in a comprehensible way.

Citizen Kane also provides a clear demonstration of how events that occur only once in the story may appear several times in the plot. In their respective flashbacks, both Leland and Susan Alexander describe the latter's debut in the Chicago premiere of *Salammbo.* Watching Leland's account (6i), we see the performance from the front; we witness the audience reacting with distaste. Susan's version (7c) shows us the performance from behind and on the stage, to suggest her humiliation. This repeated presentation of Susan's debut in the plot does not confuse us, for we understand the two scenes as depicting the same story event. ("News on the March" has also referred to Susan's opera career, in parts G and H.)

Overall, *Citizen Kane*'s narrative dramatizes Thompson's search by means of flashbacks that encourage us to seek the sources of Kane's failure and to try to identify "Rosebud." As in a detective film, we must locate missing causes and arrange events into a coherent story pattern. Through manipulations of order, duration, and frequency, the plot both assists our search and complicates it in order to provoke curiosity and suspense.

Motivation

Some critics have argued that Welles's use of the search for "Rosebud" is a flaw in *Citizen Kane,* because the identification of the word proves it to be a trivial gimmick. If indeed we assume that the whole point of *Citizen Kane* is really to identify Rosebud, this charge might be valid. But in fact, Rosebud serves a very important motivating function in the film. It creates Thompson's goal and thus focuses our attention on his delving into the lives of Kane and his associates. *Citizen Kane* becomes a mystery story; but instead of investigating a crime, the reporter investigates a character. So the Rosebud clues provide the basic motivation necessary for the plot to progress. (Of course, the Rosebud device serves other functions as well; for instance, the little sled provides a transition from the boardinghouse scene to the cheerless Christmas when Thatcher gives Charles a new sled.)

Citizen Kane's narrative revolves around an investigation into traits of character. As a result, these traits provide many of the motivations for events. (In this respect, the film obeys principles of the classical Hollywood narrative.) Kane's desire to prove that Susan is really a singer and not just his mistress motivates his manipulation of her opera career. His mother's overly protective desire to remove her son from what she considers to be a bad environment motivates her appointment of Thatcher as the boy's guardian. Dozens of actions are motivated by character traits and desires.

At the end of the film, Thompson gives up his search for the meaning of Rosebud, saying he doesn't think "any word can explain a man's life." Up to a point Thompson's statement motivates his acceptance of his failure. But if we as spectators are to accept this idea that no key can unlock the secrets of a life, we need further motivation, and the film provides this. In the scene in the newsreel projection room, Rawlston suggests that "maybe he told us all about himself on his deathbed." Immediately, one of the reporters says, "Yeah, and maybe he didn't." Already the suggestion is planted that Rosebud may not provide any adequate answers about Kane. Later Leland scornfully dismisses the Rosebud issue and goes on to talk of other things. These brief references to Rosebud help justify Thompson's pessimistic attitude in the final sequence.

The presence of the scene in which Thompson first visits Susan Alexander at the El Rancho nightclub (3) might seem puzzling at first. Unlike the other scenes in which he visits people, no flashback occurs here. Thompson learns from the waiter that Susan knows nothing about Rosebud; he could easily learn this on his second visit to her. So why should the plot include the scene at all? One reason is that it evokes curiosity and deepens the mystery around Kane. Moreover, Susan's story, when she does tell it, covers events relatively late in Kane's career. As we have seen, the flashbacks go through Kane's life roughly in order. If Susan had told her story first, we would not have all of the material necessary to understand it. But it is plausible that Thompson should start his search with Kane's ex-wife, presumably the surviving person closest to him. In Thompson's first visit, Susan's drunken refusal to speak to him motivates the fact that her flashback comes later. By that point, Bernstein and Leland have filled in enough of Kane's personal life to prepare the way for Susan's flashback. This first scene functions partly to justify postponing Susan's flashback until a later part of the plot.

Motivation makes us take things for granted in narratives. Mrs. Kane's desire for her son to be rich and successful motivates her decision to entrust him to

Thatcher, a powerful banker, as his guardian. We may just take it for granted that Thatcher is a rich businessman. Yet on closer inspection, this feature is necessary to motivate other events. It motivates Thatcher's presence in the newsreel; he is powerful enough to have been asked to testify at a congressional hearing. More important, Thatcher's success motivates the fact that he has kept a journal now on deposit at a memorial library that Thompson visits. This, in turn, justifies the fact that Thompson can uncover information from a source who knew Kane as a child.

Despite its reliance on psychological motivation, *Citizen Kane* also departs somewhat from the usual practice of the classical Hollywood narrative by leaving some motivations ambiguous. The ambiguities relate primarily to Kane's character. The other characters who tell Thompson their stories all have definite opinions of Kane, but these do not always tally. Bernstein still looks on Kane with sympathy and affection, whereas Leland is cynical about his own relationship with Kane. The reasons for some of Kane's actions remain unclear. Does he send Leland the $25,000 check in firing him because of a lingering sentiment over their old friendship or from a proud desire to prove himself more generous than Leland? Why does he insist on stuffing Xanadu with hundreds of artworks that he never even unpacks?

Parallelism

Parallelism does not provide a major principle of development in *Citizen Kane*'s narrative form, but several parallel structures are present. We have already seen important formal parallels between the newsreel and the film's plot as a whole. We have also noticed a parallel between the two major lines of action: Kane's life and Thompson's search. Rosebud serves as a summary of the things Kane strives for through his adult life. We see him repeatedly fail to find love and friendship, living alone at Xanadu in the end. His inability to find happiness parallels Thompson's failure to locate the significance of the word Rosebud. This parallel does not imply that Kane and Thompson share similar character traits. Rather, it allows both lines of action to develop simultaneously in similar directions.

Another narrative parallel juxtaposes Kane's campaign for the governorship with his attempt to build up Susan's career as an opera star. In each case he seeks to inflate his reputation by influencing public opinion. In trying to achieve success for Susan, Kane forces his newspaper employees to write favorable reviews of her performances. This parallels the moment when he loses the election and the *Inquirer* automatically proclaims a fraud at the polls. In both cases Kane fails to realize that his power over the public is not great enough to hide the flaws in his projects: first his affair with Susan, which ruins his campaign, then her lack of singing ability, which Kane refuses to admit. The parallels show that Kane continues to make the same kinds of mistakes throughout his life.

Patterns of Plot Development

The progression from beginning to ending in *Citizen Kane* leads us through two lines of action, as we have seen: Kane's life story and Thompson's investigation of it. Each of Thompson's visits during his investigation leads to a flashback that gives us a further look at Kane.

The order of Thompson's visits allows the series of flashbacks to have a clear pattern of progression. Thompson moves from people who knew Kane early in his life to those who knew him as an old man. Moreover, each flashback contains a distinct type of information about Kane. Thatcher establishes Kane's political stance;

next Bernstein gives an account of the business dealings of the newspaper. These provide the background to Kane's early success and lead into Leland's stories of Kane's personal life, where we get the first real indications of Kane's failure. Susan continues the description of his decline with her account of how he had manipulated her life. Finally, in Raymond's flashback Kane becomes a pitiable old man.

Thus even though the order of events in the story varies greatly from that given in the plot, *Citizen Kane* presents Kane's life through a steady pattern of development. The present-day portions of the narrative—Thompson's scenes—also follow their own pattern of a search. By the ending this search has failed, as Kane's own search for happiness or personal success had also failed.

Because of Thompson's failure, the ending of *Citizen Kane* remains somewhat more open than was the rule in Hollywood in 1941. True, Thompson does resolve the question of Rosebud for himself by saying that it would not have explained Kane's life. To this extent, we have the common pattern of action leading to greater knowledge. Thompson has come to understand that a life cannot be summed up in one word. Still, in most classical narrative films, the main character reaches his or her initial goal, and Thompson is the main character of this line of action.

The line of action involving Kane himself has even less closure. Not only does Kane apparently not reach his goal, but the film never specifies what that goal is to start with. Most classical narratives create a situation of conflict. The character must struggle with a problem and solve it by the ending. Kane begins his adult life in a highly successful position (happily running the *Inquirer*), then gradually falls into a barren solitude. We are invited to speculate about exactly what, if anything, would make Kane happy. *Citizen Kane*'s lack of closure in this line of action made it a very unusual narrative for its day.

The search for Rosebud does lead to a certain resolution at the end. We the audience discover what Rosebud was. The ending of the film, which follows this discovery, strongly echoes the beginning. The beginning had moved past fences toward the mansion. Now a series of shots takes us away from the house and back outside the fences, with the "No Trespassing" sign and large K insignia.

But even at this point, when we learn the answer to Thompson's question, a degree of uncertainty remains. Just because we have learned what Kane's dying word referred to, do we now have the key to his entire character? Or is Thompson's final statement *correct*—that no one word can explain a person's life? It is tempting to declare that all of Kane's problems arose from the loss of his sled and his childhood home life, but the film also suggests that this is too easy a solution. It is the kind of solution that the slick editor Rawlston would pounce on as an angle for his newsreel.

For years critics have debated whether the Rosebud solution does give us a key that resolves the entire narrative. This debate itself suggests the ambiguity at work in *Citizen Kane*. The film provides much evidence for both views and hence avoids complete closure. (You might contrast this slightly open ending with the tightly closed narratives of *His Girl Friday* and *North by Northwest* in Chapter 11. You might also compare *Citizen Kane*'s narrative with that of another somewhat open-ended film, *Do The Right Thing,* also discussed in Chapter 11.)

Narration in *Citizen Kane*

In analyzing how *Kane*'s plot manipulates the flow of story information, it is useful to consider a remarkable fact: The only time we see Kane directly and in the present is when he dies. On all other occasions, he is presented at one remove—in the newsreel, in various characters' memories. This unusual treatment makes the film something of a portrait, a study of a man seen from different perspectives.

Kane, we are told, loved only his mother—only his newspaper—only his second wife—only himself. Maybe he loved all of these, or none. It is for the audience to judge. Kane was selfish and selfless, an idealist, a scoundrel, a very big man and a very little one. It depends on who's talking about him. He is never judged with the objectivity of an author, and the point of the picture is not so much the solution of the problem as its presentation.

— Orson Welles, director

The film employs five narrators, the people whom Thompson tracks down: Thatcher (whose account is in writing), Bernstein, Leland, Susan, and the butler, Raymond. The plot thus motivates a series of views of Kane more or less restricted in their range of knowledge. In Thatcher's account (4b–4e), we see only scenes at which he is present. Even Kane's newspaper crusade is rendered as Thatcher learns of it, through buying copies of the *Inquirer.* In Bernstein's flashback (5b–5f), there is some deviation from what Bernstein witnesses, but in general his range of knowledge is respected. At the *Inquirer* party, for example, we are confined to following Bernstein and Leland's conversation while Kane dances in the background. Similarly, we never see Kane in Europe, we merely hear the contents of Kane's telegram, which Bernstein delivers to Leland.

Leland's flashbacks (6b, 6d–6j) deviate most markedly from the narrator's range of knowledge. Here we see Kane and Emily at a series of morning breakfasts, Kane's meeting with Susan, and the confrontation of Kane with Boss Gettys at Susan's apartment. In scene 6j, Leland is present but in a drunken stupor most of the time. (The plot motivates Leland's knowledge of Kane's affair with Susan by having Leland suggest that Kane told him about it, but the scenes present detailed knowledge that Leland is unlikely to possess.) By the time we get to Susan's flashback (7b–7k), however, the range of knowledge again fits the character more snugly. (There remains one scene, 7f, in which Susan is unconscious for part of the action.) The last flashback (8b) is recounted by Raymond and plausibly accords with his range of knowledge; he is standing in the hallway as Kane wrecks Susan's room.

Using different narrators to transmit story information fulfills several functions. It offers itself as a plausible depiction of the process of investigation, since we expect any reporter to hunt down information through a series of inquiries. More deeply, the plot's portrayal of Kane himself becomes more complex by showing somewhat different sides of him, depending on who's talking about him. Moreover, the use of multiple narrators makes the film like one of Susan's jigsaw puzzles. We must put things together piece by piece. The pattern of gradual revelation enhances curiosity—what is it in Kane's past that he associates with Rosebud?—and suspense—how will he lose his friends and his wives?

This strategy has important implications for film form. While Thompson uses the various narrators to gather data, the plot uses them both to furnish us with story information and to *conceal* information. The narration can motivate gaps in knowledge about Kane by appealing to the fact that no informant can know everything about anyone. If we were able to enter Kane's consciousness, we might discover the meaning of Rosebud much sooner—but Kane is dead. The multiple-narrator format thus appeals to expectations we derive from real life in order to motivate the bit-by-bit transmission of story information, the withholding of key pieces of information, and the arousing of curiosity and suspense.

Although each narrator's account is predominantly restricted to his or her range of knowledge, the plot does not treat each flashback in much subjective depth. Most of the flashbacks are rendered objectively. Some transitions from the framing episodes use a voice-over commentary to lead us into the flashbacks, but these do not represent the narrators' subjective states. Only in Susan's flashbacks are there some attempts to render subjectivity. In scene 7c we see Leland as if from her optical point of view on stage, and the phantasmagoric montage of her career (7e) suggests some mental subjectivity that renders her fatigue and frustration.

On the whole, however, the film adheres to the classical Hollywood convention of objective presentation. This, too, is functional. If we are to pursue the Rosebud mystery and to watch the unraveling of Kane's personal relationships, we need to believe that what we see and hear actually occurred in the fictional world.

Against the five character narrators, the film's plot sets another purveyor of knowledge, the "News on the March" short. We have already seen the crucial function of the newsreel in introducing us both to Kane's story and to its plot construction, with the newsreel's parts echoing the parts of the film as a whole. The newsreel also gives us a broad sketch of Kane's life and death that will be filled in by the more restricted behind-the-scenes accounts offered by the narrators. The newsreel is also highly objective, even more so than the rest of the film; it reveals nothing about Kane's inner life. Rawlston acknowledges this: "It isn't enough to tell us what a man did, you've got to tell us who he was." In effect, Thompson's aim is to add depth to the newsreel's superficial version of Kane's life.

Yet we are still not through with the narrational manipulations in this complex and daring film. For one thing, all the localized sources of knowledge—"News on the March" and the five narrators—are linked together by the shadowy reporter Thompson. To some extent, he is our surrogate in the film, gathering and assembling the puzzle pieces.

Note too that Thompson is barely characterized; we cannot even identify his face. This, as usual, has a function. If we saw him clearly, if the plot gave him more traits or a background or a past, he would become the protagonist. But *Citizen Kane* is less about Thompson than about his *search*. The plot's handling of Thompson makes him a neutral conduit for the story information that he gathers (though his conclusion at the end, "I don't think any word can explain a man's life," suggests that he has been changed by his investigation).

Thompson is not, however, a perfect surrogate for us because the film's narration inserts the newsreel, the narrators, and Thompson within a still broader range of knowledge. The flashback portions are predominantly restricted, but there are other passages that reveal an overall narrational omniscience. From the very start we are given a god's-eye-view of the action. We move into a mysterious setting that we will later learn is Kane's estate, Xanadu. We might have learned about this locale through a character's journey, the way we acquaint ourselves with Oz by means of Dorothy's adventures there. Here, however, an omniscient narration conducts the tour. Eventually we enter a darkened bedroom. A hand holds a paperweight, and over this is superimposed a flurry of snow **(3.20).** The image teases us. Is the narration making a lyrical comment, or is the image subjective, a glimpse into the dying man's mind or vision? In either case, the narration reveals its ability to command a great deal of story information. Our sense of omniscience is enhanced when, after the man dies, a nurse strides into the room. Apparently no character knows what we know.

3.20   The elusive image of the paperweight in *Citizen Kane.*

At other points in the film the omniscient narration calls attention to itself, as during Susan's opera debut in Leland's flashback (6i), we see stagehands high above reacting to her performance. (Such omniscient asides tend to be associated with camera movements, as we shall see in Chapter 10.) Most vivid, however, is the omniscient narration at the end of the film. Thompson and the other reporters leave, never having learned the meaning of Rosebud. But we linger in the vast storeroom of Xanadu. And, thanks to the narration, we learn that Rosebud is the name of Kane's childhood toy (see 10.12). We can now associate the opening's emphasis on the paperweight with the closing scene's revelation of the sled.

This narration is truly omniscient. It knew a key piece of story information at the outset, teased us with hints (the snow, the tiny cottage in the paperweight), and has finally revealed at least part of the answer to the question posed at the outset. A return to the "No Trespassing" sign reminds us of our point of entry into the film. Like *The Road Warrior,* then, the film derives its unity not only from principles of causality and time but also from a patterned narration that arouses curiosity and suspense and yields a surprise at the very end.

SUMMARY

Not every narrative analysis runs through the categories of cause–effect, story–plot differences, motivations, parallelism, progression from opening to closing, and narrational range and depth in that exact order, as we have done here. Our purpose in this examination of *Citizen Kane* has been as much to illustrate these concepts as to analyze the film's narrative. With practice, the critic becomes more familiar with these analytical tools and can use them flexibly, suiting his or her approach to the specific film at hand.

In looking at any narrative film, such questions as these may help in understanding its formal structures:

1. Which story events are directly presented to us in the plot, and which must we assume or infer? Is there any nondiegetic material given in the plot?

2. What is the earliest story event of which we learn? How does it relate through a series of causes and effects to later events?

3. What is the temporal relationship of story events? Has temporal order, frequency, or duration been manipulated in the plot to affect our understanding of events?

4. Does the closing reflect a clear-cut pattern of development that relates it to the opening? Do all narrative lines achieve closure, or are some left open?

5. How does the narration present story information to us? Is it restricted to one or a few characters' knowledge, or does it range freely among the characters in different spaces? Does it give us considerable depth of story information by exploring the characters' mental states?

6. How closely does the film follow the conventions of the classical Hollywood cinema? If it departs significantly from those conventions, what formal principle does it use instead?

Usually when we go to a movie theater, we see a live-action, fictional narrative film that conforms to classical norms to a large extent. Yet there are ways of specifying the *types* of films we see. One is by *genre,* as when we attend a Western, musical, or science-fiction film. Another way is by *mode* of filmmaking: documentary, experimental, or animation. Such films can all use narrative form, but they are made in distinctive ways, arouse specific expectations, and often employ formal principles other than narrative. We shall examine genres and modes of filmmaking in Chapters 4 and 5.

NOTES AND QUERIES

Narrative Form

An overview of the history and functions of narrative in human culture is Robert Scholes and Robert Kellogg, *The Nature of Narrative* (New York: Oxford University Press, 1966). Most conceptions of narrative are drawn from literary theory, which in the past two decades has made remarkable contributions to the study of this type of form. Good introductions are Seymour Chatman, *Story and Discourse:* *Narrative Structure in Fiction and Film* (Ithaca, N.Y.: Cornell University Press, 1978), and *Coming to Terms: The Rhetoric of Narrative in Fiction and Film* (Ithaca, N.Y.: Cornell University Press, 1990). The concepts we discuss in this chapter are congruent with this trend of contemporary theory. See also "Film-Narratology," in Robert Stam, Robert Burgoyne, and Sandy Flitterman-Lewis, *New Vocabularies in Film Semiotics: Structuralism, Post-Structuralism, and Beyond* (New York: Routledge, 1992), pp. 69–122, and

Thomas B. Leitch, *What Stories Are: Narrative Theory and Interpretation* (University Park: Pennsylvania State University Press, 1986).

For a discussion centered on film narrative's debt to literature and other arts, see John L. Fell, *Film and the Narrative Tradition* (Norman: University of Oklahoma Press, 1974). For a discussion emphasizing the theoretical aspects of film narrative, see Roy Armes, *Action and Image: Dramatic Structure in Cinema* (Manchester, England: Manchester University Press, 1994).

The Spectator

What does the spectator *do* in making sense of a narrative? Various theorists have sought to characterize the perceiver's activity. In literature, two valuable studies are Horst Ruthrof, *The Reader's Construction of Narrative* (London: Routledge & Kegan Paul, 1981) and Peter Brooks, *Reading for the Plot: Design and Intention in Narrative* (New York: Knopf, 1984). Meir Sternberg emphasizes expectation, hypotheses, and inference in his *Expositional Modes and Temporal Ordering in Fiction* (Baltimore, Md.: Johns Hopkins University Press, 1978). Sternberg's approach is close to our own assumptions in this chapter. David Bordwell proposes a model of the spectator's story-comprehending activities in chap. 3 of *Narration in the Fiction Film* (Madison: University of Wisconsin Press, 1985). Compare Edward Branigan, *Narrative Comprehension in Film* (New York: Routledge, 1992).

Narrative Time

Most theorists agree that both cause–effect relations and chronology are central to narrative. The books by Chatman and Sternberg cited above provide useful analyses of causality and temporality. For specifically cinematic discussions, see Jan Mukařovský, "Time in Film," in John Burbank and Peter Steiner, eds., *Structure, Sign, and Function: Selected Essays by Jan Mukařovský* (New Haven, Conn.: Yale University Press, 1977), pp. 191–200; Brian Henderson, "Tense, Mood, and Voice in Film (Notes after Genette)," *Film Quarterly* **26,** 4 (Summer 1983): 4–17; and Maureen Turim, *Flashbacks in Film: Memory and History* (New York: Routledge, 1989).

Our discussion of the differences between plot duration, story duration, and screen duration is necessarily simplified. The distinctions hold good at a theoretical level, but the differences may sometimes vanish in particular cases. Story duration and plot duration differ most drastically at the level of the *whole* film, as when two years of action (story duration) are shown or told about

in scenes that occur across a week (plot duration) and then that week is itself rendered in two hours (screen duration). At the level of a smaller *part* of the film, say a shot or a scene, we usually assume story and plot duration to be equal, and screen duration may or may not be equal to them. These nuances are discussed at greater length in chap. 5 of Bordwell, *Narration in the Fictional Film* (cited above). For more on films that play with the temporal dimensions of narratives, see chap. 5, on *Groundhog Day,* in Kristin Thompson, *Storytelling in the New Hollywood: Understanding Classical Narrative Technique* (Cambridge, Mass.: Harvard University Press, 1999, pp. 131–154; Christopher Nolan, *"Memento" & "Following"* (New York: Faber and Faber, 2001); and James Mottram, *The Making of "Memento"* (New York: Faber and Faber, 2002).

Narration

One approach to narration has been to draw analogies between film and literature. Novels have first-person narration ("Call me Ishmael") and third-person narration ("Maigret puffed his pipe as he walked along slowly, hands clasped behind his back"). Does film have first-person or third-person narration, too? The argument for applying the linguistic category of "person" to cinema is discussed most fully in Bruce F. Kawin, *Mindscreen: Bergman, Godard, and First-Person Film* (Princeton, N.J.: Princeton University Press, 1978). Kawin does not confine his discussion to character narrators, such as Kane's associates, who are obviously telling their tale in the first person. He suggests that entire films can be seen as proceeding from the mind of a narrator and thus warrant the label first person. This analogy seems to assume the more basic categories of range and depth, which we discuss in this chapter. A more complex approach to the problem of "I" and "you" in filmic storytelling is seen in Francesco Casetti's *Inside the Gaze: The Fiction Film and Its Spectator,* trans. Nell Andrew and Charles O'Brien (Bloomington: Indiana University Press, 1998.)

Another literary analogy is that of point of view. The best survey in English is Susan Snaider Lanser, *The Narrative Act: Point of View in Prose Fiction* (Princeton, N.J.: Princeton University Press, 1981). The applicability of point of view to film is discussed in detail in Edward Branigan, *Point of View in the Cinema: A Theory of Narration and Subjectivity in Classical Film* (New York: Mouton, 1984). See also Kristin Thompson's "Closure within a Dream? Point-of-View in *Laura*," in *Breaking the Glass Armor: Neoformalist Film Analysis* (Princeton, N.J.: Princeton University Press, 1988), pp. 162–194.

Is the Classical Hollywood Cinema Dead?

Since the early 1990s, some film historians have claimed that the classical approach to Hollywood narrative faded away during the 1970s, replaced by something variously termed postclassical, postmodern, or post-Hollywood cinema. Contemporary films are thought to be characterized by extremely simple, high-concept, premises, with the cause–effect chain weakened by a concentration on high-pitch action at the expense of character psychology. Tie-in merchandising and distribution through other media have also supposedly fragmented the filmic narrative. Other historians argue that the changes are superficial and that underlying classical principles endure.

For important early texts arguing for postclassicism, see Thomas Schatz, "The New Hollywood," in *Film Theory Goes to the Movies,* ed. Jim Collins, Hilary Radner, and Ava Preacher Collins (New York: Routledge, 1993), pp. 8–36, and Justin Wyatt, *High Concept: Movies and Marketing in Hollywood* (Austin: University of Texas Press, 1994). *Contemporary Hollywood Cinema,* ed. Steven Neale and Murray Smith (New York: Routledge, 1998), contains essays supporting (e.g., by Thomas Elsaesser, James Schamus, and Richard Maltby) and opposing (e.g., Murray Smith, Warren Buckland, Peter Kramer) this notion. For a lengthy argument against postclassicism, see Kristin Thompson, *Storytelling in the New Hollywood,* cited above.

"Rosebud"

Critics have scrutinized few films as closely as *Citizen Kane.* For a sampling, see Joseph McBride, *Orson Welles* (New York: Viking, 1972); Charles Higham, *The Films of Orson Welles* (Berkeley: University of California Press, 1970); Robert Carringer, "Rosebud, Dead or Alive: Narrative and Symbolic Structure in *Citizen Kane,*" *PMLA* (March 1976): 185–193; James Naremore, *The Magic World of Orson Welles* (New York: Oxford University Press, 1978); and Laura Mulvey, *Citizen Kane* (London: British Film Institute, 1993).

Pauline Kael, in a famous essay on the making of the film, finds Rosebud a naïve gimmick. Interestingly, her discussion emphasizes *Citizen Kane* as part of the journalist-film genre and tends not to go beyond the detective-story aspect. See *The "Citizen Kane" Book* (Boston: Little Brown, 1971), pp. 1–84. In contrast, other critics find Rosebud an incomplete answer to Thompson's search; compare particularly the Naremore and Carringer analyses above. In "Interpreting *Citizen Kane,*" in *Interpreting the Moving Image* (Cambridge: Cambridge University Press, 1998), pp. 155–165, Noël Carroll argues that the film deliberately stages a debate between the Rosebud interpretation and the enigma interpretation. Robert Carringer's *Making of "Citizen Kane,"* rev. ed. (Berkeley: University of California Press, 1996) offers the most extensive account of the film's production.

PART THREE

Types of Films

In most video stores, films are filed under different headings—by star, by period (Silent Movies), occasionally by director (Alfred Hitchcock, Woody Allen), by place of origin (Foreign Films). In order to understand how films work and how we experience them, we need to gain a sense of some significant ways audiences, filmmakers, reviewers, and film scholars sort them into groups.

One popular way of grouping fiction films is by *genre*, such as Westerns, musicals, war films, science fiction, and so on. These terms are used in everyday writing and talk, yet few stop to think how we come to share common assumptions about fitting movies into such categories. In Chapter 4 we will examine the concept of genres and consider how genre categories affect people's attitudes toward the films they see in a theater. We will look briefly at three widely recognized genres: the Western, the horror film, and the musical.

Another way we group films is based on ideas of how they were made and what effects they attempt to achieve. In Chapter 5 we will discuss three major types of filmmaking: documentary, experimental, and animation.

Documentary films, as their name implies, document some aspect of the world. They are distinguished from fiction films because they are assumed to portray real events and show the actual people involved in those events. Another particular kind of filmmaking is termed experimental. Such films play with film form and conventions in ways that are intended to confound audience expectations and provide unusual emotional appeals or intellectual challenges.

Finally, animated films are defined by the way they are made, using drawings, models, or other subjects photographed frame by frame to create illusory movements that never existed in front of the camera. Although we often think of animated films as being for children, we will see that virtually any type of film can be made using animation.

Chapter 4

Film Genres

In Chapter 1 we discussed what happens when you go to see a movie in a theater. That experience included visiting the concession stand, encountering publicity for upcoming films, and (with luck) seeing a high-quality projection of a 35mm print. But what made you go to that particular theater to see that particular film? With the spread of multiplex cinemas, viewers can have their pick of several films in any given week.

Sometimes we go to films because we like their stars. The fact that Sandra Bullock or Tom Cruise plays the protagonist is often enough to attract their fans, whatever the film is about. Movie buffs may choose a film on the basis of its director ("I'll see anything Martin Scorsese makes"), and a few directors, like Steven Spielberg and James Cameron, have become famous enough to be box-office draws for the general public. Very frequently, however, people choose to go to the movies to see a certain type of film. Types of films are commonly referred to as **genres** (pronounced "zhan-rahz").

The word *genre* is originally French and simply means kind or type. It is closely related to another word, *genus,* which is used in the biological sciences to classify large groups of similar plants or animals; a genus usually consists of several species.

Scientists can usually place plants or animals within a single genus with confidence, since a living thing's DNA will determine what category it belongs to. Defining film genres lacks that sort of scientific precision. Instead, genres are convenient terms that develop in an informal way. Filmmakers, industry decision makers, critics, and viewers all contribute to the formation of a shared sense that certain films seem to resemble one another in significant ways. Genres also change over time, as filmmakers invent new twists on old formulas. Thus, defining the precise boundaries between genres can be tricky.

A genre is easier to recognize than to define. The Western, the musical film, the action picture, the horror movie, the comedy, the romance—all these are genres. The popular cinema of most countries rests on genre filmmaking. Germany has its *Heimatfilm,* the tale of small-town life. The Hindi cinema of India produces devotionals, films centering on the lives of saints and religious figures, as well as mythologicals derived from legend and literary classics. Mexican filmmakers developed the *cabaretera,* a type of melodrama centering on prostitutes.

Since most popular filmmaking is fictional, fictional genres come to mind most readily. But there are genres of documentary as well, such as the propaganda film or the instructional film. Experimental film has genres too; the found-footage film, where the filmmaker re-edits shots from existing movies, is a common one. And in many cases genre categories cut across the basic types. The animated film *Beauty and the Beast* is also a musical, and the Japanese cartoon *Akira* is a science-fiction film. We shall examine these other types of filmmaking in the next chapter.

UNDERSTANDING GENRE

Defining a Genre

Audiences know the genres of their culture very well, and so do filmmakers. The intriguing problem comes in defining just what a genre is. What places a group of films in a genre?

Most scholars now agree that no genre can be defined in a single hard-and-fast way. Some genres stand out by their subjects or themes. A gangster film centers on large-scale urban crime. A science-fiction film features a technology beyond the reach of contemporary science. A Western is usually about life on some frontier (not necessarily the West, as *North to Alaska* and *Drums along the Mohawk* suggest).

Yet subject matter or theme is not so central to defining other genres. Musicals are recognizable chiefly by their manner of presentation: singing, dancing, or both. The detective film is partly defined by the plot pattern of an investigation that solves a mystery. And some genres are defined by the distinctive emotional effect they aim for: amusement in comedy, tension in suspense films. Apparently no strictly logical distinctions can capture the variety of factors that create the genres we have.

The question is complicated by the fact that genres can be more or less broad. There are large, blanket genre categories that fit many films. We refer commonly to thrillers, yet that term may encompass horror films, detective stories, hostage films like *Die Hard* or *Speed,* and many others. "Comedy" is a similarly broad term that includes slapstick comedies like *Liar Liar,* romantic comedies like *Groundhog Day,* parodies like the "Austin Powers" series, and gross-out comedy like *There's Something about Mary.* Thus subgenres can be devised by critics, viewers, or filmmakers to try to describe more precisely what films are like.

Still, there are limits to the precision with which the concept of genre can be applied. Any category contains both undeniable instances and fuzzy cases. *Singin' in the Rain* is a prime example of a musical, but David Byrne's *True Stories,* with its ironic presentation of musical numbers, is more of a borderline case. And an audience's sense of the core cases can change over history. For modern audiences, a gory film like *The Silence of the Lambs* probably exemplifies the thriller, whereas for audiences of the 1950s a prime example would have been an urbane Hitchcock exercise like *North by Northwest.*

In other cases, films may seem to straddle two genre classifications. Is *Groundhog Day* a romantic comedy or a fantasy? Is *Psycho* a slasher film or a detective thriller? *Minority Report* blends science fiction and a detective investigation in equal measures. *Signs* combines horror, science fiction, and family melodrama. (As we shall see, mixing formulas like this is one important source of innovation and change in genres.) And, further, some films seem so distinctive that critics and audiences have trouble assigning them to a genre. When *Being John Malkovich* appeared in

1999, TV interviewers joked with the cast and crew about how impossible the film was to describe—hinting that they simply could not place it in a genre.

How are genre categories used? They are certainly one guideline by which industry officials decide what sorts of films to make. While big-budget musicals were commonly produced in the 1960s, they are out of fashion now, and few companies would be likely to make one. On the other hand, horror and action films are currently popular, and executives would be likelier to green-light projects perceived to fit into those genres.

For the vast publicity system that exists around filmmaking, genres are a simple way to characterize film. In fact, reviewers are often central in gathering and crystallizing notions about genres. If you read popular reviews or watch television coverage of entertainment, you will notice that reporters make frequent reference to films' genres, because they know that most members of the public will easily grasp what they are referring to.

You may also find that some reviewers tend to dismiss genre films as shallow and trivial, assuming them to be simply formulaic: It's only a Western, just a horror film. Undoubtedly many films in such genres are cheaply and unimaginatively made. Yet some of the greatest films also fall into genres. *Singin' in the Rain* is a musical, but it is arguably also one of the best American films ever made. The important classic *Grand Illusion* is a war film; *Psycho* is a thriller. *The Godfather* is a gangster film. On the whole, genre is a category best used to describe and analyze films, not to evaluate them.

For viewers, genre often provides a way of finding a film they want to see. If a group plans an evening together at the movies, they may debate which film to see by expressing their preferences for a science-fiction film or a thriller or a romance and then negotiate from there. Some filmgoers consider themselves fans of a specific genre and may seek out and exchange information via magazines, Internet sites, or conventions devoted to that genre. Science-fiction aficionados are one example of such a group, with subgroups pledging allegiance to the *Star Wars* or the *Star Trek* series.

At all levels of the filmmaking and film-viewing processes, then, genres help assure that most members of a society share at least some general notions about the many films that compete for our attention.

Analyzing a Genre

As we have seen, genres are based on a tacit agreement among filmmakers, reviewers, and audiences. What gives films of a type some common identity are shared *genre conventions* which reappear in film after film.

Certain plot elements may be conventional. We anticipate an investigation in a mystery film; revenge plotlines are common in Westerns; a musical will find ways to provide song-and-dance situations. The gangster film usually centers on the gangster's rise and fall as he struggles against police and rival gangs. We expect a biographical film to trace major episodes in the main character's life. In a cop thriller, certain characters are conventional: the shifty informer, the comic sidekick, the impatient captain who despairs of getting the squad detectives to follow procedure.

Other genre conventions are more thematic, involving general meanings that are summoned up again and again. The Hong Kong martial arts film commonly celebrates loyalty and obedience to one's teacher. A standard theme of the gangster film has been the price of criminal success, with the gangster's rise to power portrayed as a hardening into egotism and brutality. The screwball comedy traditionally sets up a thematic opposition between a stiff, unyielding social milieu and characters' urges for freedom and innocent zaniness.

4.1 In *The Exorcist,* a single streetlight picks out the priest as he arrives at night, while light streams from the room where the possessed girl is confined.

Still other genre conventions involve characteristic film techniques. Somber lighting is standard in the horror film and the thriller **(4.1).** The action picture often relies on rapid cutting and slow-motion violence. In the melodrama, an emotional twist may be underscored by a sudden burst of poignant music.

As a visual medium, cinema can also define genres through conventional *iconography.* A genre's iconography consists of recurring symbolic images that carry meaning from film to film.

Objects and settings often furnish iconography for a genre. A close-up of a tommy gun lifted out of a 1920s Ford would probably be enough to identify a film as a gangster movie, while a shot of a long, curved sword hanging from a kimono would place us in the world of the samurai. The war film takes place in battle-scarred landscapes, the backstage musical in theaters and nightclubs, the space-travel film in starships and on distant planets. Even stars can become iconographic—Judy Garland for the musical, John Wayne for the Western, Arnold Schwarzenegger for the action picture, Bill Murray for comedy.

By knowing conventions, the viewer has a pathway into the film. Such landmarks allow the genre movie to communicate information quickly and economically. When we see the weak sheriff, we strongly suspect that he will not stand up to the gunslinger. We can then focus attention on the cowboy hero as he gets slowly drawn into helping the townspeople defend themselves.

Alternatively, a film can revise or reject the conventions associated with its genre. *Bugsy Malone* is a gangster musical in which children play all the traditional adult roles. *2001: A Space Odyssey* violated several conventions of the science-fiction genre: beginning with a lengthy sequence set in prehistoric times, synchronizing classical music to outer-space action, and ending with an enigmatically symbolic fetus drifting through space. Filmmakers may seek to surprise or shock viewers by breaking their expectations that a certain convention will be followed. (See Box.)

Audiences expect the genre film to offer something familiar, but they also demand fresh variations on it. The filmmaker may devise something mildly or radically different, but it will still be based on tradition. The interplay of convention and innovation, familiarity and novelty, is central to the genre film.

Genre History

Because filmmakers frequently play with conventions and iconography, genres seldom remain unchanged for very long. The broader, blanket genres like thrillers, romances, comedies, and the like may stay popular for decades, but an exemplary comedy from the 1920s will be very different from one in the 1960s. Genres change

A Contemporary Genre: The Crime Thriller

The thriller, like the comedy, is a very broad category, virtually an umbrella genre. There are supernatural thrillers (*The Sixth Sense*), political thrillers (*The Hunt for Red October*), and spy thrillers (*The Tailor of Panama*), but many revolve around crime—planned, committed, or thwarted. During the 1990s and early 2000s, many filmmaking countries have turned to making crime thrillers. With few special effects and set in contemporary city locations, they are comparatively cheap to produce. They offer showy roles to actors, and they allow writers and directors to display their ingenuity in playing with the audience's expectations. Although the genre has fuzzy edges, we can chart some core cases by considering the narrative conventions and the effects that filmmakers try to arouse.

A crime is at the center of the plot, and usually three sorts of characters are involved. There are the lawbreakers, the forces of law, and the innocent victims or bystanders. Typically the narration concentrates on one of these characters or groups. In *Double Jeopardy* a husband fakes his own murder in order to run off with his mistress. His wife is found guilty, but in prison she discovers that he's living under a new identity. Released on parole, she flees to find her son, but she is pursued by her hard-bitten parole officer. Suspense arises from the double chase and the cat-and-mouse game played by the desperate husband and his embittered wife, who can now murder him with impunity. The plot is organized around the wife: Her pursuit propels the action forward, and the narration favors her, restricting us largely to what she believes and eventually learns.

Double Jeopardy concentrates on an innocent person who is the target of the crime, and this is one common pattern in the genre. At some point the victim will usually realize that he or she cannot react passively and must fight the criminal, as in *Duel, The Fugitive, The Net, Breakdown,* and *Panic Room* **(4.2).** In *Ransom,* the father of a kidnapped boy spurns police advice and refuses to pay the ransom, offering it as a bounty on the criminals. Alternatively, the plot may center on an innocent bystander dropped unexpectedly into a struggle between the criminal and the police. Most of Hitchcock's films are built around an ordinary person who stumbles into a dangerous situation (*The 39 Steps, Shadow of a Doubt, North by Northwest, Rear Window*). In *Die Hard,* an off-duty detective is accidentally trapped in a hostage crisis, so he must fight both police and thieves to rescue the other innocents. *Red Rock West* shows a drifter who is mistaken for a paid killer by a man who wants to murder his wife. Thematically, this innocent-centered plot pattern often emphasizes characters discovering resources within themselves—courage, cleverness, even a capacity for violence.

Instead of spotlighting the innocents, the plot may concentrate on the forces of justice. The action then typically becomes an investigation, in which police or private detectives seek to capture the criminal or prevent a crime. A classic example is *The Big Heat,* in which a rogue cop seeks to avenge the death of his family by capturing the mobsters responsible. *Nick of Time, The Bodyguard,* and *In the Line of Fire* present protagonists seeking to forestall a threatened murder. The contemporary serial-killer plot may emphasize police pursuit, offering only glimpses of the criminal (*The Silence of the Lambs, Copy Cat, From Hell*). *Se7en* follows two policemen in their efforts to untangle a string of murders emblematic of the seven deadly sins. When a plot highlights the investigators, themes of the fallibility of justice tend to come to the fore. In *L.A. Confidential* three ill-matched detectives join forces to reveal how official corruption has led to the murders of prostitutes.

As another alternative, the thriller can put the criminals center stage. One subgenre is the hit-man film, following the adventures of a paid killer. Jean-Pierre Melville's *Le Samourai* is a classic instance; more recent examples are *Leon the Professional* and *Panic.* There is also the heist or caper

4.2 Innocents in jeopardy: An unusual camera position for a classic thriller situation in *Panic Room.*

film, featuring a tightly orchestrated robbery. This subgenre became a mainstay of world cinema in the 1950s, with *The Asphalt Jungle, Bob le Flambeur, Rififi,* and *Big Deal on Madonna Street,* and it has made a comeback in recent years with *Heist, The Score, Ronin,* and *Ocean's 11.* There is also what we might call the dishonor among thieves variant, in which criminals betray one another. In *Bound,* lesbian lovers try to steal $2 million from the mob. *A Simple Plan* portrays nervous and clumsy thieves, while *Jackie Brown* traces an expanding web of double crosses, as each crook tries to outsmart the others. The more emphasis placed on professional criminals, the closer the film comes to the gangster or outlaw genre. Some serial-killer films, such as *The Minus Man* and *Henry: Portrait of a Serial Killer,* make the murderer the protagonist, as do more intimate psychological tales like *The Talented Mr. Ripley.*

Sometimes the thriller will balance its plot and narration between the police and the criminal. Often this tactic draws thematic parallels between the two. In John Woo's *The Killer,* the plot alternates between showing the efforts of a hit man to quit the business, aided by his weak mentor, and showing his cop adversary, who is also under the sway of an older colleague. Michael Mann's *Heat* creates strong parallels between two robbers, each having problems with the women in their lives, and the dissolving marriage of the policeman trying to catch them. In both *The Killer* and *Heat,* the characters themselves recognize their affinities. In contrast, *Fargo* plays on the sharp differences between the sunny common sense of the policewoman and an almost pitiably blundering kidnapper.

Thrillers obviously aim to thrill us—that is, to startle, shock, and scare. How do we distinguish them from horror films, which seek similar effects? Horror aims to disgust as well as frighten, but the thriller need not involve disgust. The central character of a horror film is a monster who is both fearsome and repellent, but a thriller villain may be quite attractive (the deceptively kind men in *The Minus Man* and *Primal Fear,* the treacherous women in *Red Rock West* and *The Last Seduction*). While suspense and surprise are important in most cinematic storytelling, these responses dominate the crime thriller. The plots highlight clever plans, still more clever blocking moves, and sudden coincidences that upset carefully timed schemes. Tracing out a plan or following an investigation can yield suspense (Will the criminal succeed? How?), while unexpected twists trigger surprise, forcing us to reconsider the odds of the criminal's success.

More specifically, the thriller's effects will depend on which characters are highlighted by the plot and narration. If the

4.3 The aftermath of the mysterious dockyard explosion that triggers the investigation in *The Usual Suspects*.

protagonist is an innocent, the suspense we feel comes from the prospect that the crime will harm him or her. If the hero is a figure of justice, we become concerned that she or he will not be able to protect the innocents. When the protagonist is the criminal, one way to achieve some sympathy is to rank the lawbreakers on a scale of immorality. The most sympathetic criminals will be ones who are trying to get out of the business (*The Killer*) or those who oppose even more immoral figures. The heroes of *Out of Sight* are easygoing, good-humored thieves ripping off a white-collar embezzler and a band of sociopathic killers. Sometimes criminal protagonists can stretch our sympathies in complicated ways. In *A Simple Plan,* basically good people turn criminal after a momentary weakness, and even though they have done wrong, we may find ourselves hoping that they will succeed in their crime.

Like any genre, this can mix with others. It blends with the horror film in *From Dusk to Dawn* and with science fiction in *Blade Runner* and *Minority Report. Rush Hour* pushes the police investigation toward farce, while *Lock, Stock, and Two Smoking Barrels* piles up absurd coincidences around a quartet of petty crooks who steal ganja and money from a gang (who stole the goods from another gang).

The thriller's emphasis on suspense and surprise encourages filmmakers to mislead the audience, and this can lead to experiments with narrative form. Hitchcock pioneered this tendency by suddenly switching protagonists in *Psycho* and by letting two couples' lives intertwine in *The Family Plot.* Many recent films that play with story–plot relations (see pp. 77–79) are crime thrillers. A crime in the story may be replayed in the plot, showing different clues each time (*Snake Eyes*) or presenting different points of view (*The Killing, Jackie Brown*). *Memento* tells its investigation story in reverse order. *The Usual Suspects* creates an unreliable flashback narration, at the end turning a minor character into a major player **(4.3)**. *Bound* consists largely of flashbacks

launched from a cryptic present-time situation, a woman tied and gagged in a closet. As the crime story is revealed, we have reason to suspect that at some phase the robbery scheme she and her partner have devised will fail.

Independent filmmakers have found that general audiences will accept narrational experiments when packaged in this genre. Clever thrillers can also showcase their directors' talents; the Wachowski brothers moved from *Bound* to *The Matrix* films, and Bryan Singer went from *The Usual Suspects* to *X-Men.* For other independents, the genre offers a structure on which they can hang their personal concerns. David Mamet's interest in how people conceal their true motives surfaces in *House of Games* and *The Spanish Prisoner.* Joel and Ethan Coen set *Blood Simple* and *The Man Who Wasn't There* in bleak, small-town locales populated with losers lusting for one big chance. David Lynch uses the genre's tactics of suspense and surprise to summon up a dread-filled atmosphere that may never receive rational explanation. In *Blue Velvet, Lost Highway,* and *Mulholland Drive,* the crimes are ominous but obscure, the criminals nightmarish grotesques, and the innocents not wholly innocent.

Because crime thrillers can be shot fairly cheaply, the genre has offered Hollywood's rivals a path to international distribution. Hong Kong has exported many such films, as has France (*La Femme Nikita*), Britain (*Snatch, Sexy Beast*), Japan (*Fireworks, Cure*), Korea (*Tell Me Something, Nowhere to Hide*), and Thailand (*Bangkok Dangerous*). Audiences worldwide share similar expectations about crime thrillers, and filmmakers can innovate by injecting local cultural traditions into the genre's conventions of plot, character, and theme. Two of our sample analyses, of *Breathless* (pp. 428–433) and of *Chungking Express* (pp. 437–442), focus on non-Hollywood films that imaginatively shift the expectations we bring to the crime thriller.

over history. Their conventions change, and by mixing conventions from different genres, filmmakers create new possibilities every now and then.

Many film genres originate in part by borrowing existing conventions from the other media. The melodrama has clear antecedents in stage plays and novels like *Uncle Tom's Cabin*. Types of comedy can be traced back to stage farces or comic novels. Musicals drew on both musical comedies and variety reviews.

Yet the film medium always imposes its own distinctive qualities and circumstances on an adopted genre. For example, Western novels were already popular in the 19th century. Yet, although the cinema became commercially successful in 1895, Westerns did not become a film genre until after 1908. Why the delay? It may well have been that the greater length of films around that era (up to roughly 15 minutes), plus the rise of film studios with companies of actors under contract, encouraged more shooting on location. Using unspoiled American landscapes in turn fostered stories involving the frontier, and the Western quickly became a tremendously popular genre. It was also a notably American genre, giving U.S. films a way to compete in the growing international market. Thus film genres have their own history, combining borrowings from other arts and distinctive innovations.

Most cinema genres and subgenres become established when one film becomes successful and is widely imitated. New genres and subgenres are not, however, recognized after that first successful film, since by definition a genre consists of a group of similar films. But after several films that resemble one another appear, people begin to compare them. For example, in the late 1990s, the term gross-out came to be commonly applied to a group of films, including *Ace Ventura, Pet Detective; There's Something about Mary;* and *American Pie*. But critics then traced this "new" subgenre back to such influential comedies as *Animal House* (1978) and *Porky's* (1981).

Similarly, when the television-related fantasy *Pleasantville* appeared in 1998, some critics linked it to comparable films: *Big* (1988), *Dave* (1993), *Splash* (1984), *Peggy Sue Got Married* (1986), *Groundhog Day* (1993), *The Truman Show* (1998), and *Sliding Doors* (1998). Reviewer Richard Corliss suggested a new term for the subgenre, *fantasies of displacement*. Lisa Schwartzbaum called such films *magical comedies*. Whether these or other phrases will ever become common parlance, many viewers might recognize that these films share traits that set them apart. Such comments by reviewers are one way in which new subgenres come to be recognized.

Once a genre is launched, there seems to be no fixed pattern of development. We might expect that the earliest films in the genre are the "purest," with genre mixing coming at a late stage. But genre mixing can take place very soon. *Whoopee!* (1930), a musical from the beginning of talking pictures, is also a Western. *Just Imagine* (1930), one of the first sound science-fiction films, contains a comic song. Some historians have also speculated that a genre inevitably passes from a phase of maturity to one of parody, when it begins to mock its own conventions. Yet an early Western, *The Great K & A Train Robbery* (1926) is an all-out parody of its own genre. Early slapstick comedies often take moviemaking as their subject and ruthlessly poke fun at themselves, as in Charlie Chaplin's farcical *His New Job* (1915).

Typically genres do not remain constantly successful. Rather, they rise and fall in popularity. The periods in which a genre remains popular are called *cycles*.

A cycle is a batch of genre films that enjoy intense popularity and influence over a distinct period. Cycles can occur when a successful film produces a burst of imitations. *The Godfather* triggered a brief spate of gangster movies. During the 1970s there was a cycle of disaster movies (*Earthquake, The Poseidon Adventure*). More recently there have been cycles of comedies centering on spaced-out teenagers (*Wayne's World, Bill and Ted's Excellent Adventure,* and *Dude, Where's My Car?*), buddy-cop movies (*Lethal Weapon* and its successors), movies adapted from comic books (*Batman, Spiderman*), romantic thrillers aimed at a woman's audience (*Dead Again, Double Jeopardy*), and dramas describing coming of age in African American neighborhoods (*Boyz N the Hood, Menace II Society*). Few observers would have predicted that science-fiction movies would return in the 1970s, but *Star Wars* created a long-lasting cycle. It seems likely that a genre never dies. It may pass out of fashion for a time, only to return in updated garb. The sword-and-sandal epic set in ancient times was popular in the 1950s and 1960s, then virtually disappeared until Ridley Scott revived it to considerable acclaim in 2000 with *Gladiator*—inspiring other filmmakers to undertake similar subjects.

One of the most common ways in which genres change and develop subgenres is by the mixing of conventions and iconography. Genre mixing has been common throughout the history of popular filmmaking. The musical seems capable of blending with almost any subject matter. During the 1930s and 1940s, singing cowboys like Roy Rogers and Gene Autry combined the musical and the Western. There have been musical melodramas, such as *Yentl* and all three versions of *A Star Is Born*. *The Rocky Horror Picture Show* created a musical horror film. *Alien* mixed elements of the horror film with science fiction by treating the unknown life-form as a scary hidden creature that could strike at any time; the spaceship in effect became like the old dark house of earlier horror conventions. *Blade Runner* mixes science fiction and the detective story, while *Billy the Kid vs. Dracula* links the Western and the horror film—two genres that would have seemed pretty incompatible.

Comedy seems capable of motivating the mixture of almost any imaginable genres, as in Woody Allen's *Mighty Aphrodite*. This film inserts a tragic Greek chorus (filmed in authentic costume in ancient Greek theaters) to comment at intervals on the twists and turns of a modern-day romantic comedy concerning a man trying to help a prostitute get married and find a respectable career.

In some cases, genres influence and mix with each other across cultures. The Japanese samurai genre, with its conventions of swordplay and revenge, has blended well with a parallel genre, the Western. Sergio Leone based his Italian Western *For a Fistful of Dollars* loosely around the plot of Akira Kurosawa's *Yojimbo,* and the same Japanese director's *Seven Samurai* provided the basis of the Hollywood Western *The Magnificent Seven.* Similarly, widespread fan interest in Hong Kong movies during the 1980s and 1990s led the Wachowski brothers to mix high-tech science-fiction effects with Hong Kong martial-arts choreography in *The Matrix.*

Such mixtures are often consciously recognized by filmmakers and audiences alike. Filmmakers may take elements of two or more successful films, blend them, and spin off an entirely new concept. Similarly, spectators are used to comparing new films with existing ones. If someone who has not seen *Pleasantville* asks a friend what it is like, the reply might be "It's sort of a combination of *The Truman Show* and *Back to the Future.*" That is, it's a fantasy film dealing with television, but it also has a science-fiction element of a time machine.

The fact that genres can intermingle does not, however, mean that there are no distinctions among them. *The Matrix* does not prevent us from differentiating standard Hong Kong martial-arts films from standard Hollywood science-fiction tales. Although we cannot pin down a single description of a genre that will apply for all time, we can recognize that at a given period of film history, filmmakers, reviewers, and audiences manage to distinguish one sort of movie from another.

The Social Functions of Genres

The fact that every genre has fluctuated in popularity reminds us that genres are tightly bound to cultural factors. Why do audiences enjoy seeing the same conven-

"So it's kind of a psychic political thriller comedy with a heart."

"With a heart. And not unlike *Ghost* meets *Manchurian Candidate.*"

— Producer and screenwriter in the opening scene of Robert Altman's *The Player* tions over and over? Many film scholars believe that genres are ritualized dramas resembling holiday celebrations—ceremonies that are satisfying because they re-affirm cultural values with little variation. At the end of *Saving Private Ryan* or *You've Got Mail,* who can resist a surge of reassuring satisfaction that cherished values—self-sacrificing heroism, the desirability of romantic love—are validated? And just as one can see these ceremonies as helping participants forget the more disturbing aspects of the world, the familiar characterizations and plots of genres may also serve to distract the audience from genuine social problems.

Some scholars would argue that genres go further and actually exploit ambiva-lent social values and attitudes. The gangster film, for instance, makes it possible for audiences to relish the mobster's swaggering freedom while still feeling satis-fied when he receives his punishment. Seen from this standpoint, genre conven-tions arouse emotion by touching on deep social uncertainties but then channel those emotions into approved attitudes.

Because of the contract between filmmaker and audience, the promise of some-thing new based on something familiar, genres may also respond quickly to broad social trends. During the economic depression of the 1930s, for instance, the Warner Bros. musical films introduced social commentary into stage numbers; in *Gold Diggers of 1933* a singer asks the Depression-era audience to remember "my forgotten man," the unemployed war veteran. More recently Hollywood producers have tried to shape romantic comedies and dramas to the emergence of Generation X tastes. In Chapter 11, we will consider how another musical, *Meet Me in St. Louis,* reflects concerns of the U.S. home front during World War II.

It is common to suggest that at different points in history, the stories, themes, values, or imagery of the genre harmonize with public attitudes. For instance, do the science-fiction films of the 1950s, with hydrogen bombs creating Godzilla and other monsters, reveal fears of technology run amok? The hypothesis is that genre conventions, repeated from film to film, reflect the audience's pervasive doubts or anxieties. Many film scholars would argue that this reflectionist approach helps ex-plain why genres vary in popularity.

Social processes can also be reflected in genre innovations. Ripley, the female protagonist of *Aliens,* is a courageous, even aggressive, warrior who also has a warm maternal side **(4.4, 4.5).** This is something of a novelty in the science-fiction genre. Many commentators saw Ripley as a product of attitudes derived from the Women's Movement of the 1970s. Feminist groups argued that women could be seen as active

4.4 In *Aliens,* Ripley learns how to use a weapon . . .

4.5 . . . but can also comfort the orphaned girl the group of soldiers find.

and competent without losing positive qualities associated with feminine behavior, like gentleness and sympathy. As these ideas spread through mainstream media and social opinion, films like *Aliens* could turn traditionally masculine roles over to female characters.

Such ways of looking at genre are usually called reflectionist, because they assume that genres reflect social attitudes, as if in a mirror. But some critics would object that reflectionist readings can become oversimplified. Once we look closely at a genre film, we usually discover complexities that nuance a reflectionist account. For instance, if we look beyond Ripley, the protagonist of *Aliens,* we find that all the characters lie along a continuum running between "masculine" and "feminine" values, and the survivors of the adventure, male or female, seem to blend the best of both gender identities. Moreover, often what seems to be social reflection is simply the film industry's effort to exploit the day's headlines. A genre film may reflect not the audience's hopes and fears but the filmmakers' guess about what will sell.

The argument over whether genre conventions directly reflect social circumstances came into the open in a particularly explicit way in the late 1990s. Over the past decades there had been a gradual increase in the violent content of some action films. Such violence seemed to be popular with a broad segment of the audience—and particularly with the young people who made up much of the active filmgoing public. When a series of multiple killings at schools and other public places occurred within a short stretch of time in the late 1990s, the popular media came under scrutiny as a possible cause. In 1999, for the first time, the film industry (along with the music, television, and videogame businesses) began voluntarily to monitor their own projects with an eye to reducing violence. Was this an industry reacting to a real revulsion on the part of its audience? Or did the media and the government condemn depictions of violence as a way to avoid confronting such causes of violence as poverty and the wide availability of guns? The terrorist attacks of September 11, 2001, initially intensified public reactions against violence, yet after a short time there was also an increased interest in war films. Did such patriotic themes help justify the United States' increasing isolation from international politics? Such questions have long been raised in relation to popular genres, since they seem so familiar and closely related to society as a whole.

Whether we study a genre's history, its cultural functions, or its reflection of social trends, conventions remain our best point of departure. As examples, we look briefly at three significant genres of American fictional filmmaking.

THREE GENRES

The Western

The Western emerged early in the history of cinema, becoming well established by the early 1910s. It is partly based on historical reality, since in the American West there were cowboys, outlaws, settlers, and tribes of Native Americans. Films also based their portrayal of the frontier on songs, popular fiction, and Wild West shows. Early actors sometimes mirrored this blend of realism and myth: Cowboy star Tom Mix had been a Texas Ranger, a Wild West performer, and a champion rodeo rider.

Quite early the central theme of the genre became the conflict between civilized order and the lawless frontier. From the East and the city come the settlers who want to raise families, the schoolteachers who aim to spread learning, and the

"I knew Wyatt Earp. In the very early silent days, a couple of times a year he would come up to visit pals, cowboys he knew in Tombstone; a lot of them were in my company. I think I was an assistant prop boy then and I used to give him a chair and a cup of coffee, and he told me about the fight at the O. K. Corral. So in *My Darling Clementine,* we did it exactly the way it had been. They didn't just walk up the street and start banging away at each other; it was a clever military manoeuvre."

— John Ford, director

bankers and government officials. In the vast natural spaces, in contrast, thrive those outside civilization—not only the American Indians but also outlaws, trappers and traders, and greedy cattle barons.

Iconography reinforces this basic duality. The covered wagon and the railroad are set against the horse and canoe; the schoolhouse and church contrast with the lonely campfire in the hills. As in most genres, costume is iconographically significant, too. The settlers' starched dresses and Sunday suits stand out against Indians' tribal garb and the cowboys' jeans and Stetsons.

Interestingly, the typical Western hero stands between the two thematic poles. At home in the wilderness but naturally inclined toward justice and kindness, the cowboy is often poised between savagery and civilization. William S. Hart, one of the most popular early Western stars, crystallized the character of the "good bad man" as the most common protagonist. In *Hell's Hinges* (1916) a minister's sister tries to reform him; one shot represents the pull between two ways of life **(4.6)**.

4.6   The "good bad" hero of *Hell's Hinges* reads the Bible, a bottle of whiskey at his elbow.

The in-between position of the hero affects common Western plots. He may start out on the side of the lawless, or he may simply stand apart from the conflict. In either case, he will become uneasily attracted to the life offered by the newcomers to the frontier. Eventually the hero decides to join the forces of order, helping them fight hired gunmen, bandits, or whatever the film presents as a threat to stability and progress.

As the genre developed, it adhered to a social ideology implicit in its conventions. White populations' progress westward was considered a historic mission, while the conquered indigenous cultures were usually treated as primitive and savage. Western films are full of racist stereotypes of Native Americans and Hispanics. Yet on a few occasions filmmakers treated Native American characters as tragic figures, ennobled by their closeness to nature but facing the extinction of their way of life. The best early example is probably *The Last of the Mohicans* (1920).

Moreover, the genre was not wholly optimistic about taming the wilderness. The hero's eventual commitment to civilization's values was often tinged with regret for his loss of freedom. In John Ford's *Straight Shooting* (1917), Cheyenne Harry (played by Harry Carey) is hired by a villainous rancher to evict a farmer, but he falls in love with the farmer's daughter and vows to reform. Rallying the farmers, Harry helps defeat the rancher. Still, he is reluctant to settle down with Molly **(4.7)**.

4.7   In *Straight Shooting,* the hero stands framed in the farmhouse doorway, halfway between the lure of civilization and the call of the wilderness.

Within this set of values a great many conventional scenes became standardized— the Indians' attack on forts or wagon trains, the shy courting of a woman by the rough-hewn hero, the hero's discovery of a burned settler's shack, the outlaws' robbery of bank or stagecoach, the climactic gunfight on dusty town streets. Writers and directors could distinguish their films by novel handlings of these elements. In Sergio Leone's flamboyant Italian Westerns, every convention is stretched out in minute detail or amplified to a huge scale, as when the climactic shootout in *The Good, the Bad, and the Ugly* (1966) is filmed to resemble a bullfight **(4.8)**.

There were narrative and thematic innovations as well. After such liberal Westerns of the 1950s as *Broken Arrow* (1950), native cultures began to be treated with more respect. In *Little Big Man* (1970) and *Soldier Blue* (1970), the conventional thematic values were reversed, depicting Indian life as civilized and white society as marauding. Some films played up the hero's uncivilized side, showing him perilously out of control (*Winchester 73*, 1950), even psychopathic (*The Left-Handed Gun*, 1958). The heroes of *The Wild Bunch* (1969) would have been considered unvarnished villains in early Westerns.

The new complexity of the protagonist is evident in John Ford's *The Searchers* (1956). After a Comanche raid on his brother's homestead, Ethan Edwards sets out to find his kidnapped niece Debbie. He is driven primarily by family loyalty but

4.8   A low wall creates an arena in which the three-way shoot-out can occur at the end of *The Good, the Bad, and the Ugly.*

4.9   The closing shot of *The Searchers.*

4.10   Harry Carey's gesture in *Straight Shooting.*

also by his secret love for his brother's wife, who has been raped and killed by the raiders. Ethan's sidekick, a young man who is part Cherokee, realizes that Ethan plans not to rescue Debbie but to kill her for becoming a Comanche wife. Ethan's fierce racism and raging vengeance culminate in a raid on the Comanche village. At the film's close, Ethan returns to civilization but pauses on the cabin's threshold **(4.9)** before turning back to the desert.

The shot eerily recalls Ford's *Straight Shooting* (4.7); Ford even has John Wayne repeat Harry Carey's characteristic gripping of his forearm **(4.10)**. Now, however, it seems that the drifting cowboy is condemned to live outside civilization because he cannot tame his grief and hatred. More savage than citizen, he seems condemned, as he says of the souls of dead Comanches, "to wander forever between the winds." This bitter treatment of a perennial theme illustrates how drastically a genre's conventions can change across history.

The Horror Film

While the Western is most clearly defined by subject, theme, and iconography, the horror genre is most recognizable by its intended emotional effect on the audience. The horror film aims to shock, disgust, repel—in short, to horrify. This impulse is what shapes the genre's other conventions.

What can horrify us? Typically, a monster. In the horror film, the monster is a dangerous breach of nature, a violation of our normal sense of what is possible. The monster might be unnaturally large, as King Kong is. The monster might violate the boundary between the dead and the living, as vampires and zombies do. The monster might be an ordinary human who is transformed, as when Dr. Jekyll drinks his potion and becomes the evil Mr. Hyde. Or the monster might manifest a biology unknown to science, as with the creature in the *Alien* films. The genre's horrifying emotional effect, then, is usually created by a character convention: a threatening, unnatural monster.

Other conventions follow from this one. Our reaction to the monster may be guided by other characters who react to it in the properly horrified way. In *Cat People* (1942), a mysterious woman can, apparently, turn into a panther. Our revulsion and fear are confirmed by the reaction of the woman's husband and his coworker **(4.11)**. In contrast, we know that *E.T.* is not a horror film because, although the alien is unnatural, he is not threatening and the children do not react to him as if he is.

4.11   A shadow and a character's reaction suggest an offscreen menace in *Cat People*.

The horror plot will often start from the monster's attack on normal life. In response, the other characters must discover that the monster is at large and try to destroy it. (In some cases, as when a character is possessed by demons, others may seek to rescue him or her.) This plot can be developed in various ways—by having the monster launch a series of attacks, by having people in authority resist believing that the monster exists, or by blocking the characters' efforts to destroy it. In *The Exorcist,* for example, the characters only gradually discover that Regan is possessed; even after they realize this, they still must struggle to drive the demon out.

The genre's characteristic themes also stem from the intended response. If the monster horrifies us because it violates the laws of nature we know, the genre is well suited to suggest the limits of human knowledge. It is probably significant that the skeptical authorities who must be convinced of the monster's existence are often scientists. In other cases, the scientists themselves unintentionally unleash monsters through their risky experiments. A common convention of this type of plot has the characters concluding that there are some things that humans are not meant to know. Another common thematic pattern of the horror film plays on fears about the environment, as when nuclear accidents and other human-made disasters create mutant monsters like the giant ants in *Them!*

Not surprisingly, the iconography of the horror film includes settings where monsters might be expected to lurk. The old dark house where a group of potential victims gather was popularized by *The Cat and the Canary* in 1927 and has been used recently for *The Haunting* (1999) and *The Others* (2001). Cemeteries can yield the walking dead, scientists' laboratories the artificial human (as in *Frankenstein*). Filmmakers have played off these conventions cleverly, as when Hitchcock juxtaposed a mundane motel with a sinister, decaying mansion in *Psycho* or George Romero had humans battle zombies in a shopping mall in *Dawn of the Dead.* The slasher subgenre has made superhuman killers invade everyday settings like summer camps and suburban neighborhoods.

Heavy makeup is unusually prominent in the iconography of horror. A furry face and hands can signal transformation into a werewolf, while dried, shriveled skin indicates a mummy. Some actors have specialized in transforming themselves into many frightening figures. Lon Chaney, who played the original Phantom in *The Phantom of the Opera* (1925), was known as "the man of a thousand faces." Boris Karloff's makeup as Frankenstein's monster in the 1930 *Frankenstein* rendered him so unrecognizable that the credits of his next film informed viewers that it featured the same actor. More recently computer special effects have supplemented makeup in transforming actors into monsters. Like the Western, the horror

4.12 In *Nosferatu,* Max Schreck's makeup and acting make his Count Orlock eerily like a rat or a bat.

4.13 A tiny gleam reflected in Boris Karloff's eye signals the moment when the monster revives in *The Mummy.*

"Our formula is simple. A love story, three scenes of suggested horror and one of actual violence. Fadeout. It's all over in less than 70 minutes."

— Val Lewton, producer, *Cat People*

film emerged in the era of silent moviemaking. Some of the most important early works in the genre were German—notably *The Cabinet of Dr. Caligari* (1920) and *Nosferatu* (1922), the first adaptation of the novel *Dracula.* The angular performances, heavy makeup, and distorted settings characteristic of German Expressionist cinema conveyed an ominous, supernatural atmosphere **(4.12).**

Because a horror film can create its emotional impact with makeup and other low-technology special effects, the horror genre has long been favored by low-budget filmmakers. During the 1930s, a secondary Hollywood studio, Universal, launched a cycle of horror films. *Dracula* (1931), *Frankenstein* (1931), and *The Mummy* (1932; **4.13**) proved enormously popular and helped the studio become a major company. A decade later, RKO's B-picture unit under Val Lewton produced a cycle of literate, somber films on minuscule budgets. Lewton's directors proceeded by hints, keeping the monster offscreen and cloaking the sets in darkness. In *Cat People,* for instance, we never see the heroine transform herself into a panther, and we only glimpse the creature in certain scenes. The film achieves its effects through shadows, offscreen sound, and character reaction (4.11).

In later decades, other low-budget filmmakers were drawn to the genre. Horror became a staple of the 1960s U.S. independent production, with many films targeted at the teenage market. Similarly, George Romero's *Night of the Living Dead* (1968) was budgeted at only $114,000, but its success on college campuses helped revive the genre. *The Blair Witch Project* (1999), made for a reputed $35,000, found an even bigger audience internationally. Today, the horror film remains one of the most popular types of exploitation filmmaking.

During the 1970s, the genre acquired a new respectability, chiefly because of the prestige of *Rosemary's Baby* (1968) and *The Exorcist* (1973). These films innovated by presenting violent and disgusting actions with unprecedented explicitness. When the possessed Regan vomited in the face of the priest bending over her, a new standard for horrific imagery was set.

The big-budget horror film entered on a period of popularity that has not yet ended. Many major Hollywood directors have worked in the genre, and several horror films—from *Jaws* (1975) and *Carrie* (1976) to *The Sixth Sense* (1999) and *The Mummy* (1999)—have become huge hits. The genre's iconography pervades contemporary culture, decorating lunch boxes and theme park rides. Horror classics have been remade (*Cat People, Dracula*), and the genre conventions have been parodied (*Young Frankenstein, Beetlejuice*).

While the Western declined in popularity during the 1970s, the horror film has sustained an audience for over 30 years. Its longevity has set scholars looking for cultural explanations. Many critics suggest that the 1970s subgenre of family horror films, such as *The Exorcist* and *Poltergeist,* reflect social concerns about the breakup of American families. Others suggest that the genre's questioning of normality and traditional categories is in tune with both the post-Vietnam and the post–Cold War eras: Viewers may be uncertain of their fundamental beliefs about the world and their place in it. The continuing popularity of the teenage-oriented slasher series during the 1980s and 1990s might cater to young people's fascination with and simultaneous anxieties about sexuality and violence—enhanced by sophisticated special-effects capable of creating gory and grotesque scenes. By the late 1990s, horror-film conventions had become so familiar that parodies also became popular: *Men in Black* (1997), *Men in Black II* (2002), and the "Scary Movie" and "Scream" series. Whatever the causes, filmmakers working in the horror film have maintained that dynamic of convention and innovation that is basic to every film genre.

The Musical

If the Western was largely based around the subject matter of the American frontier and the horror film around the emotional effect on the spectator, the musical came into being in response to a technical innovation. Though there had been occasional attempts to synchronize live vocal and musical accompaniment to scenes of singing and dancing during the silent era, the notion of basing a film on a series of musical numbers did not emerge until the late 1920s with the successful introduction of recorded sound tracks. One of the earliest features to include the human voice extensively was *The Jazz Singer* (1927), which contained almost no recorded dialogue but had several songs.

At first many musicals were *revues,* programs of numbers with little or no narrative linkage between. Such revue musicals aided in selling these early sound films in foreign-language markets, where spectators could enjoy the performances even if they could not understand the dialogue and lyrics. As subtitles and dubbing solved the problems of the language barrier, musicals featured more complicated narratives. Filmmakers devised plots that could motivate the introduction of musical numbers.

Two typical plot patterns of the musical emerged during the 1930s. One of these was the *backstage musical,* with a narrative centering on singers and dancers who perform for an audience within the fiction. Warner Bros.'s successful early musical, *42nd Street* (1933), set the classic pattern for backstage musicals by casting dancer Ruby Keeler as the understudy for a big musical star who breaks her leg just before the big opening. The director tells Keeler, "You're going out a youngster, but you've *got* to come back a star!" and indeed she wins the audience's cheers **(4.14).** During the decade, Warners' elaborately choreographed Busby Berkeley musicals, MGM's pairing of the youthful Judy Garland and Mickey Rooney in a series of "let's put on a show!" plots, and RKO's elegant cycle of films starring the dance team of Fred Astaire and Ginger Rogers all established the conventions of the backstage musical. Later examples included musicals where the characters are film performers, as in *Singin' in the Rain* (1952). More recent backstage musicals are *The Commitments, That Thing You Do!,* and *What's Love Got to Do with It.*

> "[Producer Arthur Freed] came to me and said, 'What are you going to do with it?' I said, 'Well, Arthur, I don't know yet. But I do know I've gotta be singing and it's gotta be raining.' There was no rain in that picture up to then."
>
> — Gene Kelly, actor/choreographer, on *Singin' in the Rain*

4.14 Ruby Keeler hoofs her way to stardom in *42nd Street*'s title number.

4.15   The citizens of a whole town are drawn into the dance in *The Young Girls of Rochefort.*

Not all musicals take place in a show-business situation, however. There is also the *straight musical,* where people may sing and dance in situations of everyday life. Even in backstage musicals, the characters occasionally break into song in an everyday setting. Straight musicals are often romantic comedies, where characters typically trace the progress of their courtship by breaking into song to express their fears, longings, and joys. We analyze one such film, *Meet Me in St. Louis,* in Chapter 11. In 1968, a French director took the romantic musical to extremes by having his characters in *The Young Girls of Rochefort* sing most of the dialogue in the film, with dozens of passersby joining in dance numbers staged in the town's streets **(4.15).**

In both backstage and straight musicals, the numbers are often associated with romance. Often the hero and heroine realize that they form the perfect romantic couple because they perform beautifully together. This happens in *Shall We Dance* when the Ginger Rogers character sheds her original annoyance with Fred Astaire during the "Isn't It a Wonderful Day" number, and by the end they have clearly fallen in love. This plot device has remained a staple of the genre. Astaire again charms his reluctant partner, this time Cyd Charisse, in the "Dancing in the Dark" number in *The Band Wagon* (1953), and John Travolta meets his romantic match on the disco dance floor in *Saturday Night Fever* (1977).

Apart from the backstage and romantic plot patterns, the musical has also often been associated with children's stories. *The Wizard of Oz* is an early example of this. Another instance would be the musical biography *Hans Christian Andersen* (1952). Feature-length cartoons are often musicals, a convention that was established by Walt Disney in 1937 with *Snow White and the Seven Dwarfs* and has continued to the present with *The Lion King* and *Lilo and Stitch.* Indeed, by the 1980s and 1990s the live-action musical had become relatively rare and animated films had largely taken over the function of providing tales interspersed with musical numbers.

Although we tend to associate musicals with light-hearted romance and comedy, more serious, even tragic, narratives have figured in musicals. *West Side Story* involves a cross-cultural romance that ends with the death of the hero, and *Pennies from Heaven* evokes the grim atmosphere of the Depression by having its characters lip-synch to recordings from that era. Even in these cases, however, a romance—albeit one that ends unhappily—forms the basis for the action. Still, for the most part, while the Western and the horror film may often explore the darker sides of human nature, Hollywood musicals tend to celebrate typically American ideals: Ambition is rewarded (the protagonists' show succeeds!), the romance usually ends happily, and high ideals are justified. A union strike can even succeed with the leaders of the management and labor sides pairing off romantically, as in *The Pajama Game.*

The range of subject matter in musicals is so broad that it may be hard to pin down specific iconography associated with the genre. Yet the backstage musical at least had its characteristic settings: the dressing rooms and wings of a theater, the flats and backdrops of the stage (as in 4.14), the nightclub with orchestra and dance floor. Similarly, performers in these musicals are often recognizable by their distinctive stage costumes. During the 1930s, Fred Astaire wore the most famous top hat in the cinema, a hat so closely associated with his musicals that the beginning of *The Band Wagon*—where Astaire plays a washed-up movie actor—could make a joke about it. Similarly, Travolta's white suit in *Saturday Night Fever* became an icon of the disco era. The chance for novelty has always been high in the musical, however, as the musical numbers set in a factory (*The Pajama Game*) or under an elevated street (*West Side Story*) show.

The characteristic techniques of the musical are similarly diverse. Musicals tend to be brightly lit, to set off the cheerful costumes and sets and to keep the choreography of the dance numbers clearly visible. For similar reasons, color film stock was applied quite early to musicals, including Eddie Cantor's *Whoopee!* and, as we saw in Chapter 2, *The Wizard of Oz.* In order to show off the patterns formed by the dancers in musical numbers, the camera is often unusually mobile and can even be mounted on a moving crane that lifts it up into the air. One technique widely used in the musical is not usually evident to viewers: lip-synching to prerecorded songs. Throughout the history of musicals, the most common approach has been for the singers to record their musical numbers in advance. On the set, they move their lips in synchronization to a playback of the recording. This technique allows the singers to move about freely and to concentrate on their acting. Such prerecording of sound is otherwise quite rare in live-action filmmaking.

The 1935 RKO Astaire-Rogers musical *Swing Time* is one of the exemplary backstage musicals. Early in the film the hero, a gambler and tap dancer nicknamed Lucky, is trying to quit his stage act and get married. At once we sense his fiancée is not right for him; she is not a dancer (and is not even seen during the early scenes in which his colleagues try to trick him into missing the wedding). The opening scenes take place in the conventional settings of the stage, wings, and dressing room of a theater. Later, when Lucky goes to the city and meets the heroine, Penny (a name that echoes Lucky's precious "lucky quarter"), she quickly takes a strong dislike to him. An amusing scene in the dance school where she works has Lucky pretending to be hopelessly clumsy. Yet when the school's owner fires Penny, Lucky saves her job by suddenly launching into a graceful, virtuoso, and unrehearsed dance with her. By the end her animosity has disappeared and the school owner sets the two up to audition at a fashionable club.

Obstacles ensue, primarily in the form of a romantic rivalry between Lucky and the orchestra leader at the club and also Penny's mistaken belief that Lucky intends to return to his fiancée. Near the end, Penny seems about to abandon Lucky to marry the conductor. She and Lucky meet, apparently for the last time, and their talk at cross-purposes reveals the link between performance and romance:

PENNY: "Does she dance very beautifully?"

LUCKY: "Who?"

PENNY: "The girl you're in love with?"

LUCKY: "Yes—very."

4.16   After losing his suit in a card game, Lucky still wears his top hat in *Swing Time.*

4.17   Astaire and Rogers dance in the art deco nightclub set.

PENNY: "The girl you're going to marry."

LUCKY: "Oh, I don't know. I've danced with you. I'm never going to dance again."

That Fred Astaire will never dance again is the ultimate threat, and his song "Never Gonna Dance" leads into a duet that reconfirms that they are meant for each other. In the end, Lucky and Penny reconcile.

The film calls on the newly established conventions of the genre. Lucky wears Astaire's classic top hat and formal clothes in scene after scene **(4.16).** Astaire and Rogers dance in the beautiful art deco–style sets that were typical of musical design in the 1930s **(4.17).** The film departs from convention, however, in a remarkable number, "Bojangles of Harlem," where Astaire pays tribute to the great African American dancers who had influenced him during his New York stage career in the 1920s. When he appears in blackface here, it is not to exploit a demeaning stereotype but to impersonate Bill "Bojangles" Robinson, the most famous black tap dancer of the era. (The tribute is all the more unusual because Robinson was at that time employed by a rival studio, Twentieth Century Fox, costarring in Shirley Temple musicals.)

Despite its backstage settings and show-business plot, *Swing Time* contains some numbers in an everyday environment. When Lucky visits Penny's apartment, he sings "The Way You Look Tonight" as she shampoos her hair—using a convenient piano in her apartment to accompany himself (though a nondiegetic orchestra plays along as well). When the couple visits the snowy countryside, however, there is no musical accompaniment at all within the locale as they sing "A Fine Romance"—only an unseen orchestra. As we are reminded over and over in musicals, this world makes it possible for people, at any time and in any place, to express themselves through song and dance.

In studying film we often need to make explicit some things we ordinarily take for granted—those assumptions that are so fundamental that we no longer even notice them. Genres, along with more basic types of film like fiction and documentary, animation, and live action, mainstream and experimental film, are just such taken-for-granted categories. At the back of our minds whenever we watch a film, these categories shape what we expect to see and hear. They guide our reactions. They press us to make sense of a movie in certain ways. Shared by filmmakers and viewers alike, these categories are a condition for film art as we most often experience it.

Yet there are other kinds of films than live-action fictional features. There are other modes of filmmaking, which, as we saw in Chapter 1, depend on ways in which the films are made and the intentions of the filmmakers. The most common categories for these types of filmmaking are documentary, experimental, and animated cinema, and we shall examine these in the next chapter.

SUMMARY

One of the most common ways in which we approach films is by type, or genre. Genres are ways of classifying films that are largely shared across society, by filmmakers, critics, and viewers. Films are most commonly grouped into genres by virtue of similar plot patterns, similar thematic implications, characteristic filmic techniques, and recognizable iconography.

When trying to characterize a film, you can ask such questions as these:

1. Had the publicity surrounding this film already cued me to link it to a certain genre even before I watched it?

2. Have its stars appeared in other films like this over and over? If so, what kind?

3. Did I recognize some of the costumes, settings, and other elements as similar to others I had previously seen in other films?

4. If I were to describe this film to a friend, would I find it easy to compare to other films? If so, which ones? If not, how *would* I describe it?

5. Does this film fit into a genre that I typically like or one that I don't? How has that fact affected what I thought of the film?

6. Does this film seem to be combining conventions from more than one genre? If so, how does it make them compatible with each other?

NOTES AND QUERIES

Genres and Society

The conception of a genre's social function as ritual (p. 117) derives from the anthropological theory of Claude Lévi-Strauss. One version of the ritual model is Thomas Schatz, *Hollywood Genres* (New York: Random House, 1981). See also Jane Feuer, *The Hollywood Musical* (London: British Film Institute, 1982) and Rick Altman, *The American Film Musical* (Bloomington: Indiana University Press, 1987). Altman has recently refined and elaborated on his views in his *Film/Genre* (London: British Film Institute, 1999), which examines many issues relating to genre theory.

Another conception of a genre's social function holds that genre films are centrally concerned with social groups—particularly women and racial minorities—which are oppressed and feared by many in a society. The genre's stories and iconography portray those groups as threatening the majority's way of life. The film's action will then work to contain and defeat these elements. One argument for this approach can be found in Robin Wood, "An Introduction to the American Horror Film," in Bill Nichols, ed., *Movies and Methods,* vol. II (Berkeley: University of California Press, 1985), pp. 195–220. For a criticism of this otherness theory, see Noël Carroll's *The Philosophy of Horror; or, Paradoxes of the Heart* (New York: Routledge, 1990), pp. 168–206.

For a survey of approaches to genre, as well as an analysis of several Hollywood genres, see Steve Neale, *Genre and Hollywood* (London: Routledge, 2000). A variety of approaches is represented in Wheeler Winston Dixon, ed., *Film Genre 2000: New Critical Essays* (Albany: State University of New York Press, 2000).

Specific Genres

The vast array of conventions in the Western genre have been codified, along with major films and figures, in two useful reference books: *The Western,* Phil Hardy, ed. (London: Aurum, 1991) and *The BFI Companion to the Western,* Edward Buscombe, ed. (New York: Atheneum, 1988). Our discussion of the conventions of the Western has been shaped by John Cawelti's *The Six-Gun Mystique* (Bowling Green, Ohio: Bowling Green Popular Press, 1975). Howard Hughes summarizes one subgenre of the Western in *Spaghetti Westerns* (Harpenden, England: Pocket Essentials, 2001.)

Noël Carroll explores the affective aesthetics of the horror film in *The Philosophy of Horror,* cited above. Carroll's analysis, which has guided our discussion of the genre, is complemented by Cynthia A. Freeland's *The Naked and the Undead: Evil and the Appeal of Horror* (Boulder, Colo.: Westview, 2000) and by the social account offered by Andrew Tudor's *Monsters and Mad Scientists: A Cultural History of the Horror Movie* (Oxford: Blackwell, 1989). Phil Hardy, ed., *Horror* (London: Aurum, 1985) is a comprehensive reference book.

For a general history of the American musical, see Ethan Mordden, *The Hollywood Musical* (New York: St. Martin's, 1981). Essays on specific topics are included in Rick Altman, ed., *Genre: The Musical* (London: Routledge & Kegan Paul, 1981).

A survey of early Hollywood musicals that deals with the revue musicals and the more narratively oriented films of the 1930s is Richard Barrios's *A Song in the Dark: The Birth of the Musical Film* (New York: Oxford University Press, 1995). One of the most important production units concentrating on musicals, run by Arthur Freed, is discussed in Hugh Fordin, *The World of Entertainment: The Freed Unit at MGM* (New York: Doubleday, 1975).

Chapter 5

Documentary, Experimental, and Animated Films

Some of the most basic types of films line up as distinct alternatives. We commonly distinguish documentary from fiction, experimental films from mainstream fare, and animation from live-action filmmaking. In all these cases, we make assumptions about how the material to be filmed was chosen or arranged, how the filming was done, and how the filmmakers intended the finished work to affect the spectator. Chapter 3, on narrative form, drew its examples principally from fictional, live-action cinema. Now we explore these other important types of films.

DOCUMENTARY

Before we see a film we nearly always have some sense whether it is a documentary or a piece of fiction.

What Is a Documentary?

A documentary film purports to present factual information about the world outside the film. For example, *Primary* asks us to take it as a factual account of John Kennedy and Hubert Humphrey campaigning to win the 1960 Democratic presidential nomination (5.1). Documentary films are typically contrasted with fiction films (more about them shortly).

What justifies our belief that a film is a documentary? For one thing, a documentary typically comes to us labeled as such. The label leads us to assume that the persons, places, and events exist and that the information presented about them is trustworthy.

In carrying out its purpose of presenting factual information, a documentary may utilize many devices. The filmmaker may record events as they actually occur, as the cameramen did in filming the Democratic campaigns in *Primary*. But a documentary may convey information in other ways as well. The filmmaker might supply charts, maps, or other visual aids. In addition, the documentary filmmaker may stage certain events for the camera to record.

It is worth pausing on this last point. Some viewers tend to suspect that a documentary is unreliable if it manipulates the events that are filmed. It is true that, very often, the documentary filmmaker records an event without scripting or staging it. For example, in interviewing an eyewitness, the documentarist typically controls where the camera is placed, what is in focus, and so on; the filmmaker likewise controls the final editing of the images. But the filmmaker does not tell the witness what to say or how to act. The filmmaker may also have no choice about setting or lighting.

Still, both viewers and filmmakers regard some staging as legitimate in a documentary if the staging serves the larger purpose of presenting information. Suppose you are filming a farmer's daily routines. You might ask him or her to walk toward a field in order to frame a shot showing the whole farm. Similarly, the cameraman who is the central figure in Dziga Vertov's documentary *Man with a Movie Camera* is clearly performing for Vertov's camera **(5.2).**

In some cases, staging may intensify the documentary value of the film. Humphrey Jennings made *Fires Were Started* during the German bombardment of London during World War II. Unable to film during the air raids, Jennings found a group of bombed-out buildings and set them afire. He then filmed the fire patrol battling the blaze **(5.3).** Although the event was staged, the actual firefighters who took part judged it an authentic depiction of the challenges they faced under real bombing. Similarly, after Allied troops liberated the Auschwitz concentration camp near the end of World War II, a newsreel cameraman assembled a group of children and had them roll up their sleeves to display the prisoner numbers tattooed on their arms. This staging of an action arguably enhanced the film's reliability.

Staging events for the camera, then, need not consign the film to the realm of fiction. Regardless of the details of its production, the documentary film asks us to assume that it presents trustworthy information about its subject. Even if the filmmaker asks the farmer to wait a moment while the camera operator frames the shot, the film suggests that the farmer's morning visit to the field is part of the day's routine, and it is this suggestion that is set forth as reliable.

As a type of film, documentaries present themselves as factually trustworthy. Still, any one documentary may not prove reliable. Throughout film history, many documentaries have been challenged as inaccurate. One controversy involved Michael Moore's *Roger and Me.* The film presents, in sequences ranging from the heartrending to the absurd, the response of the people of Flint, Michigan, to a series of layoffs at General Motors plants during the 1980s. Much of the film shows inept efforts of the local government to revive the town's economy. Ronald Reagan visits, a television evangelist holds a mass rally, and the city officials launch expensive new building campaigns, including AutoWorld, an indoor theme park that is supposed to lure tourists to Flint.

No one disputes that all these events took place. The controversy arose when critics claimed that *Roger and Me* leads the audience to believe that the events occurred in the *order* in which they are shown. Ronald Reagan came to Flint in 1980, the TV evangelist in 1982; AutoWorld opened in 1985. These events could not have been responses to the plant closings shown early in the film because the plant closings started in 1986. Moore falsified the actual chronology, critics charged, in order to make the city government look foolish.

Moore's defense is discussed in Notes and Queries at the end of this chapter. The point for our purposes is that his critics accused his film of presenting unreliable information. Even if this charge were true, however, *Roger and Me* would not therefore turn into a fiction film. An unreliable documentary is still a documentary. Just as there are inaccurate and misleading news stories, there are inaccurate and misleading documentaries.

A documentary may take a stand, state an opinion, advocate a solution to a problem. As we shall see shortly, documentaries often use rhetorical form to persuade an audience. But, again, simply taking a stance does not turn the documentary into fiction.

5.1 John Kennedy greeting a Wisconsin crowd in *Primary.*

"There are lots of in between stages from shooting to public projection—developing, printing, editing, commentary, sound effects, music. At each stage the effect of the shot can be changed but the basic content must be in the shot to begin with."

— Joris Ivens, documentary filmmaker

5.2 Although the central figure of *Man with a Movie Camera* is a real cinematographer, his actions were staged.

5.3 A staged blaze in *Fires Were Started.*

In order to persuade us, the filmmaker marshals evidence, and this evidence is put forth as being factual and reliable. A documentary may be strongly partisan, but as a documentary it nonetheless presents itself as providing trustworthy information about its subject.

Types of Documentary

Like fiction films, documentaries also have their own genres. One common genre is the *compilation* film, produced by assembling images from archival sources. *The Atomic Cafe* compiles newsreel footage and instructional films to suggest how 1950s American culture reacted to the proliferation of nuclear weapons **(5.4).** The *interview,* or *talking heads,* documentary records testimony about events or social movements. *Word is Out* consists largely of interviews with lesbians and gay men discussing their lives.

The *direct-cinema* documentary characteristically records an ongoing event as it happens, with minimal interference by the filmmaker. Direct cinema emerged fully in the 1950s and 1960s, when portable camera and sound equipment became available and allowed films like *Primary* to follow an event as it unfolds. For this reason, such documentaries are also known as *cinéma-vérité,* French for "cinema-truth." An example is *Hoop Dreams,* which traces two aspiring basketball players through high school and into college.

Another common type is the nature documentary, such as *Microcosmos,* which used magnifying lenses to explore the world of insects. The Imax format has spawned numerous nature documentaries such as *Everest* and *Galapogos.* With increasingly unobtrusive, lightweight equipment becoming available, the portrait documentary has also become increasingly prominent in recent years. This type of film centers on scenes from the life of a compelling person. Terry Zwigoff recorded the eccentricities of underground cartoonist Robert Crumb and his family in *Crumb.* For *The Cruise,* Bennett Miller worked alone without cast or crew to depict the life of a boisterous New York tour guide. In *American Movie,* Chris Smith followed the difficulties of a Milwaukee filmmaker struggling with budgetary problems and amateur actors to make a horror film **(5.5).**

Very often a documentary pursues several of these options at once. A film may mix archival footage, interviews, and material shot on the fly, as do *Roger and Me, Harlan County, U.S.A.,* and *In the Year of the Pig.* This *synthetic* documentary format is also common in television journalism.

The Boundaries between Documentary and Fiction

By contrast with documentary, we assume that a fictional film presents imaginary beings, places, or events. We take it for granted that Don Vito Corleone and his family never existed, and that their activities, as depicted in *The Godfather,* never took place. Bambi's mother did not really get shot by a hunter because Bambi, his mother, and their forest companions are imaginary.

If a film is fictional, that does not mean that it is completely unrelated to actuality. For one thing, not everything shown or implied by a fiction film need be imaginary. *The Godfather* alludes to World War II and the building of Las Vegas, both historical events; it takes place in New York City and in Sicily, both real locales. Nonetheless, the characters and their activities remain fictional, with history and geography providing a context for the made-up elements.

Fictional films are tied to actuality in another way: They often comment on the real world. *Dave,* about an imaginary U.S. president and his corrupt administration, criticizes contemporary political conduct. In 1943 some viewers took Carl

5.4   Older documentary footage of protective gear incorporated into *The Atomic Cafe.*

5.5   Filmmaker Mark Borchardt and his friend Mike freely discussed their lives and projects with Chris Smith for *American Movie*.

Dreyer's *Day of Wrath*, a film about witch-hunts and prejudice in 17th-century Denmark, as a covert protest against the Nazis currently occupying the country. Through theme, subject, characterization, and other means, a fictional film can directly or obliquely present ideas about the world outside the film.

Sometimes our response to a fictional film is shaped by our assumptions about how it was made. The typical fictional film stages all or nearly all its events; they are designed, planned, rehearsed, filmed, and refilmed. The studio mode of production is well suited to creating fiction films, since it allows stories to be scripted and action to be staged until what is captured on film satisfies the decision makers. Similarly, in a fictional film the characters are portrayed by actors, not photographed directly (as in a documentary). The camera films not Vito Corleone but Marlon Brando portraying the Don.

This assumption about how the film was made typically comes into play when we consider historical films or biographies. *Apollo 13* and *Schindler's List* base themselves on actual events, while *Malcolm X, Heart Like a Wheel, Nixon,* and other *biopics* trace episodes in the lives of people who really existed. Are these documentaries or fictional films? In practice most such films add purely make-believe characters, speeches, or actions. But even if the films did not tamper with the record in this way, they would remain fictional according to our assumptions about how they were produced. Their events are wholly staged and the historical agents are portrayed through actors' performances. In David Lynch's *The Straight Story,* the person photographed is actor Richard Farnsworth, not Alvin Straight himself. Like plays or novels based on real-life events, historical and biographical movies convey ideas about history by means of fictional portrayal.

Sometimes, however, the ways in which the images and sounds were produced will not distinguish sharply between a fiction film and a documentary. Documentaries may include shots of prearranged or staged events, while fictions can incorporate unstaged material. Some fictional films include newsreel footage to bolster their stories. *Invaders from Mars* includes authentic footage of Army and Navy forces readying for battle, but the context makes the fictional point that the U.S. armed forces are prepared to repel Martians. Early in *The Road Warrior,* a sequence of shots from documentaries suggests an apocalyptic war that precedes the main story. Some filmmakers have made fictional films almost completely out of documentary footage. Craig Baldwin's *Tribulation 99: Alien Anomalies under America* draws extensively on newsreel footage to present a conspiracy involving space aliens living within the earth and controlling international politics. As with documentary, the overall *purpose and point* of the fictional film—to present imaginary actions and events—govern how we will take even documentary footage seen within it.

As you might expect, filmmakers have sometimes sought to blur the lines separating documentary and fiction. A notorious example is Mitchell Block's *No Lies,* which purports to present an interview with a woman who has been raped. Audiences are typically disturbed by the woman's emotional account and by the callousness of the offscreen filmmaker questioning her. A final title, however, reveals that the film was scripted and that the woman was an actor. Part of Block's purpose was apparently to show how the look and sound of *cinéma-vérité* documentary can elicit viewers' uncritical belief in what they are shown.

Most fake documentaries—a genre often referred to as *mockumentaries*—are not this serious. Often mock documentaries imitate the conventions of documentaries but do not try to fool audiences into thinking that they portray actual people or events. A classic case is Rob Reiner's *This Is Spinal Tap,* which takes the form of a behind-the-scenes documentary about a completely fictional rock band. Before its release, *The Blair Witch Project* was promoted on the Internet as if it were a documentary about three filmmakers who disappeared while investigating reports of a witch. When the film came out, some people were confused as to whether it was fictional or not.

A film may fuse documentary and fiction in other ways. For *JFK,* Oliver Stone inserted compilation footage into scenes in which actors played historical figures such as Lee Harvey Oswald. Stone also staged and filmed the assassination of Kennedy in a pseudo-documentary manner. This material was then intercut with genuine archival footage, creating constant uncertainty about what was staged and what was filmed spontaneously. An even more extreme example is *Forrest Gump,* which uses special effects to allow its hero to meet John F. Kennedy, Lyndon Johnson, and Richard Nixon **(5.6).**

Errol Morris's *The Thin Blue Line,* a documentary investigation into murder, mixes interviews and archival material with episodes performed by actors. The sequences, far from being the jittery reenactments of television true-crime shows, are shot with smooth camera work, dramatic lighting, and vibrant color **(5.7).** Several of these staged sequences dramatize witnesses' alternative versions of how the crime took place. The result is a film that not only seeks to identify the real killer but also raises questions about how fact and fiction may intermingle. (See pp. 446–452.)

Types of Form in Documentary Films

Many documentaries are organized as narratives, just as fiction films are. William Wyler's World War II–era *Memphis Belle* follows the course of a single raid over Germany, seen largely from inside a B-17 bomber. There are, however, other, nonnarrative types of documentary form. A film might be intended to convey information in a simple fashion and hence draw on what we can term **categorical form.** Or

5.7 Carefully composed shots like this from *The Thin Blue Line* emphasize that some events have been reenacted.

5.6 *Forrest Gump:* Computer-generated imagery allows the hero to meet President Kennedy.

the filmmaker may want to make an argument that will convince the spectator of something. In this case the film draws upon **rhetorical form.** Let us look at each of these types of form in turn.

Categorical Form   *Categories* are groupings that individuals or societies create to organize their knowledge of the world. Some categories are based on scientific research, and these will often attempt to account exhaustively for all the data in question. For example, scientists have developed an elaborate system to classify every known animal and plant into genus and species.

Most of the categories we use in our daily life are less strict, less neat, and less exhaustive. We tend to group the things around us based on a commonsense, practical approach or on ideological views of the world. Ordinarily, for example, we do not sort animals we see by genus and species. We use rough categories as "pets," "wild animals," "farm animals," "zoo animals," and so on. Such groupings are not logically exclusive or exhaustive (at one time or another, some animals might fit into most or all of these categories), yet they suffice for our usual purposes. Ideologically based categories are also seldom strictly logical. Societies do not naturally fall into such categories as "primitive" or "advanced," for example. These are groupings that have been developed out of complex sets of beliefs, and they may not stand up to scrutiny.

If a documentary filmmaker wants to convey some information about the world to audiences, categories and subcategories may provide a basis for organizing the film's form. A documentary film about butterflies might use scientific classification, showing one type of butterfly and giving information about its habits, then showing another, with more information, and so on. Similarly, a travelogue about Switzerland might offer a sampling of local sights and customs. Often the categories chosen will be loose, commonsense, ones that audiences can easily recognize.

One classic documentary organized categorically is Leni Riefenstahl's *Olympia,* Part 2, made in 1936 as a record of the Berlin Olympics. Its basic category is the Olympic Games as an event, which Riefenstahl had to condense and arrange into two feature-length films. Within these films, the games are broken down into subcategories—sailing events, sprinting events, and so on. Beyond this, Riefenstahl creates an overall tone, stressing the games' grandeur and the international cooperation implicit in the gathering.

The categorical film often begins by identifying its subject. Our clichéd travelogue might start with a map of Switzerland. Riefenstahl begins *Olympia*'s second part with athletes jogging and then fraternizing in their clubhouse. Thus they are not differentiated by what sports each specializes in but are only seen as participants in the Olympics. Later the individual sequences will assign the athletes to various events.

In categorical form, patterns of development will usually be simple. The film might move from small to large, local to national, personal to public, and so on. The film on butterflies, for example, might begin with smaller species and work up to large ones, or it might go from drab to colorful types. Riefenstahl organizes *Olympia* according to a large-scale ABA pattern. The early part of the film concentrates on the games as such, rather than on the competition among athletes and countries. Later she shifts to setting up more dramatic tension by focusing on some of the individual athletes and whether they will be successful in their events. Finally, in the diving sequence at the end, there is again no differentiation among participants, and the sheer beauty of the event dominates. Thus Riefenstahl achieves her thematic goal of stressing the international cooperation inherent in the Olympics.

Because categorical form tends to develop in fairly simple ways, it risks boring the spectator. If the progression from segment to segment depends too much on repetition ("And here's another example . . ."), our expectations will be easily satisfied. The challenge to the filmmaker using categorical form is to introduce variations and thereby to make us adjust our expectations.

For example, the filmmaker may choose a category that is exciting or broad or unusual enough to present many possibilities for stimulating interest. The Olympics have an innate drama because they involve competition and a potential for beauty through the way the athletes' performances are filmed. For the film that will provide our main example, *Gap-Toothed Women,* Les Blank chose a very odd category that will provoke interest and one broad enough that many different sorts of women could fit into it. Thus the film's talking heads interviews cover a range of varying viewpoints.

Another way in which the filmmaker can maintain our interest across the segments is through patterned use of film techniques. Our film about butterflies might concentrate on conveying information about types of insects, but it could also exploit the colors and shapes of the various examples to add abstract visual interest. The diving sequence at the end of *Olympia* is famous for its dazzling succession of images of divers filmed from all angles **(5.8)**.

Finally, the categorical film can maintain interest by mixing in other kinds of form. While overall the film is organized around its category, it can inject small-scale narratives. At one point *Olympia* singles out one athlete, Glen Morris, and follows him through the stages of his event, because he was an unknown athlete who unexpectedly won the decathlon. Similarly, a filmmaker might take a stance on his or her subject and try to make an ideological point about it, thus injecting a bit of rhetorical form into the film. We shall see that Les Blank hints that treating gap-teeth as a flaw reflects a society's bias about what constitutes beauty.

Categorical form is simple in principle, but filmmakers can use it to create complex and interesting films, as *Gap-Toothed Women* demonstrates.

An Example of Categorical Form: *Gap-Toothed Women*

Les Blank has been making modest, personal documentary films since the 1960s. These are often observations of a single unusual subject as seen by a variety of people, as with his *Garlic Is as Good as Ten Mothers.* Several of Blank's films use

5.8   Filmed against the sky, the divers at the end of *Olympia, Part 2,* became soaring shapes rather than individual competitors.

"The whole history of movie making has been to portray extraordinary things, and no one has felt that much confidence in looking at life itself and finding the extraordinary in the ordinary."

— Albert Maysles, documentary filmmaker

categorical organization in original ways that demonstrate how entertaining and thought-provoking this simple approach to form can be.

Gap-Toothed Women (1987) announces its main category straightforwardly in its title, and the film deals with the unlikely subject of women with spaces between their front teeth. It consists mainly of brief interviews with gap-toothed women, describing their opinions and experiences. Although Blank refrains from commenting overtly on his subject matter, the film's exploration of this supposed physical flaw ends up implying a great deal about society's narrow notions of beauty.

The opening title of *Gap-Toothed Women* announces that it is "A Film By Les Blank, Maureen Gosling, Chris Simon, and Susan Kell." Although Blank conceived the film and served as its producer, director, and cinematographer, he collaborated with this small team, with Simon as associate producer, Gosling as editor, and Kell as assistant director; all three worked as sound recordists. The result is a casual, mostly relaxed set of interviews that progress gradually in a distinct pattern.

From its opening introduction of the category, the film moves through various social attitudes, both positive and negative, toward gap-toothed women. By the end, being gap-toothed is associated with creative, active women. We can segment *Gap-Toothed Women* into these parts:

5.9 *Gap-Toothed Women:* A close view of a woman's mouth with a large gap leads to . . .

1. A pretitle sequence introducing a few gap-toothed women
2. A title segment with a quotation from Chaucer
3. Some genetic and cultural explanations for gaps
4. How American culture stigmatizes gap-teeth and efforts to correct or adjust to them
5. Careers and creativity
6. Epilogue: Gaps and life
C. Credits

These segments are punctuated with songs, as well as with still images from magazine covers and photographs that comment on the subject matter of the interviews.

Over the opening title previously quoted, we hear the sound of someone biting into an apple—an odd sound soon explained in the first interview. The opening image is a startlingly close view of a woman's mouth (**5.9**) as she recalls babysitting for her brothers and being baffled when her parents knew when she had stolen bits from forbidden sweets. She has a wide gap between her teeth, and a cut to a close view of an apple shows a bite taken out (**5.10**). The woman's voice refers to her parents' clue: "My signature, which was my teeth marks."

5.10 . . . her "signature" bite on an apple.

Blank sets up the film's category humorously, and he makes the tooth-gap distinctive and personal—a "signature." A quick series of close views of five smiling mouths follows, culminating in a shot of a woman's entire head. All show gaps and are accompanied by folksy harp music that enhances the cheerful tone. Thus the category for the entire film is quickly established.

The next segment switches to slower shots of a woman playing a harp in a garden. The light, pleasant tone of this opening will be echoed at the end by another, even more buoyant, musical performance. In between the film explores its subjects' attitudes toward being gap-toothed.

During the harpist's performance, the film's title appears in white longhand (**5.11**). This writing recalls the initial woman's reference to her gap-teeth as "my signature." The title leads to a superimposed epigraph: "'The Wife of Bath knew much about wandering by the way. She was gap-toothed, to tell the truth.'—Geoffrey Chaucer, The Canterbury Tales, 1386 A.D." This epigraph suggests that the film's central category originated long ago. Moreover, Chaucer's association of being

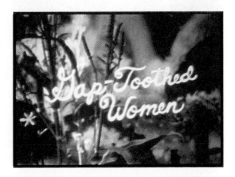

5.11 The film's title is superimposed on a garden scene.

gap-toothed and "wandering by the way," along with his addition of "to tell the truth," sounds vaguely euphemistic, so we are likely to be intrigued as to what Chaucer meant. The Wife of Bath will return as a major motif.

The film's third segment deals with where gaps come from and what they are thought to mean. In a cluster of brief interviews, three women mention that other members of their family had gap-teeth as well, so we infer that this is a natural, if unusual, feature that runs in families. All three women speak in a neutral way about gapped teeth, but the first, mentioning that her mother had worn braces, drops the first hint that some people take gapped teeth to be undesirable.

This segment then shifts its focus to how various cultures, specifically non-white societies, have interpreted gap-teeth. A young Asian woman with a gap speculates on a "stupid" myth that gap-toothed women "are supposed to be sexier." Blank then cuts to a brief clip from the fiction film *Swann in Love,* with the protagonist making love to a beautiful gap-toothed woman in a carriage. Does this confirm the myth? Or only suggest that the myth has been applied to gap-toothed women in general—since the actress is not Asian? This clip from another film introduces a tactic of juxtaposing images from art and popular culture with the interview footage, as if to suggest how pervasive ideas about gapped teeth are.

5.12 In *Gap-Toothed Women,* the image of the Wife of Bath stands out incongruously from the dignified group, with her low-cut dress and broad grin.

This motif continues as harp music and the sound of horses' hooves lead to a black-and-white engraving (by William Blake) of a group of pilgrims to Canterbury, centered on the Wife of Bath riding a horse **(5.12).** A man's voice begins to interpret what Chaucer's description of the Wife as gap-toothed meant in a medieval context, and we next see a shot of a middle-aged man continuing his interpretation. His careful pronunciation of the phrase in Middle English marks him as an expert, so we are likely to take his explanation seriously: that in medieval times being gap-toothed was associated with loving to travel but also with being of an amorous nature. The latter interpretation links back to the Asian woman's remarks on the myth of enhanced sexuality.

The expert's discussion continues over another image of the Wife of Bath, now depicted in a colorful comic-strip-style image based on the Blake original. Next a gap-toothed woman who accompanies her anecdote with sign language tells of dreaming about kissing her instructor, also gap-toothed, and having their gaps interlock. This shot ends the discussion of sexuality, which leads to a close view of an African American woman describing how overseas, gaps are seen as lucky or beautiful. She mentions Senegal as one such place, and photos of gap-toothed, smiling African women are accompanied by African singing **(5.13).**

5.13 *Gap-Toothed Women:* An image from a culture in which gaps are praised.

These lead into a brief interview with an Indian woman who says she knows of no Indian mythology concerning gaps. Indeed, she says her mother asked, "Why are they doing a film?" since half of Indian women have gap-teeth. Her words introduce the idea that in some cultures gaps are simply accepted as ordinary and hence without special meaning. The film abruptly switches to a view of a modern copy of an Egyptian sphinx, while a woman's voice claims that ancient Egyptian women believed that gaps were associated with beautiful singing. Her comment ends the discussions of cultural explanations for gaps.

The next segment centers on the idea that in modern Western cultures gaps are stigmatized as unattractive and unnatural. A French teenager declares that although in France gaps are referred to as "the teeth of happiness," she is annoyed by hers. Three panels of *Garfield* follow, with Garfield teasing his girlfriend for having a gap (which she defends as "a sign of sensitivity").

The film returns to interviews, with a brief close view of a woman's mouth as she says she has "never been real comfortable" with her gap. Another woman, seen from further away, describes how dentists have always urged her to have her teeth straightened, explaining in a mock-sultry whisper, "I'd be more attractive with my teeth closed together." This woman is clearly not entirely happy about having a gap, yet she is quite beautiful. By this point we might suspect that the filmmakers have deliberately chosen mostly beautiful or at least attractive women in order to suggest that stigmatizing gapped teeth is ludicrous.

Another song follows, making the point more explicitly: "They say they want to save your face / But they just want to take away your space / Fill your mouth with wire, your head with lies / About the smile that should go with those pretty eyes." Two magazine images of models without gaps and then a photo of a pretty little African American girl with a gap lead to a photo of Madonna, perhaps the ultimate gap-toothed glamour icon in modern society, and finally a *Vogue* cover of Lauren Hutton, the first major model with a gap **(5.14).**

5.14   *Gap-Toothed Women* integrates images from popular culture to examine social attitudes.

Despite this somewhat defiant stance, we see one more interview with a woman who seems more worried about her gap than anyone else in the film **(5.15).** She worries about her height and weight as well as her gap—"I'll probably never look at this film, because I don't want to know how I'd look on film." Yet she is one of the most conventionally beautiful women in *Gap-Toothed Women,* someone who could plausibly become a model or actress. From here the film moves into a series of more defiant opinions. A woman with a large gap poses against a waterfront setting and talks about how in magazines "you *never* see a person with gapped teeth." A mother with a gap-toothed toddler recalls how she herself had hated her own teeth until Lauren Hutton became a successful role model.

These interviews have been less playful and humorous than the opening. Now the film becomes playful again in a sequence involving Lauren Hutton herself roaming through city streets in a vain attempt to find gap-toothed people to interview. Hutton is then interviewed in her home, discussing how inner beauty and contentment lead to satisfaction with one's appearance.

5.15   A beautiful woman concerned about her physical imperfections in *Gap-Toothed Women.*

The playful tone returns with another musical interlude, folk singer Claudia Schmidt's "I'm a Little Cookie," a song about gap-toothed children, accompanied by ten photos of little girls and teenagers, all smiling, all gap-toothed. The last is the beautiful woman we had seen earlier talking about how her dentists had wanted to fix her teeth. Now she describes an elaborate—and ineffectual—rig she had concocted from rubber bands and tape for closing her gap, shortening her nose, and straightening her hair **(5.16).** Ruefully she concludes, "Here I am, still with my gap."

Another woman drolly recounts how her mother had filled her own wide gap with a bridge creating a third front tooth so that she looked like "a freak of nature." By this point the film is moving into a somewhat defiant stance against the idea of correcting gap-teeth. The woman with a blond braid who earlier discussed ancient Egyptian beliefs returns, now presenting a mock commercial **(5.17).** Another woman ridicules the idea that some people have their hair straightened at the same time that others get permanents: "It's always in the eye of the beholder anyway . . . now I'm glad I have a space between my teeth, and I would never change it." This segment of the film ends with an interview with a very elderly lady who is proud of still having all her own teeth—including a gap.

5.16   *Gap-Toothed Women:* Describing efforts to close the gap.

The next segment begins with another Claudia Schmidt song about gaps, heard over images of gap-toothed women, including Whoopi Goldberg. She sings, "You can call it diastema, call it a gap, but old Chaucer knew where the score was at"— a reintroduction of the Wife of Bath motif, which will soon become even more prominent. A shot of the cover of Schmidt's "Out of the Dark" album (from which her songs were taken) introduces Schmidt herself as an interviewee, enthusiastically

5.17 *Gap-Toothed Women:* A demonstration of an actual device designed to invisibly fill in gaps.

5.18   The Wife of Bath motif in the poster for *Gap-Toothed Women.*

5.19 *Gap-Toothed Women:* Cartoonist Dori Seda discusses active women.

recalling how defiant she used to be about having a gap. She has extolled "gap power" and met with gap-toothed people from various social spheres. Gaps now become a point of pride and a source of fellowship.

The cartoony color image of the Wife of Bath now returns, revealed as part of a group of gap-toothed historical women on the poster for the very film we are watching **(5.18).** The artist, Dori Seda, recalls how unhappy and lonely she had been as a bookkeeper. She had concluded that women are valuable for their beauty, for their wealth, or for what they do **(5.19).** She became an underground cartoonist and found a long-term boyfriend: "I'm kind of glad that my teeth are like this, because if I had nice, straight teeth, I might never have done anything."

This notion of gapped teeth as a sign of energy and creativity seems confirmed by the next series of interviews. The woman we had seen earlier at the waterfront discussing magazine images is now revealed to be creating large public sculptures and murals **(5.20).** Her discussion of how her work affects communities is the first stretch of the film in which gapped teeth are not mentioned, and this remains true for the rest of this segment, which focuses on these women's activities. We see the Indian woman again, now drawing traditional rice-paint patterns on her threshold as a welcome for a goddess. This is followed by an interview with a Hispanic woman trucker. She describes a long, difficult trip through a storm. Again her gap is not mentioned, though it is easily visible in the interview **(5.21).** Here is another image of the interesting and unusual work such women do.

Next the filmmakers interview Catherine De Santis (who worked in an assistant role in *Gap-Toothed Women*). She talks about making a Super 8mm film about a family of Arab women who regularly use a hot-wax concoction to remove body hair. Although De Santis finds this process fascinating, she also acknowledges that it is painful as well—tying back to the idea that women may inflict damage on themselves by conforming to conventional notions of beauty. She concludes, "You have to suffer to be beautiful, right?" Yet the film has hinted that some women who believe this are beautiful to begin with.

The film moves on to an interview with a heavy-metal singer who has quit her band because the audience wanted to hear only a violent message. She prefers gentle lyrics and displays a peace symbol painted on her fingernail. This leads to a photograph of a gap-toothed woman with the signs for "woman" and "peace" painted on her cheeks, as well as "No draft" written on her chin. A chorus begins singing, "They'll be marching, marching, marching when the Army comes to town," leading into the next sequence: a Salvation Army band in an auditorium. The transition is ironic, since the "marching when the Army comes to town" seems to refer to the 1960s image of a female protester, yet it actually comes from a public meeting occurring long after the era of anti-Vietnam demonstrations.

The band is playing before a speech by Supreme Court Justice Sandra Day O'Connor. We might initially be puzzled as to why the film includes O'Connor. True, she is gap-toothed (and had been pictured next to the Wife of Bath in Dori Seda's poster for the film), but the reportage-style footage of a real speech by O'Connor seems oddly out of place in a film based largely on interviews. Yet it fits in well, since she emphasizes "creativity, work, and love" as things that make life worthwhile. Since we have just seen a series of working and creative women, the thematic connection is clear. O'Connor says that when creativity is gone, "the will to live seems to go with it."

5.20 *Gap-Toothed Women:* Links gaps with creativity.

Her remark leads into the final, summarizing segment of the film. It begins with a tight shot of a woman's stomach gyrating in a belly dance. As the scene continues, we glimpse other costumed women looking on and musicians accompanying the dancer. The dancer's voice tells of how she is in remission from acute leukemia. A cut moves us to a quiet interview with the dancer, now revealed as a Caucasian woman (identified as Sharlyn Sawyer in the final credits) in everyday clothes against a simple board fence. She describes her change in attitude since facing death. Little physical problems do not bother her: "You get stepped on by a horse, fine, you know, you've got a scar on your leg. Oh, well, you know, you've got a gap between your teeth, hey, no problem!" Sawyer's spontaneity and commonsense acceptance of physical flaws and aging help put the anxieties of some of the earlier women in perspective. As if to confirm this, applause begins, and we move back to the Middle Eastern dance class, where Sawyer performs another lively dance **(5.22).** The final credits of the film begin to roll, ending over a very close photo of a smiling, anonymous gap-toothed woman's mouth. This last shot echoes the first one, confirming the film's positive depiction not only of gap-toothed women but also of creative, determined women in general. The credits end with an acknowledgment that maintains the film's exuberant tone: "Many thanks to all the wonderful Gap-Toothed women who made this film possible!"

5.21 *Gap-Toothed Women:* As the trucker lowers a photograph of her semi, the gap in her teeth becomes visible.

Gap-Toothed Women demonstrates how a documentary film organized around a category can take a stance in relation to its subject matter, create a definite tone, entertain its audience—in short, do much more than simply laying out facts. Blank and his collaborators have created a light, often humorous, film in part by choosing an unusual topic and in part by the way they use film technique to present their material. (We will analyze the style of *Gap-Toothed Women* in Chapter 10.)

Such a film can also create the four levels of meaning that we described in Chapter 2 (pp. 55–58). On the referential level, *Gap-Toothed Women* simply presents a series of gap-toothed women from different races and different cultural and class backgrounds. We may know some of their faces and names from previous experience (Madonna and Whoopi Goldberg most obviously, Claudia Schmidt and Dori Seda to fans of folk music and underground comics). We also know that *Vogue* is a fashion magazine and assume that the magazines with Russian or other foreign writing are those countries' equivalents of *Vogue.*

5.22 *Gap-Toothed Women*'s leukemia survivor leaps and spins to the applause of musicians and onlookers.

Moving to the level of explicit meaning, the interviewees display a range of reactions to gap-teeth. Some are obviously proud, some embarrassed, others more ambivalent. Some express quite directly the idea that magazines and other people often stigmatize people with gaps, while others reveal that gaps are admired in other cultures. At one point the sculptor compares the lack of gap-toothed models in magazines to the notion of black people seeing only white faces in media images. This explicitly links stereotyped attitudes about feminine beauty to racism. In most cases the filmmakers' voices are not heard; they let their interviewees make these points.

The film's form is not organized as an argument in favor of gap-teeth being a natural, even attractive, trait; yet on the level of implicit meaning, the music and photographs of smiling, gap-toothed women tend to imply just that. The choice of some very beautiful women who are worried about their gaps cues us to interpret their fears as unnecessary. Certain women's comments are clearly privileged as reflecting the ideas that the filmmakers wish to convey. Dori Seda's discussion of how important it is for women to do things helps define the film's segment on careers and creativity, and the cancer survivor's speech at the end makes anxieties about gapped teeth trivial in relation to the potential joys of life.

Beyond these three levels of meaning, we can also discern symptomatic meanings. Blank began making films in the 1960s, a period when counterculture based upon protest and distrust of authority emerged. More specifically, it was the era of women's liberation, with its demands for gender equality and the breaking down of feminine stereotypes. By 1987, when the film appeared, the counterculture of the 1960s and 1970s had died down, but many people preserved its ideals. Several of the women interviewed in Blank's film are clearly of this generation and sensibility. Moreover, one legacy of the counterculture has been widespread attention paid to society's pressures on women to conform to limiting ideals of beauty. *Gap-Toothed Women* could be interpreted as reflecting the shift of some radical attitudes of the 1960s into the mainstream during the 1980s—a situation that persists and makes Blank's film still relevant today.

Rhetorical Form   Another type of documentary film uses *rhetorical* form, in which the filmmaker presents a persuasive argument. The goal in such a film is to persuade the audience to adopt an opinion about the subject matter and perhaps to act on that opinion. This type of film goes beyond the categorical type in that it tries to make an explicit argument.

Rhetorical form is common in all the media. We encounter it frequently in daily life, not just in formal speeches but also in conversation. People often try to persuade each other by argument. Salespeople use persuasion in their jobs, and friends may argue politics over lunch. Television bombards us with one of the most pervasive uses of rhetorical form in film—commercials, which try to induce viewers to buy products or vote for candidates.

We can define rhetorical form in film by four basic attributes. First, it addresses the viewer openly, trying to move him or her to a new intellectual conviction, to a new emotional attitude, or to action. (In the latter case, we may already believe something but may need to be persuaded that the belief is important enough to act upon.)

Second, the subject of the film will usually not be an issue of scientific truth but a matter of opinion, toward which a person may take a number of equally plausible attitudes. (It would be quite possible, however, to make a film arguing against scientifically established information, such as a documentary arguing against the teaching of evolution.) The filmmaker will try to make his or her position seem the most plausible by presenting different types of arguments and evidence. Yet, because the issue cannot be absolutely proved, we may accept the position simply because the filmmaker has made a convincing case for it. Because rhetorical films deal with beliefs and arguments, they involve the expression of ideology; indeed, perhaps no type of film form centers so consistently on explicit meaning and ideological implications.

A third aspect of rhetorical form follows from this. If the conclusion cannot be proved beyond question, the filmmaker often appeals to our emotions, rather than presenting only factual evidence. And, fourth, the film will often attempt to persuade the viewer to make a choice that will have an effect on his or her everyday life. This may be as simple as what shampoo to use, or it may involve decisions about which political candidate to support or even whether a young person will fight in a war.

Films can use all sorts of arguments to persuade us to make such choices. Often, however, these arguments are not presented to us *as* arguments. The film will frequently present arguments as if they were simply observations or factual conclusions. Nor will the film tend to point out other opinions. There are three main types of arguments the film may use: relating to the source, to the subject, and to the viewer.

Arguments from source   Some of the film's arguments will usually present the film as a reliable source of information. The people who made it and those who narrate it try to give the audience the impression that they are intelligent, well informed, sincere, trustworthy, and so on. These seem just to be objective traits, but they imply an argument: This film comes from reliable people; therefore, you should allow yourself to be persuaded by it. For example, a film may use a narrator whose voice is strong and clear, rather than soft and hesitating, because if we hear a voice that seems to carry conviction, we may be likelier to take the speaker as a reliable source of information.

Subject-centered arguments   The film will also employ arguments about its subject matter. Sometimes the film appeals to beliefs common at the time in a given culture. For example, in contemporary America, a large segment of the population is said to believe that most politicians are cynical and corrupt. This may or may not be true of any one politician, but someone running for public office may appeal to that belief and tell potential voters that he or she will bring a new honesty to government.

A second approach the film may take is to use examples that support its point. Such evidence may be more or less strong. A taste-test commercial that shows one person choosing the advertiser's product seems to imply that the product really tastes better; yet there is no mention of the other people—perhaps a majority—who prefer other brands.

Further, filmmakers can back up an argument by exploiting familiar, easily accepted, argumentative patterns. Students of rhetoric call such patterns *enthymemes,* arguments that rely on widespread opinion and usually conceal some crucial premises.

For example, we might make a film to persuade you that a problem has been solved correctly. We would show that the problem had existed and then show that some action had been taken that solved it. The movement from problem to solution is such a familiar pattern of inference that you might assume that we had proved reasonably that the right thing was done. On closer analysis, however, you might discover that the film had a hidden premise, such as "On the assumption that this was the best solution, a particular course of action was taken." Perhaps other solutions would have been better, but the film does not examine them. The solution presented is not as strictly necessary as the problem–solution pattern would seem to suggest. Shortly we shall see such enthymematic patterns at work in *The River.*

Viewer-centered arguments   The film may make an argument that appeals to the emotions of the viewer. We are all familiar with politicians who pose with flag, family, and pets. Appeals to patriotism, romantic sentimentality, and other emotions are common in rhetorical films. Filmmakers often draw conventions from other films to provoke the desired reaction. Sometimes such appeals can disguise the weakness of other arguments of the film and can persuade the more susceptible audience members to accept the film's outlook.

Rhetorical form in a documentary can organize these arguments and appeals in a variety of ways. Some filmmakers will present their basic arguments first, then go on to show evidence and the problems and how they would be addressed by the solutions argued for in the film. Other films will start with the problem, describe it in detail, and then let the viewer know late in the film what change is being advocated. This second approach may create more curiosity and suspense, leading the viewer to reflect on and anticipate possible solutions. Which overall approach the filmmaker chooses will depend on judgments about how the subject can be most effectively presented.

One standard description of rhetorical form suggests that it begins with an introduction of the situation, goes on to a discussion of the relevant facts, then presents proofs that a given solution fits those facts, and ends with an epilogue that summarizes what has come before. *The River,* a documentary made in 1937 by Pare Lorentz, will be our example of rhetorical form. In laying out its overall form, the film adheres to the four-part structure just outlined.

An Example of Rhetorical Form: *The River*

Lorentz made *The River* for the U.S. government's Farm Security Administration. In 1937, the country was making progress toward pulling out of the Depression. Under the administration of Franklin Delano Roosevelt, the federal government used its powers extensively to create public works programs in order to provide jobs for the large number of unemployed workers, as well as to correct various social problems. Although many people tend now to think of Roosevelt's policies as the right ones and to credit him with bringing America out of the Depression, he faced strong political opposition at the time. *The River* hails the Tennessee Valley Authority (TVA) as the solution to the region's problems of flooding, agricultural depletion, and electrification. The film had a definite ideological slant: promoting Roosevelt's policies. Thus the film's argument was controversial at the time. It might be considered equally controversial today, when there is a movement toward getting rid of dams and restoring rivers to their original ecological states.

Let us look at how this film sets out to persuade its audience that the TVA is a good program. *The River* has eleven segments:

C.   The credits
1.   A prologue title setting forth the subject of the film
2.   A description of the rivers that flow into the Mississippi and then into the Gulf of Mexico
3.   A history of the early agricultural use of the river
4.   The problems caused in the South by the Civil War
5.   A section on lumbering and steel mills in the North and the building of urban areas
6.   The floods caused by careless exploitation of the land
7.   The current effects of these cumulative problems on people: poverty and ignorance

8. A map and description of the TVA project
9. The dams of the TVA and the benefits they bring
E. An end title

The film seems at first just to be giving us information about the Mississippi. It proceeds for quite a while before its argument becomes apparent. But, by the careful use of repetition, variation, and development, Lorentz builds up a case that really depends on all the segments working together.

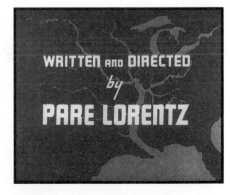

5.23 *The River* begins with a map with the Mississippi River and its tributaries exaggerated in size.

The opening credits of the film are shown over an old-fashioned picture of steamboats on the Mississippi and then over a map of the United States **(5.23).** The film immediately suggests to the audience that its makers are reliable and knowledgeable and that this will be an account based on both historical and geographical facts. The same map returns under the prologue in the brief opening segment, which states, "This is the story of a river." Such a statement disguises the rhetorical purpose of the film, implying that the film will be an objectively told story—that is, it will have features of narrative form.

Segment 2 continues the introduction with images of the sky, mountains, and rivers, with a man's voice telling us facts about how water flows into the Mississippi from as far away as Idaho and Pennsylvania. The narrator's voice is deep and authoritative, playing on culturally conventional notions of what a trustworthy person sounds like. (The narrator, who was carefully chosen for these qualities, was Thomas Chalmers, formerly a baritone with the Metropolitan Opera.) As the images show the rivers growing in size as they join together **(5.24),** the narrator begins to intone, "Down the Yellowstone, the Milk, the White, and Cheyenne . . . the Cannonball, the Musselshell, the James, and the Sioux." Many other river names follow in a rhythmically declaimed roll call. (The technique is based on the work of Walt Whitman and other American poets.) Moreover, the voice combines at most points in the film with the distinctively American musical score written by Virgil Thomson, often employing familiar folk songs. Thus the film deliberately adopts an American tone throughout. This not only appeals to the spectator's patriotic and sentimental feelings but also implies that the whole country should be united in dealing with problems that seem merely regional.

5.24 An idyllic image of nature in *The River.*

Segment 2 has established an idyllic situation, with its beautiful images of mountain and river landscapes. The overall development of the film will be toward a restoration of this beauty, but with a difference. The scene also sets up techniques to be repeated and varied in other segments.

With Segment 3, we move into the section of the film devoted to facts of American history relating to the Mississippi and the problems it causes. Segment 3 begins much as Segment 2 had, with a view of clouds. But now things begin to change. Instead of the mountains we saw earlier, we see mule teams and drivers. Again the narrator's voice begins a list: "New Orleans to Baton Rouge . . . Baton Rouge to Natchez . . . Natchez to Vicksburg." This list is part of the brief recounting of the history of the dikes built along the Mississippi in pre–Civil War days to control flooding. The narrator is confirmed as trustworthy and knowledgeable, giving us facts and dates in the nation's history. We see cotton bales loaded onto steamboats, giving a sense of the country's early strength as an exporter of goods.

So far the film has seemed to follow its initial purpose of telling a story of the river. But in Segment 4, it begins to introduce the problems that the TVA will eventually solve. The film shows the results of the Civil War: destroyed houses and dispossessed landowners, the land worn out by the cultivation of cotton, and people forced to move west. The moral tone of the film becomes apparent, and it is an appealing one. Over images of impoverished people, bleak music plays. It is based

5.25 Motifs of pines and clouds in *The River*.

5.26 The pines now transformed into stumps, the clouds into fog.

5.27 *The River*.

on a familiar folk tune, "Go Tell Aunt Rhody," which, with its line, "The old gray goose is dead," underscores the losses of the farm dwellers. The narrator's voice expresses compassion as he speaks of the South's "tragedy of land impoverished." This attitude of sympathy may incline us to accept as true other things that the film tells us. The narrator also refers to the people of the period as "we:" "We mined the soil for cotton until it would yield no more." Here the film's persuasive intent becomes evident. It was not literally *we,* you and I and the narrator, who grew this cotton. The use of *we* is a rhetorical strategy to make us feel that all Americans have a responsibility for this problem and for finding a solution.

Later segments repeat the strategies of these earlier ones. In Segment 5 the film again uses the poetically repetitious narration to describe the lumbering industry's growth after the Civil War, listing "Black spruce and Norway pine" and other trees. In the images, we see the pines against the sky, echoing the cloud motif that had opened Segments 2 and 3 **(5.25).** This creates a parallel between the riches of the agricultural and the industrial areas. A sprightly sequence of logging, accompanied by music based on the tune "Hot Time in the Old Town Tonight," again gives us a sense of America's strength. A section on coal mining and steel mills follows and enhances this impression. This segment ends with references to the growing urban centers: "We built a hundred cities and a thousand towns," and we hear a list of some of their names.

Up to this point we have seen the strengths of America associated with the river valley, with just a hint of problems that growth has sparked. But Segment 6 switches over and creates a lengthy series of contrasts to the earlier parts. It begins with the same list of trees—"Black spruce and Norway pine"—but now we see stumps against fog instead of trees against clouds **(5.26).** Another line returns, but with a new phrase added: "We built a hundred cities and a thousand towns . . . but at what a cost." Beginning with the barren hilltops, we are shown how melting ice runs off, and how the runoff gradually erodes hillsides and swells rivers into flooding torrents. Once more we hear the list of rivers from Segment 2, but now the music is sombre and the rivers are no longer idyllic. Again there is a parallel presented between the soil erosion here and the soil depletion in the South after the Civil War.

The film has gradually taken us away from a situation of natural beauty and developed the central problem around which its argument is based. Now we see scenes of real flooding, with sandbagging, destruction, people rescued and living in tent camps, and other flood problems. And, as we watch these scenes, we hear sirens and the turbulent roar of water, building up a sense of onrushing disaster. There is a considerable emotional appeal here, as we are given a sense of people being utterly unable to control the water.

By this point we understand the information the film is presenting about flooding and erosion. Still, the film witholds the solution and presents the effects of the floods on people's lives in contemporary America. Segment 7 describes government aid to flood victims in 1937 but points out that the basic problem still exists. *The River* employs a striking enthymeme here: "And poor land makes poor people—poor people make poor land." This sounds reasonable on the surface, but upon examination its meaning becomes unclear. (Didn't the rich southern plantation owners whose ruined mansions we saw in Segment 4 have a lot to do with the impoverishment of the soil?) Such statements are employed more for their poetic neatness and emotional appeal than for any rigorous reasoning they may contain. Scenes of tenant farmer families **(5.27)** appeal directly to our emotional response to such poverty. This segment picks up on motifs introduced in Segment 4, on the Civil War. Now, the film tells us, these people cannot go west, because there is no more open land there.

Now the problem has been introduced and discussed, and emotional appeals have prepared the audience to accept a solution. Segment 8 presents that solution and begins the part of the film devoted to the proofs that this solution is an effective one. In Segment 8, the map of the opening titles returns, and the narrator says, "There is no such thing as an ideal river in nature, but the Mississippi River is out of joint." Here we have another example of an enthymeme—an inference assumed to be logically valid and factually accurate. The Mississippi may be "out of joint" for certain uses, but would it present a problem to the animals and plants in its ecological system? This statement assumes that an "ideal" river would be one perfectly suited to *our* needs and purposes. The narrator goes on to give the film's most clear-cut statement of its argument: "The old River *can* be controlled. We had the power to take the Valley apart. We have the power to put it together again."

Now we can see why the film's form has been organized as it has. In early segments, especially 3 and 5, we saw how the American population built up great agricultural and industrial strengths. At the time, we might have just taken these events as simple facts of history. But now they turn out to be crucial to the film's argument. That argument might be summarized this way: We have seen that the American people have the power to build and to destroy; therefore they have the power to build again. This argument is yet another enthymeme. Perhaps the people destroyed something incapable of being rebuilt, or maybe they have lost their former power. But the film does not consider these possibilities.

The narrator continues, "In 1933 we started . . . ," going on to describe how Congress formed the TVA. This segment presents the TVA as an already implemented solution to the problem and presents no other possible solutions. Thus something that was actually controversial seems to be a matter of straightforward implementation. Here is a case where one solution, because it has so far been effective in dealing with a problem, is taken to be *the* solution. Yet, in retrospect, it is not certain that the massive series of dams built by the TVA was the single best solution to flooding. Perhaps a less radical plan combining reforesting with conservation-oriented farming would have created fewer new problems (such as the displacement of people from the land flooded by the dams). Perhaps local governments rather than the federal government would have been more efficient problem solvers. *The River* does not bother to rebut these alternatives, relying instead on our habitual inference from problem to solution.

Segment 9 contains similarities to and differences from several earlier parts of *The River*. It begins with a list of dams, which we see in progress or finished. This echoes the lists of rivers, trees, towns, and so on that we have heard at intervals. The serene shots of the artificial lakes that follow link the ending to the beginning, recalling the lyrical river shots of Segment 2 **(5.28).** The displaced, flooded-out, and unemployed people from Segment 6 seem now to be happily at work, building planned model towns on government loans. Electricity generated by the dams links these rural communities to those "hundred cities and thousand towns" we heard about earlier, bringing to the countryside "the advantages of urban life." Many motifs planted in a simple fashion are now picked up and woven together to act as proofs of the TVA's benefits. The ending shows life as being parallel to the way it was in the beginning—beautiful nature, productive people—but enhanced by modern government planning.

5.28   A beautiful lake in *The River.*

An upswell of music and a burst of views of the dams and rushing water create a brief epilogue summarizing the factors that have brought about the change—the TVA dams. Under the ending titles and credits, we see the map again. A list tells us the names of the various government agencies that sponsored the film or assisted in its making. These again seem to lend authority to the source of the arguments in the film.

The River was successful in achieving its purposes. Favorable initial response led a major American studio, Paramount, to agree to distribute the film, a rare opportunity for an independently made short documentary at that time. Reviewers and public alike greeted the film enthusiastically. A contemporary critic's review testifies to the power of the film's rhetorical form. After describing the early portions, Gilbert Seldes wrote, "And so, without your knowing it, you arrive at the Tennessee Valley—and if this is propaganda, make the most of it, because it is masterly. It is as if the pictures which Mr. Lorentz took arranged themselves in such an order that they supplied their own argument, not as if an argument conceived in advance dictated the order of the pictures."

President Roosevelt himself saw *The River* and liked it. He helped get congressional support to start a separate government agency, the U.S. Film Service, to make other documentaries like it. But not everyone was in favor of Roosevelt's policies or believed that the government should set itself up to make films that essentially espoused the views of the administration currently in office. By 1940, the Congress had taken away the U.S. Film Service's support, and documentary films were once again made only within the separate sections of the government. Such a series of results shows that rhetorical films can lead both to direct action and to controversy.

5.29   Maya Deren's *Choreography for Camera* frames and cuts a dancer's movements . . .

5.30   . . . to suggest graceful passage across different times and places.

"One of the things that goes on in *Critical Mass* (this is also true of much of the rest of my work and of the work by others I admire) is a process of training the spectator to watch the film."

— Hollis Frampton, experimental filmmaker

EXPERIMENTAL FILM

Another basic type of filmmaking is willfully nonconformist. In opposition to dominant, or mainstream, cinema, some filmmakers set out to create films which challenge orthodox notions of what a movie can show and how it can show it. These filmmakers work independently of the studio system, and often they work alone. Their films are hard to classify, but usually they are called *experimental* or *avant-garde*.

Experimental films are made for many reasons. The filmmaker may wish to express personal experiences or viewpoints in ways that would seem eccentric in a mainstream context. In *Mass for the Dakota Sioux,* Bruce Baillie suggests a despair at the failure of America's optimistic vision of history. Su Friedrich's *Damned If You Don't,* a story of a nun who discovers her sexuality, presents the theme of release from religious commitment. Alternatively, the filmmaker may seek to convey a mood or a physical quality (**5.29, 5.30**).

The filmmaker may also wish to explore some possibilities of the medium itself. Experimental filmmakers have tinkered with the medium in myriad ways. They have presented cosmic allegories, such as Stan Brakhage's *Dog Star Man,* and highly private japes, as in Ken Jacobs's *Little Stabs at Happiness.* Robert Breer's *Fist Fight* experiments with shots only one or two frames long (**5.31**); in contrast, the shots in Andy Warhol's *Eat* last until the camera runs out of film. An experimental film might be improvised or built according to mathematical plan. For *Eiga-zuke* ("Pickled Film") Japanese American Sean Morijiro Sunada O'Gara applied pickling agents to negative film and then handprinted the blotchy abstractions onto positive stock.

The experimental filmmaker may tell no story, creating poetic reveries like Willard Maas's *Geography of the Body* (**5.32**) or pulsating visual collages like *Ballet mécanique,* which we will examine later (pp. 150–157 and Chapter 10). Alternatively, the filmmaker may create a fictional story, but it will usually challenge the viewer. Yvonne Rainer's *Film about a Woman Who . . .* presents its story partly through a series of slides that a group of men and women are watching. At the same time, on the sound track, we hear anonymous voices carry on a dialogue, but we cannot confidently assign any voice to a particular character. Rainer thus forces us to weigh everything we see and hear on its own terms, outside any involvement with characters (**5.33**).

Any sort of footage may be used for an avant-garde film. Images that a documentarist might take as fragments of actuality can be mobilized for quite different purposes (**5.34**). Bruce Conner pulls footage from travelogues and newsreels to create a sweeping image of the destruction of civilization in *A Movie* (pp. 157–162). Within the experimental mode, such scavenged works are often called *found-footage films*.

Experimentalists have also used staging to express distinct feelings or ideas (**5.35**). By superimposing different portions of a kitchen scene from a fiction film, Ivan Galeta's *Two Times in One Space* creates cycles of people splitting or drifting like phantoms. There is avant-garde animation as well, seen in Breer's *Fuji* (pp. 169–171) and Red Grooms's *Tappy Toes* (**5.36**).

The freedom available to experimental film is on flamboyant display in Kenneth Anger's *Scorpio Rising*. Anger takes as his subject the motorcycle culture of the 1960s, and he includes scenes of bikers working on their machines, dressing, reveling, and racing. Alongside footage of bikers glimpsed on the streets or in parties, there are many staged incidents—chiefly around Scorpio, a James Dean figure. Anger also cuts in still photos, comic strips, old movies, and Nazi posters. In addition, each segment is accompanied by a rock-and-roll song that adds an ironic or ominous tone to the images. For example, as one young man fetishistically tunes up his bike, Anger shows the figure of death looming over him (**5.37**) and on the sound track we hear "My boyfriend's back . . . and he's coming after you." This sequence links biking to a death wish, an idea that returns in cartoons and other imagery. In such ways, *Scorpio Rising* creates elusive but powerful associations, suggesting the homoerotic dimensions of bike culture, comparing its rituals to fascism and Christianity, and evoking the possibility that people often model their behavior on images supplied by mass media.

Impossible to define in a capsule formula, avant-garde cinema is recognizable by its efforts at self-expression or experimentation outside mainstream cinema. Yet the boundary lines can be breached. Techniques associated with the avant-garde have been deployed in music videos; Conner, Anger, Derek Jarman, and other experimentalists were early pioneers of the format. And mainstream features have been continually drawing on the avant-garde for ideas and techniques. Over the history of film, the basic types have cross-fertilized each other constantly.

Types of Form in Experimental Films

Like documentaries, experimental films sometimes use narrative form. James Sibley Watson, Jr., and Melville Webber's 1928 film *The Fall of the House of Usher* evokes the atmosphere of the Poe story through expressionistic sets and lighting. And occasionally we find an experimental film organized by categories, as in Peter Greenaway's *The Falls*, a mockumentary tracing, in alphabetical order, information about a disparate group of people named Fall. Yet other types of form are characteristic of experimental films: *abstract form* and *associational form*.

Abstract Form When we watch a film that tells a story, or surveys categories, or makes an argument, we usually pay little attention to the sheer pictorial qualities of the shots. Yet it is possible to organize an entire film around colors, shapes, sizes, and movements in the images.

5.31 The stretches of single-frame shots in *Fist Fight* create a flickering effect on the screen.

5.32 In *Geography of the Body,* an ear creates an abstract, lyrical composition.

5.33 Thanks to Rainer's combination of images, sounds, and captions in *Film about a Woman Who . . . ,* the viewer is left free to imagine several possible stories.

5.34 Gianfranco Baruchello's *La Verifica inserta* scavenges frames from old features to create a flicker film, here juxtaposing shots including telephones.

5.35 James Broughton's *Mother's Day* offers static pictures of adults playing children's games.

How? Consider *Railroad Turnbridge,* by the sculptor Richard Serra. A turnbridge allows a section of railroad tracks to swivel on a central column, clearing space for tall boats passing along the river. Serra set up a camera at the center of a turnbridge and filmed the bridge's movement. The result onscreen is surprising. The bridge is swiveling, but because the camera is anchored to it, the crossed girders and powerful uprights seem monumentally static, and the landscape rotates majestically around **(5.38).** There is no argument, no survey of categories. A narrative film might

5.36 Pop-art painter Red Grooms animates cut-out figures to create the cheerful experimental film *Tappy Toes*.

5.37 Death imagery in *Scorpio Rising*.

5.38 The slowly changing background obliges the viewer to notice the symmetrical geometry of the bridge's design in *Railroad Turnbridge*.

have used the bridge for an exciting chase or fight, but Serra invites us to contemplate the bridge as a geometrical sculpture, all grids and right angles, in relation to the curves and sweeps of nature beyond. Serra asks us to notice and enjoy the slowly changing pictorial qualities of line, shape, tonalities, and movement.

Of course, all films contain these qualities. We have seen how the lyrical beauty of the river and lake shots in *The River* functions to create parallels, and the rhythm of its musical score enhances our emotional involvement in the argument being made. But in this case, an abstract pattern becomes a means to an end, always subordinate to the overall purposes of the film. It is not organized around abstract qualities but emphasizes such qualities only occasionally. In **abstract form,** the *whole* film's system will be determined by such qualities.

Abstract films are often organized in a way that we might call *theme and variations.* This term usually applies to music, where a melody or other type of motif is introduced, and then a series of different versions of that same melody follows—often with such extreme differences of key and rhythm that the original melody becomes difficult to recognize. An abstract film's form may work in a similar fashion. An introductory section will typically show us the kinds of relationships the film will use as its basic material. Then other segments will go on to present similar kinds of relationships but with changes. The changes may be slight, depending on our noticing that the similarities are still greater than the differences. But abstract films also usually depend on building up greater and greater differences from the introductory material. Thus we may find considerable contrast coming into the film, and sudden differences can help us to sense when a new segment has started. If the film's formal organization has been created with care, the similarities and differences will not be random. There will be some underlying principle that runs through the film.

The theme-and-variations principle is clearly evident in J. J. Murphy's *Print Generation.* Murphy took a series of vacation home movies, then rephotographed them over and over on a contact printer. Each succeeding duplication lost photographic quality, until the final images were unrecognizable. *Print Generation* repeats the footage 25 times, starting with the most abstract images and moving to the most recognizable ones. Then the process is reversed and the images gradually move back toward abstraction. On the sound track the progression is exactly the opposite. Murphy rerecorded the sound 25 times, but the film begins with the most

"Thematic interpretation comes from literature: it's been carried over to conventional narrative films, but it shouldn't be grafted onto experimental films, which are often a reaction against such conventions."

— J. J. Murphy, experimental filmmaker

clearly audible version. As the image clarifies, the sound deteriorates; as the image slips back into abstraction, the sound clarifies. Part of the fascination of this experimental film derives from seeing blobs of abstract color become slowly defined as people and landscapes before passing back into abstraction. The film also teases us to discover its overall formal pattern.

As *Railroad Turnbridge* and *Print Generation* indicate, by calling a film's form abstract, we do not mean that the film has no recognizable objects in it. It is true that many abstract films use pure shapes and colors, created by the filmmaker by drawing, cutting out pieces of colored paper, animating clay shapes, and the like. There is an alternative approach, however, and that is to use real objects and to isolate them from their everyday context in such a way that their abstract qualities come forward. After all, shapes, colors, rhythmic movements, and every abstract quality that the filmmaker uses exist both in nature and in human-made objects. Markings on animals, bird songs, cloud formations, and other such natural phenomena often attract us because they seem beautiful or striking—qualities similar to those that we look for in artworks. Moreover, even those objects that we create for very practical and mundane uses may have pleasing contours or textures. Chairs are made to sit on, but we will usually try to furnish our home with chairs that also look attractive to us.

Because abstract qualities are common in the world, filmmakers often start by photographing real objects. But, since the filmmakers then juxtapose the images to create relations of shape, color, and so on, the film is still using abstract organization in spite of the fact that we can still recognize the object as a bird, a face, or a spoon. And, because the abstract qualities in films are shared with real objects, such films call on skills we use in everyday life. Normally we use our ability to recognize shapes and colors in practical ways, as when we drive and have to interpret traffic signs and lights quickly. But, in watching an abstract film, we do not need to use the shapes, colors, or repetitions that we see and hear for practical purposes. Consequently we can notice them more fully and see relationships that we would seldom bother to look for during the practical activities of everyday life. In a film these abstract qualities become interesting for their own sake.

This impractical interest has led some critics and viewers to think of abstract films as frivolous. Critics may call them "art for art's sake," since all they seem to do is present us with a series of interesting patterns. Yet in doing so, such films often make us more aware of such patterns, and we may be better able to notice them in the everyday world as well. No one who has watched *Railroad Turnbridge* can see bridges in quite the same way afterward. In talking about abstract films, we might amend the phrase to "art for life's sake"—for such films enhance our lives as much as do the films of other formal types.

An Example of Abstract Form: *Ballet mécanique*

Ballet mécanique ("Mechanical Ballet"), one of the earliest abstract films ever made, was also one of the most influential. It remains a highly enjoyable avant-garde film and a classic example of how mundane objects can be transformed when their abstract qualities are used as the basis for a film's form.

Two filmmakers collaborated on *Ballet mécanique* during 1923–1924. They were Dudley Murphy, a young American journalist and aspiring film producer, and Fernand Léger, a major French painter. Léger had developed his own distinctive version of Cubism in his paintings, often using stylized machine parts. His interest in machines transferred well into the cinema, and it contributed to the central formal principles of *Ballet mécanique*.

This title suggests the paradox the filmmakers employ in creating their film's thematic material and variations. We expect a ballet to be flowing, with human dancers performing it. A classical ballet seems the opposite of a machine's movements, yet the film creates a mechanical dance. Relatively few of the many objects we see in the film are actually machines; it mostly uses hats, faces, bottles, kitchen utensils and the like. But through juxtaposition with machines and through visual and temporal rhythms, we are cued to see even a woman's moving eyes and mouth as being like machine parts.

We cannot segment *Ballet mécanique* by tracing its arguments or dividing it into scenes of narrative action. Rather, we must look for changes in abstract qualities being used at different points in the film. Going by this principle, we can find nine segments in *Ballet mécanique:*

C. A credits sequence with a stylized, animated figure of Charlie Chaplin introducing the film's title (The word "Charlot" in this introduction is Chaplin's character's name in France.)
1. The introduction of the film's rhythmic elements
2. A treatment of similar elements with views taken through prisms
3. Rhythmic movements
4. A comparison of people and machines
5. Rhythmic movements of intertitles and pictures
6. More rhythmic movements, mostly of circular objects
7. Quick dances of objects
8. A return to Charlot and the opening elements

5.39   In *Ballet mécanique*, the figure of Chaplin is highly abstract—recognizably human but also made up of simple shapes that move in a jerky fashion.

Ballet mécanique uses the theme-and-variations approach in a complex way, introducing many individual motifs in rapid succession, then bringing them back at intervals and in different combinations. There is a definite pattern of development built from elements of the earlier segments. Each new segment picks up on a limited number of the abstract qualities from the previous one and plays with these for a while.

The last segments use elements from early in the film once again, and the ending strongly echoes the opening. The film throws a great deal of material at us in a short time, and we must actively seek to make connections among motifs if we are to perceive the film's repetitions and variations.

As we have suggested, the introductory portion of an abstract film will usually give us strong cues as to what we can expect to see developed later. *Ballet mécanique*'s animated Chaplin begins this process **(5.39)**. Already we have the human figure as an object.

5.40   The opening shot of *Ballet mécanique*'s first segment.

Segment 1 surprises us by beginning with a woman swinging in a garden **(5.40)**. Yet the film's title may lead us to notice the regular rhythm of the swinging, and the puppetlike gestures as the woman repeatedly lifts her eyes and head, then lowers them, a fixed smile on her face. Certain abstract qualities already have become prominent. Suddenly a rapid succession of images appears, passing too quickly for us to be able to do more than glimpse a hat, bottles, an abstract white triangle, and other objects. Next a woman's mouth appears, smiling, then not smiling, then smiling again. The hat returns, then the smiling mouth again, then some spinning gears, then a shiny ball circles close to the camera. Next we see the woman in the swing and the camera moves back and forth with her—but now she is upside down **(5.41)**. This segment ends with the shiny ball, now swinging back and forth directly toward the camera, and we are invited to compare its movement with that of the woman in the swing. We are thus confirmed in our expectation that she is not

5.41   *Ballet mécanique.*

5.42 *Ballet mécanique:* A prism shot is recognizable as a pot lid, its round shape picking up that of both the ball and the hat of the previous segment.

5.43 A masked shot in *Ballet mécanique.*

5.44 *Ballet mécanique:* A strongly horizontal composition is contrasted with . . .

a character but an object, like the bottle or the shiny ball. The same is true of that smiling mouth, which does not suggest an emotion as much as a regularly changing shape. Shapes of objects (a round hat, vertical bottles), direction of movement (the swing, the shiny ball), textures (the shininess of both the ball and the bottles), and the rhythms of the objects' movements and the changes from object to object will be qualities that the film calls to our attention.

With these expectations set up in the short introduction section, the film goes on to vary its elements. Segment 2 sticks fairly closely to the elements just introduced by beginning with another view of the shiny ball, now seen through a prism. There follow other shots of household objects, similar to the ball in that they are also shiny and are seen through a prism **(5.42).** Here is a good example of how a mundane object can be taken out of its everyday use and its abstract qualities can create formal relations.

In the middle of the series of prism shots, we see a rapid burst of shots, alternating a white circle and a white triangle. This is yet another motif that will return at intervals, with variations. In a sense, these shapes, which are not recognizable objects, contrast with the kitchen utensils of the other shots. But they also invite us to make comparisons: The pot lid is also round, the prismatic facets are somewhat triangular. During the rest of Segment 2 we see more prism shots, interspersed with another rapid series of circles and triangles, and also with views of a woman's eyes opening and closing, a woman's eyes partially masked off by dark shapes **(5.43),** and finally the smiling/unsmiling mouth from Segment 1.

Segment 2 has further confirmed our expectations that the film will concentrate on comparisons of shapes, rhythms, or textures. We also begin to see a pattern of surprising interruptions of the segments with brief bursts of short shots. In Segment 1 interruptions had been created by shots alternating objects and a single triangle. Now we have twice seen a circle and triangle alternate. The rhythm of changing views is as important as the rhythm of movement within individual shots.

Now that such patterns are well established, the film begins to introduce greater variations in order to complicate and sometimes overturn our expectations. Segment 3 begins with shots of rows of platelike discs, alternating with spinning shapes reminiscent of a fairground game wheel. Will round shapes and movements provide the main principle of development in this segment? Suddenly the camera is moving rapidly down a twisting fairground slide. We see elements such as marching feet, cars going over the camera, and rapid shots of a carnival ride's cars spinning past. Here different rhythms succeed each other, and common shape seems less important. Relatively few of the elements from Segments 1 and 2 return. We do not see the parts of the woman's face, and many of the objects are new ones, seen out of doors. Yet, after the carnival cars, we see a relatively lengthy shot of a spinning, shiny object—not in a prism view but at least recalling the image of the kitchen utensils seen earlier. The segment ends with the familiar rapid alternation of circle and triangle.

Segment 4 gives us the film's most explicit comparison of humans and machines. We first see a carnival slide from above, picking up on an element from Segment 3 (though here the camera does not move down the slide). The slide stretches horizontally across the screen, and in quick succession a man's silhouette whizzes down it four times **(5.44).** This may seem a continuation of Segment 3's concentration on rhythm, but next we see a machine part, strongly vertical on the screen **(5.45),** with a piston moving up and down rhythmically. Again we see similarities—a tubelike object with another object moving along it—and differences—the compositions use opposing directions, and the four movements of the man are done in different shots, while the camera holds as the piston moves up and down within one shot. More shots compare the slide and machine parts, ending with one machine seen through a prism.

The familiar alternating circle and triangle return, but with differences: Now the triangle is sometimes upside down, and each shape remains on the screen slightly longer. The segment continues with more spinning shiny objects and machine parts; then it reintroduces the motif of the woman's masked eye (similar to 5.43). Now the motions of this eye are compared to machine parts.

Segment 4 closes with one of *Ballet mécanique*'s most famous and daring moments. After a shot of a rotating machine part (5.46), we see seven identically repeated shots of a laundry woman climbing a stair and gesturing (5.47). The segment returns to the smiling mouth, then gives us eleven more shots of the same view of the laundry woman, a shot of a large piston, and five more repetitions of the laundry woman shot. This insistent repetition makes the woman's movements as precise as those of the machine. Even though she is seen in a real place, we cannot see her as a character but must concentrate on her movements' rhythms. (The filmmakers have taken advantage of the cinema's own mechanical ability to multiply the same image.) Segment 4 is quite different from earlier ones, but it does bring back motifs: The prism recurs briefly (from Segment 2), spinning shiny objects recall those of Segment 3, and the woman's eyes and mouth (Segments 1 and 2) return, having been absent from Segment 3.

Segment 4 has been the culmination of the film's comparison of mechanical objects with people. Now Segment 5 introduces a strong contrast by concentrating on printed intertitles. Unlike other segments, this one begins with a black screen, which is gradually revealed to be a dark card on which a white zero is painted. We see this first as a prismed shot (once again recalling Segment 2). An unprismed view of the zero shows it shrinking.

Unexpectedly, an intertitle appears: "ON A VOLÉ UN COLLIER DE PERLES DE 5 MILLIONS" ("A pearl necklace worth 5 million has been stolen"). In a narrative film this might give us story information, but the filmmakers use the printed language as one more visual motif for rhythmic variation. There follows a series of quick shots, with large zeros, sometimes one, sometimes three, appearing and disappearing, shrinking and growing. Parts of the intertitle appear in isolation ("on a volé"), participating in this dance of letters. The film plays with an ambiguity: Is the zero really an "0," the first letter of the sentence, or is it part of the number 5,000,000, or is it a stylized representation of the pearl necklace itself? Beyond this sort of play with a visual pun, the zero recalls and varies the circle motif that has been so prominent in the film.

More punning occurs as the zero gives way to a picture of a horse collar—which resembles the zero visually but also refers to the word *collier* (which in French can mean either "necklace" or "collar"). The collar bobs about in its own little dance, and alternates with moving zeros and parts of the intertitle sentence, sometimes printed backward—to emphasize their graphic, rather than informative, function. This segment has been very different from earlier ones, but even here a couple of motifs are repeated. Just before the horse collar is introduced, we see the masked woman's eye briefly, and, in the course of the rapid flashes of intertitles, one tiny shot of a machine part is inserted.

After this point, the film begins to move toward variations that are closer to the elements of the opening segments. Segment 6 shows us rhythmic movements involving mostly circular shapes (5.48, 5.49). Once again the comparison of person and object comes forward. An abstract circular shape grows, cueing us to watch for the recurrence of this shape. A woman's face appears in a prismed view; she passes a cardboard with holes cut in it before her face, with her expression continually

5.45 . . . a strongly vertical one.

5.46 *Ballet mécanique* cuts from a machine part . . .

5.47 . . . to mechanical repetitions of a woman's movements.

5.48 *Ballet mécanique*'s series of circular shapes begins with a woman's head, eyes closed, turning . . .

5.49 . . . after which we see a wooden statue swing toward and away from the camera.

5.50 *Ballet mécanique:* A brief shot of kitchen utensils.

changing in a mechanical fashion. We see the circles and triangles alternate again, but this time these shapes are presented in four different sizes. A quick series of shots of rows of shiny kitchen utensils follows **(5.50)**, with short bursts of black film interspersed. This blackness picks up and varies the dark backgrounds of the intitles in Segment 5, and the shiny pots and other utensils reintroduce a motif that has appeared in every segment *except* 5. The motif of rows of objects had come in Segment 3, while the swinging motion of the utensils in many of these shots echoes the swinging of the woman and the shiny ball from way back in Segment 1. With this sequence and the next segment the film's development is turning back toward its beginning.

Segment 7 begins with a shot of a display window **(5.51).** The circle motif returns, leading into a series of dances that vary key motifs. Short shots make a pair of mannequin legs seem to dance **(5.52);** then the legs begin to spin within the shots. The shiny ball motif returns, but now two balls spin in opposite directions. Two very different shapes—a hat and a shoe—alternate quickly **(5.53)**, creating a conflict of shapes similar to the juxtaposition of circle and triangle earlier. The prismed shot of a woman changing expressions follows, then a profile shot similar to the one in 5.48. Two slightly different views of a face **(5.54)** quickly alternate, inducing us to see the head as nodding mechanically. Finally, quick shots of bottles make them seem to change position in another dancelike rhythm.

Interestingly, the motifs used in Segment 7 come primarily from Segments 1 and 2 (the shiny balls, hat, bottles) and from Segment 6 (the prismed face, the growing circle). Here, where the mechanical ballet becomes most explicit, the film draws together elements from its beginning, and from the previous segment, where the recapitulation of the earlier segments had begun. Segment 7 avoids motifs from the center of the film—3 through 5—and thus gives us a sense both that the film is continuing to develop and that it is coming full circle.

The final segment makes this return more obvious by showing us the Chaplin figure again. Now its movements are even less human, and at the end most of its parts seem to fall away, leaving the head alone on the screen. The spinning head may remind us of the woman's profile (5.48) seen earlier. But the film is not quite over yet. Its last shot brings back the woman from the swing in Segment 1, now standing in the same garden smelling a flower and looking around. Seen in another context, her gestures might seem ordinary to us **(5.55)**. But by now the film has trained us sufficiently for us to make the connection between this shot and what has preceded it. Our expectations have been so strongly geared to seeing rhythmic, mechanical movement that we will probably see her smiles and head gestures as *un*natural, like other motifs we have seen in the film. Léger and Murphy end their abstract film by emphasizing how much they have altered our perception of ordinary objects and people.

Associational Form Many experimental films draw on a poetic series of transitions that create what we may term **associational form.** Associational formal systems suggest expressive qualities and concepts by grouping images that may not have any immediate logical connection. But the very fact that the images and sounds are juxtaposed prods us to look for some connection—an *association* that binds them together.

Godfrey Reggio's *Koyaanisqatsi* is a very clear example of associational form. The film is built out of shots of widely different things—airplanes and buttes, subways and clouds, rockets and pedestrians. At one point, rows of frankfurters are seen pumped out of a machine and fed onto an assembly line. Reggio then cuts to fast-motion shots of commuters riding escalators. The juxtaposition has no narrative

5.51 *Ballet mécanique:* Spiral shapes seem to freeze the gyrating motions that have made up so much of the film's rhythmic play.

5.52 *Ballet mécanique:* Very short shots make mannequin legs "dance."

5.54 *Ballet mécanique:* Slight changes of composition make a face "nod."

5.53 Shapes create graphic contrast in *Ballet mécanique.*

5.55 The final shot of *Ballet mécanique.*

connection, and the pictorial qualities are not as stressed as they would be in *Ballet mécanique.* Instead, the shots evoke the idea of impersonal, routine sameness, perhaps suggesting that modern life makes people into standardized units. The filmmaker has created an association among unlike things.

Koyaanisqatsi illustrates the unique aspect of associational form. The film surely presents a process, but it does not tell a story in the manner of narrative filmmaking. It offers no continuing characters, no specific causal connections, and no temporal order among the scenes. The film has a point, perhaps several, but it does not attempt to persuade us of it through an argument, giving reasons and offering evidence to lead us to a conclusion. There is no voice-over narrator as in *The River* to define problems and marshall evidence. Nor does the film explore a clear-cut set of categories. It centers on majestic nature and destructive technology, very loose and open-ended ideas. But *Koyaanisqatsi* is not purely a pictorial exercise either, in the manner of abstract form. The connections we make among its images sometimes involve visual qualities, but these qualities are associated with broader concepts and emotions.

This process is somewhat comparable to the techniques of metaphor and simile used in lyric poetry. When the poet Robert Burns says, "My love is like a red, red rose," we do not leap to the conclusion that his love is prickly to the touch, bright red, or vulnerable to aphids. Rather we look for the possible conceptual links: Her beauty is the most likely reason for the comparison.

A similar process goes on in associational films. Here the imagery and the metaphorical connections that poetry conveys through language are presented in a more direct fashion. A filmmaker could film a woman he loved in a garden and suggest by visual juxtaposition that she is like the flowers that surround her. (Indeed, this might be an implicit meaning that viewers could assign to *Ballet mécanique*'s last shot, if it were taken out of context.)

The imagery used in associational form may range from the conventional to the strikingly original, and the conceptual connections can be readily apparent or downright mystifying. These possibilities are not necessarily linked: A highly original juxtaposition might have an obvious emotional or conceptual implication. Again, poetry offers examples. Many religious, patriotic, romantic, and laudatory poems use strings of images to create an expressive tone. In "America the Beautiful," the images of "spacious skies," "purple mountains' majesty," and "fruited plain" add up to suggest the patriotic fervor expressed in the chorus, "God shed his grace on thee."

Another poem might be more elusive in its effect, giving us less explicit statements of the associative qualities of its imagery. The Japanese poetic form called *haiku* usually juxtaposes two images in a brief three-line form, in order to create an immediate emotion in the reader. Here, for example, is a haiku by Bashō:

The eleventh moon—

Storks listlessly

Standing in a row

Bashō's images are somewhat cryptic and the purpose for connecting them somewhat mysterious. Yet, if we are willing to fill in with our imaginations, as one is supposed to do with haiku, the effect should be a mood or emotional tone—one that is not present in either individual image but that results from the juxtaposition of the two.

So far we have looked at associational form working at a fairly small-scale level: the side-by-side juxtaposition of images. Associational form also creates larger-scale patterns that can organize an entire film. Yet because associational formal systems are unlimited in their subjects and means of organization, it is impossible to define a conventional set of parts into which an associational film will fall. Some films will show us a series of amusing images, while others may offer us frightening ones. Still, we can make a start at understanding associational form by noticing that it usually accords with a few general principles.

First, the filmmaker typically groups images together in larger sets, each of which creates a distinct, unified part of the film. Each group of images can then contrast with other groups of images. This principle of grouping is also seen in abstract form, as our *Ballet mécanique* analysis shows. Second, as in other types of form, the film will use repeated motifs to reinforce associational connections. Third, associational form strongly invites interpretation, the assigning of general meanings to the film, as in the environmentalist implications of *Koyaanisqatsi*.

The associational small-scale connections, the distinct large-scale parts, the repeated motifs, and the cues for interpretation—all these factors indicate that associational organization puts demands on the viewer. This is why so many filmmakers seeking to push the boundaries of form use associational patterns. Nevertheless, although associational form may use striking, original, even puzzling, juxtapositions, it may still elicit a fairly familiar emotion or idea. The explicit point of *Koyaanisqatsi* is not particularly subtle or novel. Here, as in many associational films, the purpose is to make a familiar emotion or concept vivid by means of new imagery and fresh juxtapositions.

Other associational films are more complex and evocative. The filmmaker will not necessarily give us obvious cues to the appropriate expressive qualities or concepts. He or she may simply create a series of unusual and striking combinations and leave it up to us to tease out their relations. Kenneth Anger's *Scorpio Rising*, for instance, explicitly associates motorcycle gangs with traditional religious groups and with Nazi violence, but it also suggests, more elusively, that gang regalia and rituals have homoerotic aspects. Like other sorts of film form, associational form can offer implicit, as well as more explicit, meanings.

An Example of Associational Form: *A Movie*

Bruce Conner's film *A Movie* illustrates how associational form can confront us with evocative and mysterious juxtapositions, yet can at the same time create a coherent film and an intense impact on the viewer.

Conner made *A Movie,* his first film, in 1958. Like Léger, he worked in the visual and plastic arts and was noted for his *assemblage* pieces—collages built up of miscellaneous found objects. Conner takes a comparable approach to filmmaking. He typically uses footage from old newsreels, Hollywood movies, soft-core pornography, and the like. As a result, Conner can find two shots from widely different sources that apparently have nothing in common. Yet, if we see the two shots together, we will strive to find some connection between them. From a series of juxtapositions, our activity can create an overall emotion or concept.

A Movie uses a musical accompaniment that helps establish these emotions and ideas. As with the images, Conner chose music that already existed: three portions of Respighi's well-known tone poem *The Pines of Rome*. The music is important to the film's form, since it has distinct sections. Moreover, the overall tone of each segment is different, corresponding to the music.

We can break *A Movie* into four large-scale segments. Each segment consists of related images, marked off from other segments by a shared expressive idea and by a distinct musical accompaniment.

1. An introductory portion with the film's title and director's name and projectionists' marking
2. Quick, dynamic music with images of moving animals and vehicles on land
3. A more mysterious, tense section stressing precariously balanced objects in air and water
4. Frightening images of disaster and war interspersed with more lyrical, mysterious scenes

In only twelve minutes, *A Movie* leads us through a range of emotionally charged ideas and qualities. It also creates a distinct developmental thread. In Segments 2, 3, and 4 many shots emphasize accidents or aggressive actions, and while some of these seem funny or trivial at first, they gradually accumulate and become more serious. By Segment 4 a series of war scenes and natural disasters presents practically an apocalyptic vision. *A Movie*'s tone finally eases in its closing underwater scenes.

Segment 1   This segment does far more than give us the title and filmmaker's name, and for that reason we have numbered it as the first segment rather than separating it off as a credits sequence. At first we see blank black leader, over which the dynamic, quick opening of *The Pines of Rome* begins. This stresses the importance of the music in the film, since we hear it before seeing any images. Then the words "Bruce Conner" appear, remaining on the screen for many seconds. As we do not need that much time to read the name, we may begin to sense that the film will playfully thwart our expectations.

After the name we see black leader, then white leader, then a quick flicker effect rapidly alternating two frames of the word "A" with a blank white leader, and then the word "Movie." The word "By" appears, with more white frames, then "Bruce Conner," as before. Now a black leader appears, with markings that usually appear on the first portion of the film strip, but which are seldom projected on the screen for the audience to see: splice cues, dots, and other signs. Then, suddenly, "End of Part Four," flashes on the screen.

We might think that Conner is simply playing with the graphic qualities of titles and leader marks, as Léger and Murphy had done in Segment 5 of *Ballet mécanique* with their dance of intertitles and zeros. But here Conner uses graphics with conventional meanings: Leaders and credits usually signal the beginning, while "End of Part Four" implies we have already seen a considerable part of the film. Once again *A Movie* signals us that it will not be a conventional film—not one where the parts will follow in logical order. We must prepare our expectations for odd juxtapositions. Moreover, the flicker and leader markings stress the physical qualities of the film medium itself. The title *A Movie* reinforces this reference to the medium, cueing us to watch this assemblage of shots *as* bits of film.

The opening continues with a countdown leader, beginning with "12" and flashing other numbers at one-second intervals—again, more signals to the projectionist, but seldom seen by the audience. Is *this* the beginning, then? But after "4," we are startled to see the film's first moving image: a "nudie" shot of a woman taking off her stockings. The shot is very worn, with lines and scratches, and we surmise that Conner took it from an old stag film. Here *A Movie* helps us to focus our expectations by suggesting that it will involve more found footage of this type. After the nude shot, the countdown leader continues to "1," then the words "The End" appear. Another joke: This is the end of the leader, not of the film. Yet even this is untrue, since more leader appears, with "Movie" backward, more projectionists' signals, and a repeating number "1" that flickers in time to the music's quick tempo, then goes to black.

"Part of the creation of the sequence you're thinking about happened during the process of collecting film. I snip out small parts of films and collect them on a larger reel. Sometimes when I tail-end one bit of the film onto another, I'll find a relationship that I would have never thought about consciously—because it doesn't create a logical continuity, or it doesn't fit my concept of how to edit a film."

— Bruce Conner, experimental filmmaker

Segment 2   Although the music runs continuously over the transition, in Segment 2 we begin to see a very different kind of image. A series of twelve shots shows us mounted Indians on a hill, then chasing a fleeing wagon train, with Hopalong Cassidy recognizable as one of the cowboys. More old film footage follows, this time a clip suggesting a story situation that will continue from shot to shot: a fight between Indians and settlers. But Conner shows us this scene only to refer briefly to the conventional kind of movie he is *not* making (**5.56, 5.57**). The association here seems clear enough; we move from horses to more horses, all in rapid motion. The next change, moving toward imagery of cavalry, confirms this association among horse-drawn vehicles.

There follows a shaky shot of a charging elephant. Now we must stretch our associations to account for this: Maybe the link is through a series of rapidly moving animals? This seems safe enough to assume, as we see two more shots of horses' running legs. But the next shot shows a speeding locomotive's wheels. We must generalize the terms of the association still further—the rapid motion of animals and vehicle on land. (The "on land" idea may not seem important at this point, but it will become significant in contrast to the later segments, which often emphasize air and water.) The next series of shots, repeating these motifs and introducing a military tank, seems to confirm this overall idea of rushing movement. The segment so far has been very dynamic, with short shots, fast-moving objects, and a loud musical accompaniment in a quick tempo.

This sense of rapid activity continues into the later part of Segment 2, which moves from the tank to a series of shots of race cars speeding around tracks. Since these shots initially confirm our expectations about moving animals and vehicles, they are less challenging to us—at first. Then one race car crashes, followed by two other similar crashes; and the segment ends with the long, spectacular fall of an old-fashioned car off a cliff. The sense of movement has become less funny and exhilarating, more uncontrolled and frightening in these final shots. During the crashes the music has built up to a frenzied climax, and it cuts off abruptly as a "The End" title flashes on the screen. This parody of the ending of a conventional film suggests that the crashes have resulted from all that rushing motion earlier in the segment.

At this point, we might begin to sense that there was an underlying tone of threatening aggression and danger from the start: the attacking Indians, the cavalry, the charging elephant, the tank, and so on. This element will be intensified in Segments 3 and 4.

Segment 3   More black leader continues the transition set up by the "The End" title, and there is a pause before the music of Segment 3 begins. (As at the film's opening, it plays at first over the darkness.) But this time the music is slow, bleak, and slightly ominous. The "Movie" title and more black leader move us into a series of shots very different from those of Segment 2. Two Polynesian women carry large totemlike objects on their heads. Leader and a title interrupt once more, introducing a short series of shots of a large dirigible in flight (**5.58**) and of an acrobat couple performing on a small platform and tightrope high above a street (**5.59**). If the women and the dirigible are associated through balancing, the dirigible is linked to the acrobats not only by that but also by an emphasis on heights and danger. This portion of the segment ends with a shot of a small plane plunging downward through fleecy clouds, as if, having lost its balance, it is falling. Slow, ominous music has cued us how to react to these floating and falling objects; without the music, we might take them to be lyrical, but in context they suggest a vague threat. This passage ends with more titles: "A," "Movie," "By," and "Bruce Conner," followed by black leader.

5.56   *A Movie:* From a shot of galloping horses pulling a wagon, Conner cuts to . . .

5.57   . . . similar horses, but now pulling a fire engine on a city street.

5.58   *A Movie:* Images of heights . . .

5.59   . . . and danger.

5.60   *A Movie:* A shot from one film leads to . . .

5.61   . . . a shot from another, creating a visual joke.

5.62   An inexplicably grotesque image from *A Movie.*

The next part of the segment begins with an apparent incongruity between music and image. A series of shots shows parts of a submarine, including an officer looking through a periscope **(5.60).** The next shot seems to suggest that he sees a bikini-clad woman **(5.61).** This shot picks up the stag-film motif from Segment 1 and points out the paradox of this juxtaposition. We know the shots of the officer and the woman come from different films—yet at the same time we cannot help but interpret the shots as showing him looking at her, and thus we find the moment comic.

The same principle underlies the next shots, as the officer orders a torpedo fired, and we see it seeming to race toward the woman, creating a sexual pun. This, too, is funny, as is the atomic-bomb orgasm that seems to result. But, as in the first segment, there is an overtone of threat and aggression—now specifically sexual aggression—in these images. They move quickly from humor to disaster as additional mushroom-cloud shots undercut the joke. Moreover, the music that plays through the submarine–woman series is slow, quiet, and ethereal—*not* appropriate to the silly punning scene, but more suited to the images of the bomb blasts.

5.63   In this puzzling shot from *A Movie,* Roosevelt speaks vigorously, seemingly angry, with bared teeth.

This music carries us into a series of shots of waves and wavelike movements that seem to result from the bomb: a ship engulfed by fog or smoke, surfers and rowing teams battered by heavy waves, water skiers and motorboaters falling during stunts. During this, the music's ethereal quality gives way to a slow melody with a dynamic tempo, played on low stringed instruments; this creates a more ominous tone. The first accidents seem trivial, as when water skiers fall over. But gradually things become more disturbing. A motorboat driver plows into a pile of debris and is hurled out.

Abruptly, people are seen riding odd bicycles **(5.62).** The move from the boat to the bikes takes us briefly away from the accident series to a string of shots showing people deliberately doing things that look grotesque. Additional shots show motorcyclists riding through mud and water and a plane trying to land on a lake and flipping over.

The whole segment has developed steadily, introducing tension at the beginning and then juxtaposing the humorous (the submarine–woman scene) with the disastrous (the bomb), and trivial accidents with grotesque actions. The sequence ends in an odd way. Black leader appears after the plane crash, with the music building up toward a climax. This is followed by a close view of Theodore Roosevelt speaking vigorously, seemingly angry, with bared teeth **(5.63).** Immediately, there follows a shot of a collapsing suspension bridge, with the music swelling up as the pieces fall **(5.64)** and then fading down. Although these shots are difficult to interpret, the association of human-caused disasters with one of America's most belligerent presidents would seem to link even the toppling bridge to human, especially political, aggression.

5.64   A collapsing bridge in *A Movie.*

Segment 4   Once more *A Movie* marks off its segments clearly, with black leader again accompanying the opening of the third portion of *The Pines of Rome.* An eerie gong and low, slow chords create a distinctly ominous mood. Segments 2 and 3 had both built up toward accidents and disasters. Now Segment 4 begins with a series of images of military planes being shot out of the sky and firing on the ground, followed by a series of explosions against a dark sky.

5.65   *A Movie.*

Yet the next passage juxtaposes shots of disasters with some shots that are inexplicable in this context. All the images of planes and explosions seem associated with war and disaster. Now we see two planes flying past an Egyptian pyramid **(5.65).** As with so many of the earlier juxtapositions, we must abruptly switch our assumptions about how these shots relate to one another, since now we see *nonmilitary* planes. But immediately two shots of an erupting volcano appear. Clearly, the connection between them and the previous shot is mainly created by the pictorial similarity of mountains and pyramids. Are we back to disasters again? Seemingly not, for we next see an elaborate church ceremony, and all our expectations are thwarted. But the disaster motif returns as strongly as ever: the burning dirigible *Hindenburg,* tanks, more race car crashes, and tumbling bodies.

5.66   A brief moment of peace in *A Movie.*

All these images create tension, but the next shots we see are of people parachuting from a plane. Interestingly, this action is not threatening, and the people here are not hurt. Yet in the context of the earlier accidents and because of the ominous music, we have begun to expect some sort of disaster as the likeliest subject of each shot. Now even these innocent actions seem threatening and again may be seen as linked to military and political aggression.

The next series of shots is equally innocent in itself but takes on mysterious and ominous overtones as part of the overall segment. We see a burning balloon floating to earth, reminding us of the floating dirigible and *Hindenburg* footage. Shots of palm trees, cattle, and other glimpses follow, suggesting some idyllic Middle Eastern or African setting **(5.66).** This brief respite, however, leads into one of the film's eeriest and most striking moments, three shots of a suspension bridge writhing and buckling as if shaken by a giant hand **(5.67).** This is followed by the most intense disaster images in the whole film, including the burning *Hindenburg,* a sinking ship **(5.68),** a firing-squad execution, bodies hanging on a scaffold, dead soldiers, and a mushroom cloud. A shot of a dead elephant and hunters introduces a brief series of shots of suffering Africans. The music has built up during this, becoming steadily less ominous and more triumphant with fanfares of brass instruments.

5.67   *A Movie:* A frightening image of a buckling bridge.

After the climactic series of disaster shots, the tone shifts one more time. A relatively lengthy series of underwater shots follows a scuba diver. He explores a sunken wreck encrusted with barnacles **(5.69).** It recalls the disasters just witnessed, especially the sinking ship (5.68). The music builds to a triumphant climax as the diver swims into the ship's interior. The film ends on a long-held musical chord over more black leader and a final shot looking up toward the surface of the sea. Ironically, there is no "The End" title at this point.

A Movie has taken us through its disparate footage almost entirely by means of association. There is no argument about why we should find these images disturbing or why we should link volcanoes and earthquakes to sexual or military aggression. There are no categorical similarities between many of the things juxtaposed and no story told about them. Occasionally, as we shall see in Chapter 10, Conner does use abstract qualities to compare objects, but this is only a small-scale strategy, not one that organizes the whole film.

In building its associations, *A Movie* uses the familiar formal principles of repetition and variation. Even though the images come from different films, certain elements

5.68   *A Movie:* More disasters as a ship sinks.

5.69   *A Movie:* The diver in the final scene.

"Animators have only one thing in common. We are all control freaks. And what is more controllable than the inanimate? You can control every frame, but at a cost. The cost is the chunks of your life that the time-consuming process devours. It is as if the objects suck your time and energy away to feed their own life."

— Simon Pummell, animator

are repeated, as with the series of horse shots in Segment 1 or the different airplanes. These repetitions form motifs that help unify the whole film.

Moreover, these motifs return in a distinct pattern. We have seen how the titles and leader of the opening come back in some way in all the segments and how the *nudie* shot of Segment 1 is similar to the one used with the submarine footage in Segment 3. Interestingly, not a single motif that appears in Segment 2 returns in Segment 3, creating a strong contrast between the two. But then Segment 4 picks up and varies many of the motifs of both 2 and 3. As in so many films, the ending thus seems a development of and return to earlier portions. The dead elephant, the tanks, and the race cars all hark back to Segment 2, while the natives, the *Hindenburg* disaster, the planes, the ships, and the bridge collapse all continue motifs begun in 3. The juxtapositions that have obvious links play on repetition, while startling and obscure ones create contrast. Thus Conner has created a unified work from what would seem to be a disunified mass of footage.

The pattern of development is also strikingly unified. Segment 1 is primarily amusing, and a sense of play and exhilaration also carries through most of Segment 2, up to the car crashes. But we have seen that the subjects of all the shots in Segment 2 could also suggest aggression and violence, and they all relate in some way to the disasters to come. Segment 3 makes this more explicit but uses some humor and playfulness as well. By Segment 4, the mixture of tones has largely disappeared, and an intensifying sense of tension and doom replaces it. Now even odd or neutral events seem ominous.

Unlike the more clear-cut *Koyaanisqatsi, A Movie* withholds explicit meanings. Still, *A Movie*'s constantly shifting associations invite us to reflect on a range of implicit meanings. From one standpoint, the film can be interpreted as presenting the devastating consequences of unbridled aggressive energy. The horrors of the modern world—warfare and the hydrogen bomb—are linked with more trivial pastimes, like sports and risky stunts. We are asked to reflect on whether both may spring from the same impulse, perhaps a kind of death wish. This impulse may in turn be tied to sexual drives (the pornographic motif) and political repression (the recurring images of people of developing countries).

Another interpretation might see the film as commenting on how cinema stirs our emotions through sex, violence, and exotic spectacle. In this sense, *A Movie* is "a movie" like any other, with the important difference that its thrills and disasters are actual parts of our world.

What of the ending? The scuba diver epilogue also offers a wide range of implicit meanings. It returns to the beginning in a formal sense: Along with the Hopalong Cassidy segment, it is the longest continuous action we get. It might offer a kind of hope, perhaps an escape from the world's horrors. Or the images may suggest humankind's final death. After despoiling the planet, the human can only return to the primeval sea. Like much of *A Movie,* the ending is ambiguous, saying little but suggesting much. Certainly we can say that it serves to relax the tension aroused by the mounting disasters. In this respect, it demonstrates the power of an associational formal system: its ability to guide our emotions and to arouse our thinking simply by juxtaposing different images and sounds.

THE ANIMATED FILM

Most fiction and documentary films photograph people and objects in full-sized, three-dimensional spaces. As we have seen, the standard shooting speed for such *live-action* filmmaking is typically 24 frames per second.

Animated films are distinguished from live-action ones by the unusual kinds of work that are done at the production stage. Instead of continuously filming an ongoing action in real time, animators create a series of images by shooting one frame at a time. Between the exposure of each frame, the animator changes the subject being photographed. Daffy Duck does not exist to be filmed, but a carefully planned and executed series of slightly different drawings of Daffy can be filmed as single frames. When projected, the images create illusory motion comparable to that of live-action filmmaking. Anything in the world—or indeed the universe—that the filmmaker can manipulate can be animated by means of two-dimensional drawings, three-dimensional objects, or electronic information stored in a computer.

Because animation is the counterpart to live action, any sort of film that can be filmed live can be made using animation. There are animated fiction films, both short and feature-length. There can also be animated documentaries, usually instructional ones. Animation provides a convenient way of showing things that are normally not visible, such as the internal workings of machines or the extremely slow changes of geological formations.

5.70 Two layered cels from a Road Runner cartoon, with Wile E. Coyote on one cel and the patches of flying dust on another.

With its potential for distortion and pure design, animation lends itself readily to experimental filmmaking as well. Many classic experimental animated films employ either abstract or associational form. For example, both Oskar Fischinger and Norman McLaren made films by choosing a piece of music and arranging abstract shapes to move in rhythm to the sound track. Later in this chapter, we will examine an example of abstract animation in Robert Breer's *Fuji.*

There are several distinct types of animation. The most familiar is *drawn* animation. From almost the start of cinema, animators drew and photographed long series of cartoon images. At first they drew on paper, but copying the entire image, including the setting, over and over proved too time-consuming. During the 1910s, studio animators introduced clear rectangular sheets of celluloid, nicknamed **cels.** Characters and objects could be drawn on different cels, and these could then be layered like a sandwich on top of an opaque painted setting. The whole stack of cels would then be photographed. New cels showing the characters and objects in slightly different positions could then be placed over the same background, creating the illusion of movement **(5.70).** The cel process allowed animators to save time and to split up the labor among assembly lines of people doing drawing, coloring, photography, and other jobs. The most famous cartoon shorts made during the 1930s to the 1950s were made with cels. Warner Bros. created characters such as Bugs Bunny, Daffy Duck, and Tweety Bird; Paramount had Betty Boop and Popeye; Disney made both shorts (Mickey Mouse, Pluto, Goofy) and, beginning with *Snow White and the Seven Dwarfs* in 1937, feature-length cartoons.

5.71 A frame from *Silent Möbius.*

This system, with a few additional laborsaving techniques, is still in use today. Big-budget studio cartoons have used *full* animation, with lots of movement and detailed drawing styles. (See 6.130 and 6.132, as well as 7.142–7.144.) Cheaper productions use *limited* animation, with only small sections of the image moving from frame to frame. Limited animation is mainly used on television, although Japanese theatrical features **(5.71)** have exploited it to create flat, posterlike images.

Some independent animators have continued to draw on paper. Robert Breer, for example, uses ordinary white index cards for his witty, quasi-abstract animated films. We will examine his *Fuji* shortly.

Cels and drawings are photographed, but an animator can work without a camera as well. He or she can draw directly on the film, scratch on it, attach flat objects to it. Stan Brakhage taped moths' wings to film stock in order to create *Mothlight.* The innovative animator Norman McLaren made *Blinkety Blank* by engraving the images frame by frame, using knives, needles, and razor blades **(5.72).**

5.72 A nearly abstract but recognizable bird etched directly into the black emulsion in *Blinkety Blank.*

"You don't very often see model animation which is well lit, do you? For me, that's part of the comedy of it; I love the idea that you're making a thriller and it all looks authentic, but the lead character is in fact a Plasticine penguin."

— Nick Park, animator, on *The Wrong Trousers*

5.73   *The Adventures of Prince Achmed* (1926), the first feature-length animated film.

5.74   Household objects perform comic dances in *Frank Film.*

5.75   A flock of Plasticine hens in *Chicken Run* receive Hollywood-style lighting.

Another type of animation that works with two-dimensional images involves *cut-outs.* Sometimes filmmakers make flat puppets with movable joints. Lotte Reiniger specialized in lighting her cut-outs in silhouette to create delicate, intricate fairy tales, as in **5.73.** Animators could also manipulate cut-out images frame by frame to create moving collages; Frank Mouris's exuberant *Frank Film* presents a flickering dance of popular-culture imagery **(5.74).** A very simple form of cut-out animation involves combining flat shapes of paper or other materials to create pictures or patterns. The rudimentary shapes and unshaded colors of *South Park: Bigger, Longer & Uncut* (as well as the television series from which it derives) flaunt deliberately crude cut-out animation.

Three-dimensional objects can also be shifted and twisted frame by frame to create apparent movement. Animation of objects falls into three closely related categories: clay, model, and pixillation. *Clay animation,* often termed *claymation,* sometimes actually does involve modeling clay. But more often, Plasticine is used, since it is less messy and can be made in a wider range of colors. Sculptors create objects and characters of Plasticine, and the animator then presses the flexible material to change it slightly between exposures.

Although clay animation has been used occasionally since the early years of the 20th century, it has grown enormously in popularity since the mid-1970s. Nick Park's *Creature Comforts* parodies the talking heads documentary by creating droll interviews with the inhabitants of a zoo. His Wallace and Gromit series (*A Grand Day Out, The Wrong Trousers,* and *A Close Shave*) and feature-length *Chicken Run* (co-directed with Peter Lord; **5.75**) contain extraordinarily complex lighting and camera movement.

Model or *puppet animation* is often very similar to clay animation. As the name implies, it involves the use of figures that can be moved, using bendable wires, joints, and the like. Historically the master of this form of animation was Ladislav Starevich, who as early as 1910 baffled Russian audiences with realistic insect models acting out human dramas and comedies. Starevich's puppets display intricate movements and detailed facial expressions **(5.76).** Some of the main characters in his films had up to 150 separate interchangeable faces to render different expressions. Perhaps the most famous animated puppet was the star of *King Kong,* a small, bendable gorilla doll. If you watch *King Kong* (1933) closely, you can see the gorilla's fur rippling—the traces of the animator's fingers touching it as he shifted the puppet between exposures. The most famous feature-length puppet film of recent years is Tim Burton's *The Nightmare before Christmas* **(5.77).**

Pixillation is a term applied to frame-by-frame movement of people and of ordinary objects. For example, in 1908 Arthur Melbourne-Cooper animated toys in a miniature set to create dense layers of movement in *Dreams of Toyland* **(5.78).** Although actors ordinarily move freely and are filmed in real time, occasionally an animator pixillates them. That is, the actor freezes in a pose for the exposure of one frame, then moves slightly and freezes again for another frame, and so on. The result is a jerky, unnatural motion quite different from ordinary acting. The innovative animator Norman McLaren uses this approach to tell the story of a feud, *Neighbors,* and to show a man struggling to tame a rebellious piece of furniture in *A Chairy Tale.* Dave Borthwick's *The Secret Adventures of Tom Thumb* animates a tiny Plasticine figure of Tom as well as eerie giants played by real actors. (The humans are pixillated even in scenes without Tom.)

Computer imaging has begun a revolution in animation. On a mundane level, the computer can perform the repetitive task of making the many slightly altered images needed to give a sense of movement. On a creative level, software can be

5.76 Devil and thief puppets in *The Mascot* (1933).

5.77 In *The Nightmare before Christmas,* an attempt to blend Halloween and Christmas ends disastrously.

5.78 Animated toys in *Dreams of Toyland.*

5.79 An elaborate pattern generated by a computer for *Lapis.*

devised that enables filmmakers to create images of things that could not be filmed in the real world.

The earliest computer animation depended on intensive hand labor and could not create convincing three-dimensional compositions. James Whitney used an analogue computer to generate the elaborate and precise abstract patterns for his *Lapis* (1963–1966), but he still had to hand-prick cards to create the myriad dots of light for each frame **(5.79).**

It was not until the 1980s that computer technology advanced far enough to be used extensively in feature production. Graphic manipulation of frame-by-frame images requires enormous amounts of computer memory, and the first feature film to include computer animation, Disney's *TRON* (1982), contained only 15 minutes of

5.80   *Toy Story*'s computer-generated world.

5.81   In *Princess Mononoke,* five portions of the image (the grass and forest, the path and motion lines, the body of the Demon God, the shading of the Demon God, and Ashitaka riding away) were joined by computer, giving smoother, more complex motions than regular cel animation could achieve.

computer-generated imagery out of its running length of 96 minutes. In the 1990s, George Lucas's Industrial Light & Magic, Steve Jobs's Pixar Animation, and other firms developed banks of powerful computers and complex programs for creating animated imagery. Images generated on computers are transferred to film either by filming directly off a high-resolution monitor or by using a laser to imprint individual pixels of the images onto each frame. In 1995, Pixar's *Toy Story,* the first animated feature created entirely via computer, was released through Disney. It presented an illusion of a three-dimensional world peopled by figures that somewhat resembled Plasticine models **(5.80).** By 2000, Pixar's programs had improved computer animation's ability to render surface textures, as demonstrated in *Monsters, Inc.*

Computer animation can also be used to simulate the look of traditional cel animation. Working on a computer can make the processes of painting colors onto the cell or of joining the various layers of the image more efficient and consistent. For example, Japan's master cel animator Hayao Miyazaki adopted computer techniques for some images of his 1997 film *Princess Mononoke.* Miyazaki used morphing, multilayer compositing, and painting for about 100 of the film's total of around 1600 shots **(5.81),** yet the difference from traditional cel animation is virtually undetectable on the screen. (For more on Japanese animation, or *anime,* see Notes and Queries.)

In 1989 James Cameron's thriller *The Abyss* popularized computer animation in live-action features by creating a shimmering water creature. Since then, computer animation has allowed Forrest Gump to meet past presidents (5.6), has created dinosaurs for *Jurassic Park* (1.33), and has made the flight of bullets visible in *The Matrix* (1.37). (For a discussion of computer-generated special effects in live-action films, see Chapter 1, pp. 34–35.) Animation, which was formerly used primarily in shorts to accompany a feature-length film, is now supplying special-effects imagery for the features themselves.

Animation is sometimes mixed with live-action filming. Walt Disney's earliest success in the 1920s came with a series, "Alice in Cartoonland," which placed a little girl played by an actress in a black-and-white drawn world. Gene Kelly entered a world of cels to dance with Jerry the Mouse in *Anchors Aweigh.* Perhaps the most elaborate combination of cel animation and live action has been *Who Framed Roger Rabbit?* **(5.82).**

5.82 In *Who Framed Roger Rabbit?* a human director inhabits the same world as the cartoon characters starring in his film.

An Example of Narrative Animation: *Duck Amuck*

During the golden age of Hollywood short cartoons, from the 1930s to the 1950s, Disney and Warner Bros. were rivals. Disney animators had far greater resources at their disposal, and their animation was more elaborate and detailed than the simpler style of the Warner's product. Warner's cartoonists, despite their limited budgets, fought back by exploiting the comic fantasy possible in animated films and playing with the medium in imaginative ways.

In Warner Bros. cartoons, characters often spoke to the audience or referred to the animators and studio executives. For example, the Warner's unit's producer Leon Schlesinger appeared in *You Ought to Be in Pictures,* letting Porky Pig out of his contract so that he could try to move up to live-action features. The tone of Warner's cartoons was also very different from that of Disney. The action was often faster and more violent. The main characters, like Bugs Bunny and Daffy Duck, were wisecracking cynics rather than innocent altruists like Mickey Mouse.

The Warner's animators tried many experiments over the years, but perhaps none was so extreme as *Duck Amuck,* directed by Charles M. (Chuck) Jones in 1953. It is now recognized as one of the masterpieces of American animation. Although it was made within the Hollywood system and uses narrative form, it has an experimental feel because it asks the audience to take part in an exploration of techniques of cel animation.

As the film begins, it seems to be a swashbuckler of the sort Daffy Duck had appeared in before, such as *The Scarlet Pumpernickel* (1950)—itself a parody of Errol Flynn's most famous Warner Bros. films. The credits are written on a scroll fastened to a wooden door with a dagger, and when Daffy is first seen he appears to be a dueling musketeer. But almost immediately he moves to the left and passes the edge of the painted background **(5.83).** Daffy is baffled, calls for scenery, and exits. A giant animated brush appears from outside the frame and paints in a barnyard **(5.84).** When Daffy enters, still in musketeer costume, he is annoyed but changes into a farmer's outfit. Such quick switches continue throughout the film, with the paintbrush and a pencil eraser adding and removing scenery, costumes, props, even Daffy himself, with dizzying frequency and illogic. At times the sound cuts out, or the film seems to slip in the projector, so that we see the frameline in the middle of the screen **(5.85).**

All these tricks result in a peculiar narrative. Daffy repeatedly tries to get a plot—any plot—going, and the unseen animator constantly thwarts him. As a result, the film's principles of narrative progression are unusual. First, it gradually

"As the six-year-old boy protested when I was introduced to him as the man who draws Bugs Bunny, 'He does not! He draws pictures *of* Bugs Bunny.' "

— Chuck Jones, animator

5.83 Early in *Duck Amuck,* the background tapers off into white blankness.

5.84 An inappropriate background for a swashbuckler appears in the blank space.

5.85   *Duck Amuck:* As the image apparently slips in the projector, Daffy's feet appear at the top and his head at the bottom.

5.86   A pencil protruding into the frame finally begins to reveal *Duck Amuck's* fiendish animator.

5.87   As in many other Warner Bros. cartoons, Bugs turns and speaks to the audience after he triumphs over Daffy.

becomes apparent to us that the film is exploring various conventions and techniques of animation: painted backgrounds, sound effects, framing, music, and so on. Second, the outrages perpetrated against Daffy become more extreme, and his frustrated rage mounts steadily. Third, a mystery quickly surfaces, as we and Daffy wonder who this perverse animator is and why he is tormenting Daffy.

At the end the mystery is solved when the animator blasts Daffy with a bomb and then closes a door in his face **(5.86).** The next shot moves us to the animation desk itself, where we see Bugs Bunny, who has been the animator playing all the tricks on Daffy. He grins at us: "Ain't I a stinker?" **(5.87).** To a spectator who had never seen a Warner Bros. cartoon before, this ending would be puzzling. The narrative logic of *Duck Amuck* depends largely on knowing the character traits of the two stars. Bugs and Daffy often costarred in other Jones cartoons, and invariably the calm, ruthless Bugs would get the better of the manic Daffy.

Duck Amuck's use of animation techniques is just as unconventional as its narrative form. Because the action moves so quickly, we might fail on first viewing to note that aside from the credits title and the familiar "That's All, Folks!" logo, the film contains only four separate shots—three of which come in quick succession at the end. The bulk of the cartoon consists of a single lengthy and continuous shot—a technique that in live-action filming is termed a *long take* (see pp. 284–285). Yet the settings and situations change quickly as the paintbrush and pencil transform the image and Daffy moves in and out of the frame. Often he appears against a stark white background **(5.88).** Such moments emphasize the fact that in cel animation, the figures and background are layers that could easily be photographed separately. In *Duck Amuck,* the only certain space is that of the frame itself—a quality quite different from the clearly established locales provided in more conventional cartoons.

Similarly, the temporal flow becomes warped as Daffy moves into and out of diegetic situations, launching into one possible plotline only to find it cut short by the mystery animator. Daffy keeps assuming that he is at the beginning of the cartoon, but time is flowing inexorably by in the outer cartoon, *Duck Amuck* itself. (Traditionally, cartoons were around seven minutes long to fit into the shorts section of movie-theater programs.) At one point more than halfway through, Daffy shouts, "All right! Let's get this picture started!" Immediately a "The End" title appears, but Daffy pushes it aside and tries to take charge: "Ladies and gentlemen, there will be no further delays, so I shall attempt to entertain you in my own inimitable fashion," going into a soft-shoe routine against the blank background.

Duck Amuck also plays with what we can and cannot see on the screen. Many of the startling transformations we witness come from outside the limits of the frame. Most important, the unknown animator occupies the space from which the camera photographs the scene, with the brush and pencil coming in from under the camera. Daffy enters and exits frequently, and the frame often moves to reveal or conceal new portions of the scenery. When the sound cuts out entirely, Daffy asks to get it back (5.88), and then we hear a scratchy sound, as if from a phonograph somewhere outside the frame playing a worn record. This unseen phonograph provides inappropriate noises—a machine gun when Daffy strums the guitar, a donkey's bray when he breaks it—an elaborate joke on the fact that in animated films, the sound is never really produced by the characters and objects we see on the screen.

The most spectacular gag involving the space outside the edges of the image comes when the top of the frame seems to collapse, dripping down onto Daffy like black syrup **(5.89).** For a moment we have the contradictory situation of having the space that we know should be invisible outside the frame suddenly become visible on the screen.

The inventiveness of *Duck Amuck* sets it apart from more conventional Hollywood animated films. Yet is also motivates its play with the medium through its adherence to narrative form, the genre of comedy, and familiar characters (Bugs mistreating Daffy, as usual). It is possible to go even further in exploring the medium of animation and to depart from narrative altogether, as our second example shows.

An Example of Experimental Animation: *Fuji*

In contrast to smooth Hollywood narrative animation, Robert Breer's 1974 film *Fuji* looks disjointed and crudely drawn. It does not involve a narrative but instead, like *Ballet mécanique,* it groups images by principles of abstract form.

Fuji begins without a title or credits, with a bell ringing three times over blackness. A cut leads not to animated footage but to a shaky, fuzzy shot through a train window, with someone's face and eyeglasses partially visible at the side in the extreme foreground. In the distance, what might be rice paddies slide by. This shot and most of the rest of the film are accompanied by the clacking, rhythmic sound of a train.

More black leader creates a transition to a very different image. Against a white background, two flat shapes, like keystones with rounded corners, alternate frame by frame, one red, the other green. The effect is a rapid flicker as the two colored shapes drift about the frame in a seemingly random pattern. Another stretch of black introduces a brief, fuzzy shot of a man in a dark suit running across the shot in a strange corridor.

More black leader follows. Then, against a white background, a jagged line moves and changes shape, briefly coming together to form a crude tracing of the running man's movement, then collapsing quickly into an abstract line and reforming into a running man. During this shot, colors shift and change rapidly.

Within this spurt of images, Breer has aroused our curiosity about what kind of film we are watching. He has also introduced most of the devices that will be varied across the film to create its principles of abstract form. For one thing, the regular clack and hum of the train sets up a rhythm that will govern the movement on the screen. A flicker effect in which images change every one or two frames will recur through much of the film. Even when the same shape remains on the screen for a longer stretch, its color and outline often jumps about every few frames. In *Fuji,* shapes jitter in a rough rhythm.

Such attempts to avoid smooth movement and to explore the perceptual possibilities offered by different types of abstract drawings are common in experimental animation. *Fuji* is distinctive, however, in part because of its juxtaposition of live-action footage and animated images that are obviously sketchily traced from the live-action frames. Here Breer is manipulating a technique commonly used in Hollywood cartoons (and, more recently, Japanese anime), **rotoscoping.** The rotoscope is a machine used to project live-action footage, frame by frame, onto a drawing board, so that an animator can trace the outlines of the figures. The original purpose of rotoscoping was not to make the characters in the cartoon look exactly like those in the live-action film, for in fact their appearances are often quite different. Rather, a character's movement is usually smoother and more lifelike if traced from a live model. Disney's animated features, such as *Snow White and the Seven Dwarfs* and *Cinderella,* used extensive rotoscoping for their human characters. (Computer animation works with a similar principle but uses three-dimensional tracing and mapping.)

5.88   In *Duck Amuck,* Daffy is trapped without background or sound track.

5.89   *Duck Amuck:* Daffy struggles to preserve a bit of space for himself as the frame collapses on him

5.90 Early in *Fuji*, we see flickering images that include single frames of blurry live-action footage of the train's interior . . .

5.91 . . . alternating with single frames of parts of that same view in crude tracings of the conductor's body.

"What attracted me to the footage was the mountain in the background and the possibility for motion perspective in the foreground. The film plays with deep space and the picture plane on the screen."

— Robert Breer, animator

5.92 A simply sketched view of a mountain and passing bridge in *Fuji*.

Breer takes rotoscoping, a technique intended to create smooth motion, and uses it in quite a different way. For one thing, he often traces only part of a figure, leaving it against a blank white background instead of tracing it onto a cel and combining it with painted scenery. In other cases he traces the background itself rather than the moving figures, as with the train interior that appears in various colors. He also photographs his rough pencil drawings, rather than tracing them neatly onto cels in ink, as a Hollywood animator would do. By changing the color so often and by moving from image to image so quickly, Breer's animation avoids all sense of smoothness. (Breer uses small blank index cards for his drawings, deliberately avoiding the illusion of depth that cel animation can achieve.)

Most of the flickering images in *Fuji* are two frames long, and here Breer may be playing off the fact that in Hollywood cartoons of the studio age, each set of cels was actually photographed for two frames in a row, to save time and labor. In the Hollywood films the movement still appears smooth and continuous on the screen, while Breer creates such noticeable differences between each pair of frames that the effect looks jerky.

Perhaps most daringly, Breer includes bits of the original live-action footage from which he made his tracings. As a result, we are led to see many of the images in the film *as* tracings **(5.90, 5.91).** In effect Breer has taken one of the most realistic animation techniques, the rotoscope, and used it to create a dazzling, abstract exploration of movement and perception in cinema.

The opening section of *Fuji* is based chiefly on shapes derived from train interiors. The second, lengthier section, which forms the rest of the film, begins with a stylized series of views of a mountain that we assume from the title is Mount Fuji. Again we see shifting colors and shapes, but as before, some of the footage seems to have been traced from live-action frames. The train sound continues, and as sparsely sketched buildings, bridges, poles, and fields move jerkily past in the foreground, we are likely to take this view to be one seen from a moving train—though in this case Breer does not alternate live-action and traced footages **(5.92).**

The mountain footage creates planes in depth: Fields and buildings in the middle ground pass by, while the distant mountain remains in the same spot. At times colors or abstract shapes appear for a frame or two, and we are likely to perceive them as being in the extreme foreground, near the train and thus visible only as a blurred flash. Yet, even though the mountain remains in the same spot, its simple black outline frequently shifts slightly, and the color changes constantly, making the sky now red, now blue. The smooth sense of motion that rotoscoped footage could create is undermined, and the stable mountain actually shimmers constantly. In this way Breer simultaneously suggests realistic depth and flat, abstract shapes in the images.

To underline this contrast between conventional animation and the abstract techniques of *Fuji,* Breer includes one ordinary rotoscoped motion **(5.93).** This paper-cup shape, drawn with the simplest of perspective cues, is the only object in the film to move so smoothly. We also, however, see the cup changing color or superimposed over the more abstract, flickering images of the mountain. At other times, the cup shape is seen as just a flat blob of color. Indeed, the rounded keystone shapes near the beginning are flat, nonperspectival versions of this cup.

At other points, the neat perspective renderings of the cup suddenly twist into skewed trapezoids or fold up into straight lines. Thus even the most conventional of animated movements can collapse in this pulsating, unstable space. With this and dozens of other devices, Breer explores and displays many of the perceptual tricks on which drawn animation is based. While *Duck Amuck* flaunts the unique powers of animation in order to create comedy and deflate our narrative expectations, *Fuji,* an experimental film, takes animation techniques as its very subject. The result is a film that asks the viewer to enjoy its abstract design and reflect as well on the possibilities of animated filmmaking.

SUMMARY

In most situations, when we watch a film we have some idea of what type it will be. If we are seeing a documentary, we expect to learn something, perhaps in a way that will entertain or move us in the process. An experimental film, however, will probably challenge us, rather like a game, to figure out its patterns and strategies. Animated films that we encounter in theaters will most likely amuse and entertain us.

In watching a documentary film, we can ask ourselves just what it is trying to teach us. Does it present one or more categories of things? If so, how are these organized? Is the filmmaker trying to convey an attitude about the topic? Are there abstract or narrative portions that lend interest to its subject? Or is the topic organized as an argument? Does the filmmaker present convincing evidence or rely more on emotional appeal cloaked as logic?

As we have seen, experimental films often employ abstract or associational formal patterns. From moment to moment, try to understand what connections there are between shots or small-scale segments. Is there a similarity in shapes on the screen, in directions of movement, in colors? If so, the film probably uses abstract form. But if you detect some similarities in the subject matter that shifts in odd but evocative ways as the film progresses, associational form is probably at work.

Animated films can present narratives, can convey documentary information, or aid in experimenting with the medium. In most cases, however, you should be able to detect generally what techniques were used in making the film. Is the movement on the screen based on drawings or on moving puppets, clay figures, or flat cut-outs? Keeping in mind that most animated films are made by shooting only one or two frames at a time, you should be able to imagine the amount of work that goes into this mode of filmmaking.

5.93 *Fuji*'s most conventional animation: a paper-cup shape rolling in an arc against a white background.

NOTES AND QUERIES

Documentary Films

Bill Nichols provides an overview of types of documentaries and issues relating to them in his *Introduction to Documentary* (Bloomington: Indiana University Press, 2001). For histories of documentary, see Richard Meran Barsam, *Non-Fiction Film: A Critical History,* rev. ed. (Bloomington: Indiana University Press, 1992) and Erik Barnouw, *Documentary: A History of the Non-Fiction Film,* 2d ed. (New York: Oxford University Press, 1993). Important specific periods and types of documentary are covered in Paul Swann, *The British Documentary Film Movement, 1926–1946* (Cambridge: Cambridge University Press,

1989); Raymond Fielding, *The American Newsreel 1911–1967* (Norman: University of Oklahoma Press, 1972); Peter Ian Crawford and David Turton, ed., *Film as Ethnography* (Manchester, England: Manchester University Press, 1992); and Thomas Waugh, ed., *"Show Us Life"; Toward a History and Aesthetics of the Committed Documentary* (Metuchen, N.J.: Scarecrow, 1984).

Much contemporary work on documentary has centered on how this mode of filmmaking can be differentiated from fiction. Bill Nichols's *Representing Reality* (Bloomington: Indiana University Press, 1991) explores this question. See also Michael Renov, ed., *Theorizing Documentary* (New York: Routledge, 1993); the essays by Noël Carroll and Carl R. Plantinga in Carroll and David Bordwell, ed., *Post-Theory: Reconstructing Film Studies* (Madison: University of Wisconsin Press, 1996); Plantinga's *Rhetoric and Representation in Nonfiction Film* (Cambridge: Cambridge University Press, 1997); and Michael Tobias, ed., *The Search for Reality: The Art of Documentary Filmmaking* (Studio City, Calif.: Wiese, 1997).

For studies of some of the most historically important documentary filmmakers, see Kevin Jackson, ed., *The Humphrey Jennings Reader* (Manchester, England: Carcanet, 1993); Thomas W. Benson and Carolyn Anderson, *Reality Fictions: The Films of Frederick Wiseman* (Carbondale: Southern Illinois University Press, 1989); Gary Evans, *John Grierson and the National Film Board: The Politics of Wartime Propaganda* (Toronto: University of Toronto Press, 1984); Paul Rotha, *Robert J. Flaherty: A Biography* (Philadelphia: University of Pennsylvania Press, 1983); Randolph Lewis's *Emile de Antonio: Radical Filmmaker in Cold War America* (Madison: University of Wisconsin Press, 2000); and Douglas Kellner and Dan Streible, ed., *Emile de Antonio: A Reader* (Minneapolis: University of Minnesota Press, 2000). Joris Ivens has published his memoirs, *The Camera and I* (New York: International Publishers, 1969).

Alan Rosenthal presents case studies of several important film and television documentaries, including Barbara Koppel's *Harlan County, U.S.A.,* in *The Documentary Conscience: A Casebook in Film Making* (Berkeley: University of California Press, 1980).

On *Roger and Me*

On its release *Roger and Me* was hailed as one of the best films of 1989, winning large audiences in the United States and abroad. It seemed a likely contender for an Academy Award until a series of articles pointed out that the film diverged from the actual chronology of events. The major revelations appeared in Harlan Jacobson's interview with director Michael Moore ["Michael and Me," *Film Comment* **25,** 6 (November–December 1989): 16–30]. This often heated conversation explores different conceptions of documentary accuracy.

When challenged by Jacobson about the order of events, Moore granted that "the chronology skips around a bit. That's why I don't use dates in the film" (p. 111). He claimed that he had sought to portray the entire 1980s and that the chronology of the film was not intended to be exact. Moore also said that rearranging events made the film more entertaining and allowed him to condense a decade down to a manageable viewing length.

The controversy is discussed in Carley Cohan and Gary Crowdus, "Reflections on *Roger and Me,* Michael Moore, and His Critics," *Cinéaste* **17,** 4 (1990): 25–30. Carl Plan-

tinga finds *Roger and Me* an example of an expressive documentary, a trend that also includes the work of Errol Morris ["The Mirror Framed: A Case for Expression in Documentary," *Wide Angle* **13,** 2 (April 1991): 40–53].

Experimental Films

Good general studies of experimental cinema are *Film as Film: Formal Experiment in Film 1910–1975* (London: Hayward Gallery, 1979), P. Adams Sitney, *Visionary Film: The American Avant-Garde 1943–1978,* 2d ed. (New York: Oxford University Press, 1979); Scott MacDonald's *Avant-Garde Film: Motion Studies* (Cambridge: Cambridge University Press, 1993); and James Peterson, *Dreams of Chaos, Visions of Order: Understanding the American Avant-Garde* (Detroit: Wayne State University Press, 1993). Jan-Christopher Horak's anthology *Lovers of Cinema: The First American Film Avant-Garde, 1919–1945* (Madison: University of Wisconsin Press, 1995) deals with an earlier, often neglected, period. It contains an essay by William Moritz, "Americans in Paris: Man Ray and Dudley Murphy," that examines the background of *Ballet mécanique.* Scott MacDonald has published his interviews with many recent and current avant-garde filmmakers in his three-volume series, *A Critical Cinema: Interviews with Independent Filmmakers* (Berkeley: University of California Press, 1988, 1992, and 1998).

There are many works dealing with more specific aspects of experimental cinema. Found-footage film is discussed in William C. Wees, *Recycled Images* (New York: Anthology Film Archives, 1993) and Cecilia Hausheer and Christoph Settele, ed., *Found Footage Film* (Luzern: VIPER/zyklop, 1992). A major trend in American avant-garde cinema is covered by Jack Sargeant, ed., *Naked Lens: Beat Cinema* (London: Creating Books, 1997). Lauren Rabinovitz deals with female experimental filmmakers in *Points of Resistance: Women, Power & Politics in the New York Avant-Garde Cinema, 1943–71* (Chicago: University of Chicago Press, 1991), including material on Maya Deren. For essays spanning the history of computer-generated experimental films by one of its early practitioners, see Malcolm Le Grice, *Experimental Cinema in the Digital Age* (London: British Film Institute, 2001).

Several of the experimental filmmakers mentioned in this book have been the subject of studies. These include a large exhibition catalogue, Peter Boswell, Joan Rothfuss, and Bruce Jenkins, *2000 BC: The Bruce Conner Story Part II* (New York: Distributed Art Publishers, 1999). (In keeping with Conner's sense of humor, there is no Part I.) The work of Andy Warhol in various media has received extensive coverage, but the books most directly focused on his films include Michael O'Pray, ed., *Andy Warhol: Film Factory*

(London: British Film Institute, 1989) and Ann Abrahams, *Warhol Films* (Amsterdam: Rongwrong, 1989). See also Bill Landis, *Anger: The Unauthorized Biography of Kenneth Anger* (New York: HarperCollins, 1995); Regina Cornwell, *Snow Seen: The Films and Photographs of Michael Snow* (Toronto: Peter Martin, 1980); and Philip Monk, "Around Wavelength: The Sculpture, Film and Photo Work of Michael Snow," in *The Michael Snow Project: Visual Art 1951–1993* (Toronto: Art Gallery of Ontario, 1994).

Animated Films

The most comprehensive history of animation to date is Giannalberto Bendazzi's *Cartoons: One Hundred Years of Cinema Animation* (London: John Libbey, 1994), which is truly international in its scope. Donald Crafton concentrates on the silent era in his *Before Mickey: The Animated Film 1898–1928* (1982; 2d ed., Chicago: University of Chicago Press, 1993). John Grant's *Masters of Animation* (New York: Watson-Guptill, 2001) provides brief introductions to major international animators. A study of a major Eastern European animation studio is Ronald Holloway's *Z Is for Zagreb* (London: Tantivy, 1972).

Many histories concentrate on Hollywood animation, particularly in the era of studio-made shorts. See Leonard Maltin, *Of Mice and Magic: A History of American Animated Cartoons* (New York: New American Library, 1980) and Michael Barrier, *Hollywood Cartoons: American Animation in Its Golden Age* (New York: Oxford University Press, 1999). Jerry Beck and Will Friedwald provide a complete filmography of the Warner Bros. animation unit's output, with descriptions, in their *Looney Tunes and Merrie Melodies: A Complete Illustrated Guide to the Warner Bros. Cartoons* (New York: Holt, 1989).

Good general introductions to the various techniques of animation are Roger Noake's *Animation: A Guide to Animated Film Techniques* (London: MacDonald Orbis, 1988) and Kit Laybourne's *The Animation Book* (New York: Three Rivers, 1998). Specific types of animation are dealt with in Robert Russett and Cecile Starr, ed., *Experimental Animation: An Illustrated Anthology* (New York: Van Nostrand Reinhold, 1976), which contains an interview with Roger Breer; Lotte Reiniger's *Shadow Puppets, Shadow Theatres and Shadow Films* (Boston: Publishers Plays, 1970), dealing with silhouette animation; Michael Frearson's *Clay Animation: American Highlights 1908 to the Present* (New York: Twayne, 1994); and Christopher W. Baker's *How Did They Do It? Computer Illusion in Film and TV* (Indianapolis: Alpha Books, 1994). Peter Lord and Brian Sibley's *Creating 3-D Animation: The Aardman Book of Filmmaking* (New York: Abrams, 1998) deals with clay animation, drawing entirely on the work of the British firm Aardman, the productions of which include the Wallace and Gromit films of Nick Park; Brian Sibley's *"Chicken Run:" Hatching the Movie* (New York: Abrams, 2000) contains a brief overview of Aardman as well as a detailed production history of the firm's first feature.

Works about individual animators include Valliere T. Richard's *Norman McLaren: Manipulator of Movement* (Newark: University of Delaware Press, 1982); Donald Crafton's *Emile Cohl, Caricature, and Film* (Princeton, N.J.: Princeton University Press, 1990); Peter Hames, ed., *Dark Alchemy: The Films of Jan Săvankmajer* (Trowbridge, Wiltshire, England: Flicks Books, 1995); John Canemaker's *Tex Avery: The MGM Years, 1942–1955* (Atlanta: Turner, 1996); and Leslie Cabarga's *The Fleischer Story* (New York: Nostalgia Press, 1976), which deals with Dave and Max Fleischer (Betty Boop and Popeye). Chuck Jones has published an autobiography, *Chuck Amuck: The Life and Times of an Animated Cartoonist* (New York: Farrar Straus, and Giroux, 1989).

A rare serious consideration of the artistic properties of animation is Maureen Furniss's *Art in Motion: Animation Aesthetics* (Sydney: John Libbey, 1998).

Japanese Anime

Although many countries have made animated films, the worldwide commercial market has long been dominated by American cartoons, particularly those from the Disney studio. Until quite recently theatrical animation was so expensive that only large companies could support it. In the 1970s, however, small Japanese companies emerged as rivals to Hollywood firms. They began producing hundreds of what came to be known as *anime* (pronounced "AH-nee-may"), which quickly became part of the world's film culture.

The films came in many genres. Science-fiction efforts like *Macross, Gundam,* and *Fist of the North Star* proved particularly popular, as did postapocalyptic cyberpunk sagas, most notably *Bubblegum Crisis* and *Akira.* There were also fantasy comedies (*Urusei Yatsura, Ranma $^1/_2$*), serious dramas (*Grave of the Fireflies*), and children's films of a quiet charm rarely achieved by the brash Disneys (notably Hayao Miyazaki's *Kiki's Delivery Service* and *My Neighbor Totoro*). Some anime defies description, including the nutty *Project A-Ko* and the erotic-mythical *Urotsukidoji: Legend of the Overfiend.*

Lacking the funding of the big U.S. companies, Japanese animators learned to do more with less. They couldn't duplicate the incessant bustle and flashy depth effects which Disney preferred, so they worked with static shots enhanced by slight motions: winds rustling a dress, a tear rolling down a cheek, even just the shimmer in a character's eyes. Directors also concentrated on *mecha* figures—robots and giant machines, which with their chunky outlines and stiff movements are easier to animate than the flexible human body. When required to animate humans, the Japanese often encased them in hardbody space suits (in effect turning them into robots) or rendered them as fairly flat shapes, as in comic strips. And many works of anime explore subtle changes in color produced by light, liquid, mist, and reflections—all easier to depict than a landscape teeming with figures.

Anime is a media mix. Many of the most popular anime are derived from Japan's flourishing *manga* (comic-book) industry; in turn, successful anime become the basis for new manga. Many anime are made for television or straight-to-video release, but some are conceived as theatrical films, and popular TV series are often turned into feature-length movies. Anime soundtrack CDs have become an influential part of Japanese pop music, and one anime feature, *Perfect Blue,* offers a critical portrait of the cutthroat music industry. Many video games are derived from anime, and the computer-animated musical interludes in the *Final Fantasy* game recall techniques found in the films.

Some TV anime made their way on television in Europe and North America, and *Akira, Ghost in the Shell,* and *Pokémon: The First Movie* had successful English-language releases. Still, video has been the source of anime for Western *otaku* (obsessive fans), who hold conventions and spend hours online discussing their favorites. There are many good websites on anime, but for the most reliable information, see Helen McCarthy's, *Anime! A Beginner's Guide to Japanese Animation* (London: Titan, 1993) and *The Anime Movie Guide* (London: Titan, 1996). McCarthy has also written a detailed study of the creator of Kiki, Totoro, Princess Mononoke and the fantastic creators of *Spirited Away, Hayao Miyazaki: Master of Japanese Animation* (Berkeley: Stone Bridge, 1999). Two reference books are Gilles Poitras, *The Anime Companion: What's Japanese in Japanese Animation?* (Berkeley: Stone Bridge, 1999) and Jonathan Clements and Helen McCarthy, *The Anime Encyclopedia: A Guide to Japanese Animeation since 1917* (Berkeley: Stone Bridge, 2001). For production information on the first computer-generated anime feature, see *The Making of "Final Fantasy: The Spirits Within"* (Indianapolis: Brady, 2001). John A. Lent, ed., *Animation in Asia and the Pacific* (London: John Libbey, 2001) contains several essays on anime, as well as related Asian animation.

PART FOUR

Film Style

We are still seeking to understand the principles by which a film is put together. Chapter 2 showed that the concept of film form offers a way to do this. Chapter 3 examined how films can be organized by narrative form, and Chapter 5 showed that other types of form are often used in documentaries (categorical and rhetorical form) and experimental films (abstract and associational form).

When we see a film, though, we do not engage only with its form. We experience a *film*—not a painting or a novel. Analyzing a painting demands a knowledge of color, shape, and composition; analyzing a novel demands knowledge of language. To understand form in any art, we must be familiar with the medium that art utilizes. Consequently, our understanding of a film must also include features of the *film medium*. Part Four of this book investigates just this area. We shall look at four sets of cinematic techniques: two techniques of the shot, mise-en-scene and cinematography; the technique that relates shot to shot, editing; and the relation of sound to film images.

Each chapter will introduce a single technique, surveying the choices it offers to the filmmaker. We will suggest how you can recognize the technique and its uses. Most important, we shall concentrate on the formal functions of each technique. We will try to answer such questions as these: How may a technique guide expectations or furnish motifs for the film? How may it develop across a film? How may it direct our attention, clarify or emphasize meanings, shape our emotional response?

In Part Four, we will also discover that in any film, certain techniques tend to create a formal system of their own. Every film develops specific techniques in patterned ways. This unified, developed, and significant use of particular technical choices we shall call *style*. In our study of certain films, we shall see how each filmmaker creates a distinctive stylistic system. We can visualize the result in a diagram:

Film Form

interacts with

Formal System	⟷	Stylistic System
Narrative		Patterned and
Categorical		significant use
Rhetorical		of techniques:
Abstract		Mise-en-scene
Associational		Cinematography
		Editing
		Sound

The use a film makes of the medium—the film's style—cannot be studied apart from the film's overall form. We shall find that film style interacts with the formal system. In a narrative film, techniques can function to advance the cause–effect chain, create parallels, manipulate story–plot relations, or sustain the narration's flow of information. But also, film style may become separate from narrative or non-narrative form, attracting our attention in its own right. Some uses of film technique can call attention to patterns of style. In either event, the chapters that follow will continually return to the problem of relations between narrative and non-narrative formal systems and the stylistic system.

Chapter 6

The Shot: Mise-en-Scene

O f all the techniques of cinema, **mise-en-scene** is the one with which we are most familiar. After seeing a film, we may not recall the cutting or the camera movements, the dissolves or the offscreen sound. But we do remember the costumes in *Gone with the Wind* or the bleak, chilly lighting in Charles Foster Kane's Xanadu. We retain vivid impressions of the rainy, gloomy streets in *The Big Sleep* or the labyrinthine, fluorescent-lit lair of Buffalo Bill in *The Silence of the Lambs*. We recall Harpo Marx clambering over Edgar Kennedy's peanut wagon (*Duck Soup*), Katharine Hepburn defiantly splintering Cary Grant's golf clubs (*The Philadelphia Story*), and Michael J. Fox escaping high-school bullies on an improvised skateboard (*Back to the Future*). In short, many of our most sharply etched memories of the cinema turn out to center on mise-en-scene.

WHAT IS MISE-EN-SCENE?

In the original French, *mise-en-scene* (pronounced "meez-ahn-sen") means "putting into the scene," and it was first applied to the practice of directing plays. Film scholars, extending the term to film direction, use the term to signify the director's control over what appears in the film frame. As you would expect from the term's theatrical origins, mise-en-scene includes those aspects of film that overlap with the art of the theater: setting, lighting, costume, and the behavior of the figures. In controlling the mise-en-scene, the director *stages the event* for the camera.

Any of the types of films we have examined so far can use mise-en-scene. While the *cinéma-vérité* director tries to capture events without controlling them, makers of other sorts of documentaries often arrange at least some events, with vivid examples including *The Thin Blue Line* (5.7; we shall analyze this film in Chapter 11). Animated and abstract films may control mise-en-scene to a degree impossible with performers shot in real time—as is seen not only in drawn or puppet animation but also in computer graphics. Most often when we think of mise-en-scene, however, we think of fictional narratives, and most of our examples here will be drawn from such films.

Mise-en-scene usually involves some planning, but the filmmaker may be open to unplanned events as well. An actor may add a line on the set, or an unexpected change in lighting may enhance a dramatic effect. While filming a cavalry procession through Monument Valley for *She Wore a Yellow Ribbon,* John Ford took advantage of an approaching lightning storm to create a dramatic backdrop for the action. The storm remains part of the film's mise-en-scene even though Ford neither planned it nor controlled it; it was a lucky accident that helped create one of the film's most affecting passages. Jean Renoir, Robert Altman, and other directors have allowed their actors to improvise their performances, making the films' mise-en-scene more spontaneous and unpredictable.

REALISM

Before we analyze mise-en-scene in detail, one preconception must be brought to light. Just as viewers often remember this or that bit of mise-en-scene from a film, so they often judge mise-en-scene by standards of realism. A car may seem to be realistic for the period the film depicts, or a gesture may not seem realistic because "real people don't act that way."

Realism as a standard of value, however, raises several problems. Notions of realism vary across cultures, through time, and even among individuals. Marlon Brando's acclaimed realist performance in the 1954 film *On the Waterfront* looks stylized today. American critics of the 1910s praised William S. Hart's Westerns for being realistic, but equally enthusiastic French critics of the 1920s considered the same films to be as artificial as a medieval epic. Moreover, realism has become one of the most problematic issues in the philosophy of art. (See Notes and Queries for examples.) Most important, to insist rigidly on realism for all films can blind us to the vast range of mise-en-scene possibilities.

Look, for instance, at the frame from *The Cabinet of Dr. Caligari* (**6.1**). Such a scene certainly does not accord with our conception of normal reality. Yet to condemn the film for lacking realism would be inappropriate, because the film uses stylization to present a madman's fantasy. *The Cabinet of Dr. Caligari* borrows conventions of Expressionist painting and theater and then assigns them the function of suggesting the madman's delusion.

It is better, then, to examine the *functions* of mise-en-scene than to dismiss this or that element that happens not to match our conception of realism. While one film might indeed use mise-en-scene to create an impression of realism, others might seek very different effects: comic exaggeration, supernatural terror, understated beauty, and any number of other functions. We should analyze mise-en-scene's function in the total film—how it is motivated, how it varies or develops, how it works in relation to other film techniques.

6.1 An Expressionist rooftop scene created from jagged peaks and slanted chimneys in *The Cabinet of Dr. Caligari.*

THE POWER OF MISE-EN-SCENE

To confine the cinema to some notion of realism would indeed impoverish mise-en-scene. This technique has the power to transcend normal conceptions of reality, as we can see from a glance at the cinema's first master of the technique, Georges Méliès. Méliès's mise-en-scene enabled him to create a totally imaginary world on film.

A caricaturist and magician, Méliès became fascinated by the Lumière brothers' demonstration of their short films in 1895. (For more on the Lumières, see pp. 252–253.) After building a camera based on an English projector, Méliès

6.2   Georges Méliès's design for the rocket-launching scene in *A Trip to the Moon* and . . .

6.3   . . . the scene in the film.

6.4   *The Mermaid* created an undersea world by placing a fish tank between the camera and an actress, some backdrops, and "carts for monsters."

6.5   The telescope, globe, and blackboard are all flat, painted cut-outs in *La Lune á une mètre.*

"When Buñuel was preparing *The Discreet Charm of the Bourgeoisie,* he chose a tree-lined avenue for the recurring shot of his characters traipsing endlessly down it. The avenue was strangely stranded in open country and it perfectly suggested the idea of these people coming from nowhere and going nowhere. Buñuel's assistant said, 'You can't use that road. It's been used in at least ten other movies.' 'Ten other movies?' said Buñuel, impressed. 'Then it must be good.' "

began filming unstaged street scenes and moments of passing daily life. One day, the story goes, he was filming at the Place de l'Opéra and his camera jammed as a bus was passing. After some tinkering, he was able to resume filming, but by this time the bus had gone and a hearse was passing in front of his lens. When Méliès screened the film, he discovered something unexpected: A moving bus seemed to transform itself instantly into a hearse. The anecdote may be apocryphal, but it at least illustrates Méliès's recognition of the magical powers of mise-en-scene. He would devote most of his efforts to cinematic conjuring.

But to do so would require preparation, since Méliès could not count on lucky accidents like the bus–hearse transformation. He would have to plan and stage action for the camera. Drawing on his experience in theater, Méliès built one of the first film studios—a small, crammed affair bristling with theatrical machinery, balconies, trapdoors, and sliding backdrops. He sketched shots beforehand and designed sets and costumes. The correspondence between his detailed drawings and the finished shots is illustrated in **6.2** and **6.3**. As if this were not enough, Méliès starred in his own films (often in several roles per film). His desire to create magical effects led Méliès to control every aspect of his films' mise-en-scene.

Such control was necessary to create the fantasy world he envisioned. Only in a studio could Méliès produce *The Mermaid* (**6.4**). He could also surround himself (playing an astronomer) with a gigantic array of cartoonish cut-outs in *La Lune à un mètre* (**6.5**).

6.6 *L'Arroseur arrosé.*

6.7 The filmmakers constructed none of the setting in this shot from *Contempt,* but control of character placement and framing turn it into a nearly abstract composition.

Méliès's "Star-Film" studio made hundreds of short fantasy and trick films based on such a control over every element in the frame, and the first master of mise-en-scene demonstrated the great range of technical possibilities it offers. The legacy of Méliès's magic is a delightfully unreal world wholly obedient to the whims of the imagination.

ASPECTS OF MISE-EN-SCENE

What possibilities for selection and control does mise-en-scene offer the filmmaker? We can mark out four general areas and indicate some potential uses of each.

Setting

Since the earliest days of cinema, critics and audiences have understood that setting plays a more active role in cinema than in most theatrical styles. André Bazin writes,

> The human being is all-important in the theatre. The drama on the screen can exist without actors. A banging door, a leaf in the wind, waves beating on the shore can heighten the dramatic effect. Some film masterpieces use man only as an accessory, like an extra, or in counterpoint to nature, which is the true leading character.

Cinema setting, then, can come to the forefront; it need not be only a container for human events but can dynamically enter the narrative action. (See 6.112, 6.114, 8.135, and 8.136 for examples of settings without characters.)

The filmmaker may control setting in many ways. One way is to select an already existing locale in which to stage the action, a practice stretching back to the earliest films. Louis Lumière shot his short comedy *L'Arroseur arrosé* ("The Waterer Watered," **6.6**) in a garden, and Jean-Luc Godard filmed the exteriors for *Contempt* on the resort island of Capri, off the coast of Italy (**6.7**). At the close of World War II, Roberto Rossellini shot *Germany Year Zero* in the rubble of Berlin (**6.8**). Today filmmakers often go on location to shoot.

Alternatively, the filmmaker may choose to construct the setting. Méliès understood that shooting in a studio increased his control, and many filmmakers followed his lead. In France, Germany, and especially the United States, the possibility of

6.8 *Germany Year Zero.*

6.9 Details like hanging flypaper and posters create a tavern scene in *Greed*.

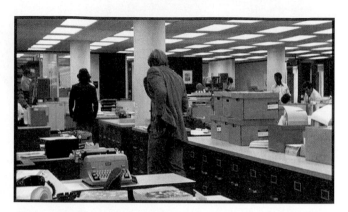

6.10 Replicating an actual newsroom in *All the President's Men*.

6.11 The Babylonian sequences of *Intolerance* combined influences from Assyrian history, 19th-century biblical illustration, and modern dance.

creating a wholly artificial world on film led to the development of several approaches to constructing setting.

Some directors have emphasized authenticity. For example, Erich von Stroheim prided himself on meticulous research into details of locale for *Greed* **(6.9)**. *All the President's Men* (1976) took a similar tack, seeking to duplicate the *Washington Post* office on a soundstage **(6.10)**. Even wastepaper from the actual office was scattered around the set. We should remember, however, that realism in settings is partly a matter of viewing conventions. What strikes us as realistic today might seem highly stylized to future audiences.

Other films have been less committed to historical accuracy. Though D. W. Griffith studied the various historical periods presented in *Intolerance*, his Babylon constitutes a personal image of that city **(6.11)**. Similarly, in *Ivan the Terrible*

6.12 In *Wings of Desire,* busy, colorful graffiti on a wall draw attention from the man lying on the ground.

6.13 *Bram Stoker's Dracula:* Apart from the candles, the setting of this scene has been obliterated by darkness.

6.14 Light, blank backgrounds focus attention on the actors' faces in many shots of *La Passion de Jeanne d'Arc.*

6.15 In *Les Vampires,* a background frame created by a large doorway . . .

6.16 . . . emphasizes the importance of an entering character.

Sergei Eisenstein freely stylized the decor of the czar's palace to harmonize with the lighting, costume, and figure movement, so that characters crawl through doorways that resemble mouseholes and stand frozen before allegorical murals.

Setting can overwhelm the actors, as in Wim Wender's *Wings of Desire* (**6.12**), or it can be reduced to nothing, as in Francis Ford Coppola's *Bram Stoker's Dracula* (**6.13**) and Dreyer's *La Passion de Jeanne d'Arc* (**6.14**). Settings need not possess realistic-looking buildings, as witness the comic-book cityscapes of such films as Tim Burton's *Batman* and Warren Beatty's *Dick Tracy.*

The overall design of a setting can shape how we understand story action. In Louis Feuillade's silent crime serial *The Vampires,* a criminal gang has killed a courier on his way to a bank. The gang's confederate, Irma Vep, is also a bank employee, and just as she tells her superior that the courier has vanished, an imposter, in beard and bowler hat, strolls in behind them (**6.15**). They turn away from us in surprise as he comes forward (**6.16**). Working in a period when cutting to closer shots was rare in a French film, Feuillade draws our attention to the man by centering him in the doorway.

Something similar happens in a more crowded setting in Juzo Itami's *Tampopo.* The plot revolves around a widow who is trying to improve the food and service she offers in her restaurant. In one scene, a truck driver (in a cowboy hat) helps her by taking her to another noodle shop to study technique. Itami has staged the scene so that the kitchen and the counter serve as two arenas for the action. At first,

6.17 *Tampopo:* At the start of the scene, the noodle counter, with only two customers, occupies the center of the action.

6.18 After the counter is full, the dramatic emphasis shifts to the kitchen when the widow moves toward the center and takes the challenge to name the customers' orders. Her red dress helps draw attention to her.

6.19 When she has triumphantly matched the orders, she gets a round of applause. By turning her from us, Itami once more emphasizes the counter area, now filled with customers.

6.20 Color links the home in *L'Argent* . . .

the widow watches the noodle-man take orders, sitting by her mentor on the edge of the kitchen **(6.17).** Quickly the counter fills with customers calling out orders. The truck driver challenges her to match the orders with the correct customers, and she steps closer to the center of the kitchen **(6.18).** After she calls out the orders correctly, she turns her back to us, and our interest shifts to the customers at the counter, who applaud her **(6.19).**

As the *Tampopo* example shows, color can be an important component of settings. The dark colors of the kitchen surfaces make the widow's red dress stand out. Robert Bresson's *L'Argent* creates parallels among its various settings by the recurrence of drab green backgrounds and cold blue props and costumes **(6.20–6.22).** In contrast, Jacques Tati's *Play Time* displays sharply changing color schemes. In the first portion of *Play Time,* the settings and costumes are mostly gray, brown, and black—cold, steely colors. Later in the film, however, beginning in the restaurant scene, the settings start to sport cheery reds, pinks, and greens. This change in the settings' colors supports a narrative development that shows an inhuman city landscape that is transformed by vitality and spontaneity.

A full-size setting need not always be built. Through much of the history of the cinema, filmmakers used miniature buildings to create fantasy scenes or simply

6.21 . . . to the school . . .

6.22 . . . and later to the prison.

6.23 *The Fifth Element* creates a collagelike city using computer graphics to join images from various sources.

to economize. Parts of settings could also be rendered as paintings and combined photographically with full-sized sections of the space. Now, digital special effects are used to fill in portions of the setting, such as cities in *The Phantom Menace* and *The Fifth Element* **(6.23).** Since such special effects also involve cinematography, we look at them in the next chapter.

In manipulating a shot's setting, the filmmaker may create *props*—short for *property*. This is another term borrowed from theatrical mise-en-scene. When an object in the setting has a function within the ongoing action, we can call it a prop. Films teem with examples: the snowstorm paperweight that shatters at the beginning of *Citizen Kane*, the little girl's balloon in *M*, the cactus rose in *The Man Who Shot Liberty Valance*, Sarah Connor's hospital bed turned exercise machine in *Terminator 2: Judgment Day*. Comedies teem with props used for humorous purposes **(6.24).**

In the course of a narrative, a prop may become a motif. The shower curtain in *Psycho* is at first an innocuous part of the setting, but when the killer enters the bathroom the curtain screens her (?) from our sight. Later, after the murder, Norman Bates uses the curtain to wrap up the victim's body. In *The Crime of M. Lange* a poster outside Batala's publishing house advertises its new dime-novel series "Javert" **(6.25),** but after the tyrannical Batala has left the company, Lange and his

"The best sets are the simplest, most 'decent' ones; everything should contribute to the feeling of the story and anything that does not do this has no place. Reality is usually too complicated. Real locations contain too much that is extreme or contradictory and always require some simplifying: taking things away, unifying colors, etc. This strength through simplicity is much easier to achieve on a built set than in an existing location."

— Stuart Craig, art director, *Notting Hill*

6.24   The irresponsible protagonist of *Groundhog Day* eats an enormous breakfast made up of props that dominate the foreground of the diner setting.

6.25   Our first view of the "Javert" poster in *The Crime of M. Lange*.

6.26   Later the window and room behind the poster are revealed . . .

6.27   . . . as it is ripped down to admit sunlight.

associates pull the poster down to reveal the window and room that have for so long been blocked from sunlight (**6.26, 6.27**).

Alexander Payne created a story motif by repeating one type of prop in *Election.* The fussy, frustrated high school teacher begins his day by cleaning out the faculty refrigerator (**6.28**). Soon afterward he picks up hallway litter (**6.29**). At a major turning point in the plot, he decides to conceal a decisive ballot, which he crumples and secretly drops into a wastebasket (**6.30**). Payne calls this the motif of trash, "of throwing things away, since that's in fact the climax of the film. . . . So we establish it early on."

When the filmmaker uses color to create parallels among elements of setting, a color motif may become associated with several props, as in Souleymane Cissé's *Finye* (*The Wind;* **6.31–6.33**). In these and other scenes, the recurrent use of orange creates a cluster of nature motifs within the narrative. Later in this chapter we shall examine in more detail how elements of setting can weave through a film to form motifs within the narrative.

Costume and Makeup

Like setting, costume can have specific functions in the total film, and the range of possibilities is huge. Erich von Stroheim, for instance, was as passionately committed to authenticity of dress as of setting, and he was said to have created underwear

6.28   As he discards spoiled leftovers, the teacher is suspiciously watched by the custodian—
who will play an important role in his downfall.

6.29   He tosses a scrap of paper into the corridor trash bin.

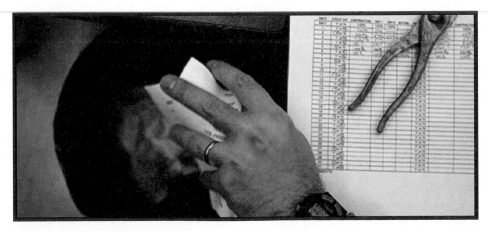

6.30   A close-up of the teacher's hand discarding the crucial vote for student council president.

6.31 *Finye* begins with a woman carrying an orange calabash as the wind rustles through weeds.

6.32 Later, the vengeful grandfather prepares to stalk his grandson's persecutor by dressing in orange and making magic before a fire.

6.33 At the end, the little boy passes his bowl to someone offscreen—possibly the couple seen earlier.

6.34 In *The Birth of a Nation,* the Little Sister realizes how shabby her dress remains despite her attempts to add festive trimming.

6.35 The sweeping folds of a priest's lightweight black robe contrast with the heavy cloak and train of the czar's finery in *Ivan the Terrible.*

that would instill the proper mood in his actors even though it was never to be seen in the film. In Griffith's *The Birth of a Nation,* a poignant moment occurs when the Little Sister decorates her dress with "ermine" made of cotton dotted with spots of soot **(6.34).** The costume displays the poverty of the defeated Southerners at the end of the Civil War.

In other films, costumes may be quite stylized, calling attention to their purely graphic qualities. Throughout *Ivan the Terrible* costumes are carefully orchestrated with one another in their colors, their textures, and even their movements. One shot of Ivan and his adversary gives their robes a plastic sweep and dynamism **(6.35).** In *Freak Orlando,* Ulrike Ottinger (herself a costume designer) boldly uses costumes to display the spectrum's primary colors in maximum intensity **(6.36).**

Costumes can play important motivic and causal roles in narratives. The film director Guido in Fellini's *8½* persistently uses his dark glasses to shield himself from the world. To think of Dracula is to recall how his billowing cape enwraps his victims. When Hildy Johnson, in *His Girl Friday,* switches from her role of aspir-

6.36 Stylized costumes in *Freak Orlando*.

6.37 Hildy's stylish hat with a low-dipping brim worn early in *His Girl Friday* . . .

6.38 . . . is replaced by a "masculine" hat with its brim pushed up, journalist-style, when she returns to work.

ing housewife to that of reporter, her hats change as well (**6.37, 6.38**). In the runaway bus section of *Speed,* during a phone conversation with Jack, the villain Howard refers to Annie as a "Wildcat"; Jack sees Annie's University of Arizona sweater and realizes that Howard has hidden a video camera aboard the bus. Thus a costume provides the clue that allows Jack to outwit Howard.

Any portion of a costume may become a prop: a pair of glasses (*Potemkin, L.A. Confidential*), shoes (*Strangers on a Train, The Wizard of Oz*), a jacket (*Le Million*). In *Titanic,* Rose's diamond pendant is both a treasure which the explorers hope to find and her romantic link with Jack.

Film genres make extensive use of costume props—the frontier six-gun, the gangster's automatic pistol, the dancer's top hat and cane. Every major film comedian has turned a specific costume into a panoply of props: Chaplin's cane and derby, Fields's cigar and top hat, Laurel and Hardy's derbies and too-tight suits, Harpo Marx's capacious pockets.

As we have already seen in *L'Argent* and *Play Time* (p. 000), costume is often coordinated with setting. Since the filmmaker usually wants to emphasize the human figures, setting may provide a more or less neutral background, while costume helps pick out the characters. Color design is particularly important here. The *Freak Orlando* costumes (6.36) stand out boldly against the neutral gray background of an artificial lake. In *The Night of the Shooting Stars,* luminous wheat fields set off the hard black-and-blue costumes of the fascists and the peasants (**6.39**). The director may instead choose to match the color values of setting and costume more closely. One shot in Fellini's *Casanova* (**6.40**) creates a color gradation that runs from bright red costumes to paler red walls, the whole composition capped by a small white accent. This "bleeding" of the costume into the setting is carried to a kind of limit in the prison scene of *THX 1138,* in which George Lucas strips both locale and clothing to stark white on white (**6.41**).

Ken Russell's *Women in Love* affords a clear example of how costume and setting can coordinate and contribute to a film's overall narrative progression. The opening scenes portray the characters' shallow middle-class life by means of highly saturated primary and complementary colors in costume and setting (**6.42**). In the middle portions of the film, as the characters discover love on a country estate, pale pastels predominate (**6.43**). The last section of *Women in Love* takes place around the Matterhorn, and the characters' ardor has cooled. Now the colors have become even paler, dominated by pure black and white (**6.44**). By integrating itself with setting, costume may function to reinforce the film's narrative and thematic patterns.

6.39 The climactic skirmish of *The Night of the Shooting Stars.*

6.40 *Casanova:* Subtle color gradations and a dramatic accent in the distance.

6.41 Heads seem to float in space as white costumes and settings blend in *THX 1138.*

6.42 Bright colors in an early scene of *Women in Love* give way . . .

6.43 . . . to the softer hues of trees and fields . . .

6.44 . . . and finally to a predominantly white-and-black scheme.

6.45 In *Heat,* Al Pacino's makeup gives him slightly rounded eyebrows and, with the help of the lighting, minimizes the bags under his eyes.

6.46 In *The Godfather Part III*, made five years before *Heat,* Pacino looks older. Not only has his hair been whitened, but the makeup, again assisted by the lighting, gives him more sunken and baggy eyes, more hollow cheeks, and a longer, flatter chin.

Many of these points about costume apply equally to a closely related area of mise-en-scene, the actors' makeup. Makeup was originally necessary because actors' faces would not register well on early film stocks. Up to the present, it has been used in various ways to enhance the appearance of actors on the screen. Over the course of film history, a wide range of possibilities has emerged. Dreyer's *La Passion de Jeanne d'Arc* was famous for its complete avoidance of makeup (6.14). This film relied on close-ups and tiny facial changes to create an intense religious drama. On the other hand, Nikolai Cherkasov did not look particularly like Eisenstein's conception of Czar Ivan IV, so he wore a wig and false beard, nose, and eyebrows for *Ivan the Terrible.* Changing actors to look like historical personages has been one common function of makeup.

Today makeup usually tries to pass unnoticed, but it also accentuates expressive qualities of the actor's face. Since the camera may record cruel details that would pass unnoticed in ordinary life, any unsuitable blemishes, wrinkles, and sagging skin will have to be hidden. The makeup artist can sculpt the face, making it seem narrower or broader by applying blush and shadow. Viewers expect that female performers will wear lipstick and other cosmetics, but the male actors are often wearing makeup too (**6.45, 6.46**).

Film actors rely on their eyes to a very great extent (see Box, p. 201), and makeup artists can often enhance that area. Eyeliner and mascara can draw attention to the eyes and emphasize the direction of a glance. Nearly every actor will also have expressively shaped eyebrows. Lengthened eyebrows can enlarge the face, while shorter brows make it seem more compact. Eyebrows plucked in a slightly rising curve add gaiety to the face, while slightly sloping ones hint at sadness. Thick, straight brows, commonly applied to men, reinforce the impression of a hard, serious gaze. Thus eye makeup can assist the actor's performance (**6.47, 6.48**).

Makeup can aim at complete realism. When Laurence Olivier blackened his skin and hair to make a film of *Othello,* he strove to be as convincing a Moor as possible. Yet it is equally possible to use make-up in nonrealistic ways. Bizarre makeup plays a major role in genres like horror and comedy. Just as they adopted distinctive costumes, famous comedians often created an amusing look using makeup (**6.49**).

In recent decades the craft of makeup has developed in response to the popularity of horror and science-fiction genres. Rubber and Plasticine compounds create bumps, bulges, extra organs, and layers of artificial skin in such films as David Cronenberg's *The Fly* (**6.50**) and Tim Burton's *Edward Scissorhands* (**6.51**). In

6.47   In *Speed,* Sandra Bullock's eyeliner, shadow, and arched brows make her eyes vivid and give her an alert expression.

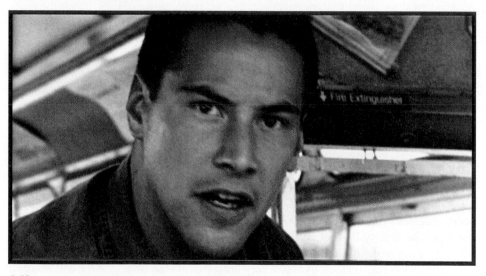

6.48   For the same scene, the eyeliner on Keanu Reeves makes the upper edges of his eyes stand out. Note also the somewhat fierce curve of the eyebrows, accentuating his slight frown.

6.49   *Horse Feathers:* Groucho Marx's instantly recognizable moustache was simply (and obviously) a patch of black paint.

6.50   Jeff Goldblum, nearly unrecognizable under grotesque makeup, during his tranformation into *The Fly.*

6.51   In *Edward Scissorhands,* the hero's scars hint that his hands, made of metal blades, are an inadvertant danger to himself and others.

such contexts, makeup, like costume, becomes important in creating character traits or motivating plot action.

Lighting

Much of the impact of an image comes from its manipulation of lighting. In cinema, lighting is more than just illumination that permits us to see the action. Lighter and darker areas within the frame help create the overall composition of each shot and thus guide our attention to certain objects and actions. A brightly illuminated patch may draw our eye to a key gesture, while a shadow may conceal a detail or build up suspense about what may be present. Lighting can also articulate textures: the soft curve of a face, the rough grain of a piece of wood, the delicate tracery of a spider's web, the sheen of glass, the sparkle of a faceted gem.

Lighting shapes objects by creating highlights and shadows. A highlight is a patch of relative brightness on a surface. The man's face in **6.52** and the edge of the fingers in **6.53** display highlights. Highlights provide important cues to the texture of the surface. If the surface is smooth, like glass or chrome, the highlights tend to gleam or sparkle; a rougher surface, like a coarse stone facing, yields more diffuse highlights.

There are two basic types of shadows, each of which is important in film composition: *attached* shadows, or *shading,* and *cast* shadows. An attached shadow occurs when light fails to illuminate part of an object because of the object's shape or surface features. If a person sits by a candle in a darkened room, patches of the face and body will fall into darkness. Most obviously, the nose often creates a patch of darkness on an adjoining cheek. This phenomenon is shading, or attached shadow. But the candle also projects a shadow on the wall behind. This is a cast shadow, because the body blocks out the light. The shadows in 6.52, for example, are cast shadows, made by bars between the actor and the light source. But, in 6.53 the small dark patches on the hand are attached shadows, for they are caused by the three-dimensional curves and ridges of the hand itself.

As these examples suggest, highlights and shadows help create our sense of a scene's space. In 6.52, a few shadows imply an entire prison cell. Animated films can use the same cues to one degree or another. In 5.82, from *Who Framed Roger Rabbit?,* human and cartoon figures display both cast shadows and attached shadows, or shading.

Lighting also shapes a shot's overall composition. One shot from John Huston's *Asphalt Jungle* welds the gang members into a unit by the pool of light cast by a hanging lamp **(6.54).** At the same time, it sets up a scale of importance, emphasizing the protagonist by making him the most frontal and clearly lit figure.

A shot's lighting affects our sense of the shape and texture of the objects depicted. If a ball is lit straight from the front, it will appear round. If the same ball is lit from the side, we will see it as a half-circle. Hollis Frampton's short film *Lemon* consists primarily of light moving around a lemon, and the shifting shadows create dramatically changing patterns of yellow and black. This film almost seems designed to prove the truth of a remark made by Josef von Sternberg, one of the cinema's masters of film lighting: "The proper use of light can embellish and dramatize every object."

For our purposes, we can isolate four major features of film lighting: its *quality, direction, source,* and *color.*

Lighting *quality* refers to the relative intensity of the illumination. *Hard* lighting creates clearly defined shadows, crisp textures, and sharp edges, whereas *soft* lighting creates a diffused illumination. In nature, the noonday sun creates hard

6.52 In *The Cheat,* Cecil B. DeMille suggested a jail cell by casting a bright light on a man's face and body through unseen bars.

6.53 Robert Bresson's *Pickpocket.*

"Light is everything. It expresses ideology, emotion, colour, depth, style. It can efface, narrate, describe. With the right lighting, the ugliest face, the most idiotic expression can radiate with beauty or intelligence."

— Federico Fellini, director

6.54 Attached shadows on faces create a dramatic composition in John Huston's *Asphalt Jungle.*

6.55 In this shot from Satyajit Ray's *Aparajito,* Apu's mother and the globe she holds are emphasized by hard lighting, while . . .

6.56 . . . in another shot from the same film, softer lighting blurs contours and textures and makes for more diffusion and gentler contrasts between light and shade.

6.57 In *La Chinoise,* frontal lighting makes the actress's shadow fall directly behind her, where we cannot see it.

6.58 In another shot from *La Chinoise,* the lighting is still frontal, but comes from slightly off to the left of the camera, creating a shadow on the wall behind the actor's head.

6.59 *Touch of Evil:* Sidelight creates sharp attached shadows by the character's nose, cheek, and lips, while long cast shadows appear on the file cabinets at the left.

6.60 In Godard's *Passion,* the lamp and window provide backlighting that presents the woman almost entirely in silhouette.

light, while an overcast sky creates soft light. The terms are relative, and many lighting situations will fall between the extremes, but we can in practice easily recognize the differences (**6.55, 6.56**).

The *direction* of lighting in a shot refers to the path of light from its source or sources to the object lit. "Every light," wrote von Sternberg, "has a point where it is brightest and a point toward which it wanders to lose itself completely. . . . The journey of rays from that central core to the outposts of blackness is the adventure and drama of light." For convenience we can distinguish among frontal lighting, sidelighting, backlighting, underlighting, and top lighting.

Frontal lighting can be recognized by its tendency to eliminate shadows. In **6.57** and **6.58,** two shots from Godard's *La Chinoise,* the result of such frontal lighting is a fairly flat-looking image. Contrast **6.59,** from *Touch of Evil,* in which Welles uses a hard **sidelight** (also called a *crosslight*) to sculpt the character's features.

Backlighting, as the name suggests, comes from behind the subject filmed. It can be positioned at many angles: high above the figure, at various angles off to the side, pointing straight at the camera, or from below. Used with no other sources of light, backlighting tends to create silhouettes, as in **6.60.** Combined with more frontal sources of light, the technique can create an unobtrusively illuminated contour. This use of backlighting is called *edge lighting* or *rim lighting* (**6.61**).

6.61   In *Wings,* a narrow line of light makes each actor's body stand out from the background.

6.62   *The Sixth Sense:* A flashlight lights the boy's face from below, enhancing our empathy with his fright as he feels the presence of a ghost.

Underlighting suggests that the light comes from below the subject. In **6.62,** the underlighting suggests an offscreen flashlight. Since underlighting tends to distort features, it is often used to create dramatic horror effects, but it may also simply indicate a realistic light source, such as a fireplace. As usual, a particular technique can function differently according to context.

Top lighting is exemplified by **6.63,** where the spotlight shines down from almost directly above Marlene Dietrich's face. Von Sternberg frequently used such a high frontal light to bring out the line of his star's cheekbones. (Our earlier example from *Asphalt Jungle* in Figure 6.54 provides a less glamorous instance of top lighting.)

Lighting can also be characterized by its *source.* In making a documentary, the filmmaker may be obliged to shoot with the light available in the actual surroundings. Most fictional films, however, use extra light sources to obtain greater control of the image's look. In most fictional films, the table lamps and streetlights you see in the mise-en-scene are not the principal sources of illumination for the filming. Such visible sources of light, however, will serve to motivate the lighting decisions made in production. The filmmaker will usually strive to create a lighting design that is consistent with the sources in the setting. In **6.64,** from *The Miracle Worker,* the window in the rear and the lantern in the right foreground are purportedly the sources of illumination, but you can see the many studio lights used in this shot reflected as tiny white dots in the glass lantern.

Directors and cinematographers manipulating the lighting of the scene will start from the assumption that any subject normally requires two light sources: a **key light** and a **fill light.** The key light is the primary source, providing the dominant illumination and casting the strongest shadows. The key light is the most directional light, and it usually corresponds to the motivating light source in the setting. A fill is a less intense illumination that "fills in," softening or eliminating shadows cast by the key light. By combining key and fill, and by adding other sources, lighting can be controlled quite exactly.

The key lighting source may be aimed at the subject from any angle, as our examples of lighting direction have indicated. As one shot from *Ivan the Terrible* shows (6.81), underlighting may be the key source, while a softer and dimmer fill falls on the setting behind the figure.

Lights from various directions can be combined in any way. A shot may use key and fill lights without backlighting. In the frame from *The Bodyguard* (**6.65**), a

"When taking close-ups in a colour picture, there is too much visual information in the background, which tends to draw attention away from the face. That is why the faces of the actresses in the old black and white pictures are so vividly remembered. Even now, movie fans nostalgically recall Dietrich . . . Garbo . . . Lamarr . . . Why? Filmed in black and white, those figures looked as if they were lit from within. When a face appeared on the screen overexposed—the high-key technique, which also erased imperfections—it was as if a bright object was emerging from the screen."

— Nestor Almendros, cinematographer

6.63 Top lighting in Josef von Sternberg's *Shanghai Express.*

6.64 Apparent and hidden light sources in *The Miracle Worker.*

6.65 Strong key and soft fill light combined in *The Bodyguard.*

6.66 *Bezhin Meadow.*

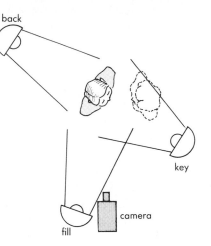

6.67 Three-point lighting, one of the basic techniques of Hollywood cinema.

6.68 The three-point system's effect as it looks on the screen in *Jezebel.*

strong key light from offscreen left throws a dramatic shadow on the wall at the right. The dim fill light inconspicuously shows the back wall and ceiling of the set, but leaves the right side of the actor's head dark.

In **6.66,** from *Bezhin Meadow,* Eisenstein uses a number of light sources and directions. The key light falling on the figures comes from the left side, but it is hard on the face of the old woman in the foreground and softened on the face of the man because a fill light comes in from the right. This fill light falls on the woman's forehead and nose.

Classical Hollywood filmmaking developed the custom of using at least three light sources per shot: key light, fill light, and backlight. The most basic arrangement of these lights on a single figure is shown in **6.67.** The backlight comes from behind and above the figure, the key light comes diagonally from the front, and a fill light comes from a position near the camera. The key will usually be closer to the figure or brighter than the fill. Typically, each major character in a scene will have his or her own key, fill, and backlight. If another actor is added (as in the dotted figure in 6.67), the key light for one can be altered slightly to form the backlight for the other and vice versa, with a fill light on either side of the camera.

In **6.68,** the Bette Davis character in *Jezebel* is the most important figure, and the **three-point lighting** centers attention on her: A bright backlight from the rear

6.69 In this shot from *The Purple Rose of Cairo*, the two figures are modeled by a strong key light from the left side, a fill light from off right of the camera, and a trace of edge lighting to pick out their clothes. The office behind the couple is lit with dimmer, softer fill light, as is typical with backgrounds.

6.70 *Back to the Future*: day . . .

6.71 . . . versus night.

upper right highlights her hair and edge-lights her left arm. The key light is off left, making her right arm brightly illuminated. A fill light comes from just to the right of the camera. It is less bright than the key. This balanced lighting creates mild shading, modeling Davis's face to suggest volume rather than flatness. (Note the slight shadow cast by her nose.) Davis's backlight and key light serve to illuminate the woman behind her at the right, but less prominently. Other fill lights, called *background* or *set lighting,* fall on the setting and on the crowd at the left rear. Three-point lighting emerged during the studio era of Hollywood filmmaking, and it is still widely used, as in **6.69,** from Woody Allen's *Purple Rose of Cairo.*

You may have already noticed that this three-point lighting system demands that the lamps be rearranged virtually every time the camera shifts to a new framing of the scene. In spite of the great cost involved, most Hollywood films will have a different lighting arrangement for each camera position. Such variations in the light sources do not conform to reality, but they do enable filmmakers to create clear compositions for each shot.

Three-point lighting was particularly well suited for the high-key lighting used in classical Hollywood cinema and other filmmaking traditions. **High-key lighting** refers to an overall lighting design that uses fill and backlight to create low contrast between brighter and darker areas. Usually, the light quality is soft, making shadow areas fairly transparent. The frames from *Jezebel* (6.68) and from *The Purple Rose of Cairo* (6.69) exemplify high-key lighting. Hollywood directors and cinematographers have relied on this for comedies, adventure films, and most dramas.

High-key lighting is not used simply to render a brightly lit situation, such as a dazzling ballroom or a sunny afternoon. High-key lighting is an overall approach to illumination that can suggest different lighting conditions or times of day. Consider, for example, two frames from *Back to the Future.* The first shot **(6.70)** uses high-key illumination matched to daylight and a brightly lit malt shop. The second frame **(6.71)** is from a scene set in a room at night, but it still uses the high-key approach, as can be seen from the lighting's softness, its low contrast, and its detail in shadow areas.

6.72 In *Kanal,* low-key lighting creates a harsh highlight on one side of the woman's face, a deep shadow on the other.

"When I started watching films in the 1940s and 1950s, Indian cinematography was completely under the influence of Hollywood aesthetics, which mostly insisted on the 'ideal light' for the face, using heavy diffusion and strong back-light. I came to resent the complete disregard of the actual source of light and the clichéd use of back-light. Using back-light all the time is like using chili powder in whatever you cook."

— Subrata Mitra, cinematographer

Low-key illumination creates stronger contrasts and sharper, darker shadows. Often the lighting is hard, and fill light is lessened or eliminated altogether. The effect is of *chiaroscuro,* or extremely dark and light regions within the image. An example is **6.72,** from Andrzej Wajda's *Kanal.* Here, the fill light and background light are significantly less intense than in high-key technique. As a result, shadow areas on the left third of the screen remain hard and opaque. In **6.73,** a low-key shot from Carax's *Mauvais sang,* the key light is hard and comes from the side. Carax eliminates both fill and background illumination, creating very sharp shadows and a dark void around the characters.

As our examples indicate, low-key lighting has usually been applied to somber or mysterious scenes. It was common in horror films of the 1930s and *films noirs* ("dark films") of the 1940s and 1950s. The low-key approach was revived in the 1980s in such films as *Blade Runner* and *Rumble Fish* and continued in the 1990s in *films noirs* like *Se7en* and *The Usual Suspects.* In *El Sur* **(6.74)** Hector Erice's low-key lighting yields dramatic chiaroscuro effects that portray the adult world as a child imagines it.

When the actors move, the director must decide whether to alter the lighting. By overlapping several different key lights, the filmmaker can maintain a constant intensity as actors move around the set. Although constant lighting is not particularly realistic, it has advantages, the main one being that distracting shadows and highlights do not move across actors. At the end of Fellini's *Nights of Cabiria,* for example, the heroine moves diagonally toward us, accompanied by a band of singing young people **(6.75, 6.76).** Alternatively, the filmmaker may have his or her figures move through patches of light and shadow. The swordfight in *Rashomon* is intensified by the contrast between the ferocious combat and the cheerfully dappled lighting pouring into the glade **(6.77).**

Like any technique, lighting can become a motif in the course of a film. Woody Allen's *Purple Rose of Cairo* presents a woman torn between a brutal, abusive marriage and her fantasy of a movie hero (who steps down from the screen to meet her). Scenes with her fictional hero are presented in moderately high-key, using the three-point system (6.69). But scenes with her husband at her home are given the harsh, hard-edged treatment characteristic of low-key technique **(6.78).**

We tend to think of film lighting as limited to two colors—the white of sunlight or the soft yellow of incandescent interior lamps. In practice, filmmakers who choose

6.73 In *Mauvais sang,* a single key light without any fill on the actress's face leaves her expression nearly invisible.

6.74 Low-key lighting in *El Sur* suggests a child's view of the adult world as full of mystery and danger.

6.75 At the end of Fellini's *Nights of Cabiria,* the heroine moves diagonally toward us, accompanied by a band of singing young people.

6.76 As she walks, the lighting on her face does not change, enabling us to notice slight changes in her expression.

6.77 Dappled lighting in *Rashomon.*

6.78 Low-key lighting creates dark shadows on actors and set in *The Purple Rose of Cairo.*

6.79 An orange filter suggests that all the light in this scene from *The Green Room* comes from candles.

to control lighting typically work with as purely white a light as they can. By use of filters placed in front of the light source, the filmmaker can color the onscreen illumination in any fashion. There may be a realistic source in the scene to motivate the hue of the light. For example, cinematographers often use filters over lighting equipment to suggest the orange tint of candlelight, as in François Truffaut's *The Green Room* **(6.79).** In Douglas Sirk's *Written on the Wind,* purplish-blue lighting is motivated as the color of night **(6.80).** But colored light can also be unrealistic in its motivation. Eisenstein's *Ivan the Terrible,* Part 2, uses a blue light suddenly cast on an actor, nondiegetically, to suggest the character's terror and uncertainty **(6.81, 6.82).** Such a shift in stylistic function—using colored light to perform a function usually confined to acting—is all the more effective because it is so unexpected.

Most film lighting is applied during shooting, but computer-generated imagery allows filmmakers to create virtual lighting designs. Powerful 3-D programs allow filmmakers to add broad overall illumination or strongly directional effects. Spotlights can sprinkle highlights on shiny metal, while "shader" tools model objects with attached shadows. In normal filming, the filmmakers must reduce the vast amount of visual information in front of the camera, using lighting to clarify and simplify the space. In contrast, digital lighting is built up little by little from simple

6.80 *Written on the Wind:* Although this scene is not particularly dark, the purple light suggests that it takes place at night.

6.81 In *Ivan the Terrible,* a character's fear registers on his face, but a blue light also suddenly and briefly shines on it . . .

6.82 . . . until it disappears and the scene continues.

elements. For this reason, it is very time-consuming; a program may need a day and a night to render moving cast shadows in a single shot. Still, new software and faster computers are likely to accelerate the work process.

We are used to ignoring the illumination of our everyday surroundings, so film lighting is also easy to take for granted. Yet the look of a shot is centrally controlled by light quality, direction, source, and color. The filmmaker can manipulate and combine these factors to shape the viewer's experience in a great many ways. No component of mise-en-scene is more important than "the drama and adventure of light."

Staging: Movement and Acting

6.83 The actors strike weary poses in *Seven Samurai.*

The director may also control the behavior of various figures in the mise-en-scene. Here the word *figures* covers a wide range of possibilities, since the figure may represent a person but could also be an animal (Lassie, the donkey Balthasar, Donald Duck), a robot (R2D2 and C3PO in the *Star Wars* series), an object (as in *Ballet mécanique*'s choreography of bottles, straw hats, and kitchen utensils), or even a pure shape (as in *Ballet mécanique*'s circles and triangles). Mise-en-scene allows such figures to express feelings and thoughts; it can also dynamize them to create various kinetic patterns.

In **6.83** (from *Seven Samurai*) the samurai have won the battle with the bandits. Virtually the only movement in the frame is the driving rain, but the slouching postures of the men leaning on their spears express their tense weariness. In contrast, in *White Heat* explosive movement and ferocious facial expression present an image of psychotic rage **(6.84).**

6.84 In *White Heat,* Cody Jarrett (James Cagney) bursts up from the prison mess table after learning of his mother's death.

In cinema, facial expression and movement are not restricted to human figures. As mentioned in Chapter 5, animation can use abstract drawings or three-dimensional objects with highly dynamic movement. For example, in science-fiction and fantasy films, monsters and robots may be given expressions and gestures through the technique of *stop-action* (also called *stop-motion*). Typically a small-scale model is made with articulated parts. In filming, it is posed as desired, and a frame or two is shot. Then the figure is adjusted slightly and another frame or two is exposed, and so on. The result on screen is a continuous, if sometimes jerky, movement. The horrendous onslaught of ED-209, the crimefighting robot in *Robocop,* was created by means of a twelve-inch miniature filmed in stop-action **(6.85).** (A full-scale but unmoving model was also built for long shots.) Stop-action can also be used for more abstract and unrealistic purposes, as in Jan Švankmajer's *Dimensions of Dialogue* **(6.86).**

6.85 A miniature used in *Robocop*.

6.86 A conversation between clay figures degenerates as they begin to claw each other to bits in *Dimensions of Dialogue*.

The filmmaker can stage action without three-dimensional figures or objects. Cel animation presents us with drawings of Aladdin or Daffy Duck. Filmmakers may also blend photographed action with animated mise-en-scene. Highly detailed computer-generated animation made it possible for James Cameron to create the outrageous metamorphoses of the cyborg in *Terminator 2: Judgment Day*. (See Notes and Queries for more on computer-generated mise-en-scene.)

Acting and Actuality   Although abstract shapes and animated figures can become important in the mise-en-scene, the most intuitively familiar cases of figure expression and movement are actors playing roles. Like other aspects of mise-en-scene, the performance is created in order to be filmed. An actor's performance consists of visual elements (appearance, gestures, facial expressions) and sound (voice, effects). At times, of course, an actor may contribute only visual aspects, as in the silent period of film history. Similarly, an actor's performance may sometimes exist only on the sound track of the film; in *A Letter to Three Wives,* Celeste Holm's character, Addie Ross, speaks a narration over the images but never appears on the screen.

Acting is often approached as a question of realism. While some broad conception of realistic behavior is probably indispensable as a first step to understanding acting, we cannot stop there. It is not always fruitful to judge an actor's performance by what would be likely behavior in the world outside the movie theater, and this is for several reasons.

For one thing, concepts of realistic acting have changed over film history. Today we may think that the performances of Russell Crowe and Al Pacino in *The Insider* or those given by Sissy Spacek and Tom Wilkinson in *In the Bedroom* are reasonably close to people's real-life behavior. Yet in the early 1950s, the New York Actors Studio style, as exemplified by Marlon Brando's performances in *On the Waterfront* and *A Streetcar Named Desire,* was also thought to be extremely realistic. Fine though we may still find Brando's work in these films, it seems deliberate, heightened, and quite unrealistic. The same might be said of the performances, by professional and amateur actors alike, in post–World War II Italian neorealist films, which were hailed when they first appeared as almost documentary depictions of Italian life but many of which now seem to us to contain polished performances suitable to Hollywood films. (In fact, one of the main neorealist actors, Anna Magnani, went to Hollywood and won an Oscar there.) Already major naturalistic performances of the 1970s, such as Robert De Niro's protagonist in *Taxi Driver,* are coming to seem quite stylized. Who can say what the acting in *The Insider, In the Bedroom,* and other recent films will look like in a few decades?

Changing views of realism are not the only reason to be wary of this as a concept for analyzing acting. Often when people call a performance unrealistic, they are evaluating it as bad. But not all films try to achieve realism. Since the performance an actor creates is part of the overall mise-en-scene, films contain a wide variety of acting styles. Instead of assuming that acting must be realistic, we should try to understand what kind of acting style the film is aiming at. If the functions of acting in the film are best served by a nonrealistic performance, that is the kind that the skillful actor will strive to present. Obvious examples of nonrealistic acting style occur constantly in *The Wizard of Oz,* for fantasy purposes. (How would a real Wicked Witch behave?) Moreover, realistic performance will always be only one option in film acting. In mass-production filmmaking from Hollywood, India, Hong Kong, and other traditions, overblown performances are a crucial source of the audience's pleasure. Viewers do not expect narrowly realistic acting from Jim Carrey or from martial arts stars like Bruce Lee or Jackie Chan.

Finally, when we watch any fictional film, we are to some degree aware that the performances on the screen are the result of the actors' skills and decisions. (See Box.) When we use the phrase "larger than life" to describe an effective performance, we seem to be tacitly acknowledging the actor's deliberate craft. In analyzing a particular film, it is usually necessary to go beyond assumptions about realism and consider the functions and purposes that the actor's craft serves.

Acting: Functions and Motivation

In 1985 a considerable controversy arose in Hollywood because Steve Martin was not nominated for an Academy Award for his acting in *All of Me.* In that film, Martin portrays a man whose body is suddenly inhabited on the right side by the soul of a woman who has just died. Martin used sudden changes of voice, along with acrobatic pantomime, to suggest a split body. In 1999, a similar outcry occurred when Jim Carrey was not nominated for an Oscar for *The Truman Show,* a comedy about a man who is unaware that his entire life has been broadcast as a sitcom on television. Neither Martin nor Carrey could be expected to perform realistically in the narrow sense of the word, since the situations they portray could not exist in the real world. Yet in the context of each of these fantasy-comedies, the actor is completely appropriate.

In films like *All of Me* and *The Truman Show,* a more muted and superficially realistic performance would clearly be inappropriate to the context established by the genre, the film's narrative, and the overall mise-en-scene. This suggests that in order to determine the acting's functions, we need to determine overall normal factors, such as narrative causality and genre conventions. In addition, if we want also to evaluate the actors' performances, we might set forth this criterion: If the actor looks and behaves in a manner *appropriate* to his or her character's *function* in the context of the film, the actor has given a good performance—whether or not he or she looks or behaves as a real person would.

As a first approximation, we can consider performance styles along two dimensions. The performance will be more or less *individualized,* and it will be more or less *stylized.* Often we have both in mind when we think of a realistic performance: It will create a unique character, and it will not seem too exaggerated or too underplayed. Yet less individualized and more stylized performances may also be appropriate to the context of a particular film's mise-en-scene.

Although we often think of good acting as creating highly individualized roles, many filmmaking traditions emphasize the creation of broader, more anonymous, *types.* Classical Hollywood narrative was built on ideologically stereotyped roles: the Irish cop on the beat, the black servant, the Jewish pawnbroker, the wisecracking waitress or showgirl. Through *typecasting,* actors were selected and directed to

The Film Actor's Toolkit

We might think that the most important task facing an actor is reading dialogue in a convincing and stirring way. Certainly voice and delivery are very important in cinema, but considered in terms of mise-en-scene the actor is always part of the overall visual design. Many film scenes contain little dialogue, and some contain none, but at every moment onscreen the actor must be in character. Film demands that the actor and director shape the performance pictorially.

At all times, film actors use their faces. This was most evident before movies had sound, and theorists of the silent film were full of praise for the subtle facial acting of Charlie Chaplin, Greta Garbo, and Lillian Gish. Since some basic facial expressions (happiness, fear, anger) are understood easily across cultures, it's not surprising that silent film could become popular around the world. Today, with mainstream fiction films using many close-ups (see pp. 327–331), actor's faces are hugely enlarged, and the performers must control their expressions minutely.

The most expressive parts of the face are the brows, the mouth, and the eyes. All work together to signal how the character is responding to the dramatic situation. In *Jerry Maguire*, the accountant Dorothy Boyd accidentally meets Jerry at an airport baggage conveyor. She has a crush on him, partly because she admires the courageous mission statement he has issued to the sports agency they work for. As he starts to back off from the statement, she eagerly quotes it from memory; Renee Zellwegger's earnest smile and steady gaze suggest that she takes the issues more seriously than Jerry does **(6.87)**. This impression is confirmed when Jerry says, "Uh-huh," and studies her skeptically, his fixed smile signaling social politeness rather than genuine pride **(6.88)**. This encounter sets up one premise of the film—that Jerry's idealistic impulses will need constant shoring up, for he might at any moment slip back into being "a shark in a suit."

The eyes hold a special place in film. In any scene, crucial story information is conveyed by the direction of a character's glance, the use of eyelids, and the shape of the eyebrows. One of Chaplin's most heartrending moments comes in *City Lights*, when the blind flower girl, now sighted, suddenly realizes that he's her benefactor. Chaplin twirls a flower in his teeth, so we can't see the shape of his mouth; we must read yearning in his brows and rapt, dark gaze **(6.89)**.

6.87 Perky and sincere, Dorothy pledges allegiance to Jerry Maguire's idealistic memo.

6.88 Jerry smiles politely but his sideways glance and brows suggest that he is a bit put off by her earnestness.

6.89 The climax of *City Lights:* By concealing his mouth with the flower he twirls nervously, Chaplin obliges us to find his hope expressed in the upper part of his face.

6.90 In *Tigre Reale*, Menichelli's right hand seizes her hair, as if pulling her head back in agony; but her body still expresses defiance, thrust forward and standing firm as the left hand grips her waist.

Normally we don't stare intently at the people we talk with. We glance away about half the time to gather our thoughts, and we blink 10 to 12 times a minute. But actors must learn to look directly at each other, locking eyes and seldom blinking. If an actor glances away from the partner in the conversation, it suggests distraction or evasion. If an actor blinks, it suggests a reaction to what is happening in the scene (surprise, or anxiety). Actors playing forceful characters often stare fixedly. Anthony Hopkins says this of playing Hannibal Lecter: "If you don't blink you can keep the audience mesmerized." (See 10.1, 10.3.) In our *Jerry Maguire* scene, the protagonists watch each other fixedly. When Jerry does close his eyes in response to Dorothy's praise, it indicates his nervousness about confronting the issues that his mission statement raised.

Actors act with their bodies as well. How a character walks, stands, or sits conveys a great deal about personality and attitude. In fact, during the 18th and 19th centuries, *attitude* was used to refer to the way a person stood. Stage acting gave early film a repertoire of postures that could express a character's state of mind. In the 1916 Italian film *Tigre Reale* (*The Royal Tigress*), the diva Pina Menichelli plays a countess with a shady past. At one point she confesses this in a florid attitude that expresses noble suffering **(6.90)**. While few actors today would resort to this stylized posture, early film audiences would have accepted it as vividly expressive, like a movement in dance. Menichelli plays the rest of the scene more quietly, but she still employs expressive attitudes **(6.91, 6.92)**.

Chaplin's and Menichelli's gestures show that hands are important tools of the film actor. Hands are to the body what eyes are to the face: They focus our attention and evoke the character's thoughts and feelings. In the doomsday thriller *Fail-Safe* Henry Fonda plays the U.S. president, who has learned that an American warplane has been accidentally sent to bomb the Soviet Union. Fonda stands erect at the phone as he hears distressing news about the plane's progress, and he hangs up with his left hand **(6.93–6.96)**. By keeping most of the shot still and bare, director Sidney Lumet has given Fonda's fingers the main role, letting them express the president's measured prudence but also suggesting the strain of the crisis.

conform to type. Often, however, skillful performers gave these conventions a freshness and vividness.

In the Soviet cinema of the 1920s, several directors used a similar principle, called *typage*. Here the actor was expected to portray a typical representative of a social class or historical movement **(6.97, 6.98)**.

Whether more or less typed, the performance can also be located on a continuum of stylization. A long tradition of film acting strives for a resemblance to what is thought of as realistic behavior. This sense of realism may be created by giving the actors small bits of business to perform while they speak their lines. Frequent gestures and movements by the actors add plausibility to the humor of Woody Allen's films **(6.99)**. More intense and explicit emotions dominate *Winchester 73*, in which James Stewart plays a man driven by a desire for revenge **(6.100)**.

Psychological motivation is less important in a film like *Trouble in Paradise*, a sophisticated comedy of manners in which the main concern is with more stereo-

6.91 As Menichelli begins to feel shame, she retreats toward the fireplace, turning from us and slumping in a way that suggests regret.

6.92 She keeps her back to the camera as she withdraws, now a pathetic figure.

6.93 In *Fail-Safe,* the president stands erect at the phone as he hears distressing news about the plane's progress, and he hangs up with his left hand.

6.94 The president pauses and rubs his fingers together thoughtfully . . .

6.95 . . . then he taps into the intercom with his right hand.

6.96 As he waits, for a brief moment his left fingers waggle anxiously.

typical characters in a comic situation. In **6.101** two women competing for the same man pretend to be friendly. Again, the performances are perfectly appropriate to the genre, narrative, and overall style of the film.

Comedy does not provide the only motivation for greater stylization. *Ivan the Terrible* is a film that heightens every element—music, costume, setting—to create a larger-than-life portrait of its hero. Nikolai Cherkasov's broad, abrupt gestures fit in perfectly with all of these other elements to create an overall unity of composition (**6.102**).

Some films may combine different degrees of stylization. *Amadeus* contrasts a grotesque, giggling performance by Tom Hulce as Mozart with Murray Abraham's suave Salieri. Here the acting sharpens the contrast between the older composer's decorous, boring music and the young man's irrepressible but offensive genius.

Films like *Caligari, Ivan the Terrible,* and *Amadeus* create stylized performances through extroversion and exaggeration. The director can also explore the

6.97   The opening of Sergei Eisenstein's *Strike* presents the cartoonish cliché of the top-hatted capitalist . . .

6.98   . . . while in contrast the workers are later presented as earnest and resolute.

6.99   Verisimilitude in acting: Mia Farrow as Hannah, Diane Wiest as her sister Holly, and Carrie Fisher as their friend April set a table, chatting about the other guests in *Hannah and Her Sisters*.

6.100   In *Winchester 73*, Jimmy Stewart's mild manner occasionally erupts into explosions of anger, revealing him as on the brink of psychosis.

6.101   The exaggerated smiles and gestures in *Trouble in Paradise* are amusing because we know that each woman is trying to deceive the other.

6.102   Nikolai Cherkasov's dramatically raised arm and thrown-back head are appropriate to the heightened style of *Ivan the Terrible*.

possibilities of very muted performances. Compared to normal practice, highly re-strained acting can seem quite stylized. Robert Bresson is noted for such restrained performances. Using nonprofessional actors and drilling them in the details of the characters' physical actions, Bresson makes his actors quite inexpressive by con-ventional standards **(6.103, 6.104).** Although these performances often upset our expectations, we soon realize that such restraint focuses our attention on details of action we never notice in most movies.

Acting in the Context of Other Techniques   By examining how an actor's perfor-mance functions in the context of the overall film, we can also notice how acting cooperates with other film techniques. For instance, the actor is always a graphic element in the film, but some films underline this fact. In *The Cabinet of Dr. Cali-gari,* Conrad Veidt's dancelike portrayal of the somnambulist Cesare makes him blend in with the graphic elements of the setting **(6.105).** As we shall see in our examination of the history of film styles, the graphic design of this scene in *Cali-gari* typifies the systematic distortion characteristic of German Expressionism.

In *Breathless,* director Jean-Luc Godard juxtaposes Jean Seberg's face with a print of a Renoir painting **(6.106).** We might think that Seberg is giving a wooden

6.103   As the heroine of *Au Hasard Balthasar,* Anna Wiazemsky looks without expression at her would-be seducer, who wants her to get in his car . . .

6.104   . . . and glances downward, still without registering her thoughts, before getting into the car.

6.105   In *The Cabinet of Dr. Caligari,* Cesare's body echoes the tilted tree trunks, his arms and hands their branches and leaves.

6.106   Jean Seberg in *Breathless:* An inexpressive performance or an enigmatic one?

performance, for she simply poses in the frame and turns her head. Indeed, her acting in the entire film may seem flat and inexpressive. Yet her face and general demeanor are visually appropriate for her role, a capricious American woman unfathomable to her Parisian boyfriend.

The context of a performance may also be shaped by the technique of film editing. Sometimes film acting is denigrated because its practitioners do not have to sustain a performance. In the theater, the actor must be able to give a single, often lengthy, presentation of a character. But a film, because it is shot over a period of time, breaks that performance up into bits. This can work to the filmmaker's advantage, since these bits can be selected and combined to build up a performance in ways that could never be accomplished on the stage. Most simply, if a scene has been filmed in several shots, with alternate takes of each shot, the editor may select the best gestures and expressions and create a composite performance better than any one sustained performance could be. Through the addition of sound and the combination with other shots, the performance can be built up still further. The director may simply tell an actor to widen his or her eyes and stare offscreen. If the next shot shows a hand with a gun, we are likely to think the actor is depicting fear. As we will see in more detail in Chapter 8, editing plays a key role in shaping a performance.

Camera techniques also create a controlling context for acting. Film acting, as most viewers know, differs from theatrical acting. At first glance, that suggests that cinema always call for more underplaying, since the camera can closely approach the actor. But actually cinema calls for a stronger interplay between restraint and emphasis.

In a theater, we are usually at a considerable distance from the actor on the stage. We certainly can never get as close to the theater actor as the camera can put us in a film. In watching a film, however, we are not necessarily seeing close views of the actor at every moment. The camera can be at *any* distance from the figure. Filmed from very far away, the actor is a dot on the screen—much tinier than an actor on stage seen from the back of the balcony. Filmed from very close, the actor's tiniest eye movement may be revealed.

Thus the film actor must behave differently than the stage actor does, but not always by being more restrained. Rather, she or he must be able to *adjust to each type of camera distance.* If the actor is far from the camera, he or she will have to gesture broadly or move around to be seen as acting at all. But if the camera and actor are inches apart, a twitch of a mouth muscle will come across clearly. Between these extremes, there is a whole range of adjustments to be made.

Basically, a scene can concentrate on either the actor's facial expression or on pantomimic gestures of the body. Clearly, the closer the actor is to the camera, the more the facial expression will be visible and the more important it will be (although the filmmaker may choose to concentrate on another part of the body, excluding the face and emphasizing gesture). But if the actor is far away from the camera, or turned to conceal the face, his or her gestures become the center of the performance.

Thus both the staging of the action and the camera's distance from it determine how we will see the actors' performances. Many shots in Bernardo Bertolucci's *The Spider's Stratagem* show the two main characters from a distance, so that their manner of walking constitutes the actors' performances in the scene **(6.107).** In conversation scenes, however, we see their faces clearly, as in **6.108.**

Turning back to some earlier examples, we see that in 6.6 the actors are placed at either side of the garden, far back from the camera. The actors are so distant in 6.11 that we see each one only as part of a moving crowd. See 6.8, 6.27, 6.35, 6.83,

"You can ask a bear to do something like, let's say, 'Stand up,' and the bear stands up. But you cannot say to a bear, 'Look astonished.' So you have him standing up, but then you have to astonish him. I would bang two saucepans, or get a chicken from a cage, then shake it so it squawked, and the bear would think, 'What was that?' and 'click' I'd have that expression."

— Jean-Jacques Annaud, director,
The Bear

6.107   In this long shot from *The Spider's Strategem,* the stiff, upright way in which the heroine holds her parasol is one of the main facets of the actress's performance . . .

6.108   . . . while in a conversation scene we can see details of her eye and lip movements.

6.109   A cat "acting" in *Aliens.*

6.101 and 6.105 for shots in which bodily behavior rather than facial expression forms the basis for the acting. Contrast these with 6.14, 6.37, 6.61, 6.63, 6.66, and 6.106, where the faces are close enough for small changes to be visible. A performance typically combines facial expression with bodily gesture, as is evident in 6.108; see also 6.13, 6.59, 6.84, 6.98, 6.100, and 6.101. In 6.53, small gestures become crucial.

Such factors of context are particularly important when the performers are not actors, or even human beings. Framing, editing, and other film techniques can make trained animals give appropriate performances. Jonesy, the cat in *Aliens,* seems threatening because his hissing movement has been emphasized by lighting, framing, editing, and the sound track **(6.109).** In animated films, the filmmaker's manipulation must go further, as in Ladislav Starevich's *The Mascot.* There a conversation between a devil and a thief includes subtle facial expressions and gestures, all created through the frame-by-frame manipulation of puppets (5.76).

As with every element of a film, acting offers an unlimited range of distinct possibilities. It cannot be judged on a universal scale that is separate from the concrete context of the entire film's form.

PUTTING IT ALL TOGETHER: MISE-EN-SCENE IN SPACE AND TIME

Setting, costume, lighting, and staging—these are the components of mise-en-scene. Yet seldom does one element appear in isolation. Each usually combines with others to create a specific system in every film. The general formal principles of unity, disunity, similarity, difference, and development will guide us in analyzing how specific elements of mise-en-scene can function together. What are some ways in which mise-en-scene affects our attention? What pulls our eye to a portion of the frame at a given moment?

Most basically, our visual system is attuned to perceiving *change,* both in time and space. Our eyes and brains are better suited for noticing differences than for concentrating on uniform, prolonged stimuli. Thus aspects of mise-en-scene will attract our attention by means of changes in light, shape, movement, and other aspects of the image.

Moreover, looking is purposeful; what we look *at* is guided by our assumptions and expectations about what to look *for*. These, in turn, are based on our previous experiences of artworks and of the real world. In viewing a film image, we frame expectations on the basis of many factors.

One general factor is the total organization of the film's form. In a narrative film, characters and their actions offer strong cues. If a shot shows a crowd, we will tend to scan it looking for a character we recognize from earlier scenes. In **6.110,** although there are several people in the foreground of this shot from *Tootsie,* we will likely notice Julie (Jessica Lange) and Dorothy Michaels (Dustin Hoffman) quickly, since they are our main characters. Similarly, we will notice Les, seen here for the first time, because he and Dorothy are exchanging smiles. Similarly, sound can become an important factor controlling our attention. As we shall see in Chapter 9, sound can draw attention to areas of the image in various ways. Written language can also shape the viewer's expectations, as when an intertitle cues us what to look for in the next shot. In what follows, we shall concentrate on another source of cues: the elements and patterns in the mise-en-scene itself. Mise-en-scene contains a host of purely spatial and temporal factors to guide our expectations and hence shape our viewing of the image.

6.110   Narrative expectations guide our eye to the main characters in *Tootsie*.

Space

We already know that cinema is involved with different sorts of space. The image projected on a screen is flat, of course, and it displays a composition within a frame, just as a still photograph or a painting would. The arrangement of the mise-en-scene creates the composition of the *screen space*. That two-dimensional composition consists of the organization of shapes, textures, and patterns of light and dark. In most films, though, the composition also represents a *three-dimensional space* in which the action occurs. Since the image projected on the screen is flat, the mise-en-scene must give the audience cues that will enable us to infer the three-dimensionality of the scene. The filmmaker uses mise-en-scene to guide our attention across the screen, shaping our sense of the space that is represented and emphasizing certain parts of it.

In cinema, our vision is attuned to changes of several kinds: *movement, color differences, balance of distinct components,* and *variations in size.* Our sensitivity to these changes allows the filmmaker to direct our notice across the two-dimensional space of the frame.

"The audience is only going to look at the most overriding thing in the frame. You must take charge of and direct their attention. It's also the principle of magic: What is the single important thing? Make it easy for them to see it, and you're doing your job."

— David Mamet, director

Almost invariably, a *moving* item draws our attention more quickly than does a static item. We are sensitive to even the slightest activity within the frame. Normally, for instance, we ignore the movement of scratches and dust on a film. But in David Rimmer's *Watching for the Queen,* in which the first image is an absolutely static photograph **(6.111),** the jumping bits of dust on the film draw our attention.

In **6.112,** from Yasujiro Ozu's *Record of a Tenement Gentleman*, many items compete for our attention. But the moment that a scrap of newspaper flaps, it immediately attracts the eye because it is the only motion in the frame. When several moving elements appear on the screen, as in a ballroom dance, we are likely to shift our attention among them, according to other cues or depending on our expectations about which one is most salient to the narrative action. In **6.113,** from John Ford's *Young Mr. Lincoln,* Lincoln is moving much less than the dancers we see in front of him. Yet he is framed centrally, he is the major character, and the dancers pass rapidly through the frame. As a result, we are likely to concentrate on his gestures and facial expressions, however slight they might be compared to the energetic action in the foreground.

The filmmaker, like the painter, can also exploit the principle of *color contrast* to shape our sense of screen space. For instance, bright colors set against a more subdued background are likely to draw the eye. Jiří Menzel exploits this principle in *Larks on a String* **(6.114).** Another pertinent principle is that when lightness values are equal, warm colors in the red-orange-yellow range tend to attract attention, while cool colors like purple and green are less prominent. In Yilmaz Güney's *Yol,* for example, the setting and the characters' outfits are already quite warm in hue,

6.111 *Watching for the Queen* emphasizes scratches and dust.

6.112 A tiny movement in *Record of a Tenement Gentleman.*

6.113 Emphasizing a background figure in *Young Mr. Lincoln.*

6.114 In *Larks on a String,* the junkyard setting provides earthy grays and blacks against which the characters' lighter clothes stand out sharply.

6.115 Warm colors guide the eye in *Yol.*

6.116 *A* uses fine-point black and white before enlivening its absurd comedy with a brief appearance of pastel flowers.

but the hot pink vest of the man in the central middle ground helps make him the primary object of attention **(6.115).**

Sometimes the filmmaker will treat color design in terms of what painters call a *limited palette.* This involves a few noncontrasting colors, perhaps along with white, browns, grays, and black. An extreme example of a limited palette is Jan Lenica's animated film *A* **(6.116).** The limited palette allows the viewer to make finer distinctions of intensity or saturation in the composition. Our earlier example from Fellini's *Casanova* (6.40) uses various shades of red. A limited palette drawing on the cooler end of the spectrum is seen in Peter Greenaway's *The Draughtsman's Contract* **(6.117).**

An extreme use of the limited palette principle is sometimes called **monochromatic** color design. Here the filmmaker emphasizes a single color, varied only in purity or lightness. We have already seen an example of monochromatic mise-en-scene in the white-on-white scene of *THX 1138* (6.41). A more common usage can be found in 1970s and 1980s action films, which often envelop battle sequences in a silver or blue-gray haze. **(6.118).** In a monochromatic design, even the slightest fleck of a contrasting color will catch the viewer's attention. The color design of *Aliens* is dominated by metallic tones, so even a dingy yellow can mark the stiltlike loader as an important prop within the narrative **(6.119).**

Black-and-white films also rely on our sensitivity to changes in tonalities. The colors of setting, costumes, lighting, and figures register on the film in shades of black, white, and gray. The differences among these provide cues for us as we scan the image. Usually lighter shapes leap to our notice while darker ones recede **(6.120).** All things being equal, if several light areas compete in the composition (6.98, 6.99), we will tend to shift our attention back and forth. Dark shapes may become prominent, however, if they are clearly defined and placed against a light background. In 6.105, the actor and the trees draw our eyes instantly because they stand out so starkly from the lighter area.

Compositional *balance* refers to the extent to which the areas of screen space have equally distributed masses and points of interest. Filmmakers often assume that the spectator will concentrate more on the upper half of the frame (probably because in most shots that is where characters' faces are placed). Thus because of viewers' prior expectations, the upper half needs less filling up than the lower.

Since the film shot is composed within a horizontal rectangle, the director usually takes care to balance the left and right halves. The extreme type of such balancing is bilateral symmetry. In the wedding banquet of *Ivan the Terrible,*

6.117 *The Draughtsman's Contract* uses a limited palette of green, black, and white.

6.118 A typical action-film color scheme in *A Better Tomorrow III.*

6.119 *Aliens* uses warm colors like yellow sparingly.

6.120 In Pudovkin's *Mother,* the spectator concentrates on the man's face rather than on the darkness surrounding it.

Eisenstein stages the action symmetrically **(6.121).** A more grandiose example is the battle scene of Chen Kaige's *Life on a String* **(6.122).**

More common than such near-perfect symmetry is a loose balancing of the shot's left and right regions. The simplest way to achieve compositional balance is to center the frame on the human body. Filmmakers often place a single figure at the center of the frame and minimize distracting elements at the sides, as in **6.123.** Many of our earlier illustrations display this sort of balance (for example, 6.14, 6.55, 6.63, 6.64, and 6.68). Other shots may balance two or more elements, encouraging our eye to move back and forth, as in **6.124.** (For other examples, see

6.121 Symmetrical mise-en-scene in *Ivan the Terrible.*

6.122 A limited palette emphasizes this symmetrical composition in *Life on a String.*

6.123 *Mars Attacks!:* Centering a single character . . .

6.124 . . . and balancing two.

6.125   This composition from *Bicycle Thieves* emphasizes the father's new job by massing most of the figures on the right.

6.126   In *Il Grido,* instead of balancing the couple, the composition centers the man. If there were no tree in the frame, the shot would still be somewhat weighted to the right, but the unexpected vertical of the trunk makes that side even heavier.

6.127   Shading and shape suggest volume in Dreyer's *La Passion de Jeanne d'Arc.*

6.35, 6.66, 6.70, 6.101, and 6.106.) The balance can be roughly equal, as in 6.101, or more unequal. In 6.83, we will most likely pick out the two standing men first, since they are at the center, and then we notice the crouching villagers at the far left. These examples suggest that compositional balance helps shape our expectations about where significant action will be located on the screen.

Balanced composition is the norm, but unbalanced shots can also create strong effects. A mild example comes from Vittorio de Sica's *Bicycle Thieves* (**6.125**). A bolder example occurs in Michelangelo Antonioni's *Il Grido* (**6.126**). In Chapter 8, we will see how editing can create balance between two relatively unbalanced compositions.

Our effort to monitor differences also affects our sense of onscreen *size.* Looking at a static shot, we will register the larger shapes first and then discriminate smaller ones. In 6.11, the huge pillars and statues of the Babylon set contribute more to our sense of the overall composition than do either the individual actors or the light and dark patches on the steps near the bottom. In 6.59 we are likely to look first at the actor's face and the paper he holds, rather than at the small white labels on the file drawers—even though the labels are just as bright and in the same centered area of the screen. Nevertheless, movement, color, or balance can override size as a compositional cue and can draw our attention quickly to very small areas of the screen. For example, if one of the file-drawer labels suddenly fluttered to the floor, we would almost certainly notice it.

Such compositional qualities guide our attention across the flat screen space, but they do more as well. In virtually all films, mise-en-scene functions to suggest a three-dimensional space, abstract or representational, real or fictitious.

The factors in the image that help create such a sense of space are broadly called *depth cues.* There is no real space extending behind the screen, of course, but depth cues prompt us to imagine that space, to construct a three-dimensional world in which the film's action takes place. Again, we develop our understanding of depth cues from our experience of space in the real world and from conventions of space in such arts as painting and theater. In cinema, depth cues are largely provided by lighting, setting, costumes, and staging.

The depth cues suggest that a space has both *volume* and several distinct *planes.* When we speak of an object as having volume, we mean that it is solid and occupies a three-dimensional area. A film suggests volume by shape, shading, and movement. In 6.106 and **6.127** (the latter from Dreyer's *La Passion de Jeanne d'Arc*), we do not think of the actors' faces as flat cutouts, like paper dolls. The shapes of those heads and shoulders suggest solid people. The attached shadows on the faces suggest the curves and recesses of the actors' features and give a modeling effect. We assume that if the actor in 6.106 turned her head, we would see a profile. Thus we use our knowledge of objects in the world to discern volume in filmic space.

An abstract film, because it can use shapes that are not everyday objects, can create compositions without a sense of volume. The shapes in **6.128** give us no depth cues for volume—they are unshaded, do not have a recognizable shape, and do not move in such a way as to reveal new views that suggest roundness.

Depth cues also pick out *planes* within the image. Planes are the layers of space occupied by persons or objects. Planes are described according to how close or far away from the camera they are: foreground, middle ground, background.

Only a completely blank screen has a single plane. Whenever a shape—even an abstract one—appears, we will perceive it as being in front of a background. In 6.128, the four red S shapes are actually painted right on the frame surface, as is the lighter, textured area. Yet the textured area seems to lie behind the four shapes.

The space here has only two planes, as in an abstract painting. This example suggests that one of the most basic depth cues is **overlap** of edges. The curling S shapes have edges which overlap the background plane, block our vision of it, and thus seem to be closer to us. In 6.125, the people overlap the ladders, so we understand that they are closer to the camera than the ladders are, while in 6.126, the tree overlaps the figure of the woman.

Through overlap a great many planes can be defined. In 6.57, from Jean-Luc Godard's *La Chinoise,* three distinct planes are displayed: the background of fashion cutouts, the woman's face that overlaps that background, and her hand, which overlaps her lower face. In the three-point lighting approach, edge-lighting accentuates the overlap of planes by emphasizing the contour of the object, thus sharply distinguishing it from the background. (See again 6.61, 6.66, and 6.68.)

Color differences also create overlapping planes. Because cool or pale colors tend to recede, filmmakers commonly use them for background planes such as setting. Similarly, because warm or saturated colors tend to come forward, such hues are often employed for costumes or other foreground elements, as in Sarah Maldoror's *Sambizanga* **(6.129).** (See also 6.31, 6.36, and 6.119.)

Animated films can achieve brighter and more saturated color than most live-action filming, so depth effects can be correspondingly more vivid. In Chuck Jones's *One Froggy Evening* **(6.130),** the luminous yellow of the umbrella and the frog's brilliant green skin make him stand out against the darker red of the curtain and the earth tones of the stage floor. In **6.131,** from *Bambi,* spatial layers are defined by contrasting pastels and darker hues: light yellow in the foreground, then pure black and white for the skunk, then milder pastels for the flowers behind him, and finally darker green and black for the backgrounds.

Because of the eye's sensitivity to differences, even quite muted color contrasts can suggest three-dimensional space. In *L'Argent* (6.20–6.22) Bresson uses a limited, cool palette and relatively flat lighting. Yet the compositions pick out several planes by means of overlapping slightly different masses of black, tan, and light blue. Our shot from *Casanova* (6.40) articulates planes by means of slightly differing shades of red. In *The Draughtsman's Contract* (6.117), much of our sense of distant space is created by strong black verticals and by horizontal strips of various shades of green. Together these colors define distinct layers in this scene.

Another depth-producing factor is suggested in 6.58, from *La Chinoise:* the *movement* of the cigarette smoke in the foreground. In cinema, movement is one of

6.128 A flat composition in Norman McLaren's *Begone, Dull Care.*

6.129 *Sambizanga:* The heroine's dress has very warm and fairly saturated colors, making it stand out distinctly against the pale background.

6.130 Vivid colors emphasize the sense of extreme depth in *One Froggy Evening.*

6.131 *Bambi* uses more muted but distinctly different colors to place the skunk in a bed of flowers.

the most important depth cues, since it strongly suggests both planes and volumes. Note also the *cast shadow* in the background of 6.58, which is another depth cue.

Aerial perspective, or the hazing of more distant planes, is yet another depth cue. Typically, our visual system assumes that sharper outlines, clearer textures, and purer colors belong to foreground elements. In landscape shots, the blurring and graying of distant planes can be caused by actual atmospheric haze, as in Güney's *The Wall* (**6.132**). Even when such haze is a minor factor, our vision typically assigns strong color contrasts to the foreground, as in the *Sambizanga* shot (6.129). In addition, very often lighting is manipulated in conjunction with lens focus to blur the background planes (**6.133**).

In **6.134,** the mise-en-scene provides several depth cues: overlap of edges, cast shadows, and **size diminution.** That is, figures and objects farther away from us are seen to get proportionally smaller; the smaller the figure appears, the farther away we believe it to be. This reinforces our sense of there being a deep space with considerable distances between the various planes.

The same illustration dramatically displays *linear perspective.* We will consider perspective relations in more detail in the next chapter, since they derive as much from properties of the camera lens as they do from mise-en-scene. For now, we can simply note that a strong impression of depth emerges when parallel lines converge at a distant vanishing point. *Off-center* linear perspective is illustrated in

6.132 Fog emphasizes the distance between the foreground and background trees in *The Wall.*

6.133 In Michael Curtiz's *The Charge of the Light Brigade,* aerial perspective is artificially created through diffused lighting of the background and a lack of clear focus beyond the foreground character.

6.134 Depth cues in Straub and Huillet's *The Chronicle of Anna Magdalena Bach.*

6.134; note that the vanishing point is not the geometrical center. *Central* perspective is exemplified in 6.117, from *The Draughtsman's Contract.*

In many of the examples already given, you may have noticed that mise-en-scene serves not simply to direct our attention to foreground elements but rather to create a dynamic relation between foreground and background. In 6.57 and 6.58, for instance, Godard keeps our attention on the whole composition by using prominent backgrounds. In 6.57, the pictures behind the actress's head lead us to scan the various small shapes quickly, while the bright red wall in 6.58 comes forward strongly, making us aware of the background even if we concentrate on the actor's face.

The last two instances both exemplify **shallow-space** compositions. In such shots, the mise-en-scene suggests comparatively little depth, and the closest and most distant planes seem only slightly separated. The opposite tendency is **deep-space** composition, in which a significant distance seems to separate planes. Our earlier example from *Chronicle of Anna Magdalena Bach* (6.134) exemplifies deep-space mise-en-scene. Often a director creates a deep-space composition by making the foreground plane quite large and the background plane quite distant **(6.135)**.

Shallow and deep mise-en-scene are relative. Most compositions present a moderately deep space, falling between the extremes we have just considered. Sometimes a composition will manipulate depth cues to make a space appear deeper or shallower than it really is—creating an optical illusion **(6.136)**.

At this point, you might want to return to shots illustrated earlier in this chapter. You will notice that these images use depth cues of overlap, movement, cast shadows, aerial perspective, size diminution, and linear perspective to create distinctive foreground/background relations.

The fact that our vision is sensitive to differences allows filmmakers to guide our understanding of the mise-en-scene. All the cues to story space interact with one another, working to emphasize narrative elements, direct our attention, and set up dynamic relations among areas of screen space. We can see this interaction clearly in two shots from Carl Dreyer's *Day of Wrath.*

In the first shot, the heroine Anne is standing before a grillwork panel **(6.137)**. She is not speaking, but since she is a major character in the film, the narrative already directs us to her. Setting, lighting, costume, and figure expression create

6.135 Several scenes of Wajda's *Ashes and Diamonds* create large foreground and distant background planes.

6.136 Leo Carax flattens space in *Boy Meets Girl* by making the actor in the foreground seem to blend into the advertisement on the wall behind.

6.137 *Day of Wrath:* Concentrating on a single figure.

6.138 *Day of Wrath:* Dividing attention between foreground and background figures.

6.139 A simple shot from *An Autumn Afternoon* employs several depth cues.

6.140 The striped smokestacks establish a color motif for *An Autumn Afternoon.*

pictorial cues that confirm our expectations. The setting yields a screen pattern of horizontal and vertical lines that intersect in the delicate curves of Anne's face and shoulders. The lighting yields a patch of brightness on the right half of the frame and a patch of darkness on the left, creating pictorial balance. Anne is the meeting point of these two areas. Her face becomes modeled by the relatively strong key lighting from the right, a little top lighting on her hair, and relatively little fill light. Coordinated with the lighting in creating the pattern of light and dark is Anne's costume—a black dress punctuated by white collar, a black cap edged with white— that again emphasizes her face.

The shot is comparatively shallow, displaying two major planes with little distance between them. The background sets off the more important element, Anne. The rigid geometrical grid in the rear makes Anne's slightly sad face the most expressive element in the frame, thus encouraging our eye to pause there. In addition, the composition divides the screen space horizontally, with the grid pattern running across the top half and the dark, severe vertical of Anne's dress dominating the lower half. As is common, the upper zone is the stronger because the character's head and shoulders occupy it. Anne's figure is positioned slightly off center, but with her face turned so as to compensate for the vacant area on the right. (Imagine how unbalanced the shot would look if she were turned to face us squarely and the same amount of space were left empty on the right.) Thus compositional balance reinforces the shot's emphasis on Anne's expression. In all, without using motion, Dreyer has channeled our attention by means of lines and shapes, lights and darks, and the foreground and background relations in the mise-en-scene.

In the second example, also from *Day of Wrath,* Dreyer coaxes our attention into a to-and-fro movement (**6.138**). Again, the plot guides us, since the characters and the cart are crucial narrative elements. Sound helps too, since Martin is at the moment explaining to Anne what the cart is used for. But mise-en-scene also plays a role. Size diminution and cast shadows establish basic foreground/background relations, with Anne and Martin on the front plane and the cart of wood in the background. The space is comparatively deep (though the foreground is not as exaggeratedly close as that in *Ashes and Diamonds,* 6.135). The prominence of the couple and the cart is reinforced by line, shape, and lighting contrasts. The figures are defined by hard edges and by dark costumes within the predominantly bright setting. Unlike most shots, this puts the human figures in the lower half of the frame, which gives that zone an unusual importance. The composition thus creates a vertical balance, counterweighting the cart with the couple. This encourages us to glance up and down between the two objects of our attention.

Similar processes are at work in color films. In one shot of Yasujiro Ozu's *An Autumn Afternoon* (**6.139**), our attention is concentrated on the woman in the center foreground. Here many depth cues are at work. Overlap locates the two figures in two foreground planes, setting them against a series of more distant planes. Aerial perspective makes the tree foliage somewhat out of focus. Movement creates depth when the bride lowers her head. Perspective diminution makes the more distant objects smaller. The figure and the bright silver, red, and gold bridal costume stand out strikingly against the muted, cool colors of the background planes. Moreover, the colors bring back a red-and-silver motif that began in the very first shot of the film (**6.140**).

In all these cases, compositional elements and depth cues have functioned to focus our attention on the narrative elements. But this need not always be the case. Bresson's *Lancelot due Lac* uses a limited palette of dark and metallic hues, and warmer colors tend to stand out (**6.141**). Such a distracting use of color becomes a stylistic motif in the film.

Time

So far we have examined some spatial factors that guide our viewing of an image. In addition, both the shot and our viewing of it take place in time.

As we will see in more detail when we consider editing (Chapter 8), the film-maker decides how long the shot will last on the screen. Within the confines of the shot's duration, the director can control the rhythm of time as it unfolds. Although the issue of rhythm in cinema is enormously complex and still not well understood, we can say roughly that it involves, at least, a *beat* or pulse, a pace (what musicians call *tempo*), and a pattern of *accents,* or stronger and weaker beats.

We are most familiar with these factors in the filming of dance. When Fred Astaire or Ann Miller performs, the bodily movements obey strongly patterned rhythms. We should recognize, though, that any movement within the mise-en-scene may involve the same rhythmic components. Movement on the screen can have a distinctive visual beat, such as the flashing of a neon sign or the steady rocking of a ship. Movement can also have a marked pace, such as the acceleration of a car in a chase scene. And visual movement can create distinctive, accented instants as well.

These factors combine to create a sense of the shot's overall rhythm. In **6.142,** from Chantal Akerman's *Jeanne Dielman, 23 quai du Commerce, 1080 Bruxelles,* the protagonist simply prepares a meal. This feminist film emphasizes the daily routine of a Belgian housewife, and many of its shots show small movements carried out slowly. Because there are no competing movements on the screen, her gestures create accented moments. Overall, the film's rhythm concentrates attention on minute variations in her habits.

A far busier shot is **6.143,** from Busby Berkeley's *42nd Street.* This overhead view presents strongly opposed movements. The central and outer rings of dancers circle in one direction, while the second ring turns in a contrary direction. The dancers also swing strips of shiny cloth back and forth. The result is a partially abstract composition, emphasized by a steady beat, rapid tempo, and strong accents—all appropriate to the shot's placement as part of a musical number.

The dancers in *42nd Street* are synchronized to a considerable degree, but **6.144,** from Tati's *Play Time,* contains movements of differing speeds, with different visual

6.141 In *Lancelot du Lac,* a group of conversing knights is centered and balanced in the foreground planes, yet a pinkish-purple saddle blanket on a passing horse momentarily draws our eyes away from the action.

6.142 Slow, quiet movement in *Jeanne Dielman, 23 quai du Commerce, 1080 Bruxelles.*

6.143   Synchronized rhythm in *42nd Street.*

6.144   Competing rhythms of movement in a busy shot from *Play Time.*

6.145   In one scene of *La Terra Trema,* Luchino Visconti's deep-space composition prepares us for activity in the left foreground . . .

6.146   . . . by having women in the family come forward to stare at the picture hanging there.

accents. Moreover, they occur on different planes and follow contrasting trajectories. These diverse movements accord with Tati's tendency to cram his compositions with gags that compete for our attention.

As we have already seen, we scan any film frame for information. This scanning brings time sharply into play. Only a very short shot forces us to try to take in the image all at once. In most shots we get an initial overall impression that creates formal expectations. These expectations are quickly modified as our eye roams around the frame.

Once again, our scanning of the shot is strongly affected by the presence of movement. A static composition, such as our first shot from *Day of Wrath* (6.137), may keep pulling our attention back to a single element (here, Anne's face). In contrast, a composition emphasizing movement becomes more time-bound because our glance may be directed from place to place by various speeds, directions, and rhythms of movements. In the second image from *Day of Wrath* (6.138) Anne and Martin are turned from us (so that expression and gesture are minimized), and they are standing still. Thus the single movement in the frame—the cart—catches our attention. But when Martin speaks and turns, we look back at the couple, then back at the cart, and so on, in a shuttling, dynamic shift of attention. In such ways mise-en-scene can control not only *what* we look at but also *when* we look at it.

Our time-bound process of scanning involves not only looking to and fro across the screen but also, in a sense, looking into its depths. A deep-space composition will often use background events to create expectations about what is about to happen in the foreground. "Composing in depth isn't simply a matter of pictorial richness," British director Alexander Mackendrick has remarked. "It has value in the narrative of the action, the pacing of the scene. Within the same frame, the director can organize the action so that preparation for what will happen next is seen in the background of what is happening now." In fact, movement can occur moving forward from depth **(6.145, 6.146)** or away into the distance within the shot **(6.147, 6.148)**.

Another fairly straightforward way to guide the viewer's attention over time is to adjust *frontality* of figure placement. All other things being equal, the viewer expects that more story information will come from a character's face than from a character's back. The viewer's attention will thus usually pass over figures that are turned away and fasten on figures that are positioned frontally. We have already seen this cue at work in our second still from *Day of Wrath* (6.138), as well as in our *Vampires* examples (6.15, 6.16, p. 181). In Hou Hsiao-hsien's *City of Sadness,* depth staging favors the woman coming to visit the hospital by turning all the other characters away from the viewer **(6.149).** This shifts our attention to the most frontally

6.147   At the height of the drama in *Naniwa Elegy,* Kenji Mizoguchi has the heroine move away from us, into depth . . .

6.148   . . . and as she passes through patches of distant darkness, our curiosity about her emotional state intensifies.

6.149   Although she is further from the camera, the woman visiting the hospital in *City of Sadness* draws our eye partly because she is the only one facing front.

6.150   In a conversation in *The Bad and the Beautiful,* our attention fastens on the studio executive on the right because the other two characters are turned away from us . . .

6.152   A striking instance of frontality in *L'Avventura:* the characters alternate . . .

6.151   . . . but when the producer turns to the camera, his centered position and frontal posture emphasize him.

6.153   . . . turning their backs on the camera.

positioned characters, even though they are the most distant. In our *Naniwa Elegy* examples (6.147, 6.148), both figures are turned from us, so other cues, such as the centrality and movement, drive our attention to the woman. The frontality cue can shift the viewer's attention according to what the filmmaker wants to stress. Like movements through a lighted volume and the filling of empty zones, the frontality cue shows mise-en-scene's indebtedness to theatrical staging **(6.150–6.153)**.

As a set of techniques, mise-en-scene helps compose the film shot in space and time. Setting, lighting, costume, and staging interact to create patterns of movement, of color and depth, line and shape, light and dark. These patterns define and develop the space of the story world and emphasize salient story information. The director's use of mise-en-scene not only guides our attention from moment to moment but also helps create the overall form of the film.

NARRATIVE FUNCTIONS OF MISE-EN-SCENE: *OUR HOSPITALITY*

Up to now we have looked at the general stylistic possibilities offered by mise-en-scene. Its potential for creating graphic compositions is vital to the abstract film and can be useful as well to the other types of formal organization. Fictional, documentary, experimental, and animated films all can use mise-en-scene to guide our attention, our understanding, and our inferences about what we see. The rest of this chapter considers how mise-en-scene can function in a fictional narrative film.

Mise-en-scene functions not only in isolated moments, but also in relation to the narrative organization of the entire film. *Our Hospitality,* like most of Buster Keaton's films, exemplifies how mise-en-scene can economically advance the narrative and create a pattern of motifs. Since the film is a comedy, the mise-en-scene also creates gags. *Our Hospitality,* then, exemplifies what we will find in our study of every film technique: An individual element almost always has *several* functions, not just one.

Consider, for example, how the settings function within the plot of *Our Hospitality.* For one thing, they help divide the film into scenes and to contrast those scenes. The film begins with a prologue showing how the feud between the McKays and the Canfields results in the deaths of the young Canfield and the husband of the McKay family. We see the McKays living in a shack and are left in suspense about the fate of the baby, Willie. Willie's mother flees with her son from their Southern home to the North (action narrated to us mainly by an intertitle).

The plot skips over several years to begin the main action, with the grown-up Willie living in New York. There are a number of gags concerning early 19th-century life in the metropolis, contrasting sharply with the prologue scene. We are led to wonder how this locale will relate to the Southern scenes, and soon Willie receives word that he has inherited his parents' home in the South. A series of amusing short scenes follows as he takes a primitive train back to his birthplace. During these scenes Keaton uses real locales, but by laying out the railroad tracks in different ways, he exploits the landscapes for surprising and unusual comic effects we shall examine shortly.

The rest of the film deals with Willie's movements in and around the Southern town. On the day of his arrival he wanders around and gets into a number of comic situations. That night he stays in the Canfield house itself. Finally, an extended chase occurs the next day, moving through the countryside and back to the Canfield house for the settling of the feud. Thus the action depends heavily on shifts of setting that establish Willie's two journeys, as baby and as man, and later his wanderings to escape his enemies' pursuit. The narration is relatively unrestricted once Willie reaches the South, shifting between him and members of the Canfield family. We usually know more about where they are than Willie does,

"The most striking aspect of the Keaton pictures was the enormous amount of trouble lavished over every gag. Production value on such a scale requires more than a simple desire to make people laugh. It is not surprising that Keaton's childhood aim was to be a civil engineer."

— Kevin Brownlow, film historian

and the narrative generates suspense by showing them coming toward the places where Willie is hiding.

Specific settings fulfill distinct narrative functions. The McKay estate, which Willie envisions as a mansion, turns out to be a tumbledown shack. The McKay house is contrasted with the Canfield's palatial plantation home. In narrative terms the Canfield home gains even more functional importance when the Canfield father forbids his sons to kill Willie on the premises: "Our code of honor forbids us to shoot him while he is a guest in our house." (Once Willie overhears this, he determines *never* to leave.) Ironically the home of Willie's enemies becomes the only safe spot in town, and many scenes are organized around the Canfield brothers' attempts to lure Willie outside. At the end of the film another setting takes on significance: the landscape of meadows, mountains, river banks, rapids, and waterfalls across which the Canfields pursue Willie. Finally, the feud ends back in the Canfield house itself, with Willie now welcomed as the daughter's husband. The pattern of development is clear: from the opening shootout at the McKay house that breaks up Willie's home to the final scene in the Canfield house with Willie becoming part of a new family. In such ways every setting becomes highly motivated by the narrative's system of causes and effects, parallels and contrasts, and overall development.

The same narrative motivation marks the film's use of costume. Willie is characterized as a city boy through his dandified suit, whereas the Southern gentility of the elder Canfield is represented through his white planter's suit. Props become important here: Willie's suitcase and umbrella succinctly summarize his role as visitor and wanderer, and the Canfields' ever-present pistols remind us of their goals of continuing the feud. Note also that a change of costume (Willie's disguising himself as a woman) enables him to escape from the Canfield household. At the end, the putting aside of the various guns by the characters signals the end of the feud.

Like setting, lighting in *Our Hospitality* has both general and specific functions. The film alternates scenes in darkness with scenes in daylight. The feuding in the prologue takes place at night; Willie's trip South and wanderings through the town occur in daylight; that night Willie comes to dinner at the Canfield's and stays as a guest; next day, the Canfields pursue him; and the film ends that night with the marriage of Willie and the Canfield daughter. More specifically, the bulk of the film is evenly lit in the three-point method. Yet the somber action of the prologue takes place in hard sidelighting (**6.154, 6.155**). Later, the murder scene is played

6.154 *Our Hospitality:* When the elder McKay flings off his hat to douse the lamp, the illumination changes from a soft blend of key, fill, and backlight . . .

6.155 . . . to a stark key light from the fireplace.

6.156 Within the same frame, we see both cause—the engineer's cheerful ignorance, made visible by frontality—and effect—the runaway disconnected cars.

6.157 The Canfield boys in the foreground make plans to shoot Willie, who overhears them in the background.

6.158 While Willie ambles along unsuspectingly in the background, one Canfield waits in the foreground to ambush him.

out in flashes of light—lightning, gunfire—that fitfully punctuate the overall darkness. Because this sporadic lighting hides part of the action from us, it helps build suspense. The gunshots themselves are seen only as flashes in the darkness, and we must wait to learn the outcome—the deaths of both opponents—until the next flash of lightning.

Most economically of all, virtually every bit of the acting functions to support and advance the cause–effect chain of the narrative. The way Canfield sips and savors his julep establishes his Southern ways; his Southern hospitality in turn will not allow him to shoot a guest in his house. Similarly, Willie's every move expresses his diffidence or resourcefulness.

Even more concise is the way the film uses staging in depth to present two narrative events simultaneously. While the engineer drives the locomotive, the other cars pass him on a parallel track **(6.156)**. In other shots, Willie's awareness or ignorance of a situation is displayed through planes of depth **(6.157, 6.158).** Thanks to such spatial arrangements, Keaton is able to pack together two story events, resulting in a tight narrative construction and in a relatively unrestricted narration. In 6.157, we know what Willie does and we expect that he will probably flee now that he understands the sons' plans. But in 6.158, we are aware, as Willie is not, that danger lurks around the corner; suspense results, as we wonder whether the Canfield boys' ambush will succeed.

All of these devices for narrative economy considerably unify the film, but some other elements of mise-en-scene function as specific motifs. For one thing, there is the repeated squabble between the anonymous husband and wife. On his way to his estate, Willie passes a husband throttling his wife. Willie intervenes to protect her; the wife proceeds to thrash Willie for butting in. On Willie's way back, he passes the same couple, still fighting, but studiously avoids them. Nevertheless, the wife aims a kick at him as he passes. The mere repetition of the motif strengthens the film's narrative unity, but it functions thematically, too, as another joke on the contradictions surrounding the idea of hospitality.

Other motifs recur. Willie's first hat is too tall to wear in a jouncing railway coach. (When it gets crushed, he trades it for the flat Keaton trademark hat.) Willie's second hat serves to distract the Canfields when Willie coaxes his dog to fetch it. There is also a pronounced water motif in the film. Water as rain conceals from us the murders in the prologue and later saves Willie from leaving the Canfield home after dinner ("It would be the death of anyone to go out on a night like this!"). Water as a river functions significantly in the final chase. And water as a waterfall appears soon after Willie's arrival in the South **(6.159)**. This waterfall initially protects Willie by hiding him **(6.160, 6.161)** but later threatens both him and the Canfield daughters as they are nearly swept over it (6.167).

Two specific motifs of setting help unify the narrative. First there is the recurrence of an embroidered sampler hanging on the Canfield wall: "Love Thy Neighbor." It appears initially in the prologue of the film, when seeing it motivates Canfield's attempt to stop the feud. It then plays a significant role in linking the ending back to the beginning. The sampler reappears at the end when Canfield, enraged that Willie has married his daughter, glances at the wall, reads the inscription, and resolves to halt the years of feuding. His change in attitude is motivated by the earlier appearance of the motif.

The film also uses gun racks as a motif. In the prologue each feuder goes to his mantelpiece to get his pistol. Later, when Willie arrives in town, the Canfields hurry to their gun rack and begin to load their pistols. Near the end of the film, when the Canfields return home after failing to find Willie, one of the sons notices that the gun rack is now empty. And, in the final shot, when the Canfields accept the marriage and lay down their arms, Willie produces from all over his person a staggering assortment of pistols taken as a precaution from the Canfields' own supply. Thus mise-en-scene motifs unify the film through their repetition, variation, and development.

Yet *Our Hospitality* is more than a film whose narrative system relates economically to patterns of mise-en-scene. It is a comedy, and one of the funniest. We should not be surprised to find, then, that Keaton uses mise-en-scene for gags. Indeed, so unified is the film that most of the elements that create narrative economy also function to yield comic effects.

The mise-en-scene bristles with many individually comic elements. Settings are exploited for amusement—the ramshackle McKay estate, the Broadway of 1830, the specially cut train tunnel that just fits the old-fashioned train and its smokestack **(6.162)**. Costume gags also stand out. Willie's disguise as a woman is exposed by a gap in the rear of his skirt; later, Willie puts the same costume on a horse to distract the Canfields. Most strongly, comedy arises from the behavior of the figures. The railroad engineer's high kick unexpectedly swipes off his conductor's hat **(6.163)**. The elder Canfield sharpens his carving knife with ferocious energy, just inches from Willie's head. When Willie lands at the bottom of the river, he stands there looking left and right, his hand shading his eyes, before he realizes where he is. Later, Willie scuds down the river, leaping out of the water like a fish and skidding across the rocks.

Perhaps the only aspect of mise-en-scene that competes with the comic brilliance of the figures' behavior is the film's use of deep space for gags. Many of the shots we have already examined function to create comedy as well: The engineer stands firmly oblivious to the separation of train cars from the engine (see 6.156) just as Willie is unaware that the Canfield boy is lurking murderously in the foreground (6.158).

Even more striking, though, is the deep-space gag that follows the demolition of the dam. The Canfield boys have been searching the town for Willie. In the meantime, Willie sits on a ledge, fishing. As the water bursts from the dam and sweeps over the cliff, it completely engulfs Willie (6.160). At that very instant, the Canfield brothers step into the foreground from either side of the frame, still looking for their victim (6.161). The water's concealment of Willie reduces him to a neutral background for the movement of the Canfields. This sudden eruption of new action into the scene surprises us, rather than generating suspense, since we

6.159 After an explosion demolishes a dam, the water spills over a cliff and creates a waterfall.

6.160 The new waterfall begins to hide Willie as he sits fishing . . .

6.161 . . . and by the time the Canfields rush into the foreground, he is invisible.

6.162   The tunnel cut to fit the old-fashioned train.

6.163   As the engineer, Keaton's father Joe used his famous high kick vaudeville stunt for this gag.

6.164   The motif begins as Willie is jerked into the water.

6.165   Tied to Willie, the Canfield boy falls off the cliff . . .

6.166   . . . and Willie braces himself to be pulled after.

6.167   Willie dangles like a fish on the end of a pole.

were not aware that the Canfield sons were so close by. Here surprise is crucial to the comedy.

However appealing the individual gags are, *Our Hospitality* patterns its comic aspects as strictly as it does its other motifs. The film's journey pattern often arranges a series of gags according to a formal principle of theme and variations. For instance, during the train trip South, a string of gags is based on the idea of people encountering the train. Several people turn out to watch it pass, a tramp rides the rods, and an old man chucks rocks at the engine. Another swift series of gags takes the train tracks themselves as its theme. The variations include a humped track, a donkey blocking the tracks, curled and rippled tracks, and finally no tracks at all.

But the most complex theme-and-variations series can be seen in the motif of "the fish on the line." Soon after Willie arrives in town, he is angling and hauls up a minuscule fish. Shortly afterward, a huge fish yanks him into the water **(6.164).** Later in the film, through a series of mishaps, Willie becomes tied by a rope to one of the Canfield sons. Many gags arise from this umbilical-cord linkage, especially one that results in Canfield's being pulled into the water as Willie was earlier.

Perhaps the single funniest shot in the film occurs when Willie realizes that since the Canfield boy has fallen off the rocks **(6.165),** so must he **(6.166).** But even after Willie gets free of Canfield, the rope remains tied around his waist. So in the film's climax Willie is dangling from a log over the waterfall **(6.167).** Here again, one element fulfills multiple functions. The fish-on-the-line device advances the narrative, becomes a motif unifying the film, and takes its place in a pattern of parallel gags involving variations of Willie on the rope. In such ways *Our Hospitality* becomes an outstanding example of the integration of cinematic mise-en-scene with narrative form.

SUMMARY

The viewer who wants to study mise-en-scene should look for it systematically. Watch, first of all, for how setting, costume, lighting, and the behavior of the figures present themselves in a given film. As a start, try to trace only one sort of element—say, setting or lighting—through a scene.

We should also reflect on the patterning of mise-en-scene elements. How do they function? How do they constitute motifs that weave their ways through the entire film? In addition, we should notice how mise-en-scene is patterned in space and time to attract and guide the viewer's attention through the process of watching the film and to create suspense or surprise.

Finally, we should try to relate the system of mise-en-scene to the large-scale form of the film. Hard-and-fast prejudices about realism are of less value here than an openness to the great variety of mise-en-scene possibilities. Awareness of those possibilities will better help us to determine the functions of mise-en-scene.

NOTES AND QUERIES

On the Origins of Mise-en-Scene

As a concept, mise-en-scene reaches back into the 19th-century theater. For a historical introduction that is relevant to film, see Oscar G. Brockett and Robert R. Findlay, *Century of Innovation* (Englewood Cliffs, N.J.: Prentice-Hall, 1973). More specialized are Brooks McNamara, "The Scenography of Popular Entertainment," *Drama Review* **18**, 1 (March 1974): 16–24; and Martin Meisel, *Realizations: Narrative, Pictorial, and Theatrical Arts in Nineteenth-Century England* (Princeton, N.J.: Princeton University Press, 1983). The standard film works are Nicolas Vardac, *Stage to Screen* (Cambridge, Mass.: Harvard University Press, 1949) and Ben Brewster and Lea Jacobs, *Theatre to Cinema: Stage Pictorialism and the Early Feature Film* (Oxford: Oxford University Press, 1997).

On Realism in Mise-en-Scene

Many film theorists have seen film as a realistic medium par excellence. For such theorists as Siegfried Kracauer, André Bazin, and V. F. Perkins, cinema's power lies in its ability to present a recognizable reality. The realist theorist thus often values authenticity in costume and setting, naturalistic acting, and unstylized lighting. "The primary function of decor," writes V. F. Perkins, "is to provide a believable environment for the action" [*Film as Film* (Baltimore, Md.: Penguin, 1972), p. 94]. André Bazin praises the Italian neorealist films of the 1940s for "faithfulness to everyday life in the scenario, truth to his part in an actor" [*What Is Cinema?* vol. 2 (Berkeley: University of California Press, 1970), p. 25].

Though mise-en-scene is always a product of selection and choice, the realist theorist may value the filmmaker who creates a mise-en-scene that *appears* to be reality. Kracauer suggests that even apparently unrealistic song-and-dance numbers in a musical can seem impromptu [*Theory of Film* (New York: Oxford University Press, 1965)], and Bazin considers a fantasy film such as *The Red Balloon* realistic because here "what is imaginary on the screen has the spatial density of something real" [*What Is Cinema?* vol. 1 (Berkeley: University of California Press, 1966), p. 48].

These theorists, then, set the filmmaker the task of representing some historical, social, or aesthetic reality through the selection and arrangement of mise-en-scene. Though this book postpones the consideration of this problem—it lies more strictly in the domain of film theory—the realist controversy is worth your examination. For arguments against a realist theory of mise-en-scene, see Noël

Burch, *Theory of Film Practice* (Princeton, N.J.: Princeton University Press, 1981), and Sergei Eisenstein, "An Unexpected Juncture," in Richard Taylor, ed., *Writings 1922–1934* (Bloomington: Indiana University Press, 1988), pp. 115–122. Christopher Williams, in *Realism and the Cinema* (London: Routledge & Kegan Paul, 1980), reviews many issues in the area.

Computer Imaging and Mise-en-Scene

In recent years, the filmmaker's control of mise-en-scene has been extended by means of computer technology. *Digital* computer animation uses a program that will itself create images. *Analog image synthesis* enables a full blend of live-action footage with computer-generated image transformations. A drawing, photograph, or videotape is scanned with a video camera, which yields an image that can be manipulated by computer. An object can be pulled out of the image and recolored, or even rotated or extended by being plotted through a series of movements. The resulting animation is rescanned onto a high-resolution television monitor, which is then filmed by a 35mm motion-picture camera. See Neil Weinstock's *Computer Animation* (Reading, Mass.: Addison-Wesley, 1986) and Thomas A. Ohanian and Michael E. Phillips, *Digital Filmmaking* (Boston: Focal Press, 1996).

Another technique is *digital compositing,* used for the T-1000 cyborg in *Terminator 2: Judgment Day.* Here a grid was painted on the actor's body and the actor was filmed executing movements. As the film was scanned, the changing grid patterns were translated into a digital code similar to that used on compact discs. Then new actions could be created on the computer frame by frame. For a discussion, see Jody Duncan, "A Once and Future War," *Cinefex* **47** (August 1991): 4–59. Since *Terminator 2,* sophisticated software programs have enabled directors to create "actors" wholly from models that can be scanned into a computer and then animated. The most famous example is the gallimimus herd in *Jurassic Park.* The phases of the imaging process for this film are explained in Jody Duncan, "The Beauty in the Beasts," *Cinefex* **55** (August 1993): 42–95. Both analog image synthesis and digital compositing were used in *The Matrix;* for background, see Kevin H. Martin, "Jacking into the Matrix," *Cinefex* **79** (October 1999): 66–89. As we shall see in Chapter 7, computers have simplified the insertion of miniature sets into live-action shots, creating a new interest in elaborate set designs, especially in science-fiction and fantasy films.

The combination of live-action filming with computer animation has created a fresh range of cinematic effects. Méliès's urge to dazzle the audience with the magical powers of mise-en-scene continues to bear fruit.

Particular Aspects of Mise-en-Scene

On costume, see Elizabeth Lees, *Costume Design in the Movies* (London: BCW, 1976), and Edward Maeder, ed., *Hollywood and History: Costume Design in Film* (New York: Thames and Hudson, 1987). Léon Barsacq, with careful assistance by Elliott Stein, has produced the best history of setting to date, *Caligari's Cabinet and Other Grand Illusions: A History of Film Design* (New York: New American Library, 1976). Other major studies of decor in the cinema are Charles Affron and Mirella Jona Affron, *Sets in Motion: Art Direction and Film Narrative* (New Brunswick, N.J.: Rutgers University Press, 1995); Beverly Heisner, *Hollywood Art: Art Direction in the Days of the Great Studios* (Jefferson, N.C.: McFarland, 1990); Dietrich Meumann, ed., *Film Architecture: Set Designs from "Metropolis" to "Blade Runner"* (Munich: Prestel, 1996); and C. S. Tashiro, *Pretty Pictures: Production Design and the History of Film* (Austin: University of Texas Press, 1998). For insightful interviews with set designers, see Vincent LoBrutto, *By Design* (New York: Praeger, 1992). The memoirs of a major set designer who worked extensively with Jean Renoir have been published: Eugene Lourie's *My Work in Films* (San Diego: Harcourt Brace Jovanovich, 1985). Collections of brief studies of major set designers are Robert S. Sennett's *Setting the Scene: The Great Hollywood Art Directors* (New York: Abrams, 1994) and Peter Ettedgui, *Production Design & Art Direction* (Woburn, Mass.: Focal Press, 1999).

A wide-ranging analysis of performance in film is Richard Dyer, *Stars* (London: British Film Institute, 1979). This book is complemented by Charles Affron, *Star Acting: Gish, Garbo, Davis* (New York: Dutton, 1977) and James Naremore, *Acting in the Cinema* (Berkeley: University of California Press, 1988). Useful practical guides are Patrick Tucker, *Secrets of Screen Acting* (New York: Routledge, 1994) and Tony Barr, *Acting for the Camera* (New York: Perennial, 1986). Michael Caine's *Acting in Film: An Actor's Take on Movie Making* (New York: Applause Books, 1990) offers excellent and detailed discussion; see also the accompanying videotape, *Michael Caine on Acting in Film.*

Two fine surveys of lighting are Kris Malkiewicz, *Film Lighting: Talks with Hollywood's Cinematographers and Gaffers* (New York: Prentice-Hall, 1986); and Gerald Millerson, *Lighting for Television & Film,* 3d ed. (Boston: Focal Press, 1991). John Alton's *Painting with Light* (New York: Macmillan, 1949) and Gerald Millerson's *Technique of Lighting for Television and Motion Pictures* (New York: Hastings House, 1972) are useful older discussions, with emphasis on classical Hollywood practices. A useful reference book is Richard K. Ferncase's *Film and Video Lighting Terms and Concepts* (Newton, Mass.: Focal Press, 1995).

One of the cinema's masters of lighting, Josef von Sternberg, has much to say on the subject in his entertaining autobiography, *Fun in a Chinese Laundry* (New York: Macmillan, 1965). Raoul Coutard discusses a different approach to lighting in "Light of Day," in Toby Mussmann, ed., *Jean-Luc Godard* (New York: Dutton, 1968), pp. 232–239. Hollywood cinematographers recall their lighting experiments in Malkiewicz, mentioned above, and in Charles Higham, *Hollywood Cameramen* (London: Thames and Hudson, 1970).

Depth

Art historians have long studied how a two-dimensional image can be made to suggest a deep space. A comprehensive introductory survey is William V. Dunning, *Changing Images of Pictorial Space: A History of Spatial Illusion in Painting* (Syracuse: Syracuse University Press, 1991). Dunning's history of Western painting emphasizes the manipulation of five techniques we have considered in this chapter: linear perspective, shading, the separation of planes, atmospheric perspective, and color perspective.

Though film directors have of course manipulated the image's depth and flatness since the beginning of cinema, critical understanding of these spatial qualities did not emerge until the 1940s. It was then that André Bazin called attention to the fact that certain directors staged their shots in unusually deep space. Bazin singled out F. W. Murnau (for *Nosferatu* and *Sunrise*), Orson Welles (for *Citizen Kane* and *The Magnificent Ambersons*), William Wyler (for *The Little Foxes* and *The Best Years of Our Lives*), and Jean Renoir (for practically all of his 1930s work). Today we would add Kenji Mizoguchi (for *Osaka Elegy, Sisters of Gion,* and others) and even Sergei Eisenstein (for *Old and New, Ivan the Terrible,* and the unreleased *Bezhin Meadow*). By offering us depth and flatness as analytical categories, Bazin increased our understanding of mise-en-scene. (See "The Evolution of the Language of Cinema," in *What Is Cinema?* vol. 1.) Interestingly, Sergei Eisenstein, who is often contrasted with Bazin, explicitly discussed principles of deep-space staging in the 1930s, as recorded by his faithful pupil, Vladimir Nizhny, in *Lessons with Eisenstein* (New York: Hill & Wang, 1962). Eisenstein asked his class to stage a murder scene in a single shot and without camera movement; the result was a startling use of extreme depth and dynamic movement toward the spectator. For a discussion, see David Bordwell, *The Cinema of Eisenstein* (Cambridge, Mass.: Harvard University Press, 1993), chaps. 4 and 6. For a general historical overview of depth in mise-en-scene, see David Bordwell's *On the History of Film Style* (Cambridge, Mass.: Harvard University Press, 1997), chap. 6.

Color Design

Two clear and readable discussions of color aesthetics in general are Luigina De Grandis, *Theory and Use of Color,* trans. John Gilbert (New York: Abrams, 1986) and Paul Zelanski and Mary Pat Fisher, *Colour for Designers and Artists* (London: Herbert Press, 1989).

Filmmakers have long considered color to be an important aspect of mise-en-scene, capable of furnishing motifs that will develop across the film. Believing that color evokes definite emotions, Rouben Mamoulian claimed that the director must develop "a complete chromatic plan for the film" ["Color and Light in Films," *Film Culture* **21** (Summer 1960): 68–79.] Carl Dreyer agreed, stressing the necessity for the director to plan the color scheme to flow smoothly, "which creates the effect of persons and objects being in constant motion and causes the colors to glide from one place to another in changing rhythms, creating new and surprising effects when they collide with other colors or melt into them" ["Color Film and Colored Films," *Dreyer in Double Reflection* (New York: Dutton, 1973), pp. 168–173].

For Stan Brakhage, cinema must break down our normal sense of color, as "closed-eye visions" produce purely subjective tonalities: "I am stating my given ability, prize of all above pursuing, to transform the light sculpted shapes of an almost dark-blackened room to the rainbow-hued patterns of light without any scientific paraphernalia" [*Metaphors on Vision* (New York: Film Culture, 1963)]. The filmmaker who theorized most extensively about color was Sergei Eisenstein. See especially "Color and Meaning," in *The Film Sense* (New York: Harcourt, Brace, 1947), pp. 113–153.

For general discussion of the aesthetics of film color, see Raymond Durgnat, "Colours and Contrasts," *Films and Filming* **15,** 2 (November 1968): 58–62; and William Johnson, "Coming to Terms with Color," *Film Quarterly* **20,** 1 (Fall 1966): 2–22. Two essays on Jean-Luc Godard exemplify how the analyst can examine a film's color system: Paul Sharits, "Red, Blue, Godard," *Film Quarterly* **19,** 4 (Summer 1966): 24–29; and Edward Branigan, "The Articulation of Color in a Filmic System," *Wide Angle* **1,** 3 (1976): 20–31. The latter contains an excellent bibliography.

Frame Composition and the Viewer's Eye

The film shot is like the painter's canvas: It must be filled up, and the spectator must be cued to notice certain things (and not to notice others). For this reason, composition in film owes much to principles developed in the graphic arts. A good basic study of composition is Donald L. Weismann, *The Visual Arts as Human experience* (Englewood Cliffs:

Prentice-Hall, 1974), which has many interesting things to say about depth as well. More elaborate discussions are to be found in Rudolf Arnheim, *Art and Visual Perception: A Psychology of the Creative Eye,* rev. ed. (Berkeley: University of California Press, 1974), and his *The Power of the Center: A Study of Composition in the Visual Arts,* 2d ed. (Berkeley: University of California Press, 1988).

André Bazin suggested that shots staged in depth and shot in deep focus give the viewer's eye greater freedom than do flatter, shallower shots: The viewer's eye can roam across the screen. [See Bazin, *Orson Welles* (New York: Harper & Row, 1978).] Noël Burch takes issue: "All the elements in any given film image are perceived as equal in importance" (*Theory of Film Practice,* p. 34). Psychological research on pictorial perception suggests, however, that viewers do indeed scan images according to specific cues. A good review of the subject, with bibliography, may be found in Julian Hochberg, "The Representation of Things and People," in E. H. Gombrich et al., *Art, Perception, and Reality* (Baltimore, Md.: Johns Hopkins University Press, 1972), pp. 47–94. In cinema, static visual cues for "when to look where" are reinforced or undermined by movement of figures or of camera, by sound track and editing, and by the overall form of the film. The psychological research is outlined in Robert L. Solso, *Cognition and the Visual Arts* (Cambridge, Mass.: MIT Press, 1994), pp. 129–156.

Chapter 7

The Shot: Cinematography

In controlling mise-en-scene the filmmaker stages an event to be filmed. But a comprehensive account of cinema as a medium cannot stop with simply what is put in front of the camera. The *shot* does not exist until light-and-dark patterns are inscribed on a strip of film. The filmmaker also controls what we will call the *cinematographic qualities* of the shot—not only *what* is filmed, but also *how* it is filmed. Cinematographic qualities involve three factors: (1) the photographic aspects of the shot, (2) the framing of the shot, and (3) the duration of the shot. This chapter surveys these three areas of control.

THE PHOTOGRAPHIC IMAGE

Cinematography (literally, "writing in movement") depends to a large extent on *photography* ("writing in light"). Sometimes the filmmaker eliminates the camera and simply works on the film itself; but even when drawing, painting, or scratching directly on film, punching holes in it, or growing mold on it, the filmmaker is creating patterns of light on celluloid. Most often the filmmaker uses a camera to regulate how light from some object will be photochemically registered on the sensitized film. In any event, the filmmaker can select the range of tonalities, manipulate the speed of motion, and transform perspective.

The Range of Tonalities

An image may seem all grays or stark black and white. It may display a range of colors. Textures may stand out clearly or recede into a haze. The filmmaker may control all these visual qualities by manipulating the film stock, exposure, and developing procedures.

Types of **film stocks** are differentiated by the chemical qualities of the emulsion. The choice of film stock has many artistic implications. For one thing, the image will have more or less *contrast* depending partly on the stock used. Contrast refers to the degree of difference between the darkest and lightest areas of the frame. A high-contrast image displays bright white highlights, stark black areas,

229

7.1   Most black-and-white films employ a balance of grays, blacks, and whites, as in this shot from *Casablanca*.

7.2   *Breaking the Waves:* Color manipulation to create bleached-out images.

7.3   The dream sequence early in Ingmar Bergman's *Wild Strawberries* uses a combination of film stock, overexposure, and laboratory processing to create a bleached-out look.

7.4   This shot from *Les Carabiniers* achieves a newsreel-like quality heightened by both the film stock and lab work that increased contrast.

"Both [cinematographer] Floyd [Crosby] and I wanted [*High Noon*] to look like a documentary, or a newsreel from the period of the 1880s, if film had existed at that time—which, of course, it did not. I believe that we came close to our goal by using flat lighting, a grainy texture in the printing and an unfiltered white sky."

— Fred Zinnemann, director

and a narrow range of grays in between. A low-contrast image possesses a wide range of grays with no true white or black areas.

As we have already seen in Chapter 6, human vision is highly sensitive to differences in color, texture, shape, and other pictorial properties. Contrasts within the image enable filmmakers to guide the viewer's eye to important parts of the frame. Filmmakers control the degree of contrast in the image in various ways. In general, a very fast stock, one which is very sensitive to reflected light, will produce a contrasty look, while a slower, less light-sensitive one, will be low in contrast. The amount of light used on the set during shooting will also affect the image's degree of contrast. Moreover, the cinematographer may choose to use particular developing procedures that increase or decrease contrast. For example, the strength and temperature of the chemicals and the length of time the film is left in the developing bath affect contrast. By manipulating the film stock, lighting factors, and developing procedures, filmmakers can achieve enormous variety in the look of the film image **(7.1–7.3).** Most black-and-white films employ a balance of grays, blacks, and whites.

Jean-Luc Godard's *Les Carabiniers* **(7.4)** offers a good example of what postfilming manipulations of film stock can accomplish. The shot's newsreel-like quality is heightened by both the film stock and lab work that increased contrast. "The positive prints," Godard has explained, "were simply made on a special Kodak high contrast stock. . . . Several shots, intrinsically too gray, were duped again

7.5 The trolley scene in *Meet Me in St. Louis* shows off the vivid colors possible with the Technicolor process.

7.6 The use of blues in *Stalker* makes the action almost seem to be taking place underwater.

7.7 Lye manipulated Gasparcolor paper stock to create pure, saturated silhouettes that split and recombine in *Rainbow Dance*.

sometimes two or three times, always to their highest contrast." The effect suggests old combat footage that has been recopied or shot under bad lighting conditions; the high-contrast look suited a film about the grubbiness of war.

Different color film stocks yield varying color contrasts. Technicolor became famous for its sharply distinct, heavily saturated hues, as seen in such films as *Meet Me in St. Louis* (**7.5**). The richness of Technicolor was achieved by means of a specially designed camera and sophisticated printing process. To take another example, Soviet filmmakers long used a domestically made stock that tends to lower contrast and give the image a murky greenish-blue cast. Andrei Tarkovsky exploited just these qualities in the monochromatic color design of his shadowy *Stalker* (**7.6**). Len Lye's abstract *Rainbow Dance* uses specific features of the English stock Gasparcolor (**7.7**).

The tonalities of color stock may also be altered by laboratory processes. The person assigned the role of *color timer* or *grader* has a wide choice about the color range of a print. A red patch in the image may be printed as crimson, pink, or almost any shade in between. Often the timer consults with the director to select a key tone that will serve as a reference point for color relations throughout the film. In addition, some prints can be made for purposes that require a different color balance. Today, most prints made for 35mm exhibition are printed somewhat dark, to create rich shadows and darker colors. But prints struck for transfer to video are made on special low-contrast stock in order to compensate for television's tendency to heighten contrast. The resulting image often has a lighter, brighter color range than seen in any theatrical print. Increasingly cinematographers are using computer grading for selected shots or even an entire film. (See Box, p. 250–251.)

Certain procedures may also add color to footage originally shot in black and white. The most widely used of these processes have been tinting and toning. *Tinting* is accomplished by dipping the already developed film into a bath of dye. The dark areas remain black and gray, while the lighter areas pick up the color (**7.8**). *Toning* works in an opposite fashion. The dye is added during the developing of the positive print. The darker areas of the frame are colored, while the lighter portions of the frame remain white or only faintly colored (**7.9**).

Both tinting and toning were common in the silent cinema. Night scenes, as in 7.9 (from *Cenere,* a 1916 Italian film) were often colored blue. Firelight was frequently colored red, while interiors were commonly amber. *The Wrath of the Gods* (1914) uses a pink tint to suggest the glow of an erupting volcano (**7.8**). Some contemporary filmmakers have revived these processes. Arrabal's *Viva la Muerte!* uses

7.8   Tinting creates a pinkish color across the entire frame in the 1914 film *The Wrath of the Gods.*

7.9   *Cenere:* The deep blue of the dark areas and nearly white patches are characteristic of toning.

7.10   A modern use of tinting in *Viva la Muerte!*

a vibrant yellow-orange tint **(7.10)**, while Vera Chytilova employs a crimson toning in *Daisies* **(7.11)**.

A rarer method of adding color is the difficult process of *hand coloring.* Here portions of black-and-white images are painted in colors, frame by frame. The ship's flag in Eisenstein's *Potemkin* was originally hand colored red against a blue sky. A modern use of hand coloring may be seen in Makavejev's *Innocence Unprotected* **(7.12)**.

There are many other ways in which the filmmaker can manipulate the image's tonalities after filming. In *Reflections on Black,* Stan Brakhage scratches off the emulsion in certain parts of the shot **(7.13)**. Lars von Trier shot *Breaking the Waves* on 35mm film, then transferred the footage to video and used digital manipulation to drain out much of the color. He transferred the result back to film, resulting in desaturated images that tremble and shimmer (7.2).

The range of tonalities in the image is most crucially affected by the *exposure* of the image during filming. The filmmaker usually controls **exposure** by regulating how much light passes through the camera lens, though images shot with correct exposure can also be overexposed or underexposed in developing and printing. We commonly think that a photograph should be well exposed—neither underexposed (too dark, not enough light admitted through the lens) nor overexposed (too bright, too much light admitted through the lens). But even correct exposure usually offers some latitude for choice; it is not an absolute.

The filmmaker can manipulate exposure for specific effects. American *films noirs* of the 1940s sometimes underexpose shadowy regions of the image in keeping with low-key lighting techniques. In *Vidas Secas,* Nelson Pereira dos Santos overexposes the windows of the prison cell to sharpen the contrast between the prisoner's confinement and the world of freedom outside **(7.14)**. In the Moria sequence, *The Lord of the Rings: The Fellowship of the Ring* uses overexposure in several shots **7.15)**.

7.11 Toning in *Daisies.*

7.12 In *Innocence Unprotected,* stylized images are created by painting multiple colors within a shot.

7.13 By scratching the emulsion, Brakhage emphasizes the eye motif that runs through *Reflections on Black.*

7.14 Deliberate overexposure of windows in *Vidas Secas.*

7.15 *The Fellowship of the Ring:* The overexposure of the wizard's staff makes the Fellowship a bright island threatened by countless orcs in the surrounding darkness.

Choices of exposure are particularly critical in working with color. For shots of *Kasba,* Kumar Shahani chooses to emphasize tones within shaded areas, and so he exposes for them and lets sunlit areas bleach out somewhat **(7.16, 7.17).**

Exposure can in turn be affected by **filters**—slices of glass or gelatin put in front of the lens of the camera or printer to reduce certain frequencies of light reaching the film. Filters thus alter the range of tonalities in quite radical ways. Before modern improvements in film stocks and lighting made it practical to shoot most outdoor night scenes at night, filmmakers routinely made such scenes by using blue filters in sunlight—a technique called *day for night* **(7.18).** Hollywood cinematographers since the 1920s sought to add glamour to close-ups, especially of women, by means of diffusion filters and silks. Filters applied during shooting or during printing can also alter the color image.

Further, exposure can be altered by the process called *flashing.* Here the film is exposed to light (often a white or gray card) before shooting or before processing. Flashing lowers contrast, since it can make shadows grayer and more transparent. Francis Ford Coppola's *Tucker: A Man and His Dream* flashed each reel differently, changing the color scheme as the film progressed. In such ways, both in filming and in laboratory work the manipulation of film stock and exposure powerfully affects the image that we see on the screen.

7.16   In *Kasbah,* the vibrant hues of the store's wares stand out, while the countryside behind is overexposed . . .

7.17   . . . and while at other moments underexposure for the shaded porches emphasizes the central outdoor area.

7.18   In *The Searchers,* this scene of the protagonist spying on an Indian camp from a bluff was shot at midday (as the shadow reveals) using day-for-night filters.

Speed of Motion

A gymnast's performance seen in slurred slow motion, ordinary action accelerated to comic speed, a tennis serve stopped in a freeze-frame—we are all familiar with the effects of the control of the speed of motion. Of course, the filmmaker who stages the event to be filmed can (within limits) dictate the pace of the action. But that pace can also be controlled by a photographic power unique to cinema: the control of the speed of movement seen on the screen.

The speed of the motion we see on the screen depends on the relation between the rate at which the film was shot and the rate of projection. Both **rates** are calculated in frames per second. In the silent era, films were shot at a variety of speeds, usually ranging from 16 to 20 frames per second, gradually getting a bit faster in the mid-1920s. Once sound was adopted in the late 1920s, it was necessary to record both sound and image at a uniform speed, so that they could be synchronized. The rate of shooting and projection for the sound cinema was standardized at 24 frames per second.

For depicted movement to look accurate, the rate of shooting must correspond to the rate of projection. For example, we are so used to seeing silent films have jerky, accelerated movements that we assume that the films always looked that way. But the jerkiness of the images is usually a result of projecting a film shot at

7.19 Cars become blurs of light when shot in fast motion for *Koyaanisqatsi.*

16 to 20 frames per second at 24 frames per second. When shown at the proper rate, silent films look completely normal. For this reason, it is best to project silent films on projectors that can run at 16 or 18 frames per second or, better, on variable speed projectors that can tailor the speed precisely to the film.

Projection usually lies outside the filmmaker's control, but he or she can control the rate of the film's movement through the camera. The camera's drive mechanism can be adjusted to vary the shooting rate. A common range on 35mm cameras today is between 8 and 64 frames per second.

With the assumption of a constant projection speed, the fewer frames per second shot, the greater the acceleration of the screen action. We are used to this *fast-motion* effect in comedies. The most famous example of it for noncomic purposes occurs in F. W. Murnau's *Nosferatu,* in which the vampire's accelerated mobility represents his supernatural power. In Godfrey Reggio's *Koyaanisqatsi,* a delirious fast motion renders the hectic rhythms of urban life **(7.19).**

Contrarily, the more frames per second shot, the slower the screen action will appear. The resulting *slow-motion* effect is used notably in Dziga Vertov's *Man with a Movie Camera* to render sports events in detail, a function that continues to be important today. The technique can also be used for expressive purposes. In Rouben Mamoulian's *Love Me Tonight* the members of a hunt decide to ride quietly home to avoid waking the sleeping deer; their ride is filmed in slow motion to create a comic depiction of noiseless movement. Today slow-motion footage often functions to suggest that the action takes place in a dream or fantasy; to express a lyrical quality; or to convey enormous power, as in a martial-arts film. Slow motion is also increasingly used for emphasis, becoming a way of dwelling on a moment of spectacle or high drama. The slow-motion scene of violence has become a cliché of the modern cinema.

To enhance expressive effects, filmmakers can change the speed of motion in the course of a shot. Often the change of speed helps create special effects. In *Die Hard* a fireball bursts up an elevator shaft toward the camera. During the filming, the fire at the bottom of the shaft was filmed at 100 fps, slowing down its progress, and then shot at faster speeds as it erupted upward, giving the impression of an explosive acceleration. For *Bram Stoker's Dracula,* director Francis Ford Coppola wanted his vampire to glide toward his prey with supernatural suddenness. Cinematographer Michael Ballhaus used a computer program to control the shutter and the speed of filming, allowing smooth and instantaneous changes from 24 fps to 8 fps and back again.

Digital postproduction allows filmmakers to create the effect of variable shooting speeds through *ramping,* shifting speed of movement very smoothly and rapidly. In an early scene of Michael Mann's *The Insider,* researcher Jeffrey Wigand leaves the tobacco company that has just fired him. As he crosses the lobby toward a revolving door, his brisk walk suddenly slows to a dreamlike drifting. The point of this very noticeable stylistic choice becomes apparent only in the film's last shot. Lowell Bergman, the TV producer who has helped Wigand reveal that addictive substances are added to cigarettes, has been dismissed from CBS. He strides across the lobby, and as he passes through the revolving door, his movement glides into sub–slow motion. The repetition of the technique points out the parallels between two men who have lost their livelihoods as a result of telling the truth—two insiders who have become outsiders.

Extreme forms of fast and slow motion alter the speed of the depicted material even more radically. *Time-lapse* cinematography permits us to see the sun set in seconds or a flower sprout, bud, and bloom in a minute. For this a very low shooting speed is required—perhaps one frame per minute, hour, or even day. For *high-speed* cinematography, which may seek to record a bullet shattering glass, the camera may expose hundreds, even thousands, of frames per second. Most cameras can be used for time-lapse shooting, but high-speed cinematography requires specially designed cameras.

After filming, the filmmaker can still control the speed of movement on the screen through various laboratory procedures. The most common means used is the optical printer (Fig. 1.5). This device rephotographs a film, copying all or part of each original frame onto another reel of film. The filmmaker can use the optical printer to skip frames (accelerating the action when projected), reprint a frame at desired intervals (slowing the action by *stretch printing*), stop the action (repeating a frame over and over, to freeze the projected image for seconds or minutes), or reverse the action. Nowadays some silent films are stretch-printed with every other frame repeated, so that they may run more smoothly at sound speed. We are familiar with freeze-framing, slow-motion, and reverse-motion printing effects from the *instant replays* of sports coverage and investigative documentaries. Many experimental films have made striking use of the optical printer's possibilities, such as Ken Jacobs's *Tom Tom the Piper's Son,* which explores the images of an early silent film by enlarging portions of its shots.

Perspective Relations

You are standing on railroad tracks, looking toward the horizon. The tracks not only recede but also seem to meet at the horizon. You glance at the trees and buildings along the tracks. They diminish by simple, systematic rule: the closer objects look larger, the farther objects look smaller—even if they are actually of uniform size. The optical system of your eye, registering light rays reflected from the scene, supplies a host of information about scale, depth, and spatial relations among parts of the scene. Such relations are called *perspective* relations.

The **lens** of a photographic camera does roughly what your eye does. It gathers light from the scene and transmits that light onto the flat surface of the film to form an image that represents size, depth, and other dimensions of the scene. One difference between the eye and the camera, though, is that photographic lenses may be changed, and each type of lens will render perspective relations in different ways. If two different lenses photograph the same scene, the perspective relations in the resulting images could be drastically different. A wide-angle lens could exaggerate the depth you see down the track or could make the trees and buildings seem to bulge; a telephoto lens could drastically reduce the depth, making the trees seem very close together and nearly the same size.

"I tend to rely on only two kinds of lenses to compose my frames: very wide angle and extreme telephoto. I use the wide angle because when I want to see something, I want to see it completely, with the most detail possible. As for the telephoto, I use it for close-ups because I find it creates a real "encounter" with the actor. If you shoot someone's face with a 200-millimeter lens, the audience will feel like the actor is really standing in front of them. It gives presence to the shot. So I like extremes. Anything in between is of no interest to me."

— John Woo, director

The Lens: Focal Length   Control of perspective relations in the image is obviously very important to the filmmaker. The chief variable in the process is the **focal length** of the lens. In technical terms the focal length is the distance from the center of the lens to the point where light rays converge to a point of focus on the film. The focal length of the lens can affect perspective relations in several ways.

The focal length alters the perceived magnification, depth, and scale of things in the image. We usually distinguish three sorts of lenses on the basis of their effects on perspective:

1. *The short-focal-length* (**wide-angle**) *lens.*   In 35mm-gauge cinematography, a lens of less than 35mm in focal length is considered a wide-angle lens. Such lenses tend to distort straight lines lying near the edges of the frame, bulging them outward. Note the distortion in two frames from a shot in Nicholas Roeg's *Don't Look Now* (**7.20, 7.21**). When a wide-angle lens is used for a medium shot or close-up, the distortion of shape may become very evident. (See **7.22**.)

The lens of short focal length has the property of exaggerating depth (**7.23**). Because distances between foreground and background seem greater, the wide-angle lens also makes figures moving to or from the camera seem to cover ground more rapidly.

2. *The middle-focal-length* (**normal**) *lens.*   A lens of medium focal length is 35 to 50mm. This normal lens seeks to avoid noticeable perspective distortion. With a normal lens, horizontal and vertical lines are rendered as straight and perpendicular. (Compare the bulging effect of the wide-angle lens.) Parallel lines should recede to distant vanishing points, as in our railroad-tracks example. Foreground and background should seem neither stretched apart (as with the wide-angle lens) nor squashed together (as with the telephoto lens). A normal lens was used for **7.24**; contrast the sense of distance among the figures achieved in 7.23.

3. *The long-focal-length* (**telephoto**) *lens.*   Whereas wide-angle lenses distort space laterally, longer lenses flatten the space along the camera axis. Cues for depth and volume are reduced. The planes seem squashed together, much as when you look through a telescope or binoculars. In **7.25,** from Chen Kaige's *Life on a String,* the long lens pushes the crowd members almost to the same plane. It also makes the rapids behind the men virtually a two-dimensional backdrop. Akira Kurosawa relies heavily on long lenses, using them for all shot scales (**7.26**).

Today, the focal length of long lenses typically ranges from around 75 to 250mm or more. They are commonly used in the filming or televising of sports events, since they allow the cinematographer to magnify action at a distance. (For this reason, long lenses are also called telephoto lenses.) In a baseball game there will invariably be shots taken from almost directly behind the umpire. You have probably noticed that such shots make catcher, batter, and pitcher look unnaturally close to one another. What a very long lens can do to space is dramatically illustrated throughout Godfrey Reggio's *Koyaanisqatsi* (**7.27**).

A long-focal-length lens also affects subject movement. Because it flattens depth, a figure moving toward the camera takes more time to cover what seems to be a small distance. The clichéd *running-in-place* shots in *The Graduate* and other films of the 1960s and 1970s were produced by lenses of very long focal length. In *Tootsie* the introduction of Michael Dorsey disguised as Dorothy Michaels occurs in a lengthy telephoto shot in order for us to recognize his altered appearance and to notice that none of the people around him find "her" unusual (**7.28–7.30**).

7.20   In *Don't Look Now,* as the camera swivels to follow the walking character, the wide-angle lens makes a street lamp he passes appear to lean rightward . . .

7.21   . . . and then leftward.

"I'm standing around waiting to see where the 50mm is going to be, or what size lens they're putting on, and in that unwritten book in my brain, I said, 'Don't ever let them shoot you full face, on a wide-angle lens, you'll end up looking like Dumbo.'"

— Tony Curtis, actor

7.22 Wide-angle distortion in Mikhail Kalatozov's *The Cranes Are Flying*.

7.23 In this scene from *The Little Foxes,* the lens makes the characters seem farther from each other than we would expect in so relatively tight a grouping.

7.24 A shot made with a normal lens in *His Girl Friday*.

7.25 The long lens in Chen Kaige's *Life on a String*.

7.26 In this medium shot from *Seven Samurai,* the figures seem close together and almost the same size, even though the two facing front are really quite far behind the foreground man.

7.27 In *Koyaanisqatsi,* an airport is filmed from a great distance, and the long lens makes it appear that a plane is landing on a crowded highway.

Lens length can distinctly affect the spectator's experience. For example, expressive qualities can be suggested by lenses that distort objects or characters. We tend to see the man in **7.31** as looming, even aggressive. Moreover, choice of the lens can make a character or object blend into the setting (7.28) or stand out in sharp relief (7.31). Filmmakers may exploit the flattening effects of the long-focal-length lens to create solid masses of space **(7.32),** as in an abstract painting.

A director can use lens length to surprise us, as Kurosawa does in *Red Beard.* When the mad patient comes into the intern's room, a long-focal-length lens filming

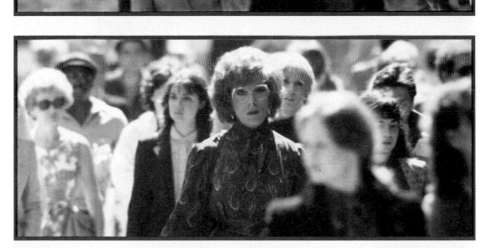

7.28   In *Tootsie,* Dorothy becomes visible among the crowd at a considerable distance from the camera . . .

7.29   . . . and after taking 20 steps seems only slightly closer until . . .

7.30   . . . she finally grows somewhat larger, after a total of about 36 steps.

7.31   Ilya Trauberg's *China Express.*

7.32   In *Eternity and a Day,* a long lens makes the beach and sea appear as two vertical blocks.

7.33   In Kurosawa's *Red Beard,* the mad patient in the background seems threateningly to approach the intern . . .

7.34   . . . until a cut reveals that she is across the room from him.

from behind him initially makes her seem to be quite close to him **(7.33).** But a cut to a more perpendicular angle shows that the patient and the intern are actually several feet apart and that he is not yet in danger **(7.34).**

There is one sort of lens that offers the director a chance to manipulate focal length and to transform perspective relations during a single shot. A **zoom lens** is optically designed to permit the continuous varying of focal length. Originally designed for aerial and reconnaissance photography, zoom lenses gradually became a standard tool for newsreel filming. It was not, however, the general practice to zoom during shooting. The camera operator varied the focal length as desired and then started filming. In the late 1950s, however, the increased portability of cameras led to a trend toward zooming while filming.

Since then, the zoom has sometimes been used to substitute for moving the camera forward or backward. However, although the zoom shot presents a mobile framing, it is not a genuine movement of the camera. During a zoom, the camera remains stationary and the lens simply increases or decreases its focal length. Onscreen, the zoom shot magnifies or demagnifies the objects filmed, excluding or including surrounding space, as in **7.35** and **7.36,** from Francis Ford Coppola's *The Conversation,* and in **7.37** and **7.38,** from *Barravento.* The zoom can produce interesting and peculiar transformations of scale and depth, as we shall see when we examine Michael Snow's *Wavelength.*

The impact that focal length can have on the image's perspective qualities is dramatically illustrated in Ernie Gehr's abstract experimental film *Serene Velocity.* The scene is an empty corridor. Gehr shot the film with a zoom lens, but he did not zoom while filming the shot. Instead, the zoom permitted him to change the lens's focal length between takes. As Gehr explains,

> [I] divided the mm range of the zoom lens in half and starting from the middle I recorded changes in mm positions. . . . The camera was not moved at all. The zoom

7.35 In the opening of *The Conversation,* a long, slow zoom-in arouses considerable uncertainty about its target . . .

7.36 . . . until it finally centers on a mime and our protagonist, surveillance technician Harry Caul.

7.37 A zoom-out in *Barravento* begins with a tight framing on the hero . . .

7.38 . . . and ends by revealing a huge bridge above him.

7.39 *Serene Velocity:* Telephoto shots of a hallway are juxtaposed to wide-angle shots taken from the same spot.

7.40 *Boyz N the Hood:* Selective focus in depth.

7.41 Harpo Marx burns the candle at both ends in *Horse Feathers.* The woman and wall behind him are out of focus.

lens was not moved during recording either. Each frame was recorded individually as a still. Four frames to each position. To give an example: I shot the first four frames at 50mm. The next four frames I shot at 55mm. And then, for a certain duration, approximately 60 feet, I went back and forth, four frames at 50mm, four frames at 55mm; four frames at 50mm, four frames at 55mm; etc. . . . for about 60 feet. Then I went to 45–60 [mm] and did the same for about 60 feet. Then to 40–65, and so on.

The resulting film presents an image whose perspective relations pulsate rhythmically—first with little difference in size and scale, but gradually with greater tension between a telephoto image and a wide-angle image (**7.39**). In a sense *Serene Velocity* takes as its subject the effect of focal length on perspective.

The Lens: Depth of Field and Focus   Focal length not only affects how shape and scale are magnified or distorted. It also affects the lens's **depth of field.** Depth of field is the range of distances before the lens within which objects can be photographed in sharp **focus.** A lens with a depth of field of 10 feet to infinity will render any object in that range clearly, but the sharpness of the image will decrease when the object moves closer to the lens (say, to 4 feet). All other things being equal, a short-focal-length (wide-angle) lens has a relatively greater depth of field than does a long-focal-length (telephoto) lens.

Depth of field should not be confused with the concept of deep space, used in Chapter 6. *Deep space* is a term for the way the filmmaker has staged the action on several different planes, *regardless of whether or not all of these planes are in focus.* In the case of *Our Hospitality* those planes usually are in sharp focus, but in other films not every plane of deep space is in focus. In this shot from *Boyz N the Hood* (**7.40**)*,* there are three planes of depth visible, but deep focus is not used. The woman in the foreground is slightly out of focus, the table and the man opposite her are in focus, and the furniture and man glimpsed in the background are distinctly out of focus. Deep space is a property of mise-en-scène, depending on how the image is composed. Depth of field is a property of the photographic lens, affecting what planes of the image are in focus.

If depth of field controls perspective relations by determining what planes will be in focus, what choices are open to the filmmaker? He or she may opt for what is usually called selective focus—choosing to focus on only one plane and letting the other planes blur. This is what John Singleton does in the *Boyz N the Hood* example.

Before 1940 it was common Hollywood practice to shoot close-ups in selective focus, making the faces sharp and the foreground and background planes hazy (**7.41**). Sometimes objects near the camera were thrown out of focus so that the sharper middle ground would claim the viewer's attention. The same stylistic choice is common today, especially when long-focal-length lenses are used (**7.42**). Selective focus typically draws the viewer's attention to the main character or object (**7.43**). The technique can be used for a more abstract compositional effect as well (**7.44**).

In Hollywood during the 1940s, partly due to the influence of *Citizen Kane,* Hollywood filmmakers began using faster film, shorter-focal-length lenses, and more intense lighting to yield a greater depth of field. The contract-signing scene from *Citizen Kane* (**7.45**) offers a famous example. This practice came to be called **deep focus.**

Deep-focus cinematography became a major stylistic option throughout the 1940s and 1950s. A typical usage is illustrated in **7.46.** The technique was even imitated in animated cartoons (6.130, from Chuck Jones's *One Froggy Evening*).

7.42 The long lens throws most foreground and background planes out of focus, leaving only one area sharp—in this case, the young hero of *A Time to Live, a Time to Die.*

7.43 Agnès Varda's *Vagabonde (Sans toi ni loi).*

7.44 Leos Carax's *Boy Meets Girl.*

7.45 *Citizen Kane:* From one plane near the lens (Bernstein's head) through several planes in the middle ground to the wall far in the distance, everything is in sharp focus.

7.46 Anthony Mann's *The Tall Target.*

During the 1970s and 1980s deep-focus cinematography was revived in Steven Spielberg's work, notably *Jaws* and *Close Encounters of the Third Kind,* and in the films of Brian De Palma **(7.47).** Today, extreme deep-focus effects can also be achieved digitally **(7.48).**

Since the lens may be refocused at various planes, the filmmaker may also adjust perspective relations while filming by **racking focus,** or *pulling focus.* A shot may begin with an object in the foreground sharply visible and the rear plane fuzzy, then rack focus so that the background elements come into crisp focus and the foreground becomes blurred. Alternatively, the focus can rack from background to foreground, as in **7.49** and **7.50,** from Bernardo Bertolucci's *Last Tango in Paris.*

Special Effects   The image's perspective relations may also be created by means of **special effects.** We have already seen (p. 28) that the filmmaker can create setting by use of models and computer-generated images. The filmmaker can also use a *glass shot.* Here portions of the setting are painted onto a pane of glass and the camera shoots through it to film action supposedly occurring in the painted setting. Glass shots were principally used in the silent era.

Alternatively, separately photographed planes of action may be combined on the same strip of film to create the illusion that the two planes are adjacent. The simplest way to do this is through **superimposition.** Either by double exposure in the camera or in laboratory printing, one image is laid over another. Méliès, whom we have already studied as an early master of mise-en-scene, was well aware of this

"If I made big-budget films, I would do what the filmmakers of twenty years ago did: use 35, 40, and 50mm [lenses] with lots of light so I could have that depth of field, because it plays upon the effect of surprise. It can give you a whole series of little tricks, little hiding places, little hooks in the image where you can hang surprises, places where they can suddenly appear, just like that, within the frame itself. You can create the off-frame within the frame."

— Benoit Jacquot, director

7.47 In *The Untouchables,* a conversation scene is played in the foreground while setting and distant figures are also kept in focus.

7.48 The small size of the chip in a digital video camera yields extreme depth of field. If this shot, from Agnès Varda's *The Gleaners and I,* had been made on film, either Varda's hand or the truck would have been far more out of focus.

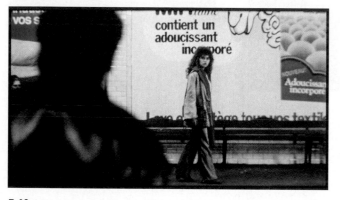

7.49 In this shot from *Last Tango in Paris,* the woman, bench, and wall in the distance are in focus, while the man in the foreground is not . . .

7.50 . . . but after the camera racks focus, the man in the foreground becomes sharp and the background fuzzy.

device. Superimposition allowed him to present the illusion of *The Man with the Rubber Head* (**7.51, 7.52**). In his time and since, filmmakers have most commonly employed double exposure to depict ghosts or to display characters' thoughts.

More complex techniques for combining strips of film to create a single shot are usually called **process,** or *composite,* **shots.** These techniques can be divided into *projection process work* and *matte process work.*

In projection process work, the filmmaker projects footage of a setting onto a screen, then films actors performing in front of the screen. Classical Hollywood filmmaking began this process in the late 1920s, as a way to avoid taking cast and crew on location. The Hollywood technique involved placing the actors against a translucent screen and projecting a film of the setting from behind the screen. The whole ensemble could then be filmed from the front (**7.53**).

Rear projection, as this system was known, seldom creates very convincing depth cues. Foreground and background tend to look starkly separate, partly because of the absence of cast shadows from foreground to background, partly because all background planes tend to seem equally diffuse (**7.54,** from Hitchcock's *Vertigo*).

Front projection, which came into use in the late 1960s, projects the setting onto a two-way mirror, angled to throw the image onto a high-reflectance screen.

7.51 Méliès inflates the head of Méliès in *The Man with the Rubber Head* . . .

7.52 . . . using superimposition and a cart to move him toward the camera.

7.53 *Boom Town.*

7.54 *Vertigo:* The seascape in the rear plane was clearly shot separately and used as a back-projected setting for an embrace filmed under studio lighting.

The camera photographs the actors against the screen by shooting through the mirror **(7.55).** The results of front projection can be clearly seen in the "Dawn of Man" sequence of *2001: A Space Odyssey,* the first film to use front projection extensively. (At one moment, a saber-toothed tiger's eyes glow, reflecting the projector's light.) Because of the sharp focus of the projected footage, front projection blends foreground and background planes fairly smoothly. The nonrealistic possibilities of front projection have been recently explored by Hans-Jürgen Syberberg. In his

7.55   A front-projection system.

7.56   In Syberberg's film of Wagner's *Parsifal,* front projection conjures up colossal, phantasmagoric landscapes.

film of Wagner's opera *Parsifal* front projection conjures up colossal, phantasmagoric landscapes **(7.56).**

Composite filming can also be accomplished by **matte work.** A *matte* is a portion of the setting photographed on a strip of film, usually with a part of the frame empty. Through laboratory printing, the matte is joined with another strip of film containing the actors. One sort of matte involves a painting of the desired areas of setting, which is then filmed. The footage is combined with footage of action, segregated in the blank portions of the painted scenery. In this way, a matte can create an entire imaginary setting for the film. Stationary mattes of this sort have made glass shots virtually obsolete and are so widely used in commercial cinema that until the late 1990s the matte painter was a mainstay of production. In recent years matte paintings have been made using computer programs, but they are used in the same way to create scenery **(7.57).**

7.57   In this shot from *The Fellowship of the Ring,* the distant part of the building, the cliffs, and the sky are all on a matte painting created by computer.

7.58   In *2001*, the spacecraft visible through the porthole is a model that has been matted into a shot of the astronaut in the control cabin (production still).

7.59   In *Rumble Fish,* a black-and-white film, Francis Ford Coppola uses traveling mattes to color the fish in an aquarium.

With a matte painting, however, the actor cannot move into the painted portions of the frame without seeming to disappear. To solve this problem, the filmmaker can use a *traveling matte.* Here the actor is photographed against a blank, usually blue, background. In laboratory printing, the moving outline of the actor is cut out of footage of the desired background. After further lab work, the shot of the actor is jigsawed into the moving gap in the background footage. It is traveling mattes that present shots of Superman's flight or of spaceships hurtling through space **(7.58).** In 6.85, the robot is combined with live action in the background by means of a traveling matte. The animated figures in our shot from *Who Framed Roger Rabbit?* (5.82) were matted into live-action footage shot separately.

You can often detect traveling mattes on the screen, because even the most expensive and carefully executed special effects do not always join the various portions of the shot perfectly. A dark contour, called a *matte line,* may shimmer around the moving sections. In *The Empire Strikes Back,* matte lines are particularly evident during the battle with the Imperial Walkers.

Before the perfecting of computer-generated imagery, traveling mattes were commonly used in all genres of mainstream cinema. Usually they function to create a realistic-looking locale or situation. But they can also generate an abstract, deliberately unrealistic, image **(7.59).**

For many films, different types of special effects will be combined. Our earlier illustration from *The Fellowship of the Ring* (7.57) includes a partial full-size set with an actor at the left, a miniature set in the middle ground, a matte painting of the background elements, and computer-animated waterfalls and falling leaves. A single shot of a science-fiction film might animate miniatures or models through stop action, convey their movements by a traveling matte, and add animated ray bursts in superimposition while a matte painting supplies a background. For the train crash in *The Fugitive,* front and rear projection were used simultaneously within certain shots.

You may have noticed that glass shots, superimpositions, projection process work, and matte work all straddle two general bodies of film techniques. These special effects all require arrangement of the material before the camera, so to some extent they are aspects of mise-en-scene. But they also require control of photographic choices (such as refilming, laboratory adjustments) and affect perspective relations, so they also involve cinematography. We have considered them here because, unlike effects employing models and miniatures, these effects are created through specifically photographic tricks. Their photographic base is hinted at in Hollywood terminology, which describes them as *optical effects.*

With the rise of computer-generated effects, the fusion of mise-en-scene and cinematography becomes even more seamless. Digital compositing allows the filmmaker to shoot some action with performers and then add backgrounds, shadows, or movement that would previously have required photographed mattes, multiple exposures, or optical printing. In *Speed,* the audience sees a city bus leap a broken freeway. The stunt was performed on a ramp designed for the jump, and the highway background was drawn digitally as a matte painting (**7.60).** With the proliferation of specialized programs, computer-generated imagery (CGI) increasingly provides convincing effects that have all but replaced traditional optical printing. (See Box.)

Like other film techniques, photographic manipulations of the shot are not ends in themselves. They function within the overall context of the film. Specific treatments of tonalities, speed of motion, or perspective should be judged less on criteria of realism than on criteria of function. For instance, many Hollywood filmmakers strive to make their rear-projection shots unnoticeable. But in Jean-Marie Straub and Danièle Huillet's *The Chronicle of Anna Magdalena Bach,* the

7.60   Computer-generated imagery created a gap in the freeway for the bus to leap in *Speed.*

From Monsters to the Mundane: Computer-Generated Imagery in *The Lord of the Rings*

The films adapted from J. R. R. Tolkien's trilogy *The Lord of the Rings (The Fellowship of the Ring, The Two Towers,* and *The Return of the King)*, show how CGI can be used for impressive special effects: huge battle scenes, realistic monsters, and magical events. Less obviously, the films also indicate how, more and more, CGI shapes many aspects of production, from the spectacular to the mundane.

The director, Peter Jackson, had started his career in horror and fantasy films in New Zealand, where he and his partner Richard Taylor formed a CGI firm, Weta Digital, in 1993. Most of the digital work for *Rings* was done at the Weta facility, although the film involved so much CGI that a few sequences were commissioned from other effects firms.

CGI was used at every stage of production. In preproduction, a sort of animated storyboard (a *previz*, for "previsualization") was made, consisting of *animatics*, or rough computer-generated versions of the scenes. Each of the three previzs was roughly as long as each finished film and helped to coordinate the work of the huge staff involved in both the digital and physical work of production.

During production of the three films, CGI helped create portions of the mise-en-scene. Many shots digitally stitched together disparate elements, blending full-size settings, miniature sets, and matte paintings (7.57). A total of 68 miniature sets were built, and computer manipulation was required in each case to make them appear real or to allow camera movements through them. Computer paint programs could generate matte paintings (often based on location still photographs) for the sky, clouds, distant cliffs, and forests that appeared behind the miniatures.

Rings also drew on the rapidly developing capacity of CGI to create characters. The war scenes were staged with a small number of actual actors in costumes, while vast crowds of CGI soldiers appeared in motion alongside them. Like many companies working on digitally sophisticated films, the Weta team had to develop its own proprietary software programs. A crucial program was Massive (for "Multiple Agent Simulation System in Virtual Environment"). Using motion capture on a few *agents* (costumed actors), the team could build a number of different military motions, assigning all of them to the thousands of crude, digitally generated figures. By giving each figure a rudimentary artificial intelligence—such as the ability to see an approaching soldier and identify it as friend or foe—Massive could generate a scene with figures moving in unpredictable patterns. (So many options were given to the soldiers that, according to the filmmakers, during one test simulation of the opening battle scene in Mordor, a band of soldiers in the distance decided to run away.) Another new program, Grunt, rendered these figures into photorealistic soldiers, again by creating a variety of options as to weight, height, and so on and letting these combine randomly for each figure **(7.61)**.

The monsters encountered by the characters during their quest were much more elaborately designed and executed than the troops. A detailed three-dimensional model of each creature was constructed and captured with a new scanning wand that could read even into recesses and folds to create a complete image from all angles. Obtaining realistic movement from these figures demanded further computer manipulation, however. A new system, Character Mapper, captured motion from a human actor, then adjusted the mass and musculature to imaginary skeletons. This was used notably in the cave-troll sequence to give an impression of the large, squat creature swinging its limbs and flexing its muscles in a believable fashion.

7.61   Vast crowds of soldiers with individualized movements were generated by the Massive program for *The Two Towers*.

Most of the speaking characters (with the important exception of the skeletal creature, Gollum) were played by actors, but even here CGI was used. The main characters had digital look-alikes who acted as stunt doubles, performing actions that were dangerous or impossible. In the cave-troll fight, the actors playing Legolas, Merry, and Pippin are all replaced by their digital doubles when they climb or jump on the troll's shoulders. A requirement specific to this story was the juxtaposition of full-size actors playing three-foot hobbits with other characters considerably taller than themselves. The size difference was often created during filming by using small doubles or by placing the hobbits further from the camera in false-perspective sets. Some scenes combining tall and short characters required camera movement, which, to avoid destroying the false perspective, was accomplished by using *motion control:* Motion control uses a camera guided by computer calculations, and here it moved the foreground and background figures at different rates, proportionate to their size and distance from the lens.

In many cases CGI created the kinds of special effects generated on an optical printer. In *The Fellowship of the Ring*, such effects include Gandalf's fireworks, the flood at the Fords of Bruinen, the avalanche that hits the Fellowship on the mountain pass, and the flaming Eye of Sauron. The Elf Legolas's superhuman speed in archery was achieved by adding digital arrows to the actor's pantomime of firing.

Cinematography also depended on CGI. For the cave-troll scene, Jackson donned a virtual-reality helmet and planned camera positions by moving around a virtual set and facing a virtual troll. The camera positions were motion-captured and reproduced in the actual filming of the sequence—which has a rough, hand-held style quite different from the rest of the scenes.

CGI was required in postproduction as well. Filmmakers erased telephone poles in location shots and helicopter blades dipping into the aerial shots of the Fellowship's voyage across mountains. Specialized programs added details, such as the ripples caused by drops of dew falling into the water in the Mirror of Galadriel and the moving water in the distant falls seen behind Rivendell.

Perhaps most important, digital grading after filming manipulated 70 percent of the shots in *Fellowship,* 100 percent in *The Two Towers*. Grading could alter the color of

7.62   In *The Fellowship of the Ring* selective digital color grading makes one figure bright white while the rest of the scene has a uniform muted blue tone.

shots, giving each major location a distinctive look, such as the autumnal shades used for Rivendell. The faces of the characters were made to look pallid in the Mines of Moria, while the early scenes in the Shire were given a yellow glow that enhanced the sunshine and green fields. The grading also utilized a specially designed program, Colossus, which allowed artists to adjust the color values of individual elements within a shot. Thus in the Lorien scene in which Galadriel shows Frodo her mirror, she glows bright white, contrasting with the deep blue tones of Frodo's figure and setting. This is achieved not only by aiming bright lights at her (which would brighten nearby parts of the set as well), but also by digitally brightening only her figure in postproduction **(7.62)**. In such ways CGI techniques can go beyond the creation of imaginary creatures and large crowds to shape the visual style of an entire film.

Commenting on the special effects in the hobbit party scene in *Fellowship*, Visual Effects Supervisor Jim Rygiel and Weta Animation Design Supervisor William Cook emphasize the range of uses for CGI. The party was shot on a set in a studio, but the treetops and sky were added by computer:

"So we ended up replacing that whole sky and some of those trees and obviously adding the fireworks dragon and the smoke elements. So the showy stuff is obviously effects, but there's a lot of stuff that's hidden, like just the background behind Ian [Holm] and Elijah [Wood], which is every bit as much of a challenge."

Such ambitious applications of CGI required enormous technical facilities. With *Fellowship*, Weta began with 192 computers devoted solely to rendering images 24 hours a day. During 2002, after the success of the first film, the firm acquired another 150 workstations. The digital information generated for the three films was around 150 terabytes. As computer memory and speed continue to develop, the applications of CGI to many aspects of filmmaking—and not just on effects-heavy films like *The Lord of the Rings*—will expand as well.

7.63   The foreground plane of this shot from *The Chronicle of Anna Magdalena Bach* shows Bach, shot straight on, playing a harpsichord—yet the back-projected building behind him is shot from a low angle.

perspective relations are yanked out of kilter by an inconsistent rear projection **(7.63).** Since the film's other shots have been filmed on location in correct perspective, this blatantly artificial rear projection calls our attention to the visual style of the entire film.

Similarly, **7.64** looks unrealistic unless we posit the man as being about two feet long. But director Vera Chytilova has used setting, character position, and deep focus to make a comic point about the two women's treatment of men. Such trick perspective was designed to be unnoticeable in *The Lord of the Rings,* where an adult actor playing a 3-foot hobbit might be placed considerably further from the camera than an actor playing a taller character, yet the two appeared to be talking face to face. (See box, p. 250.) The filmmaker chooses not only how to register light and movement photographically but also how those photographic qualities will function within the overall formal system of the film. Trick perspective of the sort used in *Daisies* or *The Lord of the Rings* depends on another factor as well: the precise framing of the image.

FRAMING

7.64   *Daisies:* Perspective cues create a comic optical illusion.

It may seem odd to talk of something as elusive as the border of the image, since it may seem merely an edge or break. (After all, literary critics do not talk of the margins of the pages in *Moby Dick.*) But, in a film, the frame is not simply a neutral border; it imposes a *certain vantage point* onto the material within the image. In cinema the frame is important because it actively *defines* the image for us.

If proof were required of the power of **framing,** we need only turn to the first major filmmaker in history, Louis Lumière. An inventor and businessman, Lumière and his brother Auguste devised one of the first practical cinema cameras **(7.65).** The Lumière camera, the most flexible of its day, also doubled as a projector. Whereas the bulky American camera invented by W. K. L. Dickson was about the size of an office desk **(7.66),** the Lumière camera weighed only 12 pounds and was small and portable. As a result of its lightness, the Lumière camera could be taken outside and could be set up quickly. Louis Lumière's earliest films presented simple events—workers leaving his father's factory, a game of cards, a family meal. But even at so early a stage of film history, Lumière was able to use framing to transform everyday reality into cinematic events.

Consider one of the most famous Lumière films, *The Arrival of a Train at La Ciotat* (1897). Had Lumière followed theatrical practice, he might have framed the shot by setting the camera perpendicular to the platform, letting the train enter the frame from the right side, broadside to the spectator. Instead, Lumière positioned the camera at an oblique angle. The result is a dynamic composition, with the train arriving from the distance on a diagonal **(7.67).** If the scene had been shot perpendicularly, we would have seen only a string of passengers' backs climbing aboard. Here, however, Lumière's oblique angle brings out many aspects of the passengers' bodies and several planes of action. We see some figures in the foreground, some in the distance. Simple as it is, this single-shot film, less than a minute long, aptly illustrates how choosing a position for the camera makes a drastic difference in the framing of the image and how we perceive the filmed event.

7.65   The Lumière camera provided flexibility in framing.

Consider another Lumière short, *Baby's Meal* (1895). Lumière selected a camera position that would emphasize certain aspects of the event. A long shot would have situated the family in its garden, but Lumière frames the figures at a medium distance, which downplays the setting but emphasizes the family's gestures and

7.66 The bulky camera of
W. K. L. Dickson.

7.67 Louis Lumière's diagonal framing
in *The Arrival of a Train at La Ciotat.*

7.68 *Baby's Meal.*

facial expressions **(7.68).** The frame's control of the scale of the event has also controlled our understanding of the event itself.

Framing can powerfully affect the image by means of (1) the size and shape of the frame; (2) the way the frame defines onscreen and offscreen space; (3) the way framing imposes the distance, angle, and height of a vantage point onto the image; and (4) the way framing can move in relation to the mise-en-scene.

Frame Dimensions and Shape

We are so accustomed to the frame as a rectangle that we should remember that it need not be one. In painting and photography, of course, images have frames of various sizes and shapes: narrow rectangles, ovals, vertical panels, even triangles and parallelograms. In cinema the choice has been more limited.

The ratio of frame width to frame height is called the **aspect ratio.** The rough dimensions of the ratio were set quite early in the history of cinema by Edison, Dickson, Lumière, and other inventors. The film frame was to be rectangular, its proportion approximately three to two, yielding an aspect ratio of 1.33:1. Nonetheless, in the silent period, some filmmakers felt that this standard was too limiting. Abel Gance shot and projected sequences of *Napoleon* (1927) in a format he called *triptychs.* This was a widescreen effect composed of three normal frames side-by-side. Gance used the effect sometimes to show a single huge expanse, sometimes to put three distinct images side by side **(7.69).** In contrast, the Soviet director

7.69 A panoramic view from *Napoleon* joined images shot with three cameras.

Sergei Eisenstein argued for a square frame, which would make compositions along horizontal, vertical, and diagonal directions equally feasible.

The coming of sound in the late 1920s altered the frame somewhat. Adding the sound track to the film strip required adjusting either the shape or the size of the image. At first, some films were printed in an almost a square format, usually about 1.17:1 **(7.70).** But in the early 1930s, the Hollywood Academy of Motion Picture Arts and Sciences established the so-called **Academy ratio** of 1.33:1. (Strictly speaking, on most prints this works out to 1.37:1, but 1.33:1 is still referred to as the standard.) The Academy ratio was standardized throughout the world until the mid-1950s **(7.71).** Outside North America and Western Europe, many films are still shot in this format. Standard television screens also are in the 1.33:1 ratio.

Since the mid-1950s, a variety of *widescreen* ratios have dominated 35mm filmmaking. The most common format in North America today is 1.85:1 **(7.72,** from *Aliens).* The 1.66:1 ratio **(7.73,** from *Une Chambre en Ville)* is more frequently used in Europe than in North America, although Steven Spielberg intended *E.T.: The Extraterrestrial* to be shown in this format. A less common ratio, also widely used in European films, is 1.75:1 **(7.74,** from *Last Tango in Paris).* A 2.35:1 ratio **(7.75,** from King Hu's *The Valiant Ones)* was standardized by the Cinema-Scope anamorphic process during the 1950s. (In contemporary practice, the 2.35:1 ratio is usually projected at 2.40:1.) The 2.2:1 ratio has been widely used for 70mm presentation **(7.76,** from *Ghostbusters),* although many projectionists prefer to present 70mm at 2:1.

The simplest way to create a widescreen image is by **masking** it at some stage in production or exhibition **(7.77).** This masking is usually called a *hard matte.* Alternatively, many contemporary films are shot full-frame (that is, between 1.33:1 and 1.17:1) in the expectation that they will be masked when the film is shown. Sometimes this results in lights or sound equipment being visible in the full-frame image. In **7.78** you can clearly see the microphone bobbing down into the shot. This would not be seen in the theater, where the top and bottom of the frame would be masked by the aperture plate in the projector. The colored lines in our illustration show a projection framing at 1.85:1.

Another way to create a widescreen image is by using an **anamorphic** process. Here a special lens squeezes the image horizontally, either during filming or in printing. A comparable lens is necessary to unsqueeze the image during projection. The image on the 35mm film strip is shown in **7.79,** while the image as projected on the screen is shown in **7.80.** The anamorphic aspect ratio, established by Cinema-Scope was 2.35:1, until the 1970s; for technical reasons it was adjusted to 2.40:1. This is the aspect ratio of Panavision, today's most frequently used anamorphic system.

Widescreen cinema, either masked or anamorphic, has significant visual effects. The screen becomes a band or strip, emphasizing horizontal compositions. The format was initially associated with genres of spectacle—Westerns, travelogues, musicals, historical epics—in which sweeping settings were important. But directors quickly learned that widescreen has value for more intimate subjects, too. The frame from Kurosawa's *Sanjuro* **(7.81)** shows how an anamorphic process (Tohoscope, the Japanese equivalent of CinemaScope) can be used to create significant foreground and background areas in a confined setting.

In some widescreen compositions, the director will draw the audience's attention to only one area of the image. A common solution is to put the important information slightly off center **(7.82),** or even sharply off center **(7.83).** Or the director may use the widescreen format to multiply points of interest. Many scenes

Common Aspect Ratios of 35mm Film

1.17:1

7.70 *Public Enemy:* The squarish aspect ratio of early sound films.

1.33 (1.37):1

7.71 *The Rules of the Game* was shot in "Academy ratio."

1.85:1

7.72 *Aliens* uses 1.85:1, a common North American ratio.

1.66:1

7.73 The 1.66:1 ratio in *Une chamber en ville.*

1.75:1

7.74 *Last Tango in Paris,* shot at 1.75:1.

2.35:1
(35mm anamorphic)

7.75 Anamorphic widescreen in *The Valiant Ones.*

2.2:1
(70mm)

7.76 *Ghostbusters.*

7.77 This frame from Agnès Varda's *Vagabond* was masked during filming or printing.

7.78 Martin Scorsese's *Raging Bull*.

7.79 A frame from Nicholas Ray's CinemaScope film *Bigger than Life* squeezed . . .

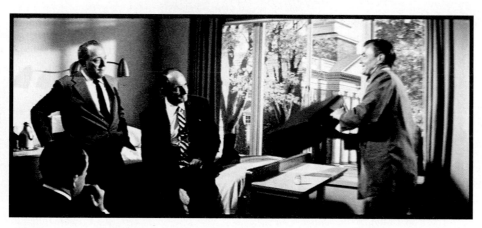

7.80 . . . and as projected.

7.81 Akira Kurosawa's *Sanjuro*.

7.82 Souleymare Cissé's *Yeelen.*

7.83 John McTiernan's *Die Hard.*

in Im Kwon-Taek's *Chunhyang* fill the frame with bustle and movement **(7.84).** Similarly, though less hectically, the shipboard sequences in Michelangelo Antonioni's *L'Avventura* pepper the frame with several points of interest **(7.85).**

The rectangular frame, while by far the most common, has not prevented filmmakers from experimenting with other frame shapes. This has usually been done by attaching **masks** over either the camera's or the printer's lens to block the passage of light. Masks were quite common in the silent cinema. A moving circular mask that opens to reveal or closes to conceal a scene is called an **iris.** In *La Roue,* Gance employed a variety of circular and oval masks **(7.86).** In **7.87,** a shot from Griffith's *Intolerance,* most of the frame is boldly blocked out to leave only a thin vertical slice, emphasizing the soldier's fall from the rampart. A number of directors in the sound cinema have revived the use of irises and masks. In *The Magnificent Ambersons* **(7.88),** Orson Welles uses an iris to close a scene; the old-fashioned device adds a nostalgic note to the sequence.

We also should mention experiments with *multiple-frame* imagery, often called *split-screen* imagery. In this process, two or more images, each with its own frame dimensions and shape, appear within the larger frame. From the early cinema onward, this device has been used to present scenes of telephone conversations **(7.89).** Split-screen phone scenes were revived for phone conversations in *Bye Bye Birdie* and other 1960s widescreen comedies. Multiple-frame imagery is also useful for building suspense, as Brian De Palma has shown in such films as *Sisters.* We gain a

7.84   In this busy scene from *Chunhyang,* our eye shuttles around the widescreen frame according to who is speaking, who is facing us, and who responds to the speaker.

7.85   Antonioni's *L'Avventura:* Items dispersed across the frame.

7.86   Gance's *La Roue.*

7.87   Griffith's *Intolerance.*

7.88   Welles's *The Magnificent Ambersons.*

7.89   Philips Smalley's 1913 *Suspense* uses a three-way split screen.

godlike omniscience as we watch two or more actions at exactly the same moment. Peter Greenaway uses split screen more experimentally in *Prospero's Books,* juxtaposing images suggested by Shakespeare's *The Tempest* **(7.90).**

As usual, the filmmaker's choice of screen format can be an important factor in shaping the viewer's experience. Frame size and shape can guide the spectator's attention. It can be concentrated through compositional patterns or masking, or it can be dispersed by use of various points of interest or sound cues. The same possibilities exist with multiple-frame imagery, which must be carefully coordinated either to focus the viewer's notice or to send it ricocheting from one image to another.

Onscreen and Offscreen Space

Whatever its shape, the frame makes the image finite. The film image is bounded, limited. From an implicitly continuous world, the frame selects a slice to show us, leaving the rest of the space *offscreen.* If the camera leaves an object or person and moves elsewhere, we will assume that the object or person is still there, outside the frame. Even in an abstract film, we cannot resist the sense that the shapes and patterns that burst into the frame come from somewhere.

Noël Burch has pointed out six zones of offscreen space: the space beyond each of the four edges of the frame, the space behind the set, and the space behind the camera. It is worth considering how many ways a filmmaker can imply the

7.90 The actor playing Ariel in *Prospero's Books* hovers over the scene in a separate space.

7.91 *Jezebel:* The heroine, Julie, greets some friends in medium shot . . .

7.92 . . . when suddenly a huge fist holding a glass appears in the left foreground.

7.93 Julie looks off at its owner and comes forward . . .

7.94 . . . and the camera retreats slightly to frame her with the man who had toasted her.

presence of things in these zones of offscreen space. A character can direct looks or gestures at something offscreen. As we shall see in Chapter 9, sound can offer potent clues about offscreen space. And, of course, something from offscreen can protrude partly into the frame. Virtually any film could be cited for examples of all these possibilities, but attractive instances are offered by films that use offscreen space for surprise effects.

In a party scene in William Wyler's *Jezebel*, the heroine, Julie, is the main focus of attention until a man's hand comes abruptly into the frame **(7.91–7.94).** The intrusion of the hand abruptly signals us to the man's presence; Julie's glance, the camera movement, and the sound track confirm our new awareness of the total space. The director has used the selective powers of the frame to exclude something of great importance and then introduce it with startling effect.

More systematically, D. W. Griffith's *Musketeers of Pig Alley* makes use of sudden intrusions into the frame as a motif developing across the whole film. When a gangster is trying to slip a drug into the heroine's drink, we are not aware that the Snapper Kid has entered the room until a plume of his cigarette smoke wafts into the frame **(7.95).** At the film's end, when the Snapper Kid receives a payoff, a mysterious hand thrusts into the frame to offer him money **(7.96).** Griffith has exploited the surprise latent in our sudden awareness that figures are offscreen.

The use of the fifth zone of offscreen space, that behind the set, is of course common; characters go out a door and are now concealed by a wall or a staircase. Somewhat rarer is the use of the sixth zone—offscreen space behind and near the camera. One lengthy example occurs in Abbas Kiarostami's *Under the Olive Trees*. The crew is shooting a film scene, and we watch through the lens of the camera. As the tensions between two young actors spoil take after take, the action is repeated many times **(7.97).** Occasional cuts show the director and his crew behind the camera **(7.98).** After several repetitions, the director walks in from that offscreen space behind the camera and tries to resolve the problem **(7.99).** Because of our awareness of the space behind the camera, throughout the many retakes we remain aware of the offscreen crew and their growing frustration. In such ways a filmmaker can turn the necessary limitations of the frame edge to advantage.

Angle, Level, Height, and Distance of Framing

The frame implies not only space outside itself but also a position from which the material in the image is viewed. Most often, of course, such a position is that of the camera filming the event, but this need not always be true. In an animated film, the position implied by the drawn frames is not necessarily the same position that the camera

7.95   *The Musketeers of Pig Alley.*

7.96   *The Musketeers of Pig Alley.*

7.97   The actors return to their positions for one of many retakes of a shot for the film-within-a-film in *Under the Olive Trees.*

7.98   Finally, a reverse shot reveals the crew behind the camera, trying to figure out what is causing the problem.

7.99   Eventually the director walks into camera range and tries to talk the actors into playing their roles as he wants them to.

occupies during the making of the film. Shots in an animated film may be framed as high or low angles, or long shots or close-ups, all of which simply result from the perspective of drawings selected to be photographed. Still, in what follows, we shall continue to speak of *camera angle, camera level, camera height,* and *camera distance,* with the understanding that these terms refer simply to what we see on the screen and need not always conform to what occurred during production.

Angle   The frame implies an **angle of framing** with respect to what is shown. It thus positions us at some angle onto the shot's mise-en-scene. The number of such

7.100   A straight-on angle in *The Chronicle of Anna Magdalena Bach.*

7.101   A high-angle framing from *Se7en.*

7.102   A low-angle framing from *Babe.*

7.103   A canted framing in *Fallen Angels.*

7.104   A startling canted framing in *The End.*

angles is infinite, since there is an infinite number of points in space that the camera might occupy. In practice, we typically distinguish three general categories: the straight-on angle, the high angle, and the low angle. The straight-on angle is the most common **(7.100).** The high-angle positions us looking down at the material within the frame **(7.101).** The low-angle framing positions us as looking up at the framed materials **(7.102).**

Level   We can also distinguish the degree to which the frame is *level.* This ultimately bears on the sense of gravity governing the filmed material and the frame. Assume that we are filming telephone poles. If the framing is level, the horizontal edges of the frame will be parallel to the horizon of the shot and perpendicular to the poles. If horizon and poles are at diagonal angles, the frame is **canted** in one manner or another.

Canted framing is relatively rare, although a few films make heavy use of it, such as Orson Welles's *Mr. Arkadin,* Carol Reed's *The Third Man,* and Wong Kar-wai's *Fallen Angels* **(7.103).** In Christopher Maclaine's *The End,* a canted framing makes a steep street in the foreground appear level and renders the houses in the background grotesquely out of kilter **(7.104).**

Height   Sometimes it becomes important to indicate that the framing gives us a sense of being stationed at a certain **height.** Camera angle is, of course, partly related to height: To frame from a high angle entails being at a vantage point higher than the material in the image.

But camera height is not simply a matter of camera angle. For instance, the Japanese filmmaker Yasujiro Ozu often positions his camera close to the ground to film characters or objects on the floor (6.139, 8.135, and 8.136). Note that this is not a matter of camera angle, for the angle is straight on; we still see the ground or floor. Filming from such a low height with a straight-on angle is an important quality of Ozu's visual style, as we shall see in Chapter 11.

Distance   The framing of the image stations us not only at a certain angle and height and on a level plane or at a cant but also at a certain distance. Framing supplies a sense of being far away or close to the mise-en-scene of the shot. This aspect of framing is usually called camera distance. In what follows, we shall use the standard measure—the scale of the human body—but any other filmed material would do as well. The examples are all from *The Third Man.*

In the **extreme long shot,** the human figure is barely visible (**7.105**). This is the framing for landscapes, bird's-eye views of cities, and other vistas. In the **long shot,** figures are more prominent, but the background still dominates (**7.106**). Shots in which the human figure is framed from about the knees up are called **medium long shots (7.107).** These are common, since they permit a nice balance of figure and surroundings.

The **medium shot** frames the human body from the waist up (**7.108**). Gesture and expression now become more visible. The **medium close-up** frames the body from the chest up (**7.109**). The **close-up** is traditionally the shot showing just the head, hands, feet, or a small object. It emphasizes facial expression, the details of a gesture, or a significant object (**7.110**). The **extreme close-up** singles out a portion of the face (eyes or lips) and isolates and magnifies a detail (**7.111**).

7.105   *The Third Man:* extreme long shot.

7.106   Long shot.

7.107   Medium long shot.

7.108   Medium shot.

7.109   Medium close-up.

7.110   Close-up.

7.111   Extreme close-up.

Note that the size of the photographed material within the frame is as important as any real camera distance. From the same camera distance, you could film a long shot of a person or a close-up of King Kong's elbow. We would not call the shot in **7.112** (from *La Passion de Jeanne d'Arc*) a close-up just because only Jeanne's head appears in the frame; the framing is that of a long shot because in scale her head is relatively small. (If the framing were simply adjusted downward, her whole body would be visible.) In judging camera distance, the relative proportion of the material framed provides the basic determinant.

Common confusions exist about framing. Categories of framing are obviously matters of degree. There is no universal measure of camera angle or distance. No precise cut-off point distinguishes between a long shot and an extreme long shot, or a slightly low angle and a straight-on angle. Moreover, filmmakers are not bound by terminology. They rightly do not worry if a shot does not fit into traditional categories. (Nevertheless abbreviations like MS for medium shot and CU for close-up are regularly used in screenplays, so filmmakers do find these terms useful in their work.) In most cases, the concepts are clear enough for us to use them in talking about films. It is not of great importance whether the shot that cuts John Wayne off slightly above his waist is to be called a "true" medium shot or a "true" medium close-up. What is important is that we use the term consistently, so that we can analyze how that framing functions in the particular film.

7.112 *La Passion de Jeanne d'Arc.*

Functions of Framing

Another problem is more important. Sometimes we are tempted to assign absolute meanings to angles, distances, and other qualities of framing. It is tempting to believe that framing from a low angle automatically presents a character as powerful and that framing from a high angle presents him or her as dwarfed and defeated. Verbal analogies are especially seductive: A canted frame seems to mean that "the world is out of kilter."

The analysis of film as art would be a lot easier if technical qualities automatically possessed such hard-and-fast meanings, but individual films would thereby lose much of their uniqueness and richness. The fact is that framings have no absolute or general meanings. In *some* films angles and distance carry such meanings as mentioned above, but in other films—probably most films—they do not. To rely on such formulas is to forget that meaning and effect always stem from the total film, from its operation as a system. The context of the film will determine the function of the framings, just as it determines the function of mise-en-scene, photographic qualities, and other techniques. Consider three examples.

At many points in *Citizen Kane,* low-angle shots of Kane do convey his looming power, but the lowest angles occur at the point of Kane's most humiliating defeat—his miscarried gubernatorial campaign **(7.113).** Note that angles of framing affect not only our view of the main figures but also the background against which those figures may appear.

If the cliché about high-angle framings were correct, **7.114,** a shot from *North by Northwest,* would express the powerlessness of Van Damm and Leonard. In fact, Van Damm has just decided to eliminate his mistress by pushing her out of a plane, and he is saying, "I think that this is a matter best disposed of from a great height." The angle and distance of Hitchcock's shot wittily prophesy how the murder is to be carried out.

Similarly, the world is hardly out of kilter in the shot from Eisenstein's *October* shown in **7.115.** The canted frame dynamizes the effort of pushing the cannon.

These three examples should demonstrate that we cannot reduce the richness of cinema to a few recipes. We must, as usual, look for the *functions* the technique performs in the particular *context* of the total film.

"I don't *like* close-ups unless you can get a kick out of them, unless you *need* them. If you can get away with attitudes and positions that show the feeling of the scene, I think you're better off using the close-up only for absolute punctuation— that's the reason you do it. And you save it—not like TV where they do *everything* in close-up.

— Howard Hawks, director

7.113 *Citizen Kane:* The low angle functions to isolate Kane and his friend against an empty background, his deserted campaign headquarters.

7.114 *North by Northwest.*

7.115 A dramatic canted framing from *October.*

7.116 The tears of Henriette in *A Day in the Country* are visible in extreme close-up.

7.117 In *Day for Night,* a close framing emphasizes the precision with which the film director positions an actor's hands.

Camera distance, height, level, and angle often take on clear-cut narrative functions. Camera distance can establish or reestablish settings and character positions, as we shall see in the next chapter when we examine the editing of the first sequence of *The Maltese Falcon.* A framing can isolate a narratively important detail **(7.116, 7.117).**

Framing also contributes to cueing us to take a shot as subjective. In Chapter 3, we saw that a film's narration may present story information with some degree of psychological depth (p. 85), and one option is a perceptual subjectivity that renders what a character sees or hears. When a shot's framing prompts us to take it as a character's vision, we call it an optically subjective shot, or a point-of-view (POV). Fritz Lang's *Fury* provides a clear example **(7.118, 7.119).**

Framings may serve the narrative in yet other ways. Across an entire film the repetitions of certain framings may associate themselves with a character or situation. That is, framings may become motifs unifying the film **(7.120).** Throughout *La Passion de Jeanne d'Arc* Dreyer returns obsessively to extreme close-up shots of Jeanne (6.14).

Alternatively, certain framings in a film may stand out by virtue of their rarity. The ominously calm effect of the shot of the birds descending on Bodega Bay in Hitchcock's film *The Birds* arises from the abrupt shift from straight-on medium shots to an extreme long shot from very high above the town (8.40 and 8.41, p. 302). In a film composed primarily of long shots and medium shots, an extreme close-up will obviously have considerable force. Similarly, the early scenes of Ridley Scott's *Alien* present few shots depicting any character's point of view. But when Kane approaches the alien egg, we see close views of it as if through his eyes, and the creature leaps straight out at us. This not only provides a sudden shock; the abrupt switch to framings that restrict us to one character's range of knowledge emphasizes a major turning point in the plot.

Even within a single sequence, camera angle, level, and distance may develop significantly. In the final sequence from Hitchcock's *Saboteur,* at the top of the Statue of Liberty, the hero is holding the coatsleeve of the saboteur, who dangles precariously. The sleeve's stitching starts to tear. Hitchcock cuts from extreme long shots, high- and low-angled, canted this way and that, of the statue to extreme close-ups of the threads ripping out one by one. The scene's suspense derives principally from the drastic difference between the broad view (emphasizing the saboteur's danger) and the focused enlargement (his fate hangs by a thread).

Framings do not function only to emphasize narrative form. They can have their own intrinsic interest as well. Close-ups can bring out textures and details we

7.118   In *Fury,* the hero in his jail cell is seen through the bars from a slightly low angle . . .

7.119   . . . while the next shot, a high angle through the window toward the street outside, shows us what he sees, from his point of view.

7.120   In *The Maltese Falcon,* Casper Gutman is frequently photographed from a low angle, emphasizing his obesity.

might otherwise ignore. We can see the smallest surreptitious gestures of a pickpocket in the medium close-up from Robert Bresson's *Pickpocket* **(7.121);** a series of similar close shots makes up a dazzling, balletlike scene in this film. Long shots can permit us to explore vistas. Much of the visual delight of Westerns, of David Lynch's *The Straight Story,* or of Werner Herzog's documentary, *Lessons of Darkness* **(7.122)** arises from long shots that make huge spaces manifest. By including a range of information, the long-shot framing encourages us to explore details or discover abstract patterns **(7.123).**

7.121   Bresson's *Pickpocket.*

Our eye also enjoys the formal play presented by unusual angles on familiar objects **(7.124).** In *La Passion de Jeanne d'Arc* the upside-down framings **(7.125)** are not motivated as a character's point of view; they exist as an exploration of framing in its own right. "By reproducing the object from an unusual and striking angle," writes Rudolf Arnheim, "the artist forces the spectator to take a keener interest, which goes beyond mere noticing or acceptance. The object thus photographed sometimes gains in reality, and the impression it makes is livelier and more arresting."

Framing may be used for comic effect, as Charlie Chaplin, Buster Keaton, and Jacques Tati have all shown. We have seen that in *Our Hospitality* Keaton stages many gags in depth. Now we can see that well-chosen camera angles and distances are also vital to the gags' success. For example, if the railroad scene shown in 6.156 (p. 222) were shot from the side and in extreme long shot, we would not see so

7.122   *Lessons of Darkness:* Helicopter shots give the desolate burning oilfields of Kuwait after the Gulf War an eerie, horrifying grandeur.

7.123 Hou Hsiao-hsien's *Summer at Grandpa's:* The boy from the city visits his disgraced uncle, and the neighborhood is presented as a welter of rooftops sheltering a spot of bright red.

7.124 René Clair in *Entr'acte* frames a ballerina from straight below, transforming the figure into an expanding and contracting flower.

clearly that the two parts of the train are on parallel tracks. Moreover, we could not see the engineer's unconcerned posture, which indicates his failure to realize what has happened. Similarly, the use of framing to create offscreen space is vital to the gag shown in 6.165 and 6.166 (p. 222). Here the gag is laid out in time rather than space. First Willie tugs on the rope; then an unseen effect of that tug becomes visible as the Canfield son hurtles past and disappears. Finally Willie reacts and is himself dragged down into the abyss below the frameline. Try to imagine these moments and others in *Our Hospitality* framed in a different way, and you will see how our reaction to Keaton's humor depends on the careful combination of mise-en-scene and framing.

Similarly, in Tati's *Play Time* mise-en-scene and camera position cooperate to create pictorial jokes **(7.126).** The visual pun issues from the precisely chosen camera angle and distance, as well as from the mise-en-scene: the man's stooping posture as well as the door handles make him look like a goat. We cannot classify all the non-narrative functions of framing; we can only suggest that camera angle, level, height, and distance have the constant possibility of sharpening our perception of purely visual qualities.

The Mobile Frame

All of the features of framing we have examined are present in paintings, photographs, comic strips, and other sorts of pictures. All images furnish instances of aspect ratios, in-frame and out-of-frame relations, angle, level, height, and distance of the frame's vantage point. But there is one resource of framing that is specific to cinema (and video). In film it is possible for the frame to *move* with respect to the framed material.

Mobile framing means that, within the image, the framing of the object changes. The mobile frame thus produces changes of camera angle, level, height, or distance *during* the shot. Further, since the framing orients us to the material in the image, we often see ourselves as moving *along with* the frame. Through such framing we may approach the object or retreat from it, circle it, or move past it.

Types of Mobile Framing   We usually refer to the ability of the frame to be mobile as *camera movement.* Very often the term is accurate, for usually mobility of framing is achieved by moving the camera physically during production. The camera, as

7.125   *La Passion de Jeanne d'Arc.*

7.126 *Play Time:* M. Hulot reacts with a start when he notices that a man locking a door seems suddenly to have sprouted horns (the door handles).

we know, usually rests on a support while filming, and this support may be designed to move the camera. There are several kinds of camera movement, each a specific effect onscreen.

The **pan** (short for *panorama*) movement rotates the camera on a vertical axis. The camera as a whole does not move to a new position. Onscreen, the pan gives the impression of a frame horizontally scanning space. It is as if the camera "turns its head" right or left **(7.127, 7.128).**

The **tilt** movement rotates the camera on a horizontal axis. It is as if the camera's head were swiveling up or down. Again, the entire camera does not change position. Onscreen, the tilt movement yields the impression of unrolling a space from top to bottom or bottom to top **(7.129, 7.130).**

In the **tracking,** or **dolly** or *trucking,* **shot,**, the camera as a whole does change position, traveling in any direction along the ground—forward, backward, circularly, diagonally, or from side to side **(7.131, 7.132).** Note how the figures remain in the same basic relationship to the frame as they stroll along a sidewalk, while the front of the house that they hope to buy remains visible behind them.

In the **crane shot** the camera moves above ground level. Typically, it rises or descends, often thanks to a mechanical arm that lifts and lowers it. The mourning scene in *Ivan the Terrible* begins with a crane downward **(7.133, 7.134).** A crane shot may move not only up and down, like an elevator, but forward and backward or from side to side **(7.135, 7.136).** For *The Thin Red Line,* Terence Malick used a crane with a 72-foot arm to let the camera slither over tall grass during battle scenes. Variations of the crane shot are helicopter and airplane shots.

7.127   During a shot in Dreyer's *Ordet,* the camera pans right . . .

7.128   . . . to keep the figures in frame as they cross a room.

7.129   François Truffaut's *The Bride Wore Black* begins with a tilt down a church spire . . .

7.130   . . . to the church door.

7.131   During this lateral tracking shot in Erich von Stroheim's *Greed,* the camera moves rightward . . .

7.132   . . . along with the two characters.

7.133   *Ivan the Terrible:* From a high-angle view of the bier, the camera cranes down . . .

7.134   . . . to end with a straight-in framing of Ivan seated at the bier's base.

7.135   At the end of Karel Reisz's *Morgan!,* the camera moves diagonally up . . .

7.136   . . . and back to reveal that the hero's apparently innocuous flower garden proclaims his Communist sympathies.

Pans, tilts, tracking shots, and crane shots are the most common framing movements, but virtually any kind of camera movement can be imagined (somersaulting, rolling, and so on). The pan resembles a lateral tracking shot, and the tilt resembles a vertical crane shot. But a little practice in viewing makes the differences easy to spot. In both the pan and the tilt, the body of the camera does not change position; it simply swivels left or right, up or down. For example, in 7.127 the framing is fairly close to the central man, showing him in profile. If the camera were tracking along with him, it would continue to show him roughly in profile—yet 7.128 shows him at a greater distance and from behind—indicating that the camera has turned but not moved along with the character. In the lateral tracking shot and the vertical crane shot, the camera moves horizontally or vertically, as if you were gliding along with a character or swooping up over a landscape. As we shall see, though, types of camera movements can be combined.

Camera movements have held an appeal for filmmakers and audiences since the beginnings of cinema. Why? Visually, camera movements have several arresting effects. They often increase information about the space of the image. Objects become more vivid and sharper than in stationary framings. New objects or figures are usually revealed. Tracking shots and crane shots supply continually changing perspectives on passing objects as the frame constantly shifts its orientation. Objects appear more solid and three-dimensional when the camera arcs (i.e., tracks along a curved path) around them. Pan and tilt shots present space as continuous, both horizontally and vertically.

Moreover, it is difficult not to see camera movement as a substitute for *our* movement. The objects do not seem to swell or shrink. We seem to approach or retreat from them. We are not, of course, completely fooled. We never forget that we are watching a film in a theater. But camera movement provides several convincing cues for movement through space. Indeed, so powerful are these cues that filmmakers often make camera movements subjective—motivated narratively to represent the view through the eyes of a moving character. That is, camera movement can be a powerful cue that we are watching a POV shot.

In commercial film production today, many camera movements are made with the camera on a dolly. Before the 1970s, it was standard practice to mount the dolly on rails for lengthy movements (hence the term *tracking*). In recent decades, however, a simple and popular means is a gimbal-balanced camera mount patented as the Steadicam. This mount attaches the camera to the operator's body by means of a brace. The operator can walk with the camera, guiding the framing by minimal hand movements while viewing the image on a video monitor. Another operator adjusts focus by remote control.

The balancing mechanism allows the Steadicam to produce mobile shots of great smoothness. It allows fluidity in tracking with actors climbing stairs, entering rooms, and riding bicycles or motorcycles (**7.137, 7.138**). Recently directors have used a Steadicam on the set to supplement the principal camera by providing moving shots that can be cut into longer views. Some directors have taken advantage of the Steadicam to create elaborate moving shots lasting several minutes and traversing a series of spaces, as in the openings of Brian De Palma's *The Bonfire of the Vanities* and *Snake Eyes.* (For a Steadicam in use, see Fig. 7.210.)

In creating certain special effects, the camera's movement may be governed by electronic means. **Motion-control** techniques use computer programs to plot the camera's movements and execute them precisely. The movements can then be repeated for different elements of a composite shot. For example, a track toward a spacecraft can be repeated to enlarge the background within which the miniature will be matted. Motion control can also blend camera movements filmed on location with those made in a studio. When the makers of *Clear and Present Danger* could not get permission to film Harrison Ford in a car inside the White House gates, a motion-control device recorded the pan from the deserted gate to the building. Back in California, Ford was filmed in a car beside a replica of the gate, and the motion-control program reproduced the original panning movement. The two shots were then blended by digital compositing.

Sometimes the filmmaker does not want smooth camera movements, preferring a bumpy, jiggling image. Commonly this sort of image is achieved through use of the **hand-held** camera. That is, the operator does not anchor the machine on

"It's a compulsion of mine to move the camera, and I now know why. It enhances three-dimensionality. It puts you in the space, and if you move the camera the audience becomes aware of the space."

— George Miller, director

7.137 In Martin Scorsese's *Raging Bull,* the Steadicam follows the protagonist out of his dressing room . . .

7.138 . . . and through a crowd up to the boxing ring.

7.139 Don Pennebaker hand-holds the camera while filming his *Keep on Rocking.*

a tripod or dolly but instead uses his or her body to act as the support without benefit of compensating equipment **(7.139).** This sort of camera movement became common in the late 1950s, with the growth of the *cinéma-vérité* documentary. One of the most famous early handheld traveling shots was in *Primary,* when a cameraman held the camera above his head and followed John F. Kennedy through a milling crowd (see 5.1).

Handheld shots have appeared in many fiction films as well. Because the technique originated in documentary filming, it can lend an air of authenticity to mockumentaries like *The Blair Witch Project.* In other instances, the handheld camera movement functions to create subjective point of view **(7.140).** Sometimes the handheld shot intensifies a sense of abrupt movement, as if the action were glimpsed on the fly. For *julien donkey-boy,* Harmony Korine used lightweight, bouncy mini-DV cameras to shoot Julian shuffling through his neighborhood **(7.141).**

Camera movement is the most common way of making the frame mobile, but it is not the only way. In animation, the camera stays in one position, but through the drawing of individual cels frame by frame, the animator can create the effect of camera movement **(7.142–7.144).** Alternatively, a mobile frame effect can be achieved by photographing a still picture or a stopped frame of film and gradually enlarging or reducing any portion of that image, as is frequently done in optical

7.140 In Samuel Fuller's *The Naked Kiss,* a handheld subjective camera heightens the impact of a fight.

7.141 As Julien walks, the handheld camera's jerky pace complements the explosions of color created by printing video up to 35mm.

7.142 A pan shot simulated by animation in *Peter Pan* begins with Peter and Captain Hook near a mast. Peter swings in to kick Hook . . .

7.143 . . . and the framing pans to follow as the two fly rightward . . .

7.144 . . . across the deck.

printing. Iris masking can open up to reveal a vista or close down to isolate a detail. The zoom lens can also be used to provide a mobile framing.

The differences between the laboratory or zoom sorts of mobile framing and some kinds of mobile framing created by camera movement during filming are difficult to illustrate on the printed page. How, for instance, can we as viewers distinguish between a zoom-in and a forward tracking shot, or a crane shot back and a change in framing created on the optical printer? In general, animation, special effects, and the zoom lens make the frame mobile by reducing or blowing up some portion of the image. Although the tracking shot and the crane shot do enlarge or reduce portions of the frame, this is not *all* that they do. In the genuine camera movement, static objects in different planes pass one another at different rates. We see different sides of objects, and backgrounds gain volume and depth.

Consider some examples. In Alain Resnais's *La Guerre est finie,* a tracking shot **(7.145, 7.146)** gives the objects considerable volume. The wall has lost none of its bulk or solidity. Moreover, the street sign has not simply been enlarged; its orientation has also changed with respect to the camera's vantage point. Similarly, in **7.147–7.149,** a forward tracking movement from Ron Howard's *The Paper,* the figures and the settings through which they move retain their three-dimensional volume. Note, for example, how the window frames, fan, and actors shift positions in relation to the Coke machine in the room at the rear.

7.145 In *La Guerre est finie,* a street sign tilted slightly up on its right side . . .

7.146 . . . is tilted up distinctly at the left by the end of the track-in.

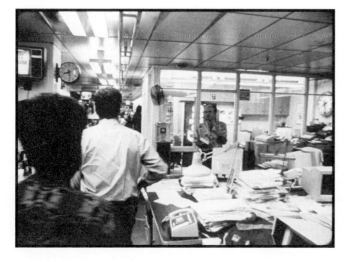

7.147 As the protagonist of *The Paper* and his assistant pass through a newsroom, we see another character at the rear, while the window frame partially blocks the Coke machine at the rear.

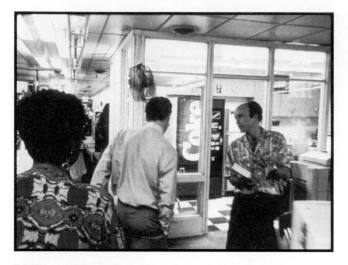

7.148   As the pair pass their colleague, he is seen from a different vantage, and the window frame is no longer in front of the Coke machine.

7.149   As the protagonist approaches the door of the snack room, he and his assistant are to the right of the machine, and the fan now partially blocks it.

7.150   A distant view of a statue on a barge in *Ulysses' Gaze* . . .

7.151   . . . is enlarged by a zoom-in.

With the zoom and optical printer enlargement, however, the mobile frame does not alter the aspects or positions of the objects filmed. In **7.150** and **7.151,** from Theo Angelopoulos's *Ulysses' Gaze,* a zoom enlarges our view of a large, broken statue of Lenin floating on a barge. Our vantage point on the statue is the same at the end of the shot as at the beginning: The top of the statue is still seen against the bottom of a row of small trees and its feet are in exactly the same place in relation to the railing on the ship's prow. As the zoom occurs, the barge gradually looks closer to the line of trees than it had at the beginning. In sum, when the camera moves, we sense our own movement through the space. When the lens zooms, a bit of the space seems magnified or demagnified.

So far, we have isolated these different sorts of mobile framings in fairly pure states. But filmmakers frequently combine such framings within a single shot: The camera may track and pan at the same time or crane up while zooming. Still, every instance can be identified as a combination of the basic types.

Functions of Frame Mobility   Our catalog of the types of mobile framings is of little use without a consideration of how such framing strategies function systematically within films. How does mobile framing relate to cinematic space? To cinematic time? How do mobile framings create certain patterns of their own? Such questions demand that we examine how mobile framing interacts with the form of the film.

1. *The mobile frame and space.* The mobile frame affects onscreen and offscreen space considerably. A forward tracking shot or zoom puts onscreen space offscreen. Other camera movements and optical effects may reveal fresh offscreen areas. In many films, the camera moves back from a detail and brings something unexpected into the shot's space. This is what happens in our earlier example from *Jezebel* (7.91–7.94); after the hand with the glass intrudes into close-up, the camera tracks back to frame the man standing in the foreground. The mobile frame also continually affects the angle, level, height, or distance of the framing. A crane up may change the angle from a low one to a high one; a track-in may change the distance from long shot to close-up.

We can, in general, ask several questions about how the mobile frame relates to space. Do the frame's movements depend on figure movement? For example, one of the commonest functions of camera movement is **reframing.** If a character moves in relation to another character, often the frame will slightly pan or tilt to adjust to the movement. In *His Girl Friday* director Howard Hawks strives to balance his compositions through reframing **(7.152–7.154).** Since reframings are motivated by figure movement, they tend to be relatively unnoticeable. When you do start to notice them, you may be surprised at how frequently they appear. A modern film like *Jerry Maguire* uses nearly constant small reframings in conversation scenes.

Reframing is only one way that the mobile frame may depend on figure movement. The camera may also displace itself in order to follow figures or moving objects. A camera movement that is more than just a reframing and that follows a figure's movement is termed—logically enough—a **following shot,** as in 7.147 to 7.149. A pan may keep a racing car centered, a tracking shot may follow a character from room to room, or a crane shot may pursue a rising balloon. In such cases frame mobility functions primarily to keep our attention fastened on the subject of the shot, and it subordinates itself to that subject's movement.

A following shot can become quite complex. Michelangelo Antonioni's *Cronaca di un amore (Story of a Love Affair)* contains many scenes in which several characters are present. Typically the camera follows one figure moving to meet another, then follows the second character's movement to another spot, where he or she meets someone else, then traces the third character's movement, and so on. The card-party sequence in *Cronaca* is a superb example of the camera's restlessly following character after character in rapid succession.

Still, the mobile frame need not be subordinate to the movement of figures at all. It can move independently of them, too. Often, of course, the camera moves away from the characters to reveal something of significance to the narrative. The most banal examples are movements that point out an overlooked clue, a sign that comments on the action, an unnoticed shadow, or a clutching hand. The moving camera can establish a locale the characters will eventually enter. This is what happens at the start of Otto Preminger's *Laura,* when the camera glides through Waldo Lydecker's sitting room, establishing him as a man of wealth and taste, before revealing the detective MacPherson. In Renoir's *Crime of M. Lange* the moving camera characterizes Lange by leaving him and panning around to survey his room **(7.155–7.159).** Lange is shown to be a fantasist, living in the world of Western lore he draws on for his cowboy stories.

Whether dependent on figure movement or independent of it, the mobile frame can profoundly affect how we perceive the space within the frame and off-screen. Different sorts of camera movements create different conceptions of space. In *Last Year at Marienbad* Resnais often tracks into corridors and through doorways, turning a fashionable resort hotel into a maze. Alfred Hitchcock has produced some of the most famous single camera movements in film history. One track-and-crane shot moves from a high-angle long shot of a ballroom over the heads of the dancers to an extreme close-up of a drummer's blinking eyes (*Young and Innocent*). In *Vertigo,* an especially tricky combination track-*out* and zoom-*in* plastically distorts the shot's perspective and conveys the protagonist's dizziness. The device reappears in Spielberg's *Jaws,* when Sheriff Brody at the beach suddenly realizes that the shark has attacked a child. Simultaneously tracking and zooming in opposite directions has become a cliché of modern Hollywood filmmaking (what director Sam Raimi calls the "warp-o cam"). In films such as *The*

7.152   In *His Girl Friday,* when Hildy crosses from the left . . .

7.153   . . . to sit on a desk, the camera pans right to reframe her . . .

7.154   . . . and when Walter swivels his chair to face her, the camera reframes slightly leftward.

7.155   *The Crime of M. Lange:* Although the camera begins on Lange at work . . .

7.156   . . . it soon leaves him to show his cowboy pistols and hat . . .

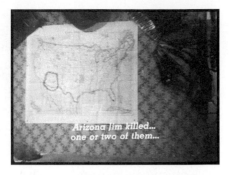

7.157   . . . keeps going to show a map with Arizona outlined . . .

7.158   . . . pans past more guns . . .

7.159   . . . before returning to the excited author writing his Western tales.

Red and the White, Miklós Janscó specialized in lengthy camera movements that roam among groups of people moving across a plain. His shots use all of the resources of tracking, panning, craning, zooming, and racking focus to sculpt ever-changing spatial relations.

For his experimental film *La Région centrale* Michael Snow built the machine pictured in **7.160.** Since all of the moving arms could pivot the camera in several ways in response to a remote-control device, the machine produced a varied series of rotational camera movements—everything from elaborate corkscrew spiralings to huge, Ferris-wheel spins. Snow set up his machine in a barren Canadian landscape, and the film that resulted transforms that landscape into a series of uniquely mobile views. A set of variations on the possibilities of the camera's speed and direction of movement provides the basis of this film's abstract form. This is an example of how one film technique can largely determine the form of a long and complex film.

All of these examples illustrate various ways in which frame mobility affects our sense of space. Of any mobile framing we can ask, How does it function to reveal or conceal offscreen space? Is the frame mobility dependent on figure movement or independent of it? What particular trajectory does the camera pursue? Such questions will best be answered by considering how spatial effects of the camera movement function with respect to the film's overall form.

2. *The mobile frame and time.* Frame mobility involves time as well as space, and filmmakers have realized that our sense of duration and rhythm is affected by

7.160   One of the most elaborate camera mounts ever devised created complex patterns for Snow's *La Région centrale.*

the mobile frame. The importance of duration in camera movement, for example, can be sensed by comparing two Japanese directors, Yasujiro Ozu and Kenji Mizoguchi. Ozu prefers short camera movements in a single direction, as in *Early Summer* and *The Flavor of Green Tea over Rice.* Mizoguchi, alternatively, cultivates the leisurely, drawn-out tracking shot, often combining it with panning. That camera movements simply take less time in Ozu's films than in Mizoguchi's constitutes a major difference between the two directors' styles.

Since a camera movement consumes time on screen, it can create an arc of expectation and fulfillment. In the pan shot across M. Lange's study (7.155–7.159), Renoir makes us wonder why the camera strays from the main character, then answers the question by indicating Lange's fascination with the American West. Later in this chapter we shall examine how our expectations are manipulated over time in the opening camera movements of Welles's *Touch of Evil.*

The velocity of frame mobility is important, too. A zoom or a camera movement may be relatively slow or fast. Richard Lester's *A Hard Day's Night* and *Help!* started a fad in the 1960s for very fast zoom-ins and -outs. In comparison, one of the most impressive early camera movements, D. W. Griffith's monumental crane shot in Belshazzar's feast in *Intolerance,* gains majesty and suspense through its inexorably slow descent toward the immense Babylonian set (6.11).

In general, a camera movement may create particular effects of its own. If the camera pans quickly from an event, we may be prompted to wonder what has happened. If the camera abruptly tracks back to show us something in the foreground that we had not expected, as in our earlier *Jezebel* example (7.91–7.94), we are taken by surprise. If the camera slowly moves in on a detail, gradually enlarging it but delaying the fulfillment of our expectations, the camera movement has contributed to suspense. In a narrative film, the velocity of mobile framing can be motivated by narrational needs. A quick track-in to a significant object can underline a key piece of story information.

"One thing I hate in films is when the camera starts circling characters. If three people are sitting at a table talking, you'll often see the camera circling them. I can't explain why, but I find it totally fake."

— Takeshi Kitano, director

Sometimes the speed of the mobile framing functions rhythmically. In Will Hindle's *Pastorale d'été* a gentle, bouncing beat is created by zooming in and slightly tilting up and down in time to Honegger's music. Often musical films make use of the speed of camera movement to underline qualities of a song or dance. During the "Broadway Rhythm" number in *Singin' in the Rain,* the camera cranes quickly back from Gene Kelly several times, and the speed of the movement is timed to accentuate the lyrics. Frame velocity can also create expressive qualities—a camera movement can be fluid, staccato, hesitant, and so forth. In short, the duration and speed of the mobile frame can significantly control our perception of the shot over time.

3. *Patterns of mobile framing.* The mobile frame can create its own specific motifs within a film. For example, Hitchcock's *Psycho* begins and ends with a forward movement of the frame. In the film's first three shots, the camera pans right and then zooms in on a building in a cityscape **(7.161).** Two forward movements finally carry us under a window blind and into the darkness of a cheap hotel room **(7.162–7.164).** The camera's movement inward, the penetration of an interior, is repeated throughout the film, often motivated as a subjective point of view as when various characters move deeper and deeper into Norman Bates's mansion. The next-to-last shot of the film shows Norman sitting against a blank white wall, while we hear his interior monologue **(7.165).** The camera again moves forward into a close-up of his face **(7.166).** This shot is the climax of the forward movement initiated at the start of the film; the film has traced a movement into

7.161   The opening shot of *Psycho.*

7.162   The second shot concentrates on one building . . .

7.163   . . . as the camera moves lower and closer to a window . . .

7.164   . . . and reveals the heroine and her boyfriend in a lunchtime tryst.

7.165   *Psycho's* next-to-last shot begins at a distance from Norman . . .

7.166   . . . and moves in so that we see his expression as we hear his thoughts.

Norman's mind. Another film that relies heavily on a pattern of forward, penetrating movements is *Citizen Kane,* which depicts the same inexorable drive toward the revelation of a character's secret.

Other kinds of movements can repeat and develop across a film. Max Ophuls's *Lola Montès* uses both 360° tracking shots and constant upward and downward crane shots to contrast the circus arena with the world of Lola's past. In Michael Snow's ⟷ (usually called *Back and Forth*), the constant panning to and fro across a classroom, Ping-Pong fashion, determines the basic formal pattern of the film. It comes as a surprise when, near the very end, the movement suddenly becomes a repeated tilting up and down. In these and many other films the mobile frame sets up marked repetitions and variations.

Functions of Mobile Framing: Grand Illusion *and* Wavelength

By way of summary we can look at two films that illustrate possible relations of the mobile frame to narrative form. These two films constitute a pertinent contrast in that one uses the mobile frame in order to strengthen and support the narrative, whereas the other subordinates narrative form to an overall frame mobility.

Jean Renoir's *Grand Illusion* is a war film in which we almost never see the war. Heroic charges and doomed battalions, the staple of the genre, are absent. World War I remains obstinately offscreen. Instead, Renoir concentrates on life in a German POW camp to suggest how relations between nations and social classes are affected by war. The prisoners Maréchal and Boeldieu are both French; Rauffenstein is a German. Yet the aristocrat Boeldieu has more in common with Rauffenstein than with the mechanic Maréchal. The film's narrative form traces the death of the Boeldieu-Rauffenstein upper class and the precarious survival of Maréchal and his pal Rosenthal—their flight to Elsa's farm, their interlude of peace there, and their final escape back to France and presumably back to the war as well.

Within this framework, camera movement has several functions, all directly supportive of the narrative. First, and most usual, is its tendency to adhere to figure movement. When a character or vehicle moves, Renoir often pans or tracks to follow. The camera follows Maréchal and Rosenthal walking together after their escape; it tracks back when the prisoners are drawn to the window by the sound of marching Germans below. But it is the movements of the camera *independent* of figure movement that make the film more unusual.

When the camera moves on its own in *Grand Illusion,* we are conscious of it actively interpreting the action, creating suspense or giving us information which the characters do not have. For example, in one scene a prisoner is digging in an escape tunnel and tugs a string signaling that he needs to be pulled out (**7.167**). Independent camera movement builds suspense by showing that the other characters have missed the signal and have not realized that he is suffocating (**7.168, 7.169**). Camera movement thus helps create a somewhat unrestricted narration.

Sometimes the camera is such an active agent that Renoir will use repeated camera movements to create patterns of narrative significance. One such pattern is the movement to link characters with details of their environment. Often a sequence begins on a close-up of some detail, and the camera moves back to anchor this detail in its larger spatial and narrative context (**7.170, 7.171**).

More complicated is the scene of the Christmas celebration at Elsa's that begins on a close-up of the crèche and tracks back to show, in several stages, the interplay of reactions among the characters. Such camera movements are not simply decoration; beginning on a scenic detail before moving to the larger context makes narrative points economically, constantly emphasizing relationships among elements of Renoir's mise-en-scene. So does the rarer track-in to a detail at the *end*

7.167   A can used as a signal is initially seen sitting on a shelf . . .

7.168   . . . then is pulled over. It lands on a pillow and so makes no sound . . .

7.169   . . . and the camera pans left to reveal that the characters have not noticed it.

7.170   Renoir begins the scene of Boeldieu and Maréchal discussing escape plans by framing a close-up of a caged squirrel . . .

7.171   . . . before tracking back to reveal the men beside the cage, thus creating a clear narrative parallel.

of a scene, as when after Boeldieu's death, Rauffenstein cuts the geranium, the one flower in the prison **(7.172, 7.173).**

Characters are tied to their environment by some even more ambitious moving-camera shots, which function to stress important narrative parallels. For example, tracking shots compare actions in two officers' bars, one French **(7.174–7.176),** one German **(7.177–7.179).** Through his camera movements Renoir indicates a similarity between the two warring sides, blurring their national differences and stressing common desires. The camera movements, repeated in a systematic pattern, create the narrative parallel.

Or consider how two parallel tracking shots compare the war of the aristocrats and the war of the lower-class people. We are introduced to Rauffenstein's new position as commander of a prisoner-of-war camp through a lengthy tracking shot **(7.180–7.187).** During this movement Renoir presents, wordlessly, the military mystique of grace on the battlefield that characterizes the aristocrat's war.

Late in the film, however, a parallel shot criticizes this one **(7.188–7.190).** That Elsa's war has none of Rauffenstein's glory is conveyed chiefly through a parallel created by the repeated camera movement. Moreover, these camera movements work together with mise-en-scene, as the narrative parallel is reinforced by the subtle use of objects as motifs—the crucifixes in 7.180 and 7.190, the photographs in 7.181 and 7.188, and the tables that end both shots. (Note the subtle use of the empty chairs upended on the table to reinforce the absence of Elsa's husband.)

7.172   As Rauffenstein moves to the geranium in the window . . .

7.173   . . . Renoir tracks in to a close shot of the flower as he cuts it.

7.174   In the first scene, as Maréchal leaves the French officers' bar . . .

7.175   . . . Renoir pans and tracks left from the door to reveal pin-ups (just coming into the frame at the right) . . .

7.176   . . . and a poster.

Another function of moving the camera independently of figure movement is to link characters with one another. Again and again in the prison camps, the camera moves to join one man to his comrades, spatially indicating their shared condition. When the prisoners ransack the collection of women's clothes, one man decides to dress up in them. When he appears, a stillness falls over the men. Renoir tracks silently over the prisoners' faces, each one registering a reticent longing.

A more elaborate linking movement occurs in the scene of the prison vaude-ville show, when the men learn that the French have recaptured a city. Renoir presents the shot as a celebration of spatial unity, with the camera moving among the men as they begin defiantly to sing the "Marseillaise" **(7.191–7.197).** This complex camera movement circulates freely among the prisoners, suggesting their patriotic courage and unity in disobeying their captors.

In Elsa's cottage as well as in the prison, camera movement links characters. Recall the shot that moves from Elsa and Rosenthal inside through the window to Maréchal outside. The culmination of the linking movement comes near the film's end, when Renoir pans from the Germans on one side of the border **(7.198)** to the distant French escapees on the other **(7.199, 7.200).** Even on this scale, Renoir's camera refuses to honor national divisions.

A remark of André Bazin's is pertinent here: "Jean Renoir found a way to re-veal the hidden meaning of people and things without destroying the unity that is

7.177 One scene later, in the German officers' bar, a similar camera movement, this time toward the right, leaves the characters . . .

...two of Rhine wine, one of champagne and a half-bottle of Martell....

7.178 . . . and explores on its own . . .

7.179 . . . discovering some similar decorations.

natural to them." By placing emphasis and making comparisons, the mobile frame in *Grand Illusion* becomes as important as the mise-en-scene. The camera carves into space to create connections that enrich the film's narrative form. Renoir has found imaginative ways to make the mobile frame sustain and elaborate a system of narrative relationships.

In Michael Snow's experimental film *Wavelength,* the relation of narrative to the mobile frame is quite different. Instead of supporting narrative form, frame mobility dominates narrative, even deflecting our attention from narrative. The film begins with a long-shot framing of a loft apartment, facing one wall and window **(7.201).** In the course of the film the camera zooms in abruptly a short distance and then holds that framing. It zooms in a bit more and then holds that **(7.202).** And so it goes throughout the film's 45-minute length. By the end a photograph of ocean waves on the distant wall fills the frame in close-up.

Thus *Wavelength* is structured primarily around a single kind of frame mobility—the zoom-in. Its pattern of progression and development is not a narrative one, but that of an exploration, through deliberately limited means, of how the zoom transforms the space of the loft. The sudden zooms create frequent abrupt shifts of perspective relations. In excluding parts of the room, the zoom-in also magnifies and flattens what we see; every change of focal length gives us a new set of spatial relations. The zoom places more and more space offscreen. The sound track, for the most part, reinforces the basic formal progression by emitting a single humming tone that rises consistently in pitch as the zoom magnifies more and more.

Within *Wavelength*'s basic pattern, though, there are two contrasting systems. The first is a series of filtered tints that plays across the image as abstract fields of color. These tints often work against the depth represented in the shot of the loft.

The second system evokes a sketchy narrative. At various intervals characters enter the loft and carry on certain activities (talking, listening to the radio, making phone calls). There is even a mysterious death (a body lies on the floor in **7.203).** But these events remain unexplained in cause–effect terms and inconclusive as to closure (although at the film's end we do hear a sound that resembles a police siren). Furthermore, none of these actions swerves the mobile framing from its predetermined course. The jerkily shifting and halting zoom continues, even when it will exclude important narrative information. Thus *Wavelength* pulls in bits and pieces of narrative, but these fragments of action remain secondary, operating within the temporal progression of the zoom.

7.180   Renoir begins on a crucifix and . . .

7.181   . . . tilts down to a military portrait on an altar, underlining the irony of a chapel commandeered as a bivouac.

7.182   The camera tracks past whips, spurs, and swords . . .

7.183   . . . to a servant preparing Rauffenstein's gloves.

7.184   He then walks away from the camera to close a window before returning . . .

7.185   . . . into the foreground as the camera pans left and tracks back to reveal . . .

7.186   . . . a breakfast table . . .

7.187   . . . at which Rauffenstein is revealed to be sitting.

7.188   This shot also begins on an object, a photograph of Elsa's dead husband . . .

7.189   . . . before tracking left past Elsa . . .

7.190   . . . to reveal the kitchen table, where her daughter Lotte sits alone as Elsa remarks offscreen, "Now the table is too large."

7.191   As the lead "female" singer whips off his wig and requests the "Marseillaise" from the musicians . . .

7.192   . . . the camera moves right as the singer turns toward the audience . . .

7.193   . . . and further right as others onstage sing along.

7.194   A tilt down shows two worried German guards . . .

7.195   . . . and a track back to the left reveals a row of French prisoners in the audience on their feet, singing.

7.196   The camera tracks forward past them to the musicians and singer again . . .

7.197   . . . then pans quickly left to face the entire audience.

7.198   As the Germans realize that Maréchal and Rosenthal have crossed over into Switzerland . . .

7.199   . . . Renoir pans to the right across the invisible border . . .

7.200   . . . to the two escapees, tiny dots in the huge landscape.

7.201   Early in *Wavelength,* much of the apartment is visible.

7.202   Near the end, the sporadic zoom-ins have made details of the far wall visible.

7.203   The zoom-ins in *Wavelength* will soon eliminate the body on the floor from the frame.

From the standpoint of the viewer's experience, *Wavelength*'s use of frame mobility arouses, delays, and gratifies unusual expectations. What plot there is arouses curiosity (What are the people up to? What has led to the man's death, if he does die?) and surprise (the apparent murder). But in general, a story-centered suspense is replaced by a *stylistic* suspense: What will the zoom eventually frame? From this standpoint, the colored tints and even the plot work with the spasmodic qualities of the zoom to delay the forward progress of the framing. When the zoom finally reveals its target, our stylistic anticipations have come to fulfillment. The film's title stands revealed as a multiple pun, referring not only to the steadily rising pitch of the sound track but also to the distance that the zoom had to cross in order to reveal the photo—a "wavelength."

Grand Illusion and *Wavelength* illustrate, in different ways, how frame mobility can guide and shape our perception of a film's space and time. Frame mobility may be motivated by larger formal concerns, as in Renoir's film, or it may itself become the principal formal concern, motivating other systems, as in Snow's film. What is important to realize is that by attention to how filmmakers use the mobile frame within specific contexts, we can gain a fuller understanding of how our experience of a film is created.

DURATION OF THE IMAGE: THE LONG TAKE

In our consideration of the film image, we have emphasized spatial qualities—how photographic transformations can alter the properties of the image, how framing defines the image for our attention. But cinema is an art of time as well as of space, and we have seen already how mise-en-scene and frame mobility operate in temporal as well as spatial dimensions. What we need to consider now is how the duration of the shot affects our understanding of it.

There is a tendency to consider the shot as recording real duration. A runner takes three seconds to clear a hurdle. If we film the runner, our projected film will also consume three seconds—or so the assumption goes. One film theorist, André Bazin, made it a major tenet of his aesthetic that cinema records real time. (See Notes and Queries for a discussion of Bazin's position.) What must be noted, though, is that the relation of shot duration to the time consumed by the filmed event is not so simple.

First, obviously, the duration of the event on the screen may be manipulated by adjustments in the camera's or printer's drive mechanism, as we discussed earlier in this chapter. Slow-motion or fast-motion techniques may present the runner's jump in twenty seconds or two. Second, narrative films often permit no simple equivalence of real duration with screen duration. As Chapter 3 pointed out (p. 75–76), story duration can differ considerably from plot duration and screen duration.

7.204   A scene in *The Only Son* moves from night . . .

7.205   . . . to day in a single shot.

Consider a shot from Ozu's *The Only Son*. It is well past midnight and we have just seen a family awake and talking; this shot shows a dim corner of the family's apartment, with none of the characters onscreen **(7.204)**. But soon the light changes. The sun is rising. By the end of the shot it is morning **(7.205)**. This transitional shot consumes about a minute of screen time. It plainly does not record the duration of the story events; that duration would be at least five hours. To put it another way, by manipulating screen duration, the film's plot has condensed a story duration of several hours into a minute or so. More recent films use tracking movements to compress longer passages of time in a continuous shot. In *Notting Hill,* the protagonist's walk through the Portobello street market moves through autumn, winter, and spring. The final shot of *Signs* moves away from an autumn view through a window (itself an echo of the opening shot's track-back from a window) and through a room, to reveal a winter landscape outside another window. Months of story time have passed during the tracking movement. In the next chapter we shall examine how editing one shot with another can expand or contract screen duration. Here we need only note that it is possible to manipulate screen duration *within a single shot* as well. There need be no one-to-one correspondence between the onscreen duration of the shot and the duration of the story events represented.

Functions of the Long Take

Every shot has some measurable screen duration, but in the history of cinema, directors have varied considerably in their choice of short or lengthy shots. In general, early cinema (1895–1905) tended to rely on shots of fairly long duration, since there was often only one shot in each film. With the emergence of continuity editing in the period of 1905–1916, shots became shorter. In the late 1910s and early 1920s, an American film would have an average shot length of about 5 seconds. After the coming of sound, the average stretched to about 10 seconds.

But throughout the history of the cinema, some filmmakers have consistently preferred to use shots of greater duration than the average. In various countries in the mid-1930s there was a tendency to increase the length of the shots, and this tendency continued throughout the next 20 years. The causes of this change are complex and not fully understood, but film scholars agree that the use of unusually lengthy shots—**long takes,** as they are called—constitutes a major resource for the filmmaker.

Long take is not the same as *long shot;* the latter term refers to the apparent distance between camera and object. As we saw in examining film production (p. 29), a *take* is one run of the camera that records a single shot. Calling a shot of notable length a long take rather than a long shot prevents ambiguity, since the latter term refers to a distanced framing, not to shot duration. In the films of Jean Renoir, Kenji Mizoguchi, Orson Welles, Carl Dreyer, or Miklós Jancsó, a shot may go on for several minutes, and it would be impossible to analyze these films without an awareness of how the long take can contribute to form and style. One long take in Andy Warhol's *My Hustler* follows the seductive exchange of two gay men as they groom themselves in a bathroom **(7.206).** The shot, which runs for about 30 minutes, constitutes virtually the second half of the film.

7.206   A long take in *My Hustler.*

Usually, we can regard the long take as an alternative to a series of shots. The director may choose to present a scene in one or a few long takes or to present the scene through several shorter shots. When an entire scene is rendered in only one shot, the long take is known by the French term ***plan-séquence,*** or *sequence shot.*

Most commonly, filmmakers use the long take selectively. One scene will rely heavily on editing, another will be presented in a long take. This permits the director to associate certain aspects of narrative or non-narrative form with the different stylistic options. A vivid instance occurs in the first part of Humberto Solanas and Octavio Gentiño's *Hour of the Furnaces.* Most of the film relies on editing of newsreel and staged shots to describe how European and North American ideologies penetrate developing nations. But the last shot of the film is a slow zoom-in to a photograph of the corpse of Che Guevera, symbol of guerrilla resistance to imperialism. Solanas makes the shot a long take, holding it for three minutes to force the viewer to dwell on the cost of resistance **(7.207).**

7.207   The final three-minute shot of *Hour of the Furnaces.*

Mixing long takes and shorter shots also creates parallels and contrasts among scenes. André Bazin pointed out that *Citizen Kane* oscillates between long takes in the dialogue scenes and rapid editing in the "News on the March" newsreel and other sequences. Hitchcock, Mizoguchi, Renoir, and Dreyer often vary shot duration, depending on the scene's function in the entire film.

Alternatively, the filmmaker may decide to build the entire film out of long takes. Hitchcock's *Rope* is famous for containing only eight shots, each running the full length of a reel of film in the camera. Similarly, each scene in *Winterwind, Agnus Dei, Red Psalm,* and other films by Miklós Jancsó is a *plan-séquence.* In such cases, the long take becomes a large-scale part of a film. And in such a context editing can have great force. After a seven- or eight-minute shot, an elliptical cut can prove quite disorienting, as Jancsó's films show.

Could a feature-length movie consist of one long take? Many directors have dreamed of this possibility, but the lengths of film reels have prevented it. A 35mm camera reel typically runs for about 11 minutes, so Hitchcock tried to hide his seven obligatory cuts in *Rope*. Extended 16mm reels of the type Warhol used in *My Hustler* (7.206) can run up to 30 minutes. With digital video, however, it is possible to shoot for over two hours on a single tape, and the Russian director Aleksander Sokurov seized this opportunity in his *Russian Ark*. The film consists of a single shot nearly 90 minutes long, as a Steadicam follows over 2000 actors in period costume through St. Petersburg's immense Winter Palace. *Russian Ark* takes us through several eras of Russian history, culminating in a stupendous ballroom dance and a crowd drifting off into a wintry night **(7.208–7.210).** Sokurov rehearsed *Russian Ark* for several months and completed a satisfactory take on the third try.

The Long Take and the Mobile Frame

If the long take often replaces editing, it should surprise no one that the long take is frequently allied to the mobile frame. The long take may use panning, tracking, craning, or zooming to present continually changing vantage points that are comparable in some ways to the shifts of view supplied by editing.

Very often frame mobility breaks the long-take shot into significant smaller units. In Mizoguchi's *Sisters of Gion,* one long take shows a young woman, Omocha, luring a businessman into becoming her patron **(7.211–7.216).** Though there is no cutting, the camera and figure movements have demarcated important stages of the scene's action.

As in this example, long takes tend to be framed in medium or long shots. The camera lingers on a fairly dense visual field, and the spectator has more opportunity to scan the shot for particular points of interest. This is recognized by Steven Spielberg, not a director who exploits lengthy takes:

> I'd love to see directors start trusting the audience to be the film editor with their eyes, the way you are sometimes with a stage play, where the audience selects who they would choose to look at while a scene is being played. . . . There's so much cutting and so many closeups being shot today I think directly as an influence from television.

As we have seen in the previous chapter, however, the director can guide the audience's scanning of the frame through all of the technical resources of mise-en-scene. This is another way of saying that using the long take often puts more emphasis on performance, setting, lighting, and other mise-en-scene factors.

7.208   In *Russian Ark,* one episode takes place in the palace theater, with Catherine the Great pronouncing the rehearsal satisfactory.

7.209   An hour or so later, still within the same shot, hundreds of aristocrats and officers descend a staircase toward the impending devastation of the Russian Revolution.

7.210 *Crew members moving through the Hermitage Museum, filming* Russian Ark *with a digital camera mounted on a Steadicam (photography by Alexander Belenkiy).*

The example from *Sisters of Gion* illustrates another important feature of the long take. Mizoguchi's shot reveals a complete internal logic—a beginning, middle, and end. As a large-scale part of a film, the long take can have its own formal pattern, its own development, its own trajectory and shape. Suspense develops; we start to ask how the shot will continue and when it will end.

The classic example of how the long take can constitute a formal pattern in its own right is the opening sequence of Welles's *Touch of Evil* **(7.217–7.228).** This opening shot makes plain most of the features of the long take. It offers an alternative to building the sequence out of many shots, and it stresses the cut that finally comes (the sudden cut on the sound of the explosion to the burning car).

Most important, the shot has its own internal pattern of development. We expect that the bomb shown at the beginning will explode at some point, and we wait for that explosion through the duration of the long take. The shot establishes the geography of the scene (the border between Mexico and the United States). The camera movement, alternately picking up the car and the walking couple, weaves together two separate lines of narrative cause and effect that intersect at the border station. Vargas and Susan are thus drawn into the action involving the bombing. Our expectation is fulfilled when the end of the shot coincides with the explosion (offscreen) of the bomb. The shot has guided our response by taking us through a suspenseful process of narrative development. The long take can present, in a single chunk of time, a complex pattern of events moving toward a goal, and this ability shows that shot duration can be as important to the image as photographic qualities and framing are.

7.211   *Sisters of Gion:* The long take begins with Omocha and the businessman seated. The camera follows as . . .

7.212   . . . she moves to the opposite end of the room . . .

7.213   . . . and sits at a small table facing him.

7.214   A second phase of the shot begins as she begins to appeal to his sympathy and he moves to the table . . .

7.215   . . . and sits down to console her.

7.216   Finally the camera moves into a tighter shot as she sits beside him and he succumbs to her advances.

7.217   The opening shot of *Touch of Evil* begins with a close-up of a hand setting the timer of a bomb.

7.218   The camera tracks immediately right to follow first the shadow . . .

7.219   . . . and then the figure of an unknown assassin planting the bomb in a car.

7.220   The camera then cranes up to a high angle as the assassin flees and the victims arrive and set out in the car.

7.221   As the camera rounds the corner, the camera circles back, rejoins the car, and tracks back to follow it.

7.222   The car passes Vargas and his wife, Susan, and the camera starts to follow them, losing the car and tracking diagonally backward with the couple through the crowd.

7.223   The camera tracks backward until both the occupants of the car and Susan and Vargas meet again . . .

7.224   . . . and a brief scene with the border guard ensues.

7.225   After tracking left with the car, the camera again encounters Susan and Vargas and tracks forward toward them . . .

7.226   . . . bringing them into medium shot as they begin to kiss.

7.227   Their embrace is interrupted by the offscreen sound of an explosion, and they turn to look leftward.

7.228   The next shot zooms in to show the car in flames.

SUMMARY

The film shot, then, is a very complex unit. Mise-en-scene fills the image with material, arranging setting, lighting, costume, and figure behavior within the formal context of the total film. Within that same formal context, the filmmaker also controls the cinematographic qualities of the shot—how the image is photographed and framed, how long the image lasts on the screen.

You can sensitize yourself to these cinematographic qualities in much the same way that you worked on mise-en-scene. Trace the progress of a single technique—say, camera angle—through an entire scene or film. Become conscious of when a shot begins and ends, observing how the long take may function to shape the film's form. Watch for camera movements, especially those that follow the action (since those are usually the hardest to notice). In short, once you are aware of cinematographic qualities, you can move to an understanding of their various possible functions within the total film.

Film art offers still other possibilities for choice and control. Chapters 6 and 7 have focused on the shot. The filmmaker may also juxtapose one shot with another through editing, and that is the subject of Chapter 8.

NOTES AND QUERIES

General Works

The standard contemporary references on cinematography are Rob Hummel, ed., *The American Cinematographer Manual,* 8th ed. (Hollywood: American Society of Cinematographers, 2001); and Kris Malkiewicz, *Cinematography: A Guide for Film Makers and Film Teachers,* 2d ed. (Englewood Cliffs, N.J.: Prentice-Hall, 1989). An excellent introduction to all phases of 8 and 16mm cinematography is David Cheshire, *The Book of Movie Photography* (New York: Knopf, 1979). Cinematographers can be articulate about their craft, and we can learn a lot from their interviews. See Vincent LoBrutto, *Principal Photography: Interviews with Feature Film Cinematographers* (Westport, Conn.: Praeger, 1999); Pauline Rogers, *Contemporary Cinematographers on Their Art* (Boston: Focal Press, 1999); Benjamin Bergery, *Reflections: Twenty-One Cinematographers at Work* (Hollywood: ASC Press, 2002), and Peter Ettedgui, *Cinematography: Screencraft* (Hove, England: RotoVision, 1998). In the Rogers collection, Dean Cundey recalls that the camera movements in *Who Framed Roger Rabbit?* posed problems for adding animation. "If Roger was to go from one part of the room to another, hopping onto a chair, we had to find a way for the camera operator to track that movement. We developed full-size rubber characters to stage the action. The operator could then see

movement in real time. He would associate movement with dialogue." A monthly magazine, *American Cinematographer,* contains detailed articles on current cinematography around the world. For historical information, see Brian Coe, *The History of Movie Photography* (London: Ash & Grant, 1981); Leonard Maltin, *The Art of the Cinematographer* (New York: Dover, 1978); and David Bordwell, Janet Staiger, and Kristin Thompson, *The Classical Hollywood Cinema: Film Style and Mode of Production to 1960* (New York: Columbia University Press, 1985).

Alternative points of view on cinematography may be found in Stan Brakhage, "A Moving Picture Giving and Taking Book," in *Brakhage Scrapbook: Collected Writings 1964–1980,* ed. Robert A. Haller (New Paltz, N.Y.: Documentext, 1982), pp. 53–77; Dziga Vertov, *Kino-Eye: The Writings of Dziga Vertov,* ed. Annette Michelson (Berkeley: University of California Press, 1984); and Maya Deren, "An Anagram of Ideas on Art, Form, and Film," and "Cinematography," in George Amberg, ed., *The Art of Cinema* (New York: Arno, 1972).

Color versus Black and White

Today most films are shot on color stock and most viewers have come to expect that movies will be in color. At many points in film history, however, color and black-and-white film have been used to carry different meanings. In 1930s and 1940s American cinema, color tended to be reserved for fantasies (for example, *The Wizard of Oz*), historical films or films set in exotic locales (*Becky Sharp, Blood and Sand*), or very lavish musicals (*Meet Me in St. Louis*). Black and white was then considered more realistic. But now that most films are in color, filmmakers can call on black and white to suggest a historical period (as witnessed by two such different films as Straub and Huillet's *Chronicle of Anna Magdalena Bach* and Tim Burton's *Ed Wood*). Such rules of thumb as "color for realism" have no universal validity; as always, it is a matter of context, the function of color or black-and-white tonalities within a specific film.

For more data on the principles of color photography, see Society of Motion Picture and Television Engineers, *Elements of Color in Professional Motion Pictures* (New York: SMPTE, 1957). A brief but well-illustrated history of color in motion pictures may be found in Roger Manvell, ed., *The International Encyclopedia of Film* (New York: Crown, 1972); this article demonstrates conclusively that radically different color ranges can all be accepted as realistic. A basic history is R. T. Ryan, *A History of Motion Picture Color Technology* (New York: Focal Press, 1977). The most influential early process is considered in Fred E. Basten's *Glorious Technicolor: The Movies' Magic Rainbow* (San Diego: A. S. Barnes, 1980). Len Lye explains the elaborate process behind the color design of *Rainbow Dance* in Wystan Curnow and Roger Horrocks, eds., *Figures of Motion: Len Lye/Selected Writings* (Auckland: Auckland University Press, 1984), pp. 47–49.

Film theorists have debated whether color film is artistically less pure than black and white. One argument against color may be found in Rudolf Arnheim, *Film as Art* (Berkeley: University of California Press, 1957). How is Arnheim's argument disputed by V. F. Perkins in *Film as Film* (Baltimore: Penguin, 1972)?

Special Effects

Part of the reason that major film studios tout themselves as the "magic factories" is that special-effects cinematography demands the complexity and expense that only a big firm can support. Special effects—rear projection, matte work, superimposition, and other procedures—require the time, patience, and rehearsal afforded by control over mise-en-scene. It is, then, no surprise that Méliès, the first person to exploit fully the possibilities of studio filmmaking, excelled at special-effects cinematography. Nor is it surprising that when UFA, the gigantic German firm of the 1920s, became the best-equipped film studio in Europe, it invested heavily in new special-effects processes. Similarly, as

Hollywood studios grew from the mid-1910s on, so did their special-effects departments. Engineers, painters, photographers, and set designers collaborated to contrive fantastic visual novelties. In these magic factories most of the history of special effects has been made.

But such firms were not motivated by sheer curiosity. The costs of elaborate back projection and matte work were usually investments. First, expensive as they were, such tricks often saved money in the long run. Instead of building a huge set, one could photograph the actors through a glass with the setting painted on it. Instead of taking players to the desert, one could film them against a back projection of the pyramids. Second, special effects made certain film genres possible. The historical epic whether set in Rome, Babylon, or Jerusalem—was unthinkable unless special effects were devised to create huge vistas and crowds. The fantasy film, with its panoply of ghosts, flying horses, and invisible or incredibly shrinking people, demanded the perfection of superimposition and matte processes. The science-fiction film genre could scarcely exist without a barrage of special effects. For the major studios, the "factory" principle was responsible for the "magic."

The best survey of the subject is Richard Rickitt's sumptuously illustrated *Special Effects: The History and the Technique* (New York: Billboard, 2000). See also John Culhane, *Special Effects in the Movies: How They Do It* (New York: Ballantine, 1981) and Christopher Finch's *Special Effects: Creating Movie Magic* (New York: Abbeville, 1984). Illuminating case studies can be found in Linwood G. Dunn and George E. Turner, eds., *The ASC Treasury of Visual Effects* (Hollywood: American Society of Cinematographers, 1983). See also Mark Cotta Vaz and Patricia Rose Duignan, *Industrial Light & Magic: Into the Digital Realm* (New York: Ballantine, 1996). An extensive and well-illustrated history of matte paintings, including the move to the digital creation of environments, is Mark Cotta Vaz and Craig Barron's *The Invisible Art: The Legends of Movie Matte Painting* (San Francisco: Chronicle Books, 2002); this book includes a CD-ROM with examples of matte paintings by themselves and as parts of final compositions.

As of 2002, the top special-effects firms were Digital Domain (*Titanic, Apollo 13*), Industrial Light and Magic (*Star Wars, The Abyss*), Rhythm & Hues (*Babe*), Sony Pictures Imageworks (*Cast Away, Spider-Man*), and Weta Digital (*The Lord of the Rings*). On the first of these, see Piers Bizony, *Digital Domain: The Leading Edge of Visual Effects* (New York: Billboard Books, 2001). Articles on particular films' use of special effects appear regularly in *American Cinematographer* and *Cinefex*.

Aspect Ratio

In Jean-Luc Godard's film *Contempt,* the director Fritz Lang (playing himself) laments that "CinemaScope is good only for filming funerals and snakes." *Contempt,* of course, is an anamorphic widescreen film (using the Franscope widescreen system).

The aspect ratio of the film image has been debated since the inception of cinema. The Edison-Lumière ratio (1.33:1) was not generally standardized until 1911, and even after that other ratios were explored. Many cinematographers believed that 1.33:1 was the perfect ratio (perhaps not aware that it harks back to the "golden section" of academic painting). With the large-scale innovation of widescreen cinema in the early 1950s, cries of distress were heard. Most camera operators hated it. Lenses often were not sharp, lighting became more complicated, and as Lee Garmes put it, "We'd look through the camera and be startled at what it was taking in." Yet some directors—Nicholas Ray, Akira Kurosawa, Samuel Fuller, François Truffaut, Jean-Luc Godard—created fascinating compositions in the widescreen ratio. The systems are exhaustively surveyed in Robert E. Carr and R. M. Hayes's *Wide Screen Movies: A History and Filmography of Wide Gauge Filmmaking* (Jefferson, N.C.: McFarland, 1988).

The most detailed defense of the aesthetic virtues of the widescreen image remains Charles Barr's "CinemaScope: Before and After," *Film Quarterly* **16,** 4 (Summer 1963): 4–24. To what extent does Barr's argument rest on an assumption that new technological possibilities create new formal and functional possibilities? *Velvet Light Trap* **21** (1985) contains several articles on the history and aesthetics of widescreen cinema, including an article on Barr's essay and second thoughts by Barr. See Notes and Queries for Chapter 1 for sources on widescreen films on video.

During the 1980s, two variants on traditional film gauges were designed in response to widescreen demands. One innovation is Super 35mm, which expands the image area within the traditional 35mm format. It allows filmmakers to make a release print at either 2.40:1 (anamorphic) ratio or 1.85:1 matted. For small-budget projects there is Super 16mm, which can be blown up to make 35mm release prints more easily than normal 16mm. Super 16mm provides 40 percent more image area and creates a wider frame that can be matted to the 1.85:1 aspect ratio favored in 35mm exhibition. Pioneered on Robert Young's *Ballad of Gregorio Cortez* and Robert Altman's *Come Back to the Five and Dime, Jimmy Dean, Jimmy Dean,* Super 16mm was used frequently during the 1990s, as on Mike Figgis's *Leaving Las Vegas.*

The Subjective Shot

Sometimes the camera, through its positioning and movements, invites us to see events through the eyes of a character. Some directors (Howard Hawks, John Ford, Kenji Mizoguchi, Jacques Tati) seldom use the subjective shot, but others (Alfred Hitchcock, Alain Resnais) use it constantly. As 7.140 indicated, Samuel Fuller's *Naked Kiss* starts with shocking subjective shots:

> We open with a direct cut. In that scene, the actors utilized the camera. They held the camera; it was strapped on them. For the first shot, the pimp has the camera strapped on his chest. I say to [Constance] Towers, "Hit the camera!" She hits the camera, the lens. Then I reverse it. I put the camera on her, and she whacks the hell out of him. I thought it was effective. [Quoted in Eric Sherman and Martin Rubin, *The Director's Event* (New York: Signet, 1969), p. 189.]

Historically, filmmakers began experimenting with the "first-person camera" or the "camera as character" quite early. *Grandma's Reading Glass* (1901) features subjective point-of-view shots. Keyholes, binoculars, and other apertures were often used to motivate optical point of view. In 1919 Abel Gance used many subjective shots in *J'accuse.* The 1920s saw many filmmakers taking an interest in subjectivity, seen in such films as E. A. Dupont's *Variety* (1925), F. W. Murnau's *The Last Laugh* (1924), with its famous drunken scene, and Abel Gance's *Napoleon* (1927). Some believe that in the 1940s the subjective shot—especially the subjective camera movement—got completely out of hand in Robert Montgomery's *Lady in the Lake* (1946). For almost the entire film the camera represents the vision of the protagonist, Philip Marlowe; we see him only when he glances in mirrors. "Suspenseful! Unusual!" proclaimed the advertising. "YOU accept an invitation to a blonde's apartment! YOU get socked in the jaw by a murder suspect!"

The history of the technique has teased film theorists into speculating about whether the subjective shot evokes identification from the audience. Do we think we *are* Philip Marlowe? The problem of audience identification with a point-of-view shot remains a difficult one in film theory. A useful discussion is Edward Branigan's *Point of View in the Cinema: A Theory of Narration and Subjectivity in Classical Film* (New York: Mouton, 1984).

Real Time and the Long Take

When the camera is running, does it record real time? If so, what artistic implications follow from that?

It was André Bazin who took the theoretical initiative in viewing cinema as an art which depends on actual duration. Like photography, Bazin argued, cinema is a *recording process*. The camera registers, photochemically, the light reflected from the object. Like the still camera, the movie camera records space. But unlike the still camera, the movie camera can also record *time.* "The cinema is objectivity in time. . . . Now, for the first time, the image of things is likewise the image of their duration, change mummified as it were" [*What Is Cinema?* Vol. 1 (Berkeley: University of California Press, 1966), pp. 14–15]. On this basis, Bazin saw editing as an intrusive interruption of the natural continuity of duration. He thus praised long-take directors such as Jean Renoir, Orson Welles, William Wyler, and Roberto Rossellini as artists whose styles respected concrete moment-to-moment life.

Bazin should be credited with calling our attention to the possibilities latent in the long take at a time when other film theorists considered it theatrical and uncinematic. Yet the problem of real time in film seems more complicated than Bazin thought. The most productive avenues that Bazin's ideas opened up have involved the analysis of different directorial *styles* rather than analysis of the most realistic ways to shoot a scene. That is, analysts no longer tend to ask whether Renoir's long takes are more faithful to reality than Eisenstein's short shots; we ask instead about the shots' different formal functions in each director's films.

Chapter 8

The Relation of Shot to Shot: Editing

Since the 1920s, when film theorists began to realize what **editing** can achieve, it has been the most widely discussed film technique. This has not been all to the good, for some writers have mistakenly found in editing the key to good cinema (or even *all* cinema). Yet many films, particularly in the period before 1904, consist of only one shot and hence do not depend on editing at all. Experimental films sometimes deemphasize editing by making each shot as long as the amount of film a camera will hold, as with Michael Snow's *La Région centrale* and Andy Warhol's *Eat, Sleep,* and *Empire.* Such films are not necessarily less *cinematic* than others that rely heavily on editing.

Still, one can see why editing has exercised such an enormous fascination for film aestheticians, for as a technique it is very powerful. The ride of the Klan in *The Birth of a Nation,* the Odessa Steps sequence in *Potemkin,* the hunt sequence in *The Rules of the Game,* the shower murder in *Psycho,* the train crash in *La Roue,* the diving sequence in *Olympia,* Clarice Starling's discovery of the killer's lair in *The Silence of the Lambs,* the tournament sequence in *Lancelot du Lac*—all of these celebrated moments derive much of their effect from editing.

Perhaps even more important, however, is the role of editing within an entire film's stylistic system. An ordinary Hollywood film typically contains between 1000 and 2000 shots; an action-based movie can have 3000 or more. This fact alone suggests that editing strongly shapes viewers' experiences, even if they are not aware of it. Editing contributes a great deal to a film's organization and its effects on spectators.

WHAT EDITING IS

Editing may be thought of as the coordination of one shot with the next. As we have seen, in film production a shot is one or more exposed frames in a series on a continuous length of film stock. The film editor eliminates unwanted footage, usually by discarding all but the best take. The editor also cuts superfluous frames, such as those showing the clapboard (p. 29), from the beginnings and endings of shots. She or he then joins the desired shots, the end of one to the beginning of another.

These joins can be of different sorts. A **fade-out** gradually darkens the end of a shot to black, and a **fade-in** accordingly lightens a shot from black. A **dissolve** briefly superimposes the end of shot A and the beginning of shot B **(8.1–8.3).** In a

wipe, shot B replaces shot A by means of a boundary line moving across the screen, as in *Seven Samurai* **(8.4).** Here both images are briefly on the screen at the same time, but they do not blend, as in a dissolve. In the production process, fades, dissolves, and wipes are optical effects and are marked as such by the editor. They are typically executed in the laboratory.

The most common means of joining two shots is the **cut.** Until the rise of digital editing in the 1990s, a cut was made by splicing two shots together by means of cement or tape. Some filmmakers "cut" during filming by planning that the film would emerge from the camera ready for final showing. Here the physical junction from shot to shot is created in the act of shooting. Such editing in the camera, however, is rare and is mainly confined to experimental and amateur filmmaking. Editing after shooting is the norm. Today much editing is done by means of video transfers stored on discs or a hard drive, so that the cuts (or *edits,* in video terminology) can be made without touching film. Nevertheless the final version of the film is prepared for printing by cutting and splicing the negative footage.

As viewers, we perceive a shot as an uninterrupted segment of screen time, space, or graphic configurations. Fades, dissolves, and wipes are perceived as gradually interrupting one shot and replacing it with another. Cuts are perceived as instantaneous changes from one shot to another.

Consider an example of cutting, four shots from the first attack on Bodega Bay in Alfred Hitchcock's film *The Birds* **(8.5–8.8):**

1. *Medium shot, straight-on angle.* Melanie, Mitch, and the Captain standing by the restaurant window talking. Melanie on extreme right, bartender in background (8.5).
2. *Medium close-up.* Melanie by Captain's shoulder. She looks to right (out offscreen window) and up, as if following with eyes. Pan right with her as she turns to the window and looks out (8.6).
3. *Extreme long shot.* Melanie's point of view. Gas station across street, phone booth in left foreground. Birds dive-bomb attendant, right to left (8.7).
4. *Medium close-up.* Melanie, profile. Captain moves right into shot, blocking out bartender; Mitch moves right into extreme foreground. All in profile look out window (8.8).

Each of these four shots presents a different segment of time, space, and pictorial information. The first shot shows three people talking. An instantaneous change—a cut—shifts us to a medium close-up shot of Melanie. (Hitchcock could have used a fade, dissolve, or wipe instead, with a slower change from shot to shot,

"Editing is the basic creative force, by power of which the soulless photographs (the separate shots) are engineered into living, cinematographic form."

— V. I. Pudovkin, director

"You can definitely help performances in the cutting room, by intercutting reaction, maybe rerecording lines, adding lines over reaction shots. And you can help a film's structure by moving sequences about and dropping scenes that hold up pacing. And sometimes you can use bits and pieces from different takes, which also helps a lot. What you can do in the editing room to help a film is amazing."

— Jodie Foster, actor and director

8.1 The first shot of *The Maltese Falcon* leads to . . .

8.2 . . . a dissolve to . . .

8.3 . . . the second shot.

8.4 A wipe joins the last shot of one scene with the first of the next in *Seven Samurai.*

8.5 *The Birds:* Shot 1.

8.6 Shot 2.

8.7 Shot 3.

8.8 Shot 4.

or he could have handled the scene as one continuous shot, as we shall see presently.) In the second shot, space has changed (Melanie is isolated and larger in the frame), time is continuous, and the graphic configurations have changed (the arrangements of the shapes and colors vary). Another cut takes us instantly to what she sees. The gas station shot (8.7) presents a very different space, a successive bit of time, and a different graphic configuration. Another cut returns us to Melanie (8.8), and again we are shifted instantly to another space, the next slice of time, and a different graphic configuration. Thus the four shots are joined by three cuts.

Hitchcock could have presented the *Birds* scene without editing. Imagine a camera movement that frames the four people talking, tracks in and rightward to Melanie as she turns, pans rightward to the window to show the dive-bombing gull, and pans leftward back to catch the group's expressions. This would constitute one shot, although the camera movements, no matter how fast, would not present the marked and abrupt shifts that cuts produce. Now imagine a deep-space composition that presents Mitch in the foreground, Melanie and the window in the middle ground, and the gull attack in the distance. Again, the scene could now be played in one shot, for we would have no abrupt change of time or space or graphics. And the movements of the figures would not yield the jumps in time, space, and composition provided by editing.

Although some films are shot with several cameras running simultaneously, throughout film history most sequences have been shot with only one camera. In *The Birds* scene, for example, the shots were taken at different times and places—one (shot 3) outdoors, the others in a sound stage (and these perhaps on different days). A film editor thus must assemble a large and varied batch of footage. To ease this task, most filmmakers plan for the editing phase during the preparation and shooting phases. Shots are taken with an idea of how they will eventually fit together. In fictional filming, scripts and storyboards help plan editing, while documentary filmmakers often shoot with an eye to how the footage will be cut.

DIMENSIONS OF FILM EDITING

Editing offers the filmmaker four basic areas of choice and control:

1. Graphic relations between shot A and shot B
2. Rhythmic relations between shot A and shot B
3. Spatial relations between shot A and shot B
4. Temporal relations between shot A and shot B

Graphic and rhythmic relationships are present in the editing of any film. Spatial and temporal relationships may be irrelevant to the editing of films using abstract form, but they are present in the editing of films built out of nonabstract images (that is, the great majority of motion pictures). Let us trace the range of choice and control in each area.

Graphic Relations between Shot A and Shot B

The four shots from *The Birds* may be considered purely as graphic configurations, as patterns of light and dark, line and shape, volumes and depths, movement and stasis—*independent of* the shot's relation to the time and space of the story. For instance, Hitchcock has not drastically altered the overall brightness from shot to shot. But he could have cut from the uniformly lit second shot (8.6, Melanie turning to the window) to a shot of the gas station swathed in darkness. Moreover, Hitchcock has usually kept the most important part of the composition roughly in the center of the frame. (Compare Melanie's position in the frame with that of the gas station in 8.7.) He could, however, have cut from a shot in which Melanie was in, say, upper frame left to a shot locating the gas station in the lower right of the frame.

Hitchcock has also played off certain color differences. Melanie's hair and outfit make her a predominantly yellow and green figure, whereas the shot of the gas station is dominated by drab bluish grays set off by touches of red in the gas pumps. Alternatively, Hitchcock could have cut from Melanie to another figure composed of similar colors. Furthermore, the movement in Melanie's shot—her turning to the window—does not blend into the movements of either the attendant or the gull in the next shot, but Hitchcock could have echoed Melanie's movement in speed, direction, or frame placement by movement in the next shot.

In short, editing together any two shots permits the interaction, through similarity and difference, of the *purely pictorial* qualities of those two shots. The four aspects of mise-en-scene (lighting, setting, costume, and the behavior of the figures in space and time) and most cinematographic qualities (photography, framing, and camera mobility) all furnish potential graphic elements. Thus every shot provides possibilities for purely graphic editing, and every cut creates some sort of graphic relationship between two shots.

At one level we perceive all film images as configurations of graphic material, and every film manipulates those configurations. Indeed, even in a film that is not pure abstraction, graphic editing can be a source of interest to filmmaker and audience.

Graphics may be edited to achieve smooth continuity or abrupt contrast. The filmmaker may link shots by graphic similarities, thus making what we can call a **graphic match.** Shapes, colors, overall composition, or movement in shot A may be picked up in the composition of shot B. A minimal instance is the cut that joins the first two shots of David Byrne's *True Stories* **(8.9, 8.10).** Similarly, in the "Beautiful Girl" song in Stanley Donen and Gene Kelly's *Singin' in the Rain,* amusing graphic matches are achieved through dissolves from one fashionably dressed woman to another, each figure posed and framed quite similarly from shot to shot.

More dynamic graphic matches appear in Akira Kurosawa's *Seven Samurai.* After the samurai have first arrived at the village, an alarm sounds and they race to discover its source. Kurosawa cuts together six shots of different running samurai, which he dynamically matches by means of composition, lighting, setting, figure movement, and panning camera movement **(8.11–8.16).**

Filmmakers often call attention to graphic matches at transitional moments **(8.17–8.22).** Such precise graphic matching is relatively rare. Still, an approximate graphic continuity from shot A to shot B is typical of most narrative cinema. The

8.9 A shot from *True Stories* with the Texas horizon midway up the frame is graphically matched . . .

8.10 . . . with a shot where the waterline of ancient seas is in the same position.

8.11 *Seven Samurai.*

8.12 *Seven Samurai.*

8.13 *Seven Samurai.*

8.14 *Seven Samurai.*

8.15 *Seven Samurai.*

8.16 *Seven Samurai.*

8.17 *Aliens:* The curved outline of Ripley's sleeping face . . .

8.18 . . . is graphically matched by means of a dissolve . . .

8.19 . . . to the outline of the earth.

8.20 Satyajit Ray's *World of Apu* ends one scene with a view of a movie screen, then dissolves . . .

8.21 . . . to the rectangular window of a taxicab . . .

8.22 . . . with the camera then moving back to show Apu and his wife riding home from the theater.

director will usually strive to keep the center of interest roughly constant across the cut, to maintain the overall lighting level, and to avoid strong color clashes from shot to shot. In Juzo Itami's *Tampopo,* an aspiring cook is trying to learn the secret of good noodles, and she questions a successful cook. Their confrontation is presented through head-on framings. Alternating shots keep each main character's face on the right side of each frame **(8.23, 8.24).**

Editing need not be graphically continuous. Mildly discontinuous editing may appear in widescreen compositions organized around characters facing one another. (Later we will study this editing pattern as *shot/reverse-shot cutting*). A scene from Quentin Tarantino's *Pulp Fiction* places the two hitmen opposite each other in a restaurant booth, each framed distinctly off-center **(8.25, 8.26).** Compared to the *Finye* example, the cut here creates greater graphic discontinuity. Note, however, that the cut does balance the frame area from shot to shot: Each man fills the space left empty in the previous shot. In addition, each man's face is just above the horizontal center of each frame, so that the spectator's eye can easily adjust to the changing composition. If asked afterward, many viewers would probably not recall that these compositions were unbalanced.

Graphically discontinuous editing can be more noticeable. Orson Welles frequently strives for a clash from shot to shot, as in *Citizen Kane* when the dark long shot of Kane's bedroom is followed by the bright opening title of the "News on the March" reel. Similarly, in *Touch of Evil,* Welles dissolves from a shot of Menzies looking out a window on frame right **(8.27)** to a shot of Susan Vargas looking out a different window on frame left **(8.28).** The clash is further accentuated by contrasting screen positions of the window reflections. Alain Resnais's *Night and Fog* began something of a fad by utilizing an extreme but apt graphic conflict: Color footage of an abandoned concentration camp today is cut together with black-and-white newsreel shots of the camps in the period 1942–1945. Even here, though, Resnais found striking similarities in shape, as when a tracking shot of fence posts graphically matches a low-angle shot of marching Nazi legs.

A director may call on editing to create a graphic conflict between color qualities. In *Paris, Texas,* the protagonist discovers his wife working in an erotic peepshow. Wim Wenders follows the couple's conversation by cutting from the customer's side of the glass to the performer's **(8.29, 8.30).** Although both people are visible in each shot, the cutting stresses their separation by harsh color contrasts.

8.23   The woman and her friend, the cowboy truck driver . . .

8.24   . . . confront the enraged cook and his assistants. The key characters are made prominent by being placed in the same area of each shot.

8.25   As Tarantino cuts between Jules and . . .

8.26   . . . Vincent, our eye must move back and forth across the screen.

8.27   *Touch of Evil:* graphic discontinuity.

8.28   *Touch of Evil.*

Later in the *Birds* sequence discussed above, Hitchcock puts graphic conflict to good use. Gasoline spurting from the pump has flowed across the street to a parking lot, and Melanie, along with several other people at the restaurant window, has seen a man accidentally set the gasoline alight. His car ignites, and an explosion of flame engulfs him. What we see next is Melanie watching helplessly as the flame races along the trail of gas toward the station. Hitchcock cuts the shots as shown in **8.31–8.41:**

8.29 In *Paris, Texas,* the wife's light-blue, almost washed-out, stage setting, as seen from the husband's side of the glass, clashes . . .

8.30 . . . with the blackness and the aluminum-foil reflections in the next shot.

Shot 30.	(ls)	High angle. Melanie's POV. Flaming car, spreading flames (8.31).	73 frames
Shot 31.	(mcu)	Straight-on angle. Melanie, immobile, looking off left, mouth open (8.32).	20 frames
Shot 32.	(ms)	High angle. Melanie's POV. Pan with flames moving from lower right to upper left of trail of gasoline (8.33).	18 frames
Shot 33.	(mcu)	as 31. Melanie, immobile, staring down center (8.34).	16 frames
Shot 34.	(ms)	High angle. Melanie's POV. Pan with flames moving from lower right to upper left (8.35).	14 frames
Shot 35.	(mcu)	as 31. Melanie, immobile, looking off right, staring aghast (8.36).	12 frames
Shot 36.	(ls)	Melanie's POV. Gas station. Flames rush in from right. Mitch, sheriff, and attendant run out left (8.37).	10 frames
Shot 37.	(mcu)	as 31. Melanie, immobile, stares off extreme right (8.38).	8 frames
Shot 38.	(ls)	as 36. Melanie's POV. Cars at station explode (8.39).	34 frames
Shot 39.	(mcu)	as 31. Melanie covers her face with her hands (8.40).	33 frames
Shot 40.	(els)	Extreme high angle on city, flaming trail in center. Gulls fly into shot (8.41).	

In graphic terms, Hitchcock has exploited two possibilities of contrast. First, although each shot's composition centers the action (Melanie's head, the flaming trail), the movements thrust in different directions. In shot 31 Melanie looks to the lower left, whereas in shot 32 the fire moves to the upper left. In shot 33 Melanie is looking down center, whereas in the next shot the flames still move to the upper left, and so on.

8.31 *The Birds:* Shot 30.

8.32 *The Birds:* Shot 31.

8.33 *The Birds:* Shot 32.

8.34 *The Birds:* Shot 33.

8.35 *The Birds:* Shot 34.

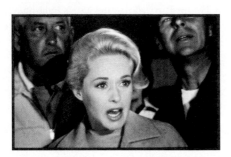

8.36 *The Birds:* Shot 35.

8.37 *The Birds:* Shot 36.

8.38 *The Birds:* Shot 37.

8.39 *The Birds:* Shot 38.

8.40 *The Birds:* Shot 39.

8.41 *The Birds:* Shot 40.

More important—and what makes the sequence impossible to recapture on the printed page—is a crucial contrast of mobility and stasis. The shots of the flames present movement of both the subject (the flames rushing along the gas) and of the camera (which pans to follow). But the shots of Melanie could almost be still photographs, since they are absolutely static. She does not turn her head within the shots, and the camera does not track in or away from her. Interestingly too, instead of showing her turning to watch the flames, Hitchcock presents only static stages of her action, and so we must infer the progress of her attention. By making movement conflict with countermovement and with stillness, Hitchcock has powerfully exploited the graphic possibilities of editing.

Rhythmic Relations between Shot A and Shot B

Each shot, being a strip of film, is of a certain length, measured in frames, feet, or meters. And the shot's physical length corresponds to a measurable duration on-screen. As we know, at sound speed, 24 frames last one second in projection. A shot can be as short as a single frame, or it may be thousands of frames long, running for many minutes when projected. Editing thus allows the filmmaker to determine the duration of each shot. When the filmmaker adjusts the length of shots in relation to one another, she or he is controlling the **rhythmic** potential of editing.

As we have already seen (pp. 217–218), rhythm in cinema includes many factors—principally accent, beat, and tempo. And cinematic rhythm as a whole derives not only from editing but from other film techniques as well. The filmmaker also relies on movement in the mise-en-scene, camera position and movement, the rhythm of sound, and the overall context to determine the editing rhythm. Nevertheless, the patterning of shot lengths contributes considerably to what we intuitively recognize as a film's rhythm.

Sometimes the filmmaker will use shot duration to create a stressed, accented, moment. In one sequence of *The Road Warrior,* a ferocious gang member butts his head against that of a victim. At the moment of contact, director George Miller cuts in a few frames of pure white. The result is a sudden flash that suggests violent impact. Alternatively, a shot's duration can be used to deaccentuate an action. During test screenings of *Raiders of the Lost Ark,* Steven Spielberg discovered that after Indiana Jones shoots the gigantic swordsman, several seconds had to be added to allow the audience's reaction to die down before the action could resume.

More commonly, the rhythmic possibilities of editing emerge when several shot lengths form a discernible pattern. A steady, metrical, beat can be established by making all of the shots approximately the same length. The filmmaker can also create a dynamic pace. Steadily lengthening shots can generate a gradually slowing tempo, while successively shorter shots can create an accelerating one.

Consider how Hitchcock handles the tempo of the first gull attack in *The Birds.* Shot 1, the medium shot of the group talking (8.5), consumes almost a thousand frames, or about 41 seconds. But shot 2 (8.6), which shows Melanie looking out the window, is much shorter—309 frames (about 13 seconds). Even shorter is shot 3 (8.7), which lasts only 55 frames (about $2\frac{1}{3}$ seconds). The fourth shot (8.8), showing Melanie joined by Mitch and the Captain, lasts only 35 frames (about $1\frac{1}{2}$ seconds). Clearly Hitchcock is accelerating the pace at the beginning of what will be a tense sequence.

In what follows, Hitchcock makes the shots fairly short, but subordinates the length of the shot to the internal rhythm of the dialogue and the movement in the images. As a result, shots 5 through 29 (not shown here) have no fixed pattern of lengths. But once the essential components of the scene have been established, Hitchcock returns to strongly accelerating cutting.

In presenting Melanie's horrified realization of the flames racing from the parking lot to the gas station, shots 30 through 40 (8.31–8.41) climax the rhythmic intensification of the sequence. As the description on p. 301 shows, after the shot of the spreading flames (shot 30, 8.31), each shot decreases in length by two frames, from 20 frames ($^4/_5$ of a second) to 8 frames ($^1/_3$ of a second). Two shots, 38 and 39, then punctuate the sequence with almost identical durations (a little less than $1^1/_2$ seconds apiece). Shot 40 (8.41), a long shot that lasts over 600 frames, functions as both a pause and a suspenseful preparation for the new attack. The scene's variations in rhythm alternate between rendering the savagery of the attack and generating suspense as we await the next onslaught.

We have had the luxury of counting frames on the actual strip of film. The theater viewer cannot do this, but she or he does feel and recognize the shifting tempo in this sequence because of the changing shot durations. In general, by controlling editing rhythm, the filmmaker controls the amount of time we have to grasp and reflect on what we see. A series of rapid shots, for example, leaves us little time to think about what we are watching. In the *Birds* sequence, Hitchcock's editing impels the viewer's perception to move at a faster and faster pace. Quickly grasping the progress of the fire and understanding Melanie's changes in position become essential factors in the rising excitement of the scene.

Hitchcock is not, of course, the only director to use rhythmic editing. Its possibilities were initially explored by such directors as D. W. Griffith (especially in *Intolerance*) and Abel Gance. In the 1920s the French Impressionist filmmakers and the Soviet Montage school explored the rhythmic possibilities of strings of short shots (pp. 475–477, 478–481). When sound films became the norm, pronounced rhythmic editing survived in dramas such as Lewis Milestone's *All Quiet on the Western Front* as well as in musical comedies and fantasies such as René Clair's *À Nous la liberté* and *Le Million,* Rouben Mamoulian's *Love Me Tonight,* and Busby Berkeley's dance sequences in *42nd Street* and *Footlight Parade.* In classical Hollywood cinema the rhythmic use of dissolves became crucial to the *montage sequence,* which we shall discuss shortly. Rhythm remains a fundamental resource of the editor, most notably in the use of fast cutting to build up excitement during an action sequence, a television advertisement, or a music video.

Spatial Relations between Shot A and Shot B

Editing usually serves not only to control graphics and rhythm but also to construct film space as well. Exhilaration in this newly discovered power can be sensed in the writings of such filmmakers as the Soviet director Dziga Vertov: "I am Kino-eye. I am builder. I have placed you . . . in an extraordinary room which did not exist until just now when I also created it. In this room there are twelve walls, shot by me in various parts of the world. In bringing together shots of walls and details, I've managed to arrange them in an order that is pleasing."

Such elation is understandable. Editing lets an omniscient range of knowledge become visible as omnipresence, the ability to move from one spot to any other. Editing permits the filmmaker to relate *any* two points in space through similarity, difference, or development.

The director might, for instance, start with a shot that establishes a spatial whole and follow this with a shot of a part of this space. This is what Hitchcock does in shot 1 and shot 2 of the *Birds* sequence (8.5, 8.6): a medium long shot of the group of people followed by a medium shot of only one, Melanie. Such analytical breakdown is a very common editing pattern, especially in classical continuity editing.

"I noticed a softening in American cinema over the last twenty years, and I think it's a direct influence of TV. I would even say that if you want to make movies today, you'd be better off studying television than film because that's the market. Television has diminished the audience's attention span. It's hard to make a slow, quiet film today. Not that *I* would want to make a slow, quiet film anyway!"

— Oliver Stone, director

Alternatively, the filmmaker could construct a whole space out of component parts. Hitchcock does this later in the *Birds* sequence. Note that in 8.5 through 8.8 and in shots 30–39 (8.31–8.40) we do not see an establishing shot including Melanie *and* the gas station. In production the restaurant window need not have been across from the station at all; they could have been filmed in different cities or countries. Yet we are compelled to believe that Melanie is across the street from the gas station. The bird cry offscreen and the mise-en-scene (the window and Melanie's sideways glance) contribute considerably as well. It is, however, primarily the editing that creates the spatial whole of restaurant-and-gas-station.

Such spatial manipulation through cutting is fairly common. In documentaries compiled from newsreel footage, for example, one shot might show a cannon firing, and another shot might show a shell hitting its target; we infer that the cannon fired the shell (though the shots may show entirely different battles). Again, if a shot of a speaker is followed by a shot of a cheering crowd, we assume a spatial coexistence.

The possibility of such spatial manipulation was examined by the Soviet filmmaker Lev Kuleshov, who during the 1920s shot and cut "experiments" in constructing spatial relations by eliminating establishing shots. The most famous of these involved the cutting of neutral shots of an actor's face with other shots (variously reported as shots of soup, nature scenes, a dead woman, a baby). The reported result was that the audience immediately assumed not only that the actor's expression changed but also that the actor was reacting to things present in the same space as himself. Similarly, Kuleshov cut together shots of actors, "looking at each other" but on Moscow streets miles apart, then meeting and strolling together—and looking at the White House in Washington. Although filmmakers had used such cutting before Kuleshov's work, film scholars call the *Kuleshov effect* any series of shots that *in the absence of an establishing shot* prompts the spectator to infer a spatial whole on the basis of seeing only portions of the space.

The Kuleshov effect can conjure up robust cinematic illusions. In Corey Yuen's *Legend of Fong Sai-Yuk,* a martial-arts bout between the hero and an adept woman begins on a platform but then moves into the audience—or rather, onto the audience, for the two fight while balancing on the heads and shoulders of the crowd. Yuen's rapid editing conveys the scene's point by means of the Kuleshov effect **(8.42, 8.43).** (In production, this meant that the combatants could be hung on wires or bars suspended outside the frame, as in 8.43.) Across many shots, Yuen provides only a few brief full-figure framings showing Fong Sai-Yuk and the woman.

8.42 *The Legend of Fong Sai-Yuk:* A shot of the woman's upper body is followed by . . .

8.43 . . . a shot of her legs and feet, supported by unwilling bystanders.

"Editing is very interesting and absorbing work because of the illusions you can create. You can span thirty years within an hour and a half. You can stretch a moment in slow motion. You can play with time in extraordinary ways."

— Paul Hirsch, editor

8.44   *Hiroshima mon amour:* A view of the protagonist's Japanese lover asleep is followed by . . .

8.45   . . . a shot of her looking at him, leading to . . .

8.46   . . . a flashback of her dead German lover's hand.

While the viewer doesn't normally notice the Kuleshov effect, a few films call attention to it. Carl Reiner's *Dead Men Don't Wear Plaid* mixes footage filmed in the present with footage from Hollywood movies of the 1940s. Thanks to the Kuleshov effect, *Dead Men* creates unified scenes in which Steve Martin converses with characters who were originally featured in other films. In *A Movie,* Bruce Conner makes a joke of the Kuleshov effect by cutting from a submarine captain peering through a periscope to a woman gazing at the camera, as if they could see each other (5.60, 5.61, p. 160).

In the Kuleshov effect, editing cues the spectator to infer a single locale. Editing can also emphasize action taking place in separate places. In *Intolerance,* D. W. Griffith cuts from ancient Babylon to Gethsemane, from France in 1572 to America in 1916. Such parallel editing, or **crosscutting,** is a common way films construct a variety of spaces.

More radically, the editing can present spatial relations as being ambiguous and uncertain. In Carl Dreyer's *La Passion de Jeanne d'Arc,* for instance, we know only that Jeanne and the priests are in the same room. Because the neutral white backgrounds and the numerous close-ups provide no orientation to the entire space, we can seldom tell how far apart the characters are or precisely who is beside whom. We shall see later how films can create even more extreme spatial discontinuities.

Temporal Relations between Shot A and Shot B

Like other film techniques, editing can control the time of the action denoted in the film. In a narrative film especially, editing usually contributes to the plot's manipulation of story time. You will recall that Chapter 3 pointed out three areas in which plot time can cue the spectator to construct the story time: order, duration, and frequency. Our *Birds* example (8.5–8.8) shows how editing reinforces all three areas of control.

First, there is the *order* of presentation of events. The men talk, then Melanie turns away, then she sees the gull swoop, then she responds. Hitchcock's editing presents these story events in the 1-2-3-4 order of his shots. But he could have shuffled the shots into a different order. Transposing shot 2 and shot 3 would be unusual, but it is possible to put the shots in any order at all, even reverse (4-3-2-1). This is to say that the filmmaker may control temporal succession through the editing.

As we saw in Chapter 3, such manipulation of events leads to changes in story–plot relations. We are most familiar with such manipulations in **flashbacks,** which present one or more shots out of their presumed story order. In *Hiroshima mon amour,* Resnais uses the protagonist's memory to motivate a violation of temporal order. Three shots (**8.44–8.46**) suggest visually that the position of her current lover's hand triggers a recollection of another lover's death years before. In contemporary cinema, brief flashbacks to key events may brutally interrupt present-time action. *The Fugitive* uses this technique to return obsessively to the murder of Dr. Kimball's wife, the event that initiated the story's action. In Errol Morris's documentary *The Thin Blue Line,* present-day interrogations of suspects and witnesses are interspersed with reenactments that function as flashbacks to the central crime.

A much rarer option for reordering story events is the **flashforward.** Here the editing moves from the present to a future event and then returns to the present. A small-scale instance occurs in *The Godfather.* Don Vito Corleone talks with his sons Tom and Sonny about their upcoming meeting with Solozzo, the gangster who is asking them to finance his narcotics traffic. As the Corleones talk in the present, shots of them are interspersed with shots of Solozzo going to the meeting in the future (**8.47–8.49**). The editing is used to provide exposition about Solozzo

8.47   In *The Godfather*, the Corleones discuss their upcoming meeting with Solozzo.

8.48   Flashforward: Solozzo arrives at the meeting, greeted by Sonny.

8.49   The next shot returns us to the family conversation, where Don Vito ponders what he will tell Solozzo.

while also moving quickly to the Don's announcement, at the gangsters' meeting, that he will not involve the family in the drug trade.

Filmmakers may use flashforwards to tease the viewer with glimpses of the eventual outcome of the story action. The end of *They Shoot Horses, Don't They?* is hinted at in brief shots that periodically interrupt scenes in the present. Such flashforwards create a sense of a narration with a powerful range of story knowledge.

We may assume, then, that if a series of shots traces a 1-2-3 order in the presentation of story events, it is because the filmmaker has chosen to do that, not because of any necessity of following this order. Editing also offers ways for the filmmaker to alter the *duration* of story events as presented in the film's plot.

In our sample sequence from *The Birds,* the duration of the story events is presented whole. Melanie's act of turning consumes a certain length of time, and Hitchcock does not alter the duration of the event in his editing. Nevertheless, he could have. Imagine cutting from shot 1 (the men talking and Melanie standing by) to a shot of Melanie already turned and looking out the window. The time it took her to turn to the window would be eliminated by the cut. Thus editing can create a temporal **ellipsis.**

Elliptical editing presents an action in such a way that it consumes less time on the screen than it does in the story. The filmmaker can create an ellipsis in three principal ways.

Suppose that a director wants to show a man climbing a flight of stairs, but does not want to show the entire duration of his climb. The director could use a conventional *punctuation* shot change, such as a dissolve or a wipe or a fade; in the classical filmmaking tradition, such a device signals that some time has been omitted. Our director could simply dissolve from a shot of the man starting at the bottom of the stairs to a shot of him reaching the top.

Alternatively, the filmmaker could show the man at the bottom of the staircase and let him walk up out of the frame, hold briefly on the empty frame, then cut to an empty frame of the top of the stairs and let the man enter the frame. The *empty frames* on either side of the cut cover the elided time.

Also, the filmmaker can create an ellipsis by means of a *cutaway:* a shot of another event elsewhere that will not last as long as the elided action. In our example, the director might start with the man climbing but then cut away to a woman in her apartment. We could then cut back to the man much further along in his ascent.

In our *Birds* example, Hitchcock could also have controlled the duration of the action by *expansion,* the opposite of ellipsis. For example, he might have extended shot 1 so as to include the beginning of Melanie's act of turning, then shown her beginning to turn in shot 2 as well. This would have prolonged the action, stretching it out past its story duration. The Russian filmmakers of the 1920s made frequent use of temporal expansion through such **overlapping editing,** and no one mastered it more thoroughly than Sergei Eisenstein. In *Strike* when factory workers bowl over a foreman with a large wheel hanging from a crane, two shots expand the action **(8.50–8.52).** In *October* Eisenstein overlaps several shots of rising bridges in order to stress the significance of the moment. In *Ivan the Terrible* friends pour golden coins down on the newly crowned Ivan in a torrent that seems never to cease. In all of these sequences the duration of the action is prolonged through noticeably overlapping the movements from shot to shot.

8.50 *Strike:* A wheel swings toward the foreman . . .

8.51 . . . then swings toward him again . . .

8.52 . . . and then again before striking him.

So much for order and duration in editing. What about *frequency?* Returning once more to the temporal relations in the *Birds* segment, we note that in the story Melanie turns to the window only once and the gull swoops only once. And Hitchcock presents these events on the screen the same number of times that they occur in the story. But, of course, Hitchcock could have repeated any of these shots. Melanie could have been shown turning to the window several times; this would be not merely overlapping a phase of an action but rather full-scale repetition.

If this sounds peculiar, it is doubtless because we are accustomed to seeing a shot present the action only once. Yet its very rarity may make repetition a powerful editing resource. In Bruce Conner's *Report* there is a newsreel shot of John and Jacqueline Kennedy riding a limousine down a Dallas street. The shot is systematically repeated, in part or in whole, over and over, building up tension in our expectations as the shot seems to move by tiny increments closer to the moment of the inevitable assassination. Occasionally in *Do The Right Thing,* Spike Lee cuts together two takes of the same action, as when we twice see a garbage can fly through the air and break the pizzeria window at the start of the riot. Jackie Chan often shows his most virtuosic stunts three or four times in a row from different angles to allow the audience to marvel at his daring and dexterity **(8.53–8.55).**

8.53   *Police Story:* Chasing the gangsters through a shopping mall, Jackie Chan leaps onto a pole several stories above them . . .

8.54   . . . and slides down in a shower of exploding lights.

8.55   Cut to a new angle: Jackie leaps again, leading to an instant replay of the risky stunt.

Graphics, rhythm, space, and time, then, are at the service of the filmmaker through the technique of editing. Our brief survey should suggest that the potential range of these areas of control is virtually unlimited. Yet most films we see make use of a very narrow set of editing possibilities—so narrow, indeed, that we can speak of a dominant editing style throughout Western film history. This is what is usually called **continuity editing.** Still, the most familiar way to edit a film is not the only way to edit a film, and so we will also consider some alternatives to continuity editing.

CONTINUITY EDITING

Around 1900–1910, as filmmakers started to use editing, they sought to arrange their shots so as to tell a story coherently and clearly. Thus editing, supported by specific strategies of cinematography and mise-en-scene, was used to ensure *narrative continuity.* So powerful is this style that, even today, anyone working in narrative filmmaking around the world is expected to be thoroughly familiar with it.

The basic purpose of the continuity system is to create a smooth flow from shot to shot. All of the possibilities of editing we have already examined are turned to this end. First, graphic qualities are usually kept roughly continuous from shot to shot. The figures are balanced and symmetrically deployed in the frame; the overall lighting tonality remains constant; the action occupies the central zone of the screen.

Second, the rhythm of the cutting is usually made dependent on the camera distance of the shot. Long shots are left on the screen longer than medium shots, and medium shots are left on longer than close-ups. The assumption is that the spectator needs more time to take in the shots containing more details. In scenes of physical action like the fire in *The Birds,* accelerated editing rhythms may be present, but the shorter shots will tend to be closer views.

Since the continuity style seeks to present a story, however, it is chiefly through the handling of space and time that editing furthers narrative continuity.

Spatial Continuity: The 180° System

In the continuity style the space of a scene is constructed along what is called variously the **axis of action,** the *center line,* or the *180° line.* The scene's action—a person walking, two people conversing, a car racing along a road—is assumed to take place along a discernible, predictable line. This axis of action determines a half-circle, or 180° area, where the camera can be placed to present the action. Consequently, the filmmaker will plan, film, and edit the shots so as to respect this center line. The camera work and mise-en-scene in each shot will be manipulated to establish and reiterate the 180° space.

Consider the bird's-eye view in **8.56.** We have a girl and a boy conversing. The axis of action is that imaginary line connecting the two people. Under the continuity system, the director would arrange the mise-en-scene and camera placement so as to establish and sustain this line. The camera can be put at any point as long as it stays on the same *side* of the line (hence the 180° term). A typical series of shots would be: (1) a medium shot of the girl and boy; (2) a shot over the girl's shoulder, favoring the boy; (3) a shot over the boy's shoulder, favoring the girl. But to cut to a shot from camera position X, or from any position within the tinted area, would be considered a violation of the system because it *crosses* the axis of action. Indeed, some handbooks of film directing call shot X flatly wrong. To see why, we need to examine what happens if a filmmaker follows the **180° system.**

The 180° system ensures that relative positions in the frame remain consistent. In the shots taken from camera positions 1, 2, and 3, the characters remain in the same positions in the frame relative to each other. Even though we see them from different angles, the girl is always on the left and the boy is always on the right. But if we cut to shot X, the characters will switch positions in the frame. An advocate of traditional continuity would claim that shot X confuses us: Have the two characters somehow swiveled around each other?

"The way Hawks constructs a continuity of space is remarkable, and generally holds you 'inside' it. There is no possible way of escape, unless the film decides to provide you with one. My theory is that his films are captivating because they build a sense of continuity which is so strong that it allows the complete participation of the audience."

— Slobodan Sijan, director

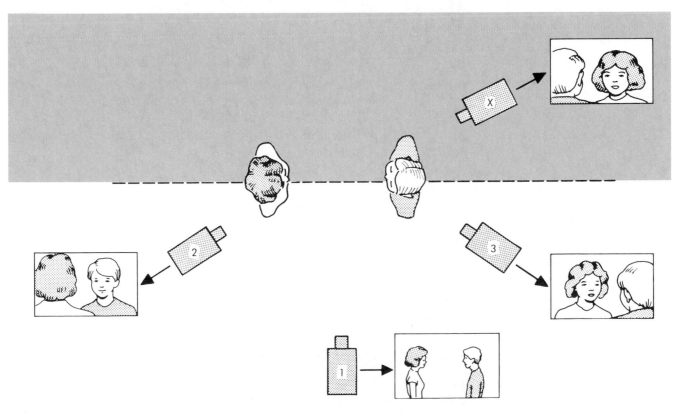

8.56   A conversation scene and the axis of action.

" . . . what I call "new brutalism" in cinema . . . is a form of naïveté, because it's made by people who I think don't really have a grasp of cinema's history. It's the MTV kind of editing, where the main idea is that the more disorienting it is, the more exciting. And you see it creeping into mainstream cinema more and more. You look at something like *Armageddon* and you see all the things that would have been forbidden in classical cinema, like crossing the line, camera jumping from side to side. It is a way to artificially generate excitement, but it doesn't really have any basis to it. And I find it kind of sad, because it's like an old man trying to dress like a teenager."

— John Boorman, director

The 180° system ensures consistent eyelines. In shots 1, 2, and 3, the girl is looking right and the boy is looking left. Shot X violates this pattern by making the girl look to the left.

The 180° system ensures consistent screen direction. Imagine now that the girl is walking left to right; her path constitutes the axis of action. As long as our shots do not cross this axis, cutting them together will keep the **screen direction** of the girl's movement constant, from left to right. But if we *cross* the axis and film a shot from the other side, the girl will now appear on the screen as moving from *right to left.* Such a cut could be disorienting.

Consider a similar situation to that in 8.56, a standard scene of two cowboys meeting for a shootout on a town street **(8.57)**. Cowboy A and Cowboy B form the 180° line, but here A is walking from left to right and B is approaching from right to left, both seen in the shot taken from camera position 1. A closer view, from camera position 2, shows B still moving from right to left. A third shot, from camera position 3, shows A walking, as he had been in the first shot, from left to right.

But imagine that this third shot was instead taken from position X, on the opposite side of the line. A is now seen as moving from right to left. Has he taken fright and turned around while the second shot, of B, was on the screen? The filmmakers may want us to think that he is still walking toward his adversary, but the change in screen directions could make us think just the opposite. A cut to a shot taken from any point in the colored area would create this change in direction. Such breaks in continuity can be confusing.

8.57 A Western shootout and the axis of action.

Even more disorienting would be crossing the line while establishing the scene's action. In our shootout, if the first shot shows A walking from left to right and the second shot shows B (from the other side of the line) also walking left to right, we would probably not be sure that they were walking toward each other. The two cowboys would seem to be walking in the same direction at different points on the street, as if one were following the other. We would very likely be startled if they suddenly came face to face within the same shot.

The 180° system prides itself on delineating space clearly. The viewer should always know *where the characters are* in relation to one another and to the setting. More important, the viewer always knows *where he or she is* with respect to the story action. The space of the scene, clearly and unambiguously unfolded, does not jar or disorient, because such disorientation, it is felt, will distract the viewer from the center of attention: the narrative chain of causes and effects.

Continuity Editing: A Case Study

We saw in Chapter 3 that the classical Hollywood mode of narrative subordinates time, motivation, and other factors to the cause–effect sequence. We also saw how mise-en-scene and camera work may present narrative material. Now we can note how, on the basis of the 180° principle, filmmakers have developed the continuity system as a way to build up a smoothly flowing space that remains subordinate to narrative action. Let us consider a concrete example, the opening of John Huston's film *The Maltese Falcon.*

8.58   *The Maltese Falcon:* Shot 1a.

The scene begins in the office of detective Sam Spade. In the first two shots this space is established in several ways. First, there is the office window (shot 1a, **8.58**), from which the camera tilts down to reveal Spade (shot 1b, **8.59**) rolling a cigarette. As Spade says, "Yes, sweetheart?" shot 2 **(8.60)** appears. This is important in several respects. It is an **establishing shot,** delineating the overall space of the office: the door, the intervening area, the desk, and Spade's position. Note also that shot 2 establishes a 180° line between Spade and his secretary, Effie; Effie could be the girl in 8.56, and Spade could be the boy. The first phase of this scene will be built around staying on the same side of this 180° line.

Once laid out for us in the first two shots, the space is analyzed into its components. Shots 3 **(8.61)** and 4 **(8.62)** show Spade and Effie talking. Because the 180° line established at the outset is adhered to (each shot presents the two from the same side), we know their location and spatial relationships. In cutting together medium shots of the two, however, Huston relies on two other common tactics within the 180° system.

8.59   *The Maltese Falcon:* Shot 1b.

8.60   *The Maltese Falcon:* Shot 2.

8.61   *The Maltese Falcon:* Shot 3.

8.62   *The Maltese Falcon:* Shot 4.

The first is the **shot/reverse-shot** pattern. Once the 180° line has been established, we can show first one end point of the line, then the other. Here we cut back and forth from Effie to Spade. A reverse shot is not literally the reverse of the first framing. It is simply a shot of the opposite end of the axis of action, usually showing a three-quarters view of the subject. In our bird's-eye view diagram (8.56), shots 2 and 3 form a shot/reverse-shot pattern, as 8.61 and 8.62 do here. Earlier examples in this chapter of shot/reverse-shot cutting are 8.23, 8.24 and 8.25, 8.26.

The second tactic Huston uses here is the **eyeline match.** That is, shot A presents someone looking at something offscreen; shot B shows us what is being looked at. In neither shot are *both* looker and object present. In the *Maltese Falcon* opening, the cut from the shot of Effie (shot 3, 8.61) to the shot of Spade at his desk (shot 4, 8.62) is an eyeline match. The shots from *The Birds* of Melanie watching the bird attack and fire also create eyeline matches, as do the examples of editing balancing frame compositions (8.23, 8.24 and 8.25, 8.26).

Note that shot/reverse-shot editing need not employ eyeline matches. You could film both ends of the axis in a shot/reverse-shot pattern without showing the characters looking at each other. One character might have her hands over her eyes, the other might have his back to her. (Note that in 8.62, Spade is not looking at Effie.) On the whole, however, most shot/reverse-shot cuts also utilize the eyeline match.

The eyeline match is a simple idea but a powerful one, since the *directional* quality of the eyeline creates a strong spatial continuity. To be looked at, an object must be near the looker. The eyeline match presumably created the effects Kuleshov identified in his construction of false spaces through editing. That is, the expressionless actor seems to be looking at whatever is in the next shot, and the audience assumes that the actor is reacting accordingly.

Within the 180° system, the eyeline match, like constant screen direction, can stabilize space. Note how in shot 3, Effie's glance off right reiterates Spade's position even though he is not onscreen. And though Spade does not look up after the cut to shot 4, the camera position remains adamantly on the same side of the axis of action (indeed, the position is virtually identical to that in shot 1b). We know that Effie is offscreen left. Thus the breakdown of the scene's space is completely consistent, this consistency ensured by adherence to the 180° system. Thanks to the shot/reverse-shot pattern and the eyeline match, we understand the characters' locations even when they are not in the same frame.

The spatial consistency is reaffirmed in shot 5, which presents the same framing as did shot 2. The office is shown again (shot 5a, **8.63**), when the new character, Brigid O'Shaughnessy, enters. Spade stands to greet her, and the camera reframes his movement by a slight tilt upward (shot 5b, **8.64**). Shot 5 is a **reestablishing shot,** since it reestablishes the overall space that was analyzed into shots 3 and 4. The pattern, then, has been *establishment/breakdown/reestablishment*—one of the most common patterns of spatial editing in the classical continuity style.

Let us pause to examine how this pattern has functioned to advance the narrative. Shot 1 has suggested the locale and, more important, has emphasized the protagonist by linking him to the sign on the window. Offscreen sound and Spade's "Yes, sweetheart?" motivate the cut to shot 2. This establishing shot firmly anchors shot 1 spatially. It also introduces the source of the offscreen sound—the new character, Effie. The shot changes at precisely the moment when Effie enters. We are thus unlikely to notice the cut, because our expectations lead us to want to see what happens next. The space near the door has been shown when the cause–effect chain makes it important, not before.

Shots 3 and 4 present the conversation between Spade and Effie, and the shot/reverse shot and the eyeline match reassure us as to the characters' locations. We may not even notice the cutting, since the style works to emphasize the dra-

8.63 *The Maltese Falcon:* Shot 5a.

8.64 *The Maltese Falcon:* Shot 5b.

matic flow of the scene—what Effie says and how Spade reacts. In shot 5 the over-all view of the office is presented again, precisely at the moment when a new character enters the scene, and this in turn situates her firmly in the space. Thus the narrative—the dialogue, the entrance of new characters—is emphasized by adhering to the 180° system. The editing subordinates space to action.

We can trace the same procedures, with one additional variation, in the shots that follow. In shot 5 Brigid O'Shaughnessy enters Spade's office. Shot 6 presents a reverse angle on the two of them as she comes toward him (shot 6a, **8.65**). She sits down alongside his desk (shot 6b, **8.66**). Up to this point the 180° line ran between Spade and the doorway. Now the axis of action runs from Spade to the client's chair by his desk. Once established, this new line will not be violated.

The extra factor here is a third tactic for ensuring spatial continuity—the **match on action,** a very powerful device. Assume that a person starts to stand up in shot 1. We can wait until the character is standing up and has stopped moving before cutting to shot 2. But we can instead show the person's movement *beginning* in shot 1, and then we can cut to shot 2, which shows the continuation of the movement. We would then have a match on action, the editing device that carries a movement across the break between two shots.

To appreciate the skill involved in making a match on action, recall that most films are shot with a single camera. In filming shots whose action will be matched at the editing stage, it is possible that the first shot, in which the movement starts, will be filmed hours or days apart from the second, in which the movement is continued. Thus matching action is not simply a matter of cutting together two complete versions of the same scene from different vantage points. The process involves keeping notes about matters of camera work, mise-en-scène, and editing so that all the details can be fitted together in the assembly phase of production.

In the *Maltese Falcon* scene, the cut from the end of shot 5 (8.64) to the beginning of shot 6 (8.65) uses a match on action, the action being Brigid's walk toward Spade's desk. Again, the 180° system aids in concealing the match, since it keeps screen direction constant: Brigid moves from left to right in both shots. As one would expect, the match on action is a tool of narrative continuity. It takes a practiced eye to spot a smooth match on action; so powerful is our desire to follow the action flowing across the cut that we ignore the cut itself.

Except for the match on action, the editing in the rest of the scene uses the same tactics we have already seen. When Brigid sits down, a new axis of action has been established (shot 6b, 8.66). This enables Huston to break down the space into closer shots (shots 7 through 13, **8.67–8.73**). All of these shots use the shot/reverse-shot tactic: The camera frames, at an oblique angle, one end point of the 180° line, then frames the other. (Note the shoulders in the foreground of shots 7, 8, and 10—8.67, 8.68, and 8.70). Here again, the editing of space presents the dialogue action simply and unambiguously.

Beginning with shot 12, Huston's cuts also create eyeline matches. Spade looks off left at Brigid (shot 12, 8.72). She looks off left as the door is heard opening (shot 13, 8.73). Archer, just coming in, looks off right at them (shot 14, **8.74**), and they both look off at him (shot 15, **8.75**). The 180° rule permits us always to know who is looking at whom.

What is the function of the analytical cutting in this part of the scene? Huston could have played the entire conversation in one long take, remaining with shot 6b (8.66). Why has he broken the conversation into seven shots? Most evidently, the analytical breakdown controls our attention. We will look at Brigid or Spade at exactly the moment Huston wants us to. In the long take and the more distant framing, Huston would have to channel our attention in other ways, perhaps through composition or sound.

8.65 *The Maltese Falcon:* Shot 6a.

8.66 *The Maltese Falcon:* Shot 6b.

8.67   *The Maltese Falcon:* Shot 7.

8.68   *The Maltese Falcon:* Shot 8.

8.69   *The Maltese Falcon:* Shot 9.

8.70   *The Maltese Falcon:* Shot 10.

8.71   *The Maltese Falcon:* Shot 11.

8.72   *The Maltese Falcon:* Shot 12.

8.73   *The Maltese Falcon:* Shot 13.

8.74   *The Maltese Falcon:* Shot 14.

8.75   *The Maltese Falcon:* Shot 15.

Furthermore, the shot/reverse-shot pattern emphasizes the development of Brigid's story and Spade's reaction to it. As she gets into details, the cutting moves from over-the-shoulder shots (8.67, 8.68) to framings that isolate Brigid (8.69 and 8.71) and eventually one that isolates Spade (8.72). These shots come at the point when Brigid, in an artificially shy manner, tells her story, and the medium close-ups arouse our curiosity about whether she is telling the truth. The shot of Spade's reaction (8.72) suggests that he is skeptical. In short, the analytical editing cooperates with framing and figure behavior to focus our attention on Brigid's tale, to let us study her demeanor, and to get a hint as to Spade's response.

When Archer enters, the breakdown of the space stops for a moment, and Huston reestablishes the locale. Archer is integrated into the action by means of a rightward pan shot (shots 16a and 16b, **8.76** and **8.77**). His path is consistent with the scene's first axis of action, that running between Spade and the doorway. More-

8.76 *The Maltese Falcon:* Shot 16a.

8.77 *The Maltese Falcon:* Shot 16b.

8.78 *The Maltese Falcon:* Shot 17.

over, the framing on him is similar to that used for Brigid's entrance earlier. [Compare shot 16b with 6a (8.77 and 8.65).] Such repetitions allow the viewer to concentrate on the new information, not the manner in which it is presented.

Now firmly established as part of the scene, Archer hitches himself up onto Spade's desk. His position puts him at Spade's end of the axis of action (shot 17, **8.78**). The rest of the scene's editing analyzes this new set of relationships without ever crossing the 180° line.

The viewer is not supposed to notice all this. Throughout, the shots present space to emphasize the cause–effect flow—the characters' actions, entrances, dialogue, reactions. The editing has economically organized space to convey narrative continuity.

The continuity system, in exactly these terms, remains in force today. Most narrative films still draw on 180° principles **(8.79, 8.80).**

8.79 In Ron Howard's *Parenthood,* eyeline matched shot/reverse shots present a conversation . . .

Continuity Editing: Some Fine Points

The continuity system can be refined in various ways. If a director arranges several characters in a circular pattern, say, sitting around a dinner table, then the axis of action will probably run between the characters of greatest importance at the moment. In **8.81** and **8.82,** from Howard Hawks's *Bringing Up Baby,* the important interaction is occurring between the two men, so we can cut from one side of the woman in the foreground to the other side in order to get consistent shot/reverse shots. When one man leaves the table, however, a semicircular arrangement of figures in space is created, so that a new axis of action can be established between the two women. Now we can get shot/reverse-shot exchanges running down the length of the table **(8.83, 8.84).**

Both the *Maltese Falcon* and the *Bringing Up Baby* examples show that in the course of a scene the 180° line may shift as the characters move around the setting. In some cases, the filmmaker may create a new axis of action that allows the camera to take up a position that would have been across the line in an earlier phase of the scene.

A simple example occurs in Georges Franju's *Eyes without a Face.* The daughter, who wears a mask to hide her disfigured face, is talking with her father's housekeeper. The housekeeper is shown in an over-the-shoulder medium shot, with the axis of action running from the right foreground to the left middle ground **(8.85).** If Franju wanted us to see the daughter's reaction, the continuity rules would oblige him to take a shot over the housekeeper's right shoulder, showing the daughter facing leftward. Instead, the housekeeper moves rightward into depth, the camera panning to keep her in the frame **(8.86).** From the right rear she turns to look leftward

8.80 . . . with the women in the foreground establishing the axis of action.

8.81 *Bringing Up Baby:* Shot/reverse
shot between the man on the right . . .

8.82 . . . and the left gives way to . . .

8.83 . . . shot/reverse shot between the
woman on the left . . .

8.84 . . . and the one on the right.

at the daughter **(8.87)**. This creates an axis of action running from the foreground
left to the background right. Now Franju gives us a three-quarter reverse shot of
the young woman looking rightward **(8.88)**. Had Franju cut from the first camera
position (8.85) to this position, he would have violated the original axis of action.
(This would essentially present us with shot X in 8.56.) The housekeeper's move to
the right created a new axis that made this angle and eyeline permissible.

Alternatively, even if the actors remain in place, the filmmaker can create a
new axis by tracking the camera across the line. Going back to our bird's-eye view
in 8.56, suppose that shot 2, showing the boy, continued while the camera circled
the couple clockwise and ended up in the shaded area, still facing him but now angled over the girl's left shoulder. Then a new 180° line would be set up, showing
the boy looking screen right. And now shot X, showing the girl looking left, would
be in correct continuity. The camera movement would have established a new axis
of action.

The power of the axis of action and the eyelines it can create is so great that
the filmmaker may be able to eliminate an establishing shot, thus relying on the
Kuleshov effect. In Spike Lee's *She's Gotta Have It,* Nola Darling holds a Thanksgiving dinner for her three male friends. Lee never presents a shot showing all four
in the same frame. Instead he uses medium long shots including all the men (for
example, **8.89**), over-the-shoulder shot/reverse shots among them (for example,
8.90), and eyeline-matched medium close-ups of them. Nola is given her own
medium close-ups **(Fig. 8.91)**.

Through eyelines and body orientations, the editing keeps the spatial relations
completely consistent. For example, each man looks in a different direction when

8.85 *Eyes without a Face:* The older woman on the left of the shot moves . . .

8.86 . . . past the young woman in the foreground . . .

8.87 . . . ending up on her right . . .

8.88 . . . so that the young woman looks at her offscreen right.

addressing Nola **(8.92, 8.93).** This cutting pattern enhances the dramatic action by making all the men equal competitors for her. They are clustered at one end of the table, and none is shown in the same frame with her. In addition, by organizing the angles around her overall orientation to the action (as in **8.94**), Lee reinforces Nola as the pivotal character. Further, the longer shot and her separate medium close-ups intensify the progression of the scene: The men are on display, and Nola is coolly judging each one's behavior.

Another felicity in the 180° system is the **cheat cut.** Sometimes a director may not have perfect continuity from shot to shot because he or she has composed each shot for specific reasons. Must the two shots match perfectly? Again, narrative motivation decides the matter. Given that the 180° system emphasizes narrative causality, the director has some freedom to "cheat" mise-en-scene from shot to shot—that is, to mismatch slightly the positions of characters or objects.

Consider two shots from William Wyler's *Jezebel.* Neither character moves during either shot, but Wyler has blatantly cheated the position of Julie **(8.95, 8.96).** Yet most viewers would not notice the discrepancy since it is the dialogue that is of paramount importance in the scene; here again, the similarities between shots outweigh the differences of position. Moreover, a change from a straight-on angle to a slightly high angle helps hide the cheat. There is, in fact, a cheat in the *Maltese Falcon* scene, too, between shots 6b and 7. In 6b (8.66), as Spade leans forward,

8.89 *She's Gotta Have It.*

8.90 *She's Gotta Have It.*

8.91 *She's Gotta Have It.*

8.92 *She's Gotta Have It.*

8.93 *She's Gotta Have It.*

8.94 *She's Gotta Have It.*

8.95 In this shot from *Jezebel,* the top of Julie's head is even with the man's chin . . .

8.96 . . . but in the second shot she seems to have grown several inches.

the back of his chair is not near him. Yet in shot 7 (8.67), it has been cheated to be just behind his left arm. Here again, the primacy of the narrative flow overrides such a cheat cut.

One more fine point in spatial continuity is particularly relevant to a film's narration. We have already seen that a camera framing can strongly suggest a character's optical point of view, as in our earlier example from *Fury* (7.118, 7.119). That example depends on a cut from the person looking (7.118) to what he sees (7.119). We have also seen an instance of POV cutting in the *Birds* sequence discussed on pp. 295–296. Now we are in a position to see how optical POV is consistent with continuity editing, creating a variety of eyeline-match editing known as *point-of-view cutting.*

Consider Alfred Hitchcock's *Rear Window,* which is built around the situation of the solitary photographer Jeff watching events taking place in an apartment across the courtyard. Hitchcock uses a standard eyeline-match pattern, cutting from a shot of Jeff looking (**8.97**) to a shot of what he sees (**8.98**). Since there is no establishing shot that shows both Jeff and the opposite apartment, the Kuleshov effect operates here: Our mind connects the two images. More specifically, the second shot represents Jeff's optical viewpoint, and this is filmed from a position on his end of the axis of action (**8.99**). We are strongly restricted to what Jeff sees and what (he thinks) he knows.

As *Rear Window* goes on, the subjectivity of the POV shots intensifies. Becoming more eager to examine the details of his neighbor's life, Jeff begins to use binoculars and a photographic telephoto lens to magnify his view. By using shots taken with lenses of different focal lengths, Hitchcock can show how each new tool enlarges what Jeff can see (**8.100–8.103**). Hitchcock's cutting adheres to spatial continuity rules and exploits their POV possibilities in order to arouse curiosity and suspense.

8.97   In *Rear Window,* Jeff looks out his window and . . .

8.98   . . . the next shot shows what he sees from his optical POV.

More Refinements: Crossing the Axis of Action

Most continuity-based filmmakers prefer not to cut across the axis of action. They would rather move the actors around the setting and create a new axis, as in our example from *Eyes without a Face* (8.85–8.88). Still, can you ever legitimately cut across an established axis of action? Yes, sometimes. A scene occurring in a doorway, on a staircase, or in other symmetrical settings may occasionally break the line. Another way to get across the center line is to cut away to a character who is offscreen. By then moving that character up to the main action, perhaps following the character with a camera movement, the filmmakers can establish a different axis of action.

Sometimes too the filmmakers can get across the axis by taking one shot *on the line itself* and using it as a transition. This strategy is rare in dialogue sequences, but

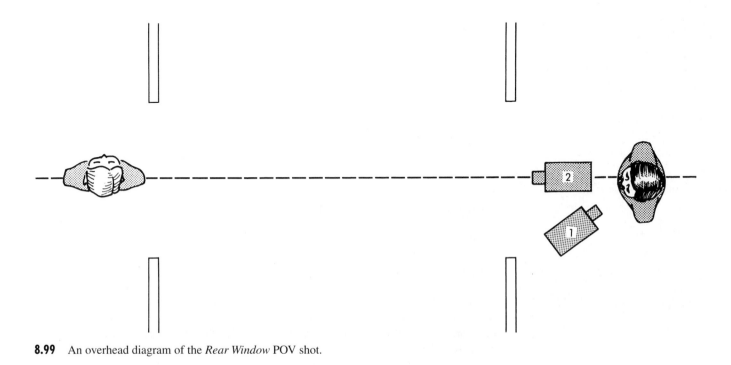

8.99   An overhead diagram of the *Rear Window* POV shot.

8.100   When Jeff looks through his binoculars . . .

8.101   . . . we see a telephoto POV shot of his neighbor.

8.102   When he employs a powerful photographic lens . . .

8.103   . . . the resulting POV shot enlarges his neighbor's activities even more.

"I saw David Lynch and asked him: 'What's this about crossing the axis?' And he burst out laughing and said, 'That always gets me.' And I asked if you could do it, and he gave me this startled look and said, 'Stephen, you can do anything. You're a director.' Then he paused and said, 'But it doesn't cut together.'"

— Stephen King, novelist, on directing his first film, *Maximum Overdrive*

it can be seen in chases and outdoor action. By filming on the axis, the filmmaker presents the action as moving directly toward the camera (a *head-on* shot) or away from it (a *tail-on* shot). The climactic chase of *The Road Warrior* offers several examples. As marauding road gangs try to board a fleeing gasoline truck, George Miller uses many head-on and tail-on shots of the vehicles (**8.104** to **8.108**).

Also, we should note that continuity-based films occasionally violate screen direction without confusing the viewer. This usually occurs when the scene's action is very well defined. For example, during a chase in John Ford's *Stagecoach,* there is no ambiguity about the Ringo Kid's leaping from the coach to the horses (**8.109, 8.110**). We would not be likely to assume that the coach had turned around suddenly, as in the possible misinterpretation of the shootout scene with the two cowboys (8.57).

Crosscutting

Continuity editing illustrates how editing can endow the film's narration with a great range of knowledge. A cut can take us to any point on the correct side of the axis of action. Editing can even create omniscience, that godlike knowledge that some films seek to present. The outstanding technical device here is *crosscutting,* first extensively explored by D. W. Griffith in his last-minute rescue scenes. In *The Battle at Elderbush Gulch,* a cavalry troop is riding to rescue some settlers trapped in a cabin and battling the Indians outside (**8.111–8.114**). After 11 additional shots of the cavalry, various parts of the cabin interior, and the Indians outdoors, a 12th shot shows the cavalry riding in from the distance behind the cabin.

8.104   Near the climax of the chase in *The Road Warrior,* Max is driving left to right along the road . . .

8.105   . . . and soon he is still driving toward the right. An attacking thug perched on the front of the truck turns and looks off right in horror . . .

8.106   . . . realizing that another vehicle, moving right to left, is coming toward them on a collision course.

8.107   Several quick shots facing head-on to the vehicles show the crash . . .

8.108   . . . and a long shot shows the truck again, now moving right to left.

Crosscutting gives us an unrestricted knowledge of causal, temporal, or spatial information by alternating shots from one line of action in one place with shots of other events in other places. Crosscutting thus creates some spatial discontinuity, but it binds the action together by creating a sense of cause and effect and temporal simultaneity. In *Jerry Maguire,* for example, crosscutting interweaves the action of sports agent Jerry and his rival racing to sign up the same clients **(8.115–8.118).**

Fritz Lang's *M* goes further, intercutting three lines of action. While the police seek the child murderer, gangsters prowl the streets looking for him as well, and we also occasionally see the murderer himself. Crosscutting ties together the different lines of action, bringing out a temporal simultaneity and the causal process of the pursuit. The crosscutting also gives us a range of knowledge greater than that of any one character. We know that the gangsters are after the murderer, but the police and the murderer do not. Crosscutting also builds up suspense, as we form expectations that are only gradually clarified and fulfilled. It may also create parallels, and Lang exploits this possibility by suggesting analogies between the police and the crooks. Whatever other functions it may have, though, crosscutting remains primarily a means of presenting narrative actions that are occurring in several locales at roughly the same time.

8.109 *Stagecoach:* In a long shot where all movement is toward the right, the hero begins leaping from the driver's seat down onto the horse team . . .

8.110   . . . and in the next shot both he and the coach are moving leftward.

8.111   In *The Battle of Elderbush Gulch,* Griffith cuts from a shot of the cavalry . . .

8.112   . . . to a view inside the besieged cabin . . .

8.113   . . . back to the cavalry . . .

8.114   . . . and returning to the cabin.

All the devices of spatial continuity show how film technique draws the spectator into an active process. We assume that setting, character movement, and character position will be consistent and coherent. Our prior knowledge of filmic conventions lets us form strong expectations about what shot will follow the one we are seeing. We also make inferences on the basis of cues, so that when Brigid and Spade look off left we infer that someone is entering the room and we expect to see a shot of that person.

8.115 *Jerry Maguire:* From a shot of Jerry looking anxious . . .

8.116 . . . there is a cut to his confident-looking rival . . .

8.117 . . . and then back to Jerry placing a phone call . . .

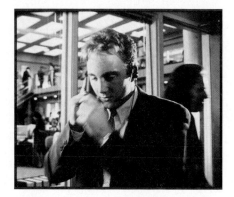

8.118 . . . and his rival doing the same.

What makes the continuity system invisible is its ability to draw on a range of skills that we have learned so well that they seem automatic. This makes spatial continuity editing a powerful tool for the filmmaker who wishes to reinforce habitual expectations. In recent decades, Hollywood filmmakers have developed ways to make traditional continuity techniques more forceful. (See Box.) Because continuity editing has been so widely used for so long, it also becomes a central target for the filmmaker who wants to use film style to challenge or change our normal viewing activities.

Temporal Continuity: Order, Frequency, Duration

In the classical continuity system, time, like space, is organized according to the development of the narrative. We know that the plot's presentation of the story typically involves manipulation of time. Continuity editing seeks to support and sustain this temporal manipulation.

To get specific, recall our distinction among temporal order, frequency, and duration. Continuity editing typically presents the story events in a 1-2-3 order (for example, Spade rolls a cigarette, then Effie comes in, then he answers her, and so on). The most common violation of this order is a flashback, signaled by a cut or dissolve.

Intensified Continuity: *L.A. Confidential* and Contemporary Editing

By the 1930s, the continuity system was the standard approach to editing in most of the world's commercial filmmaking. But it underwent changes over the years. Today's editing practices abide by the principles of continuity but amplify them in certain ways.

Most obviously, mainstream films are now cut much faster than in the period between 1930 and 1960. Then, a film typically consisted of 300–500 shots, but in the years after 1960, the cutting pace picked up. Today an average film might have over 1200 shots, and action films routinely contain 2000, 3000, or more. (*Armageddon* contains over 3700.) Partly because of the faster editing, scenes are built out of relatively close views of individual characters, rather than long-shot framings. Establishing shots tend to be less common, sometimes appearing only at the end of a scene. Telephoto lenses, which enlarge faces, help achieve tight framings, and modern widescreen formats allow two or more facial close-ups to occupy the screen. Also, the camera tends to move very frequently, picking out one detail after another.

The accompanying shots from *L.A. Confidential* show several of these tendencies at work. After arresting three black suspects, Lieutenant Ed Exley prepares to wring a confession from them. The scene takes less than a minute but employs nine shots, two with significant camera movement. (The film contains nearly 2000 shots, an average of four seconds apiece.) Director Curtis Hanson shifts the emphasis among several key characters by coordinating his editing with anamorphic widescreen, staging in depth, close-ups and medium-close-ups, rack-focus, and mobile framing **(8.119–8.130)**. Interestingly, the actors make no expressive use of their hands or bodies; the performances are almost completely facial.

Why did this intensified form of continuity become so common? Some historians trace it to the influence of television. Movies were broadcast by TV networks in the 1960s, transmitted by cable and satellite in the 1970s, and available on home video in the 1980s and 1990s. As people saw movies on home screens rather than in theaters, filmmakers reshaped their techniques.

8.119 *Shot 1:* The scene begins by presenting only a portion of the space. A reflection shows Exley waiting and his colleagues milling about outside the interrogation room. This image singles out the core dramatic action to come—Exley's brutal confrontation with the suspects.

Constantly changing the image by cutting and camera movement could keep the viewer from switching channels or picking up a magazine. On smaller screens, faster cutting is easier to follow, and closer views look better than long shots, which tend to lose detail. Intensified continuity was shaped by many factors, such as the arrival of computer-based editing, but television was a major influence.

8.120 *Shot 2:* A match on Exley's action of turning gives us a fuller view of the policemen and establishes two other main characters: Jack Vincennes on the left, Bud White in the background, watching. This is only a partial establishing shot; a later camera movement will acquaint us with the layout of the interrogation rooms.

8.121 *Shot 3:* Hanson underscores White's presence by cutting to a telephoto shot of him saying that the suspects killed his partner.

8.122 *Shot 4:* In an echo of the opening framing, Exley now stands at the second interrogation room, with another reflection. The shot also reiterates Vincennes's presence, which will provide an important reaction later.

8.123 The camera tracks with Exley moving right to study the suspect in the third room. White's reflection can be seen in frame center. The camera movement has linked the three main detectives on the case while also establishing the three rooms as being side by side. At the end of the camera movement, Exley turns, and . . .

8.124 *Shot 5:* . . . a two-shot establishes his superior, Dudley, on the scene. As Dudley explains that the suspects' shotguns put them at the murder scene, the camera racks focus to him, putting Exley out of focus.

8.125 *Shot 6:* A cutaway to White listening—again, a tight facial shot taken with a telephoto lens—reminds us of his presence. He is only an observer in this phase of the scene, but as the questioning heats up, he will burst in to attack a suspect.

8.126 *Shot 7:* Returning to the two-shot shows Dudley demanding that Exley make the men confess.

8.127 *Shot 8:* A reverse-angle on Exley, the first shot in the scene devoted to his face alone, underscores his determination: "Oh, I'll break them, sir."

8.128 *Shot 9:* A cut back to the two-shot supplies Dudley's reaction.

8.129 Exley turns away. The lens shifts focus to catch his grim face in the foreground, preparing us for the brutality he will display.

8.130 Exley walks out of the shot. The camera tilts down slightly and racks focus to display Vincennes's skeptical expression. The telephoto lens, accentuated by the rack-focus, has supplied close views of Dudley, then Exley, and then Vincennes in a single shot.

Furthermore, classical editing also often presents only *once* what happens *once* in the story; in continuity style, it would be a gross mistake for Huston to repeat the shot of, say, Brigid sitting down (8.66). Again, though, flashbacks are the most common way of motivating the repetition of a scene already witnessed. So chronological sequence and one-for-one frequency are the standard methods of handling order and frequency within the continuity style of editing. There are occasional exceptions, as we saw in our examples from *The Godfather, Do The Right Thing* and *Police Story* (pp. 306, 309–310).

What of duration? In the classical continuity system, story duration is seldom expanded; that is, screen time is seldom made greater than story time. Usually, duration is in complete continuity (plot time equaling story time) or is elided (story time being greater than plot time). Let us first consider complete continuity, the most common possibility. Here a scene occupying five minutes in the story also occupies five minutes when projected on the screen.

"Now nobody trusts the actor's performance. If an actor has a scene where they are sitting in the distance, everybody says, 'What are you shooting? It has to be close-up!' This is ridiculous. You have the position of the hand, the whole body—this is the feeling of a movie. I hate movies where everybody has big close-ups all the time. . . . This is television. I have talking heads on my television set in my home all the time."

— Miroslav Ondříček, Editor

The first scene of *The Maltese Falcon* displays three cues for *temporal continuity*. First, the narrative progression of the scene has no gaps. Every movement by the characters and every line of dialogue is presented. Second, there is the sound track. Sound issuing from the story space (what we call *diegetic* sound) is a standard indicator of temporal continuity, especially when, as in this scene, the sound bleeds over each cut. Third, there is the match on action between shots 5 and 6. So powerful is the match on action that it creates both spatial *and* temporal continuity. The reason is obvious: If an action carries across the cut, the space and time are assumed to be continuous from shot to shot. In all, an absence of ellipses in the story action, diegetic sound overlapping the cuts, and matching on action are three primary indicators that the duration of the scene is continuous.

Sometimes, however, a second possibility will be explored: *temporal ellipsis.* The ellipsis may, of course, omit seconds, minutes, hours, days, years, or centuries. Some ellipses are of no importance to the narrative development and so are concealed. To take a common example: A classical narrative film typically does not show the entire time it takes a character to dress, wash, and breakfast in the morning. Shots of the character going into the shower, putting on shoes, or frying an egg might be edited so as to eliminate the unwanted bits of time, with the plot presenting in seconds a process that might have taken an hour in the story. As we saw on p. 308, optical punctuations, empty frames, and cutaways are frequently used to cover short temporal ellipses.

But other ellipses are important to the narrative. The viewer must recognize that time has passed. For this task the continuity style has built up a varied repertoire of devices. Often, dissolves, fades, or wipes are used to indicate an ellipsis between shots. Thus from the last shot of one scene we dissolve, fade, or wipe to the first shot of the next scene. (The Hollywood rule is that a dissolve indicates a brief time lapse and a fade indicates a much longer one.) In some cases contemporary filmmakers use a cut for such transitions. For example, in *2001* Kubrick cuts directly from a bone spinning in the air to a space station orbiting the earth, one of the boldest graphic matches in narrative cinema. The cut eliminates millions of years of story time.

In other cases it is necessary to show a large-scale process or a lengthy period—a city waking up in the morning, a war, a child growing up, the rise of a singing star. Here classical continuity uses another device for temporal ellipsis: the **montage sequence.** (This should not be confused with the concept of *montage* in Sergei Eisenstein's film theory.) Brief portions of a process, informative titles (for example, "1865" or "San Francisco"), stereotyped images (such as the Eiffel Tower), newsreel footage, newspaper headlines, and the like, can be swiftly joined by dissolves and music to compress a lengthy series of actions into a few moments.

We are all familiar with the most clichéd montage ellipses—calendar leaves fluttering away, newspaper presses churning out an Extra, clocks ticking portentously—but in the hands of deft editors such sequences become small virtuoso pieces in themselves. Slavko Vorkapich's montages of American life in *Mr. Smith Goes to Washington,* Jack Killifer's tracing of a society across two decades in *The Roaring Twenties,* and Edward Curtis's brutal depictions of a gangster's rise in *Scarface* illustrate the powers of the device. The montage sequence is still used in Hollywood films, though it tends to be more restrained stylistically than in the 1930s and 1940s. *Jaws,* for example, simply uses a series of unmatched shots of vacationers arriving at the beach to indicate a time shift to the beginning of the tourist season. Music is still used as an accompaniment, however, as when a song accompanies a series of magazine covers in a scene from *Tootsie* that traces the hero's rise to success as a soap-opera star. A montage sequence in *The Silence of the Lambs* presents brief shots of Clarice Starling training at the FBI academy and researching Hannibal Lecter's past.

In sum, the continuity style uses the temporal dimension of editing primarily for narrative purposes. Through prior knowledge, the spectator expects the editing to present story events in chronological order, with only occasional rearrangement through flashbacks. The viewer expects that editing will respect the frequency of story events. And the viewer assumes that actions irrelevant to story causality will be omitted or at least abridged by judicious ellipses.

At least, this is how the classical Hollywood continuity system has treated storytelling. Like graphics, rhythm, and space, time is organized to permit the unfolding of cause and effect, the arousal of curiosity, suspense, and surprise. But there are many alternatives to the continuity style of editing, and these are worth a look.

ALTERNATIVES TO CONTINUITY EDITING

Graphic and Rhythmic Possibilities

Powerful and pervasive as it is, the continuity style remains only *one* style, and many filmmakers have explored other editing possibilities.

Films using abstract or associational form have frequently granted the graphic and rhythmic dimensions of editing great weight. Instead of joining shot 1 to shot 2 primarily on the basis of the spatial and temporal functions that the shot fulfills in presenting a story, you could join them on the basis of purely graphic or rhythmic qualities—independent of the time and space they represent. In films such as *Anticipation of the Night, Scenes from under Childhood,* and *Western History,* experimentalist Stan Brakhage uses purely graphic means of joining shot to shot: Continuities and discontinuities of light, texture, and shape motivate the editing. Similarly, parts of Bruce Conner's *Cosmic Ray, A Movie,* and *Report* cut together newsreel footage, old film clips, leader, and black frames on the basis of graphic patterns of movement, direction, and speed.

Many non-narrative films have completely subordinated the space and time presented in each shot to the rhythmic relations among shots. *Single-frame films* (in which each shot is only one frame long) are the most extreme examples of this overriding rhythmic concern. Two famous examples are Robert Breer's *Fist Fight* (5.31) and Peter Kubelka's *Schwechater.*

The preeminence of graphic and rhythmic editing in non-narrative cinema is not, however, as recent a phenomenon as these examples might suggest. As early as 1913, some painters were contemplating the pure-design possibilities offered by film, and many works of the European avant-grade movements of the 1920s combined an interest in abstract graphics with a desire to explore rhythmic editing. Perhaps the most famous of these is the Fernand Léger–Dudley Murphy film *Ballet mécanique* (see Chapter 5, pp. 150–155). In Chapter 10 we shall see how *Ballet mécanique* juxtaposes its shots on the basis of graphic and rhythmic qualities.

Important as the graphic and rhythmic possibilities of editing have been to the non-narrative cinema, their powers have not been wholly neglected in the story film. Although the continuity style seeks an overall graphic continuity, this is usually subordinated to a concern with mapping narrative space and tracing narrative time. Some narrative filmmakers, however, occasionally subordinate narrative concerns to graphic pattern. The most famous examples are probably the films for which Busby Berkeley choreographed elaborate dance numbers. In *42nd Street,*

8.131   In *An Autumn Afternoon,* Ozu cuts from one man drinking sake directly . . .

8.132   . . . to another caught in almost exactly the same position, costume, and gesture.

8.133   Later he cuts from one man to another, maintaining very similar compositions. Even their beer bottles . . .

8.134   . . . sit precisely in the same position on frame left, their labels graphically matched as well.

Gold Diggers of 1933, Footlight Parade, Gold Diggers of 1935, and *Dames,* the narrative periodically grinds to a halt and the film presents intricate dances that are arranged, shot, and edited with a concern for the pure configuration of dancers and background (6.143, from *42nd Street*).

More complexly related to the narrative is the graphic editing of Yasujiro Ozu. Ozu's cutting is often dictated by a much more precise graphic continuity than we find in the classical continuity style. In two scenes from *An Autumn Afternoon,* Ozu creates graphic matches on men sitting opposite each other in restaurants **(8.131–8.134).** In *Ohayu* Ozu uses color for the same purpose, cutting from laundry on a line to a domestic interior and matching on a red shape in the upper left of each shot (a shirt, a lamp; **8.135, 8.136**).

Some narrative films have momentarily subordinated spatial and temporal editing factors to rhythmic ones. In the 1920s both the French Impressionist school and the Soviet avant-garde frequently made story progression secondary to purely rhythmic editing. In such films as Abel Gance's *La Roue,* Jean Epstein's *Coeur fidèle* and *La Glace à trois faces,* and Ivan Mosjoukin's *Kean,* accelerated editing renders the tempo of an onrushing train, a whirling carousel, a racing automobile, and a drunken dance. In Epstein's *Fall of the House of Usher* a poetic sequence of Usher strumming a guitar and singing organizes the length of the shots in accord with a songlike pattern of verse and refrain. Kuleshov's *The Death Ray* and, as we shall see, Eisenstein's *October* occasionally make rhythm dominate narrative space and time. More recently, we can find strong passages of rhythmic editing in the Busby Berkeley musicals, Rouben Mamoulian's *Love Me Tonight,* René Clair's *Le Million,* and several films of Ozu and Hitchcock, as well as in *Assault on Precinct 13* and *The Terminator.* Pulsating rhythmic editing is prominent in films influenced by music videos, such as *The Crow* and *Romeo + Juliet.* As we saw with graphics, rhythmic editing may override the spatial and temporal dimensions; when this happens, narrative becomes proportionately less important.

Spatial and Temporal Discontinuity

Non-narrative films may sometimes avoid using the continuity style, but what about *narrative* alternatives? How can one tell a story without adhering to the continuity rules? Let us sample some ways particular filmmakers have created distinct editing styles by use of what might be considered spatial and temporal discontinuities.

One option is to use spatial continuity in ambiguous ways. In *Mon Oncle d'Amérique*, Resnais intercuts the stories of his three main characters with shots of each character's favorite star, taken from French films of the 1940s. At one point, as René's pesky office mate calls to him, we get the coworker in one shot (**8.137**). But Resnais cuts to a shot of Jean Gabin in an older film, turning to him in reverse shot (**8.138**). Only then does Resnais supply a shot of René turning to meet his questioner (**8.139**). The film does not definitely present the Gabin shot as a fantasy image; we cannot tell whether René imagines himself as his star confronting his coworker, or whether the film's narration draws the comparison independent of René's state of mind. The cut relies on the cues of shot/reverse-shot but uses them to create a momentarily jarring discontinuity that triggers narrational ambiguity.

More drastically, a filmmaker could violate or ignore the 180° system. The editing choices of filmmakers Jacques Tati and Yasujiro Ozu are based on what we might call 360° space. Instead of an axis of action that dictates that the camera be placed within an imaginary semicircle, these filmmakers work as if the action were not a line but a point at the center of a circle and as if the camera could be placed at any point on the circumference. In *Mr. Hulot's Holiday, Play Time,* and *Traffic,* Tati systematically films from almost every side; edited together, the shots present multiple spatial perspectives on a single event. Similarly, Ozu's scenes construct a 360° space that produces what the continuity style would consider grave editing errors. Ozu's films often do not yield consistent relative positions and screen directions; the eyeline matches are out of joint and the only consistency is the *violation* of the 180° line. One of the gravest sins in the classical continuity style is to match on action while breaking the line, yet Ozu does this comfortably in *Early Summer* (**8.140, 8.141**). (See Chapter 11 for a discussion of space and time in Ozu's *Tokyo Story.*)

Such spatially discontinuous cutting affects the spectator's experience as well. The defender of classical editing would claim that spatial continuity rules are necessary for the clear presentation of a narrative. But anyone who has seen a film by Ozu or Tati can testify that no narrative confusion arises from their continuity violations. Though the spaces do not flow as smoothly as in the Hollywood style (this is indeed part of the films' fascination), the cause–effect chains remain intelligible. The inescapable conclusion is that the continuity system is only one way to tell a story. Historically, this system has been the dominant one, but aesthetically it has no priority over other styles.

There are two other notable devices of discontinuity. In *Breathless* Jean-Luc Godard violates conventions of spatial, temporal, and graphic continuity by his systematic use of the **jump cut.** Though this term is often loosely used, its primary meaning is this: When two shots of the same subject are cut together but are not sufficiently different in camera distance and angle, there will be a noticeable jump

8.135 In *Ohayu,* Ozu creates a playful graphic match by cutting from an outdoor scene with a bright red sweater in the upper left . . .

8.136 . . . to an interior with a vivid red lampshade in the same position.

8.137 *Mon Oncle d'Amérique.*

8.138 *Mon Oncle d'Amérique.*

8.139 *Mon Oncle d'Amérique.*

8.140   In *Early Summer,* Ozu cuts on the grandfather's gesture of drinking . . .

8.141   . . . directly to the opposite side of the characters.

on the screen. Classical continuity avoids such jumps by generous use of shot/reverse shots and by the *30° rule* (advising that every camera position be varied by at least 30° from the previous one). But an examination of shots from *Breathless* suggests the consequences of Godard's jump cuts **(8.142, 8.143).** Far from flowing unnoticeably, such cuts are very visible, and they disorient the spectator.

A second violation of continuity is created by the **nondiegetic insert.** Here the filmmaker cuts from the scene to a metaphorical or symbolic shot that is not part of the space and time of the narrative. Clichés abound here **(8.144, 8.145).** More complex examples occur in the films of Eisenstein and Godard. In Eisenstein's *Strike* the massacre of workers is intercut with the slaughter of a bull. In Godard's *La Chinoise,* Henri tells an anecdote about the ancient Egyptians who, he claims, thought that "their language was the language of the gods." As he says this **(8.146),** Godard cuts in two close-ups of relics from the tomb of King Tutankhamen **(8.147, 8.148).** As nondiegetic inserts, coming from outside the story world, these shots construct a running, often ironic, commentary on the action, and they prompt the spectator to search for implicit meanings. (Do the relics corroborate or challenge what Henri says?)

Though both the jump cut and the nondiegetic insert can be used in a narrative context (as in the *Fury* example), they tend to weaken narrative continuity. The jump cut interrupts the story with abrupt gaps, while the nondiegetic insert sus-

8.142   *Breathless:* In the jump cut from this shot of Patricia . . .

8.143   . . . to this one, the background has changed and some story time has gone by.

8.144   In *Fury,* Lang cuts from housewives gossiping . . .

8.145   . . . to shots of clucking hens.

8.146 A diegetic shot in *La Chinoise* is followed by . . .

8.147 . . . nondiegetic shots of the lion bed of King Tutankhamen . . .

8.148 . . . and his golden mask.

pends story action altogether. It is no accident that both devices have been prominently used by the contemporary filmmaker most associated with the challenge to classical narrative, Jean-Luc Godard. In Chapter 11 we shall examine the nature of this challenge by analyzing *Breathless*.

There are still other alternatives to classical continuity, especially in the temporal dimension. Although the classical approach to order and frequency of story events may seem the best option, it is only the most familiar. Story events do not have to be edited in 1-2-3 order. In Resnais's *La Guerre est finie*, scenes cut in conventional continuity are interrupted by images that may represent flashbacks, or fantasy episodes, or even future events. Editing can also play with variable frequency for narrative purposes; the same event can be shown repeatedly. In *La Guerre est finie*, the same funeral is depicted in different hypothetical ways (the protagonist is present, or he is not).

Again, Godard offers a striking example of how editing can manipulate both order and frequency. In *Pierrot le fou*, as Marianne and Ferdinand leave her apartment fleeing gangsters, Godard scrambles the order of the shots (**8.149–8.152**). Godard also plays with frequency by repeating one gesture—Ferdinand jumping into the car—but showing it *differently* each time. Such manipulation of editing blocks our normal expectations about story and forces us to concentrate on the very process of piecing together the film's narrative action.

8.149 *Pierrot le fou:* Initially Ferdinand jumps into the car as Marianne pulls away . . .

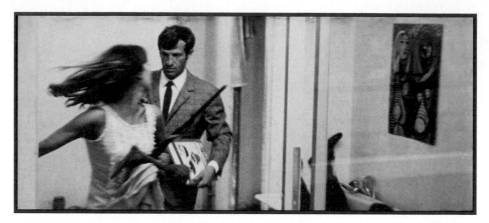

8.150   . . . but then the couple are seen back in their apartment.

8.151   Next the car races down a street . . .

8.152   . . . and then Marianne and Ferdinand climb onto a rooftop.

The editing may also take liberties with story duration. Although complete continuity and ellipsis are the most common ways of rendering duration, expansion—stretching a moment out, making screen time greater than story time—remains a distinct possibility. Truffaut uses such expansions in *Jules and Jim* to underscore narrative turning points (Catherine lifting her veil or jumping off a bridge). In Chabrol's *La Femme infidèle,* when the outraged husband strikes his wife's lover with a statuette, Chabrol overlaps shots of the victim falling to the floor.

Filmmakers have found creative ways to rework the most basic tenets of the continuity system. We have indicated, for example, that a match on action strongly suggests that time continues across the cut. Yet Alain Resnais creates an impossible continuous action in *Last Year at Marienbad.* Small groups of guests are standing around the hotel lobby; one medium shot frames a blonde woman beginning to turn away from the camera **(8.153).** In the middle of her turn, there is a cut to her, still turning but in a different setting **(8.154).** The smooth match on action, along with the woman's graphically matched position in the frame, imply that she is moving continuously, yet the change of setting contradicts this impression. In Chapter 5, we saw how Deren's *Choreography for Camera* cuts together two shots of a dancer's leap; as in *Marienbad,* we have a match on action—yet in two different locales (5.29, 5.30).

Our examples indicate that certain discontinuities of temporal order, duration, and frequency can become perfectly intelligible in a narrative context. On the other hand, with the jump cut, the nondiegetic insert, and the inconsistent match on action, such temporal dislocations can also push away from traditional notions of story altogether and create ambiguous relations among shots.

As an example of the power of spatial and temporal discontinuities in editing, we shall look at a single example: Sergei Eisenstein's *October.*

Functions of Discontinuity Editing: *October*

For many Soviet filmmakers of the 1920s, editing was a major means of organizing the entire form of the film; it did not simply serve the narrative progression, as in the continuity system. Eisenstein's early films—*Strike, Potemkin, October,* and *Old and New*—all constitute attempts to build a film on the basis of certain editing devices. Rather than subordinate his editing patterns to the mapping out of a story, Eisenstein conceives of these films as editing constructions.

8.153   *Last Year at Marienbad:* A match on action . . .

8.154   . . . across two settings.

Eisenstein deliberately opposed himself to continuity editing, seeking out and exploiting what Hollywood would consider discontinuities. He staged, shot, and cut his films for the maximum *collision* from shot to shot, sequence to sequence, since he believed that only through being forced to synthesize such conflicts could the viewer participate in actively understanding the film.

To this end, Eisenstein wrote his film by a juxtaposition of shots. No longer bound by conventional dramaturgy, Eisenstein's films roam freely through time and space to construct an intricate pattern of images calculated to stimulate the viewer's senses, emotions, and thinking. He dreamed of filming Marx's *Capital,* of writing an essay by means of film editing. Needless to say, the intricacy of Eisenstein's editing cannot be wholly conveyed here; a single sequence of an Eisenstein film could take up a chapter. Let us, however, briefly indicate how Eisenstein uses editing discontinuities in a short sequence from *October.*

The sequence is the third one in the film (and comprises no fewer than 125 shots). The story action is simple. The bourgeois Provisional Government has taken power in Russia after the February Revolution, but instead of withdrawing from World War I, the government has continued to support the Allies. This maneuver has left the Russian people no better off than under the czar. Now, in classical Hollywood cinema, this story might be shown through a montage sequence of newspaper headlines smoothly linked to a scene wherein a protagonist complains that the Provisional Government has not changed a thing. *October*'s protagonist, though, is not one person but the entire Russian people, and the film does not usually use dialogue scenes to present its story points. Rather, *October* seeks to go beyond a simple presentation of story events by making the audience actively interpret those events. To this end, the film confronts the audience with a disorienting and disjunctive set of images.

The sequence begins with shots showing the Russian soldiers on the front casting down their rifles and fraternizing freely with German soldiers **(8.155).** Eisenstein then cuts back to the Provisional Government, where a flunky extends a document to an unseen ruler **(8.156);** this document pledges the government to aid the Allies. The soldiers' fraternization is suddenly disrupted by a bombardment **(8.157).** The soldiers run back to the trenches and huddle as dirt and bomb fragments rain down on them. Eisenstein then cuts to a series of shots of a cannon being lowered off a factory assembly line. For a time the narration crosscuts these images with the soldiers on the battlefield **(8.158, 8.159).** In the last section of the sequence, the shots of the cannon are crosscut with hungry women and children standing in breadlines

8.155 In *October,* Russian and German soldiers talk, drink, and laugh together on the battlefield.

8.156 *October:* At the Provisional Government's headquarters.

8.157 *October:* A bombardment at the front.

in the snow **(8.160)**. The sequence ends with two intertitles: "All as before . . . "/ "Hunger and war."

Graphically, there are some continuities and many strong discontinuities. When the soldiers fraternize, many shots closely resemble one another graphically, and one shot of a bursting bomb is graphically matched in its movement with men bustling into a trench. But the graphic *dis*continuities are more noteworthy. Eisenstein cuts from a laughing German soldier facing right to a menacing eagle statue, facing left, at the government headquarters **(8.161 8.162)**. There is a bold jump cut: The flunky is bowing; then suddenly he is standing up **(8.163, 8.164)**. A static shot of rifles thrust into the snow cuts to a long shot of a bursting shell **(8.165, 8.166)**. When the soldiers race back to the trenches, Eisenstein often

8.158   *October:* A cannon in a factory intercut . . .

8.159   . . . with soldiers at the front.

8.160   *October:* A breadline intercut with the war scenes.

8.161   *October.*

8.162   *October.*

8.163   *October.*

8.164   *October.*

8.165   *October.*

8.166   *October.*

opposes their direction of movement from shot to shot. Moreover, the cutting contrasts shots of the cannon slowly *descending* with shots of the men crouching in the trenches looking *upward* (8.158, 8.159). In the last phase of the sequence, Eisenstein juxtaposes the misty, almost completely static shots of the women and children with the sharply defined, dynamically moving shots of factory workers lowering the cannon. Such graphic discontinuities recur throughout the film, especially in scenes of dynamic action, and stimulate perceptual conflict in the audience. To watch an Eisenstein film is to submit oneself to such percussive, pulsating graphic editing.

Eisenstein also makes vigorous use of temporal discontinuities. The sequence as a whole is opposed to Hollywood rules in its refusal to present the order of events unambiguously. Does the crosscutting of battlefield and government, factory and street indicate simultaneous action? (Consider, for example, that the women and children are seen at night, whereas the factory appears to be working in the daytime.) It is impossible to say if the battlefield events take place before or after or during the women's vigil. Eisenstein has sacrificed the delineation of 1-2-3 order so that he can present the shots as emotional and conceptual units.

Duration is likewise variable. The soldiers fraternize in fairly continuous time, but the Provisional Government's behavior presents drastic ellipses; this permits Eisenstein to identify the government as the unseen cause of the bombardment that ruptures the peace. At one point, Eisenstein uses one of his favorite devices, a temporal expansion: There is an overlapping cut as a soldier drinks from a bottle. Recall the expanded sequence of the wheel knocking over the foreman in *Strike* (8.50–8.52). At another point, the gradual collapse of the women and children waiting in line is elided. We see them standing, then later lying on the ground. Even frequency is made discontinuous: It is difficult to say if we are seeing several cannons lowered off the assembly line or only one descending cannon shown several times. Again, Eisenstein seeks a specific *juxtaposition* of elements, not obedience to a timeline. Editing's manipulation of order, duration, and frequency subordinates straightforward story time to specific logical relationships. Eisenstein creates these relationships by juxtaposing disparate lines of action through editing.

Spatially, the *October* sequence runs from rough continuity to extreme discontinuity. Although at times the 180° rule is respected (especially in the shots of women and children), never does Eisenstein begin a section with an establishing shot. Reestablishing shots are rare, and rarely are the major components of the locales shown together in one shot.

Throughout, the classical continuity of space is broken by the intercutting of the different locales. To what end? By violating space in this manner, the film invites us to make emotional and conceptual connections. For example, crosscutting to the Provisional Government makes it the source of bombardment, a meaning reinforced by the way the first explosions are followed by the jump cut of the government flunky.

8.167 *October.*

More daringly, by cutting from the crouching soldiers to a descending cannon, Eisenstein powerfully depicts the men being crushed by the warmaking apparatus of the government. This is reinforced by a false eyeline match from soldiers looking upward, *as if* at the lowering cannon—false because of course the two elements are in entirely separate settings (8.158, 8.159). By then showing the factory workers lowering the cannon (**8.167**), the cutting links the oppressed soldiers to the oppressed proletariat. Finally, as the cannon hits the ground, Eisenstein crosscuts images of it with the shots of the starving families of the soldiers and the workers.

They too are shown as crushed by the government machine. As the cannon wheels come slowly to the floor, we cut to the women's feet in the snow, and the machine's heaviness is linked by titles ("one pound," "half a pound") to the steady starvation of the women and children. Although all of the spaces are in the story, such discontinuities make the film's plot a running political commentary on the story events.

In all, then, Eisenstein's spatial editing, like his temporal and graphic editing, constructs correspondences, analogies, and contrasts that *interpret* the story events. The interpretation is not simply handed to the viewer; rather, the editing discontinuities force the viewer to work out implicit meanings. This sequence, like others in *October,* demonstrates that there are powerful alternatives to the principles of classical continuity.

SUMMARY

When any two shots are joined, we can ask several questions:

1. How are the shots graphically continuous or discontinuous?

2. What rhythmic relations are created?

3. Are the shots spatially continuous? If not, what creates the discontinuity? (Crosscutting? Ambiguous cues?) If the shots are spatially continuous, how does the 180° system create the continuity?

4. Are the shots temporally continuous? If so, what creates the continuity? (For example, matches on action?) If not, what creates the discontinuity? (Ellipsis? Overlapping cuts?)

More generally, we can ask the question we ask of every film technique. How does this technique *function* with respect to the film's narrative or non-narrative form? Does the film use editing to lay out the narrative space, time, and cause–effect chain in the manner of classical continuity? Or does the film use other editing patterns that enter into a different interplay with the narrative? If the film is not a narrative one, how does editing function to engage our formal expectations?

Some practical hints: You can learn to notice editing in several ways. If you are having trouble noticing cuts, try watching a film or television show and tapping with a pencil each time a shot changes. Once you recognize editing easily, watch any film with the sole purpose of observing one editing aspect—say, the way space is presented or the control of graphics or time. Sensitize yourself to rhythmic editing by noting cutting rates; tapping out the tempo of the cuts can help. Watching 1930s and 1940s American films can introduce you to classical continuity style; try to predict what shot will come next in a sequence. (You will be surprised at how often you are right.) When you watch a film on video, try turning off the sound; editing patterns become more apparent this way. When there is a violation of continuity, ask yourself whether it is accidental or serves a purpose. When you see a film that does not obey classical continuity principles, search for its unique editing patterns. Use the slow-motion, freeze, and reverse controls on a videocassette machine or DVD player to analyze a film sequence as this chapter has done. (Almost any film will do.) In such ways as these, you can considerably increase your awareness and understanding of the power of editing.

NOTES AND QUERIES

What Editing Is

Professional reflections on the work of the film editor include Ralph Rosenblum, *When the Shooting Stops . . . The Cutting Begins: A Film Editor's Story* (New York: Penguin, 1980); Edward Dmytryk, *On Film Editing* (Boston: Focal Press, 1984); Vincent Lo Brutto, *Selected Takes: Film Editors on Film Editing* (New York: Praeger, 1991); Gabriella Oldham, *First Cut: Conversations with Film Editors* (Berkeley: University of California Press, 1992); and Declan McGrath, *Editing and Post-Production* (Hove, England: RotoVision, 2001). See also Sam O'Steen, *Cut to the Chase: Forty-Five Years of Editing America's Favorite Movies* (Studio City, Calif.: Wiese, 2001).

Walter Murch, one of the most thoughtful and creative editors in history, provides a rich array of ideas in *In the Blink of an Eye: A Perspective on Film Editing,* 2d ed. (Los Angeles: Silman-James, 2001). Murch, who worked on *American Graffiti, The Godfather, Apocalypse Now,* and *The English Patient,* has always conceived image and sound editing as part of the same process. He shares his thoughts in a dialogue with prominent novelist Michael Ondaatje in *The Conversations: Walter Murch and the Art of Editing Film* (New York: Knopf, 2002).

General discussions of film editing may be found in Rudolf Arnheim's *Film as Art* (Berkeley: University of California Press, 1967), pp. 87–102, and Béla Belázs, *Theory of the Film* (New York: Dover, 1970), pp. 118–138. For a wide-ranging examination of editing aesthetics, see Ken Dancyger, *The Technique of Film and Video Editing* (Boston: Focal Press, 1993). See also several essays in Noël Carroll, *Theorizing the Moving Image* (Cambridge: Cambridge University Press, 1996).

We await a large-scale history of editing, but André Bazin sketches a very influential account in "The Evolution of Film Language," in *What Is Cinema?* Vol. 1 (Berkeley: University of California Press, 1967), pp. 23–40. Editing in early U.S. cinema is carefully analyzed by Charlie Keil in *Early American Cinema in Transition: Story, Style, and Filmmaking, 1907–1913* (Madison: University of Wisconsin Press, 2001). Professional editor Don Fairservice offers a thoughtful account of editing in the silent and early sound eras in *Film Editing: History, Theory and Practice* (Manchester, England: Manchester University Press, 2001). Several sections of Barry Salt's *Film Style and Technology: History and Analysis* (London: Starword, 1992) are devoted to changes in editing practices.

Editing has often been seen as an alternative to mise-en-scene and camera work. Instead of cutting to a close-up of the hero's face, we can have him come closer to the camera, or we can track into a close-up. Early film theory argued that editing was more inherently *cinematic* than the more *theatrical* technique of mise-en-scene; see in this connection Arnheim and Balázs, cited above. But the aesthetic prominence of editing was disputed by the film theorist André Bazin, who argued that editing ruptures and falsifies the spatiotemporal continuum of reality. (See not only the Bazin essay cited above but also "The Virtues and Limitations of Montage," pp. 41–52 of the same volume.) Bazin claimed that concrete reality is better respected by cinematography and mise-en-scene techniques. This debate has been taken up by others, notably Charles Barr in "CinemaScope: Before and After," *Film Quarterly* **16,** 4 (Summer 1963): 4–24, and Christian Metz in *Film Language* (New York: Oxford University Press, 1974), pp. 31–91.

Documentary films characteristically rely on editing, perhaps more than fictional films do. A set of cutting conventions has developed. For example, it is common to intercut talking head shots of conflicting experts as a way of representing opposing points of view. Interestingly, in making *The Thin Blue Line,* Errol Morris instructed his editor Paul Barnes to avoid cutting between the two main suspects. "He didn't want the standard documentary good guy/bad guy juxtaposition. . . . He hated when I intercut people telling the same story, or people contradicting or responding to what someone has just said" (Oldham, *First Cut,* p. 144). Morris apparently wanted to give each speaker's version a certain integrity, letting each stand as an alternative account of events.

Dimensions of Film Editing

Very little has been written on graphic aspects of editing. See Vladimir Nilsen, *The Cinema as a Graphic Art* (New York: Hill & Wang, 1959); Sergei Eisenstein, "The Dramaturgy of Film Form," in Richard Taylor, ed., *Selected Works,* Vol. I: *Writings 1922–1934* (Bloomington: Indiana University Press, 1988), pp. 161–180; and Jonas Mekas, "An Interview with Peter Kubelka," *Film Culture* **44** (Spring 1967): 42–47.

What we are calling rhythmic editing incorporates the categories of metric and rhythmic montage discussed by Eisenstein in "The Fourth Dimension in Cinema," in *Selected Works,* Vol. I, pp. 181–194. For a sample analysis of a film's rhythm, see Lewis Jacobs, "D. W. Griffith," in *The Rise of the American Film* (New York: Teachers College Press, 1968), chap. 11, pp. 171–201. Television commercials are useful to study for rhythmic editing, for their highly stereotyped imagery permits the editor to cut the shots to match the beat of the jingle on the sound track.

For a good discussion of spatial and temporal editing, see Noël Burch, *Theory of Film Practice* (Princeton, N.J.: Princeton University Press, 1981), especially pp. 3–16, 32–48; and Vladimir Nizhny, *Lessons with Eisenstein* (New York: Hill & Wang, 1962), pp. 63–92.

The Kuleshov experiments have been variously described. The two most authoritative accounts are in V. I. Pudovkin, *Film Technique* (New York: Grove, 1960), and Ronald Levaco, trans. and ed., *Kuleshov on Film: Writings of Lev Kuleshov* (Berkeley: University of California Press, 1974), pp. 51–55. For a summary of Kuleshov's work, see Vance Kepley, Jr., "The Kuleshov Workshop," *Iris* **4,** 1 (1986): 5–23. Can the effect actually suggest an expressionless character's emotional reaction? Two film researchers tried to test it, and their skeptical conclusions are set forth in Stephen Prince and Wayne E. Hensley, "The Kuleshov Effect: Recreating the Classic Experiment," *Cinema Journal* **31,** 2 (Winter 1992): 59–75. During the 1990s, two Kuleshov experiments, one complete and one fragmentary, were discovered. For a description and historical background on one of them, see Yuri Tsivian, Ekaterina Khokhlova, and Kristin Thompson, "The Rediscovery of a Kuleshov Experiment: A Dossier," *Film History* **8,** 3 (1996): 357–367.

Continuity Editing

For a historical discussion of continuity editing, see Chapter 12 and the chapter's bibliography. The hidden selectivity that continuity editing can achieve is well summarized in a remark of Thom Noble, who edited *Fahrenheit 451* and *Witness:* "What usually happens is that there are maybe seven moments in each scene that are brilliant. But they're all on different takes. My job is to try and get all those seven moments in and yet have it look seamless, so that nobody knows there's a cut in there" [quoted in David Chell, ed., *Moviemakers at Work* (Redmond, Wash.: Microsoft Press, 1987), pp. 81–82].

Many sources enumerate the rules of continuity. See Karel Reisz and Gavin Millar, *The Technique of Film Editing* (New York: Hastings House, 1973); Daniel Arijohn, *A Grammar of the Film Language* (New York: Focal Press, 1978); and Edward Dmytryk, *On Screen Directing* (Boston: Focal Press, 1984). Our diagram of a hypothetical axis of action has been adapted from Edward Pincus's concise discussion in his *Guide to Filmmaking* (New York: Signet, 1969), pp. 120–125.

For analyses of the continuity style, see Ramond Bellour, "The Obvious and the Code," *Screen* **15,** 4 (Winter 1974–75): 7–17; Vance Kepley, Jr., "Spatial Articulation in the Classical Cinema: A Scene from *His Girl Friday,*" *Wide Angle* **5,** 3 (1983): 50–58; André Gaudreault, "Detours in Film Narrative: The Development of Cross-Cutting," *Cinema Journal* **19,** 1 (Fall 1979): 35–59; and William Simon, "An Approach to Point of View," *Film Reader* **4** (1979): 145–151. Joyce E. Jesionowski presents a detailed study of Griffith's distinctive version of early continuity editing in *Thinking in Pictures: Dramatic Structure in D. W. Griffith's Biograph Films* (Berkeley: University of California Press, 1987). David Bordwell's *Planet Hong Kong: Popular Cinema and the Art of Entertainment* (Cambridge, Mass.: Harvard University Press, 2000) considers how Hollywood continuity was used by another national cinema.

Contemporary Editing and Intensified Continuity

Taught in film schools and learned on the job by beginning filmmakers, the principles of continuity editing still dominate cinema around the world. As we suggested on p. 327, however, there have been some changes in the system. Shots tend to be shorter (*Moulin Rouge* contains over 4000) and framed closer to the performers. The medium shots in older filmmaking traditions display the hands and upper body fully, but intensified continuity concentrates on faces, particularly the actor's eyes. Film editor Walter Murch says, "The determining factor for selecting a particular shot is frequently: 'Can you register the expression in the actor's eyes?' If you can't, the editor will tend to use the next closer shot, even though the wider shot may be more than adequate when seen on the big screen."

This trend is discussed more extensively in Salt, *Film Style and Technology* (cited above), chap. 2, and David Bordwell, "Intensified Continuity: Visual Style in Contemporary American Film," *Film Quarterly* **55,** 3 (Spring 2002): 16–28.

Alternatives to Continuity Editing

Eisenstein remains the chief source in this area. A highly introspective filmmaker, he bequeathed us a rich set of ideas on the possibilities of non-narrative editing; see the essays in *Selected Works,* Vol. 1. For further discussion of editing in *October,* see the essays by Annette Michelson, Noël Carroll, and Rosalind Krauss in the special "Eisenstein/Brakhage" number of *Artforum* **11,** 5 (January 1973): 30–37, 56–65. For a more general view of Eisenstein's editing, see David Bordwell, *The Cinema of Eisenstein* (Cambridge, Mass.: Harvard University Press, 1993). The writings of another Russian, Dziga Vertov, are also of interest. See Annette Michelson, ed., *Kino-Eye: The Writings of Dziga Vertov* (Berkeley: University of California Press, 1984). Good discussions of Vertov's montage practice are Stephen Crofts and Olivia Rose, "An Essay toward *Man with a Movie Camera*," Screen **18,** 1 (Spring 1977): 9–58, and Seth R. Feldman, *Evolution of Style in the Early Work of Dziga Vertov* (New York: Arno, 1977). For a detailed consideration of Godard's play with continuity cues, see Jacques Aumont, "This Is Not a Textual Analysis (Godard's *La Chinoise*)," *Camera Obscura* 8-9-10 (1982): 131–161. On Ozu's manipulation of discontinuities, see David Bordwell, *Ozu and the Poetics of Cinema* (Princeton, N.J.: Princeton University Press, 1988); Kristin Thompson, "Late Spring and Ozu's Unreasonable Style," in *Breaking the Glass Armor: Neoformalist Film Analysis* (Princeton, N. J.: Princeton University Press, 1988), pp. 317–352; and Edward Branigan, "The Space of Equinox Flower," in Peter Lehman, ed., *Close Viewings: An Anthology of New Film Criticism* (Sarasota: University of Florida Press, 1990), pp. 73–108.

Experimental and avant-garde filmmakers have taken the biggest steps toward constructing alternatives to the continuity style. Apart from the sources listed in the Notes and Queries for Chapter 5, see David Curtis's *Experimental Cinema* (New York: Delta, 1971) and Gregory Battcock, ed., *The New American Cinema* (New York: Dutton, 1967).

Chapter 9

Sound in the Cinema

Most films create the impression that the people and things onscreen simply produce an appropriate noise. But, as we have seen in Chapter 1, in the process of film production the sound track is constructed separately from the images, and it can be manipulated independently. This makes sound as flexible and wide-ranging as other film techniques.

Yet sound is perhaps the hardest technique to study. We are accustomed to ignoring many of the sounds in our environment. Our primary information about the layout of our surroundings comes from sight, and so in ordinary life sound is often simply a background for our visual attention. Similarly, we speak of watching a film and of being movie viewers or spectators—all terms that suggest the sound track is a secondary factor. We are strongly inclined to think of sound as simply an accompaniment to the real basis of cinema, the moving images.

Moreover, we cannot stop the film and freeze an instant of sound, as we can study a frame to examine mise-en-scene and cinematography. Nor can we lay out the sound track for our inspection as easily as we can examine the editing of a string of shots. In film, the sounds and the patterns they form are elusive. This elusiveness accounts for part of the power of this technique: Sound can achieve very strong effects and yet remain quite unnoticeable. To study sound, we must learn to listen to films.

Fortunately, many viewers are becoming more sensitive to the way movies sound. The film industry has heavily promoted improvements in sound recording, mixing, and reproduction. These developments include Dolby noise-reduction processes and four- and six-track theater sound. *Star Wars,* with its stereo and surround channels, demonstrated that audiences appreciated better sound tracks. During the early 1990s digital sound mixing and reproduction became routine attractions of big-budget pictures.

Although theatrical reproduction remains the weak link in the sound chain, many exhibitors are upgrading their equipment and paying more attention to the auditorium's acoustic design. George Lucas's THX theater-certification program promotes high-quality sound-design systems. Audiences who have become used to digital compact-disc music have also embraced stereo-encoded videocassettes and surround-encoded DVDs. Not since the first talkies of the late 1920s have filmgoers been so aware of cinema sound, and filmmakers now compete in creating rich and engaging sound tracks.

THE POWERS OF SOUND

Whether noticed or not, sound is a powerful film technique for several reasons. For one thing, it engages a distinct sense mode. Our visual attention is accompanied by aural attention. Even before recorded sound was introduced in 1926, silent films were accompanied by orchestra, organ, or piano. At a minimum, the music filled in the silence and gave the spectator a more complete perceptual experience. More significantly, the engagement of hearing opens the possibility of what the Soviet director Sergei Eisenstein called "synchronization of senses"—making a single rhythm or expressive quality unify both image and sound.

Also, sound can actively shape how we perceive and interpret the image. In one sequence of *Letter from Siberia* **(9.1–9.4),** Chris Marker demonstrates the power of sound to alter our understanding of images. Three times Marker shows the same footage—a shot of a bus passing a car on a city street, three shots of workers paving a street. But each time the footage is accompanied by a completely different sound track. Compare the three versions tabulated alongside the sequence **(Table 9.1).** The verbal differences are emphasized by the identical images; the audience will construe the same images differently, depending on the sound track.

The *Letter from Siberia* sequence demonstrates another advantage of sound: Film sound can direct our attention quite specifically within the image. When the commentator describes the "blood-colored buses," we are likely to look at the bus and not at the car. When Fred Astaire and Ginger Rogers are executing an intricate step, chances are that we watch their bodies and not the silent nightclub spectators looking on. In such ways, sound can guide us through the images, pointing to things to watch.

This possibility becomes even more fertile when you consider that the sound cue for some visual element may *anticipate* that element and relay our attention to it. Suppose we have a close-up of a man in a room and we hear the creaking of a door opening. If the next shot shows the door, now open, the viewer's attention will probably shift to that door, the source of the offscreen sound. But if the second shot shows the door still closed, the viewer will likely ponder his or her interpretation of the sound. (Maybe it wasn't a door, after all?) Thus the sound track can clarify image events, contradict them, or render them ambiguous. In all cases, the sound track can enter into an active relation with the image track.

This example of the door opening suggests another advantage of sound. It cues us to form expectations. If we hear a door creaking, we anticipate that someone has entered a room and that we will see that person in the next shot. But if the film draws on conventions of the horror genre, the camera might stay on the man, staring fearfully. We would then be in suspense as to the appearance of the monster offscreen. Horror and mystery films often use the power of sound from an unseen source to engage the audience's interest, but all types of films can take advantage of this aspect of sound. During the town meeting in *Jaws,* the characters hear a grating sound and turn to look offscreen; a cut reveals Quint's hand scraping on a blackboard—creating a dramatic introduction to this character. We shall see as well several cases in which the use of sound can creatively cheat or redirect the viewer's expectations.

In addition, sound gives a new value to silence. A quiet passage in a film can create almost unbearable tension, forcing the viewer to concentrate on the screen and to wait in anticipation for whatever sound will emerge. Just as color film makes black and white into grades of color, so the use of sound in film will include all the possibilities of silence.

"The most exciting moment is the moment when I add the sound. . . . At this moment, I tremble."

— Akira Kurosawa, director

TABLE 9.1 *Letter from Siberia* Footage

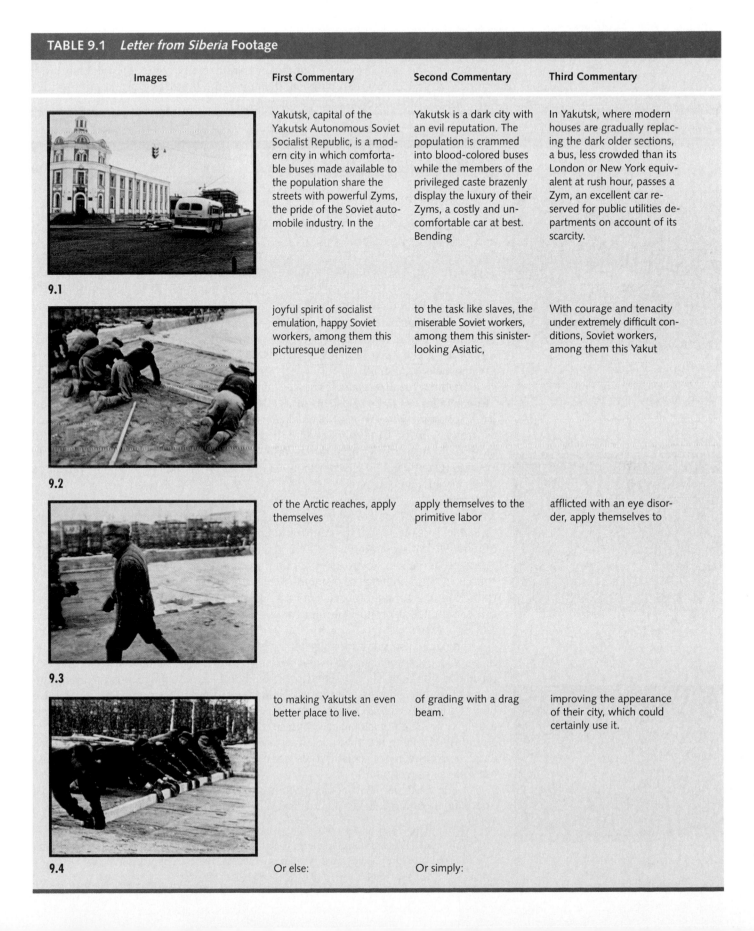

Images	First Commentary	Second Commentary	Third Commentary
9.1	Yakutsk, capital of the Yakutsk Autonomous Soviet Socialist Republic, is a modern city in which comfortable buses made available to the population share the streets with powerful Zyms, the pride of the Soviet automobile industry. In the	Yakutsk is a dark city with an evil reputation. The population is crammed into blood-colored buses while the members of the privileged caste brazenly display the luxury of their Zyms, a costly and uncomfortable car at best. Bending	In Yakutsk, where modern houses are gradually replacing the dark older sections, a bus, less crowded than its London or New York equivalent at rush hour, passes a Zym, an excellent car reserved for public utilities departments on account of its scarcity.
9.2	joyful spirit of socialist emulation, happy Soviet workers, among them this picturesque denizen	to the task like slaves, the miserable Soviet workers, among them this sinister-looking Asiatic,	With courage and tenacity under extremely difficult conditions, Soviet workers, among them this Yakut
9.3	of the Arctic reaches, apply themselves	apply themselves to the primitive labor	afflicted with an eye disorder, apply themselves to
9.4	to making Yakutsk an even better place to live. Or else:	of grading with a drag beam. Or simply:	improving the appearance of their city, which could certainly use it.

Yet another advantage: Sound bristles with as many creative possibilities as editing. Through editing, one may join shots of any two spaces to create a meaningful relation. Similarly, the filmmaker can mix any sonic phenomena into a whole. With the introduction of sound cinema, the infinity of visual possibilities was joined by the infinity of acoustic events.

FUNDAMENTALS OF FILM SOUND

Perceptual Properties

Several aspects of sound as we perceive it are familiar to us from everyday experience and are central to film's use of sound.

Loudness   The sound we hear results from vibrations in the air. The amplitude, or breadth, of the vibrations produces our sense of loudness, or volume. Film sound constantly manipulates volume. For example, in many films a long shot of a busy street is accompanied by loud traffic noises, but when two people meet and start to speak, the volume of the traffic drops. Or a dialogue between a soft-spoken character and a blustery one is characterized as much by the difference in volume as by the substance of the talk.

Loudness is also related to perceived distance; often the louder the sound, the closer we take it to be. This sort of assumption seems to be at work in the street-traffic example already mentioned: The couple's dialogue, being louder, is sensed as in the acoustic foreground, while the traffic noise sinks to the background. In addition, a film may startle the viewer by exploiting abrupt and extreme shifts in volume (usually called changes in *dynamics*), as when a quiet scene is interrupted by a very loud noise.

Pitch   The frequency of sound vibrations affects pitch, or the perceived highness or lowness of the sound. Certain instruments, such as the tuning fork, can produce pure tones, but most sounds, in life and on film, are complex tones, batches of different frequencies. Nevertheless pitch plays a useful role in picking out distinct sounds in a film. It helps us distinguish music and speech from noises. It also serves to distinguish among objects. Thumps can suggest hollow objects, while higher-pitched sounds (like those of jingle bells) suggest smoother or harder surfaces and denser objects.

Pitch can also serve more specific purposes. When a young boy tries to speak in a man's deep voice and fails (as in *How Green Was My Valley*), the joke is based primarily on pitch. Marlene Dietrich's vocal delivery often depends on a long upward-gliding intonation that makes a statement sound like a question. In the coronation scene of *Ivan the Terrible,* Part I, a court singer with a deep bass voice begins a song of praise to Ivan, and each phrase rises dramatically in pitch (**9.5–9.7**). When Bernard Herrmann obtained the effects of shrill, birdlike shrieking in Hitchcock's *Psycho,* even many musicians could not recognize the source: violins played at extraordinarily high pitch.

When Julianne Moore was planning her performance as the protagonist of Todd Haynes's *Safe,* she took pitch and other vocal qualities into account:

> My first key to her was her voice, her vocal patterns. I started with a very typical Southern California speech pattern. It's almost a sing-song rhythm, you know—it's referred to as the "Valley quality" that travelled across the country and became a uni-

9.5   In *Ivan the Terrible,* Eisenstein emphasizes changes in vocal pitch by cutting from medium-long shot . . .

9.6   . . . to medium shot . . .

9.7   . . . to close-up of the singer.

versal American vocal pattern. It was important to me that her voice would have that kind of melody to it. And then I would put question marks at the end of the sentence all the time—that way she never makes a statement; it makes her very unsure and very undefined. I also went above my own chords, because I wanted the sensation of her voice not being connected at all to her body—that's why her voice is so high. This is someone who's completely disconnected from any kind of physicality, from any sense of being herself, from really knowing herself. In that sense, I guess the vocal choices are somewhat metaphorical.

Timbre   The harmonic components of sound give it a certain color, or tone quality—what musicians call timbre. Timbre is actually a less fundamental acoustic parameter than amplitude or frequency, but it is indispensable in describing the texture of "feel" of a sound. When we call someone's voice nasal or a certain musical tone mellow, we are referring to timbre. In everyday life, the recognition of a familiar sound is largely a matter of various aspects of timbre.

Filmmakers manipulate timbre continually. Timbre can help articulate portions of the sound track, as when it differentiates musical instruments from one another. Timbre also comes forward on certain occasions, as in the clichéd use of oleaginous saxophone tones behind seduction scenes. More subtly, in the opening sequence of Rouben Mamoulian's *Love Me Tonight,* people starting the day on a street pass a musical rhythm from object to object—a broom, a carpet beater—and the humor of the number springs in part from the very different timbres of the objects. In preparing the sound track for Peter Weir's *Witness,* the editors drew on sounds recorded twenty or more years before, so that the less modern timbre of the older recordings would evoke the rustic seclusion of the Amish community.

Loudness, pitch, and timbre interact to define the overall sonic texture of a film. For example, these qualities enable us to recognize different characters' voices. Both John Wayne and James Stewart speak slowly, but Wayne's voice tends to be deeper and gruffer than Stewart's querulous drawl. This difference works to great advantage in *The Man Who Shot Liberty Valance,* where their characters are sharply contrasted. In *The Wizard of Oz* the disparity between the public image of the Wizard and the old charlatan who rigs it up is marked by the booming bass of the effigy and the old man's higher, softer, more quavering voice.

Loudness, pitch, and timbre also shape our experience of a film as a whole. *Citizen Kane,* for example, offers a wide range of sound manipulations. Echo chambers alter timbre and volume. A motif is formed by the inability of Kane's wife Susan to sing pitches accurately. Moreover, in *Citizen Kane* the plot's shifts between times and places are covered by continuing a sound thread and varying the basic acoustics. A shot of Kane applauding dissolves to a shot of a crowd applauding (a shift in volume and timbre). Leland beginning a sentence in the street cuts to Kane finishing the sentence in an auditorium, his voice magnified by loudspeakers (a shift in volume, timbre, and pitch).

Recent noise-reduction techniques, multitrack reproduction, and digital sound have yielded wider ranges of frequency and volume, as well as crisper timbres. Today sound editors can individualize voice or noise to a surprising degree. For *The Thin Red Line,* every character's distinctive breathing sounds were recorded for use as ambient noise. Randy Thoms, sound designer for *Cast Away,* sought to characterize different sorts of wind—breezes from the open sea, winds in a cave. Sound even announces a shift in wind direction crucial to one of the hero's plans. "We can use the wind in a very musical way," Thoms notes.

"The Empire spaceship sounded a certain way as compared to the Imperial fleet; that was a deliberate style change. Everybody in the Empire had shrieking, howling, ghostlike, frightening sounds. . . . You hear it—you jump with fear. Whereas the rebel forces had more junky-sounding planes and spaceships. They weren't quite as powerful; they tended to pop and sputter more."

— Ben Burtt, sound editor, on *Star Wars*

Selection, Alteration, and Combination

Sound in the cinema is of three types: *speech, music,* and *noise* (also called *sound effects*). Occasionally a sound may cross categories—is a scream speech or noise? Is electronic music also noise?—and filmmakers have freely exploited these ambiguities. In *Psycho,* when a woman screams, we expect to hear a human voice and instead hear screaming violins. Nevertheless, in most cases the distinctions hold. Now that we have an idea of some basic acoustic properties, we must consider how speech, music, and noise are selected and combined for specific functions within films.

Choosing and Manipulating Sounds

The creation of the sound track resembles the editing of the image track. Just as the filmmaker may pick the best image from several shots, he or she may choose what exact bit of sound will best serve the purpose. Just as footage from disparate sources may be blended into a single visual track, so too sound that was not recorded during filming may be added freely. Moreover, just as a shot may be rephotographed on the optical printer or tinted in color or jigsawed into a composite image, so too may a bit of sound be processed to change its acoustic qualities. And just as the filmmaker may link or superimpose images, so may he or she join any two sounds end to end or place one over another (as with commentary over music). Though we are not usually as aware of sonic manipulations, the sound track demands as much choice and control as does the visual track.

Sometimes the sound track is conceived before the image track. Studio-made animated cartoons typically record music, dialogue, and sound effects before the images are filmed, so that the figures may be synchronized with the sound frame by frame. For many years Carl Stalling created frantically paced jumbles of familiar tunes, weird noises, and distinctive voices for the adventures of Bugs Bunny and Daffy Duck. Experimental films, especially those using abstract or associational form, also frequently build their images around a preexisting sound track. Some filmmakers have even argued that abstract cinema is a sort of "visual music" and have tried to create a synthesis of the two media.

As with other film techniques, sound guides the viewer's attention. Normally, this means clarifying and simplifying the sound track so that important material stands out. Dialogue, the transmitter of story information, is usually recorded and reproduced for maximum clarity. Important lines should not have to compete with music or background noise. Sound effects are usually less important. They supply an overall sense of a realistic environment and are seldom noticed; if they were missing, however, the silence would be distracting. Music is also subordinate to dialogue, entering during pauses in dialogue or effects.

Dialogue does not always rank highest in importance. Sound effects are usually central to action sequences, while music can dominate dance scenes, transitional sequences, or emotion-laden moments without dialogue. And some filmmakers have shifted the weight conventionally assigned to each type of sound. Charles Chaplin's *City Lights* and *Modern Times* eliminate dialogue, letting sound effects and music come to the fore. The films of Jacques Tati and Jean-Marie Straub retain dialogue but still place great emphasis on sound effects. Later in this chapter we will consider how music and noise in Robert Bresson's *A Man Escaped* fill out a sparse dialogue track by evoking offscreen space and creating thematic associations.

In creating a sound track, then, the filmmaker must select sounds that will fulfill a particular function. In order to do this, usually the filmmaker will provide a clearer, simpler sound world than that of everyday life. Normally, our perception filters out irrelevant stimuli and retains what is most useful at a particular moment. As you read this, you are attending to words on the page and (to various degrees)

ignoring certain stimuli that reach your ears. But if you close your eyes and listen
attentively to the sounds around you, you will become aware of many previously
unnoticed sounds—distant voices, the wind, footsteps, a radio playing. Any amateur recordist knows that if you set up a microphone and tape recorder in even a
quiet environment, those normally unnoticed sounds suddenly become obtrusive.
The microphone is unselective; like the camera lens, it does not automatically filter
out what is distracting. Sound studios, camera blimps to absorb motor noise, directional and shielded microphones, sound engineering and editing, and libraries of
stock sounds all allow the filmmaker to choose exactly what the sound track requires. Unless a filmmaker actually wants the ambient noise of a scene, simply
holding out a microphone while filming will rarely be selective enough.

By choosing certain sounds, the filmmaker guides our perception of the image
and the action. In one scene from Jacques Tati's *Mr. Hulot's Holiday,* vacationers
at a resort hotel are relaxing (**9.8**). Early in the scene, the guests in the foreground
are murmuring quietly, but Hulot's Ping-Pong game is louder; the sound cues us to
watch Hulot. Later in the scene, however, the same Ping-Pong game makes *no*
sound at all, and our attention is drawn to the muttering card players in the foreground. The presence and absence of the sound of the Ping-Pong ball guides our
expectations. If you start to notice how such selection of sound shapes our perception, you will also notice that filmmakers often use sound quite unrealistically, in
order to shift our attention to what is narratively or visually important.

Our scene from *Mr. Hulot's Holiday* also points up the importance of how a
chosen sound may have its acoustic qualities transformed for a particular purpose.
Thanks to a manipulation of volume and timbre, the Ping-Pong game gains in
vividness and clarity. Similarly, a character speaking will usually sound about as
loud in long shot as in close-up, even though this is a flagrant violation of realism.

At the limit, wholly new sounds may be made of old ones. The noises emitted
by the demonically possessed girl in *The Exorcist* blended screams, animal thrash-
ings, and English spoken backward. To create the roar of a *Tyrannosaurus rex* for
Jurassic Park, sound engineers fused a tiger's roar, a baby elephant's trumpeting at
midrange frequencies, and an alligator's growl for the lower tones. Even jet planes'
roars typically include cries of animals—not only lions and elephants but monkeys
as well.

Nowadays, film sound is normally reprocessed to yield exactly the qualities
desired. A *dry recording* of the sound in a fairly nonreflective space will be manipulated electronically to yield the desired effect. For instance, the voice of someone
on the telephone is typically treated with filters to make it more tinny and muffled.
(In Hollywood parlance, this is called "futzing" the sound.) The almost nonstop
rock-and-roll music of *American Graffiti* used two recordings of the music: a dry
one for moments when the music was to dominate the scene and had to be of high
sonic quality, and a more ambient one for background noise. The latter was derived
from a tape recorder simply playing the tune in a backyard.

Sound Mixing
Guiding the viewer's attention, then, depends on selecting and reworking particular sounds. It also depends on **mixing,** or *combining* them. It is useful to think of the sound track not as a set of discrete sound units but as an ongoing
stream of auditory information. Each sonic event takes its place in a specific pattern.
This pattern both links events in time and layers them at any given moment.

We can easily see how the sound track offers a stream of auditory information
by considering a scene cut according to classical continuity principles. When filmmakers edit conversations in shot/reverse shot, they often use a **dialogue overlap**
to smooth down the visual change of shot. In a dialogue overlap the filmmaker

9.8 *Mr. Hulot's Holiday:* In the
foreground, guests quietly play cards
while in the depth of the shot, Mr. Hulot
is frantically playing Ping-Pong.

"[Tati's] films don't look much like
anyone else's . . . And they sure as
hell don't sound like anyone else's.
Half the time they don't even sound
like films. They sound as though
someone were holding a radio to your
ear and slowly spinning the dial."

— Anthony Lane in the *New Yorker*

"Is it better to say, 'I love you,' bang,
then cut to the reaction? Or is it
better to say, 'I love you,' hang on
it a beat to show the emotion of the
person delivering the line, then go for
the reaction? It's a matter of choice.
Either way, there's a different result
for the audience looking at it. Are
their sympathies with the guy who
said the line, or the girl who said
the line? Or is the audience saying,
'Don't believe him, he's going to
screw you over!' . . . If you find the
frame to cut on at *that* right moment,
the audience will be totally satisfied."

— Tom Rolf, editor

continues a line of dialogue across a cut. During a conversation in John McTiernan's *The Hunt for Red October,* we get the following shots and dialogue:

1. (ms) Over political officer's shoulder, favoring Captain Ramius **(9.9).**

    Officer: "Captain Tupalev's boat."

    Ramius: "You know Tupalev?"

    Officer: "I know he descends . . ."

2. (ms) Reverse angle over Ramius's shoulder, favoring officer **(9.10).**

    Officer (continuing): " . . . from aristocracy, and that he was your student. It's rumored he has a special . . ."

3. (mcu) Reverse angle on Ramius **(9.11).**

    Officer (continuing): " . . . place in his heart for you."

    Ramius: "There's little room in Tupalev's heart for anyone but Tupalev."

Here the officer's chatter provides an auditory continuity that distracts from the shot changes. Moreover, by cutting to a closer view of the listener before a sentence is finished, the sound and editing concentrate our attention on Ramius's response. As a Hollywood editor puts it, "The minute a telling word or a question is

9.9   *The Hunt for Red October,* Shot 1.

9.10   *The Hunt for Red October,* Shot 2.

9.11 *The Hunt for Red October,* Shot 3.

posed . . . I go for a reaction to see . . . how they are trying to formulate the answer in their face or dialogue." The principle of dialogue overlap can be used with noise as well. In the *Red October* scene just mentioned, sounds of a spoon clinking in a tea cup and of papers being riffled also carry over certain cuts, providing a continuous stream of sonic information.

This stream can involve more than simply linking one line of dialogue or bit of noise to another. We have already seen that in production, combining sounds is usually done after shooting, in the mixing process. For example, in *Jurassic Park* Steven Spielberg manipulates volume unrealistically for purposes of narrative clarity. After a live cow has been lowered into the velociraptors' pen, the South African hunter gives important information about the habits of these predators, and his voice comes through louder than those of characters closer to the camera **(9.12)**. The mixer can precisely control the volume, duration, and tone quality of each sound. In modern filmmaking, a dozen or more separate tracks may be mixed in layers at any moment. The mix can be quite dense, as when an airport scene combines the babble of several distinct voices, footsteps, luggage trolleys, Muzak, and plane engines. Or the mix can be very sparse, with an occasional sound emerging against a background of total silence. Most cases will fall somewhere between these extremes. In our *Red October* scene, a distant throbbing engine and slight brushings of fabric form a muted background to the dialogue exchange.

The filmmaker may create a mix in which each sound blends smoothly with the others. This is commonly the case when music and effects are mixed with speech. In classical Hollywood cinema of the 1930s, the musical score may become prominent in moments in which there is no dialogue, and then it is likely to fade unnoticeably down just as the characters begin to talk. (In studio parlance, this is called *sneaking in* and *sneaking out.*) Sometimes the mix will associate sounds evocatively. In *The English Patient,* when the nurse feeds the patient a plum, a distant churchbell rings, suggesting a peaceful refuge from the war.

Alternatively, the acoustic stream may contain much more abrupt contrasts. Contemporary Hollywood films often exploit the dynamic range of Dolby technology to fill chase sequences with startling shifts between low, rumbling engines and whining sirens or squealing tires. In *The Godfather,* just as Michael Corleone is steeling himself to shoot the rival gangster Solozzo, we hear a loud metallic screech, presumably from a nearby elevated train. The sound suggests impending danger, both for the victim and for Michael himself: After the murder, his life will change irrevocably **(9.13).**

9.12 *Jurassic Park:* Although Hammond and Ellie are closer to the camera than anything else in the shot, their dialogue is an unintelligible murmur, while the exposition about velociraptors given by the hunter in the background is clearly audible.

9.13 As Michael sits opposite Solozzo, the sudden rumble and whine of an offscreen train sound all the more harsh when compared with the calm expression on Michael's face.

A Dramatic Sound Stream: Seven Samurai   The ways in which sounds may combine to create an ongoing stream of information is well illustrated by the final battle sequence of Akira Kurosawa's *Seven Samurai.* In a heavy rain, marauding bandits charge into a village defended by the villagers and the samurai. The torrent and wind form a constant background noise throughout the scene. Before the battle, the conversation of the waiting men, footsteps, and the sound of swords being drawn are punctuated by long pauses in which we hear only the drumming rain. Suddenly distant horses' hooves are heard offscreen. This draws our attention from the defenders to the attackers. Then Kurosawa cuts to a long shot of the bandits; their horses' hooves become abruptly louder. (The scene employs vivid sound perspective: The closer the camera is to a source, the louder the sound.) When the bandits burst into the village, yet another sound element appears—the bandits' harsh battle cries, which increase steadily in volume as they approach.

The battle begins. The muddy, storm-swept mise-en-scene and rhythmic cutting gain effect from the way in which the incessant rain and splashing are explosively interrupted by brief noises—the screams of the wounded, the splintering of a fence one bandit crashes through, the whinnies of horses, the twang of one samurai's bowstring, the gurgle of a speared bandit, the screams of women when the bandit chieftain breaks into their hiding place. The sudden intrusion of certain sounds marks abrupt developments in the battle. Such frequent surprises heighten our tension, since the narration frequently shifts us from one line of action to another.

The scene climaxes after the main battle has ended. Offscreen horses' hooves are cut short by a new sound—the sharp crack of a bandit's rifle shot, which fells one samurai. A long pause, in which we hear only the driving rain, emphasizes the moment. The samurai furiously flings his sword in the direction of the shot and falls dead into the mud. Another samurai races toward the bandit chieftain, who has the rifle; another shot cracks out and he falls back, wounded; another pause, in which only the relentless rain is heard. The wounded samurai kills the chieftain. The other samurai gather. At the scene's end, the sobs of a young samurai, the distant whinnies and hoofbeats of riderless horses, and the rain all fade slowly out.

The relatively dense mix of this sound track gradually introduces sounds that turn our attention to new narrative elements (hooves, battle cries) and then modulates these sounds into a harmonious stream. This stream is then punctuated by abrupt sounds of unusual volume or pitch associated with crucial narrative actions (the archery, women's screams, the gunshots). Overall, the combination of sounds enhances the unrestricted, objective narration of this sequence, which shows us what happens in various parts of the village rather than confining us to the experience of a single participant.

Sound and Film Form   The choice and combination of sonic materials can also create patterns that run through the film as a whole. This is most readily seen by examining how the filmmaker uses a musical score. Sometimes the filmmaker will select preexisting pieces of music to accompany the images, as Bruce Conner does in using portions of Respighi's *Pines of Rome* as the sound track for *A Movie.* In other cases the music will be composed for the film, and here the filmmaker and the composer make several choices.

The rhythm, melody, harmony, and instrumentation of the music can strongly affect the viewer's emotional reactions. In addition, a melody or musical phrase can be associated with a particular character, setting, situation, or idea. *Local Hero,* a film about a confused young executive who leaves Texas to close a business deal in a remote Scottish village, uses two major musical themes. A rockabilly tune is heard in the urban Southwest, while a slower, more poignantly folkish, melody is associated with the seaside village. In the final scenes, after the young man has returned to Houston, he recalls Scotland with affection, and the film plays the two themes simultaneously. In contrast, a single musical theme can change its quality when associated with different situations. In *Raising Arizona,* the hapless hero has a terrifying dream in which he envisions a homicidal biker pursuing him, and the accompanying music is appropriately ominous. But at the film's end, the hero dreams of raising dozens of children, and now the same melody, reorchestrated and played at a lilting tempo, conveys peace and comfort.

By reordering and varying musical motifs, the filmmaker can subtly compare scenes, trace patterns of development, and suggest implicit meanings. A convenient example is Georges Delerue's score for François Truffaut's *Jules and Jim.* Overall, the film's music reflects the Paris of 1912–1933, the years during which the action takes place; many of the melodies resemble works by Claude Debussy and Erik Satie, two of the most prominent French composers of that era. Virtually the entire score consists of melodies in $3/4$ meter, many of them in waltz time, and all the main themes are in keys related to A major. These rhythmic and harmonic decisions help unify the film.

More specifically, musical themes are associated with particular aspects of the narrative. For instance, Catherine's constant search for happiness and freedom outside conventional boundaries is conveyed by her singing the "Tourbillon" ("Whirlwind") song, which says that life is a constant changing of romantic partners. Settings are also evoked in musical terms. One tune is heard every time the characters are in a café. As the years go by, the tune changes from a mechanical player-piano rendition to a jazzier version played by a black pianist.

The characters' relations become more strained and complicated over time, and the score reflects this in its development of major motifs. A lyrical melody is first heard when Jules, Jim, and Catherine visit the countryside and bicycle to the beach **(9.14)**. This "idyll" tune will recur at many points when the characters reunite, but as the years pass it will become slower in tempo and more sombre in instrumentation and will shift from a major to a minor mode. Another motif that reappears in different guises is a "dangerous love" theme associated with Jim and Catherine. This grave, shimmering waltz is first heard when he visits her apartment and watches her pour a bottle of vitriol down the sink **(9.15)**. (The acid, she says, is "for lying eyes.") Thereafter, this harmonically unstable theme, which resembles one of Satie's *Gymnopédies* for piano, is used to underscore Jim and Catherine's vertiginous love affair. At times it accompanies scenes of passion, but at other times it accompanies their growing disillusionment and despair.

The most varied theme is a mysterious phrase first heard on the flute when Jules and Jim encounter a striking ancient statue **(9.16)**. Later they meet Catherine and discover that she has the statue's face; a repetition of the musical motif confirms the comparison. Throughout the film, this brief motif is associated with the enigmatic side of Catherine. In the film's later scenes, this motif is developed in an intriguing way. The bass line (played on harpsichord or strings) that softly accompanied the woodwind tune now comes to the fore, creating a relentless, often harsh, pulsation. This "menace" waltz underscores Catherine's fling with Albert and accompanies her final vengeance on Jim: driving her car, with him as passenger, into the river.

Once musical motifs have been selected, they can be combined to evoke associations. During Jim and Catherine's first intimate talk after the war, the bass-line-dominated version of the enigma waltz is followed by the love theme, as if the latter could drown out the menacing side of Catherine's character. The love theme accompanies long tracking shots of Jim and Catherine strolling through the woods.

"It's a lot like writing an opera. There's a lot of form and structure. We're very conscious that LOTR is one story that has been broken into three parts. My score is a complex piece that has to be structured carefully, musically and thematically, so that all the parts relate to one another."

—Howard Shore, composer,
The Lord of the Rings

"So, given this mood-altering potential of music, it becomes a great source of fun, as well as a chance to make a scene that works OK work a whole lot better—to bring out the point of a scene that you haven't captured in the shooting of it, to excite the audience, to create the impression that something is happening when something isn't, and also to create little emotional touchstones which you can draw upon as the story changes—so that the music that seemed so innocent and sweet earlier, in new circumstances brings on a whole other set of feelings."

— Jonathan Demme, director

9.14   In *Jules and Jim,* an idyllic bicycle ride in the country introduces the main musical theme associated with the three characters' relations.

9.15   Catherine discards the vitriol, which she has said is "for lying eyes."

9.16   The camera slowly arcs around the statue as a new musical motif is introduced.

9.17   The sadness of the ending is undercut by the lilting whirlwind waltz.

But at the scene's end, as Jim bids Catherine farewell, the original woodwind version of her theme recalls her mystery and the risk he is running by falling in love with her. Similarly, when Jim and Catherine lie in bed, facing the end of their affair, the voice-over narrator says: "It was as if they were already dead" as the dangerous love theme plays. This sequence associates death with their romance and foreshadows their fate at the film's end.

A similar sort of blending can be found in the film's final scene. Catherine and Jim have drowned, and Jules is overseeing the cremation of their bodies. As shots of the coffins dissolve into detailed shots of the cremation process, the enigma motif segues into its sinister variant, the menace motif. But as Jules leaves the cemetery and the narrator comments that Catherine had wanted her ashes to be cast to the winds, the string instruments glide into a sweeping version of the whirlwind waltz **(9.17)**. The film's musical score thus concludes by recalling the three sides of Catherine that attracted the men to her: her mystery, her menace, and her vivacious openness to experience. In such ways, a musical score can create, develop, and associate motifs that enter into the film's overall formal system.

DIMENSIONS OF FILM SOUND

We have seen what sounds consist of and how the filmmaker can take advantage of the widely different kinds of sounds available. In addition, the way in which the sounds relate to other film elements gives them several other dimensions. First, because sound occupies a duration, it has a *rhythm*. Second, sound can relate to its perceived source with greater or lesser *fidelity*. Third, sound conveys a sense of the *spatial* conditions in which it occurs. And, fourth, the sound relates to visual events that take place in a specific time, and this relationship gives sound a *temporal* dimension. These categories reveal that sound in film offers a great many creative possibilities to the filmmaker.

Rhythm

Rhythm is one of the most powerful aspects of sound, for it works on our bodies at deep levels. We have already considered it in relation to mise-en-scene (p. 217) and editing (p. 303). As we suggested, rhythm involves, minimally, a *beat* or pulse, a *tempo* or pace, and a pattern of *accents,* or stronger and weaker beats. In the realm of sound, all of these features are naturally most recognizable in film music, since there beat, tempo, and accent are basic compositional features. In our examples from *Jules and Jim* (pp. 357–359), the motifs can be characterized as having a $^3/_4$ metrical pulse, putting an accent on the first beat, and displaying variable tempo—sometimes slow, sometimes fast.

Speech also has rhythm. People can be identified by voice prints that show not only characteristic frequencies and amplitudes but also distinct patterns of pacing and syllabic stress. In fictional films, speech rhythm is a matter for the performer's control, but the sound editor can also manipulate it at the dubbing phase.

Sound effects have distinct rhythmic qualities as well. The plodding hooves of a farmhorse differ from a cavalry company riding at full speed. The reverberating tone of a gong may offer a slowly decaying accent, while a sudden sneeze provides a brief one. In a gangster film, a machine gun's fire creates a regular, rapid beat, while the sporadic reports of pistols may come at irregular intervals.

Rhythm in Sound and Image: Coordination

Any consideration of the rhythmic uses of sound is complicated by the fact that the movements in the images have a rhythm as well, distinguished by the same principles of beat, tempo, and accent. In addition, the editing has a rhythm. As we have seen, a succession of short shots helps create a rapid tempo, whereas shots held longer tend to slow down the rhythm.

In most cases the rhythms of editing, of movement within the image, and of sound all cooperate. Possibly the most common tendency is for the filmmaker to match visual and sonic rhythms to each other. In a dance sequence in a musical, the figures move about at a rhythm determined by the music. But variation is always possible. In the "Waltz in Swing Time" number in *Swing Time,* the dancing of Astaire and Rogers moves quickly in time to the music. But no fast cutting accompanies this scene. Indeed, the scene consists of a single long take from a long-shot distance.

Another prototype of close coordination between screen movement and sound comes in the animated films of Walt Disney in the 1930s. Mickey Mouse and other Disney characters often move in exact synchronization with the music, even when they are not dancing. (As we have seen, such exactness was possible because the sound track was recorded in advance of the drawing of the cels.) Matching movement to music came to be known as *Mickey Mousing.* Films other than musicals and cartoons, however, often exploit correspondences among musical and pictorial rhythms. (See Box.)

Rhythm in Sound and Image: Disparities

The filmmaker may also choose to create a disparity among the rhythms of sound, editing, and image. One of the most common options is to edit dialogue scenes in ways that cut against natural speech rhythms. In our specimen of dialogue overlap from McTiernan's *The Hunt for Red October* (9.9–9.11), the editing does not coincide with accented beats, cadences, or pauses in the officer's speech. By cutting "against" the rhythm of his lines, the editing smoothes over the changes of shot and emphasizes the words and facial expressions of Captain Ramius. If the filmmaker wants to emphasize the speaker and the speech, the cuts usually come at pauses or natural stopping points in the line. McTiernan uses this sort of rhythmic cutting at other points in the film.

The filmmaker may contrast the rhythm of sound and picture in more noticeable ways. For instance, if the source of sound is primarily offscreen, the filmmaker can utilize the behavior of onscreen figures to create an expressive counter-rhythm. Toward the end of John Ford's *She Wore a Yellow Ribbon,* the

Rythym on Two Tracks: A Dance of Death in *The Last of the Mohicans*

It isn't only musicals and cartoons that exploit correspondences among musical and pictorial rhythms. The climax of Michael Mann's *The Last of the Mohicans* uses a dance to accompany a violent action sequence (9.18–9.26). The hero Hawkeye, his father Chingachgook, and his brother Uncas rescue Cora from a Huron village and pursue the ruthless Magua, who has taken Cora's sister Alice along a cliff. Although the sequence lasts over eight minutes, only one word is heard. The sound track is dominated by music, against which sounds of running feet and clashing weapons stand out. Instead of the typical thunderous action score, full of roaring brass and pounding drums, Mann's composer Trevor Jones supplies a grave Scottish quarter-time dance.

The music fulfills several functions. Uncas is trying to rescue Cora because he loves her. So the main musical motif here recalls an earlier love scene at the fort, where the same tune was heard at a gathering. By presenting the pursuit and combat as a dance, the score also invests the warriors' trim movements with extra grace. Overall, the sequence gains in propulsive excitement by the implacable beat and some close synchronization between melodic turns, actors' gestures, and cutting. The action and the editing are often timed to the music, so that a new shot—such as the sudden cut to a mountain landscape as the pursuit moves upland—may coincide with a musical accent. While not minimizing the ferocity of the combat, the score evokes unfulfilled love, as poignant melodic material weaves in and out of the relentless pulse.

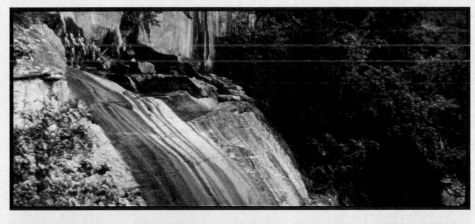

9.18   The first part of the sequence, scored for fiddle, mandolin, and harpsichord, presents a throbbing $^4/_4$ beat and a rapid dancelike tune as Hawkeye, Cora, and Uncas race up the mountain.

9.19   The crosscutting alternates shots of the pursuers with shots of Magua's band. When the chase moves to the mountain ledge, the whole orchestra joins in.

9.20 Uncas charges the lead warriors, and sharp blows stand out against the music's implacable beat.

9.21 The tempo of the fight between Uncas and Magua slows, and the fiddle is submerged in drawn-out string chords, as if time is winding down.

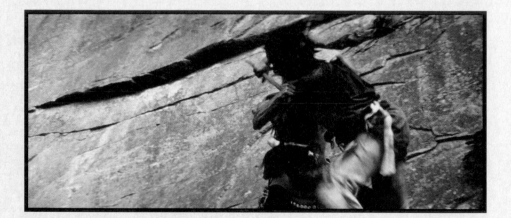

9.22 After Magua has slit Uncas's throat and shoved him off the ledge, somber chords repeat a seesaw pulse, as if time has halted. Alice sidles to the ledge, and in slow motion she turns to look down. She will soon leap off, following Uncas in death.

9.23 As Chingachgook and Hawkeye race even more urgently toward Magua's band, the rapid fiddling returns, now accompanied by full orchestration. Unlike the time-stretching in the passage of Uncas's death, Mann depicts their charge with elliptical editing, accelerating their drive for vengeance.

9.24 Chingachgook's attack on Magua consists of four precise blows of his battle-ax, and each blow coincides with the third beat in a series of musical measures.

9.25 In the final moment of their combat, when the two warriors stand frozen opposite one another, the shot lasts three beats. Then, on the fourth beat, Chingachgook delivers the fatal blow.

9.26 As Magua topples over, the music's pulse becomes a prolonged string chord.

aging cavalry captain, Nathan Brittles, watches his troops ride out of the fort just after he has retired. He regrets leaving the service and desires to go with the patrol. The sound of the scene consists of two elements: the cheerful title song sung by the departing riders, and the quick hoofbeats of their horses. Yet only a few of the shots show the horses and singers, who ride at a rhythm matched to the sound. Instead, the scene concentrates our attention on Brittles, standing almost motionless by his own horse. The contrast of brisk musical rhythm and the static images of the solitary Brittles functions expressively to emphasize his regret at having to stay behind for the first time in many years.

At times, accompanying music might even seem rhythmically inappropriate to the images. At intervals in *Four Nights of a Dreamer* Robert Bresson presents shots of a large, floating nightclub cruising the Seine. The boat's movement is slow and smooth, yet the sound track consists of lively calypso music. (Not until a later scene do we discover that the music comes from a band aboard the boat.) The strange combination of fast sound tempo with the slow passage of the boat creates a languorous, mysterious effect.

Jacques Tati does something similar in *Play Time.* In a scene outside a Parisian hotel, tourists climb aboard a bus to go to a nightclub. As they file slowly up the steps, raucous jazzy music begins. The music startles us because it seems inappropriate to the images. In fact, it primarily accompanies action in the next scene, in which some carpenters awkwardly carrying a large plate-glass window seem to be dancing to the music. By starting the fast music over an earlier scene of slower visual rhythm, Tati creates a comic effect and prepares for a transition to a new locale.

In Chris Marker's *La Jetée* the contrast between image and sound rhythms dominates the entire film. *La Jetée* is made up almost entirely of still shots; except for one tiny gesture, all movement within the images is eliminated. Yet the film utilizes voice-over narration, music, and sound effects of a generally rapid, constantly accented, rhythm. Despite the absence of movement, the film does not seem uncinematic, partly because it offers a dynamic interplay of audio-visual rhythms.

These examples suggest some of the ways in which rhythms may be combined. But of course most films also vary their rhythms from one point to another.

A change of rhythm may function to shift our expectations. In the famous battle on the ice in *Alexander Nevsky,* Sergei Eisenstein develops the sound from slow tempos to fast and back to slow. The first twelve shots of the scene show the Russian army anticipating the attack of the German knights. The shots are of moderate length, and they contain very little movement. The music is comparably slow, consisting of short, distinctly separated, chords. Then, as the German army rides into sight over the horizon, both the visual movement and the tempo of the music increase quickly, and the battle begins. At the end of the battle Eisenstein creates another contrast with a long passage of slow, lamenting music, majestic tracking shots, and little figure movement.

Fidelity

By fidelity we do not mean the quality of recording. In our sense, fidelity refers to the extent to which the sound is faithful to the source as we conceive it. If a film shows us a barking dog and we hear a barking noise, that sound is faithful to its source; the sound maintains fidelity. But if the picture of the barking dog is accompanied by the sound of a cat meowing, there enters a disparity between sound and image—a lack of fidelity.

From our standpoint, fidelity has nothing to do with what originally made the sound in production. As we have seen, the filmmaker may manipulate sound independently of image. Accompanying the image of a dog with the meow is no more difficult than accompanying the image with a bark. If the viewer takes the sound to be coming from its source in the diegetic world of the film, then it is faithful, regardless of its actual source in production.

Fidelity is thus purely a matter of expectation. Even if our dog emits a bark on screen, perhaps in production the bark came from a different dog or was electronically synthesized. We do not know what laser guns really sound like, but we accept the whang they make in *Return of the Jedi* as plausible. (In production, their sound was made by hammering guy wires that anchored a radio tower.)

When we do become aware that a sound is unfaithful to its source, that awareness is usually used for comic effect. In Jacques Tati's *Mr. Hulot's Holiday* much humor arises from the opening and closing of a dining room door. Instead of simply recording a real door, Tati inserts a twanging sound like a plucked cello string each time the door swings. Aside from being amusing in itself, this sound functions to emphasize the rhythmic patterns created by waiters and diners passing through the door. Because many of the jokes in *Mr. Hulot's Holiday* and other Tati films are based on quirkily unfaithful noises, his films are good specimens for the study of sound.

Another master of comically unfaithful sound is René Clair. In several scenes of *Le Million* sound effects occur that are not faithful to their sources. When the hero's friend drops a plate, we hear not shattering crockery but the clash of cymbals. Later, during a chase scene, when characters collide, the impact is portrayed by a heavy bass drum beat. Similar manipulations of fidelity commonly occur in animated cartoons. In Chapter 5, we saw how in *Duck Amuck* Daffy's guitar seems to emit the sounds of a machine gun and a donkey's bray (5.88).

But as with low- or high-angle framings, we have no recipe that will allow us to interpret every manipulation of fidelity as comic. Some nonfaithful sounds have serious functions. In Hitchcock's *The Thirty-Nine Steps* a landlady discovers a corpse in an apartment. A shot of her screaming face is accompanied by a train whistle; then the scene shifts to an actual train. Though the whistle is not a faithful sound for an image of a screaming person, it provides a dramatic transition.

In some cases fidelity may be manipulated by a change in volume. A sound may seem unreasonably loud or soft in relation to other sounds in the film. Curtis Bernhardt's *Possessed* alters volume in ways that are not faithful to the sources. The central character is gradually falling deeper into mental illness. In one scene she is alone, very distraught, in her room on a rainy night, and the narration restricts us to her range of knowledge. But sound devices enable the narration to achieve subjective depth as well. We begin to hear things as she does; the ticking of the clock and dripping of raindrops gradually magnify in volume. Here the shift in fidelity functions to suggest a psychological state, a movement from the character's heightened perception into sheer hallucination.

Space

Sound has a spatial dimension because it comes from a *source.* Our beliefs about that source have a powerful effect on how we understand the sound.

Diegetic Versus Nondiegetic Sound   For purposes of analyzing narrative form, we described events taking place in the story world as *diegetic* (p. 71). For this reason, **diegetic sound** is sound that has a source in the story world. The words spoken by the characters, sounds made by objects in the story, and music represented as coming from instruments in the story space are all diegetic sound.

Diegetic sound is often hard to notice as such. It may seem to come naturally from the world of the film. But as we saw in the sequence of the Ping-Pong game in *Mr. Hulot's Holiday,* the filmmaker may manipulate diegetic sound in ways that are not at all realistic.

Alternatively, there is **nondiegetic sound,** which is represented as coming from a source outside the story world. Music added to enhance the film's action is the most common type of nondiegetic sound. When Roger Thornhill is climbing Mount Rushmore in *North by Northwest* and tense music comes up, we do not expect to see an orchestra perched on the side of the mountain. Viewers understand that *movie music* is a convention and does not issue from the world of the story. The same holds true for the so-called omniscient narrator, the disembodied voice that gives us information but does not belong to any of the characters in the film. An example is *The Magnificent Ambersons,* in which the director Orson Welles speaks the nondiegetic narration.

Nondiegetic sound effects are also possible. In *Le Million* various characters all pursue an old coat with a winning lottery ticket in the pocket. The chase converges backstage at the opera, where the characters race and dodge around one another, tossing the coat to their accomplices. But instead of putting in the sounds coming from the actual space of the chase, Clair fades in the sounds of a football game. Because the maneuvers of the chase do look like a scrimmage, with the coat serving as a ball, this enhances the comedy of the sequence **(9.27).** Although we hear a crowd cheering and a referee's whistle, we do not assume that the characters present are making these sounds. (Thus this is not a manipulation of fidelity, as with the earlier cases from *Le Million.*)

Entire films may be made with completely nondiegetic sound tracks. Conner's *A Movie,* Kenneth Anger's *Scorpio Rising,* and Derek Jarman's *War Requiem* use only nondiegetic music. Similarly, many compilation documentaries include no diegetic sound; instead, omniscient voice-over commentary and orchestral music guide our response to the images.

As with fidelity, the distinction between diegetic and nondiegetic sound does not depend on the real source of the sound in the filmmaking process. Rather, it

9.27 Nondiegetic sound effects create comedy in *Le Million* by creating a sort of audio-visual pun.

depends on our understanding of the conventions of film viewing. We know that certain sounds are represented as coming from the story world, while others are represented as coming from outside the space of the story events. Such viewing conventions are so common that we usually do not have to think about which type of sound we are hearing at any moment.

At many times, however, a film's narration deliberately blurs boundaries between different spatial categories. Such a play with convention can be used to puzzle or surprise the audience, to create humor or ambiguity, or to achieve other purposes.

Resources of Diegetic Sound   We know that the space of the narrative action is not limited to what we can see on the screen at a given moment. If we already understand that several people are present in a room, we can see a shot that shows only one person without assuming that the other people have left. We simply have a sense that those people are offscreen. And if one of those offscreen people speaks, we still assume that the sound is coming from part of the story space. Thus diegetic sound can be either *onscreen* or *offscreen,* depending on whether its source is within the frame or outside the frame.

A shot shows a character talking, and we hear the sound of his or her voice. Another shot shows a door closing, and we hear a slam. A person plays a fiddle, and we hear its notes. In each case the source of the sound is in the story (diegetic) and visible within the frame (onscreen). But the shot may show only a person listening to a voice without the speaker being seen. Or a shot might show a character running down a corridor and the sound of an unseen door slamming. Or an audience can be shown listening while the sound of a fiddle is heard. In all of these instances, the sounds come from within the story (again diegetic) but are now in a space outside the frame (offscreen).

At first this may seem a trivial distinction, but we know from our study of framing in Chapter 7 how powerful offscreen space can be. Offscreen sound can suggest space extending beyond the visible action. In *American Graffiti,* a film that plays heavily on the distinction between diegetic and nondiegetic music, offscreen sounds of car radios often suggest that all of the cars on a street are tuned to the same radio station.

Offscreen sound may also control our expectations about offscreen space. In *His Girl Friday* Hildy goes into the pressroom to write her final story. As she chats with the other reporters, a loud clunk comes from an unseen source. Hildy glances offscreen left, and immediately a new space comes to our attention. She walks to the window and sees a gallows being prepared for an execution. Here offscreen sound initiates the discovery of a new area of action.

Offscreen sound can make the film's narration less restricted. In John Ford's *Stagecoach,* the stagecoach is desperately fleeing from a band of Indians. The ammunition is running out, and all seems lost until a troop of cavalry suddenly arrives. Yet Ford does not present the situation this baldly. He shows a medium close-up of one of the passengers, Hatfield, who has just discovered that he is down to his last bullet (**9.28**). He glances off right and raises his gun (**9.29**). The camera pans right to a woman, Lucy, praying. During all this, orchestral music, including bugles, plays nondiegetically. Unseen by Lucy, the gun comes into the frame from the left as Hatfield prepares to shoot her to prevent her from being captured by the Indians (**9.30**). But before he shoots, an offscreen gunshot is heard, and Hatfield's hand and gun drop down out of the frame (**9.31**). Then bugle music becomes somewhat more prominent. Lucy's expression changes as she says, "Can you hear it? Can you hear it? It's a bugle. They're blowing the charge" (**9.32**). Only then does Ford cut to the cavalry itself racing toward the coach.

"[Sound] doesn't have to be in-your-face, traditional, big sound effects. You can especially say a lot about the film with ambiences—the sounds for things you don't see. You can say a lot about where they are geographically, what time of day it is, what part of the city they're in, what kind of country they're in, the season it is. If you're going to choose a cricket, you can choose a cricket not for strictly geographic reasons. If there's a certain cricket that has a beat and a rhythm to it, it adds to the tension of a scene."

— Gary Rydstrom, sound editor

9.28 *Stagecoach.*

9.29 *Stagecoach.*

9.30 *Stagecoach.*

9.31 *Stagecoach.*

9.32 *Stagecoach.*

Rather than showing the cavalry riding to the rescue, the film's narration uses offscreen sound to restrict our awareness to the initial despair of the passengers and their growing hope as they hear the distant sound. The sound of the bugle also emerges imperceptibly out of the nondiegetic music. Only Lucy's line tells us that this is a diegetic sound that signals their rescue, at which point the narration becomes far less restricted.

Diegetic sound harbors other possibilities. Often a filmmaker uses sound to represent what a character is thinking. We hear the character's voice speaking his or her thoughts even though that character's lips do not move; presumably other characters cannot hear these thoughts. Here the narration uses sound to achieve subjectivity, giving us information about the mental state of the character. Such spoken thoughts are comparable to mental images on the visual track. A character may also remember words, snatches of music, or events as represented by sound effects. In this case the technique is comparable to a visual flashback.

The use of sound to enter a character's mind is so common that we need to distinguish between **internal** and **external diegetic sound.** External diegetic sound is that which we as spectators take to have a physical source in the scene. Internal diegetic sound is that which comes from inside the mind of a character; it is subjective. (Nondiegetic and internal diegetic sounds are often called **sound over** because they do not come from the real space of the scene.)

In the Laurence Olivier version of *Hamlet,* for example, the filmmaker presents Hamlet's famous soliloquies as interior monologues. Hamlet is the source of the thoughts we hear represented as speech, but the words are only in his mind, not in his objective surroundings. David Lynch makes interior monologue a central device in *Dune,* in which nearly every major character is given passages of internal diegetic observations. These are not lengthy soliloquies but rather brief phrases slipped into pauses in normal conversation scenes. The result is an omniscient narration that unexpectedly plunges into mental subjectivity. The characters' voiced thoughts sometimes interweave with the external dialogue so tightly that they create a running commentary on a scene's action.

A more complex use of internal diegetic sound occurs in Wim Wenders's *Wings of Desire.* Dozens of people are reading in a large public library **(9.33).** Incidentally, this sequence also constitutes an interesting exception to the general rule that one character cannot hear another's internal diegetic sound. The film's premise is that Berlin is patrolled by invisible angels who can tune in to humans' thoughts. This is a good example of how the conventions of a genre (here, the fantasy film) and the film's specific narrative context can modify a traditional device.

9.33 As the camera tracks past the readers in *Wings of Desire,* we hear their thoughts as a throbbing murmur of many voices in many languages.

9.34 In this scene from *The Magnificent Ambersons,* the woman with the teacup makes a remark about Isabel Amberson's future children . . .

To summarize: Sound may be diegetic (in the story space) or nondiegetic (outside the story space). If it is diegetic, it may be onscreen or offscreen, and internal (subjective) or external (objective).

Playing with the Diegetic/Nondiegetic Distinction

In most sequences, the sources of the sounds are clearly diegetic or nondiegetic. But some films blur the distinction between diegetic and nondiegetic sound, as we saw in the cavalry-rescue scene of *Stagecoach.* Since we are used to identifying a sound's source easily, a film may try to cheat our expectations.

At the beginning of Mel Brooks's *Blazing Saddles,* we hear what we think is nondiegetic musical accompaniment for a cowboy's ride across the prairie—until he rides past Count Basie and his orchestra. This joke depends on a reversal of our expectations about the convention of nondiegetic music. A more elaborate example is the 1986 musical version of *Little Shop of Horrors.* There a trio of female singers strolls through many scenes, providing musical commentary on the action without any of the characters noticing them. (To complicate matters, the three singers also appear in minor diegetic roles and only then do they interact with the main characters.)

More complicated is a moment in *The Magnificent Ambersons* when Welles creates an unusual interplay between the diegetic and nondiegetic sounds. A prologue to the film outlines the background of the Amberson family and the birth of the son, George. We see a group of townswomen gossiping about the marriage of Isabel Amberson, and one predicts that she will have "the worst spoiled lot of children this town will ever see" **(9.34).** This scene has presented diegetic dialogue. After this conversation ends, the nondiegetic narrator resumes his description of the family history. Over a shot of the empty street, he says, "The prophetess proved to be mistaken in a single detail merely; Wilbur and Isabel did not have *children.* They had only one." But at this point, still over the shot of the street, we hear the gossiper's voice again: "Only one! But I'd like to know if he isn't spoiled enough for a whole carload" **(9.35).** After her line, the narrator goes on, "Again, she found none to challenge her. George Amberson Minifer, the Major's one grandchild, was a princely terror." During this description, a pony cart comes up the street, and we see George for the first time **(9.36).** In this exchange the woman seems to reply to the narrator, even though we must assume that she cannot hear what he says. (After all, she is a character in the story and he is not.) Here Welles playfully departs from conventional usage to emphasize the arrival of the story's main character and the hostility of the townspeople to him.

9.35 . . . that the nondiegetic narrator's voice corrects in the next shot.

9.36 As the woman seems to reply to the narrator, Isabel's son moves into view.

This passage from *The Magnificent Ambersons* juxtaposes diegetic and nondiegetic sounds in a disconcerting way. In other films a single sound may be ambiguous because it could fall into either category. In the opening of *Apocalypse Now,* the throbbings of the ceiling fan and the helicopter blades are clearly diegetic, but Coppola accompanies these with The Doors' song "The End." This might be taken as either a subjective part of the character's Vietnam fantasy or as nondiegetic, an external commentary on the action in the manner of normal movie music.

Similarly, at a major point in Paul Thomas Anderson's *Magnolia,* several characters are shown in different locations, each singing softly along with an Aimee Mann song, "Save Me." When the sequence begins in Claudia's apartment, the song might be taken as diegetic and offscreen, since she has been listening to Aimee Mann music in an earlier scene. But then Anderson cuts to other characters elsewhere singing along, even though they cannot be hearing the music in Claudia's apartment. It would seem that the sound is now nondiegetic, with the characters accompanying it as they might do in a musical. The sequence underlines the parallels among several suffering characters and gives the sequence an eerie sense of disparate people for once on the same emotional wavelength. The sound also works with the crosscutting to pull the characters together for the climax, when their lives will converge more directly.

A more disturbing uncertainty about whether a sound is diegetic or not often crops up in the films of Jean-Luc Godard. He narrates some of his films in nondiegetic voice-over, but in other films, such as *Two or Three Things I Know about Her,* he seems also to be in the story space, whispering questions or comments whose sound perspective makes them seem close to the camera. Godard does not claim to be a character in the action, yet the characters on the screen sometimes behave as though they hear him. This uncertainty as to diegetic or nondiegetic sound sources enables Godard to stress the conventionality of traditional sound usage.

Sound and Perspective

One characteristic of diegetic sound is the possibility of suggesting the **sound perspective.** This is a sense of spatial distance and location analogous to the cues for visual depth and volume that we get with visual perspective. "I like to think," remarks sound designer Walter Murch, "that I not only record a sound but the space between me and the sound: The subject that generates the sound is merely what causes the surrounding space to resonate."

Sound perspective can be suggested by volume. A loud sound tends to seem near; a soft one, more distant. The horses' hooves in the *Seven Samurai* battle and the bugle call from *Stagecoach* exemplify how rising volume suggests closer distance. Sound perspective is also created by timbre. The combination of directly registered sounds and sounds reflected from the environment creates a timbre specific to a given distance. Such timbre effects are most noticeable with echoes. In *The Magnificent Ambersons* the conversations that take place on the baroque staircase have a distinct echo, giving the impression of huge, empty spaces around the characters.

Multichannel recording and reproduction tremendously increase the filmmaker's ability to suggest sound perspective. In most 35mm theaters equipped with multitrack sound systems, three speakers are located behind the screen. The center speaker transmits most of the onscreen dialogue, as well as the most important effects and music. The left and right speakers are stereophonic, carrying not only important dialogue but also sound effects, music, and minor dialogue. These channels can suggest a region of sound within the frame or just offscreen. Surround channels principally carry minor sound effects, and they are divided among several speakers arranged along the sides and in the back of the theater.

By using stereophonic and surround tracks, a film can more strongly imply a sound's distance and placement. In farcical comedies like *The Naked Gun* and *Hot Shots,* stereophonic sound can suggest collisions and falls outside the frame. Without the greater localization offered by the stereophonic channels, we might scan the frame for sources of the sounds. Even the center channel can be used to localize an offscreen object. In the climactic scene of *The Fugitive,* Richard Kimble is sneaking up on the friend who has betrayed him, and he reaches down past the lower frame line. As he slides his arm to the right, we hear a rolling clank telling us that there is an iron bar below the image.

In addition, stereo reproduction can specify a moving sound's direction. In David Lean's *Lawrence of Arabia,* for instance, the approach of planes to bomb a camp is first suggested through a rumble occurring only on the right side of the screen. Lawrence and an officer look off right, and their dialogue identifies the source of the sound. Then, when the scene shifts to the besieged camp itself, the sound slides from channel to channel, suggesting the planes swooping overhead.

With stereophonic and surround channels, a remarkably convincing three-dimensional sound environment may be created within the theater. Sound sources can alter in position as the camera pans or tracks through a locale. The *Star Wars* series uses multiple-channel sound to suggest space vehicles whizzing not only across the screen but also above and behind the spectators.

Like other techniques, sound localization in the theater need not be used for realistic purposes. *Apocalypse Now* divides its six-track sound among three channels in the rear of the theater and three in the front. In the film's first sequence, mentioned above, the protagonist Ben Willard is seen lying on his bed. Shots of his feverish face are superimposed on shots of U.S. helicopters dropping napalm on the Vietnamese jungle. The sound oscillates between internal and external status, as Willard's mind turns the whoosh of a ceiling fan into the whir of helicopter blades. These subjective sounds issue from both the front and the back of the theater.

Abruptly, a POV shot tracking toward the window suggests that Willard has gotten to his feet and is walking. As the camera moves, the noises fade from all rear speakers and become concentrated in the front ones at screen left, right, and center. Then, as Willard's hand opens the venetian blinds to reveal his vision of the street outside, the sound fades out of the left and right front speakers and is heard only from the center channel. Our attention has been narrowed: As we leave Willard's mind, the sound steers us back to the outside world, which is rendered as unrealistically monophonic. In addition, the disparity in acoustic dimensions suggests that the protagonist's wraparound memory of jungle destruction is richer than the pallid environment of Saigon.

Time

Sound also permits the filmmaker to represent time in various ways. This is because the time represented on the sound track may or may not be the same as that represented in the image.

The most straightforward audio-visual relations involve sound–image synchronization. The matching of sound with image in projection creates **synchronous sound.** In that case we hear the sound at the same time as we see the source produce the sound. Dialogue between characters is normally synchronized so that the lips of the actors move at the same time that we hear the appropriate words.

When the sound does go out of synchronization during a viewing (often through an error in projection or lab work), the result is quite distracting. But some filmmakers have obtained imaginative effects by putting **asynchronous,** or out-of-sync,

sound into the film itself. One such effect occurs in a scene in the musical by Gene Kelly and Stanley Donen, *Singin' in the Rain.* In the early days of Hollywood sound filming, a pair of silent screen actors have just made their first talking picture, *The Dueling Cavalier.* Their film company previews the film for an audience at a theater. In the earliest days of talkies, sound was often recorded on a phonograph record to be played along with the film; hence the chances of the sound's getting out of synchronization with the picture were much greater than they are today. This is what happens in the preview of *The Dueling Cavalier.* As the film is projected, it slows down momentarily, but the record keeps running. From this point all the sounds come several seconds before their sources are seen in the image. A line of dialogue begins, *then* the actor's lips move. A woman's voice is heard when a man moves his lips and vice versa. The humor of this disastrous preview in *Singin' in the Rain* depends on our realization that the synchronization of sound and image is an illusion produced by mechanical means.

A lengthier play with our expectations about synchronization comes in Woody Allen's *What's Up, Tiger Lily?* Allen has taken an Asian spy film and dubbed a new sound track on, but the English-language dialogue is not a translation of the original. Instead, it creates a new story in comic juxtaposition with the original images. Much of the humor results from our constant awareness that the words are not perfectly synchronized with the actors' lips. Allen has turned the usual problems of the dubbing of foreign films into the basis of his comedy.

Synchronization relates to screen duration, or *viewing* time. As we have seen in Chapter 3, narrative films can also present *story* and *plot* time. To recall the distinction: Story time consists of the order, duration, and frequency of all the events pertinent to the narrative, whether they are shown to us or not. Plot time consists of the order, duration, and frequency of the events actually represented in the film. Plot time shows us selected story events but only refers to others. Thus it usually covers a shorter span than the complete story does.

Story and plot time can be manipulated by sound in two principal ways. If the sound takes place at the same time as the image in terms of the story events, it is **simultaneous sound.** This is by far the most common usage. When characters speak onscreen, the words we hear are occurring at the same moment in the plot's action as in story time.

But it is possible for the sound we hear to occur earlier or later in the story than the events that we see in the image. In this manipulation of story order, the sound becomes **nonsimultaneous.** The most common example of this is the sonic flashback. For instance, we might see a character onscreen in the present but hear another character's voice from an earlier scene. By means of nonsimultaneous sound, the film can give us information about story events without showing them to us. And nonsimultaneous sound may, like simultaneous sound, have either an external or internal source—that is, a source in the objective world of film or the subjective realms of the character's mind.

As these categories suggest, temporal relationships in the cinema are complex. To help distinguish them, **Table 9.2** sums up the possible temporal and spatial relationships that image and sound can display.

Diegetic Sound   Because the first and third of these possibilities are comparatively uncommon, we start by commenting on the second, most common, option.

2. *Sound simultaneous in story with image.* This is by far the most common temporal relation that sound has in fiction films. Noise, music, or speech that comes from the space of the story almost invariably occurs at the same time as

TABLE 9.2   Temporal Relations of Sound in Cinema

Time	Space of Source	
	Diegetic (story space)	Nondiegetic (nonstory space)
1. Nonsimultaneous: sound from *earlier* in story than image	Sound flashback; image flashforward; sound bridge	Sound marked as past put over images (e.g., sound of a John Kennedy speech put over images of United States today)
2. Sound *simultaneous* in story with image	*External:* dialogue, effects, music *Internal:* thoughts of character heard	Sound marked as simultaneous with images put over images (e.g., a narrator describing events in the present tense)
3. Nonsimultaneous: sound from *later* in story than image	Sound flashforward; image flashback with sound continuing in the present; character narrates earlier events; sound bridge	Sound marked as later put over images (e.g., reminiscing narrator of *The Magnificent Ambersons*)

the image. Like any other sort of diegetic sound, simultaneous sound can be either external (objective) or internal (subjective).

1. *Sound earlier in story than image.* Here the sound comes from an earlier point in the story than the action currently visible onscreen. A clear example occurs at the end of Joseph Losey's *Accident.* Over a shot of a driveway gate, we hear a car crash. The sound represents the crash that occurred at the *beginning* of the film. Now if there were cues that the sound was internal—that is, that a character was recalling it—it would not strictly be coming from the past, since the memory of the sound would be occurring in the present. Late in *The Sixth Sense,* for example, the protagonist recalls a crucial statement that his young patient had made to him, causing him to realize something that casts most of the previous action in an entirely new light. The boy's voice is clearly coming from the protagonist's mind at the moment of his recollection. But in the scene from *Accident,* no character is remembering the scene, so we have a fairly pure case of a sonic flashback. In this film, an unrestricted narration makes an ironic final comment on the action.

Sound may belong to an earlier time than the image in another way. The sound from one scene may linger briefly while the image is already presenting the next scene. This is called a **sound bridge.** Sound bridges of this sort may create smooth transitions by setting up expectations that are quickly confirmed, as in a scene change in Jonathan Demme's *The Silence of the Lambs* (**9.37, 9.38**).

Sound bridges can also make our expectations more uncertain. In Tim Hunter's *The River's Edge,* three high school boys are standing outside school, and one of them confesses to having killed his girlfriend. When his pals scoff, he says, "They don't believe me." There is a cut to the dead girl

9.37 One scene of *The Silence of the Lambs* ends with Clarice Starling on the telephone, as she mentions a location called the "Your Self storage facility . . ."

9.38 . . . and her voice continues, ". . . right outside central Baltimore" over the first shot of the next scene, the sign for the Your Self warehouse.

lying in the grass by the river, while on the sound track we hear one of his friends respond to him by calling it a crazy story that no one will believe. For an instant we cannot be sure whether a new scene is starting or we are seeing a cutaway to the corpse, which could be followed by a shot returning to the three boys at school. But the shot dwells on the dead girl, and after a pause we hear, with a different sound ambience: "If you brought us. . . ." Then there is a cut to a shot of the three youths walking through the woods to the river, as the same character continues, " . . . all the way out here for nothing. . . ." The friend's remark about the crazy story belongs to an earlier time than the shot of the corpse, and it is used as an unsettling sound bridge to the new scene.

3. *Sound later in story than image.* Nonsimultaneous diegetic sound may also occur at a later time than that depicted by the images. Here we are to take the images as occurring in the past and the sound as occurring in the present or future. A simple prototype occurs in many trial dramas. The testimony of a witness in the present is heard on the sound track, while the image presents a flashback to an earlier event. The same effect occurs when the film employs a reminiscing narrator, as in John Ford's *How Green Was My Valley.* Aside from a glimpse at the beginning, we do not see the protagonist Huw as a man, only as a boy, but his narration accompanies the bulk of the plot, which is set in the distant past. Huw's present-time voice on the sound track creates a strong nostalgia for the past and constantly reminds us of the pathetic decline that the characters will eventually suffer.

Since the late 1960s, it has become somewhat common for the sound from the next scene to begin while the images of the last one are still on the screen. Like the instances mentioned above, this transitional device is a sound bridge. In Wim Wenders's *American Friend,* a nighttime shot of a little boy riding in the back seat of a car is accompanied by a harsh clacking. There is a cut to a railroad station, where the timetable board flips through its metal cards listing times and destinations. Since the sound over the shot of the boy comes from the space of the later scene, this portion is nonsimultaneous.

If the sound bridge is not immediately identifiable, it can surprise or disorient the audience, as in this *American Friend* transition. A more recognizable sonic lead-in can create more clear-cut expectations about what we will see in the next scene. Federico Fellini's $8^1/_2$ takes place in a town famous for its health spa and natural springs, and several scenes have shown an outdoor orchestra playing to entertain the tourists and guests. Midway through the film a scene ends with the closing of a window on a steam bath. Near the end of the shot, we hear an orchestral version of the song "Blue Moon." There is a cut to an orchestra playing the tune in the center of the town's shopping area. Even before the new scene has established the exact locale of the action, we can reasonably expect that the musical bridge is bringing us back to the public life of the spa.

In principle, one could also have a sound flashforward. The filmmaker could, say, use the sounds that belong with scene 5 to accompany the images in scene 2. In practice, such a technique is very rare. In Godard's *Band of Outsiders,* the sound of a tiger's roar is heard as sound over, not as sound off, several scenes before we see the tiger. A more ambiguous case can be found in Godard's *Contempt.* A husband and wife quarrel, and the scene ends with her swimming out to sea while he sits quietly on a rock formation. On the sound track we hear her voice, closely miked, reciting a letter in which she tells him she has driven back to Rome with another man. Since the husband has not yet received the letter, and perhaps the wife has not yet written it, the letter and its recitation presumably come from a later point in the story. Here the sound flashforward sets up strong expectations that a later scene confirms: We see the wife and the husband's rival stopping for gas on the road. In fact, we never see a scene in which the husband receives the letter.

Nondiegetic Sound   Most nondiegetic sound has no relevant temporal relationship to the story. When mood music comes up over a tense scene, it would be irrelevant to ask if it is happening at the same time as the images, since the music has no place in the world of the action. But occasionally the filmmaker may use a type of nondiegetic sound that does have a defined temporal relationship to the story. Welles's narration in *The Magnificent Ambersons,* for instance, speaks of the action as having happened in a long-vanished era of American history.

As we watch a film, we do not mentally slot each sound into each of these spatial and temporal categories. But our categories do assist us in analysis. They offer us ways of noticing important aspects of films—especially films that play with our expectations about sounds. By becoming aware of the rich range of possibilities, we are less likely to take a film's sound track for granted and are likelier to notice unusual sound manipulations.

One such manipulation comes early in Alain Resnais's *Providence.* As the film begins, we see a mysterious house and men hunting down a wounded old man. Suddenly we are in a courtroom, where a prosecutor is interrogating a young man **(9.39).** The scene than returns to the hunt, during which the old man was apparently murdered **(9.40).** A cut returns us to the courtroom, where the prosecutor continues his sarcastic questioning **(9.41).** The young man justifies his act by saying that the man was not only dying but also turning into an animal **(9.42);** in 9.40 we had seen the man's hairy face and clawlike hands, so now we begin to see the links between the scenes. The prosecutor pauses, astonished: "Are you suggesting some kind of actual metamorphosis?" He pauses again, and a man's voice whispers, "A werewolf." The prosecutor then asks, "A werewolf, perhaps?" **(9.43).**

The whispered words startle us, for we cannot immediately account for them. Are they whispered by an unseen character offscreen? Are they subjective, conveying the thoughts of the prosecutor or witness? Are they perhaps even nondiegetic, coming from outside the story world? Only much later in the film do we find out

9.39   The prosecuting attorney in *Providence* questions a man accused of murder . . .

9.40   . . . and we see the accused confronting the old man who was killed.

9.41   The prosecuter is seen again . . .

9.42   . . . and then the accused man, who explains his actions.

9.43   The prosecutor seems to respond to a mysterious whispered voice that no one else hears.

whose voice whispered these words, and why. The whole opening of *Providence* provides an excellent extended case of how a filmmaker can play with the conventions about sound sources.

In the *Providence* sequence, we are aware of the ambiguity immediately, and it points our expectations forward, arousing curiosity as to how the whisperer can be identified. The filmmaker can also use sound to create a retrospective awareness of how we have *mis*interpreted something earlier. This occurs in Francis Ford Coppola's *The Conversation,* a film that is virtually a textbook on the manipulation of sound and image.

The plot centers on Harry Caul, a sound engineer specializing in surveillance. Harry is hired by a mysterious corporate executive to tape a conversation between a young man and woman in a noisy park. Harry cleans up the garbled tape, but when he goes to turn over the copy to his client, he suspects foul play and refuses to relinquish it.

Now Harry obsessively replays, refilters, and remixes all his tapes of the conversation. Flashback images of the couple—perhaps in his memory, perhaps not—accompany his reworking of the tape. Finally Harry arrives at a good dub, and we hear the man say, "He'd kill us if he could."

The overall situation is quite mysterious. Harry does not know who the young couple are (is the woman his client's wife or daughter?). Nevertheless Harry suspects that they are in danger from the executive. Harry's studio is ransacked, the tape is stolen, and he later finds that the executive has it. Now more than ever Harry feels that he is involved in a murder plot. After a highly ambiguous series of events, including Harry's bugging of a hotel room during which a killing takes place, Harry learns that the situation is not as he had thought.

Without giving away the revelation of the mystery, we can say that in *The Conversation* the narration misleads us by suggesting that certain sounds are objective when at the film's end we are inclined to treat them as subjective, or at least ambiguous. The film's surprise, and its lingering mysteries, rely on unsignaled shifts between external and internal diegetic sound.

The two films just discussed point to a second justification for our set of categories. These categories seem to correspond to tacit assumptions and inferences that spectators actually make. The films and our reactions to them suggest that we quickly learn to distinguish between internal and external, diegetic and nondiegetic, simultaneous and nonsimultaneous sound. We are surprised or amused when films violate these categories; we are puzzled or misled when a sound source shifts from one category to another. If these categories did not tally with our assumptions, such films as *Providence* and *The Conversation* would not have the power to undermine our expectations, to create suspense or surprise or ambiguity. Our taxonomy, then, is offered both as a tool for film analysis and as an outline of viewers' ordinary intuitions.

FUNCTIONS OF FILM SOUND: *A MAN ESCAPED*

Robert Bresson's *A Man Escaped (Un Condamné à mort c'est échappé)* illustrates how a variety of sound techniques can function throughout an entire film. The story takes place in France in 1943. Fontaine, a Resistance fighter arrested by the Germans, has been put in prison and condemned to die. But while awaiting his execution, he works at an escape plan, loosening the boards of his cell door and making ropes. Just as he is ready to put his plan in action, a boy named Jost is put into his cell. Deciding to trust that Jost is not a spy, Fontaine reveals his plan to him, and they are both able to escape.

Throughout the film, sound has many important functions. As in all of his films, Bresson emphasizes the sound track, rightly believing that sound may be just as cinematic as images. At certain points in *A Man Escaped,* Bresson even lets his sound technique dominate the image; throughout the film, we are compelled to *listen.* Indeed, Bresson is one of a handful of directors who create a complete interplay between sound and image.

Fontaine's Commentary

A key factor in guiding our perception of the action is the commentary spoken over by Fontaine himself. The voice-over is nonsimultaneous, since it occurs at a time later than the images. But it could be either internal or external sound, since we never learn whether he is simply thinking back over these events or telling them to someone.

Fontaine's narration has several functions: The commentary helps clarify the action. Certain temporal cues suggest how long Fontaine spends in prison. As we see him working at his escape plan, his voice-over tells us, "One month of patient work and my door opened." At other points he gives us additional indications of time. His commentary is particularly important during the final escape scene, where hours of action occupy only 15 minutes of viewing time and the narration is narrowly limited to what Fontaine could know. Fontaine's voice calmly tells us of his and Jost's patient, cautious progress toward freedom.

We receive other vital information through the commentary. Sometimes the narration simply states facts: that the pin Fontaine obtains came from the women's wing of the prison or that certain prison officials' quarters were at various places in the building. More strikingly, Fontaine often tells what his thoughts had been. After being beaten and put in his first cell, he wipes the blood from his face and lies down. On the track we hear his voice say, "I'd have preferred a quick death." Often the actor does not register such thoughts visually.

At some points the sound even corrects an impression given by the image. After Fontaine has been sentenced to death, he is led back to his cell and flings himself down on the bed. We might take him to be crying, but the commentary says, "I laughed hysterically. It helped." Thus the commentary adds a degree of depth to the film's narration by allowing us glimpses into Fontaine's mental states.

Yet at first much of the commentary may seem unnecessary, since it often tells us something that we can also see in the image. In one scene Fontaine wipes the blood from his face, and his voice tells us, "I tried to clean up." Again and again in the film Fontaine describes his actions as we see him perform them or just before or after them. But this use of sound is not redundantly supporting the visuals. One major function of the past-tense commentary and even the apparently redundant remarks is to emphasize the prison event as having *already* happened. Instead of simply showing a series of events in the present, the commentary places the events in the past.

Indeed, certain phrases emphasize the fact that the commentary is a remembering of events. As we see Fontaine lie down in his cell after having been beaten, his commentary says, "I believe that I gave up and wept," as if the passage of time has made him uncertain. After meeting another prisoner, Fontaine narrates, "Terry was an exception; he was allowed to see his daughter. I learned this later." Again we are aware that the meeting we see on the screen occurred at a point in the past.

Because of this difference in time between image and commentary, the narrative indicates to us that Fontaine will eventually escape rather than be executed. (The title also indicates this.) This final *result* of the narrative cause–effect chain is known. As a result, our suspense is centered on the *causes*—not *whether* Fontaine will escape, but *how* he will escape. The film guides our expectations toward the minute details of Fontaine's work to break out of prison. The commentary and the sound effects draw our attention to tiny gestures and ordinary objects that become crucial to the escape.

Furthermore, the narrative stresses that work alone is not enough, that Fontaine and the other prisoners can survive, both mentally and physically, only through their efforts to help one another. Fontaine receives aid and comfort from his fellow prisoners. His neighbor Blanchet gives him a blanket to make his ropes; another prisoner who also tries to escape, Orsini, provides vital information about how to get over the walls. Finally, Fontaine himself must extend trust to his new cellmate, Jost, by taking him along in spite of suspicions that he may be a spy planted by the Germans.

Sound Effects and Narration

The interplay between the sounds and images in *A Man Escaped* does not pertain solely to the commentary. The ability to focus our attention on details works with sound effects as well, where each object gains a specific timbre. In the long middle portion of the film, in which Fontaine works on breaking through his door and making the implements of escape, this concentration on details becomes particularly prominent. A close-up shows Fontaine's hands sharpening a spoon handle into a chisel; the loud scraping intensifies our perception of this detail. We hear distinctly the rubbing of the spoon against the boards of the door, the ripping of cloth with a razor to make ropes, even the swish of straw against the floor as Fontaine sweeps up slivers of wood. We also become intensely aware that such sounds could alert the guards to Fontaine's activities.

The concentration on details follows a general pattern in the narration of *A Man Escaped*. The narration is unusually restricted. We learn nothing that Fontaine does not know. As Fontaine looks around his cell for the first time he names the items it contains—a slop bucket, a shelf, a window. *After* he mentions each, the camera moves to give us a glimpse of it. At another point Fontaine hears a strange sound outside his cell. He moves to the door, and we get a point-of-view shot through the peephole in his door; a guard is winding the crank of a skylight in the hall. For the first time Fontaine becomes aware of the skylight, which eventually becomes his escape route.

Indeed, at times we know less than Fontaine does. When he attempts to escape from the car in the opening scene, the camera holds on his empty seat rather than moving to follow him and show his recapture. Sound aids in restricting our knowledge by controlling what we see. Later, in prison, Fontaine's neighbor Blanchet falls down during their daily walk to empty their slop buckets. We first hear the sound of his fall as the camera remains on a medium shot of Fontaine reacting in surprise. Then there is a cut to Blanchet as Fontaine moves to help him up. While the image restricts our knowledge, the sound anticipates and guides our expectations.

At times, sound in *A Man Escaped* goes beyond controlling the image; sometimes it partially *replaces* it. Several of the film's scenes are so dark that sound must play a large part in conveying information about the action. After Fontaine falls asleep in prison for the first time, there is a fade-out. While the screen is still dark, we hear his voice-over saying, "I slept so soundly, my guards had to awaken me." This is followed by the loud sound of a bolt and hinge. The light let in by the door allows us to see a faint image of a guard's hand shaking Fontaine, and we hear a voice tell him to get up. In general, the film contains many fade-outs in which the sound of the next scene begins before the image does. By putting sound over a black screen or dark image, Bresson allows the sound track an unusually prominent place in his film.

The reliance on sound culminates in the final escape scene. During much of the last 15 or 20 minutes of the film, the action takes place outdoors at night. There are no establishing shots to give us a sense of the space of the roofs and walls which Fontaine and Jost must scale. We get glimpses of gestures and settings, but often sound is our main guide to what is happening. This has the effect of intensifying the spectators' attention greatly. We must strain to understand the action from what we can glimpse and hear. We judge the pair's progress from the church bells heard tolling the hour. The train outside the walls helps cover the noise the fugitives make. Each strange noise suggests an unseen threat.

In one remarkable shot Fontaine stands in darkness by a wall, listening to the footsteps of a guard walking up and down offscreen. Fontaine knows that he must kill this man if his escape is to succeed. We hear his voice-over explaining where the guard is moving and mentioning how hard his own heart is beating. There is little movement. All we see is Fontaine's dim outline and a tiny reflection of light in his eye. Again, throughout this scene the sound concentrates our attention on the characters' most minute reactions and gestures.

"The eye solicited alone makes the ear impatient, the ear solicited alone makes the eye impatient. *Use these impatiences.*"

— Robert Bresson, director

Sound Motifs

We have discussed how a filmmaker controls not only what we hear, but also the qualities of that sound. Bresson has achieved a considerable variety in *A Man Escaped*. Every object in the film is assigned a distinct pitch. The volumes of sounds range from very loud to almost inaudible, as the opening scene illustrates. The first few shots of Fontaine riding to prison in a car are accompanied only by the soft hum of the motor. But as a streetcar blocks the road, Fontaine seeks to use the streetcar's uproar to conceal his dash from the car. The moment Fontaine leaps from the car, Bresson eliminates the streetcar noise, and we hear running feet and gunshots offscreen. Later, in the final escape, the film alternates sounds offscreen (trains, bells, bicycle, and so on) with stretches of silence. The film's sparse sound mix effectively isolates specific sounds for our attention.

Certain sounds not only are very loud but also have an echo effect added to give them a distinctive timbre. The voices of the German guards as they give Fontaine orders are reverberant and harsh compared to the voices of the French prisoners. Similarly, the noises of the handcuffs and bolts of the cell doors are magnified for the same echo effect. These manipulations suggest Fontaine's own perceptual subjectivity. Thus our reactions to Fontaine's imprisonment are intensified through the manipulation of timbre.

These devices all help focus our attention on the details of Fontaine's prison life. But there are other devices that help unify the film and sustain its narrative and thematic development. These are the sound *motifs,* which come back at significant moments of the action.

One set of auditory motifs emphasizes the space outside Fontaine's cell. We see a streetcar in the opening scene, and the bell and motor of a streetcar are heard offscreen every time Fontaine speaks to someone through his cell window. We are always aware of his goal of reaching the streets beyond the walls. During the second half of the film the sounds of trains also become important. When Fontaine is first able to leave his cell and walk in the hall unobserved, we hear a train whistle. It returns at other moments when he leaves his cell clandestinely, until the train provides the noise to cover the sounds Fontaine and Jost make during their escape.

Since the prisoners depend on one another, certain sound motifs call attention to Fontaine's interactions with the other men. For example, the daily gathering of the men to wash in a common sink becomes associated with running water. At first, the faucet is seen onscreen, but later Bresson presents the scrubbing of the prisoners in closer shots, with the sound of the water offscreen.

Some motifs become associated with defiance of the prison rules. Fontaine uses his handcuffs to tap on the wall to signal his neighbors. He coughs to cover the sound of scraping, and coughs among the prisoners become signals. Fontaine defies the guards' orders and continues to talk to the other men. There are other sound motifs in the film (bells, guns, whistles, children's voices), which share certain functions already noted: dynamizing Fontaine's escape, calling our attention to details, and guiding what we notice.

Music

Yet another auditory motif involves the only nondiegetic sound in the film, passages from a Mozart mass. The music is motivated clearly enough, since the film's plot action refers continually to religious faith. Fontaine tells another prisoner that he prays but does not expect God to help him if he does not work for his own liberty. But the pattern of the uses of the music is less clear.

We may be unable at first to form any consistent expectations about the music, and its recurrences are likely to take us by surprise. After it is heard over the credits, the music does not return for some time. Its first use over the action occurs during the first walk Fontaine takes with the men to empty their slop buckets. As the music plays, Fontaine's commentary explains the routine: "Empty your buckets and wash, back to your cell for the day." The juxtaposition of ceremonial church music with the emptying of slop buckets in a prison is an incongruous one. Yet the contrast is not ironic. Not only are these moments of movement important to Fontaine's life in the prison but they also provide his main means of direct contact with other prisoners.

The music, which comes back seven more times, emphasizes the narrative development. Fontaine meets the other men, wins their support, and finally plans to share his escape. The music reappears whenever Fontaine makes contact with another prisoner (Blanchet, Orsini) who will affect his escape. Later washing scenes have no music; these are scenes in which Fontaine's contact is cut off because Orsini decides not to go along. The music returns as Orsini attempts his own escape plan. He fails but is able to give Fontaine vital information he will need in his own attempt. The music reappears when Blanchet, once opposed to Fontaine's plan, contributes his blanket to the rope making.

Eventually the music becomes associated with the boy, Jost. It plays again as Fontaine realizes that he must either kill Jost or take him along. The final use of music comes over the very end of the film, as the two leave the prison and disappear into the night. The nondiegetic music has traced Fontaine's developing trust in the other men on whom his endeavor depends.

The musical motif constitutes the only major appearance of a relatively unrestricted narrational element—the principal moments when we move briefly outside of our limitation to Fontaine's knowledge. Thus the music is crucial in suggesting a general implicit meaning beyond what Fontaine tells us explicitly. If we follow the pattern of the music's recurrences, we might interpret the motif as suggesting the importance of trust and interdependence among the people of the prison. It is not simply the conventional mood music that accompanies the action of many films. Indeed, its very incongruity as an accompaniment to mundane actions should cue us to seek an implicit meaning of this type.

A Sample Sequence

Let us look at a brief scene from *A Man Escaped* in order to see how silence and shifts between sounds that are internal and external, simultaneous and nonsimultaneous, guide our expectations. The eleven shots indicated by **9.44–9.54** in **Table 9.3** constitute the scene in which the boy Jost is put into Fontaine's cell.

The use of silence and the oscillations between Fontaine's internal and external speech dominate the scene. We have not seen Jost before and do not know what is happening as the scene begins. Fontaine's internal commentary tells us that a new threat has appeared. Offscreen footsteps and Fontaine's gaze indicate that someone has entered his room, but the camera lingers on Fontaine. Bresson delays the cut to the newcomer for a surprisingly long time. (This first shot is as long as the other three shots combined.) The delay creates special effects. It restricts the narration considerably, since we do not know what Fontaine is reacting to. Our access to his mental state through the commentary only hints at the threat: The "he" referred to could be either a guard or another prisoner. This is one of the many small moments of suspense the narration creates.

The fact that we wait to see Jost also functions to emphasize the importance of his appearance. It directs our expectations to Fontaine's reaction (conveyed largely

TABLE 9.3 Sound and Silence in *A Man Escaped*

	Shot	Voice	Effects	Action/Camera

(1) 27 sec

9.44

F. (over): But then once again . . .

Lock rattles off

Rattle continues off — F. turns

9.45

. . . I thought I was lost.

Footsteps off — F. turns head left

Watches off left, turning head

Moves left and slightly forward; camera pans with his actions

9.46

(Over): In French and German uniform, he looked repulsively filthy.

Lock closing off
One retreating footstep off — Catches door as it closes

9.47

(Over): He seemed barely sixteen.

Echoing of locks and doors, off

Two footsteps, off

Shot	Voice	Effects	Action/Camera

9.48

F. (aloud): Are you German?

(2) 10 sec

French? What is your name?

9.49

Jost lifts head, looks off right

Jost: Jost, François Jost.

F. (over): Had they planted a spy?

9.50

(3) 10 sec

F. (over): Did they think I was ready to talk?

F. lowers eyes

9.51

TABLE 9.3   Sound and Silence in *A Man Escaped* (continued)

Shot	Voice	Effects	Action/Camera
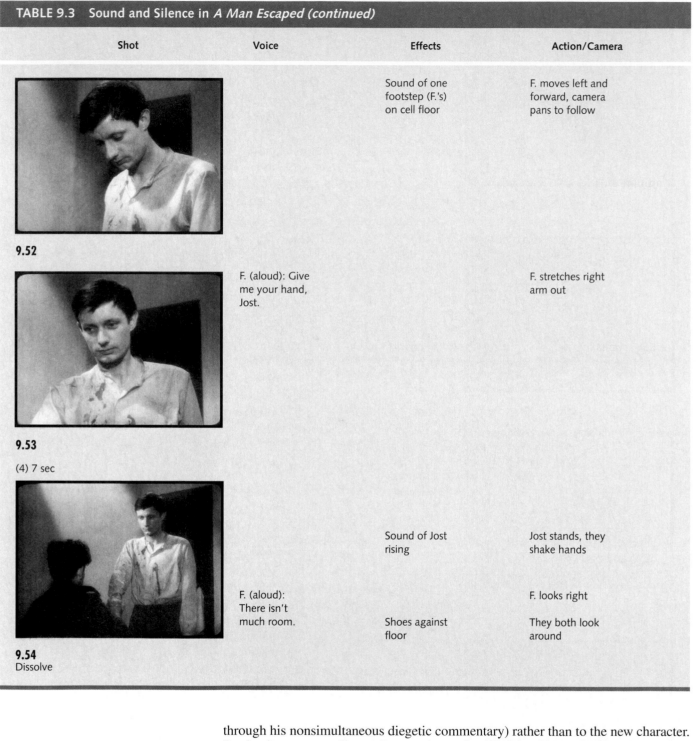**9.52**		Sound of one footstep (F.'s) on cell floor	F. moves left and forward, camera pans to follow
9.53 (4) 7 sec	F. (aloud): Give me your hand, Jost.		F. stretches right arm out
9.54 Dissolve	F. (aloud): There isn't much room.	Sound of Jost rising Shoes against floor	Jost stands, they shake hands F. looks right They both look around

through his nonsimultaneous diegetic commentary) rather than to the new character. By the time we actually see Jost, we know that Fontaine feels threatened by him and disturbed by his part-German uniform. The first words Fontaine speaks in the scene emphasize his doubt. Rather than stating a decisive attitude, he simply seeks information. Again his commentary returns as he makes clear the dilemma he is in: Jost may be a spy planted by the prison officials. Yet his words to Jost contrast with this inner doubt as he shakes hands and converses in a friendly fashion. Thus the interplay of simultaneous dialogue and nonsimultaneous narration allows the film-maker to present contrasting psychological aspects of the action.

The sound effects mark significant actions and develop the narrative progression. Fontaine's footstep is heard as he moves toward Jost after his initial reserve, and Jost's rising accompanies their first gesture of trust, the handshake. Finally, their shoes scrape against the floor as they relax and begin to speak of their situation.

This scene is very brief, but the combination of different types of sound within a few shots indicates the complexity of the film's sound track. The track, though, cannot be considered apart from its place in the entire film, functioning in interaction with other techniques and with narrative form. Through Bresson's control of what sounds we hear, what qualities these sounds have, and what relationships exist among those sounds and between sound and image, he has made this technique an important factor in shaping our experience of the whole film.

SUMMARY

As usual, both extensive viewing and intensive scrutiny will sharpen your capacity to notice the workings of film sound. You can get comfortable with the analytical tools we have suggested by asking several questions about a film's sound.

1. What sounds are present—music, speech, noise? How are loudness, pitch, and timbre used? Is the mixture sparse or dense? Modulated or abruptly changing?

2. Is the sound related rhythmically to the image? If so, how?

3. Is the sound faithful or unfaithful to its perceived source?

4. *Where* is the sound coming from? In the story's space or outside it? Onscreen or offscreen?

5. *When* is the sound occurring? Simultaneously with the story action? Before? After?

6. How are the various sorts of sounds organized across a sequence or the entire film? What patterns are formed, and how do they reinforce aspects of the film's overall formal system (narrative or non-narrative)?

7. For each of questions 1–6, what *purposes* are fulfilled and what *effects* are achieved by the sonic manipulations?

Practice at trying to answer such questions will familiarize you with the basic uses of film sound. As always, though, it is not enough to name and classify. These categories and terms are most useful when we take the next step and examine how the types of sound we identify *function* in the total film.

NOTES AND QUERIES

For material on how sound is created in film production, see Notes and Queries to Chapter 1. A delightful essay on the development of film sound is Walter Murch's "Sound Design: The Dancing Shadow," in John Boorman et al., eds., *Projections 4* (1995), pp. 237–251. The essay includes a brilliant behind-the-scenes discussion of sound mixing in *The Godfather*.

Articles on particular aspects of sound recording and reproduction in Hollywood are published in *Recording Engineer/Producer* and *Mix*. See also Jeff Forlenza and Terri Stone, eds., *Sound for Picture* (Winona, Minn.: Hal Leonard, 1993); Tom Kenny, *Sound for Picture: Film Sound through the 1990s* (Vallejo, Calif.: Mix Books, 2000); David Lewis Yewdall, *Practical Art of Motion Picture Sound*

(Boston: Focal Press, 1999); David Sonnenschein, *Sound Design: The Expressive Power of Music, Voice, and Sound Effects in Cinema* (Studio City, Calif.: Wiese, 2001); and Vincent Lo Brutto, *Sound-on-Film: Interviews with Creators of Film Sound* (New York: Praeger, 1994). Walter Murch, Hollywood's principal sound designer, explains many contemporary sound techniques in Roy Paul Madsen, *Working Cinema: Learning from the Masters* (Belmont, Calif.: Wadsworth, 1990), pp. 288–313. Our quotation on p. 370 comes from the latter source, p. 294.

A useful introduction to the psychology of listening is Robert Sekuler and Randolph Blake, *Perception,* 3d ed. (New York: McGraw-Hill, 1994). Charles Eidsvik offers rich reflections on how ambient sound works psychologically in "Background Tracks in Recent Cinema" in Joseph and Barbara Anderson, eds., *Moving Image Theory: Ecological Considerations* (Carbondale: Southern Illinois University Press, forthcoming).

The Power of Sound

Of all directors Sergei Eisenstein has written most prolifically and intriguingly about sound technique. See in particular his discussion of audio-visual polyphony in *Nonindifferent Nature,* trans. Herbert Marshall (Cambridge: Cambridge University Press, 1987), pp. 282–354. (For his discussion of music in particular, see below.) In addition, there are cryptic comments in Robert Bresson's *Notes on Cinematography,* trans. Jonathan Griffin (New York: Urizen, 1977).

The aesthetic potential of film sound is discussed in two anthologies: John Belton and Elizabeth Weis, eds., *Film Sound: Theory and Practice* (New York: Columbia University Press, 1985) and Rick Altman, ed., *Sound Theory Sound Practice* (New York: Routledge, 1992) and in "Sound and Music in the Movies," *Cinéaste* **21,** 1–2 (1995): 46–80. Critical analyses of sound in particular films include Noël Carroll, "Lang, Pabst, and Sound," *Cinétracts* **5** (Fall 1978): 15–23; Kristin Thompson, *Eisenstein's "Ivan the Terrible": A Neoformalist Analysis* (Princeton, N.J.: Princeton University Press, 1981), pp. 203–260; Alan Williams, "Godard's Use of Sound," *Camera Obscura* 8-9-10 (1982): 193–208; Robert Self, "The Sounds of *MASH*," in Peter Lehman, ed., *Close Viewings: Readings in New Film Criticism* (Sarasota: University of Florida Press, 1990), pp. 141–157; and Donald Kirihara, "Sound in *Les Vacances de Monsieur Hulot*," in Lehman, pp. 158–170. Lindley Handlon's *Fragments: Bresson's Film Style* (Rutherford, N.J.: Fairleigh Dickinson University Press, 1986) has chapters on sound in *Mouchette* and *Lancelot du Lac.*

The most prolific researcher into aesthetics of film sound is the French critic Michel Chion. His ideas are summarized in his *Audio-Vision,* trans. Claudia Gorbman (New York: Columbia University Press, 1994).

On sounds and picture editing, see Vincent Lo Brutto's *Selected Takes: Film Editors on Editing* (New York: Praeger, 1991), p. 95. Dialogue overlap is explained in detail in Edward Dmytryk, *On Film Editing* (Boston: Focal Press, 1984), pp. 47–70.

As the *Letter from Siberia* extract suggests, documentary filmmakers have experimented a great deal with sound. For other cases, watch Basil Wright's *Song of Ceylon* and Humphrey Jennings's *Listen to Britain* and *Diary for Timothy.* Analyses of sound in these films may be found in Paul Rotha, *Documentary Film* (New York: Hastings House, 1952), and Karel Reisz and Gavin Millar's *Technique of Film Editing* (New York: Hastings House, 1968), pp. 156–170.

Voice-over narration is discussed in Bill Nichols, "Documentary Theory and Practice," *Screen* **17,** 4 (Winter 1976–77): 34–48, and Eric Smoodin, "The Image and the Voice in the Film with Spoken Narration," *Quarterly Review of Film Studies* **8,** 4 (Fall 1983): 19–32. The most detailed study of fictional cinema's use of nondiegetic commentary is Sarah Kozloff's *Invisible Storytellers: Voice-Over Narration in American Fiction Film* (Berkeley: University of California Press, 1988).

Experimental films also exploit unusual aspects of sound. See Norman McLaren's "Notes on Animated Sound," *Film Quarterly* **7,** 3 (Spring 1953): 223–229 (an article on hand-drawn sound tracks), and Robert Russell and Cecile Starr, *Experimental Animation* (New York: Van Nostrand, 1976).

A wide-ranging discussion of various sound recording and reproducing systems is Stephen Handzo's "A Narrative Glossary of Film Sound Technology," in Belton and Weis, *Film Sound: Theory and Practice.* On stereophonic technology see also Michael Arick, "The Sound of Money: In Stereo!" *Sight and Sound* **57,** 1 (Winter 1987–88): 35–42, and Ronald Haver, "The Saga of Stereo in the Movies," *Perfect Vision* **1,** 1 (Winter 1986–87): 64–73. *Perfect Vision* and *Widescreen Review* report developments in modern sound reproduction.

Silent Film versus Sound Film

On the transition from silent to sound film in American cinema, see Harry M. Geduld, *The Birth of the Talkies: From Edison to Jolson* (Bloomington: Indiana University Press, 1975); Alexander Walker, *The Shattered Silents* (New York: Morrow, 1979); and chap. 23 of David Bordwell, Janet Staiger, and Kristin Thompson, *The Classical Hollywood Cinema: Film Style and Mode of Production to 1960* (New York: Columbia University Press, 1985).

It has long been assumed that cinema is predominantly a visual medium, with sound forming at best a supplement and at worst a distraction. In the late 1920s many film aestheticians protected against the coming of talkies, feeling that synchronized sound spoiled a pristine mute art. In the bad sound film, René Clair claimed, "The image is reduced precisely to the role of the illustration of a phonograph record, and the sole aim of the whole show is to resemble as closely as possible the play of which it is the 'cinematic' reproduction. In three or four settings there take place endless scenes of dialogue which are merely boring if you do not understand English but unbearable if you do" [*Cinema Yesterday and Today* (New York: Dover, 1972), p. 137]. Rudolf Arnheim, who saw the artistic potential of cinema as its inability to reproduce reality perfectly, asserted that "the introduction of the sound film smashed many of the forms that the film artists were using in favor of the inartistic demand for the greatest possible 'naturalness' (in the most superficial sense of the word)" [*Film as Art* (Berkeley: University of California Press, 1957), p. 154].

It is easy to find such beliefs anachronistic, but we must recall that many early sound films relied simply on dialogue for their novelty; both Clair and Arnheim welcomed sound effects and music but warned against talkiness. In any event, the inevitable reaction was led by André Bazin, who argued that a greater overall realism was possible in the sound cinema. See his *What Is Cinema?* Vol. 1 (Berkeley: University of California Press, 1967). Even Bazin, however, seemed to believe that sound was secondary to vision in cinema. This view is also put forth by Siegfried Kracauer in *Theory of Film* (New York: Oxford University Press, 1965). "Films with sound live up to the spirit of the medium only if the visuals take the lead in them" (p. 103).

Today, many filmmakers and filmgoers would agree with Francis Ford Coppola's remark that sound is "half the movie . . . at least." One of the major advances of film scholarship of the 1970s and 1980s was the increased and detailed attention to the sound track. The results can be seen in writings cited throughout these Notes and Queries.

Film Music

Of all the kinds of sound in cinema, music has been the most extensively discussed. The literature is voluminous, and with a recent surge of interest in film composers, many more recordings of film music have become available.

A basic introduction to music useful for film study is William S. Newman, *Understanding Music* (New York: Harper, 1961). Classic studies of film music are Kurt London, *Film Music* (New York: Hastings House, 1970); Aaron Copland, "Film Music," in *What to Listen for in Music* (New York: Signet, 1957), pp. 152–157; and Hanns Eisler's

attack on Hollywood film scoring, *Composing for the Films* (London: Dobson, 1947). A more up-to-date and detailed production guide is Fred Karlin and Rayburn Wright's *On the Track: A Guide to Contemporary Film Scoring* (New York: Schirmer, 1990). Karlin's *Listening to Movies* (New York: Schirmer, 1994) offers a lively discussion of the Hollywood tradition.

The history of film scoring is handled in lively and unorthodox ways in Russell Lack, *Twenty-Four Frames Under: A Buried History of Film Music* (London: Quartet, 1997). For Hollywood-centered histories see Roy M. Prendergast, *Film Music: A Neglected Art* (New York: Norton, 1977) and Gary Marmorstein, *Hollywood Rhapsody: Movie Music and Its Makers 1900–1975* (New York: Schirmer, 1997). See also Martin Miller Marks, *Music and the Silent Film: Contexts and Case Studies 1895–1924* (New York: Oxford University Press, 1997). Contemporary film composers are interviewed in Michael Schelle, *The Score* (Los Angeles: Silman-James, 1999); David Morgan, *Knowing the Score* (New York: HarperCollins, 2000); and Mark Russell and James Young, *Film Music* (Hove, England; Rota, 2000).

In English, the principal study of the theory of film music is Claudia Gorbman, *Unheard Melodies: Narrative Film Music* (Bloomington: Indiana University Press, 1987). A highly informed, wide-ranging meditation on the subject is Royal S. Brown, *Overtones and Undertones: Reading Film Music* (Berkeley: University of California Press, 1994). Jonathan Romney and Adrian Wootton's *Celluloid Jukebox: Popular Music and the Movies since the 50s* (London: British Film Institute, 1995) is an enjoyable collection of essays. See also Chuck Jones, "Music and the Animated Cartoon," *Hollywood Quarterly* **1,** 4 (July 1946): 364–370. A sampling of Carl Stalling's amazing cartoon sound tracks (p. 352) is available on two compact discs (Warner Bros. 9-26027-2 and 9-45430-2).

Despite the bulk of material on film music, there have been fairly few analyses of music's functions in particular films. The most famous (or notorious) is Sergei Eisenstein's "Form and Content: Practice," in *The Film Sense* (New York: Harcourt, Brace, 1942), pp. 157–216, which examines sound/image relations in a sequence from *Alexander Nevsky*. (See also Thompson, *Eisenstein's "Ivan the Terrible,"* cited above.) Claudia Gorbman has offered detailed image/sound analyses in "Music as Salvation: Notes on Fellini and Rota," *Film Quarterly* **28,** 2 (Winter 1974–75): 17–25; in "*Cleo from Five to Seven:* Music as Mirror," *Wide Angle* **4,** 4 (1981): 38–49; and in several chapters of her book *Unheard Melodies,* cited above. For other sensitive work on film music, see Graham Bruce, *Bernard Herrmann: Film Music and Narrative* (Ann Arbor: University of Michigan, 1985); Kathryn Kalinak, *Settling the Score:*

Music and the Classical Hollywood Film (Madison: University of Wisconsin Press, 1992); Jeff Smith, *The Sounds of Commerce: Marketing Popular Film Music* (New York: Columbia University Press, 1998); and Pamela Robertson Wojcik and Arthur Knight, eds., *Soundtrack Available: Essays on Film and Popular Music,* (Durham, N.C.: Duke University Press, 2001).

Dubbing and Subtitles

People beginning to study cinema may express surprise (or annoyance) that films in foreign languages are usually shown with subtitled captions translating the dialogue. Why not, some viewers ask, use dubbed versions of the films, i.e., versions in which the dialogue has been rerecorded in the audience's language? In many countries dubbing is very common. (Germany and Italy have traditions of dubbing almost every imported film.) Why, then, do most people who study movies prefer subtitles?

There are several reasons. Dubbed voices usually have a bland studio sound. Elimination of the original actors' voices wipes out an important component of their performance. (Partisans of dubbing ought to look at dubbed versions of English-language films to see how a performance by Katharine Hepburn, Orson Welles, or John Wayne can be hurt by a voice that does not fit the body.) With dubbing, all of the usual problems of translation are multiplied by the need to synchronize specific words with specific lip movements. Most important, with subtitling viewers still have access to the original sound track. By eliminating the original voice track, dubbing simply destroys part of the film.

For a survey of subtitling practice, see Jan Ivarsson and Mary Carroll, *Subtitling* (Simrishamn, Sweden: TransEdit, 1998).

Chapter 10

Style as a Formal System

At the beginning of Part Two, we saw how the different parts of a film relate to one another dynamically within its overall *form*. We have already examined one major aspect of a film's form: its organization into a categorical, rhetorical, abstract, associational, or narrative system. Now, having examined each category of techniques of the film medium, we may go on to see how these techniques interact to create another formal system of the film, its **style.** These two systems—style and narrative/non-narrative form—in turn interact within the total film.

At this point we can recall the diagram we introduced at the start of Part Four:

Film Form

interacts with

Formal System
  Narrative
  Categorical
  Rhetorical
  Abstract
  Associational

Stylistic System
  Patterned and
  significant use
  of techniques:
    Mise-en-scene
    Cinematography
    Editing
    Sound

In this diagram, we see that stylistic patterns are a major part of any film. Sometimes, though, we talk about style in several films by the same filmmaker. When we discussed sound in *A Man Escaped,* we characterized Bresson as a director who makes sound particularly important in many of his films; we analyzed several important ways in which sound related to image in *A Man Escaped.* This use of sound is one aspect of Bresson's unique style. Similarly, we looked at *Our Hospitality* in terms of how its comic mise-en-scene is organized around a consistent use of long shots; this is part of Keaton's style in other films too. Both Bresson and Keaton have distinctive filmmaking styles, and we can become familiar with those styles by analyzing the way in which they utilize techniques within whole filmic systems.

"It's what you call style in retrospect only. At the point of actually making the movie, it's just about making individual choices . . ."

— Ethan Coen, producer/writer

". . . about the best way to tell the story, scene by scene. You make specific choices that you think are appropriate or compelling or interesting for that particular scene. Then, at the end of the day, you put it all together and somebody looks at it and, if there's some consistency to it, they say, 'Well, that's their style.'"

— Joel Coen, director/writer

Further, we can also speak of a *group style*—the consistent use of techniques across the work of several filmmakers. We can speak of a German Expressionist style, or a Soviet Montage style. In Part Six, we will consider some significant group styles that have emerged in film history.

Style and the Filmmaker

No single film uses all the technical possibilities we have discussed. For one thing, historical circumstances limit the choices that filmmakers have open to them. Before 1928, for example, most filmmakers did not have the choice of using synchronized dialogue. Even today, when the range of technical choices seems far broader, there are still limits. Filmmakers cannot use the now obsolete orthochromatic film stock of the silent era, although in some respects it was superior to contemporary stocks. Similarly, a successful system for creating three-dimensional cinema images without the necessity for spectators to wear 3-D glasses has not yet been invented.

There is another reason why only some technical possibilities may be realized in a single film. Within a concrete production situation, the filmmaker must choose what techniques to employ. Typically, the filmmaker makes certain technical choices and adheres to them throughout the film. Across the film, a filmmaker will characteristically use three-point lighting, or continuity editing, or diegetic sound. A few segments might stand out as varying from the film's normal usage, but in general a film tends to rely on consistent usage of certain techniques. The film's style results from a combination of historical constraints and deliberate choice.

Filmmakers also deliberately select techniques that will point out story parallels. Piotr Sobocinski, cinematographer for Krystyf Kieslowski, says that in *Three Colors: Red,* a crane shot down to a fashion show was designed to recall an earlier camera movement, when the camera craned down as a book fell into the street. Similarly, in filming *Viva Zapata!,* Elia Kazan tracked in on Zapata, who is ignoring the fact that a crowd of peasants is marching with him: "We had to go close on that shot and dolly [i.e., track] because what I wanted to show was his expression or lack of expression. We later contrasted that with a similar dolly shot on the police chief beginning to notice what was happening. The point was to contrast those two attitudes."

Many filmmakers plan the overall style of the film to reflect the progression of the story. In the newspaper comedy–drama *The Paper,* the pace picks up as deadlines loom and personal conflicts intensify. To communicate this to the viewer, director Ron Howard not only began to cut faster but also developed a pattern of increasingly nervous camera movements. In the early part of the film the camera tracks gracefully (7.147–7.149); later, the camera is mounted on a Steadicam, which gives it more mobility but still maintains some smoothness; at the climax, many shots are hand-held and the camera movements are jerky. For *Dead Man Walking,* Tim Robbins and his cinematographer Roger Deadkins worked out a visual pattern to convey the increasing intimacy between the characters played by Susan Sarandon and Sean Penn, who talk to each other in a string of interviews spread across the film. Early scenes were shot to emphasize the wire mesh between the two, keeping it in focus and the Penn character more distant. Later, using longer lenses and slow tracking shots, the scenes minimize the barrier. Ultimately, when the characters are communicating through a cell door, reflections in the window make each one visible in the other's shot.

Style and the Viewer

The spectator has a relation to style as well. Although we are seldom conscious of the fact, we tend to have expectations about style. If we see two characters in a long shot, we expect a cut-in to a closer view. If the actor walks rightward, as if about to leave the frame, we expect the camera to pan or track right to keep the person in the shot. If a character speaks, we expect to hear diegetic sound that is faithful to its source.

Like other kinds of expectations, stylistic ones derive both from our experience of the world generally (people talk, they don't tweet) and our experience of film and other media. The specific film's style can confirm our expectations, or modify them, or cheat, or challenge them.

Many films use techniques in ways that conform to our expectations. For example, the conventions of the classical Hollywood cinema and of specific genres provide a firm basis for reinforcing our prior assumptions. Other films ask us to readjust our expectations somewhat. Keaton's *Our Hospitality* accustoms us to expect deep-space manipulations of figures and objects, while Renoir's *Grand Illusion* builds up specific expectations about the likelihood of camera movements. Still other films make highly unusual technical choices, and to follow them we must construct stylistic expectations to which we are unaccustomed. The editing discontinuities in Eisenstein's *October* and the use of minute offscreen sounds in Bresson's *A Man Escaped* ask us to notice stylistic manipulation.

In other words, a director directs not only the cast and crew. A director directs us, directs our attention, shapes our reaction. Thus the filmmaker's technical decisions make a difference in what we perceive and how we respond.

Style, then, is that formal system of the film that organizes film techniques. Any one film will tend to rely on particular technical options in creating its style, and these are chosen by the filmmaker within the constraints of historical circumstances. We may also extend the term style to describe the characteristic use of techniques made by a single filmmaker or group of filmmakers. The spectator may not consciously notice film style, but it nonetheless makes an important contribution to the film's meanings and effects.

ANALYZING FILM STYLE

As viewers, we register the effects of film style but seldom notice it. If we want to understand how these effects are achieved, we need to look and listen more carefully than we usually do. Since the previous four chapters have shown how we can pay attention to stylistic features, we can now set forth four general steps in analyzing style.

1. Determine the organizational structure of the film, its narrative or non-narrative formal system.

The first step is to understand how the film is put together as a whole. If it is a narrative film, it will draw on all the principles we have discussed in Chapter 3. That is, it will have a plot that cues us to construct a story; it will manipulate causality, time, and space; it will have a distinct pattern of development from opening to closing; it may use parallelism; its narration will choose between restricted and more unrestricted knowledge at various points.

If the film is not a narrative, the analyst should seek to understand what other type of formal organization it uses. (See Chapter 5.) Is the film unified as a set of categories, or an argument, or a stream of associations? Or is it structured by an abstract set of technical features? In understanding either narrative or non-narrative form, making a segmentation is usually helpful. Grasping the logic that underlies the whole film supplies a context for its use of film techniques.

2. *Identify the salient techniques used.*

Here the analysis will draw on our survey of technical possibilities in Chapters 6 through 9. You need to be able to spot things such as color, lighting, framing, cutting, and sound, which most viewers don't consciously notice. Once you notice them, you can identify them as techniques—such as nondiegetic music or as a low-angle framing.

But noting and naming are only the beginning of stylistic analysis. The analyst must develop an eye for *salient* techniques. Salience will partly be determined by what techniques the film relies heavily on. The jerky forward zoom in *Wavelength* and the rapid, discontinuous editing of *October* invite scrutiny because they play a central role in the overall effect of the film.

In addition, what is salient depends on the analyst's purpose. If you want to show that a film's style is typical of one approach to filmmaking, you may focus on how the technique conforms to stylistic expectations. The 180° editing of *The Maltese Falcon* is not obvious or emphasized, but adherence to rules of classical continuity is a characteristic aspect of the film's style. Our purpose in Chapter 8 was to show that the film is typical in this respect. If, however, you want to stress unusual qualities of the film's style, you can concentrate on the more unexpected technical devices. Bresson's use of sound in *A Man Escaped* is unusual, representing choices that few filmmakers would make. It was the originality of these sonic devices that we chose to stress in Chapter 9. From the standpoint of originality, costume in *A Man Escaped* is not as salient a stylistic feature as sound because it is more in accord with conventional practice. The analyst's decision about what techniques are salient will thus be influenced partly by what the film emphasizes and partly by the analyst's purpose.

3. *Trace out patterns of techniques within the whole film.*

Once you have identified salient techniques, you can notice how they are patterned. Techniques will be repeated and varied, developed and paralleled, across the whole film or within a single segment. Chapters 6 through 9 have shown how this occurs in some films.

You can zero in on stylistic patterns in two ways. First, you can reflect on your responses. If a scene begins with a track-in, do you expect that it will end with a track-out? If you see a character looking left, do you assume that someone or something is offscreen and will be revealed in the next shot? If you feel a mounting excitement in an action scene, is that traceable to a quickening tempo in the music or to accelerating editing?

A second tactic for noticing stylistic patterns is to look for ways in which style reinforces patterns of formal organization. Filmmakers often deliberately design the film's stylistic system to underscore developments in the drama. We have seen how shifting color schemes reflect three stages of the plot's development in *Women in Love* (6.42–6.44). For *Amistad,* Steven Spielberg and his cinematographer Janusz Kaminski traced the slaves' progress toward freedom by lighting and shooting the four courtroom scenes in markedly different ways, from greenish, smoky light and somewhat scattershot camerawork to a final scene in the Supreme Court, with crisp illumination and smooth camera movements. In designing *Portrait of a Lady,* Jane

Campion and her cinematographer Stuart Dryburgh keyed colors to the protagonist's maturation. Isabel starts as an idealistic and somewhat headstrong young woman, and the background is an English summer, with bright green and yellow tones dominating. In Siena, as she becomes captivated by the sinister fortune hunter Ormond, the palette is richer and warmer, with orange and coral. Years later, she is unhappily married to Ormond, and the color scheme is steeped in pale blues. The closing scenes return to the English countryside, recalling the opening, but now, as the wiser, remorseful Isabel confronts her future, the snowy landscape is bathed slightly in blue, suggesting that memories of her marriage still haunt her.

Even within a shorter span, style can create a subtle sense of narrative progression. A scene will usually have a dramatic pattern of encounter, conflict, and outcome, and the style will often reflect this, with the cutting becoming more marked and the shots coming closer to the characters as the scene progresses. In *The Silence of the Lambs,* for example, the scenes between Clarice Starling and Hannibal Lecter tend to begin with conventional shot/reverse-shot conversations. The characters, filmed in medium shot, look off to the right or left of the camera **(10.1, 10.2).** As their conversations become more intense and intimate, the camera positions move closer to each one and shift subtly toward the axis of action until each person is looking directly into the lens **(10.3, 10.4).**

As we saw in *Grand Illusion* (pp. 277–283), style may create associations between situations, as when the camera movements suggest the prisoners' unity. It may also reinforce parallels, as do the tracking shots comparing Rauffenstein's war trophies and Elsa's. Later we shall see how style can also reinforce the organization of non-narrative films.

Sometimes, however, stylistic patterning will not respect the non-narrative or narrative structure of the film. Style can claim our attention in its own right. Since most stylistic devices have several functions, a technique may interest the analyst for different reasons. In 8.35 and 8.36 a cut from a washline to a living room acts as a transition between scenes. But the cut is of more interest for other reasons, since we do not expect a narrative film to treat objects as flat patches of color to be compared across shots. Such attention to graphic play is a convention of abstract form. Here, in a passage from Ozu's *Ohayu,* a stylistic choice comes forward because it goes beyond its narrative function. Even here, though, stylistic patterns continue to call on the viewer's expectations and to draw the spectator into a dynamic process. Anyone who notices the graphic match on red objects in *Ohayu* will most likely be intrigued at such an unconventional way of editing. And, if stylistic patterns do swerve off on their own, we still need a sense of the film's narrative or non-narrative organization in order to show how and when that happens.

4. Propose functions for the salient techniques and the patterns they form.

Here the analyst looks for the role that style plays in the film's overall form. Does the use of camera movement tend to create suspense by delaying the revelation of story information, as in the opening of *Touch of Evil* (pp. 287–289)? Does the use of discontinuous editing create a narrational omniscience, as in the sequence we analyzed in *October* (pp. 339–343)? Does the composition of the shot tend to make us concentrate on a particular detail (6.137, the shot of Anne's face in *Day of Wrath*)? Does the use of music or noise create surprise?

A direct route to noticing function is to notice the effects of the film. Style may enhance *emotional* aspects of the film. Rapid cutting in *The Birds* evokes shock and horror, while the Mozart music in *A Man Escaped* ennobles the communal routine of emptying slop buckets.

10.1 During the initial conversation in *The Silence of the Lambs,* shooting in depth with the foreground character's head prominent in the frame . . .

10.2 . . . emphasizes the distance between the pair.

10.3 Later in the scene, closer shots . . .

10.4 . . . deemphasize that distance.

> "There's no scene in any movie that fifty different directors couldn't have done fifty different ways."
>
> — Paul Mazursky, director

Style also shapes *meaning.* For example, in *Grand Illusion* the contrast between Rauffenstein and Elsa is heightened by Renoir's parallel tracking shots. We should, however, avoid reading isolated elements atomistically, taking them out of context. As we argued on p. 263, a high angle does not automatically mean "defeat," just as a low angle does not automatically mean "power." There is no dictionary to which you can turn to look up the meaning of a specific stylistic element. Instead the analyst must scrutinize the whole film, the patterns of the techniques in it, and the specific effects of film form.

Meaning is only one type of effect, and there is no reason to expect that every stylistic feature will possess a thematic significance. One part of a director's job is to direct our attention, and so style will often function simply *perceptually*—to get us to notice things, to emphasize one thing over another, to misdirect our attention, to clarify, intensify, or complicate our understanding of the action.

One way to sharpen our sense of the functions of specific techniques is to *imagine alternatives* and reflect on what differences would result. Suppose the director had made a different technical choice; how would this create a different effect? *Our Hospitality* creates its gags by putting two or more elements into the same shot and letting us observe the comic juxtaposition. Suppose Keaton had instead isolated each element in a single shot and then linked the two elements by editing. The meaning might be the same, but the perceptual effects would vary: Instead of a simultaneous presentation that lets our attention shuttle to and fro, we would have a more "programmed" pattern of building up the gags and paying them off. Or, suppose that Huston had handled the opening scene of *The Maltese Falcon* as a single take with camera movement. How would he then have drawn our attention to Brigid O'Shaughnessy's and Spade's facial reactions, and how would this have affected our expectations? By focusing on effects and imagining alternatives to the technical choices that were made, the analyst can gain a sharp sense of the particular functions of style in the given film.

The rest of this chapter provides a series of illustrations of how we can analyze film style. Our specimens are the films whose narrative and non-narrative systems were analyzed in Chapters 3 and 5: *Citizen Kane* (narrative form); *Gap-Toothed Women,* Part Two (categorical form); *The River* (rhetorical form); *Ballet mécanique* (abstract form); and *A Movie* (associational form). Our analyses are the results of following all four steps in stylistic analysis. Since these earlier chapters have discussed the films' organizational structures, we will concentrate here on identifying salient techniques, locating patterns, and proposing some functions for style in each case.

STYLE IN *CITIZEN KANE*

In analyzing *Citizen Kane*'s narrative, we discovered that the film is organized as a search; a detective-like figure, the reporter Thompson, tries to find the significance of Kane's last word, "Rosebud." But even before Thompson appears as a character, we, the spectators, are invited to ask questions about Kane and to seek the answers.

The very beginning of the film sets up a mystery. After a fade-in reveals a "No Trespassing" sign, in a series of craning movements upward, the camera travels over a set of fences, all matched graphically in the slow dissolves that link the shots. There follows a series of shots of a huge estate, always with the great house in the distance **(10.5).** (This sequence depends largely on special effects; the house itself is a series of paintings, combined through matte work with three-dimensional

10.5 The opening of *Citizen Kane.*

10.6 As this scene of *Citizen Kane* begins, the camera frames a poster of Susan Alexander on an outside wall of the nightclub . . .

miniatures in the foreground.) The gloomy lighting, the deserted setting, and the ominous music give the opening of the film the eerie uncertainty that we associate with mystery stories. These opening shots are connected by dissolves, making the camera seem to draw closer to the house although there is no forward camera movement. From shot to shot the foreground changes, yet the single lighted window remains in almost exactly the same position on the screen. Graphically matching the window from shot to shot already focuses our attention on it; we assume (rightly) that whatever is in that room will be important in initiating the story.

This pattern of our penetration into the space of a scene returns at other points in the film. Again and again, the camera moves toward things that might reveal the secrets of Kane's character, as in the spectacular crane up the side of a nightclub to a skylight as Thompson goes to interview Susan Alexander **(10.6–10.9).** As the camera reaches the skylight, a dissolve and a crack of lightning shift the scene inside to another craning movement down to Susan's table. (Actually, some of what seem to be camera movements were created in the laboratory using special effects; see Notes and Queries.)

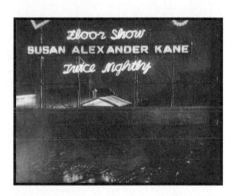

10.7 . . . then moves up the wall to the roof . . .

The opening scene and the introduction to El Rancho have some striking similarities. Each begins with a sign ("No Trespassing" and the publicity poster), and each moves us into a building to reveal a new character. The first scene uses a series of shots, whereas the second depends more on camera movement, but these different techniques are working to create a consistent pattern that becomes part of the film's style. Later, Thompson's second visit to Susan repeats the crane shots of the first. The second flashback of Jed Leland's story begins with another movement into a scene. The camera is initially pointed at wet cobblestones. Then it tilts up and tracks in toward Susan coming out of a drugstore. Only then does the camera pan right to reveal Kane standing, splashed with mud, on the curb. This pattern of gradual movement into the story space not only suits the narrative's search pattern but also uses film technique to create curiosity and suspense.

As we have seen, films' endings often contain variations of their beginnings. Toward the end of *Citizen Kane,* Thompson gives up his search for Rosebud. But after the reporters leave the huge storeroom of Xanadu, the camera begins to move over the great expanse of Kane's collections. It cranes forward high above the crates and piles of objects **(10.10),** then moves down to center on the sled from Kane's

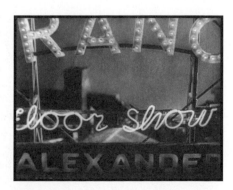

10.8 . . . forward and through the "El Rancho" sign . . .

10.9   . . . and over to the skylight.

10.10   A crane shot near the end of *Citizen Kane* . . .

10.11   . . . moves down to center on Kane's sled.

10.12   Another forward camera movement brings the sled into close-up.

childhood **(10.11).** Then there is a cut to the furnace, and the camera again moves in on the sled as it is tossed into the fire. At last we are able to read the word "Rosebud" on the sled **(10.12).** The ending continues the pattern set up at the beginning; the film techniques create a penetration into the story space, probing the mystery of the central character.

After our glimpse of the sled, however, the film reverses the pattern. A series of shots linked by dissolves leads us back outside Xanadu, the camera travels down to the "No Trespassing" sign again, and we are left to wonder whether this discovery really provides a resolution to the mystery about Kane's character.

Our study of *Kane*'s organization in Chapter 3 also showed that Thompson's search was, from the standpoint of narration, a complex one. At one level, our knowledge is restricted principally to what Kane's acquaintances know. Within the flashbacks, the style reinforces this restriction by avoiding crosscutting or other techniques that would move toward a more unrestricted range of knowledge. Many of the flashback scenes are shot in fairly static long takes, strictly confining us to what participants in the scene could witness. When the youthful Kane confronts Thatcher during the *Inquirer* crusade, Welles could have cut away to the reporter in Cuba sending Kane a telegram or could have shown a montage sequence of a day in the life of the paper. Instead, because this is Thatcher's tale, Welles handles the scene in a long take showing Kane and Thatcher in a face-to-face standoff, which is then capped by a close-up of Kane's cocky response.

We have also seen that the film's narrative requires us to take each narrator's version as objective within his or her limited knowledge. Welles reinforces this by avoiding shots that suggest optical or mental subjectivity. (Contrast Hitchcock's optical point-of-view angles in *The Birds* and *Rear Window,* pp. 301–302 and 320–322).

Welles also uses deep-focus cinematography that yields an external perspective on the action. The shot in which Kane's mother signs her son over to Thatcher is a good example. Several shots precede this one, introducing the young Kane. Then there is a cut to what at first seems a simple long shot of the boy **(10.13).** But the camera tracks back to reveal a window, with Kane's mother appearing at the left and calling to him **(10.14).** Then the camera continues to track back, following the adults as they walk to an adjoining room **(10.15).** Mrs. Kane and Thatcher sit at a table in the foreground to sign the papers, while Kane's father remains standing farther away at the left, and the boy plays in the distance **(10.16).**

Welles eliminates cutting here. The shot becomes a complex unit unto itself, like the opening of *Touch of Evil* discussed in Chapter 7. Most Hollywood directors would have handled this scene in shot/reverse shot, but Welles keeps all of the implications of the action simultaneously before us. The boy, who is the subject of the discussion, remains framed in the distant window through the whole scene; his game leads us to believe that he is unaware of what his mother is doing.

The tensions between the father and mother are conveyed not only by the fact that she excludes him from the discussion at the table but also by the overlapping sound. His objections to signing his son away to a guardian mix in with the dialogue in the foreground, and even the boy's shouts (ironically, "The Union Forever!") can be heard in the distance. The framing also emphasizes the mother in much of the scene. This is her only appearance in the film. Her severity and tensely controlled emotions help motivate the many events that follow from her action here. We have had little introduction to the situation prior to this scene, but the combination of sound, cinematography, and mise-en-scene conveys the complicated action with an overall objectivity.

Every director directs our attention, but Welles does so in unusual ways. *Kane* offers a good example of how a director chooses between alternatives. By giving

10.13 A progressively deeper shot in *Citizen Kane* begins as a long shot of the young Kane . . .

10.14 . . . becomes an interior view as the camera reveals a window . . .

10.15 . . . and moves backward with Mrs. Kane . . .

up cutting, Welles cues our attention by using deep-space mise-en-scene (figure behavior, lighting, placement in space) and sound. We can watch expressions because the actors play frontally (10.16). In addition, the framing emphasizes certain figures by putting them in the foreground or in dead center (**10.17**). And of course our attention bounces from one character to another as they speak lines. Even if Welles avoids the classical Hollywood convention of cutting in such scenes, he still uses film techniques to prompt us to make the correct assumptions and inferences about the story's progression.

Kane's narration also embeds the narrators' objective but restricted versions within broader contexts. Thompson's investigation links the various tales, so we learn substantially what he learns. Yet he must not become the protagonist of the film, for that would remove Kane from the center of interest. Welles makes a crucial stylistic choice here. By the use of low-key selective lighting and patterns of staging and framing, Thompson is made virtually unidentifiable. His back is to us, he is tucked into the corner of the frame, and he is usually in darkness. The stylistic handling makes him the neutral investigator, less a character than a channel for information.

More broadly still, we have seen that the film encloses Thompson's search within a more omniscient narration. Our discussion of the opening shots of Xanadu is relevant here: Film style is used to convey a high degree of non-character-centered knowledge. But when we enter Kane's death chamber, the style also suggests the narration's ability to plumb characters' minds. We see shots of snow covering the frame (for example, **10.18**), which hint at a subjective vision. Later in the film, the camera movements occasionally remind us of the broader range of narrational knowledge, as in the first version of Susan's opera premiere, shown during Leland's story in Segment 6. There the camera moves to reveal something neither Leland nor Susan could know about (**10.19–10.21**). The final sequence, which at least partially solves the mystery of "Rosebud," also uses a vast camera movement to give us an omniscient perspective. The camera cranes over objects from Kane's collection, moving forward in space but backward through Kane's life to concentrate on his earliest memento, the sled. A salient technique again conforms to pattern by giving us knowledge no character will ever possess.

In looking at the development of the narrative form of *Citizen Kane*, we saw how Kane changes from an idealistic young man to a friendless recluse. The film sets up a contrast between Kane's early life as an editor and his later withdrawal from public life after Susan's opera career fails. This contrast is most readily apparent in the mise-en-scene, particularly the settings of the *Inquirer* office and Xanadu.

10.16 . . . keeping the boy in extreme long shot throughout the rest of the scene.

10.17 Depth and centering in *Citizen Kane*.

10.18   *Citizen Kane:* snow inside and outside the glass ball.

10.19   In *Citizen Kane*'s first opera scene, the camera cranes up from the stage . . .

10.20   . . . through the rigging above . . .

10.21   . . . to reveal a stagehand pinching his nose to comment on Susan's singing.

10.22   *Citizen Kane:* Deep-focus photography and rear projection exaggerate the depth of the *Inquirer* office, making the characters seem far apart.

The *Inquirer* office is initially an efficient but cluttered place. When Kane takes over, he creates a casual environment by moving in his furniture and living in his office. The low camera angles tend to emphasize the office's thin pillars and low ceilings, which are white and evenly, brightly lit. Eventually Kane's collection of crated antiquities clutters his little office. Xanadu, on the other hand, is huge and sparsely furnished. The ceilings are too high to be seen in most shots, and the few furnishings stand far apart. The lighting often strikes figures strongly from the back or side, creating a few patches of hard light in the midst of general darkness. The expanded collection of antiquities and mementoes now is housed in cavernous storerooms.

The contrast between the *Inquirer* office and Xanadu is also created by the sound techniques associated with each locale. Several scenes at the newspaper office (Kane's initial arrival and his return from Europe) involve a dense sound mix with a babble of overlapping voices. Yet the cramped space is suggested by the relative lack of resonance in timbre. In Xanadu, however, the conversations sound very different. Kane and Susan speak their lines to each other slowly, with pauses between. Moreover, their voices have an echo effect that combines with the setting and lighting to convey a sense of huge, empty space.

The transition from Kane's life at the *Inquirer* to his eventual seclusion at Xanadu is suggested by a change in the mise-en-scene at the *Inquirer.* As we have just seen, while Kane is in Europe, the statues he sends back begin to fill up his little office. This hints at Kane's growing ambitions and declining interest in working personally on his newspaper. This change culminates in the last scene in the *Inquirer* office, Leland's confrontation with Kane. The office is being used as a campaign headquarters. With the desks pushed aside and the employees gone, the room looks larger and emptier than it had in earlier scenes. Welles emphasizes this by placing the camera at floor level and shooting from a low angle (7.113). The Chicago *Inquirer* office, with its vast, shadowy spaces, also picks up this pattern **(10.22),** as do later conversation scenes in the huge rooms of Xanadu (10.17).

Contrast these scenes with one near the end of the film. The reporters invade Kane's museumlike storeroom at Xanadu **(10.23).** Though the echo of Xanadu conveys its cavernous quality, the reporters transform the setting briefly by the same sort of dense, overlapping dialogue that characterized the early *Inquirer* scenes and the scene after the newsreel. By bringing together these reporters and Kane's final surroundings, the film creates another contrasting parallel emphasizing the changes in the protagonist.

Parallelism is an important feature throughout *Citizen Kane,* and most of the salient techniques work to create parallels in the ways we have already seen. For

10.23 *Citizen Kane:* Deep focus in the final scene.

10.24 The contract scene in *Citizen Kane* . . .

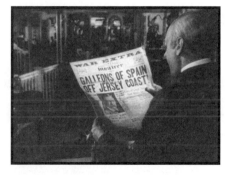

10.25 . . . echoes this earlier scene's composition . . .

example, the use of deep focus and deep space to pack many characters into the frame can create significant similarities and contrasts. Late in Thatcher's account (Segment 4), a scene presents Kane's financial losses in the Depression. He is forced to sign over his newspaper to Thatcher's bank. The scene opens on a close-up of Kane's manager, Bernstein, reading the contract **(10.24).** He lowers the paper to reveal Thatcher, now much older, seated opposite him. We hear Kane's voice off-screen, and Bernstein moves his head slightly, the camera reframing a little. Now we see Kane pacing beyond them in a huge office or boardroom (7.45). The scene is a single take in which the dramatic situation is created by the arrangement of the figures and the image's depth of field. The lowering of the contract recalls the previous scene, in which we first get a real look at the adult Kane as Thatcher puts down the newspaper that has concealed him **(10.25, 10.26).** There Thatcher had been annoyed, but Kane could defy him. Now Thatcher has gained control and Kane paces restlessly, still defiant, but stripped of his power over the *Inquirer* chain. The use of a similar device to open these two scenes sets up a contrasting parallel between them.

10.26 . . . and revelation of Kane.

Editing patterns can also suggest similarities between scenes, as when Welles compares two moments at which Kane seems to win public support. In the first scene, Kane is running for governor and makes a speech at a mammoth rally. This scene is principally organized around an editing pattern that shows one or two shots of Kane speaking, then one or two close shots of small groups of characters in the audience (Emily and their son, Leland, Bernstein, Gettys), then another shot of Kane. The cutting establishes the characters who are important for their views of Kane. Boss Gettys is the last to be shown in the scene, and we expect him to retaliate against Kane's denunciation.

After his defeat, Kane sets out to make Susan an opera star and thus justify his interest in her to the public. In the scene that parallels Kane's election speech, Susan's debut, the organization of shots is similar to that of the political rally. Again the figure on the stage, Susan, serves as a pivot for the editing. One or two shots of her are followed by a few shots of the various listeners (Kane, Bernstein, Leland, the singing teacher), then back to Susan, and so on **(10.27, 10.28).** General narrative parallels and specific stylistic techniques articulate two stages of Kane's power quest: first on his own, then with Susan as his proxy.

As we have seen in Chapter 9, music can bring out parallels as well. For example, Susan's singing is causally central to the narrative. Her elaborate aria in the opera *Salammbo* contrasts sharply with the other main diegetic music, the little song about "Charlie Kane." In spite of the differences between the songs, there is a

10.27 *Citizen Kane:* Susan onstage in her opera debut . . .

10.28 . . . and Kane in the audience.

10.29 *Citizen Kane.*

parallel between them, in that both relate to Kane's ambitions. The "Charlie Kane" ditty seems inconsequential, but its lyrics clearly show that Kane intends it as a political song, and it does turn up later as campaign music. In addition, the chorus girls who sing the song wear costumes with boots and Rough Rider hats, which they place on the heads of the men in the foreground **(10.29).** Thus Kane's desire for war with Spain has shown up even in this apparently simple farewell party for his departure to Europe. When Kane's political ambitions are dashed, he tries to create a public career for his wife instead, but she is incapable of singing grand opera. Again, the songs create narrative parallels between different actions in Kane's career.

As we saw in examining *Citizen Kane*'s narrative, the newsreel is a very important sequence, partly because it provides a map to the upcoming plot events. Because of its importance, Welles sets off the style of this sequence from the rest of the film by distinctive techniques that do not appear elsewhere in *Citizen Kane.* Also, we need to believe that this is a real newsreel in order to motivate Thompson's search for the key to Kane's life. The realistic newsreel sequence also helps establish Kane's power and wealth, which will be the basis of much of the upcoming action.

Welles uses several techniques to achieve the look and sound of a newsreel of the period. Some of these are fairly simple. The music is that of actual newsreels, and the insert titles, outmoded in regular narrative films, were still a convention in newsreel films. But beyond this, Welles employs a number of subtle cinematographic techniques to achieve a documentary quality. Since some of the footage in the newsreel is supposed to have been taken in the silent period, he uses several different film stocks to make it appear that the different shots have been assembled from widely different sources. Some of the footage has been printed so as to achieve the jerkiness of silent film run at sound speed. Welles has also scratched and faded this footage to give it the look of old, worn film. This, combined with the makeup work, creates a remarkable impression of documentary footage of Kane with Teddy Roosevelt, Adolf Hitler **(10.30),** and other historical figures. In the latter scenes of Kane being wheeled around his estate, the hand-held camera, the slats and barriers **(10.31),** and the high angle imitate the effects of a newsreel reporter surreptitiously filming Kane. All of these documentary conventions are enhanced by the use of a narrator whose booming voice also mimics the commentary typical in newsreels of the day.

One of *Citizen Kane*'s outstanding formal features is the way its plot manipulates story time. As we have seen, this process is motivated by Thompson's inquiry and the order in which he interviews Kane's acquaintances. Various techniques assist in the manipulation of order and duration. The shift from a narrator's present recounting to a past event is often reinforced by a *shock cut.* A shock cut creates a jarring juxtaposition, usually by means of a sudden shift to a higher sound volume and a considerable graphic discontinuity. *Citizen Kane* offers several instances: the abrupt beginning of the newsreel after the deathbed shot, the shift from the quiet conversation in the newsreel projection room to the lightning and thunder outside the El Rancho, and the sudden appearance of a screeching cockatoo in the foreground as Raymond's flashback begins **(10.32).** Such transitions create surprise and sharply demarcate one portion of the plot from another.

The transitions that skip over or drastically compress time are less abrupt. Recall, for instance, the languid images of Kane's sled being gradually covered by snow. A more extended example is the breakfast-table montage (Segment 6) that elliptically traces the decline of Kane's first marriage. Starting with the newlyweds' late supper, rendered in a track-in and a shot/reverse-shot series, the sequence moves

10.30   *Citizen Kane:* Costume, makeup, and . . .

10.31   . . . cinematography simulate newsreel footage.

10.32   A shock cut in *Citizen Kane.*

through several brief episodes, consisting of shot/reverse-shot exchanges linked by whip pans. (A **whip pan** is a very rapid pan that creates a blurring sidewise motion across the screen. It is usually used as a transition between scenes.) In each episode, Kane and Emily become more sharply hostile. The segment ends by tracking away to show the surprising distance between them at the table.

The music reinforces the sequence's development as well. The initial late supper is accompanied by a lilting waltz. At each transition to a later time, the music changes. A comic variation of the waltz follows its initial statement and then a tense one; then horns and trumpets restate the Kane theme. The final portion of the scene, with a stony silence between the couple, is accompanied by a slow, eerie variation on the initial theme. The dissolution of the marriage is stressed by this theme-and-variations accompaniment. A similar sort of temporal compression and sonic elaboration can be found in the montage of Susan's opera career (Segment 7).

Our brief examination of *Citizen Kane*'s style has pointed out only a few of the major patterns in the film. You will be able to find others: the musical motif associated with Kane's power; the "K" motif appearing in Kane's costumes and in Xanadu's settings; the way the decor of Susan's room in Xanadu reveals Kane's attitude toward her; the changes in the acting of individuals as their characters age in the course of the story; and the playful photographic devices, such as the photos that become animated or the many superimpositions during montage sequences. Again and again, in *Citizen Kane* such stylistic patterns sustain and intensify the narrative development and shape the audience's experience in particular ways.

STYLE IN *GAP-TOOTHED WOMEN*

Although *Gap-Toothed Women* incorporates a number of different kinds of footage, it concentrates on a series of interviews with women with gapped teeth. It recalls the familiar talking heads type of documentary, where experts or witnesses are shown discussing aspects of the subject at hand. A series of such talking heads risks becoming visually monotonous, and filmmakers often mix in different types of documentary footage with their interviews to lend variety. Les Blank follows this tactic, bringing in shots of magazine covers, posters, and some on-location footage of activities. His style also plays off the conventions of the interview documentary in clever ways.

In making *Gap-Toothed Women,* Blank controlled many aspects of filmic technique. Although he did not tell his subjects what to say, he had some choice about

10.33   *Gap-Toothed Women:* We strain to see this woman's gap as she smiles at the camera.

10.34   *Gap-Toothed Women* freezes the frame after the line, "You've got a gap between your teeth, hey, no problem."

10.35   A handheld camera in *Gap-Toothed Women.*

the settings for the interviews, and he and his crew could place the camera where they wanted it in most shots. Blank and his collaborators also controlled the editing and the sound track.

Gap-Toothed Women uses unusually close framings in many of the interviews. Usually interviews in documentaries are shot in a range from medium-long shot to medium close-up, staying far enough back to show part of the interviewee's body and some of the surroundings. Blank uses such framings, but he also includes many extreme close-ups, all centering on the subjects' mouths. The film opens with a very close framing of a woman talking about her gap as her "signature" (5.9). Viewers of interview documentaries usually focus their attention on the subjects' faces in general, but here the framing and the subject matter induce us to concentrate on these women's mouths. This happens both in the extreme close-ups and in the more conventional medium close-up and medium-shot framings, where we try to catch glimpses of the women's gaps as they speak or smile. The concentration on mouths is emphasized in a scene with an elderly woman whose smile reveals little of her gap, and Blank (in one of his few offscreen comments retained in the film) coaxes her to grin more broadly **(10.33).**

These close framings are enhanced by other cinematographic techniques. Often Blank will slowly zoom in ever closer toward the mouth as a woman speaks, as in the first shot (5.9). A number of shots during the interviews end with freeze frames, often to emphasize a comment by the interviewee. As we saw in Chapter 5, the last interview, with leukemia survivor Sharlyn Sawyer, gives her comments special weight; when she dismisses small physical flaws as unimportant, the frame freezes on her cheerful face **(10.34),** marking that comment as particularly significant.

Aside from close framings and related techniques, Blank varies the interviews with a few scenes shot using completely different camera techniques. He highlights Lauren Hutton's importance as a figure who brought gapped teeth into fashion magazines by devoting a segment to her roaming the streets looking for gap-toothed passersby. This distinctive scene uses Hutton's good-natured cooperation to turn the usual show-business interview on its head. Here the celebrity pursues and tries to talk to ordinary people, and the point is underlined by the use of a hand-held camera **(10.35).** The hand-held camera returns in the late scene of Justice Sandra Day O'Connor's addressing a Salvation Army audience on the importance of creativity **(10.36).** Here Blank did not have control over the staging of the event, and the footage simply captures a real speech from a camera placed in the audience.

The very tight framings on women's mouths reflects a stylistic playfulness that also emerges in the editing. Blank cuts freely from documentary interview footage to images from other sources. These images, many of popular magazine covers, photos, and ads, comment on the overall subject of gapped teeth and society's image of ideal feminine beauty. For example, the young woman who tells of having been ashamed of having gapped teeth until she saw images of model Lauren Hutton includes a brief passage where interview and photographs alternate **(10.37–10.40).** Blank creates a bit of humor by not simply having the woman describe things but also including images of what she mentions. The result is a version of Eisensteinian intellectual montage (see pp. 339–343) that Blank uses at several points to suggest his own approval of the women who have accepted gaps as natural and even attractive.

Despite the fact that *Gap-Toothed Women* is a documentary, Blank has controlled the mise-en-scene to a considerable extent. For example, although there are many locales used for the interviews, some of the same backgrounds are used for more than one interview. In particularly, one distinctive, brightly striped wall hanging returns several times, and two women are interviewed in front of what looks like the same blue wall. The repeated use of these settings hints not only that Blank has arranged many of the aspects of the mise-en-scene but also that he wants us to be aware of that fact. More obviously, he has chosen the various magazine covers, photographs, and drawings that form the subjects for many of his shots.

It also seems likely that Blank controlled where the women looked when responding to his questions. Most of them face toward the offscreen interviewer to the right or left of the camera. Only Sharlyn Sawyer speaks at length directly into the lens, and her spontaneous ease on camera is one more factor that privileges her comments.

Finally, Blank controlled the sound track. In most cases he eliminated the questions he and the other filmmakers asked the women, so that the interviewee's comments and anecdotes become the main source for ideas about gaps and standards of beauty. The filmmakers' attitudes, as we have seen, come from the film's form and style rather than from any straightforward statements. Thanks to music and montages of photographs, the film can comment indirectly on gapped teeth. For example, a passage from Claudia Schmidt's cheerful song about being gap-toothed, "I'm a Little Cookie," is heard over a series of ten photographs of smiling, cute little girls **(10.41)**. Blank also bookends the film with quietly cheerful harp music under the credits and livelier Middle Eastern dance music in the final scene. These interludes echo the tone of the film's final acknowledgment to the "wonderful gap-toothed women" that are its subject. (That final written statement is as close as the

10.36   Reportage-style footage of a speech in *Gap-Toothed Women.*

10.37   In *Gap-Toothed Women,* a young woman recalls being teased as a child and compared to Howdy Doody . . .

10.38   . . . and a photograph of the gap-toothed puppet briefly appears, followed by . . .

10.39   . . . another shot of the woman praising Lauren Hutton as inspirational, which leads to . . .

10.40   . . . a glamorous magazine cover photo of Hutton smilingly revealing her gap.

10.41 *Gap-Toothed Women:* An image from the "I'm a Little Cookie" montage sequence.

10.42 *Gap-Toothed Women:* "My father has a gap, about as wide as mine is; my mom has a gap that's a little smaller."

film gets to an overt statement in praise of gapped teeth, but it might also simply refer to the interviewees' "wonderful" cooperation in the making of the film.)

In Chapter 5 we discussed *Gap-Toothed Women* as an example of categorical form. In addition, the film's style evokes other types of formal interest. For one thing, the gaps seen in women's teeth, both during the interviews and in the photographs, create a certain abstract pictorial interest. Some gaps are wide, some narrow, some in between, and we are invited to study the various gaps and compare them. Early in the film, during Segment 3 (the discussions of genetic and cultural explanations for gaps), a young woman mentions the sizes of her parents' gaps **(10.42),** and the varying width of gaps becomes a visual motif, again ensuring that we will watch the women's mouths more closely than is usual in a talking heads documentary. This motif and the shifting colorful backgrounds of the interviews lend some abstract qualities to the overall categorical form.

Similarly, the abrupt cuts to photographs and other visual materials during and between interviews take on an associational quality, as Blank tries in a subtle way to suggest ideas about the women's comments without overtly expressing them. The use of gap-toothed celebrities' photographs, for example, suggests a link between gapped teeth and success and beauty. Thus associational links created by style enhance the film's main theme.

STYLE IN *THE RIVER*

As we saw in Chapter 5, *The River*'s formal development depends on a simple argument. The Mississippi Valley, we are told, was beautiful in the past, and the people's strength made it productive. That strength and productivity damaged the land. Now, with programs like the Tennessee Valley Authority, that strength can be used to repair the damage while enhancing the valley's productivity.

Stylistic systems in the film help create this argument. Motifs of camera work, sound, and editing set up the parallels we have noted among the various segments and work to suggest that by the end of the film, the TVA has helped re-create a situation similar to the pristine nature we saw at the beginning. But the film also sets up vivid contrasts between segments showing the country's beauty and strengths and other segments showing the problems created by careless exploitation of resources. Differences in the use of filmic technique strengthen the contrasts and contribute to the film's persuasive power.

The River includes a large amount of information: a summary of decades of American history, explanations of the causes of erosion and flooding, a description of the situation in 1937, and a look at the activities of the TVA. Yet we are able to keep all these matters straight and grasp the relations among them because of the film's clear form and its stylistic repetitions. For example, some segments begin by combining camerawork and editing to show us landscapes against a cloudy sky. The very first shots after the prologue introduce this motif, with mountains against the sky. At the beginning of Segment 3, we see low-height shots of the mule teams against more clouds, and in Segment 4, we first see the pine forests against the sky (5.25). This sets up an expectation that such sky shots are associated with the beauty and strength of the Mississippi Valley, and the filmmakers later use this association in order to draw parallels.

During the flood in Segment 6 and the description of the problems flooding causes, such framings are less prominent. But after the introduction of the TVA, they return **(10.43–10.45).** Thus the film satisfies our expectations about this visual

10.43 *The River:* Men going to work are framed in low angle against the sky.

10.44 *The River:* Soon after this, one shot begins on a hillside, also against the sky, then tilts down . . .

10.45 . . . to reveal the model town.

motif by bringing it back in association with the new beauty and strength created by the TVA. This repetition also ties the ending back to the beginning. We have returned to an idyllic land, a development that confirms the film's claim that the TVA was the correct solution to the problem.

By way of contrast, other scenes either eliminate the sky motif or vary it considerably. Thus Segment 4, on the Civil War, begins with a printed announcement quoting Robert E. Lee's surrender statement, with flames superimposed over the writing. This is very different from the earlier segments' openings, marking Segment 4 off as introducing the problems with which the film will deal. As we saw in Chapter 5, the segment devoted to erosion and flooding shows stumps against fog (5.26)—an obvious contrast with the earlier cloud-filled shots of trees (5.25).

The River creates other parallels by means of rhythms within the editing and the sound track. Virgil Thomson's famous musical score plays a more active role than do the scores of most documentary films, and the careful mixing of voice and music enhances the images they accompany. After the prologue, a fanfare introduces the mountain-and-cloud shots, and then the authoritative narrator's voice enters, all combining to suggest the stateliness and splendor of nature in the Mississippi Valley. Later scenes employ faster rhythms, as when a bouncy version of "Hot Time in the Old Town Tonight" plays over shots of logs hurtling down chutes into the river. Here the music is important in cueing us how to react. The logging shots could connote destruction of natural beauty, but the accompaniment suggests that this industry is part of the building of American strength.

In the next scene, Segment 6, the filmmakers create a sharp contrast. Now we are cued to take the logging activities as having harmful side effects. A long series of shots creates a slow, inexorable rhythm building up to the turbulent, dangerous movements of the floodwaters. The segment begins with slow shots of the fog-shrouded stumps (5.26), with little movement. Rhythmic, threatening, dissonant chords make up the musical accompaniment. The narrator speaks more slowly and deliberately. Dissolves, rather than straight cuts, connect the shots, slowing down the visual rhythm still further. The segment begins to build up tension. One shot shows a stump with icicles on it and, instead of going on to other stumps, as the sequence had been doing, the next shot is a cut-in to emphasize the icicles dripping **(10.46).** A sudden dissonant trumpet chord signals us to expect some threat. Then, in a series of close shots of the earth, we see more and more water gathering, first in trickles **(10.47),** later in streams, washing the unprotected soil away. By now the

10.46   In *The River,* shots of icicles dripping lead to a segment on erosion.

10.47   *The River.*

10.48   *The River.*

10.49   *The River.*

10.50   *The River.*

sound is very rhythmic; quiet tom-tom-like beats punctuate the shots. The narrator begins supplying dates, one over each shot: "Nineteen-seven" **(10.48);** "Nineteen-thirteen" **(10.49);** "Nineteen-sixteen" **(10.50);** and so on, up to 1937. By the "1916" shot (10.50), we see a small waterfall forming, and in successive shots the creeks become rivers swelling over their banks.

As the storm and flood sequence intensifies, brief shots of lightning bolts are intercut with shots of raging water. Here the dramatic music becomes overwhelmed by loud sirens and whistles. The stylistic techniques have combined to build up to a climax of rising tension, convincing us of the flood's threat. Were we not to grasp that threat, both factually and emotionally, the film's overall argument would probably affect us less. Throughout *The River,* voice, music, editing, and movement within the shot are used to build up a rhythm for just such rhetorical purposes.

Such uses of style encourage us to make comparisons between different segments of the film. In addition, *The River* employs techniques on a small scale to enhance each individual scene's impact. Since the film does not present a narrative with continuing characters and action, it need not use the continuity editing system or keep its style unobtrusive. For example, graphic discontinuity may create a striking transition. Lorentz cuts from a shot of a mud-filled, mule-drawn sledge moving from right to left **(10.51)** to a similarly framed shot of a plow going from left to right **(10.52).** This cut leads from the first portion of Segment 3, on the building of the dike, to a new portion on cotton farming. The differences between these shots suggest the transition, but their similarities might also lead us to expect some connection between these two topics.

10.51 *The River* creates graphic contrast between a sledge . . .

10.52 . . . and a plow.

10.53 A canted framing in *The River.*

Camerawork can function in an equally striking way. *The River* uses canted framings occasionally, as when we see a montage sequence of workers loading cotton bales onto a steamboat **(10.53).** The off-balance composition makes the bales seem to roll downhill almost effortlessly. Combined with sprightly banjo music, this series of shots cues us to take the scene as a positive depiction of the South's productivity in earlier years. Interestingly, the use of style here discourages us from considering whether these black workers are slaves. This is an important issue in U.S. history, but the film excludes it from its argument, preferring instead to speak of a general "we," a united people responsible for the despoiling of the Mississippi.

As we saw in Chapter 5, appeals to our emotions play a large part in rhetorical form. If a film can make us feel strongly about its subject, we may be more inclined to accept its arguments as valid. *The River*'s use of technique enhances its emotional impact. Even today, when the issues involved in Pare Lorentz's arguments are no longer topical, the film's style can powerfully affect us.

STYLE IN *BALLET MÉCANIQUE*

When we first analyzed *Ballet mécanique* in Chapter 5, we necessarily looked at some aspects of its style—its short bursts of shots, its swinging camera movements, its graphic discontinuities. Style is crucial to the abstract organization of form. Indeed, we often refer to the emphasis on abstract qualities of recognizable objects as *stylization*. But now that we have surveyed the techniques of the film medium, we can be more specific about how style functions in *Ballet mécanique*.

In general, the film reverses our normal expectations about the nature of movement. The purpose is to make objects dance and to make human movement seem mechanistic. We have already seen how the film's form is calculated to bring out these pictorial qualities. Now we can see that the film uses each film technique in ways that function in this context.

Most of the objects are familiar from everyday life, but the mise-en-scene takes them out of their familiar context and makes us see them in a new way. For example, many of the shots show faces or objects against black or white backgrounds (5.46 and 5.53). In a few cases, the backgrounds themselves have abstract white-and-black patterns **(10.54).** The swinging or turning objects, especially the machine movements in Segment 4, also emphasize the mechanical ballet pattern. Even

10.54   The shot of the swinging ball near the end of Segment 2 of *Ballet mécanique.*

10.55   A horse collar in *Ballet mécanique.*

10.56   *Ballet mécanique:* A shot of a woman with open eyes.

makeup, which we usually associate with films involving characters, acts to render abstract relations more prominent. In the shot of the woman's profile (5.48), heavy makeup combines with her lack of expression and stiff swiveling movement to point up her resemblance to a mannequin. Similarly, human figure movement imitates that of the machines.

The cinematographic properties of the shot heighten these qualities and add new abstract elements to the imagery. Any framing creates a composition, of course, but the filmmaker can emphasize or deemphasize the abstract aspects of shapes on the screen. In *Ballet mécanique,* shot scale often makes shape a prominent element of the shot. The film has a high proportion of medium close-ups, close-ups, and even extreme close-ups. In combination with the blank backgrounds, such close framings function to isolate and draw attention to shapes: the round hat (5.53), the zerolike horse collar **(10.55),** the round profile (5.48). Such close framings also make texture easier to discern, as with the shiny pots and bottles.

Other aspects of framing work in similar ways. Masks change the screen's shape to emphasize one portion, as with the repeated shots of a woman's eye (5.43). Upside-down framing is used to present the swinging woman in Segment 1 (5.41) and the rows of swinging pans in Segment 6 (5.50). A special effect may organize the small-scale form of a whole segment, as when prismatic shots dominate Segment 2, and then recur as a motif in later portions. Further, mobile framing functions prominently in the creation of the film's rhythm. The short, regular pans in the upside-down shot of the swinging woman begin this process, recurring in the rapid succession of brief, repetitive pan shots of fairground-ride cars in Segment 3.

Editing is a very important technique for creating abstract relations in *Ballet mécanique.* This film provides a good example of how filmmakers may work entirely outside the continuity editing system and create dynamic, highly organized patterns between shots. One of the film's most striking and amusing moments depends on a precise graphic match. In Segment 2 we see an extreme close-up of a woman's wide-open eyes **(10.56).** She closes them, leaving her heavily made-up eyes and brows as dark crescents against her white skin. A cut presents us with the same composition, now upside down **(10.57).** The eyes and brows are now reversed, but in identical positions. When the eyes pop open **(10.58),** we are momentarily surprised to find their positions switched; the match is so close as to make the cut almost invisible. The surprise is enhanced by a quick cutting rate that does not allow us to really examine the shots closely. Humorous touches like this occur throughout *Ballet mécanique* and make it as enjoyable to watch now as it must have been when it was first shown over 70 years ago.

Graphic matches, however, are rare in the film. Usually the shapes we are to compare do not appear in successive shots. Thus in Segment 5, the dance of intertitles and pictures, the large zero **(10.59)** and the horse collar (10.55) are graphically similar, and each recurs in many shots. Yet they are never juxtaposed in a graphic match. However, a great many cuts contrast elements through strong graphic discontinuity. The circle and triangle alternation that recurs so regularly is one example. True, the shapes are both white, and both are seen against black backgrounds. But the difference in their shapes is what we notice most readily in these passages. Such an obvious contrast cues us to look for others.

Graphic contrast can be enhanced by accelerated editing. In the hat/shoe alternation in Segment 7 (5.53), we see the striking differences in shape right away. But as the lengthy series of short shots continues, we notice variations. About a third of the way through, the directions are switched: The shoe protrudes in from the left briefly, and the hat also flips. Then they return to their original positions, and the editing rhythm accelerates. By the end, the shots are so short that we seem almost to see a single white object pulsating, rapidly changing from circle to lozenge and back again. Here the filmmakers are pointing out how the apparent-motion phenomenon makes us see movement in a strip of slightly different still images. This is the process that makes cinema itself possible. (See Chapter 1.)

Even when there are no specific graphic similarities or contrasts, *Ballet mécanique*'s editing suggests other comparisons. By placing a shot of a woman's eye next to that of a machine, or by punctuating a laundry woman's repeated stair-climbing with a rhythmically rotating shaft, the film creates a metaphorical similarity between human and mechanized motion. Such repeated comparisons help to organize the overall development of the film's form.

Rhythmic figure movement, rhythmic framing mobility, and rhythmic editing function to set objects scampering across the screen. It is difficult to resist seeing the quick shots of mannequins' legs (5.52) in Segment 7 as executing a dance, even though most of the individual shots contain no movement. This passage differs greatly from the simple shot of the woman swinging that we saw at the beginning. Yet, without any use of language beyond the title itself to direct our expectations, *Ballet mécanique* has employed film techniques to guide us to see a similarity between two such contrasting movements. Random objects seem to belong together, and a mechanical rhythm pulses through objects and humans alike.

STYLE IN *A MOVIE*

We have already seen that the overall form of Bruce Conner's *A Movie* is associational. In this context, film style fulfills three general types of functions. Across the whole film, stylistic techniques help break the form into parts and create relations among those parts. On a local level, individual techniques enhance the links between different objects and draw us to form expectations on the basis of the comparison. The style also offers us cues as to how to respond, emotionally and intellectually.

Conner controlled neither the original mise-en-scene nor the cinematography of the films from which he took the shots for *A Movie* nor the composition of the music that forms its sound track. Yet, by selection and arrangement, he made use of these elements as they already existed, and we can find techniques of mise-en-scene, camerawork, sound, and editing all at work in fulfilling the three types of functions.

Perhaps the most noticeable characteristic of the mise-en-scene of *A Movie* is its great variety. By choosing material from so many different film types, Conner cues us to seek more and more generalized associations to explain the links among the objects we see. Galloping cowboys and Indians from a fiction film, atomic-bomb blasts from documentary, and nudie shots from pornography do not add up to a story or an argument, and we must find some common association, like aggressivity and disaster, to make sense of this barrage of heterogeneous images.

Our ability to follow the comparisons being made from shot to shot also depends on the fact that Conner found similar types of elements from different films and juxtaposed them, putting a stock-car crash next to a race-car crash or a water-skier's fall next to a surfer's wipeout. *A Movie* also makes use of the mise-en-scene of its different shots to guide our emotional reaction. The plane crashes or firing-squad shots evoke horror, while the more quietly ominous sections of the film contain some images of considerable beauty, such as the first shot of the *Hindenburg* floating over a city (5.58). Mise-en-scene elements contribute to the overall form

10.57 By the last frame of the same shot, her eyes are closed, and the first frame of the next shows her upside down . . .

10.58 Later in the second shot she opens her eyes.

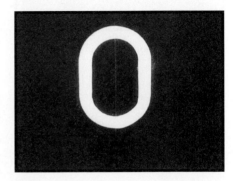

10.59 *Ballet mécanique* invites us to see this 0 as part of a motif of oval objects.

10.60   In *A Movie*, a long tilt . . .

10.61   . . . follows the fall of a car down a cliff.

10.62   *A Movie:* The brief series of shots of the buckling suspension bridge begins with mask moving aside.

10.63   Optical printing in *A Movie* creates . . .

10.64   . . . a zoom-in toward a volcano.

of the film, since visual motifs are repeated and varied. As we saw in Chapter 5, motifs from Segments 2 and 3 are picked up again in the fourth and final part.

Cinematography works in similar ways in *A Movie.* There is a great variety in the types of techniques found in the original footage: wartime aerial photography of planes being fired on, panning documentary shots that follow race cars and motor boats, and more static framings of staged scenes, as in the pornography shots. Again, this variety enhances the contrasts among elements and encourages us to make comparisons on a very general level. Yet, *A Movie* also uses as motifs the similar types of cinematography found in different films. Thus the series of different plane disasters at the beginning of Segment 4 all use aerial photography, and this links them with the aerial shots of the *Hindenburg* early in Segment 3. Cinematography can also enhance emotional response. The series of panning shots of crashing race cars late in Segment 2 builds up a relatively regular rhythm of disasters, a pattern to be intensified in later parts of the film. Similarly, the long tilt down following the old car falling over a cliff at the end of this segment (**10.60, 10.61**) emphasizes the length of that fall and provides an emotional climax to the series of car crashes.

At a few points in *A Movie,* Connor also manipulates cinematography by using laboratory-made special effects to alter shots. A few shots in Segment 4 begin or end with black masks that move to reveal or conceal the mise-en-scene of the shot (**10.62**). Such moments stress Conner's own manipulation of the found footage and perhaps function similarly to the repeated insertions of the titles "Movie," "Bruce Conner," and so on, at other points in the film.

There is also a brief series of shots early in Segment 4 that are linked by dissolves and optically printed zoom-ins that enlarge the frames. From the planes in front of the pyramid (5.65), a dissolve moves us to the beginning of the first volcano shot (**10.63**). You can see the edges of this frame as Conner prints it small at first, then optically enlarges it frame by frame to achieve a zooming effect (**10.64**). After a straight cut to a closer volcano shot (also with an optical zoom-in), there is a dissolve to the coronation (**10.65**), which is also optically enlarged (**10.66**), followed by another dissolve to the burning *Hindenburg,* and a final dissolve and zoom-in to a moving line of army tanks. In a film that usually manipulates the original shots only through editing and sound, this brief segment stands out by contrast. The effect of the quick dissolves and zooms is partly to seem to move us in toward the disasters and other scenes. But, more strikingly, each scene seems to emerge out of the previous one—the volcano coming forward from the pyramid, the church official blending briefly with the smoke of the volcano and growing larger, and so on. This series creates a strong linkage among the disparate elements, enhancing our sense of the inevitable, rhythmic flow of these ominous images.

Sound is crucial to *A Movie*'s various effects. In Chapter 5 we saw how the divisions between Segments 2, 3, and 4 coincide with pauses between parts of Respighi's *Pines of Rome.* The considerable differences in tone among those parts also give us strong cues as to how to react to the images. The shots that open Segment 3—the women carrying totems, the *Hindenburg,* the acrobats—take on their eerie, slightly ominous, quality almost solely because of the musical accompaniment. Moreover, the music intensifies our emotional response. While the series of disasters in Segment 4 are horrendous in themselves, the ponderous, driving music makes them merge into one plunging, apocalyptic rush.

The sound is all nondiegetic, and we hear no voices or sound effects from the individual scenes. Yet Conner has edited his shots very carefully to create corresponding rhythms in image movement, cutting, and music. For example, the frenzied buildup of the fast passage in *The Pines of Rome* toward the end of Segment 2 accompanies the series of race-car crashes. Blaring, dissonant phrases begin to punctuate the music at regular intervals. Conner times these to coincide with the individual car crashes, considerably enhancing their visual effectiveness. Later, in Segment 4, the shot of the flute player (5.66) coincides with a passage of flute and oboe music, so that we almost sense for a moment that the sound has become diegetic. This impression enhances the idyllic quality of these exotic shots, just before the return to the disaster footage. Thus, although Conner chose an existing piece of music, he has tailored it closely to his images and used it to help create the tone and form of *A Movie.*

Editing was the only visual technique in *A Movie* that Conner controlled completely, and it is the source of many spectacular effects. Of course, the basic associational comparisons are made by cutting together series of shots from different sources. But Conner does not stop with juxtaposing events by cutting. He exploits the graphic, spatial, and temporal relations between shots as well.

Some cuts use principles of continuity to fit together shots that really could not be in the same space, thus creating an impossible continuity that gives the film much of its humor. We can see now that the joke of the submarine officer looking at the bikini-clad woman (5.60, 5.61) comes from the fact that it is a false optical point-of-view shot. Similarly, the various racing horses, elephants, and tanks in the first part of Segment 2 are linked partly by their common screen direction. Most of the movement is from left to right on the screen, or coming directly toward the camera, both directions that would cut together correctly in the continuity editing system. Thus we can imagine all these vehicles and animals racing along together in some vast space. Yet the obvious impossibility of the juxtaposition makes this notion amusing. Later, in Segment 3, Conner varies this technique by cutting together various water-skiers and motorboats, some with similar directions of movement, some with opposed directions, but all compared through the general similarities of the series of shots.

Like *Ballet mécanique, A Movie* uses graphic matches to create comparisons. During the same series of fast movements cut together in Segment 2, we see first a shot of a wagon moving over the camera (**10.67**) and then a graphically similar shot of a tank filmed from a low camera height (**10.68**). Combined with the quick tempo of the editing rhythm, such moments contribute to the frenzied exhilaration that this segment generates. By finding similarities of this type between shots taken from different sources, Conner also enhances the associational connections between shots. Stylistic links cue us to find emotional and conceptual links as well.

10.65 *A Movie:* Another optical zoom . . .

10.66 . . . during a ceremony.

10.67 A graphic match in *A Movie* links wagon . . .

10.68 . . . and tank.

The overall formal organization of *A Movie,* developing from humor toward a threatening tone and ultimate disaster, depends heavily on the repeated use of film techniques. Editing juxtaposes elements, mise-en-scene and cinematography emphasize the similarities and contrasts among them, and music develops and unifies the emotional tone. As a result, even a very short film can elicit a wide range of responses from the viewer. Here, as in all the types of non-narrative form, we can see that style plays a crucial role in the total form of a film and in the spectator's experience.

This concludes our discussion of film form and film technique. As we have emphasized, no single set of rules will allow you to understand every film automatically. Any film creates a unique form from an interplay of overall structure and film style, and each individual element (each formal part or stylistic technique) functions according to its place within that system. Analyzing the nature of that formal system and the functions of individual devices is the goal of the critic. Part Five of this book consists of a series of analyses showing how a critic may understand the workings of widely differing kinds of films.

NOTES AND QUERIES

The Concept of Film Style

Sometimes the concept of style is used evaluatively, to imply that something is inherently good ("Now that's got real style!"). We are using the term descriptively. From our perspective, all films have style, because all films make *some* use of the techniques of the medium, and those techniques will necessarily be organized in some way.

For discussion of the concept of style in various arts, see Monroe C. Beardsley, *Aesthetics: Problems in the Philosophy of Criticism* (New York: Harcourt Brace and World, 1958); J. V. Cunningham, ed., *The Problem of Style* (Greenwich, Conn.: Fawcett, 1996); and Berel Lang, ed., *The Concept of Style,* rev. ed. (Ithaca, N.Y.: Cornell University Press, 1987).

Pioneering studies of style in the cinema are Erwin Panofsky, "Style and Medium in the Moving Pictures" (originally published in 1937), in Daniel Talbot, ed., *Film: An Anthology* (Berkeley: University of California Press, 1970), pp. 13–32; Raymond Durgnat, *Films and Feelings* (Cambridge, Mass.: MIT Press, 1967); and Raymond Bellour, "Pour une stylistique du film," *Revue d'esthétique* **19,** 2 (April–June 1966): 161–178. Most of the works cited in Notes and Queries to chapters in Part Four offer concrete studies of aspects of film style.

A shot-by-shot analysis of *Ballet mécanique* may be found in Standish Lawder, *The Cubist Cinema* (Berkeley: University of California Press, 1975).

An entire book has been written on the production of *Citizen Kane,* shedding much light on how its style was created: Robert L. Carringer's *The Making of Citizen Kane* (Berkeley: University of California Press, 1985). Among other things, Carringer reveals the degree to which Welles and his collaborators used special effects for many of the film's scenes. A tribute to the film, and a reprinting of Gregg Toland's informative article on the film, "Realism for *Citizen Kane,*" is available in *American Cinematographer* **72,** 8 (August 1991): 34–42. Graham Bruce illuminates Bernhard Herrmann's musical score for *Citizen Kane* in *Bernard Herrmann: Film Music and Narrative* (Ann Arbor, Mich.: UMI Research Press, 1985), pp. 42–57. See also Steven C. Smith, *A Heart at Fire's Center: The Life and Music of Bernard Herrmann* (Berkeley: University of California Press, 1991). A detailed analysis of the film's sound is Rick Altman, "Deep-Focus Sound: *Citizen Kane* and the Radio Aesthetic," *Quarterly Review of Film and Video* **15,** 3 (December 1994): 1–33.

PART FIVE

Critical Analysis of Films

Criticism is not an activity limited to those people who write articles or books about films. Any person who seeks actively to understand a film he or she sees is engaged in a process of criticism. You may be unsure, for example, why one scene was included in a film; your search for the function of that scene in the context of the whole is a first step in a critical examination. People who discuss a film they have seen are participating in criticism.

Up to this point, we have looked at concepts and definitions that should enable a filmgoer to analyze a film systematically. The critic approaches a film already knowing that formal patterns, such as repetitions and variations, will probably be important and should be examined. The critic will also be alert for principles of narrative and non-narrative form, and she or he will watch for salient uses of the various film techniques. The critic will also ground his or her claims in specific evidence from the film.

So far, we have looked at all the techniques that constitute a film; we have also laid out basic principles that govern a film's narrative or non-narrative form. Our examples and analyses have shown how elements of a film function in an overall system. But the only

way to gain an ability to analyze films is through practice in viewing and perhaps writing about films critically and through reading analyses by other critics. For this reason, we conclude our look at films as formal systems with a series of brief sample essays on individual films.

An analyst usually scrutinizes a film with some sort of purpose in view. You may want to understand a film's perplexing aspects, reveal the process that created a pleasurable response, or convince someone that the film is worth seeing. Our sample analyses have two primary purposes. First, we want to illustrate how film form and film style work together in a variety of films. Second, we seek to provide models of short critical analyses, exemplars of how an essay might illuminate some aspects of a film's workings.

Because an analyst is limited by his or her purposes, there is little chance of getting everything, of accounting for each facet of a film. As a result, these analyses do not exhaust the films. You might study any one of them and find many more points of interest than we have been able to present here. Indeed, whole books can be and have been written about single films without exhausting the possibilities for enriching our experience of those films.

413

Chapter 11

Film Criticism: Sample Analyses

Each of the four major sections of this chapter emphasizes different aspects of various films. We begin by discussing three classical narrative films: *His Girl Friday, North by Northwest,* and *Do the Right Thing.* Since classically constructed films are familiar to most viewers, it is important to study closely how they work.

We move to three films that represent alternatives to classical norms. *Breathless* relies on ambiguity of character motivation and on stretches of rambling action, all presented through loose, casual techniques. In contrast, *Tokyo Story* uses selective deviations from classical stylistic norms in order to create a highly rigorous style. In *Chungking Express,* the viewer's expectation that two groups of characters will converge is rechanneled to focus interest on narrative parallels.

Documentary films can go beyond direct recording and suggest a wide range of meanings. This section considers two examples of how formal and stylistic processes can expand a documentary's implications. The first, *Man with a Movie Camera,* documents a day in the life of the Soviet Union, but it also celebrates the power of cinema to transform reality. *The Thin Blue Line* tells the story of a miscarriage of justice; at the same time, it invites us to reflect on the difficulties of responsibly investigating and solving any crime.

Finally, we move to analyses that emphasize social ideology. Our first example, *Meet Me in St. Louis,* is a film that accepts a dominant ideology and reinforces the audience's belief in that ideology. In contrast, *Raging Bull* shows how a film can display ambiguity in its ideological implications.

We could have emphasized different aspects of any of these films. *Meet Me in St. Louis,* for example, is a classical narrative film and could be considered from that perspective. Similarly, *Man with a Movie Camera* could be seen as offering an alternative to classical continuity editing. And any of the films represents an ideological position that could be analyzed. Our choices suggest only certain angles of approach; your own critical activities will discover many more.

Those activities are the focus of the "Film Viewer's Guide" that accompanies this book. There we suggest some ways in which you can prepare, organize, and write a critical analysis of a film. We draw on the following sample analyses for various strategies that you can apply in your own writing.

THE CLASSICAL NARRATIVE CINEMA

His Girl Friday

1940. Columbia. Directed by Howard Hawks. Script by Charles Lederer from the play *The Front Page* by Ben Hecht and Charles MacArthur. Photographed by Joseph Walker. Edited by Gene Harlick. Music by Morris W. Stoloff. With Cary Grant, Rosalind Russell, Ralph Bellamy, Gene Lockhart, Porter Hall.

The dominant impression left by *His Girl Friday* is that of speed: It is often said to be the fastest sound comedy ever made. Let us therefore slow it down analytically. By breaking the film into parts and seeing how the parts relate to one another logically, temporally, and spatially, we can suggest how classical narrative form and specific film techniques are used to create this whirlwind experience.

His Girl Friday can be segmented into 13 scenes, set in the following locales: (1) the *Morning Post* offices; (2) the restaurant; (3) the Criminal Courts pressroom; (4) Walter's office; (5) Earl Williams's cell; (6) the pressroom; (7) a precinct jail; (8) the pressroom; (9) the sheriff's office; (10) the street outside the prison; (11) the pressroom; (12) the sheriff's office; (13) the pressroom. All of these scenes are marked off by dissolves except for the transition between 8 and 9, which is simply a cut.

Within these scenes, smaller units of action occur. Note, for example, that scene 1, occupying almost 14 minutes of screen time, introduces almost all of the major characters and sets two plotlines in motion. Or, consider scene 13: Almost every major character appears in it, and it runs for about 33 minutes.

We could go on to break the longer scenes into smaller parts on the basis of changing character interactions. Thus scene 1 comprise (a) our introduction to the newspaper office; (b) the first conversation between Hildy and Bruce; (c) Walter's discussion of the past with Hildy; (d) Walter's conference with Duffy about the Earl Williams case; (e) Hildy's telling Walter that she's remarrying; and (f) Walter's introduction to Bruce. To grasp the construction of other lengthy scenes, you may divide them into similar segments. It may be, in fact, that the somewhat theatrical feel of the film comes from its practice of segmenting its scenes by character entrances and exits (rather than, say, by frequent shifts of locale). In any event, the developing patterns of character interaction contribute a great deal to the hubbub and speed of the film.

The scenes function, as we would expect, to advance the action. As we saw in Chapter 3 (pp. 89–90), classical Hollywood cinema often constructs a narrative around characters with definite traits who want to achieve specific goals. The clash of these characters' contrasting traits and conflicting goals propels the story forward in a step-by-step process of cause and effect. *His Girl Friday* has two such cause–effect chains:

1. *The romance.*   Hildy Johnson wants to quit newspaper reporting and settle down with Bruce Baldwin. This is her initial goal. But Hildy's editor and ex-husband, Walter Burns, has a different goal: He wants her to continue as his reporter and to remarry him. Given these two goals, the characters enter into a conflict in several stages. First, Walter lures Hildy by promising a nest egg for the couple in exchange for her writing one last story. But Walter also plots to have Bruce robbed. Learning of this, Hildy tears up her story. Walter continues to delay Bruce, however, and eventually wins Hildy through her renewed interest in reporting. She changes her mind about marrying Bruce and stays with Walter.

2. *Crime and politics.* Earl Williams is to be hanged for shooting a policeman. The city's political bosses are relying on the execution to ensure their reelection. This is the goal shared by the mayor and the sheriff. But Walter's goal is to induce the governor to reprieve Williams and thus unseat the mayor's party at the polls. Through the sheriff's stupidity, Williams escapes and is concealed by Hildy and Walter. In the meantime, a reprieve does arrive from the governor; the mayor bribes the messenger into leaving. Williams is discovered, but the messenger returns with the reprieve in time to save Williams from death and Walter and Hildy from jail. Presumably the mayor's machine will be defeated at the election.

The crime-and-politics line of action is made to depend on events in the romance line at several points. Walter uses the Williams case to lure Hildy back to him, Hildy chases the Williams story instead of returning to Bruce, Bruce's mother reveals to the police that Walter has concealed Williams, and so on. More specifically, the interplay of the two lines of action alters the goals of various characters. In Walter's case, inducing Hildy to write the story fulfills his goals of embarrassing the politicos and of tempting Hildy back. Hildy's goals are more greatly changed. After she destroys her article, her decision to cover Earl Williams's jailbreak marks her acceptance of Walter's goal. Her later willingness to hide Williams and her indifference to Bruce's plea firmly establish her goals as linked to Walter's. In this way the interaction of the two plotlines advances Walter's goals but radically alters Hildy's.

Within this general framework, the cause–effect sequencing is very complex and deserves a closer analysis than space permits here. But consider, for example, the various ways in which Walter's delaying tactics (involving his confederates Duffy, Louie, and Angie) set up short-term chains of cause and effect in themselves. Also interesting is the way Bruce is steadily shouldered out of the romance plot, becoming more and more passive as he is shuttled in and out of precinct jails. In this regard Earl Williams undergoes a parallel experience as he is manipulated by Hildy, the sheriff, the psychologist, and Walter. We could also consider the function of the minor characters, such as Molly Malloy (Williams's platonic sweetheart), Bruce's mother, the other reporters, and especially Pettibone, the delightful emissary from the governor.

We could also note how the scenes hook into each other: An event at the end of one scene is seen as a cause leading to an effect, that is, the event that begins the next scene. For example, at the end of the first scene, Walter offers to take Bruce and Hildy to lunch; scene 2 starts with the three of them arriving at the restaurant. This exemplifies the linearity of classical narrative: Almost every scene ends with a dangling cause, the effect of which is shown at the beginning of the next scene. In *His Girl Friday,* this linear pattern helps keep the plot action moving rapidly forward, setting up each new scene quickly at the end of the previous one.

The cause–effect logic of the film illustrates yet another principle of classical narrative structure: closure. No event is uncaused. (Even Pettibone's arrival is no lucky accident, for we know that the governor is under pressure to decide about the case.) More important, both lines of action are clearly resolved at the end. Williams is saved and the politicians are disgraced. Bruce, having gone home with mother, leaves Walter and Hildy preparing for a second honeymoon no less hectic than their first.

So much for causality. What of narrative time? Classical Hollywood cinema typically subordinates time to the narrative's cause–effect relations, and one common way is to set a deadline for the action. Thus a temporal goal is wedded to a causal one, and the time becomes charged with cause–effect significance. The deadline is, of course, a convention of the newspaper genre, adding a built-in time and suspense factor. But in *His Girl Friday* each of the two plots has its own deadlines as well. The mayor and

"If you'll ever listen to some people who are talking, especially in a scene of any excitement, they all talk at the same time. All it needs is a little extra work on the dialogue. You put a few words in front of somebody's speech and put a few words at the end, and they can overlap it. It gives you a sense of speed that actually doesn't exist. And you can make the people talk a little faster."

— Howard Hawks, director

sheriff face an obvious deadline: Earl Williams must be hanged before next Tuesday's election and before the governor can reprieve him. In his political strategizing, Walter Burns faces the other side of the same deadline: He wants Williams reprieved. What we might not expect is that the romance plot has deadlines as well.

Bruce and Hildy are set to leave on a train bound for Albany and for marriage at four o'clock that very day. Walter's machinations keep forcing the couple to postpone their departure. Add to this the fact that when Bruce comes to confront Hildy and Walter, he exits with the defiant ultimatum: "I'm leaving on the nine o'clock train!" (Hildy misses that train as well.) The temporal structure of the film, then, depends on the cause–effect sequence. If Earl Williams were to be hanged next month, or if the election were two years off, or if Bruce and Hildy were planning a marriage at some distant future date, the sense of dramatic pressure would be lacking. The numerous overlapping deadlines under which all of the characters labor have the effect of squeezing together all the lines of action and sustaining the breathless pace of the film.

Another aspect of *His Girl Friday*'s patterning of time reinforces this pace. Though the plot presents events in straightforward chronological order, it takes remarkable liberties with story duration. Of course, since the action consumes about nine hours (from around 12:30 P.M. to around 9:30 P.M.), we expect that certain portions of time *between* scenes will be eliminated. And so they have been. What is unusual is that the time *within* scenes has been accelerated.

At the start of the very first scene, for example, the clock in the *Post* office reads 12:36; after 12 minutes of screen time have passed, the same clock reads 12:57. It's important to note that there have been no editing ellipses in the scene; the story duration has simply been compressed. If you clock scene 13, you will find even more remarkable acceleration. People leave on long trips and return less than 10 minutes later. Again, the editing presents continuity of duration: It is story time that goes faster than screen time. This temporal compression combines with frenetically rushed dialogue and occasionally accelerated rhythmic editing (for example, the reporters' cries just before Williams's capture) to create the film's breakneck pace.

Space, like time, is here subordinate to narrative cause and effect. Hawks's camera moves unobtrusively to reframe the characters symmetrically in the shot. (Watch any scene silent to observe the subtle balancing act that goes on during the dialogue scenes. An example is shown in 7.152–7.154.) Straight-on camera angles predominate, varied by an occasional high-angle shot down on the prison courtyard or on Williams's cell bars. Why, we might ask in passing, does the prison receive this visual emphasis in the camera angle and the lighting?

The restriction of the action to very few locales might seem a handicap, but the patterns of character placement are remarkably varied and functional. Walter's persuading Hildy to write the story is interesting from this standpoint (**11.1, 11.2;** note the reframing). And spatial continuity in the editing anticipates each dramatic point by judiciously cutting to a closer shot or smoothly matching on action so that we watch the movements and not the cuts (**11.3, 11.4**). The change in the position of Walter's arms, so apparent in our illustrations, goes unnoticed in the rapid action of the scene. Virtually every scene, especially the restaurant episode and the final scene, offers many fine examples of classical continuity editing. In all, space is used to delineate the flow of the cause–effect sequence.

We might highlight for special attention one specific item of both sound and mise-en-scene. It is plausible that newspapermen in 1939 use telephones, but *His Girl Friday* makes the phone integral to the narrative. Walter's duplicity demands phones. At the restaurant he pretends to be summoned away to a call; he makes and breaks promises to Hildy via phones; he directs Duffy and other minions by phone. More generally, the pressroom is equipped with a veritable flotilla of

11.1   In *His Girl Friday,* as Walter and Hildy pace in a complete circuit around the desk . . .

11.2   . . . Walter assumes dynamic and comic postures.

11.3   In the opening scene of *His Girl Friday,* Hildy's action of throwing her purse at Walter . . .

11.4   . . . is matched at the cut to a more distant framing.

11.5   *His Girl Friday.*

phones, enabling the reporters to contact their editors. And, of course, Bruce keeps calling Hildy from the various police stations in which he continually finds himself. The telephones thus constitute a communications network that permits the narrative to be relayed from point to point.

But Hawks also visually and sonically orchestrates the characters' use of the phones. There are many variations. One person may be talking on the phone, or several may be talking in turn on different phones, or several may be talking at once on different phones, or a phone conversation may be juxtaposed with a conversation elsewhere in the room, and so on. In scene 11, there is a polyphonic effect of reporters coming in to phone their editors, each conversation overlapping with the preceding one. Later, in scene 13, while Hildy frantically phones hospitals, Walter screams into another phone **(11.5).** And when Bruce returns for Hildy, a helter-skelter din arises that eventually sorts itself into three sonic lines: Bruce begging Hildy to listen, Hildy obsessively typing her story, and Walter yelling into the phone for Duffy to clear page one ("No, no, leave the rooster story—that's human interest!"). Like much in *His Girl Friday,* the telephones warrant close study for the complex and various ways in which they are integrated into the narrative, and for their contribution to the rapid tempo of the film.

North by Northwest

1959. MGM. Directed by Alfred Hitchcock. Script by Ernest Lehman. Photographed by Robert Burks. Edited by George Tomasini. Music composed by Bernard Herrmann. With Cary Grant, Eva Marie Saint, James Mason, Leo G. Carroll, Jesse Royce Landis.

Hitchcock long insisted that he made thrillers, not mystery films. For him, creating a puzzle was less important than generating suspense and surprise. While there are important mystery elements in films like *Notorious* (1946), *Stage Fright* (1950), and *Psycho* (1960), *North by Northwest* stands as almost a pure example of Hitchcock's belief that the mystery element can serve as merely a pretext for intriguing the audience. The film's tight causal unity enables Hitchcock to create an engrossing plot that obeys the norms of classical filmmaking. This plot is presented through a narration that continually emphasizes suspense and surprise. (For more on thrillers, see pp. 112–114.)

Like most spy films, *North by Northwest* has a complex plot, involving two major lines of action. In one line, a gang of spies mistakes advertising-agency executive Roger Thornhill for an American agent, George Kaplan. Although the spies fail to kill him, he becomes the chief suspect in a murder which the gang commits. He must flee the police while trying to track down the real George Kaplan. Unfortunately, Kaplan does not exist; he is only a decoy invented by the United States Intelligence Agency (USIA). Thornhill's pursuit of Kaplan leads to the second line of action: his meeting and falling in love with Eve Kendall, who is really the mistress of Philip Van Damm, the spies' leader. The spy-chase line and the romance line further connect when Thornhill learns that Eve is actually a double agent, secretly working for the USIA. He must then rescue her from Van Damm, who has discovered her identity and has resolved to kill her. In the course of all this, Thornhill also discovers that the spies are smuggling government secrets out of the country in pieces of sculpture.

From even so bare an outline it should be evident that the film's plot presents many conventional patterns to the viewer. There is the search pattern, seen when Thornhill sets out to find Kaplan. There is also a journey pattern: Thornhill and his pursuers travel from New York to Chicago and then to Rapid City, South Dakota, with side excursions as well. In addition, the last two-thirds of the plot is organized around the romance between Thornhill and Eve. Moreover, each pattern develops markedly in the course of the film. In the course of his search, Thornhill must often assume the identity of the man he is trailing. The journey pattern gets varied by all the vehicles Thornhill uses—cabs, train, pickup truck, police car, bus, ambulance, and airplane.

Most subtly, the romance line of action is constantly modified by Thornhill's changing awareness of the situation. Believing that Eve wants to help him, he falls in love with her. But then he learns that she sent him to the murderous appointment at Prairie Stop, and he becomes cold and suspicious. When he discovers her at the auction with Van Damm, his anger and bitterness impel him to humiliate her and make Van Damm doubt her loyalty. Only after the USIA chief, the "Professor," tells him that she is really an agent does Thornhill realize that he has misjudged and endangered her. Each step in his growing awareness alters his romantic relation to Eve.

This intricate plot is unified and made comprehensible by other familiar strategies. It has a strict time scheme, comprising four days and nights (followed by a brief epilogue on a later night). The first day and a half take place in New York; the second night on the train to Chicago; the third day in Chicago and at Prairie Stop; and the fourth day at Mount Rushmore. The timetable is neatly established early in the film. Van Damm, having abducted Roger as Kaplan, announces, "In two days you're due at the Ambassador East in Chicago, and then at the Sheraton Johnson Hotel in Rapid City, South Dakota." This itinerary prepares the spectator for the shifts in action that will occur in the rest of the film. Apart from the time scheme, the film also unifies itself through the characterization of Thornhill. He is initially presented as a resourceful liar when he steals a cab from another pedestrian. Later, he will have to lie in many circumstances to evade capture. Similarly, Roger is established as a heavy drinker, and his ability to hold his liquor will enable him to survive Van Damm's attempt to force him to kill himself when driving while drunk.

A great many motifs are repeated and help make the film cohere. Roger is constantly in danger from heights: His car hangs over a cliff, he must sneak out on the ledge of a hospital, he has to clamber up Van Damm's modernistic clifftop house, and he and Eve wind up dangling from the faces on Mount Rushmore. Thornhill's constant changing of vehicles also constitutes a motif that Hitchcock varies. A subtler example is the motif that conveys Thornhill's growing suspicion of Eve **(11.6, 11.7)**.

Still, narrative unity alone cannot explain the film's strong emotional appeal. In Chapter 3's discussion of narration, we used *North by Northwest* as an example of a hierarchy of knowledge (pp. 82–86). We suggested that as the film progresses, sometimes we are restricted only to what Roger knows, whereas at other times we know significantly more than he does. At still other moments, our range of knowledge, while greater than Roger's, is not as great as that of other characters. Now we are in a position to see how this constantly changing process helps create suspense and surprise across the whole film.

The most straightforward way in which the film's narration controls our knowledge is through the numerous optical point-of-view (POV) shots Hitchcock employs. This device yields a degree of subjective depth: We see what a character sees more or less as she or he sees it. More important here, the optical POV shot restricts us only to what that character learns at that moment. Hitchcock gives almost every major character a shot of this sort. The very first optical POV we see in the film is taken from the position of the two spies who are watching Roger apparently respond to the paging of George Kaplan **(11.8, 11.9)**. Later, we view events

11.6　On the train, when Thornhill and Eve kiss, his hands close tenderly around her hair, but . . .

11.7　. . . later in her hotel room, when she tries to embrace him after his narrow escape from death, his hands freeze in place, as if he fears touching her.

11.8 Early in *North by Northwest,* a shot of two spies looking off left is followed by . . .

11.9 . . . a shot of Thornhill from their POV.

through the eyes of Eve, of Van Damm, of his henchman Leonard, and even of a clerk at a ticket counter.

Nevertheless, by far the greatest number of POV shots are attached to Thornhill. Through his eyes we see his approach to the Townsend mansion, the mail he finds in the library, his drunken drive along the cliff, and the airplane that is "crop dusting where there ain't no crops." Some of the most extreme uses of optical POV give us Roger's experience directly (**11.10, 11.11**).

Thornhill's optical POV shots function within a narration that is often restricted not only to what he *sees* but also to what he *knows.* The plane attack at Prairie Stop, for example, is confined wholly to Roger's range of knowledge. Hitchcock could have cut away from Roger waiting by the road in order to show us the villains plotting in their plane, but he does not. Similarly, when Roger is searching for George Kaplan's room and gets a phone call from the two henchmen, Hitchcock could have used crosscutting to show the villains phoning from the lobby. Instead, we learn that they are in the hotel no sooner than Roger does. And when Thornhill and his mother hurry out of the room, Hitchcock does not use crosscutting to show the villains in pursuit. This makes it more startling when Roger and his mother get on the elevator and discover the two men there already. In scenes like these, confining us to Thornhill's range of knowledge sharpens the effect of surprise.

Sometimes the same effect comes from the film's restricting us to Roger's range of knowledge and then giving us information that he does not at the moment have. On page 419 we suggested that this sort of surprise occurs when the plot shifts us from Roger's escape from the United Nations murder to the scene at the USIA office, where the staff discuss the case. At this point we learn that there is no George Kaplan—something that Roger will not discover for many more scenes to come.

The abrupt shifts from Roger's range of knowledge yield a similar effect during the train trip from New York to Chicago. During several scenes, Eve Kendall helps Thornhill evade the police. Finally, they are alone and relatively safe in her compartment. At this point the narration shifts the range of knowledge. A message is delivered to another compartment. Hands unfold a note: "What do I do with him in the morning?" The camera then moves back to show us Leonard and Van Damm reading the message. Now we know that Eve is not merely a sympathetic stranger but someone working for the spy ring. Again, Roger will learn this much later. In such cases, the move to a less restricted range of information lets the narration put us a notch higher than Thornhill in the hierarchy of knowledge.

Such moments evoke surprise, but we have already noted that Hitchcock claimed in general to prefer to generate suspense (p. 84). Suspense is created by giving the spectator more information than the character has. In the scenes we have

11.10 An advancing truck as seen by Thornhill.

11.11 A trooper's fist coming toward the camera, again from Thornhill's POV.

just mentioned, once the effect of surprise has been achieved, the narration can use our superior knowledge to build suspense across several sequences. After the audience knows that there is no George Kaplan, every attempt by Thornhill to find him will build up suspense about whether he will discover the truth. Once we learn that Eve is working for Van Damm, her message to Roger on behalf of Kaplan will make us uncertain as to whether Roger will fall into the trap.

In these examples, suspense arises across a series of scenes. Hitchcock also uses unrestricted narration to build up suspense within a single scene. His handling of the U.N. murder differs markedly from his treatment of the scene showing Roger and his mother in Kaplan's hotel room. In the hotel scene, Hitchcock refused to employ crosscutting to show the spies' pursuit. At the United Nations, however, he crosscuts between Roger, who is searching for Townsend, and Valerian, one of the thugs following him. Just before the murder, a rightward tracking shot establishes Valerian's position in the doorway (something of which Roger is wholly unaware). Here crosscutting and camera movement widen our frame of knowledge and create suspense as to the scene's outcome.

The sequence in Chicago's Union Station is handled similarly. Here crosscutting moves us from Roger shaving in the men's room to Eve talking on the phone. Then another lateral tracking shot reveals that she is talking to Leonard, who is giving her orders from another phone booth. We now are certain that the message she will give Roger will endanger him, and the suspense is increased accordingly. (Note, however, that the narration does not reveal the conversation itself. As often happens, Hitchcock conceals certain information for the sake of further surprises.)

Thornhill's knowledge expands as the lines of action develop. On the third day, he discovers that Eve is Van Damm's mistress, that she is a double agent, and that Kaplan doesn't exist. He agrees to help the Professor in a scheme to clear Eve of any suspicion in Van Damm's eyes. When the scheme (a faked shooting in the Mount Rushmore restaurant) succeeds, Roger believes that Eve will leave Van Damm. Once more, however, he has been duped (as we have). The Professor insists that she must go off to Europe that night on Van Damm's private flight. Roger resists, but he is knocked out and held captive in a hospital. His escape leads to the final major sequence of the film.

Here the plot resolves all its lines of action, and the narration continues to expand and contract our knowledge for the sake of suspense and surprise. This climactic sequence comprises almost 300 shots and runs for several minutes, but we can conveniently divide the sequence into three subsegments.

In the first subsegment, Roger arrives at Van Damm's house and reconnoiters. He clambers up to the window and learns from a conversation between Leonard and Van Damm that the piece of sculpture they bought at the auction contains microfilm. More important, he watches Leonard inform Van Damm that Eve is an American agent. This action is conveyed largely through optical POV (**11.12, 11.13**; also 3.14–3.16). At two moments, as Leonard and Van Damm face one another, the narration gives us optical POV shots from each man's standpoint (**11.14, 11.15),** but these are enclosed, so to speak, within Roger's ongoing witnessing of the situation. For the first time in the film, Roger has more knowledge of the situation than any other character. He knows how the smuggling has been done, and he discovers that the villains intend to murder Eve.

The second phase of the sequence can be said to begin when Roger enters Eve's bedroom. She has gone back downstairs and is sitting on a couch. Again, Hitchcock emphasizes the restriction to Thornhill's knowledge by means of optical POV shots (**11.16, 11.17).** In order to warn Eve, he uses his ROT monogrammed

11.12 In *North by Northwest*, Thornhill watches in dismay . . .

11.13 . . . as Leonard betrays Eve to Van Damm.

11.14 When Van Damm reacts by hitting Leonard, he is seen from Leonard's POV . . .

11.15 . . . and then Leonard is seen from his POV.

11.16 Later, Thornhill's glance down at the living room is followed by . . .

11.17 . . . a high-angle POV framing appropriate to his position on the balcony upstairs.

11.18 When Eve notices the matchbook, she is seen from Thornhill's viewpoint upstairs.

matchbook (a motif set up on the train as a joke). He tosses the matchbook down toward Eve. This initiates still more suspense when Leonard sees it, but he unconcernedly puts it in an ashtray on the coffee table. When Eve notices the matchbook, Hitchcock varies his handling of optical POV from the first subsegment. There he was willing to show us the face-off between Van Damm and Leonard (11.14, 11.15). Now he does not show us Eve's eyes at all. Instead, through Roger's eyes, we see her back stiffen; we *infer* that she is looking at the matchbook **(11.18)**. Again, though, Roger's range of knowledge is the broadest, and his optical POV encloses another character's. On a pretext Eve returns to her room, and Roger warns her not to get on the plane.

As the spies make their way to the landing field outside, Roger starts to follow. Now Hitchcock's narration shifts again to show Van Damm's housekeeper spotting Roger's reflection in a television set. As earlier in the film, we know more than Roger does, and this generates suspense when she walks out . . . and returns with a pistol aimed at him.

The third subsegment takes place outdoors. Eve is about to get in the plane when a pistol shot distracts the spies' attention long enough for her to grab the statuette and race to the car Roger has stolen. This portion of the sequence confines us to Eve's range of knowledge, accentuating it with shots from her optical POV. The pattern of surprise interrupting a period of suspense—here, Roger's escape from the house interrupting Eve's tense walk to the plane—will dominate the rest of the sequence.

The last portion of the sequence depicts the chase across the presidents' faces on Mount Rushmore. Some crosscutting informs us of the spies' progress in following the couple, but on the whole the narration restricts us to what Eve and Thornhill know. As usual, some moments are heightened by optical POV shots, as when Eve watches Roger and Valerian roll down what seems to be a sheer drop. At the climax, Eve is dangling over the edge while Roger is clutching one of her hands and Leonard grinds his foot into Roger's other hand. It is a classic, not to say conventional, situation of suspense. Again, however, the narration reveals the limits of our knowledge. A rifle shot cracks out and Leonard falls to the ground. The Professor has arrived and captured Van Damm, and a marksman has shot Leonard. Once more, a restricted range of knowledge has enabled the narration to spring a surprise on the audience.

The same effect gets magnified at the very end. In a series of optical POV shots, Roger pulls Eve up from the brink. But this gesture is made continuous, in both sound and image, with that of him pulling her up to a train bunk. The narration ignores the details of their rescue in order to cut short the suspense of Eve's plight. Such a self-conscious transition is not completely out of place in a film that has taken time for offhand jokes. (During the opening credits, Hitchcock himself is shown being shut out of a bus. As Roger strides into the Plaza Hotel, about to be plunged into his adventure, the Muzak is playing "It's a Most Unusual Day.") This concluding twist shows once again that Hitchcock's moment-by-moment manipulation of our knowledge yields a constantly shifting play between the probable and the unexpected, between suspense and surprise.

Do the Right Thing

1989. Forty Acres and a Mule Filmworks (distributed by Universal). Directed and scripted by Spike Lee. Photographed by Ernest Dickerson. Edited by Barry Alexander Brown. Music by Bill Lee et al. With Danny Aiello, Ossie Davis, Ruby Dee, Giancarlo Esposito, Spike Lee, Bill Nunn, John Turturro, Rosie Perez.

At first viewing, Spike Lee's *Do the Right Thing,* with its many brief, disconnected scenes, restlessly wandering camera, and large number of characters without goals might not seem a classical narrative film. And, indeed, as we shall see, in some ways it does depart from classical usage. Yet it has the redundantly clear action and strong forward impetus to the plot that we associate with classical filmmaking. It also fits into a familiar genre of American cinema—the social problem film. Moreover, closer analysis reveals that Lee has also drawn on many traits of classicism to give an underlying unity to this apparently loosely constructed plot.

Do the Right Thing takes place in the predominantly African American Bedford–Stuyvesant section of Brooklyn during a heat wave. Sexual and racial tensions rise as Mookie, an irresponsible pizza delivery man, tries to get along with his Puerto Rican girlfriend, Tina, and with his Italian American boss, Sal. An elderly drunk, Da Mayor, sets out to ingratiate himself with his sharp-tongued neighbor, Mother Sister. An escalating quarrel between Sal and two customers, Buggin' Out and Radio Raheem, leads to a fight in which Radio Raheem is killed by police. The pizzeria is burned in the ensuing riot.

Do the Right Thing has many more individual sequences than, say, *His Girl Friday,* with its neatly delineated 13 scenes (p. 415). Even lumping together some of the very briefest scenes, there are at least 42 segments. Laying out a detailed segmentation of *Do the Right Thing* might be useful for another analysis, but here we want to concentrate on how Lee weaves his many scenes into a whole.

One important means of unifying the film is its setting. The entire narrative is played out on one block in Bedford–Stuyvesant. Sal's Famous Pizzeria and the Korean market opposite create a spatial anchor at one end of the block, and much of

"In *North by Northwest* during the scene on Mount Rushmore I wanted Cary Grant to hide in Lincoln's nostril and have a fit of sneezing. The Parks Commission of the Department of Interior was rather upset at this thought. I argued until one of their number asked me how I would like it if they had Lincoln play the scene in Cary Grant's nose. I saw their point at once."

— Alfred Hitchcock, director

the action takes place there. Other scenes are played out in or in front of the brown-stone buildings that line most of the rest of the street. Encounters among members of this neighborhood provide the causality for the narrative.

To match the limited setting, the action takes place in a restricted time frame—from one morning to the next. Structuring a film around a brief slice of the life of a group of characters is rare but not unknown in American filmmaking, as with *Street Scene, Dead End, American Graffiti, Nashville,* and *Magnolia.*

The radio DJ Mister Señor Love Daddy provides a running motif that also binds the film's events together. He appears in close-up in the first shot of the opening scene, and this initial broadcast provides important information about the setting and the weather—a heat wave that will intensify the characters' tensions and contribute to the final violent outbreak. As the DJ speaks, the camera tracks slowly out and cranes up to reveal the street, still empty in the early morning. At intervals throughout the film, Mister Señor Love Daddy also provides commentary on the action, as when he tells a group of characters spewing racist diatribes to "chill out." The music he plays creates sound bridges between otherwise unconnected scenes, since the radios in different locations are often tuned to his station. The end of the film echoes the beginning, as the camera tracks with Mookie in the street and we hear the DJ's voice giving a similar spiel to the one on the previous morning, then dedicating the final song to the dead Radio Raheem.

As the setting and the use of the neighborhood radio station suggest, *Do the Right Thing* centers more on the community as a whole than on a few central characters. On the one hand, there are older traditions that are worth preserving, represented by the elderly characters: the moral strength of the matriarch Mother Sister, the decency and courage of Da Mayor, the wit and common sense of the three chatting men, ML, Sweet Dick Willie, and Coconut Sid. On the other hand, the younger people need to create a new community spirit by overcoming sexual and racial conflict. The women are portrayed as trying to make the angry young African American men more responsible. Tina pressures Mookie to pay more attention to her and to their son; Jade lectures both her brother Mookie and the excitable Buggin' Out, telling the latter he should direct his energies toward doing "something positive in the community." The emphasis on community is underscored by the fact that most of the characters address each other by their nicknames.

One of the main conflicts in the film arises when Sal refuses to add some pictures of African American heroes to his "Hall of Fame" photo gallery of Italian Americans. Sal might have become a sort of elder statesman in the community, where he has run his pizzeria for 25 years. He seems to like the kids who eat his pizza, but he also views the restaurant as entirely his domain, emphatically declaring that he's the boss. Thus he reveals his lack of real integration into the community and ends by goading the more hot-headed elements into attacking him.

In creating its community, *Do the Right Thing* includes an unusually large number of characters for a classical film. Again, however, a closer examination shows that only eight of them provide the main causal action: Mookie, Tina, Sal, Sal's son Pino, Mother Sister, Da Mayor, Buggin' Out, and Radio Raheem. The others, intriguing or amusing as they may be, are more peripheral, mainly reacting to the action set in motion by these characters' conflicts and goals. (Some modern American screenwriting manuals recommend seven to eight important characters as the maximum for a clearly comprehensible film, so Lee is not departing from tradition as much as it might seem.) Moreover, the main causal action falls into two related lines, as in traditional Hollywood films: one involves the community's relations to Sal and his sons, the other deals with Mookie's personal life. Mookie becomes the pivotal figure, linking the two lines of action.

We have suggested that *Do the Right Thing* departs from classical narrative conventions in some ways. One such departure comes with respect to characters' goals. Usually the main characters of a film formulate clear-cut, long-range goals that bring them into conflict with each other. In *Do the Right Thing,* most of the eight main characters create goals only sporadically; the goals are sometimes introduced fairly late in the film, and some are vague.

Buggin' Out, for example, demands that Sal put up pictures of some black heroes on the pizzeria wall. When Sal refuses and throws him out, he shouts to the customers to boycott Sal's. Yet a little while later, when he tries to persuade his neighbors to participate in the boycott, they all refuse, and his project seems to sputter out. Then, later in the film, Radio Raheem and the mentally retarded Smiley agree to join him. Their visit to the pizzeria to threaten Sal then precipitates the climactic action. Ironically, Buggin' Out's goal is briefly achieved when Smiley puts a photograph of Malcolm X and Martin Luther King Jr. on the wall of the burning pizzeria—but by that point Buggin' Out is on his way to jail.

Mookie's goal is hinted at when we first see him. He is counting money, and he constantly emphasizes that he just wants to work and get paid. His repeated reference to the fact that he is due to be paid in the evening creates the film's only appointment, helping to emphasize the compressed time scheme. Yet his purpose remains unclear. Does he simply want the money so that he can move out of his sister's apartment, as she demands? Or does he also plan to help Tina care for their son?

Sal's goal is similarly vague—to keep operating his pizzeria in the face of rising tensions. Da Mayor articulates one of the few really clear-cut goals in the film when he tells Mother Sister that someday she will be nice to him. After he persistently acts courteously and bravely, she does in fact relent and become his friend. Sal's virulently racist son Pino has a goal—trying to convince his father that they should sell the pizzeria and get out of the black neighborhood. Perhaps he will get his desire at the end, although the narrative leaves open the question of whether Sal will rebuild.

In traditional classical films, clear-cut goals generate conflict, since the characters' desires often clash with each other. Lee neatly reverses this pattern by playing down goals but creating a community that is full of conflict from the very beginning of the film. Racial and sexual arguments break out frequently, and insults fly. Such conflict is tied to the fact that *Do the Right Thing* is a social problem film. Its didactic message gives it much of its overall unity. Everything that happens relates to a central question: With the community riven with such tensions, what can be done to heal it?

The characters' goals and actions suggest some of the possible ways of reacting to the situation. Some of the characters desire simply to avoid or escape this tense atmosphere—Pino by leaving the neighborhood, Da Mayor by overcoming Mother Sister's animosity. Mookie attempts to stay out of trouble by not siding with either Sal or his black friends in their escalating quarrel; only the death of Radio Raheem drives him to join in, and indeed initiate, the attack on Sal's pizzeria.

Other characters attempt to solve their problems. One central goal is Tina's desire to get Mookie to behave more responsibly and spend time with her and with their child. There is a suggestion at the end that she may be succeeding to some extent. Mookie gets his pay from Sal and says that he will get another job and that he's going to see his son. The last shot shows him walking down the now-quiet street, hinting that he may really visit his son more regularly in the future.

The central question in the film, however, is not whether any one character will achieve his or her goals. It is whether the pervasive conflicts can be resolved peacefully or violently. As the DJ says on the morning after the riot, "Are we gonna live together—together are we gonna live?"

"It's funny how the script is evolving into a film about race relations. This is America's biggest problem, always has been (since we got off the boat), always will be. I've touched upon it in my earlier works, but I haven't yet dealt with it head on as a primary subject."

— Spike Lee, from the production journal of *Do the Right Thing*

Do the Right Thing leaves unanswered questions at the end. Will Sal rebuild? Is Mookie really going back to see his son? Most important, though the conflict that flared up has died down, it is still present in the community, waiting to resurface. The old problem of how to tame it remains, and so the film does not achieve complete closure. Indeed, such an ending is typical of the social problem film. While the immediate conflict may be resolved, the underlying dilemma that caused it remains.

That is also why there is a deliberate ambiguity at the end. Just as we are left at the end of *Citizen Kane* to wonder whether the revelation of the meaning of "Rosebud" explains Kane's character, in *Do the Right Thing* we are left to ponder what "the right thing" is. The film continues after the final story action, with two nondiegetic quotations from Martin Luther King Jr. and Malcolm X. The King passage advocates a nonviolent approach to the struggle for civil rights, while Malcolm X condones violence in self-defense.

Do the Right Thing refuses to suggest which leader is right—although the narrative action and use of the phrase "by any means necessary" at the end of the credits seem to weight the film's position in favor of Malcolm X. Still, the juxtaposition of the two quotations, in combination with the open-ended narrative, also seems calculated to spur debate. Perhaps the implication is that each position is viable under certain circumstances. The line of action involving Sal's pizzeria ends in violence; yet at the same time Da Mayor is able to win Mother Sister's friendship gently and patiently.

As in its narrative structure, the style of *Do the Right Thing* stretches the traditional techniques of classical filmmaking. It begins with a credits sequence during which Rosie Perez performs a vigorous and aggressive dance to the rap song "Fight the Power." The editing here is strongly discontinuous, as she wears sometimes a red dress, sometimes a boxer's outfit, and sometimes a jacket and pants. One moment she is on the street; then she suddenly appears in an alley. This brief sequence, which is not part of the narrative, recalls music videos, employing the flashy style made familiar by MTV and television commercials.

Nothing in the rest of *Do the Right Thing* is quite as discontinuous or extreme as the credits sequence, but Lee uses a loose version of the traditional continuity system. Veteran film editor Dede Allen has referred to "an extreme MTV cutting" in some modern Hollywood films. Lee himself has made both music videos and commercials. He draws on a broad range of techniques, handling some scenes in virtuosic long takes, others with shot/reverse shot, others with extensive camera movements. In two cases, he even cuts together two takes of the same action, so that the plot presents a single important story event twice: when Mookie first kisses Tina and when the garbage can hits Sal's window. One result of this varied style is a suggestion of the vigor and variety of the community itself.

Despite the many quick changes of locale, Lee uses continuity devices to establish space clearly. As we saw in Chapter 8, he is adept at using shot/reverse shot without breaking the axis of action (8.89–8.94, from *She's Gotta Have It*, p. 320). *Do the Right Thing* similarly contains many shot/reverse-shot conversations where the eyelines are consistent **(11.19, 11.20).** Yet Lee opts to handle other conversations without any editing. The lengthy conversation in which Pino asks Sal to sell the pizzeria is handled in one long take **(11.21–11.23).**

Cinematic technique frequently emphasizes the community as a whole. Indeed, one reason why the film has so many segments is that there are frequent cuts from one action to another. The narration is largely unrestricted, flitting from one group of characters to another, seldom lingering with any individual. Similarly, complex camera movements follow characters through the street, catching glimpses

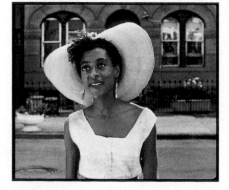

11.19   In *Do the Right Thing*, this shot/reverse-shot conversation between Jade and . . .

11.20   . . . Buggin' Out uses correct eyeline directions.

11.21 This long take in *Do The Right Thing* begins with a track in . . .

11.22 . . . toward Sal and Pino and lasts . . .

11.23 . . . until Smiley appears outside and Pino chases him away.

11.24 Da Mayor and Mother Sister talk and then move out into her front room, the camera tracking with them and . . .

11.25 . . . passing through the window as they reach it, craning down . . .

11.26 . . . to a close view of Mookie, on the way to the pizzeria.

of other activities going on in the background. Other camera movements slide away from one line of action to another. For example, on the morning after the riot, Da Mayor wakes up in Mother Sister's apartment **(11.24–11.26).**

The dense sound track helps characterize the community. As Mookie walks past a row of houses, the sounds of radios turned to different stations fade up and down, hinting at the offscreen presence of the inhabitants. The music broadcast by the DJ plays a large role in drawing the many brief scenes together, with the same song carrying over various exchanges of dialogue. The different ethnic groups are characterized by the types of music they listen to.

Style also stresses the underlying problems in the community. Radio Raheem's threatening demeanor is emphasized in some scenes by his direct address into a wide-angle lens **(11.27).** Mookie's self-absorption and lack of interest in the neighborhood is suggested in a visual motif of high-angle views showing him stepping unheedingly on a cheerful chalk picture of a house that a little girl is drawing on the pavement **(11.28).** Sound contributes to the racial tensions, as in the scenes where Radio Raheem annoys people by playing his rap song at high volume.

Thus *Do the Right Thing,* despite its stretching of traditional Hollywood conventions, remains a good example of a contemporary approach to classical filmmaking. Its style reflects the looser techniques that became conventions of post-1960s cinema—an era when the impact of television and European art films

11.27 Radio Raheem orders a slice of pizza from Sal, who has ordered him to turn his radio off.

11.28   One shot from a motif of Mookie walking across a chalk drawing.

inspired filmmakers to incorporate somewhat more variety into the Hollywood system. Even the plot's departures from tradition are somewhat motivated because Lee adopts the basic purpose of the social problem film—to make us think and to stir debate.

NARRATIVE ALTERNATIVES TO CLASSICAL FILMMAKING

Breathless (À Bout de souffle)

1960. Les Films Georges de Beauregard, Impéria Films and Société Nouvelle de Cinéma. Directed by Jean-Luc Godard. Story outline by François Truffaut, dialogue by Godard. Photographed by Raoul Coutard. Edited by Cécile Decugis. Music by Martial Solal. With Jean-Paul Belmondo, Jean Seberg, Daniel Boulanger, Henri-Jacques Huet, Van Doude, Jean-Pierre Melville.

In some ways, *Breathless* imitates a 1940s Hollywood trend, the *film noir,* or "dark film." Such films dealt with hard-boiled detectives, gangsters, or ordinary men tempted into crime. Often a seductive femme fatale lured the protagonist into a dangerous mission for hidden purposes of her own (for example, *The Maltese Falcon, Double Indemnity*). *Breathless*'s plot links it to a common *noir* vehicle—the outlaw movie involving young criminals on the run (such as *They Live by Night, Gun Crazy*).

The bare-bones story could serve as the basis of a Hollywood script. A car thief, Michel, kills a motorcycle cop and flees to Paris in order to get money to escape to Italy. He also tries to convince Patricia, an American art student and aspiring writer with whom he had a brief affair, to go with him. After equivocating for nearly two days, she agrees. Just as Michel is about to receive the cash he needs, Patricia calls the police, and they kill him.

Yet Godard's presentation of this story could never pass for a polished studio product. For one thing, Michel's behavior is presented as driven *by* the very movies that *Breathless* imitates. He rubs his thumb across his lips in imitation of his idol Humphrey Bogart. Yet he is a petty thief whose life spins out of control. He can only fantasize himself as a romantic Hollywood tough guy.

The film's ambivalent attitude toward Hollywood cinema also pervades form and technique. As we've seen, the norms of classical style and storytelling promote narrative clarity and unity. In contrast, *Breathless* appears awkward and casual, almost amateurish. It makes character motivations ambiguous and lingers over incidental dialogue. Its editing jumps about frenetically. And, whereas *films noirs* were made largely in the studio, where selective lighting could swathe the characters in a brooding atmosphere, *Breathless* utilizes location shooting with available lighting.

These strategies make Michel's story quirky, uncertain, and deglamorized. They also ask the audience to enjoy the film's rough-edged reworking of Hollywood formulas. An opening title (missing from American prints) dedicates the film to Monogram Pictures, a Poverty Row studio that churned out ramshackle B-movies. The title seems to announce a film that is indebted to Hollywood but not wholly bound by its norms.

Like many protagonists in classical Hollywood films, Michel has two main goals. In order to leave France, he must search for his friend Antonio, the only one who can cash a check for him. He also hopes to persuade Patricia to go with him, and it becomes apparent as the action progresses that, despite his flippant attitude, his love for her outweighs his desire to escape.

In a classical film, these goals would drive the action along fairly steadily. Yet in *Breathless* the plot moves in fits and starts. Brief scenes—some largely unconnected to the goals—alternate with long stretches of seemingly irrelevant dialogue. Most of *Breathless*'s 22 separate segments run four minutes or less. One 43-second scene consists simply of Michel pausing in front of a theater and looking at a picture of Bogart.

Scenes containing crucial action are sometimes brief and confusing. The murder of the traffic cop, an event that triggers much of what follows, is handled in a very elliptical fashion. In long shot, we see the officer approaching Michel's car, parked in a side road. In medium long shot Michel reaches into the car for the gun. A close shot of his head follows, as the cop's voice is heard saying, "Don't move or I'll drill you" **(11.29)**. Two very brief close-ups pan along Michel's arm and along the gun **(11.30, 11.31)**, with the sound of a gunshot. We then get a glimpse of the cop falling into some underbrush **(11.32)**, followed by an extreme long shot of Michel, running far across a field. So much action has been left out that we can barely comprehend what is happening, let alone judge whether Michel shot deliberately or by accident.

In contrast to the whirlwind presentation of this key action, a lengthy conversation in the middle of the film brings the narrative progression almost to a standstill. For nearly 25 minutes Michel and Patricia chat in her bedroom. At some points Michel attempts to further his goals, trying vainly to phone Antonio and to persuade Patricia to come to Rome. Most of the conversation, however, is trivial, as when Michel criticizes the way Patricia puts on lipstick or when she asks whether he prefers records or the radio. The pair try to outstare each other, and they discuss Patricia's new poster. So rambling is their exchange that some critics have assumed that the dialogue was improvised (although Godard attests that it was all scripted).

At one point, Patricia suggests that she will not run off with him because she does not know if she loves him. Michel: "When will you know?" Patricia: "Soon." Michel: "What does that mean—soon? In a month, in a year?" Patricia: "Soon means soon." So although the pair make love, by the end of the long scene (which occupies nearly a third of this 89-minute film) we still do not have a definite step forward or backward in Michel's courting of Patricia, and he has made no progress toward escaping. Such scenes make him seem more like a wandering, easily distracted delinquent than the desperate, driven hero of a *film noir*.

It is not until the scene outside the *Tribune* office that another decisive causal action occurs. A passerby (played by Godard) recognizes Michel from a newspaper photograph and tells the police. This triggers a chain of events that will lead to Michel's death. Yet immediately the plot meanders once more. In the next scene, Patricia participates in a news conference with a famous novelist, a character unrelated to the main action. Most of the questions asked by the reporters deal with the differences between men and women, but the novelist's responses seem more playful than meaningful. Finally Patricia asks him his greatest ambition, and he replies enigmatically, "To become immortal and then to die." Patricia's puzzled glance into the camera that ends the scene hints at the ambiguity that will linger at the film's end.

After Detective Vital questions Patricia at the *Tribune* office, she and Michel realize that the police are on his trail. Now *Breathless* begins to progress in a somewhat more conventional way. In the next scene, Patricia says that she loves Michel "enormously," and they steal a car. Here Michel seems to reach his romantic goal, as Patricia commits herself to fleeing with him. When Antonio agrees to bring the cash the next morning, Michel moves toward his second goal. We might anticipate

11.29 In *Breathless*'s murder scene, brief shots . . .

11.30 . . . give glimpses of Michel's actions . . .

11.31 . . . in pointing a gun . . .

11.32 . . . and the death of the cop, without showing anything clearly.

possible outcomes: The pair will escape, or one or both will be killed in the attempt. The next morning, however, Patricia confounds our expectations by betraying Michel to Vital. Even then Michel has a last chance. Antonio arrives just before the police, with money and a getaway car—yet Michel cannot bring himself to leave Patricia.

The ending is particularly enigmatic. As Michel lies bleeding to death, Patricia looks down at him. He slowly makes the same playful faces at her that he had made during their bedroom conversation. Muttering, "That's really disgusting" ("C'est vraiment dégueulasse"), he dies. Patricia asks Detective Vital what he said, and Vital misreports Michel's last words: "He said, 'You are really a bitch'" ("Il a dit, 'Vous êtes vraiment une dégueulasse'"). (Unfortunately, the English subtitles suggest that Vital reports Michel's words accurately.) We are left to ponder what Michel thought was disgusting—Patricia's betrayal, his own last-minute failure to flee, or simply his death. In the final shot, Patricia looks out at the camera, asks what "dégueulasse" means, rubs her lips with the Bogart-inspired gesture that Michel has used throughout the film **(11.33),** and abruptly turns her back on us as the image fades out.

Breathless achieves a degree of closure: Michel fails to achieve his goals. But we are left with many questions. Although Michel and Patricia talk constantly about themselves, we learn remarkably little about why they act as they do. Unlike characters in classical films, they do not have a set of clearly defined traits. The film begins with Michel saying, "All in all, I'm a dumb bastard," and in a way his actions bear this out. Yet we never learn background information which would explain his decisions. Why did he become a car thief? Since he casually leaves his female accomplice early in the film, what makes him willing to risk death to stay with Patricia, a woman whom he has known only briefly? Because dying for the love of an unworthy woman is what a would-be Hollywood hero is supposed to do?

Patricia's traits and goals are even more amorphous and ambiguous. When Michel first finds her selling newspapers on the Champs Elysées, she is far from welcoming. Yet at the scene's end she runs back to give him a kiss. She keeps saying she wants to get a job as a *Tribune* reporter and to write a novel, yet she seems to throw these ambitions away when she thinks she loves Michel. Patricia also tells Michel she is pregnant by him, but she has not received the final test results, and she never raises this as a reason why she should stay in Paris. She often says that she is scared, yet after she and Michel steal a car, she remarks, "It's too late now to be scared." This hints that she has resolved her own doubts and has thrown her lot definitively in with Michel. When she suddenly betrays him, she does not intend that he should be killed but simply wants to force him to leave her. Still, her speech about why she informed on Michel seems not really to explain her abrupt change of heart. Just as Michel is ill suited to be a tough guy, Patricia is too naive and indecisive to play the role of the classic femme fatale.

In the outlaw *film noir,* the characters are intensely committed to one another; here Michel and Patricia seem to have few strong feelings about what they do. When the treacherous woman deceives the *noir* hero, he often becomes bitterly disillusioned; but Michel apparently does not blame Patricia for betraying him. It is as if these ambivalent, diffident, confused characters are unable to play out the desperately passionate roles that the Hollywood tradition has assigned to them.

Breathless's elliptical, occasionally opaque, narrative is presented through techniques that are equally unconventional. As we have seen, Hollywood films use a three-point lighting system of key, fill, and back light, carefully controlled in a film studio (pp. 194–195). *Breathless* was shot entirely on location, even for interiors.

11.33 Patricia's enigmatic gesture at the end of *Breathless.*

11.34 When Patricia sits against a window and lights a cigarette, the natural light of the scene illuminates her only from behind.

11.35 Michel's first meeting with Patricia as she strolls along the Champs Elysées selling papers occurs in a three-minute take.

11.36 When Michel visits a travel agent trying to claim his check, the framing glides and turns with ease as he moves around the desks and through the corridors.

Godard and cinematographer Raoul Coutard opted not to add any artificial light in the settings. As a result, the characters' faces sometimes fall into shadow **(11.34)**.

Filming on location, especially in small apartments, would ordinarily make it difficult to obtain a variety of camera angles and movements. But taking advantage of new portable equipment, Coutard was able to film while handholding the camera. Several lengthy tracking shots follow the characters **(11.35)**. Coutard apparently sat in a wheelchair to film this shot, as well as more elaborate movements that follow the characters in interiors **(11.36)**. Such shots recall the location shooting of many *films noirs,* such as the final airport scenes of Stanley Kubrick's *The Killing,* but the low camera position and the passersby who turn to look at the actors (as with the man at the right in 11.35) call attention to the technique in a way that departs from Hollywood usage.

Even more striking than the mise-en-scene is Godard's editing. Again he sometimes follows tradition but at other points he breaks away. Standard shot/reverse-shot cutting organizes several scenes **(11.37, 11.38)**. Similarly, when Michel spots the man examining the telltale photo in the newspaper, Godard supplies correctly matched glances. Since this is a turning point in the plot, the adherence to the 180° rule makes it evident that the man has spotted Michel and may inform on him.

Yet what makes the film still quite jolting today are its violations of continuity editing. If there is one type of cut that the Hollywood editor deplores, it is the jump cut, in which a segment of time is eliminated without the camera being moved to a new vantage point (p. 335–336). Yet *Breathless* employs jump cuts throughout. In an early scene, when Michel visits an old girlfriend, jump cuts shift their positions abruptly **(11.39, 11.40)**. We have seen another example, when Godard presents a series of jump cuts of Patricia during a conversation in a car (8.142, 8.143, again showing the last and first frames of contiguous shots).

Even when Godard shifts the camera position between cuts, he may drop out a bit of time or mismatch the actors' positions. At many cuts the action seems to jerk forward, like a needle skipping on a phonograph record. One effect of this jumpy editing is to enliven the rhythm. At times, as during the murder of the police officer, we have to be very alert to follow the action. This fast pace is reinforced by the fact that, as we have seen, most of the individual scenes run for under four minutes. The elliptical editing also makes certain scenes stand out by contrast: the lengthy single-take scenes with moving camera and the rambling 25-minute conversation in Patricia's apartment.

11.37 When Michel pauses in front of a movie theater and looks at a photo on display . . .

11.38 . . . Bogart seems to look back at him in reverse shot.

11.39   The last frame of one shot during Michel's visit to an old girlfriend . . .

11.40   . . . and the first of the next shot, creating a jump cut.

11.41   In the first shot, Patricia moves from left to right . . .

11.42   . . . and in the next, she is walking right to left, a flagrant violation of conventional screen direction.

> "On *À Bout de Souffle,* he'd (Godard) ask the script-girl what kind of shot was required next to fulfill the requirements of traditional continuity. She'd tell him, and then he'd do the exact opposite."
>
> — Raoul Coutard, cinematographer

Aside from avoiding matches on action, Godard often flaunts the moments when he does not adhere to the 180° rule, as when Patricia walks along reading a paper **(11.41, 11.42)**. In the opening scene, as Michel's accomplice points out a car he wants to steal, the eyelines are quite unclear, and we get little sense of where the two are in relation to each other.

The film's sound often reinforces these editing discontinuities. When the characters' dialogue and other diegetic sounds continue over the jump cuts, we are forced to notice the contradiction: Time is apparently omitted from the visual track but not from the sound track. The location shooting also created situations in which ambient noises intrude on the dialogue. A passing siren outside Patricia's apartment nearly overwhelms her conversation with Michel during the long central scene. Later the press conference with Parvulesco inexplicably takes place on an airport observation platform, where the loud whines of nearby planes drown out conversation. Such scenes lack the balance of volumes of the well-mixed Hollywood sound track.

Godard's break with the rules of smooth sound and picture steers *Breathless* away from the glamorous portrayals seen in the Hollywood crime film. The stylistic awkwardness suits the pseudo-documentary roughness of filming in an actual, hectic Paris. The discontinuities are also consistent with other nontraditional techniques, like the motif of the characters' mysterious glances into the camera. In addition, the jolts in picture and sound create a self-conscious narration that makes the viewer aware of its stylistic choices. In making the director's hand more apparent, the film presents itself as a deliberately unpolished revision of tradition.

Godard did not set out to criticize Hollywood films. Instead, he took genre conventions identified with 1940s America and gave them a contemporary Parisian setting and a modern, self-conscious treatment. He thereby created a new type of hero and heroine. Aimless, somewhat banal, lovers on the run became central to later outlaw movies such as *Bonnie and Clyde, Badlands,* and *True Romance.* More broadly, Godard's film became a model for directors who wished to create exuberantly offhand homages to, and reworkings of, Hollywood tradition. This attitude would be central to the stylistic movement that *Breathless* helped launch, the French New Wave. (See Chapter 12, pp. 486–489.)

Tokyo Story (Tokyo Monogatari)

1953. Shochiku/Ofuna, Japan. Directed by Yasujiro Ozu. Script by Ozu and Kogo Noda. Photographed by Yuharu Atsuta. With Chishu Ryu, Chieko Higashiyama, So Yamamura, Haruko Sugimura, Setsuko Hara.

We have seen how the classical Hollywood approach to filmmaking created a stylistic system (continuity) in order to establish and maintain a clear narrative space and time. The continuity system is a specific set of guidelines that a filmmaker may follow. But some filmmakers do not use the continuity system. They may flaunt the guidelines by violating them, as Godard does in *Breathless,* creating a casual, lively film. Or they may develop a set of alternative guidelines—at least as strict as Hollywood's—that allows them to make films that are quite distinct from classical films.

Yasujiro Ozu is one such filmmaker. His approach to the creation of a narrative differs from that used in more classical films like *His Girl Friday* or *North by Northwest.* Instead of making narrative events the central organizing principle, Ozu tends to decenter narrative somewhat. As a result, spatial and temporal structures come forward and create their own interest. *Tokyo Story,* the first Ozu film to make a considerable impression in the West, offers an enlightening introduction to some of Ozu's characteristic filmmaking strategies.

Tokyo Story presents a simple narrative of an elderly provincial couple who visit their grown children in Tokyo, only to find themselves treated as inconvenient nuisances. The narrative is quiet and contemplative, yet Ozu's style does not simply conform to some characteristically spiritual Japanese system of filmmaking. Indeed, Japanese filmmakers and critics found his nonclassical approach as puzzling as did Western audiences. By creating a systematic alternative method of shaping spatial and temporal relations, Ozu sought to engage the spectator's attention more deeply. While in Hollywood style is subservient to narrative, Ozu makes it an equal partner. We watch the narrative action, the spatial relations, and the temporal relations unfold simultaneously, and all are equally dramatic and engaging. As a result, even a simple narrative like that of *Tokyo Story* becomes fresh and fascinating.

Tokyo Story's narration is, by classical standards, rather oblique. Sometimes we learn of important narrative events only after they have occurred. The last portion of *Tokyo Story,* for example, involves a series of events surrounding the sudden illness and death of the grandmother of the family. Although the grandparents are the film's two central characters, we do not see the grandmother falling ill. We hear about it only when her son and daughter receive telegrams with the news. Similarly, the grandmother's death occurs between scenes. In one scene her children are gathered by her bedside, and in the next scene they are mourning her.

Yet these ellipses are not evidence of a fast-paced film such as *His Girl Friday,* which must cover a lot of narrative ground in a hurry. On the contrary, the sequences of *Tokyo Story* often linger over details: the melancholy conversation between the

11.43   In *Tokyo Story,* a shot of Noriko at her desk . . .

11.44   . . . leads to a shot of a building . . .

11.45   . . . and then another of construction . . .

11.46   . . . before shifting to the locale for the next scene.

"I don't think the film has a grammar. I don't think film has but one form. If a good film results, then that film has created its own grammar."

— Yasujiro Ozu

grandfather and his friends in a bar as they discuss their disappointment in their children or the grandmother's walk on a Sunday with her grandchild. The result is a shift in the narrative balance. Key narrative events are deemphasized by means of ellipses, whereas narrative events that we do see in the plot are simple and understated.

Accompanying this shift away from a presentation of the most highly dramatic events of the narrative is a sliding away from narratively significant space. Scenes do not begin and end with shots that frame the most important narrative elements in the mise-en-scene. Instead of the usual transitional devices, such as dissolves and fades, Ozu typically employs a series of separate transitional shots linked by cuts. And these transitional shots often show spaces not directly connected with the action of the scene; the spaces are usually *near* where that action will take place. The opening of the film, for example, has five shots of the port town of Onomichi—the bay, schoolchildren, a passing train—before the sixth shot reveals the grandparents packing for their trip to Tokyo. Although a couple of important motifs make their first appearances in these first five shots, no narrative causes occur to get the action underway. (Compare the openings of *His Girl Friday* and *North by Northwest.*) Nor do these transitional shots appear only at the beginning. Several sequences in Tokyo start with shots of factory smokestacks, even though no action ever occurs in these locales.

These transitions have only a minimal function as establishing shots. Sometimes the transitions do not establish space at all but tend to confuse the space of the upcoming scene. After the daughter-in-law, Noriko, gets a phone call at work telling her of the grandmother's illness, the scene ends in a medium shot of her sitting pensively at her desk; the only diegetic sound is the loud clack of typewriters **(11.43).** A nondiegetic musical transition comes up in this shot. Then there is a cut to a low-angle long shot of a building under construction **(11.44).** Riveting noises replace the typewriters, with the music continuing. The next shot is another low angle of the construction site **(11.45).**

A cut changes the locale to the clinic belonging to the eldest son, Dr. Hirayama. The sister, Shige, is present. The music ends and the new scene begins **(11.46).** In this segment, the two shots of the construction site are not necessary to the action. The film does not give us any indication where the building under construction is. We might assume that it is outside Noriko's office, but the riveting sound is not audible in the interior shots.

As usual, we should look for the functions of such stylistic devices. It is hard to assign such transitional shots either explicit or implicit meanings. For example, someone might propose that the transitional shots symbolize the new Tokyo that is alien to the visiting grandparents from a village reminiscent of the old Japan. But

11.47 In the beauty salon, systematic cutting moves from one side of the axis of action . . .

11.48 . . . to the other side . . .

11.49 . . . and back again.

often the transitional spaces do not involve outdoor locales, and some shots are within the characters' homes. A more systematic function, we suggest, is narrational, having to do with the flow of story information.

Ozu's narration alternates between scenes of story action and inserted portions that lead us to or away from them. As we watch the film, we start to form expectations about these wedged-in shots. Ozu emphasizes stylistic patterning by creating anticipation about when a transition will come and what it will show. The patterning may delay our expectations and even create some surprise.

For example, early in the film Mrs. Hirayama, the doctor's wife, argues with her son, Minoru, over where to move his desk to make room for the grandparents. This issue is dropped, and there follows a scene of the grandparents' arrival. This ends on a conversation in an upstairs room. Transitional music again comes up over the end of the scene. The next shot frames an empty hallway downstairs that contains Minoru's school desk, but no one is in the shot. There follows an exterior long shot of children running along a ridge near the house; these children are not characters in the action. Finally, a cut back inside reveals Minoru at his father's desk in the clinic portion of the house, studying. Here the editing creates a very indirect route between two scenes, going first to a place where we expect a character to be (at his own desk) but is not; then the scene moves completely away from the action, outdoors. Only then, in the third shot, does a character reappear and the action continue. In these transitional passages, a kind of game emerges, one that asks us to form expectations not only about story action but about the editing and mise-en-scene.

Within scenes, Ozu's editing patterns are as systematic as those of Hollywood, but they tend to be sharply opposed to continuity rules. For example, Ozu does not observe the 180° line, the axis of action. Nor is his violation of these rules occasional, as Ford's is in *Stagecoach* (p. 322). Ozu frequently cuts 180° across the line to frame the scene's space from the opposite direction. This, of course, violates rules of screen direction, since characters or objects on the right in the first shot will appear on the left in the second, and vice versa. At the beginning of a scene in Shige's beauty salon, the initial interior medium shot frames Shige from opposite the front door **(11.47).** Then a 180° cut reveals a medium long shot of a woman under a hair dryer; the camera now faces the rear of the salon **(11.48).** Another cut 180° presents a new long shot of the room, again oriented toward the door, and the grandparents come into the salon **(11.49).** Rather than being an isolated violation of continuity rules, this is Ozu's typical way of framing and editing a scene.

Ozu is a master of matching on action, but he often does so in unusual ways. For example, as Noriko and the grandmother walk toward the door of Noriko's apartment, there is a 180° cut **(11.50, 11.51).** The women's movements are closely

11.50 From this head-on view of Noriko and the grandmother . . .

11.51 . . . there is a cut to a tails-on view of them.

11.52 *Tokyo Story.*

11.53 *Tokyo Story.*

11.54 *Tokyo Story.*

11.55 *Tokyo Story.*

11.56 *Tokyo Story.*

11.57 *Tokyo Story.*

matched, but because the consistent camera height and distance create such similar framings, the effect at the cut is to make it seem momentarily that the pair bump into themselves. Their screen positions, left to right, are also abruptly reversed, something that is usually considered an error in continuity. A classical filmmaker would most likely avoid such an unusual cut, but Ozu uses it here and in other films as part of his distinctive style.

As these examples illustrate, Ozu does not restrict his camera and editing patterns to the semicircular space on one side of the axis of action. He cuts in a full circle around the action, usually in segments of 90° or 180°. This means that backgrounds change drastically, as in both previous examples. In a Hollywood film, the camera rarely crosses the axis of action to look at the fourth wall. Because surroundings change more frequently in *Tokyo Story,* they become more prominent in relation to the action; the viewer must pay attention to setting or become confused.

The transitional shots that prolong or thwart the viewer's hypotheses and the 360° space that asks us to notice surroundings can work together. When the grandparents visit a spa at Atami, the scene begins with a long shot along a hallway **(11.52).** Latin-style dance music plays offscreen, and several people walk through the hall. The next shot **(11.53)** is a long shot of another hallway upstairs, with a maid carrying a tray; two pairs of slippers are just visible by a doorway at the lower left. Next comes a medium long shot of a hallway by a courtyard **(11.54).** More people bustle through. A medium shot of a mah-jongg game follows **(11.55);** there is a loud sound of talking and moving pieces about. Then Ozu cuts 180° across the axis, framing another mah-jongg table **(11.56).** The first table is now in the background, viewed from the opposite side. The next cut returns to the medium long shot along the courtyard hallway **(11.57).** In all of these shots, we have not yet seen the grandparents, who are the only major characters present at the spa.

Finally, there is a medium shot of the two pairs of slippers by the door in the upper hallway **(11.58),** suggesting that this is the grandparents' room. The panes of glass in the wall reflect the lively movement of the offscreen party, and the loud music and talk are still audible. A medium shot of the Hirayamas in bed, trying to sleep through the noise, finally reveals the narrative situation, and a conversation begins between the couple **(11.59).** For seven shots the film slowly explores the space of the scene, gradually letting us discover the situation. The presence of the slippers in the second shot (11.53) is almost unnoticeable. It hints that the grandparents are there, but the revelation of their whereabouts is then put off for several more shots.

In these ways Ozu draws our attention away from the strictly causal functions of space and makes space important in its own right. He does the same with the flat space of the screen as well. (Examples of graphic matches from Ozu films are found in 8.131–8.136.) The stylistic device is characteristic of Ozu, who seldom uses the graphic match for any narrative purpose. In *Tokyo Story* a conversation situation leads to a shot/reverse-shot pattern but again with cuts 180° across the axis of action. The two men speaking are framed so that each looks off right. (In Hollywood, upholders of the continuity system would claim that this implies that both are looking off toward the same thing.) Because they are positioned similarly in the frame, the result is a strong graphic match from one shot to another **(11.60, 11.61).** In this respect, Ozu's style owes something to abstract form (see Chapter 5, pp. 147–157 and Chapter 10, pp. 407–409). It is as if he sought to make a narrative film that would still make graphic similarities as evident as they are in an abstract film like *Ballet mécanique.*

The use of space and time in *Tokyo Story* is not willfully obscure, nor does it have a symbolic function in the narrative. Rather, it suggests a different relationship among space, time, and narrative logic than exists in the classical film. Space and time no longer simply function unobtrusively to create a clear narrative line. Ozu brings them forward and makes them into prominent aesthetic elements in their own right. A large part of the film's appeal lies in its strict but playful treatment of figures, settings, and movement. Ozu does not eliminate narrative, but he opens it out. *Tokyo Story* and his other films allow other stylistic devices to exist independently alongside narrative. The result is that the viewer is invited to look at his films in a new way, to participate in a play of space and time.

Chungking Express (Chung Hing sam lam)

1994. Jet Tone, Hong Kong. Directed by Wong Kar-wai. Script by Wong Kar-wai. Photographed by Andrew Lau Wai-keung and Christopher Doyle. With Brigitte Lin Ching-hsia, Takeshi Kaneshiro, Tony Leung Chiu-wai, Faye Wong Jingwen.

Contemporary Hollywood filmmaking has sometimes explored what has been called the *web-of-life plot.* Instead of two primary lines of action, as in *His Girl Friday* or *North by Northwest,* some recent films weave together a large number of plotlines, often involving many characters. Precedents for this can be found in *Grand Hotel* (1932) and *Nashville* (1976), but in the 1990s such films as *Short Cuts, Pulp Fiction, Time Code, Magnolia,* and *Traffic* made this sort of plotting more common. The plotlines may at first seem completely isolated from one another, but usually they converge, revealing unexpected causal connections. In *Magnolia,* the characters are linked through television (all are connected in one way or another to the television producer Earl Partridge) and through chance encounters (as when the police patrolman meets Partridge's unhappy daughter). In *Pulp Fiction,* the line of action involving the two hitmen and their boss is eventually linked

11.58   *Tokyo Story.*

11.59   *Tokyo Story.*

11.60   A graphic match created by cutting across the line from the grandfather . . .

11.61   . . . to his friend as they converse.

to that of the boxer Butch, and at the very end the opening diner scene is connected with the fates of Jules and Vincent.

The audience expects a web-of-life plot to reveal unforeseen relations among the disparate characters. Seen from this standpoint, *Chungking Express* constitutes an intriguing experiment in nonclassical form. It has only about six major characters, but it is broken into two distinct stories, each organized around a different batch of characters and presented one after the other. One question viewers commonly ask is What has director Wong Kar-wai accomplished by putting these two stories in the same film?

In the first tale, Officer 223 (for ease of recall, we'll call him Officer 1) has just broken up with his girlfriend and lives in hope that she'll take him back before May 1, his 25th birthday. Wandering the city at night, he runs into a mysterious woman in dark glasses and a blonde wig. He doesn't know that she runs a drug-smuggling outfit. She has hired some Indian down-and-outs to swallow bags of cocaine and fly out of the country, but they have defected with the drugs. She must find them or face the wrath of her boss, a Westerner who runs a bar. Officer 1 meets her in a bar and takes her to a cheap hotel, where she sleeps off her drinking and he eats snacks. In the morning he leaves her; she posts an affectionate message on his pager before returning to the bar and shooting her boss dead.

The second and longer tale introduces Officer 633 (Officer 2), who is happy with his girlfriend, a flight attendant. But one day she leaves him. He is still trying to get over their affair when Faye, a counterwoman at his favorite fast-food spot, Midnight Express, takes an interest in him. The flight attendant leaves Officer 2's keys at the Midnight Express for him to pick up, and Faye uses them to explore his apartment while he's out. She tidies it up and redecorates it to try to cheer him up, leaving fresh soap and towels and filling his aquarium with fish. After catching her in the apartment, he realizes she's flirting with him; and he packs up his girlfriend's things and sets off to meet Faye for a date. But she stands him up, leaving for California—the place she had always hoped to visit. A year later, he has bought the Midnight Express and is renovating it when she returns. Now *she's* a flight attendant, and there is a hint that their romance might finally begin.

What links the two parts? Both employ hand-held camerawork, moody music, and voice-over commentaries drifting in and out, but a common style is normally not enough to justify putting two stories together. Since both protagonists are policemen, we might expect them to encounter one another, but they never do; the first is a plain-clothes detective, the second pounds a beat. Nor does the mysterious blonde's drug smuggling ever impinge on the cops' activities; Officer 1 is happily ignorant of her racket, and Officer 2 doesn't, for instance, investigate the murder of the bar owner, as he might in another kind of plot. The two strands do share one locale: Both Officer 1 and Officer 2 hang out at Midnight Express. Nonetheless, this doesn't connect the parts causally, since Officer 1 meets Faye only once, and he never becomes a rival for her affections. As if to tease sharp-eyed repeat viewers, Wong inserts into the first part a brief, distant shot of each main character who will appear in the second part— Officer 1, the flight attendant, and Faye **(11.62).** But they are unknown to us on the initial viewing, and they aren't presented as shaping the story action in the first part.

It is as if Wong has juxtaposed the two stories in such a way to demand that we find our own connections between them. By analyzing narrative form and style, we can bring to light some intriguing similarities and differences, which in turn point to a set of themes that unify the film.

In broad narrative terms, the two parts stand in sharp contrast. The first takes place on the Kowloon peninsula of Hong Kong, in and around Chungking Mansions, a decaying block of cheap guest quarters, shops, and Indian restaurants. (The

11.62 While the mysterious blonde woman lounges outside a shop, Faye (whom we do not meet until part two) leaves with a stuffed toy (perhaps destined for Officer 2's apartment).

Cantonese title of the film translates as "Chungking Jungle," and it may tease the local viewer into believing that eventually the second story will return to this neighborhood.) The second part takes place on Hong Kong Island, across the bay from Kowloon, in the vicinity of the Midnight Express. The Kowloon of part one teems with crime; Officer 1 chases suspects down at gunpoint, while the blonde works for a drug cartel. Part two presents a far less threatening world, where romance can blossom and the cop on the beat drops in for snacks. The English-language title of the film fuses the basic locales of each part, balancing Chungking Mansions with Midnight Express in a single phrase.

The two parts offer very different time schemes as well. The first part takes place over a short span, about four days, and the action labors under deadlines. Officer 1 has given May, his ex-girlfriend, the month of April to come back to him. The blonde's deadline for the smuggling operation has been set by her boss, and she meets it by shooting him and flying out of Hong Kong on May 1. The second part has a much looser time frame and no strong deadlines. Over a period of weeks, Officer 2's girlfriend leaves him, Faye invades his apartment, he transfers his beat, and after a series of casual encounters they finally make a date . . . that Faye ignores, suddenly departing. The action concludes a year later when she flies back to Hong Kong.

Yet within these broad contrasts some echoes do emerge. Each man is coming out of a love affair; each meets a woman by chance; quickly or slowly he becomes attached to her; the woman abruptly departs. The characters' goals are also revealing. Officer 1 seeks a new woman to love, and although Officer 2 is content to drift, Faye seems to try to ease his broken heart. These goals are presented more vaguely and pursued more erratically than in a Hollywood film, but the parallels suggest that *Chungking Express* revolves around romance. The more closely we look at cause–effect chains, motifs, and visual style, the more evidence we find that the film is comparing ways in which people try to find love.

The two policemen's romantic problems shape their attitudes toward time. Neither man reflects on the ways in which love affairs must adjust to change. In part one, ruled by fast pace and deadlines, Officer 1 has been pining for a month and now wants to find a new girlfriend immediately. Officer 2, suddenly dumped by his girlfriend, can't summon up the energy to restart his love life. Both men fill their stretches of waiting with cycles of repetitive behavior. Officer 1 badgers May's family and then calls old girlfriends to ask for a date. Officer 2 repeatedly visits Midnight Express, first to pick up snacks for himself and his girlfriend, then simply to brood; once he switches his shift, he frequents a food stall on another street. Although one wants a sudden adventure and the other falls back on routine, both are caught in spirals of inactivity. Wong emphasizes this through parallel images of each man moping in his apartment **(11.63, 11.64)**.

They need a change, or according to the film's most pervasive motif, a change of menu. Food is central to both stories, announced at the start in the headlong tracking shots through Chungking Mansions, the cafés filled with eaters. Officer 1 measures the time he waits for May (who loved pineapple) in pineapple cans, each day buying one with a May 1 expiration date. On the last day he gorges himself, emptying the thirty cans he has saved. When he meets the blonde, he asks if she likes pineapple. Similarly, Officer 2 always orders chef's salads at the Midnight Express. In contrast, women are presented as craving varied menus. As the blonde studies Officer 1 in the bar, her voice-over commentary remarks, "Knowing someone doesn't mean keeping them. People change. A person may like pineapple today and something else tomorrow." When Officer 2 brings home pizza and fish and chips, his girlfriend leaves him. He muses that she realized that she had a choice of lovers as well as dinners.

The food motif goes on to define the men's attitudes toward change. While the blonde sleeps in a Chungking Mansions hotel room, Officer 1 stuffs himself with hamburgers, salads, and fries. Once outside, he thinks that she has forgotten him, but her pager message ("Happy birthday") leads him to wish that the expiration date on his memory of her will last forever. No longer treating a girlfriend as a fast-food snack, Officer 1's sense of time has expanded; instead of seeking a new future, he treasures a moment in the past **(11.65)**.

As the countergirl Faye invades Officer 2's life, she replaces his cheap tinned fish with another brand, spikes his water jug to help his sleep, and pushes him out of his self-pity (in which he imagines his towel crying and his soap wasting away.) When she misses their date, she leaves him a fake boarding pass she inks onto a napkin; at first he discards it but then, in a composition paralleling that of Officer 1's meditation on his pager message, he dries it in a snack-shop rotisserie **(11.66)**. A year later, Officer 2 has embraced a varied menu. He has bought the Midnight Express, and when Faye returns he persuades her to write him a new pass. Before he had been reluctant to travel with her, but now, when she asks where he wants to fly, he replies, "Wherever you want to take me." He has broken out of routine and is willing to accept change.

This last scene sums up another motif, airplane flight, which runs through both parts and marks parallels. Both are associated with women's desire for change. In

11.63 Officer 1 at home, disconsolate.

11.64 Officer 2 broods about his lost love.

the first part, the blonde prepares her drug mules for a flight, and she escapes her crime by taking an early plane out. In the second part, Officer 2's air hostess is replaced by Faye, who, when she first meets her rival, measures herself against her (11.67). Musical motifs also signal the importance of change. The repeated reggae song in the first part states, "It's not every day that's gonna be the same way, there must be a change somehow." The second part highlights the song, "What a difference a day makes," and repeats the Mamas and Papas' "California Dreamin'," which expresses a wish to leave for sunnier surroundings. Several pictorial motifs link the two main women, including their shoes, their dark glasses, and their habit of slipping into reverie (11.68, 11.69).

If the film's primary theme is indeed the acceptance of change as part of love, then the two parts are cunningly designed to lead the audience toward it indirectly. The first part begins with the blonde hurrying through Chungking Mansions, then shows Officer 1 racing after a criminal and colliding with her before moving on. Her femme fatale disguise and the drug deal suggests that this is the start of a crime thriller (see pp. 112–114). But soon the smuggling situation is overwhelmed by Officer 1's romantic yearnings, and the blonde woman's abrupt shooting of her boss ends the crime line of action. The second tale begins, and Officer 2's placid routine

11.65 After his morning run, Officer 1 gets the pager message wishing him a happy birthday.

11.66 Officer 2 had discarded the mock boarding pass Faye had left him; now he waits for it to dry so he can read it.

11.67 Faye, who will become a flight attendant, measures herself against the woman who dumped Officer 2.

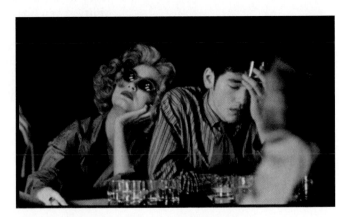

11.68 The blonde woman of part one muses . . .

11.69   . . . in a posture similar to that of Faye in part two.

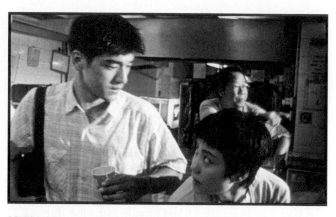

11.70   Part one of *Chungking Express* ends with Officer 1 bumping into Faye at Midnight Express.

11.71   Part two begins with Officer 2 approaching Midnight Express; he will replace Officer 1 as the film's male protagonist.

and personal problems take over. The thriller elements have served largely as bait, luring us to study the characters before the plot switches genres and becomes an open-ended romantic comedy.

Wong signposts the genre shift through a stylistic parallel. As Officer 1 collides with the blonde, the frame freezes, and his voice-over commentary says, "Fifty-seven hours later I fell in love with this woman." When at the end of the first part Officer 1 revisits Midnight Express, he bumps into Faye **(11.70).** His commentary remarks, "Six hours later . . . ," the image fades out and fades in on Officer 2 approaching the snack bar **(11.71),** and we hear Officer 1 continue, ". . . She fell in love with another man." We will never see Officer 1 again. These voice-over remarks (highly implausible on grounds of realism—how could Officer 1 know that Faye falls in love with Officer 2?) mark the film's romantic parallels explicitly.

Since the lines of action in the two parts aren't linked causally, the film may at first disappoint the viewer's expectations. But Wong's strategy invites the audience to seek other connections. The parallel situations point to the idea that change is as necessary to love as varied diet is to food. The thematic implications are reinforced by mise-en-scene, cinematography, music, and voice-over commentary. Yet, *Chungking Express* is not heavy-handed, partly because it slides cleverly from crime movie to stop-and-start romance, partly because it invites us to appreciate its playful artifice.

11.72   Vertov's regular cinematographer, Mikhail Kaufman, as the cameraman in *Man with a Movie Camera.*

11.73   Vertov alters an ordinary street scene by exposing each side of the image separately, with the camera canted in opposite directions.

11.74   A crayfish executes a little dance in the course of this shot.

DOCUMENTARY FORM AND STYLE

Man with a Movie Camera (Chelovek s kinoapparatom)

Made 1928, released 1929. VUFKU, Union of Soviet Socialist Republics. Directed by Dziga Vertov. Photographed by Mikhail Kaufman. Edited by Elizaveta Svilova.

In some ways, *Man with a Movie Camera* might seem to be a straight reportorial documentary, yet it does not try to give the impression that the reality it presents is unaffected by the medium of film. Instead, Dziga Vertov proclaims the manipulative power of editing and cinematography to shape a multitude of tiny scenes from everyday reality into a highly idiosyncratic, even somewhat experimental, documentary.

Vertov's name is usually linked to the technique of editing; in Chapter 8 (p. 304), we quoted a passage in which he equated the filmmaker with an eye, gathering shots from many places and linking them creatively for the spectator. Vertov's theoretical writings also compare the eye to the lens of the camera, in a concept he termed the "kino eye." (*Kino* is the Russian word for "cinema," and one of his earlier films is called *Kino-Glaz,* or "Cinema-Eye.")

Man with a Movie Camera takes this idea—the equation of the filmmaker's eye with the lens of the camera—as the basis for the entire film's associational form. The film becomes a celebration of the documentary filmmaker's power to control our perception of reality by means of editing and special effects. The opening image shows a camera in close-up. Through a double-exposure effect, we see the cameraman of the film's title suddenly climb, in extreme long shot, onto the top of the giant camera **(11.72)**. He sets up his own camera on a tripod and films for a bit, then climbs down again. This play with shot scale within a single image emphasizes at once the power the cinema has to alter reality in a seemingly magical way.

Cinematographic special effects of this sort appear as a motif throughout the film. These are not intended to be unnoticeable, as in a science-fiction film. Instead, they flaunt the fact that the camera can alter everyday reality. A typical example is shown in **11.73**. Later Vertov uses pixillation to animate real objects **(11.74)**. In another scene Vertov conveys the sound of a radio by superimposing images of a dancer and of a hand playing a piano against a single black background **(11.75)**. This motif of virtuosic special effects culminates in the famous final shot **(11.76)**.

11.75   Superimposition to suggest sound.

11.76   *Man with a Movie Camera* ends with an eye superimposed over the camera lens, staring straight out at us.

11.77 The animated camera comes out of its box, climbs onto the tripod, and demonstrates how its various parts work.

At several points in the film, the camera is also personified, associated by editing with the actions of human beings. One brief segment shows the camera lens focusing and then a blurry shot of flowers coming into sharp focus. This is followed immediately by a comic juxtaposition rapidly intercutting two elements: a woman's fluttering eyelids as she dries her face with a towel, and a set of venetian blinds opening and closing. Finally another shot shows the camera lens with a diaphragm closing and opening. A human eye is like venetian blinds, the lens is like an eye—all can open and close, admitting or keeping out light. Later, pixillation allows the camera to move by itself **(11.77)** and finally walk off on three legs.

Man with a Movie Camera belongs to a genre of documentaries that first became important during the 1920s: the *city symphony.* There are many ways of making a film about a city, of course. One might use categorical form to lay out its geography or scenic attractions, as in a travelogue; rhetorical form could make arguments about aspects of city planning or government policies that need changing. A narrative might stress a city as the backdrop for many characters' actions, as in Rossellini's *Rome Open City* or Jules Dassin's semidocumentary crime drama *The Naked City.* Early city symphonies, however, established the convention of taking candid (or occasionally staged) scenes of city life and linking them, usually without commentary, through associations to suggest emotions or concepts. Associational form is evident in such early examples of the genre as Alberto Cavalcanti's *Rien que les heures* (1926) and Walter Ruttmann's *Berlin, Symphony of a Great City* (1927). More recent films like Godfrey Reggio's *Koyaanisqatsi* (1983) and *Powaqqatsi* (1988) use similar techniques, avoiding voice-over narration in favor of a musical accompaniment that along with juxtapositions of images creates particular moods and evokes certain concepts. (See pp. 154–157.)

In *Man with a Movie Camera*'s opening, we see a camera operator filming, then passing between the curtains of an empty movie theater, and moving toward the screen. Then we see the theater opening, the spectators filing in, the orchestra preparing to play, and the film commencing. The film that we and the audience watch seems at first to be a city symphony laying out a typical day in the life of a town (as Ruttmann's *Berlin* does). We see a woman asleep, mannequins in closed shops, empty streets. Soon a few people appear, and the city wakes up. Indeed, much of *Man with a Movie Camera* follows a rough principle of development that progresses from waking up through work time to leisure time. But early in the waking-up portion, we also see the cameraman again, setting out with his equipment, as if starting his workday. This action creates the first of many deliberate inconsistencies. The cameraman now appears in his own film, and Vertov emphasizes this by cutting back immediately to the sleeping woman who had been the first thing we saw in the film-within-a-film.

Throughout *Man with a Movie Camera,* we will see the same actions and shots being filmed, edited, and viewed by the onscreen audience, all in scrambled order. Toward the end of the film, in fact, we see the audience in the theater watching the cameraman on the screen, filming from a moving motorcycle. Moreover, in this late portion of the film, many motifs from all the earlier parts of the day return, many now in fast motion; the simple order of the ordinary city symphony is broken and jumbled. Vertov creates an impossible time scheme, once more emphasizing the extraordinary manipulative powers of the cinema. The film also refuses to show only one city, instead mixing footage filmed in Moscow, Kiev, and Odessa, as if the cameraman hero can move effortlessly back and forth in space during this "day" of filming. Vertov's view of the cinema's relation to the cityscape is well conveyed in one shot that uses an extraordinary deep-focus composition to place the camera in the foreground, looming over the distant buildings **(11.78)**. In sum, *Man with a Movie Camera* may be a city symphony, but it goes beyond the genre as well.

11.78 The camera pans madly about to capture various views of the city.

Apart from its exuberant celebration of the powers of cinema, Vertov's film contains many explicit and implicit meanings, some of which may be missed by viewers who do not read Russian. Explicitly, the film seeks to praise and criticize aspects of Soviet society a decade after the Revolution. Many of the film's juxtapositions involve machines and human labor. Under Stalin, the USSR was beginning a major push toward industrialization, and the mechanized factories are portrayed as fascinating places full of bustling movement **(11.79).** The camera operator scales a huge factory smokestack or swings suspended over a dam to capture all this activity. Workers are seen not as oppressed, but as participating cheerfully in the country's growth, as when one young woman laughs and chats as she folds cigarette boxes on an assembly line.

11.79 Framing and lighting enhance the dynamism of throbbing, gleaming machine parts.

Vertov also points out weak spots in contemporary life, such as lingering class inequalities. Shots in a beauty shop suggest that some bourgeois values have survived the Revolution, and the leisure-time sequence near the end contrasts workers involved in outdoors sports with chubby women exercising in a weight-loss gym. Vertov also takes pains to criticize drunkenness, a major social problem in the USSR. One of the first shots within the inner film shows a derelict sleeping outdoors, juxtaposed with a huge bottle advertising a café. A shop front that we repeatedly see advertises wine and vodka, and later there is a scene where the cameraman visits this bar. When he leaves, we see shots of workers' clubs, converted from former churches. The contrast between these two places where workers can spend their leisure time is made clear through associational crosscutting: A woman shooting at targets in one of the clubs seems to be shooting away bottles of beer that disappear (through stop-motion) from a crate in the bar. During the 1920s, government officials instituted an explicit policy whose goal was to use the cinema and workers' clubs to replace both the tavern and the church in the lives of Soviet citizens. (Since the government's biggest source of income came from its monopoly on vodka sales, the policy also aimed at making cinema a major alternative source of revenue.) Thus *Man with a Movie Camera* seems to be subtly promoting this policy by using playful camera techniques to make both the cinema and the clubs seem attractive.

Implicitly, *Man with a Movie Camera* can be seen as an argument for Vertov's approach to filmmaking. He opposed narrative form and the use of professional actors, preferring that films use the techniques of the camera and the editing table to create their effects on the audience. He was not, however, entirely against controlling the mise-en-scene, and several scenes of this film—particularly the woman waking up and washing—clearly would have had to be staged. Throughout *Man with a Movie Camera,* associational juxtapositions compare the work of making a film with the other sorts of work depicted. The camera operator awakes and goes to work in the morning, like other workers. Like them, he uses a machine in his craft; the camera's crank is at various points compared with the crank on a cash register or with moving parts on factory equipment. The moving parts of the projector in the theater also resemble parts of the factory machines we see in various sequences.

Vertov further demonstrates how the film that we and the audience within the film are watching is a product of specific labor. We see the editor at work (Elizaveta Svilova, Vertov's wife and the actual editor of *Man with a Movie Camera*). Her gestures of scraping the film and putting cement on it with a brush to make a splice are cut in with shots in a beauty parlor, where a manicurist wields a nail file and a similar brush. At various times in the film we see many of the same shots in different contexts: on our screen, on the screen within the movie theater, in freeze frame, being filmed, being cut apart or spliced by the editor, in fast-motion, and so on. We must therefore view them not only as moments of recorded reality but also as pieces of a whole that is put together through much effort on the part of these film workers. Finally, the camera operator has to resort to various means, sometimes dangerous, to obtain his shots; he not only climbs a huge smokestack but also crouches across the tracks to film an oncoming train and rides a motorcycle one-handed as he cranks the camera to capture the action of a race.

Filmmaking is thus presented as a job or craft, rather than an elite-oriented art. Judging from the delighted reactions of the audience we see in the theater, Vertov hoped that the Soviet public would find his celebration of filmmaking interesting and entertaining.

This implicit meaning relates to a symptomatic meaning we can also see in the film. During the late 1920s, the Soviet authorities wanted films that would be easily understandable and would convey propagandistic messages to a far-flung, often illiterate, populace. They were increasingly critical of filmmakers like Eisenstein and Vertov, whose films, though celebrating revolutionary ideology, were extremely complex. In Chapter 8 we saw how Eisenstein adopted a dense, discontinuous style of editing. While Vertov disagreed in many ways with Eisenstein, particularly over the latter's use of narrative form, both belonged to a larger stylistic movement called Soviet Montage, whose history we shall examine in Chapter 12 (pp. 478–481). Both used very complex editing that they hoped would create predictable reactions in their audiences. With its contradictory time scheme and rapid editing (it contains over 1700 shots, more than twice what most Hollywood films of the same period had), *Man with a Movie Camera* is unquestionably a difficult film, especially for an audience unaccustomed to the conventions of filmmaking. Perhaps more Soviet spectators would have learned over time to enjoy such films as *October* and *Man with a Movie Camera* and to react to them with the delight evident in the audience in Vertov's film. Over the next few years, however, authorities increasingly criticized Vertov and his colleagues, limiting their ability to experiment with concepts like the kino eye. Vertov was constrained in his later projects, but *Man with a Movie Camera* eventually came to be recognized, in the Soviet Union and abroad, as a classic experiment in using associational form within documentary.

The Thin Blue Line

1988. An American Playhouse production (PBS). Directed by Errol Morris. Photographed by Stefan Czapsky, Robert Chappell. Edited by Paul Barnes. Music by Philip Glass.

On a west Dallas highway one night in 1976, a police officer named Robert Wood was fatally shot by a driver he had pulled over. His partner Teresa Turko saw the killer drive off, but it took months of investigation for the police to discover that the car had been stolen by David Harris. Harris, a 16-year-old from the small town of Vidor, admitted to being in the car but said that the killer was Randall Adams, a man with whom he had hung around that day. Adams was tried for murder, found guilty, and sentenced to death. Eventually through an appeal process, his sentence was commuted to life imprisonment. Harris, because of his age and his cooperation with the police, was given a suspended sentence.

In 1985, documentary filmmaker Errol Morris met Randall Adams while he was researching a film on a prominent Dallas psychiatrist known as "Dr. Death" because of his record of submitting evidence that sent defendants to the electric chair. Morris became convinced that Adams had been unjustly convicted, and over the next three years he prepared a film on the case.

The Thin Blue Line illustrates how a documentary can use narrative form, for at bottom it tells the story of events leading up to and following the murder of Officer Wood. Yet the film's narration enriches that basic story. By juggling time, inserting many details, developing the reenactments of the killing into a powerful pattern, and subtly engaging our sympathy for Randall Adams, Morris not only takes us through a criminal case but also suggests how difficult the search for truth can be.

The overall plot guides us through the story events, but not in a wholly linear way. The film breaks fairly clearly into 31 sequences, although many will contain brief flashbacks to the interrogation and the crime, and some contain fairly lengthy reenactments. (The longer reenactments are signaled on our segmentation.)

C. Opening credits.

1. Dallas, Randall Adams, and David Harris introduced.

2. The shooting of Officer Wood. *First shooting reenactment*

3. Arrest and interrogation of Adams. *First interrogation reenactment*

4. Police describe the interrogation and the beginning of the investigation. *Second interrogation reenactment*

5. Police describe the two officers' states of mind. *Second shooting reenactment*

6. Police search for the car, even using hypnotism. *Third shooting reenactment*

7. The big break: David Harris discovered in Vidor, Texas.

8. Harris accuses Randall Adams of the shooting.

9. Adams responds to Harris's charge.

10. Adams interrogated. *Third interrogation reenactment*

11. Police explain the mistaken auto identification.

12. Adams's two lawyers introduced and describe their inquiry into Harris's hometown.

13. Adams's lawyers discuss Harris as criminal; the judge describes his attitude toward police.

14. Adams recounts Harris's version of events. *Fourth shooting reenactment*

15. Adams explains his alibi.

16. Trial: Officer Turko testifies, implicating Adams. *Fifth shooting reenactment*

17. Trial: New witnesses emerge. Mr. and Mrs. Miller claim to have seen Adams shoot Wood. *Sixth shooting reenactment*

18. Adams's lawyers and Mrs. Carr rebut the Miller couple's testimony.

19. Trial: Third new witness, Michael Randell, claims to have seen Adams shoot. *Seventh shooting reenactment*

20. Trial: Jury declares Adams guilty.

21. Trial: Judge sentences Adams to death.

22. Adams's reaction to the death sentence.

23. Adams's lawyers petition for retrial and lose.

24. Adams's appeal supported by U.S. Supreme Court; his sentence commuted to life in prison.

25. Vidor detective explains: Harris arrested again.

26. Rethinking the case: Witnesses reflect, and Harris hints that he has lied. *Eighth shooting reenactment*

27. Vidor detective explains: Harris has committed a murder in town.

28. Adams: "The kid scares me;" he reflects on the mistake of letting Harris go free.

29. Harris, now on death row, reflects on his childhood.

30. Final interview on audiotape: Harris calls Adams a "scapegoat" and virtually confesses.

31. Title: Current situation of the two men.

E. Closing credits.

11.80   The questioning of Randall Adams, staged so that its status as a reenactment is unmistakable.

Segments 1–3 form a prologue, introducing the essential information and arousing our curiosity and concern. The opening sequence presents the city of Dallas, the two main characters, Randall Adams and David Harris, and their current situation: Both men are in jail. What has brought them there? They tell of meeting each other and spending the day drinking, smoking marijuana, and going to a drive-in movie. Segment 2 is the first of many shocking reenactments of the brutal shooting of Officer Wood at the murky roadside. Here, as in all the others, actors play the participants and the framing often conceals their faces, concentrating instead on details of action or setting. The third sequence depicts Adams's arrest and interrogation, which he describes as intimidating and which is shown in a reenactment **(11.80)**.

Then the film's plot provides a lengthy flashback to the period before Adams's arrest. This section (segments 4–11) concentrates on the police investigation, as recounted to us by the detectives and as documented in newspapers and other materials. The investigation leads to David Harris, who names Randall Adams as the killer (segment 8). Despite Adams's claims of innocence, he is arrested, and, for the third time, we see him interrogated (segment 10), bringing us back to the initial situation. The confusion about the make of the car is finally cleared up (11), a coda implying that the police conducted a muddled investigation. Throughout this part Morris has interspersed two more reenactments of Adams's questioning and two more reenactments flashing still further back to the murder of Officer Wood.

The longest stretch of the film (segments 12–24) centers on Randall Adams's confrontation with the courts. His trial and appeal filings are treated chronologically. We are introduced to his lawyers (12) and the judge in the case (13). Then the two conflicting versions of events, Adams's and Harris's, are presented (14–15). The curiosity and suspense aroused by the trial sequences (16–21) are intensified by the surprise entry of three eyewitnesses, Mr. and Mrs. Miller and the salesman Michael Randell, all of whom identify Adams (17–19). Each is interviewed by Morris, who restates their testimony. In the middle of this passage Morris rebuts the Millers' testimony by introducing Mrs. Carr, who claims that they bragged to her about trying to earn a reward (18). Once more, the interviews are broken up by reenactments of the crime. The jury finds Adams guilty (20), and the judge sentences him to death (21). Now Morris lets Adams tell about how it feels to be condemned to the electric chair (21). Adams's lawyers seek a retrial and then appeal the case; eventually the U.S. Supreme Court finds grounds for a retrial, but the local district attorney bypasses the verdict and Adams is resentenced to life in prison, with no possibility of a new trial (23–24).

The film has answered one question posed at the outset: Now we know how Randall Adams got to prison. But what of David Harris, who is also serving time? The final large section of the film continues the story after the trial, concentrating on Harris's criminal career. Harris is arrested for other crimes (25), and then Morris inserts a sequence (26) designed to suggest his guilt in the Woods case. The surprise eyewitnesses are shown to be unreliable, confused, and having things to hide, and most tellingly Harris explains, "Of course I picked out Randall Adams." In the next sequence a detective in Harris's hometown of Vidor explains how Harris invaded a man's home, violently abducted his girlfriend, and fatally shot the man (27). Harris, now revealed as a polite and pleasant sociopath, reflects on his childhood, when his brother drowned and his father seemed to become more distant (29). But whatever sympathy he might arouse is undercut by his final acknowledgment, captured by Morris on audiotape, that Randall Adams is innocent (30). A title explains that Adams is still serving his life sentence, while Harris is on death row (31).

In outline, then, this is a straightforward tale of crime and injustice. The film's explicit meaning was clear enough to trigger a new inquiry into the case, and Adams was freed in 1989. But Morris's film is more than a brief for the defense. It demands a great deal of the viewer; it does not spell out its message in the manner of most documentaries. We tend to side with Randall Adams and to distrust the police, prosecutors, and "eyewitnesses" aligned against him, but Morris does not explicitly favor Adams and criticize the others. The film's form and style shape our sympathies rather subtly. At another level, the film denies the viewer many of the usual aids for determining what happened on that night in 1976. Instead it asks us to heighten our attention, to concentrate on details, and to weigh the incompatible information we are given. Morris's detective story asks us to reflect on the obstacles to arriving at the truth about any crime.

The film's materials are for the most part the stuff of any true-crime report. Morris uses talking head interviews, newspaper headlines, maps, archival photos, and other documents to present information about the crime. He also includes reenactments of key events, signaled as such. Nonetheless, other documentary conventions are missing. There is no voice-over narrator explaining the situation, and no captions identify the speakers or provide dates. The reenactments don't carry the "Dramatization" caption seen in television documentaries. As a result, we are forced to evaluate what we see and hear without help. This extra responsibility is intensified by a framing that is rare in most documentary interviews: Several of the speakers look straight out at the camera **(11.81).** This somewhat unnerving direct address (which is even more prominent in other films by Morris) puts us in the position of detectives, forcing us to judge each person's testimony. Moreover, the use of paper documents is fairly cryptic: The film doesn't always specify their source, and the extreme close-ups often show only fragments of text. (One shot of a news article frames us these partial phrases: " . . . ved to be a 1973 . . . earing texas licens . . . with the letters H . . .) And Philip Glass's repetitive score is hardly conventional documentary music, especially for a true-crime story. With its mournful unresolved harmonies and nervously oscillating figures, the music arouses tension, but it also creates an eerie distance from the action: It throbs on, unchanged whether it accompanies an empty city landscape or a violent murder.

Other formal and stylistic qualities complicate the plot. For example, when an interviewee mentions a particular place, Morris tends to insert a quick shot of that locale **(11.82).** Such abrupt interruptions wouldn't be used in a normal documentary, since they don't really give us much extra information. It's as if Morris wants to suggest the vast number of tiny pieces of information that assault any investigator. Similarly, during the reenactments, the participants' faces aren't shown. Instead, the scenes are built out of many close-ups: fingers resting on a steering wheel, a milkshake flying through the air in slow motion, the popcorn machine at a drive-in **(11.83).** Again, Morris stresses the apparently trivial details that can affect our sense of what really happened on the highway. Yet, carefully composed and lit in high-key, the details also become evocative motifs. Some inserts comment ironically on

"I wanted to make a film about how truth was difficult to know, not impossible to know."

— Errol Morris, director

11.81 A police detective gives his version of Adams's interrogation.

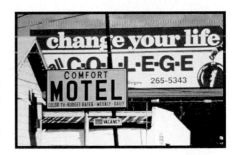

11.82 The motel where Adams stayed; in light of Adams's fate, the billboard in the background becomes ironic.

11.83 The popcorn machine at the drive-in, filmed ominously in the foreground while the clock serves as the basis for David Harris's testimony.

11.84   While Harris the teenager is associated with popcorn, Adams the panicked victim is associated with an ashtray full of cigarettes.

11.85   An echo of *film noir:* In a reenactment, Officer Wood is shown approaching the car.

the situation (11.82). Others, such as the ever-present clocks and watches, indicate the ominous passing of time; even the slowly shattering flashlight and the milkshake dribbling onto the pavement suggest the life pumping out of the fatally wounded officer. Morris's systematic withholding of information invites us to fill in parts of the story, and by amplifying apparently minor details he also invites us to build up implicit meanings.

Central to those meanings are our attitudes toward the people presented in the film. By and large the plot is shaped to build up our sympathies for Randall Adams. He is the first person we see, and Morris immediately makes him appealing by letting him explain that he was grateful to find a good job immediately after coming to Dallas. "It's as if I was meant to be here." Morris presents him as a decent, hardworking man assaulted by the justice system. The interrogation of Adams is associated with filled ashtrays, making him seem nervous and vulnerable **(11.84),** as do the repeated close-ups of newspaper photos of his frightened eyes. When the accusers state their case, Morris keeps us on Adams's side by letting him rebut them. In segment 9, Adams replies to Harris's charge that he was the shooter; in segment 15, Adams presents his alibi in reply to Harris's claims about the time frame of events. By the end, Adams becomes the authoritative commentator. In segment 28, after Harris has committed another murder, Adams reminds us that a life could have been saved if the Dallas police hadn't released Harris. At this point our sympathies for Adams are strong, and we understand why he reverses his judgment on Dallas: It's now "hell on earth."

Our acceptance of Adams's account is subtly reinforced by the many reenactments of the murder. They are clearly set off as reconstructions by their use of techniques more associated with the fiction film, particularly *film noir* (**11.85;** also 5.7) They also distinguish themselves from the restagings shown on true-crime television shows, which tend to include the faces of actors and which are usually shot in a loose, hand-held style suggesting that we are witnessing the real event.

The reenactments present different versions of the crime in accord with different witnesses' recollections. By presenting contradictory versions of what happened that night, Morris may seem to be suggesting that everyone involved saw things from his or her own perspective and so there is no final fact of the matter. But the overall progression of the film leads us to a likely conclusion: that David Harris, on his own, killed Wood. Rather than suggesting that truth is relative, the incompatible reconstructions dramatize the conflicting testimony. Like jurors or courtroom spectators, we will have to decide on the most plausible version, and the plot develops the reenactments in a strongly suggestive pattern.

In the segments devoted to the police investigation, the restagings emphasize matters of procedure. Did Officer Turko identify the car correctly? No, the police detectives eventually decide; but both before and after they arrive at this conclusion, Morris shows us two alternative cars, making the options visually concrete. The other key question is just as important: Did Turko back up Officer Wood according to procedure, or did she remain in the car? Morris dramatizes both possibilities, but he leads us to infer that she probably was inside the car drinking her milkshake, since in the crime-scene sketch spilled chocolate liquid was found near the car. It is a matter of probabilities, and we can never be certain; but on the evidence we have, we infer that she probably did not back up Wood.

The reenactments of Officer Wood's murder in the investigation section have concentrated on police procedure, but during the trial section, the reenactments suggest different versions of what was happening in the killer's car. Was David Harris ducking down in the front seat? Was Adams's bushy silhouette confused with a fur-lined coat collar? When the surprise witnesses are introduced, Morris shows reenactments that present their cars passing the murder scene. Again, the reconstructions present the alternatives neutrally, but some become more plausible than others, especially once the eyewitnesses are rebutted by other testimony or betrayed by their own evasive answers. The last reenactment, presented in the section devoted to David Harris, shows how Harris could have committed the murder, and, significantly, it is accompanied by his voice-over commentary virtually confessing to it. Now, after many other reenactments, this one is presented as most worthy of our belief. Morris carefully refrains from saying explicitly that Harris was the killer. But the development of the reconstructions, eliminating the most questionable versions and focusing more and more on the identity of the driver, pushes us toward accepting this as the likeliest account.

As in any narrative film, then, the manner of storytelling, the play with narration and knowledge, shapes our attitudes toward the characters. By letting Adams comment on other characters, and by arranging the reenactments so as to point eventually toward David Harris's guilt, the film aligns us with Randall Adams, the innocent victim. Correspondingly, Morris uses other stylistic devices to make us mistrust the forces set against Adams. The film does not present the Dallas law officers as brutal villains; all are soft-spoken and articulate, and Judge Metcalfe comes across as calm and patient. But the editing gives Adams's account prominence and allows him to answer their charges, so we are inclined to appraise their words cautiously.

Most overtly critical of the authorities are two nearly comic digressions close to the sort of associational form exploited by Bruce Conner in *A Movie* (pp. 157–162, 409–412). Judge Metcalfe recalls that he grew up with a great respect for law and order because his father was present when FBI agents shot the gangster John Dillinger. Morris cuts to a scene from a Hollywood crime movie that presents Dillinger's death (as if to recall an earlier tradition of the sort of reenactment he undertakes). Metcalfe also supplies background trivia about the woman who betrayed Dillinger, and when he says she was sent back to her native Rumania, Morris cuts to a map of Bucharest (a moment of self-parody, since he has used maps many times in the course of the film). A parallel montage appears during the remarks of Mrs. Miller, who says she always imagined herself as a girl detective who helped out investigators, as in 1950s TV shows. Morris lets her voice-over commentary run during a clip from a B-film in which a young woman helps a detective capture a crook. These sequences encourage us to see Adams's adversaries as holding a naive, romanticized conception of crimefighting derived from popular movies.

The color motifs that evoke police authority and duplicity are subtler. The first few shots of the film show skyscrapers and other architectural structures, each with a single blinking red light. After a cut to Randall Adams beginning his tale, the screen goes dark and we see the rotating red light of a police car, an image that will recur elsewhere in the film, before cutting to David Harris's account of how he came to Dallas. The motif of redness links Dallas and the police as forces aligned against Adams, and it suggests an explanation for why in the opening title credit, the word *Blue* is lettered in red. The film's title is taken from Judge Metcalfe's reference to the prosecutor's summation, which called the police the "thin blue line" between civilization and anarchy. By coloring the line red, Morris not only evokes bloodshed, but he links the police blue to the ominous blinking red lights of the opening. The motif expands even further into Judge Metcalfe's account of the death of Dillinger, who was betrayed by the notorious "woman in red." Metcalfe claims that in fact she wasn't actually wearing red; her orange dress merely looked red in a certain light. David Harris, throughout his interviews in the film, is shown wearing an orange prison uniform, suggesting that he is another figure of betrayal and perhaps hinting at his relationship to the red of the police-car light. Morris probably did not dictate what outfit Harris wore, but he did create other images that emphasize the color motif, and he did decide to retain Metcalfe's (fairly irrelevant) remarks about the woman in red. Like many documentarists, Morris highlighted certain aspects of existing footage to bring out thematic implications.

The story of Randall Adams's unjust imprisonment is presented as an intersection of several people's lives. Instead of simplifying the case for the sake of clarity, Morris treats it as a point where many stories crisscross—the private lives of the eyewitnesses, the professional rivalries among lawyers, the Dillinger tale, TV crime dramas, scenes from the drive-in movie Adams and Harris attended. Any crime, the film suggests, will consist of this tangle of threads. Any crime will seem buried in an avalanche of details (license numbers, car makes, spilled milkshakes, TV schedules), and it will engender many alternative scenarios about what really happened. *The Thin Blue Line* builds these aspects of an investigation into its very structure and style. The narration grants each version of the shooting its time onscreen (but finally guides us to eliminate the implausible ones), dwells on trivial details (but finally discards certain ones as less important), and shows many people's fates drawn together (which can confuse things, but which can eventually be sorted out). The film presents itself as both an account of what really happened on that Texas highway and a meditation on how persistent inquirers can eventually arrive at truth.

FORM, STYLE, AND IDEOLOGY

Meet Me in St. Louis

> 1944. MGM. Directed by Vincente Minnelli. Script by Irving Brecher and Fred F. Finklehoffe, from the book by Sally Benson. Photographed by George Folsey. Edited by Albert Akst. Music by Hugh Martin and Ralph Blane. With Judy Garland, Margaret O'Brien, Mary Astor, Lucille Bremer, Leon Ames, Tom Drake.

"I don't shoot elegant pictures. Mr. Vincente Minnelli, *he* shot elegant pictures."

— Billy Wilder, director

Just over halfway through *Meet Me in St. Louis,* Alonzo Smith announces to his assembled family that he has been transferred to a new job in New York City. "I've got the future to think about—the future for all of us. I've got to worry about where the money's coming from," he tells the dismayed group. These ideas of family and future, central to the form and style of the film, also create an ideological framework within which the film gains meaning and impact.

All of the films we have already analyzed could be examined for their ideological standpoints. Any film combines formal and stylistic elements in such a way as to create an ideological stance, whether overtly stated or tacit. We have chosen to stress the ideology of *Meet Me In St. Louis* because it provides a clear example of a film that does not seek to change people's ways of thinking. Instead it tends to reinforce certain aspects of a dominant social ideology. In this case *Meet Me in St. Louis,* like most Hollywood films, seeks to uphold what are conceived as characteristically American values of family unity and home life.

Meet Me in St. Louis is set during the preparations for the Louisiana Purchase Exposition in St. Louis, with the fair itself becoming the culmination of the action. The film displays its form in a straightforward way, with a title card announcing each of its four sections with a different season, beginning with "Summer, 1903." In this way the film simultaneously suggests the passage of time (equated with a movement toward the spring 1904 fair, which will bring the fruits of progress to St. Louis) and the unchanging cycle of the seasons.

The Smiths, living in a big Victorian house, form a large but closely knit family. The seasonal structure allows the film to show the Smiths at the traditional times of family unity, the holidays; we see them celebrating Halloween and Christmas. At the end, the fair becomes a new sort of holiday, the celebration of the Smiths' decision to remain in St. Louis.

The opening of the film quickly introduces the idea of St. Louis as a city on the boundary between tradition and progress. The fancy candy-box title card for Summer forms a vignette of white and red flowers around an old-fashioned black-and-white photo of the Smiths' house. As the camera moves in, color fades into the photo, and it comes to life. Slow, subdued chords over the title card give way to a bouncy tune more in keeping with the onscreen movement. Horse-drawn beer wagons and carriages move along the road, but an early model automobile (a bright red, which draws our eye) passes them. Already the motif of progress and inventions becomes prominent; it will develop quickly into the emphasis on the upcoming fair.

As Lon Smith, the son, arrives home by bicycle, a dissolve inside to the kitchen launches the exposition. One by one we meet the family members as they go about their daily activities through the house. The camera follows the second youngest daughter, Agnes, as she goes upstairs singing "Meet Me in St. Louis." She encounters Grandpa, who takes up the song as the camera follows him briefly. By means of close matches on action on the characters' passing the song along, the image track yields a flow of movement that presents the house as full of bustle and music. Grandpa hears offscreen voices singing the same song. He moves to a window, and a high-angle shot from over his shoulder shows the second oldest sister, Esther, stepping out of a buggy. Her arrival brings the sequence full circle back to the front of the house.

The house remains the main image of family unity throughout most of the film. Aside from the expedition of the young people on the trolley to see the construction of the fair, the Christmas dance, and the final fairground sequence, the entire action of the film takes place in or near the Smith house. Although Mr. Smith's job provides the reason to move to New York, we never see him at his office. In the opening sequence, the family members return home one by one, until they all gather around the dinner table. Every section of the film begins with a similar candy-box title card and a move in toward the house. In the film's ideology the home appears to be a self-sufficient place; other social institutions become peripheral, even threatening.

This vision of the unified family within an idealized household places the women at the center. The narration does not restrict our knowledge to a single character's range, but it tends to concentrate on what the Smith women know. Mrs. Smith, Rose, the youngest daughter, Tootie, and in particular Esther are the characters around which the narration is organized. Moreover, women are portrayed as the agents of stability. The action in the story constantly returns to the kitchen, where the mother and maid, Katie, work calmly in the midst of various small crises. The men present the threat to the family's unity. Mr. Smith wants to take the family to New York, thereby destroying its ties with the past. Lon goes away to the East, to college at Princeton. Only the grandfather, as representative of the older generation, sides with the women in their desire to stay in St. Louis. In general, the narrative's causality makes any departure from the home a threat—an example of how a narrative's principles of development can generate an ideological premise.

Within the family there are minor disagreements, but the members cooperate. The two older sisters, Rose and Esther, help each other in their flirtations. Esther is in love with the boy next door, John Truitt, and marriage to him poses no threat to the family unity. Several times in the film she gazes across at his house without having to leave her own home. First, she and Rose go out onto the porch to try to attract his attention; then, she sits in the window to sing, "The Boy Next Door." Finally, much later, she sits in a darkened bedroom upstairs and sees John pull his shade just after they have become engaged. That the girls might want to travel, or to educate themselves beyond high school, is never considered. By concentrating on the round of small incidents in the household and neighborhood, the film blocks consideration of any alternative way of living—except the dreaded move to New York.

Many stylistic devices build up a picture of a happy family life. The Technicolor design contributes greatly to the lushness of the mise-en-scene, making the costumes, the surroundings, and the characters' hair color stand out richly (7.5). The characters wear bright clothes, with Esther often in blue. She and Rose wear red and green, respectively, to the Christmas dance. This strengthens the association of the family unity with holidays and incidentally makes the sisters easy to pick out in the swirling crowd of pastel-clad dancers. In 7.5, the shot from the trolley scene, Esther is conspicuous because she is the only woman in black amidst the generally bright-colored dresses.

Meet Me in St. Louis is a musical, and music plays a large part in the family life. Songs come at moments of romance or gatherings. Rose and Esther sing "Meet Me in St. Louis" in the parlor before dinner. When the father interrupts them on returning from work—"For heaven's sake, stop that screeching!"—he is immediately characterized as opposed to the singing and to the fair. Esther's other songs show that her romance with John Truitt is a safe and reasonable one. A woman does not have to leave home to find a husband: She can find him right in her own neighborhood ("The Boy Next Door") or by riding the trolley ("The Trolley Song"). Other songs accompany the two parties, and Esther sings "Have Yourself a Merry Little Christmas" to Tootie, the youngest sister, after the Christmas dance. Here she tries to reassure Tootie that life in New York will be all right if the family can remain together.

But already there is a sense that such unity is in danger. "Someday soon we all will be together, if the Fates allow / Until then we'll have to muddle through somehow." We know already that Esther has achieved her romantic goal and become engaged to John Truitt. If the Smiths do move to New York, she will have to decide between him and her family. By this point, the plot has reached an impasse; whichever way she decides, the old way of life will be destroyed. The narrative needs a resolution, and Tootie's hysterical crying in reaction to the song leads Mr. Smith to reconsider his decision.

Tootie's destruction of the snow people after Esther's song is a striking image of the threat to family unity posed by the move to New York. As the winter season section opened, the children were building the snow people (and a dog) in the yard. In effect they had created a parallel to their own family, with statues of different sexes and sizes. At first these snow people were part of the comic scene in which Esther and Katie persuade Lon and Rose to go to the Christmas dance together. But when Tootie becomes hysterical at the prospect of leaving St. Louis, she runs down in her nightgown to smash the snow people. The scene is almost shocking, since Tootie seems to be killing the doubles of her own family. This moment has to be strong, even hysterical, because it must motivate the father's change of mind. He realizes that his desire to move to New York threatens the family's internal ties. This realization leads to his decision to stay in St. Louis.

Two other elements of the mise-en-scene create motifs that stress the family's comfortable life. The Smiths live surrounded by food. In the initial scene the women are making ketchup, which is shortly served at the family dinner. After the scene in which Rose's boyfriend fails to propose to her by phone, the tensions are reconciled, and the maid serves large slices of corned beef.

In the Halloween scene the connection between the plentiful food and family unity becomes even more explicit. At first, the children gather around to eat cake and ice cream, but the father arrives home and makes his announcement about moving to New York. The family members depart without touching their food. Only when they hear the mother and father singing at the piano do they gradually drift back to eat. The words of the song, "Time may pass, but we'll be together," accompany their actions. The use of food as a motif associates the family's life in the house with plenty and with the individual's place as part of a group. At the fair in the last sequence, they decide to visit a restaurant together. Thus the food motif returns at the moment of their reaffirmation of their life together in St. Louis.

Another motif of family unity involves light. The house is ablaze much of the time. As the family sits together at dinner, the low evening sun sends bright yellow rays through the white curtains. Later, one of the loveliest scenes involves Esther's request that John accompany her through the downstairs to help her turn out the lights. This action is primarily accomplished in one long take, with a crane shot following the characters from room to room. At each pause, the brightly lit chandelier is framed in the upper portion of the screen. As the rooms darken and the couple moves out to the hall, the camera cranes down to a height level with their faces. The shot contains a remarkable shift of tone. It begins with Esther's comically contrived excuse ("I'm afraid of mice") to keep John with her and develops gradually toward a genuinely romantic mood.

The Halloween sequence takes place entirely at night and makes light a central motif. The camera initially moves in toward the house's glowing yellow windows. Tense, slightly eerie, music makes the house seem an island of safety in the darkness. As Tootie and Agnes go out to join the other children in playing tricks, they are silhouetted against the flames of the bonfire the group has gathered around. At first the fire seems threatening, contradicting the earlier associations of light with safety and unity, but this scene actually harmonizes with the previous uses of light. Tootie is excluded from the group activities because she is "too little." After she proves herself worthy, she is allowed to help feed the flames along with the others. Note particularly the long track-back as Tootie leaves the fire to play her trick; the fire remains in the background of the shot, appearing as a haven she has left behind. Indeed, the first sequence of the Halloween section of the film becomes a sort of miniature working out of the entire narrative structure. Tootie's position as a part of the group is abandoned as she moves away from the fire, then triumphantly affirmed as she returns to it.

Similarly, light plays an important part in the resolution of the threat to the family's unity. Late on Christmas Eve, Esther finds Tootie awake. They look out the window at the snow people standing in the yard below. A strip of yellow light falls across the snow, suggesting the warmth and safety of the house they plan to leave. Tootie's hysterical crying, however, leads the father to reconsider his decision. As he sits thinking, he holds the match, with which he was about to light his cigar, unnoticed in his hand until it burns his fingers. Combined with the slow playing of the "Meet Me in St. Louis" theme, the flame serves to emphasize his distraction and his gradual change of mind.

As he calls his family down to announce his decision not to move, he turns up all the lights. The dim, bleak halls full of packing boxes become again the scene of busy activity as the family gathers. The lamps' glass shades are red and green, identifying the house with the appropriate Christmas colors. The announcement of the decision leads directly to the opening of the presents, as if to emphasize that staying in St. Louis will not create any financial hardship for the family.

As night falls in the final fair sequence, the many lights of the buildings come on, dazzlingly reflected in lakes and canals. Here the film ends, with the family gazing in awe at the view. Once more light signifies safety and family enjoyment. These lights also bring the other motifs of the film together. The father had originally wanted to move to New York as a provision for his family's future. In deciding to stay in St. Louis, he had told them: "New York hasn't got a copyright on opportunity. Why, St. Louis is headed for a boom that'll make your head swim. This is a great town." The fair confirms this. St. Louis allows the family to retain its unity, comfort, and safety and yet have all the benefits of progress. The film ends with the following dialogue:

MOTHER: There's never been anything like it in the whole world.

ROSE: We don't have to come here in a train or stay in a hotel. It's right in our own hometown.

TOOTIE: Grandpa, they'll never tear it down, will they?

GRANDPA: Well, they'd better not.

ESTHER: I can't believe it. Right here where we live. Right here in St. Louis.

These lines do not *create* the film's ideology, which has been present in the narrative and stylistic devices throughout. The dialogue simply makes explicit what has been implicit all along. (Compare this with the line "There's no place like home" in *The Wizard of Oz*—another MGM musical made five years earlier.)

The fair solves the problems of the future and family unity. The family is able to go to a French restaurant without going away from home. The ending also restores the father's position as at least the titular head of the family. Only he is able to remember how to get to the restaurant and prepares to guide the group there.

Understanding a film's ideology typically involves analyzing how form and style create meaning. As Chapter 2 suggested, meaning can be of four general types: referential, explicit, implicit, and symptomatic. Our analysis of *Meet Me in St. Louis* has shown how all four types work to reinforce a social ideology—in this case, the values of tradition, home life, and family unity. The referential aspects of the film presuppose that the audience can grasp the difference between St. Louis and New York and that it knows about international expositions, American family customs, national holidays, and so on. These address the film to a specifically American audience. The explicit meaning of the film is formulated by the final exchange we have just considered, in which the small city is discussed as the perfect fusion of progress and tradition.

We have also traced out how formal construction and stylistic motifs contribute to one major implicit meaning: the family and home as creating a "haven in a heartless world," the central reference point for the individual's life. What, then, of symptomatic meanings?

Generally, the film expresses one tendency of many social ideologies in its attempt to naturalize social and cultural behavior: Chapter 2 mentioned that systems of value and belief may seem unquestionable to the social groups that hold them. One way that groups maintain such systems is to assume that certain things are beyond human choice or control, that they are simply natural. Historically, this habit of thought has often been used to justify oppression and injustice, as when women, minority groups, or the poor are thought to be naturally inferior. *Meet Me in St. Louis* participates in this general tendency, not only in its characterization of the

Smith women (Esther and Rose are simply presumed to want husbands) but in the very choice of a white, upper-middle-class household as an emblem of American life. A more subtle naturalization is evident in the film's overall formal organization. The natural cycle of the seasons is harmonized with the family's life, and the conclusion of the plot takes place in the spring, the period of renewal.

We can also focus on more historically specific symptomatic meanings. The film was released during 1944, late in World War II. The audience for this film would have consisted largely of women and children whose adult male relatives had been absent for extended periods, often overseas. Families were often forced apart, and the people who remained behind had to make considerable sacrifices for the war effort. At a period when many women had been required to work in defense plants, factories, and offices (and many were enjoying the experience), there appears a film that restricts the range of women's experiences to home and family, and yearns for a simpler time when family unity was paramount.

Meet Me in St. Louis can thus be seen as a symptom of a nostalgia for prewar, pre-Depression America. Parents of young fighting men in a 1944 audience would remember the 1903–1904 period as part of their own childhoods. All of the formal devices—narrative construction, seasonal segmentation, songs, color, and motifs— can thus be seen as reassuring the viewers. If the women and others left at home can be strong and hold their families together against threats of disunity, harmony will eventually return. By setting forth this ideology at a time when so many people had been forced to leave home, *Meet Me in St. Louis* upholds dominant conceptions of American family life and may even propose an ideal of family unity for the postwar future.

Raging Bull

1980. United Artists. Directed by Martin Scorsese. Script by Paul Schrader and Mardik Martin. From the book *Raging Bull* by Jake La Motta, with Joseph Carter and Peter Savage. Photographed by Michael Chapman. Edited by Thelma Schoonmaker. With Robert De Niro, Cathy Moriarty, Joe Pesci, Frank Vincent, Nicholas Colasanto, Theresa Saldana.

In analyzing *Meet Me in St. Louis,* we argued that the film upholds a characteristically American ideology. It is also possible for a film made in Hollywood to take a more ambivalent attitude toward ideological issues. Martin Scorsese's *Raging Bull* does so by taking violence as its central theme.

Violence is widespread in American cinema, often serving as the basis for entertainment. In recent decades, extreme violence has become central to several genres, such as science-fiction and horror films. Such genres often rely in part on making their violence very stylized, and hence minimally disturbing. A series of gory deaths, enhanced by elaborate special effects, may constitute the main narrative action. *Raging Bull* uses a different tactic, drawing on conventions of cinematic realism to make violence visceral and disturbing. Thus even though it is in some ways less savage than many other films of its era—not a single death occurs, for instance—it contains several scenes that are hard to bear. Not only the brutal boxing matches but also the equally harsh quarrels in everyday life bring violence to the fore.

Scorsese's subject is loosely based on the actual career of boxer Jake La Motta, who became the world middleweight champion in 1949. *Raging Bull* uses the boxing scenes (based on real fights) as emblematic of the violence that pervades Jake's life. Indeed, he seems incapable of dealing with people without picking quarrels, making threats, or becoming abusive. His two marriages, especially that with his second wife, Vickie, are full of bickering and domestic abuse. Although his closest relationship is apparently to his brother Joey, who initially manages his career, Jake eventually thrashes Joey in a jealous rage and permanently alienates him. Moreover, while Jake's actions hurt others, he also wreaks havoc on himself, driving away everyone he loves and leading him to a pathetic career as an overweight stand-up comic and then as an actor reciting poems and speeches from famous plays and films.

How are we to understand the ideology of a film that makes such a vicious bully its hero? We might be tempted to posit either/or interpretations. Either the film celebrates Jake's murderous rage, or it condemns him as a pathological case. Yet in settling on one of these simple notions, we would fail to confront the film's uneasy balance of sympathy and revulsion toward its central character. We suggest that *Raging Bull* uses a variety of strategies, both of narrative and style, to make Jake a case study in the role of violence in American life. Scorsese thus creates a complex context within which Jake's actions must be judged.

This context can be best approached by examining the formal structure of *Raging Bull*'s narrative. If we were to segment the film into its individual scenes, we would come up with a long list. Although there are some lengthy sequences, most are quite short. In all there are 46, including the opening credits and the closing quotation title. We can usefully group some of the shorter scenes together. This procedure yields 12 segments:

1. The opening credits, shown over a lengthy shot of Jake warming up alone in a boxing ring.
2. Backstage in a nightclub, 1964. Jake practices a poem he will recite.

   Flashback begins:

3. 1941. Expository scenes of Jake losing a match, fighting with his wife, seeing Vickie, and having his first date with her.
4. 1943. Two matches with Sugar Ray Robinson, separated by a love scene between Jake and Vickie.
5. A montage sequence alternating a series of fights, 1944 to 1947, and home movies of Jake's private life.
6. A lengthy series of scenes in 1947, including three in the Copacabana nightclub, establishing Jake's jealousy over Vickie and hatred of the mob. He ends by throwing a fight for them.
7. 1949. An argument with Vickie, followed by Jake's winning the middleweight champion bout.
8. 1950. Jake beats up Vickie and his brother Joey in an unjustified jealous rage. He defends his title and fights Robinson again.
9. 1956. Jake retires and buys a nightclub in which he does comedy routines. Vickie leaves him and he is arrested on a morals charge.
10. 1958. Jake does his comedy act in a cheap strip joint; he fails to persuade Joey to reconcile with him.

    Flashback ends.

11. 1964. Jake prepares to go onstage to perform his recital.
12. A black title with a Biblical quotation and the film's dedication.

The beginning and ending of the film are vital in shaping our attitude to Jake's career. The first image shows him warming up in the ring before an unspecified fight (**11.86**). Several filmic devices create our initial impressions of the protagonist. He bounces up and down in place, in slow motion. This slow tempo is accompanied by languid classical music, suggesting that his boxing warm-up is like a dance. The deep-space staging places the ring's ropes prominently in the foreground and makes the ring seem huge, emphasizing Jake's solitude. This long take continues through the main credits, establishing boxing as both a beautiful and a lonely sport. The image remains abstract and remote: It is the only scene in the narrative that does not take place in a year specified by a superimposed title.

11.86   The slow-motion opening shot of *Raging Bull.*

A straight cut to Segment 2 shows Jake, suddenly fat and old, again practicing. He is going over his lines for a one-man show that consists of readings from famous literature and of a poem he has written about himself: "So give me a stage / Where this bull here can rage / And though I can fight / I'd much rather recite— That's entertainment!" This episode takes place quite late in the story, after the long struggles of his boxing career. Not until Segment 11 will the plot return to this moment in the story, with Jake continuing to rehearse his lines. In Segment 11, as the manager summons him onstage, he does some boxer-style warm-up punches to build his confidence, muttering rapidly over and over, "I'm the boss, I'm the boss."

By framing most of the story as a flashback, Scorsese links violence with entertainment. Jake's gesture of spreading his arms as he says, "That's entertainment!" in Segment 2 resembles the triumphant raising of his glove-clad hands whenever he wins a fight in the lengthy central flashback. Correspondingly, *Raging Bull* ignores Jake's early life and concentrates on two periods: his boxing career and his turn to stand-up comedy and literary recitations. Both periods present him as trying to control his life and the people around him. "I'm the boss," the last line spoken in the film, sums up Jake's attitude.

The plot structure we have outlined also traces a rise-and-fall pattern of development. After Segment 7, Jake's high point, his life runs downhill and his violence appears more and more savagely self-destructive. In addition, certain motifs highlight the role of violence in his life and the lives of those around him. During a rest period in his very first prizefight (Segment 3), a fistfight breaks out in the stands— suggesting at the outset that violence spills beyond the ring. Domestic relations are expressed through aggression, as in the tough-guy shoving between Jake and Joey and in Joey's disciplining his son by threatening to stab him. Most vividly, violence is again and again turned against women. Both Jake and Joey insult and threaten their wives, and Jake's beating of both his wives forms a grim counterpoint to his battles in the ring. During the first scene at the Copacabana, women emerge as targets of abuse. Jake accuses Vickie of flirting with other men, he insults a boxer and a mob member by suggesting that both are like women, and even the comedian onstage mocks women in the audience. Scene by scene, the organization of incidents and motifs suggests that aggression and pain pervade American life.

Scorsese puts Jake's violence in context by means of film techniques. In general, by appealing to conventions of realism, the film's style makes the violence in *Raging Bull* disturbing. Many of the fights are filmed with the camera on a Steadicam brace, which yields ominous tracking movements or close shots emphasizing grimaces. Backlighting, motivated by the spotlights around the ring, highlight droplets of sweat or blood that spray off the boxers as they are struck (**11.87**). Rapid editing, often with ellipses, and loud, stinging cracks intensify the physical force of punches. Special makeup creates effects of blood vessels in the boxers' faces spurting grotesquely. Scorsese treats the violent scenes outside the ring differently, favoring long shots and less vivid sound effects.

He creates a realistic social and historical context by using other conventions. One of these is a series of superimposed titles that identify each boxing match by

11.87   Realistic violence in the boxing scenes.

11.88   A graphic match moves the film from the end of the 1964 opening . . .

11.89   . . . to Jake in 1941.

11.90   Jake's point of view during a fight.

date, locale, and participants. This narrational ploy yields a quasidocumentary quality.

The most important factor creating realism, however, is probably the acting. Aside from Robert De Niro, the cast was chosen from virtually unknown actors or nonactors. As a result, they did not bring glamorous star associations to the film. De Niro was known mainly for his grittily realistic performances in Scorsese's *Mean Streets* and *Taxi Driver,* as well as Michael Cimino's *The Deer Hunter.* In *Raging Bull,* the actors speak with thick Bronx accents, repeat or mumble many of their lines, and make no attempt to create likable characters. In the publicity surrounding the film, much was also made of the fact that De Niro actually gained sixty pounds in order to play Jake as an older man. The film emphasizes De Niro's transformation by cutting straight from a medium close-up of Jake at the end of Segment 2, in 1964 **(11.88),** to a similar framing of him in the ring in 1941 **(11.89).** Such realism in the acting and other techniques makes it difficult for us to accept the film's violence casually, as we might in a conventional horror or crime film.

Through its narrative structure and its use of the stylistic conventions of realism, the film thus offers a criticism of violence in American life, both in the ring and in the home. Yet the film does not permit us to condemn Jake as merely a raging bull. It also presents violence as fascinating and ambiguous. Jake's brutality is made disturbingly attractive.

The main indicator of this attitude is the fact that narration concentrates far more on the perpetrators of violence than on its victims. In particular the three important female characters—Jake's first wife, Joey's wife Lenore, and Vickie—have little to do in the action except take abuse or rail ineffectually against it. We never learn why they are initially attracted to the violent men they marry or why they stay with them so long. At first Vickie seems to admire Jake for his fame and his flashy car, but her willingness to sustain their marriage for so long is not explained. Indeed, her sudden decision to leave him after 11 years has no specific motivation.

Such victims of Jake's violence serve chiefly to provoke him to respond. One portion of the action focuses on his pummeling of a "pretty" fighter to whom he thinks Vickie is attracted. Another deals with Jake's violent reaction to his irrational belief that Joey and Vickie have had an affair. It is notable that after this crisis, when Jake beats Joey up, Joey becomes as peripheral a figure as Vickie. We glimpse him briefly watching Jake's bloody title defeat and then see a short scene of him resisting Jake's offer of reconciliation. The film thus offers no positive counterweight to Jake's excesses.

Another indication of the narration's fascination with Jake's violence is the degree to which we are encouraged to identify with him. Several scenes show events from his point of view, using slow motion to suggest that we are seeing not just what he sees but how he reacts subjectively to it. This technique becomes especially vivid when Jake sees Vickie with other men and becomes jealous. Similarly, in the final fight with Robinson, Jake's vision of his opponent is shown via a point-of-view framing. The POV imagery also incorporates a combined track forward and zoom out to make the ring seem to stretch far into the distance, while a decrease in the frontal light makes Robinson appear even more menacing **(11.90).** Other deviations from realism, such as the thunderous throbbing on the sound track during Jake's major victory bout, also suggest that we are entering Jake's mind.

In part Scorsese justifies the film's fascination with violence by emphasizing how self-destructive Jake is. However much he hurts other people, he injures himself at least as much. He also quickly regrets having hurt people, as several parallel scenes show. In Segment 3, Jake has a vicious argument with his first wife in which he threatens to kill her but then immediately says, "Come on, honey, let's be—let's be friends. Truce, all right?" Later, after he has beaten Vickie up for her imagined infidelities, he apologizes and persuades her to stay with him. These domestic reconciliations are echoed in the big title fight where he defeats the current champion, Cerdan, then walks to his opponent's corner and magnanimously embraces him.

Sympathy for Jake is reinforced by other means. *Raging Bull* suggests that he is strongly masochistic, using his aggression to induce others to inflict pain on him. This notion is emphasized in the love scene in Segment 4. There he childishly asks Vickie to caress and kiss the wounds from his triumph over Sugar Ray Robinson (**11.91**). Soon Jake denies himself sexual gratification by pouring ice water into his shorts. The scene then leads directly into a fight in which Sugar Ray Robinson defeats him.

This defeat is paralleled in Segment 8, another boxing scene, when Jake simply stands and goads Robinson into beating him to a pulp. The motif of masochism comes to a climax in Segment 9, when Jake is thrown into solitary confinement in a Dade County jail. A long, disturbing take has Jake beating his head and fists against the prison wall, as he asserts that he is not an animal and berates himself as stupid.

More implicitly, the film suggests a strain of repressed homosexuality in Jake's aggressiveness. His embrace of the defeated opponent, Cerdan, in his title fight, as well as his urging of Robinson to attack him in his final bout, suggest such an interpretation. In Segment 6, when Jake sits down at a nightclub table and jokes about how pretty his upcoming opponent is, he tauntingly offers him as a sex partner to a mobster he suspects of being in love with Vickie. In Segment 8, one scene begins with an erotically suggestive slow-motion shot of seconds' hands massaging Jake's torso. In general, there is a hint that Jake's fascination with boxing and his refusal to deal with his domestic life stem from an unacknowledged homosexual urge. Such an implication goes against the usual ideology of Hollywood, which assumes that a heterosexual romance is the basis for most narratives.

Ultimately the ideological stance that *Raging Bull* offers is far from being as straightforward as that of *Meet Me in St. Louis*. Instead of displaying an idealized image of American society, the film criticizes one pervasive aspect of that society: its penchant for unthinking violence. Yet it also displays a considerable fascination with that violence and with its main embodiment, Jake.

The film's ambiguity intensifies at the end. In Segment 12, a biblical quotation appears: "So, for the second time, [the Pharisees] summoned the man who had been blind and said: 'Speak the truth before God. We know this fellow is a sinner.' 'Whether or not he is a sinner, I do not know,' the man replied. 'All I know is this: once I was blind and now I can see.'"

As this quotation emerges line by line, we are cued to relate it to the protagonist. Has Jake achieved some sort of enlightenment through his experiences? Several factors suggest not. Despite being a poor actor, he continues to perform literary recitals, trying to regain his public ("I'm the boss"). Furthermore, the speech he practices at the end is the famous "I could have been a contender" passage from *On the Waterfront*. In that film, a failed boxer blamed his brother for his lack of a chance to succeed. Is Jake now blaming Joey or someone else for his decline? Or is it possible that he has become aware enough of his faults to ironically recall a film in which the hero also comes to realize his mistakes?

After the biblical quotation, there appears Scorsese's dedication of the film: "Remembering Haig R. Manoogian, teacher, May 23, 1916–May 26, 1980, With Love and resolution, Marty." Now the biblical quotation may equally apply to Scorsese, himself from the tough Italian neighborhoods of New York. Were it not for people like this teacher, he might have ended up somewhat like Jake. And perhaps the professor, who helped him "to see," enabled him to present Jake with a mixture of detachment and sympathy.

11.91 A close-up links violence and sexuality as Jake asks Vickie to kiss his bruises.

"I was fascinated by the self-destructive side of Jake La Motta's character, by his very basic emotions. What could be more basic than making a living by hitting another person on the head until one of you falls or stops? . . . I put everything I knew and felt into that film and I thought it would be the end of my career. It was what I call a kamikaze way of making movies: pour everything in, then forget about it and go find another way of life."

— Martin Scorsese, director

As a cinema student, Scorsese was well aware of innovative foreign films like *Breathless* and *Tokyo Story,* so it is not surprising that his own work invites differing interpretations. The film's ending places *Raging Bull* in a tradition of Hollywood films (such as *Citizen Kane*) that avoid complete closure and opt for a degree of ambiguity, a denial of either/or answers. Such ambiguity can render the film's ideology equivocal, generating contrasting and even conflicting implicit meanings.

NOTES AND QUERIES

Specimens of Film Analysis

Many of the critical studies we have cited in the Notes and Queries to Parts Two and Three repay attention as instances of film analysis. Here are some others that exemplify diverse approaches: Thomas W. Benson and Carolyn Anderson, *Reality Fictions: The Films of Frederick Wiseman* (Carbondale: Southern Illinois University Press, 1989); David Bordwell, *The Films of Carl-Theodor Dreyer* (Berkeley: University of California Press, 1981); Noël Burch, *In and Out of Sync: The Awakening of a Cine-Dreamer* (London: Scholar Press, 1991); Robert Burgoyne, *Bertolucci's "1900": A Narrative and Historical Analysis* (Detroit: Wayne State University Press, 1991); Noël Carroll, *Interpreting the Moving Image* (Cambridge: Cambridge University Press, 1998); Philip Drummond, "Textual Space in *Un Chien andalou,*" *Screen* **18,** 3 (Autumn 1977): 55–119; Helmut Färber, *"A Corner in Wheat* by D. W. Griffith, 1909: A Critique." *Griffithiana* **59** (May 1997): 6–87; Stephen Heath, "Film and System: Terms of Analysis," *Screen* **16,** 1 (Spring 1975): 7–77, and **16,** 2 (Summer 1975): 91–113; Sandy Flitterman-Lewis, *To Desire Differently: Feminism and the French Cinema* (Urbana: University of Illinois Press, 1990); Lea Jacobs, *The Wages of Sin: Censorship and the Fallen Woman Film, 1928–1942* (Madison: University of Wisconsin Press, 1991); Annette Kuhn, "The Camera I—Observations on Documentary," *Screen* **19,** 2 (Summer 1978): 61–83; Thierry Kuntzel, "The Film-Work, 2," *Camera Obscura* **5** (1980): 7–68; William Malyszko, *The Godfather* (London: York, 2001); Judith Mayne, *The Woman at the Keyhole: Feminism and Women's Cinema* (Bloomington: Indiana University Press, 1990); Vlada Petrić, "Two Lincoln Assassinations by D. W. Griffith," *Quarterly Review of Film Studies* **3,** 3 (Summer 1978): 345–369; Bill Simon, "'Reading' *Zorns Lemma,*" *Millennium Film Journal* **1,** 2 (Spring–Summer 1978): 38–49; P. Adams Sitney, *Modernist Montage: The Obscurity of Vision in Cinema and Literature* (New York: Columbia University Press, 1990); and Kristin Thompson, *Breaking the Glass Armor: Neoformalist Film Analysis* (Princeton, N.J.: Princeton University Press, 1988); David Wills, ed. *Jean-Luc Godard's "Pierrot le fou"* (Cambridge: Cambridge University Press, 2000); and Peter Wollen, *Singin' in the Rain* (London: British Film Institute, 1992).

Two rich collections of film analyses are *Enclitic*'s special number **5,** 2/**6,** 1 (Fall 1981–Spring 1982), and Peter Lehman, ed., *Close Viewings: An Anthology of New Film Criticism* (Tallahassee: Florida State University Press, 1990).

Feminist filmmaker Lizzie Borden's personal perspective on *Raging Bull,* "Blood and Redemption," *Sight and Sound* **5,** 2 (NS) (February 1995): 61, offers an interesting supplement to our analysis.

PART SIX

Film History

Chapter 12

Film Form and Film History

"Not everything is possible at all times." This aphorism of art historian Heinrich Wölfflin might serve as a slogan for the final chapter of this book. So far, our survey of film art has examined various formal and stylistic possibilities, and we have drawn our examples from the entire range of film history. But film forms and techniques do not exist in a timeless realm, equally accessible to all filmmakers. In particular historical circumstances, certain possibilities are present while others are not. Griffith could not make films as Godard does, nor could Godard make films as Griffith did. This chapter asks, What are some ways in which film art has been treated in some particular historical contexts?

These contexts will be defined, first, by period and by nation. Although there are other equally good tools for tracing change, period and nation remain useful ways of organizing historical problems. Second, in some of our cases, we shall look for what are typically called *film movements*. A film movement consists of

1. Films that are produced within a particular period and/or nation and that share significant traits of style and form

2. Filmmakers who operate within a common production structure and who share certain assumptions about filmmaking

There are other ways of defining a historical context (for example, biographical study, genre study), but the category of *movement* corresponds most closely to the emphasis of this book. The concepts of formal and stylistic systems permit us to compare films within a movement and to contrast them with films of other movements.

Our range of choice will be narrowed still further. We are concerned with Hollywood and selected alternatives. We shall trace the development of the commercial narrative cinema while contrasting it to other approaches to style and form.

Since a film movement consists of not only films but also the activities of specific filmmakers, we must go beyond noting stylistic and formal qualities. For each period and nation, we shall also sketch relevant factors that affect the cinema. These factors include the state of the film industry, artistic theories held by the filmmakers themselves, pertinent technological features, and elements of the socioeconomic context of the period. Such factors necessarily help explain how a particular movement began, what shaped its development, and what affected its decline. However brief, such material will also provide a context for particular films we have already discussed; for example, the following section on early cinema situates Lumière and Méliès in the context of their period.

Needless to say, what follows is drastically incomplete. The writing of serious film history is in its early stages, and we must often rely on secondary sources that will eventually be superseded. This chapter reflects only current states of knowledge; there are doubtless important films, filmmakers, and movements that await discovery. Moreover, there are many unfortunate omissions. Important filmmakers who do not relate to a movement (for example, Tati, Bresson, Kurosawa) are absent, as are certain important film movements, such as French populist cinema of the 1930s and Brazil's Cinema Nôvo movement of the early 1960s. What follows simply seeks to show how certain possibilities of film form and style were explored within a few typical and well-known historical periods.

EARLY CINEMA (1893–1903)

In order to create the illusion of movement, still pictures must appear in rapid succession. To prepare them and display them at the right rate, certain technologies are necessary. Most basically, there must be a way of recording a long series of images on some sort of support. In principle one could simply draw a string of images on a strip of paper or a disk. But photography offered the cheapest and most efficient way to generate the thousands of images needed for a reasonably lengthy exhibition. Thus the invention of photography in 1826 launched a series of discoveries that made cinema possible.

Early photographs required lengthy exposures (initially hours, later minutes) for a single image; this made photographed motion pictures, which need 12 or more frames per second, impossible. Faster exposures, of about 1/25 second, became possible by the 1870s, but only on glass plates. Glass plates were not usable for motion pictures since there was no practical way to move them through a camera or projector. In 1878 Eadweard Muybridge, an American photographer, did make a series of photographs of a running horse by using a series of cameras with glass plate film and fast exposure, but he was primarily interested in freezing phases of an action, not re-creating the movement by projecting the images in succession.

In 1882 another scientist interested in analyzing animal movement, the Frenchman Étienne-Jules Marey, invented a camera that recorded 12 separate images on the edge of a revolving disc of film. This constituted a step toward the motion-picture camera. In 1888 Marey built the first camera to use a strip of flexible film, this time on paper. Again, the purpose was only to break down movement into a series of stills, and the movements photographed lasted a second or less.

In 1889 George Eastman introduced a crude flexible film base, celluloid (one type of which still forms the base of film stock today). Once this base was improved and camera mechanisms had been devised to draw the film past the lens and expose it to light, the creation of lengthy series of frames became possible.

Projectors had existed for many years and had been used to show slides and other shadow entertainments. These magic lanterns were modified by the addition of shutters, cranks, and other devices to become early motion-picture projectors.

One final device was needed if films were to be projected. Since the film stops briefly while the light shines through each individual frame, there had to be a mechanism to create an *intermittent* motion of the film. Marey used a Maltese cross gear on his 1888 camera, and this became a standard part of early cameras and projectors.

12.1 The Kinetoscope held film in a continuous loop threaded around a series of bobbins.

12.2 Placing a magic lantern behind the Lumière camera turned it into a projector.

The combination of a flexible, transparent film base, a fast exposure time, a mechanism to pull the film through the camera, an intermittent device to stop the film, and a shutter to block off light was achieved by the early 1890s. After several years, inventors working independently in many countries had developed several different film cameras and projection devices. The two most important firms were Edison in America and Lumière in France.

By 1893 Thomas A. Edison's assistant, W. K. L. Dickson, developed a camera that made short 35mm films. Interested in exploiting these films as a novelty, Edison hoped to combine them with his phonograph to show sound movies. He had Dickson develop a peep-show machine, the *Kinetoscope* (**12.1**), to display these films to individual viewers.

Since Edison believed that movies were a passing fad, he did not develop a system to project films onto a screen. This was left to the Lumière brothers, Louis and Auguste. They invented their own camera independently; it exposed a short roll of 35mm film and also served as a projector (**12.2**). On December 28, 1895, the Lumière brothers held one of the first public showings of motion pictures projected on a screen, at the Grand Café in Paris.

There had been several earlier public screenings, including one on November 1 of the same year, by the German inventor Max Skladanowsky. But Skladanowsky's bulky machine required two strips of wide-gauge film running simultaneously and hence had less influence on the subsequent technological development of the cinema. Although the Lumières did not invent cinema, they largely determined the specific form the new medium was to take. Edison himself was soon to abandon Kinetoscopes and form his own production company to make films for theaters.

The first films were extremely simple in form and style. They usually consisted of a single shot framing an action, usually at long-shot distance. In the first film studio, Edison's Black Maria (**12.3**), vaudeville entertainers, famous sports figures, and celebrities (for example, Annie Oakley) performed for the camera. A hinged portion of the roof opened to admit a patch of sunlight, and the entire building

12.3 The hinged portion of the Black Maria's roof, at the center, swung open for filming.

12.4   Méliès's glass-sided studio admitted sunlight from a variety of directions.

turned on a circular rail (visible in 12.3) to follow the sun's motion. The Lumières, however, took their cameras out to parks, gardens, beaches, and other public places to film everyday activities or news events, as in their *Arrival of a Train at La Ciotat* (7.67).

Until about 1903 most films showed scenic places or noteworthy events, but narrative form also entered the cinema from the beginning. Edison staged comic scenes, like one copyrighted 1893 in which a drunken man struggles briefly with a policeman. The Lumières made a popular success with *L'Arroseur arrosé* (*The Waterer Watered,* 1895), also a comic scene, in which a boy tricks a gardener into squirting himself with a hose (6.6).

After the initial success of the new medium, filmmakers had to find more complex or interesting formal properties to keep the public's interest. The Lumières sent camera operators all over the world to show films and to photograph important events and exotic locales. But after making a huge number of films in their first few years, the Lumières' output diminished, and they ceased filmmaking altogether in 1905.

In 1896 Georges Méliès purchased a projector from the British inventor Robert William Paul and soon built a camera based on the same mechanism. Méliès's first films resembled the Lumières' shots of everyday activities. But as we have seen (p. 177–179), Méliès was also a magician, and he discovered the possibilities of simple special effects. In 1897 Méliès built his own studio. Unlike Edison's Black Maria, Méliès's studio was glass-sided like a greenhouse, so that the studio did not have to move with the sun **(12.4).**

Méliès also began to build elaborate settings to create fantasy worlds within which his magical transformations could occur. We have already seen how Méliès thereby became the first master of mise-en-scene technique (6.2–6.5). From the simple filming of a magician performing a trick or two in a traditional stage setting, Méliès progressed to longer narratives with a series of tableaux. Each consisted of one shot, except when the transformations occurred. These were created

"In conjuring you work under the attentive gaze of the public, who never fail to spot a suspicious movement. You are alone, their eyes never leave you. Failure would not be tolerated . . . . While in the cinema . . . you can do your confecting quietly, far from those profane gazes, and you can do things thirty-six times if necessary until they are right. This allows you to travel further in the domain of the marvellous."

— Georges Méliès, magician and filmmaker

12.5   G. Albert Smith's *Santa Claus* (1898).

by cuts designed to be imperceptible on the screen. He also adapted old stories, such as *Cinderella* (1899) or wrote his own. All these factors made Méliès's films extremely popular and widely imitated.

During this early period, films circulated freely from country to country. The French phonograph company Pathé Frères moved increasingly to filmmaking from 1901 on, establishing production and distribution branches in many countries. Soon it was the largest film concern in the world, a position it retained until 1914, when the beginning of World War I forced it to cut back production. In England, several entrepreneurs managed to invent or obtain their own filmmaking equipment and made scenics, narratives, and trick films from 1895 into the early years of the 20th century. Members of the Brighton School (primarily G. Albert Smith and James Williamson), as well as others like Cecil Hepworth, shot their films on location or in simple open-air studios (as in **12.5**). Their innovative films circulated abroad and influenced other filmmakers. Pioneers in other countries invented or bought equipment and were soon making their own films of everyday scenes or fantasy transformations.

From about 1904 on, narrative form became the most prominent type of filmmaking in the commercial industry, and the worldwide success of the cinema continued to grow. French, Italian, and American films dominated world markets. Later, World War I was to restrict the free flow of films from country to country, and Hollywood emerged as the dominant industrial force in world film production contributing to the creation of distinct differences in the formal traits of individual national cinemas.

THE DEVELOPMENT OF THE CLASSICAL HOLLYWOOD CINEMA (1908–1927)

Edison's determination to exploit the money-making potential of his company's invention led him to try to force competing filmmakers out of business by bringing patents-violation suits against them. One other company, American Mutoscope & Biograph, managed to survive by inventing cameras that differed from Edison's patents. Other firms kept operating while Edison fought them in court. In 1908 Edison conceded with Biograph to bring these other companies under control by forming the Motion Picture Patents Company (MPPC), a group of ten firms based primarily in Chicago, New York, and New Jersey. Edison and Biograph were the only stockholders and patent owners. They licensed other members to make, distribute, and exhibit films.

The MPPC never succeeded in eliminating its competition. Numerous independent companies were established throughout this period. Biograph's most important director from 1908 on, D. W. Griffith, formed his own company in 1913, as did other filmmakers. The United States government brought suit against the MPPC in 1912; in 1915 it was declared a monopoly.

Around 1910, film companies began to move permanently to California. Eventually Hollywood and other small towns on the outskirts of Los Angeles became the site of widespread film production. Some historians claim that the independent companies fled west to avoid the harassment of the MPPC, but some MPPC companies also made the move. Among the advantages of Hollywood were the climate, which permitted shooting year-round, and the great variety of terrains—mountains, ocean, desert, city—available for location shooting.

The demand for films was so great that no single studio could meet it. This was one of the factors that had led Edison to accept the existence of a group of other companies, although he tried to control them as much as possible through his licensing procedure. Before 1920, the American industry assumed the structure that would continue for years: a few large studios with individual artists under contract and a peripheral group of small independent producers. In Hollywood, the studios developed a factory system, with each production under the control of the producer, who usually did not work on the actual making of the films. Even an independent director like Buster Keaton, with his own studio, had a business manager and distributed his films through larger companies, first Metro and then United Artists.

Gradually, through the 1910s and 1920s, the smaller studios merged to form the large firms that still exist today. Famous Players joined with Jesse L. Lasky and then formed a distribution wing, Paramount. By the late 1920s, most of the major companies existed—MGM (a merger of Metro, Goldwyn, and Mayer), Fox Film Corporation (merged with 20th Century in 1935), Warner Bros., Universal, and Paramount. Though in competition with one another, these studios tended to cooperate to a degree, realizing that no one firm could satisfy the market.

Within this system of mass-production studios, the American cinema became definitively oriented toward narrative form. One of Edison's directors, Edwin S. Porter, made some of the first films to use principles of narrative continuity and development (as opposed to the series of tableaux or the filmed vaudeville-style skits that made up early, preclassical narrative films). Among these was *The Life of an American Fireman* (1903), which showed the race of the firefighters to rescue a mother and a child from a burning house. Although this film used several important classical narrative elements (a fireman's premonition of the disaster, a series of shots of the horse-drawn engine racing to the house), it still had not worked out the logic of temporal relations in cutting. Thus we see the rescue of a mother and her child twice, from both inside and outside the house. Porter had not realized the possibility of intercutting the two locales within the action or matching on action to convey narrative information to the audience.

In 1903, Porter made *The Great Train Robbery,* in some ways a prototype for the classical American film. Here the action develops with a clear linearity of time, space, and logic. We follow each stage of the robbery **(12.6),** the pursuit, and the final defeat of the robbers. In 1905, Porter also created a simple parallel narrative in *The Kleptomaniac,* contrasting the fates of a rich woman and a starving woman who are both caught stealing.

British filmmakers were working along similar lines. Indeed, many historians now believe that Porter derived some of his editing techniques from films like James Williamson's *Fire!* (1901) and G. A. Smith's *Mary Jane's Mishap* (1903). The most famous British film of this era was Lewin Fitzhamon's 1905 film *Rescued by Rover* (produced by a major British firm, Cecil Hepworth), which treated a kidnapping in a linear fashion similar to that of *The Great Train Robbery.* After the kidnapping, we see each stage of Rover's journey to find the child, his return to fetch the child's father, and their retracing of the route to the kidnapper's lair. All the shots along the route maintain consistent screen direction, so that the geography of the action is completely intelligible.

In 1908, D. W. Griffith began his directing career. In the next five years, he was to make hundreds of one- and two-reelers (running about 15 and 30 minutes, respectively). These films created relatively complex narratives in short spans. Griffith certainly was not the initiator of all the devices with which he has been credited, but he did give many techniques strong narrative motivation. For example, a few other filmmakers had used simple last-minute rescues with crosscutting between the rescuers and victims, but Griffith is famous for developing and popularizing this technique (8.111–8.114). By the time he made *The Birth of a Nation*

"The cinema knows so well how to tell a story that perhaps there is an impression that it has always known how."

— André Gaudreault, film historian

12.6 The robbers in the telegraph office in *The Great Train Robbery,* preparing to board the train seen through the window.

12.7 The opening scene of *The Cheat* introduces the branding motif . . .

12.8 . . . that returns later when the villain brands the heroine.

12.9 In Fred Niblo's *The Three Musketeers*, a long shot of the group leads to . . .

12.10 . . . a cut-in to the central character, played by Douglas Fairbanks.

(1915) and *Intolerance* (1916), Griffith was creating lengthy sequences by cutting between several different locales. During the early teens, he also directed his actors in an unusual way, concentrating on subtle changes in facial expression (6.34). To catch such nuances, he set up his camera closer than did many of his contemporaries, placing his actors in medium long shot or medium shot. Griffith's films were widely influential. In addition, his dynamic, rapid editing in the final chase scenes of *Intolerance* was to have a considerable impact on the Soviet Montage style of the 1920s.

The refinement of narratively motivated cutting occurs in the work of a number of important filmmakers of the period. One of these was Thomas H. Ince, a producer and director responsible for many films between 1910 and the end of World War I. He devised a unit system, whereby a single producer could oversee the making of several films at once. He also called for tight narratives, with no digressions or loose ends. *Civilization* (1915) and *The Italian* (1915) are good examples of films directed or supervised by Ince. He also supervised the popular Westerns of William S. Hart (p. 119), who directed many of his own films.

Another prolific filmmaker of this period (and later years as well) was Cecil B. De Mille. Not yet engaged in the creation of historical epics, De Mille made a series of feature-length dramas and comedies. His *The Cheat* (1915) reflects important changes occurring in the studio style between about 1914 and 1917. During that period, the glass-roofed studios of the earlier period began to give way to studios dependent on artificial lighting rather than mixed daylight and electric lighting. *The Cheat* used spectacular effects of chiaroscuro, with only one or two bright sources of light and no fill light. According to legend, De Mille justified this effect to nervous exhibitors as *Rembrandt lighting*. This so-called Rembrandt, or *north,* lighting was to become part of the classical repertoire of lighting techniques. *The Cheat* also greatly impressed the French Impressionist filmmakers, who occasionally used similar stark lighting effects.

Like many American films of the teens, *The Cheat* also uses a linear pattern of narrative. The first scene **(12.7)** introduces the hard lighting but also quickly establishes the Japanese businessman as a ruthless collector of objects; we see him burning his brand onto a small statue. The initial action motivates a later scene in which the businessman brands the heroine, who has fallen into his power by borrowing money from him **(12.8).** *The Cheat* was evidence of the growing formal complexity of the Hollywood film.

The period 1909–1917 saw the development of the basic continuity principles. Eyeline matches occur with increasing frequency from 1910 on. The match on action developed at about the same time and was in common use by 1916. It appears in such Douglas Fairbanks films as *The Americano* (1916) and *Wild and Woolly* (1917). Shot/reverse shot was used only occasionally between 1911 and 1915, but it became widespread by 1916–1917; instances occur in such films as De Mille's *The Cheat* (1915), Hart's Western *The Narrow Trail* (1917), and Griffith's *A Romance of Happy Valley* (1919). During this period, films rarely violated the axis-of-action rule in using these techniques.

By the 1920s, the continuity system had become a standardized style that directors in the Hollywood studios used almost automatically to create coherent spatial and temporal relations within narratives. A match on action could provide a cut to a closer view in a scene **(12.9, 12.10).** A three-way conversation around a table would no longer be handled in a single frontal shot. Note the clear spatial relations in **12.11–12.15,** shots from *Are Parents People?* (Malcolm St. Clair, 1925). At the period, screen direction was usually respected, as in this case. When an awkward match might have resulted from the joining of two shots, the filmmakers could cover it by inserting a dialogue title.

12.11 In an establishing shot from *Are Parents People?,* the daughter sits down at the table.

12.12 In the medium shot she looks leftward toward her father . . .

12.13 . . . who looks rightward at her in the reverse shot.

12.14 The daughter then turns to look to the right at her mother . . .

12.15 . . . who also returns her gaze in reverse shot.

Keaton's *Our Hospitality* (1923), which we examined in Chapter 6, provides another example of a classical narrative. Keaton's mastery of classical form and style are evident in the carefully motivated recurrences of the various narrative elements and in the straightforward causal development from the death of Willie McKay's father in the feud to Willie's final resolution of the feud.

By the end of the silent period, in the late 1920s, the classical Hollywood cinema had developed into a sophisticated movement, but the Hollywood product was remarkably standardized. All of the major studios used the same production system, with a similar division of labor at each. Independent production was less important. Some independent firms made low-budget films, often Westerns, for small and rural theaters. Even powerful Hollywood stars and producers had trouble remaining independent. Keaton gave up his small studio in 1928 to go to MGM under contract; there his career declined, due partly to the incompatibility of his old working methods with the rigid production patterns of the huge studio. Griffith, Mary Pickford, Fairbanks, and Charles Chaplin were better off. Forming a distributing corporation of their own, United Artists, in 1919, they were able to continue independent production at small companies under their umbrella corporation, though Griffith's company soon failed, and the careers of Fairbanks and Pickford declined soon after the introduction of sound.

There were alternative kinds of films being made during these years—most of them in other countries. After examining these alternative movements, we shall return to a brief examination of the classical Hollywood cinema after the coming of sound.

"That evening I tried to increase my knowledge of motion-picture technique by going to the movies. I sat with a stop watch and notebook and tried to estimate the number of cuts or scenes in a thousand-foot reel, the length of individual scenes, the distance of the subject from the camera, and various other technical details."

— King Vidor, director, recalling the night before he began directing his first film, c. 1912

GERMAN EXPRESSIONISM (1919–1926)

At the start of World War I, the output of the German film industry was relatively small, though some impressive pictures were made there. Germany's 2000 movie theaters were playing mostly French, American, Italian, and Danish films. Although America and France banned German films from their screens immediately, Germany was not even in a solid enough position to ban French and American films, for then the theaters would have had little to show.

In order to combat imported competition, as well as to create its own propaganda films, the German government began to support the film industry. In 1916 film imports were banned except from neutral Denmark, whose film industry had close ties to that of Germany. Production increased rapidly; from a dozen small companies in 1911, the number grew to 131 by 1918. But government policy encouraged these companies to band together into cartels.

The war was unpopular with many in Germany, and rebellious tendencies increased after the success of the Russian Revolution in 1917. Widespread strikes and antiwar petitions were organized during the winter of 1916–1917. In order to promote pro-war films, the government, the Deutsche Bank, and large industrial concerns combined several small film firms to create the large company UFA (short for Universumfilm Aktiengesellschaft) in late 1917. Backed by these essentially conservative interests, UFA was a move toward control of not only the German market but the postwar international market as well.

With this huge financial backing, UFA was able to gather superb technicians and build the best-equipped studios in Europe. These studios later attracted foreign filmmakers, including the young Alfred Hitchcock. During the 1920s, Germany co-produced many films with companies in other countries, thus helping to spread German stylistic influence abroad.

In late 1918, with the end of the war, the need for overt militarist propaganda disappeared. Although mainstream dramas and comedies continued to be made, the German film industry concentrated on three genres. One was the internationally popular adventure serial, featuring spy rings, clever detectives, or exotic settings. Another was a brief sex exploitation cycle, which dealt "educationally" with such topics as homosexuality and prostitution. Also, UFA set out to copy the popular Italian historical epics of the pre-war period.

This last type of film proved financially successful for UFA. In spite of continued bans and prejudice against German films in America, England, and France, UFA finally was able to break into the international market. In September 1919 Ernst Lubitsch's *Madame Dubarry,* an epic of the French Revolution **(12.16),** inaugurated the magnificent UFA Palast theater in Berlin. This film helped reopen the world film market to Germany. Released as *Passion* in the United States, this film was extremely popular and won critical acclaim in many other countries as well. It was less enthusiastically received in France, however, where its premiere was considerably delayed by charges that it was anti-French propaganda. But it did well in most markets, and other Lubitsch historical films were soon exported. In 1923, he became the first German director to be hired by Hollywood.

Some small companies briefly remained independent. Among these was Erich Pommer's Decla (later Decla-Bioscop). In 1919, the firm undertook to produce an unconventional script by two unknowns, Carl Mayer and Hans Janowitz. These young writers wanted the film to be made in an unusually stylized way. The three designers assigned to the film—Hermann Warm, Walter Reimann, and Walter Röhrig—suggested that it be done in an Expressionist style. As an avant-garde

12.16 *Madame Dubarry:* A crowd scene in the Tribunal of the French Revolution.

movement, Expressionism had first been important in painting (starting about 1910) and had been quickly taken up in theater, then in literature, and in architecture. Now company officials consented to try it in the cinema, apparently believing that this might be a selling point in the international market.

This belief was vindicated when the inexpensively made film, *The Cabinet of Dr. Caligari* (1920), created a sensation in Berlin and then in the United States, France, and other countries. Because of its success, other films in the Expressionist style soon followed. The result was a stylistic movement in cinema that lasted several years.

The success of *Caligari* and other Expressionist films kept Germany's avant-garde directors largely within the industry. A few experimental filmmakers made abstract films, like Viking Eggeling's *Diagonal-symphonie* (1923), or Dada films influenced by the international art movement, like Hans Richter's *Ghosts before Breakfast* (1928). Big firms such as UFA (which absorbed Decla-Bioscop in 1921), as well as smaller companies, invested in Expressionist films because these films would compete with those of America. Indeed, by the mid-1920s, the most prominent German films were widely regarded as among the best in the world.

The first film of the movement, *Caligari,* is also one of the most typical examples. One of its designers, Warm, claimed, "The film image must become graphic art." *Caligari,* with its extreme stylization, was indeed like a moving Expressionist painting or woodcut print. In contrast to French Impressionism, which bases its style primarily on cinematography and editing, German Expressionism depends heavily on mise-en-scene. Shapes are distorted and exaggerated unrealistically for expressive purposes. Actors often wear heavy makeup and move in jerky or slow, sinuous patterns. Most important, all of the elements of the mise-en-scene interact graphically to create an overall composition. Characters do not simply exist within a setting but rather form visual elements that merge with the setting. We have already seen an example of this in 6.105, where the character Cesare collapses in a stylized forest, his body and outstretched arms echoing the shapes of the trees' trunks and branches.

In *Caligari,* the Expressionist stylization functions to convey the distorted viewpoint of a madman. We see the world as the hero does. This narrative function of the settings becomes explicit at one point, as the hero enters an asylum in his pursuit of Caligari. As he pauses to look around, he stands at the center of a pattern of radiating black-and-white lines that run across the floor and up the walls **(12.17).** The world of the film is literally a projection of the hero's vision.

Later, as Expressionism became an accepted style, filmmakers did not motivate Expressionist style as the narrative point of view of mad characters. Instead, Expressionism often functioned to create stylized situations for fantasy and horror stories (as with *Waxworks,* 1924, and *Nosferatu,* 1922) or historical epics (as with *The Nibelungen,* 1923–1924). Expressionist films depended greatly on their designers. In the German studios, a film's designer received a relatively high salary and was often mentioned prominently in the advertisements.

A combination of circumstances led to the disappearance of the movement. The rampant inflation of the early 1920s in Germany actually favored Expressionist filmmaking, partly by making it easy for German exporters to sell their films cheaply abroad. Inflation discouraged imports, however, for the tumbling exchange rate of the mark made foreign purchases prohibitively expensive. But in 1924 the U.S. Dawes Plan helped to stabilize the German economy, and foreign films came in more frequently, offering a degree of competition unknown in Germany for nearly a decade. Expressionist film budgets, however, were climbing. The last major films of the movement, Murnau's *Faust* (1926) and Lang's *Metropolis* (1927),

"Everything is composition; any image whatsoever could be stopped on the screen and would be a marvellously balanced painting of forms and lights. Also, it is one of the films which leaves in our memories the clearest visions—precise and of a slightly static beauty. But even more than painting, it is animated architecture."

— François Berge, French critic, on Fritz Lang's *The Nibelungen*

12.17 The insane asylum set of *The Cabinet of Dr. Caligari.*

12.18 *Metropolis* contained many large Expressionistic sets, including this garden, with pillars that appear to be made of melting clay.

were costly epics that helped drive UFA deeper into financial difficulty, leading Erich Pommer to quit and try his luck briefly in America **(12.18).** Other personnel were lured away to Hollywood as well. Murnau left after finishing *Faust,* his last German film. Major actors (like Conrad Veidt and Emil Jannings) and cinematographers (such as Karl Freund) went to Hollywood as well. Lang stayed on, but after the criticisms of *Metropolis*'s extravagance on its release, he formed his own production company and turned to other styles in his later German films. At the beginning of the Nazi regime in 1933, he too left the country.

Trying to counter the stiffer competition from imported Hollywood films after 1924, the Germans also began to imitate the American product. The resulting films, though sometimes impressive, diluted the unique qualities of the Expressionist style. Thus by 1927, Expressionism as a movement died out. But as Georges Sadoul has pointed out, an expressionist (spelled with a small "e" to distinguish it from the Expressionist movement proper) tendency lingered on in many of the German films of the late 1920s and even into such 1930s films as Lang's *M* (1930) and *Testament of Dr. Mabuse* (1932). And because so many of the German filmmakers came to the United States, Hollywood films also displayed expressionist tendencies. Horror films, such as *Son of Frankenstein* (1939), and *films noirs* have strong expressionist touches in their settings and lighting. Although the German movement lasted only about seven years, expressionism has never entirely died out as a trend in film style.

FRENCH IMPRESSIONISM AND SURREALISM (1918–1930)

During the silent era, a number of film movements in France posed major alternatives to classical Hollywood narrative form. Some of these alternatives—abstract cinema, Dada filmmaking—are not specifically French and constituted instead a part of the growing international avant-garde. But two alternatives to the American mode remained quite localized. Impressionism was an avant-garde style that operated largely within the film industry. Most of the Impressionist filmmakers started out working for major French companies, and some of their avant-garde works proved financially successful. In the mid-1920s, most formed their own independent companies but remained within the mainstream commercial industry by renting studio facilities and releasing their films through established firms. The other alternative movement, Surrealism, lay largely outside the film industry; allied with the Surrealist movement in other arts, these filmmakers relied on their own means and private patronage. France in the 1920s thus offers a striking instance of how different film movements may coexist in similar circumstances.

Impressionism

World War I struck a serious blow to the French film industry. Personnel were conscripted, many film studios were shifted to wartime uses, and much export was halted. Yet since the two major firms, Pathé Frères and Léon Gaumont, also controlled circuits of theaters, they needed to fill vacant screens, and so in 1915 American films began increasingly to flood into France. Represented by Pearl White, Douglas Fairbanks, Chaplin and Ince films, De Mille's *The Cheat,* and William S. Hart (affectionately named "Rio Jim" by the French), the Hollywood cinema dominated the market by the end of 1917. After the war, French filmmaking never fully recovered: In the 1920s, French audiences saw eight times more Hollywood footage than domestic footage. The film industry tried in several ways to recapture the market, mostly through imitation of Hollywood production methods and genres. Artistically, however, the most significant move was the firms' encouragement of younger French directors: Abel Gance, Louis Delluc, Germaine Dulac, Marcel L'Herbier, and Jean Epstein.

These directors differed from their predecessors. The previous generation had regarded filmmaking as a commercial craft. More theoretical and ambitious, the younger filmmakers wrote essays proclaiming cinema to be an art comparable to poetry, painting, and music. Cinema should, they said, be purely itself and should not borrow from the theater or literature. Impressed by the verve and energy of the American cinema, the young theorists compared Chaplin to Nijinsky and the films of Rio Jim to *The Song of Roland.* Cinema should, above all, be (like music) an occasion for the artist to express feelings. Gance, Delluc, Dulac, L'Herbier, Epstein, and other more tangential members of the movement sought to put this aesthetic into practice as filmmakers.

Between 1918 and 1928, in a series of extraordinary films, the younger directors experimented with cinema in ways that posed an alternative to the dominant Hollywood formal principles. Given the centrality of emotion in their aesthetic, it is no wonder that the intimate psychological narrative dominated their filmmaking practice. The interactions of a few characters, usually a love triangle [as in Delluc's *L'Inondation* (1924), Epstein's *Coeur fidèle* (1923) and *La Belle nivernaise* (1923), and Gance's *La Dixième symphonie* (1918)], would serve as the basis for the filmmaker's exploration of fleeting moods and shifting sensations.

As in the Hollywood cinema, psychological causes were paramount, but the school gained the name Impressionist because of its interest in giving narration considerable psychological depth, revealing the play of a character's consciousness. The interest falls not on external physical behavior but on *inner* action. To a degree unprecedented in international filmmaking, Impressionist films manipulate plot time and subjectivity. To depict memories, flashbacks are common; sometimes the bulk of a film will be one flashback or a series of them. Even more striking is the films' insistence on registering characters' dreams, fantasies, and mental states.

"Another period arrived, that of the psychological and impressionist film. It would seem stupid to place a character in a given situation without penetrating into the secret realm of his inner life, and the actor's performance is explained by the play of thoughts and of visualized sensations."

— Germaine Dulac, director

12.19 In *Coeur fidèle,* the heroine looks out a window, and a superimposition of the foul jetsam of the waterfront conveys her dejection at working as a barmaid in a dockside tavern.

12.20 In *El Dorado,* a man's tipsiness is conveyed by means of a curved mirror that stretches his body sideways.

Dulac's *The Smiling Mme. Beudet* (1923) consists almost entirely of the main character's fantasy life, her imaginary escape from a dull marriage. Despite its epic length (over five hours), Gance's *La Roue* (1922) rests essentially on the erotic relations among only four people, and the director seeks to trace the development of each character's feelings in great detail. Impressionism's emphasis on personal emotion gives the films' narratives an intensely psychological focus.

The Impressionist movement earned its name as well for its use of film style. The filmmakers experimented with ways of rendering mental states by new uses of cinematography and editing. In Impressionist films, irises, masks, and superimpositions function as traces of characters' thoughts and feelings **(12.19).** In *La Roue,* the image of Norma is superimposed over the smoke from a locomotive, representing the fantasy of the engine driver, who is in love with her.

To intensify the subjectivity, the Impressionists' cinematography and editing present characters' perceptual experience, their optical impressions. These films use a great deal of point-of-view cutting, showing a shot of a character looking at something, then a shot of that thing, from an angle and distance replicating the character's vantage point. When a character in an Impressionist film gets drunk or dizzy, the filmmaker renders that experience through distorted or filtered shots or vertiginous camera movements. In **12.20,** from L'Herbier's *El Dorado* (1920), a man is drinking in a cabaret.

The Impressionists also experimented with pronounced rhythmic editing to suggest the pace of an experience as a character feels it, moment by moment. During scenes of violence or emotional turmoil, the rhythm accelerates—the shots get shorter and shorter, building to a climax, sometimes with shots only a few frames long. In *La Roue* a train crash is presented in accelerating shots ranging from 13 frames down to 2, and a man's last thoughts before he falls from a cliff are rendered in a blur of many single-frame shots (the first known use of such rapid editing). In *Coeur fidèle* lovers at a fair ride in whirling swings, and Epstein presents their giddiness in a series of shots 4 frames, then 2 frames, long. Several Impressionist films use a dance to motivate a markedly accelerated cutting rhythm. More generally, their comparison of cinema to music encouraged the Impressionists to explore rhythmic editing. In such ways subjective shooting and editing patterns function within Impressionist films to reinforce the narrative treatment of psychological states.

Impressionist form created certain demands on film technology. Gance, the boldest innovator in this respect, used his epic *Napoléon* (1927) as a chance to try new lenses (even a 275mm telephoto), multiple frame images (called Polyvision), and widescreen ratio (the celebrated triptychs; see 7.69). The most influential Impressionist technological innovation was the development of new means of frame mobility. If the camera was to represent a character's eyes, it should be able to move with the ease of a person. Impressionists strapped their cameras to cars, carousels, and locomotives. For Gance's *Napoléon,* the camera manufacturer Debrie perfected a hand-held model that let the operator move on roller skates. Gance put the machine on wheels, cables, pendulums, and bobsleds. In *L'Argent* (1928), L'Herbier had his camera gliding through huge rooms and even plummeting straight down toward the crowd from the dome of the Paris stock exchange in an effort to convey the traders' frenzied excitement.

Such formal, stylistic, and technological innovations had given French filmmakers the hope that their films could win the popularity granted to Hollywood's product. During the 1920s, the Impressionists in fact operated somewhat independently; they formed their own small production companies and leased studio facilities from Pathé and Gaumont in exchange for distribution rights. Some Impressionist films did prove moderately popular with French audiences. But by 1929 most foreign audiences had not taken to Impressionism; its experimentation was attuned to elite tastes. Moreover, although production costs were rising, the Impressionists (especially Gance and L'Herbier) became even more free-spending. As a result, filmmakers' companies either went out of business or were absorbed by the big firms. Two behemoth productions of the decade, *Napoléon* and *L'Argent*, failed and were reedited by the producers; they were among the last Impressionist films released. With the arrival of the sound film, French industry tightened its belt and had no money to risk on experiments.

Impressionism as a distinct movement may be said to have ceased by 1929. But the influences of Impressionist form—the psychological narrative, subjective camera work, and editing—were more long-lived. They continued to operate, for example, in the work of Alfred Hitchcock and Maya Deren, in Hollywood montage sequences, and in certain American genres and styles (the horror film, *film noir*).

Surrealism

Whereas the French Impressionist filmmaker worked within the commercial film industry, the Surrealist filmmakers relied on private patronage and screened their work in small artists' gatherings. Such isolation is hardly surprising, since Surrealist cinema was a more radical movement, producing films that perplexed and shocked most audiences.

Surrealist cinema was directly linked to Surrealism in literature and painting. According to its spokesperson, André Breton, "Surrealism [was] based on the belief in the superior reality of certain forms of association, heretofore neglected, in the omnipotence of dreams, in the undirected play of thought," Influenced by Freudian psychology, Surrealist art sought to register the hidden currents of the unconscious, "in the absence of any control exercised by reason, and beyond any aesthetic and moral preoccupation."

Automatic writing and painting, the search for bizarre or evocative imagery, the deliberate avoidance of rationally explicable form or style—these became features of Surrealism as it developed in the period 1924–1929. From the start, the Surrealists were attracted to the cinema, especially admiring films that presented untamed desire or the fantastic and marvelous (for example, slapstick comedies, *Nosferatu*, serials about mysterious supercriminals). In due time, painters such as Man Ray and Salvador Dalí and writers such as Antonin Artaud began dabbling in cinema, while the young Spaniard Luis Buñuel, drawn to Surrealism, became its most famous filmmaker.

Surrealist cinema is overtly anti-narrative, attacking causality itself. If rationality is to be fought, causal connections among events must be dissolved. *The Seashell and the Clergyman* (1928; scripted by Artaud, filmed by the Impressionist Germaine Dulac) begins with the protagonist pouring liquids from flasks and then systematically breaking each one **(12.21)**. In Dalí and Buñuel's *Un Chien andalou* (*An Andalusian Dog*, 1928) the hero drags two pianos, stuffed with dead donkeys, across a parlor. In Buñuel's *L'Age d'or* (1930) a woman begins obsessively sucking the toes of a statue.

Many Surrealist films tease us to find a narrative logic that is simply absent. Causality is as evasive as in a dream. Instead, we find events juxtaposed for their disturbing effect. The hero gratuitously shoots a child (*L'Age d'or*), a woman closes her eyes only to reveal eyes painted on her eyelids (Ray's *Emak Bakia*, 1927), and—most famous of all—a man strops a razor and deliberately slits the eyeball of an unprotesting woman (*Un Chien andalou*, **12.22**). An Impressionist film would

12.21 *The Seashell and the Clergyman:* The clergyman's distorted view of a threatening military officer, inexplicably dressed in baby's clothes.

12.22 The shocking eye-slitting scene in *Un chien andalou.*

motivate such events as a character's dreams or hallucinations, but in these films character psychology is all but nonexistent. Sexual desire and ecstasy, violence, blasphemy, and bizarre humor furnish events that Surrealist film form employs with a disregard for conventional narrative principles. The hope was that the free form of the film would arouse the deepest impulses of the viewer. Buñuel called *Un Chien andalou* "a passionate call to murder."

The style of Surrealist cinema is eclectic. Mise-en-scene is often influenced by Surrealist painting. The ants in *Un Chien andalou* come from Dalí's pictures, whereas the pillars and city squares of *The Seashell and the Clergyman* hark back to the Italian painter Giorgio de Chirico. Surrealist editing is an amalgam of some Impressionist devices (many dissolves and superimpositions) and some devices of the dominant cinema. The shocking eyeball slitting at the start of *Un Chien andalou* relies on some principles of continuity editing (and indeed on the Kuleshov effect). However, discontinuous editing is also commonly used to fracture any organized temporal-spatial coherence. In the same film, the heroine locks the man out of a room only to turn to find him inexplicably behind her. On the whole, Surrealist film style refused to canonize any particular devices, since that would order and rationalize what had to be an "undirected play of thought."

The fortunes of Surrealist cinema shifted with changes in the art movement as a whole. By late 1929, when Breton joined the Communist Party, Surrealists were embroiled in internal dissension about whether communism was a political equivalent of Surrealism. Buñuel left France for a brief stay in Hollywood and then returned to Spain. The chief patron of Surrealist filmmaking, the Vicomte de Noailles, supported Jean Vigo's *Zéro de Conduite* (1933), a film of Surrealist ambitions, but then stopped sponsoring the avant-garde. Thus as a unified movement, French Surrealism was no longer viable after 1930. Individual Surrealists continued to work, however. The most famous was Buñuel, who continued to work in his own brand of the Surrealist style for 50 years. His later films, such as *Belle de Jour* (1967) and *The Discreet Charm of the Bourgeoisie* (1972), continue the Surrealist tradition.

SOVIET MONTAGE (1924–1930)

Despite the victory of the Russian Revolution in October of 1917, the new Soviet government faced the difficult task of controlling all sectors of life. Like other industries, the film production and distribution systems took years to build up a substantial output that could serve the aims of the new government.

Although the pre-Revolutionary Russian film industry had not figured prominently in world cinema, there were a number of private production companies operating in Moscow and Petersburg. With most imports cut off during the war, these companies had done quite well making films for the domestic market. The most distinctive Russian films made during the mid-1910s were slow-paced melodramas that concentrated on bravura performances by actors playing characters caught in extremely emotional situations. Such films showcased the talents of Ivan Mozhukin and other popular stars and were aimed mainly at the large Russian audience, seldom being seen abroad.

These film companies resisted the move made directly after the Revolution to nationalize all private property. They simply refused to supply films to theaters operating under the control of the government. In July 1918 the government's film subsection of the State Commission of Education put strict controls on the existing supplies of raw film stock. As a result, producers began hoarding their stock; the largest firms took all the equipment they could and fled to other countries. Some companies made films commissioned by the government, while hoping that the Reds would lose the Civil War and that things would return to pre-Revolutionary conditions.

In the face of shortages of equipment and difficult living conditions, a few young filmmakers made tentative moves that would result in the development of a national cinema movement. Dziga Vertov began working on documentary footage of the war; at age 20, he was placed in charge of all newsreels. Lev Kuleshov, teaching in the newly founded State School on Cinema Art, performed a series of experiments by editing footage from different sources into a whole that creates an impression of continuity. In this sense, Kuleshov was perhaps the most conservative of the young Soviet filmmakers, since he was basically trying to systematize principles of editing similar to the continuity practices of the classical Hollywood cinema. Thus even before they were able to make films, Kuleshov and his young pupils were working at the first film school in the world and writing theoretical essays on the new art form. This grounding in theory would be the basis of the Montage style.

In 1920 Sergei Eisenstein worked briefly in a train carrying propaganda to the troops in the Civil War. He returned that year to Moscow to stage plays in a workers' theater. In May 1920, Vsevolod Pudovkin made his acting debut in a play presented by Kuleshov's State Film School. He had been inspired to go into filmmaking by seeing Griffith's *Intolerance,* which was first shown widely in Russia in 1919. American films, particularly those of Griffith, Douglas Fairbanks, and Mary Pickford, which kept circulating to fill the void left by the low output of new Soviet productions, were a tremendous influence on the filmmakers of the emerging Soviet movement.

None of the important filmmakers of the Montage style was a veteran of the pre-Revolutionary industry. All came from other fields (for example, Eisenstein from engineering, Pudovkin from chemistry) and discovered the cinema in the midst of the Revolution's ferment. The Czarist-era filmmakers who remained active in the USSR in the 1920s tended to stick to older traditions. One popular director of the Czarist period, Yakov Protazanov, went abroad briefly after the Revolution but returned to continue making films whose style and form owed almost nothing to the theory and practice of the new filmmakers.

Protazanov's return coincided with a general loosening of government restrictions on private enterprise. In 1921 the country was facing tremendous problems, including a widespread famine. In order to facilitate the production and distribution of goods, Lenin instituted the New Economic Policy (NEP), which for several years permitted private management of business. For film, the NEP meant a sudden reappearance of film stock and equipment belonging to the producers who had not emigrated. Slowly Soviet production began to grow as private firms made more films. The government attempted, with little success, to control the film industry by creating a central distribution company, Goskino, in 1922.

"Of all the arts, for us the cinema is the most important," Lenin stated in 1922. Since Lenin saw film as a powerful tool for education, the first films encouraged by the government were documentaries and newsreels such as Vertov's newsreel series *Kino-Pravda,* which began in May 1922. Fictional films were also being made from 1917 on, but it was not until 1923 that a Georgian feature, *Red Imps,* became the first Soviet film to compete successfully with the foreign films predominant on Soviet screens. (And not until 1927 did the Soviet industry's income from its own films top that of the films it had imported.)

The Soviet Montage style displayed tentative beginnings in 1924, with Kuleshov's class from the State Film School presenting *The Extraordinary Adventures of Mr. West in the Land of the Bolsheviks.* This delightful film, along with

"Everyone who has had in his hands a piece of film to be edited knows by experience how neutral it remains, even though a part of a planned sequence, until it is joined with another piece, when it suddenly acquires and conveys a sharper and quite different meaning than that planned for it at the time of filming."

— Sergei Eisenstein, director

Kuleshov's next film, *The Death Ray* (1925), showed that Soviet directors could apply Montage principles and come up with amusing satires or exciting adventures as entertaining as the Hollywood product.

Eisenstein's first feature, *Strike,* was released early in 1925 and initiated the movement proper. His second, *Potemkin,* premiered later in 1925, was successful abroad, and drew the attention of other countries to the new movement. In the next few years Eisenstein, Pudovkin, Vertov, and the Ukrainian Alexander Dovzhenko created a series of films that are classics of the Montage style.

The theoretical writings and filmmaking practice of these directors were based on editing. They all declared that a film does not exist in its individual shots but only in their combination through editing into a whole. We should remember here that since the primitive cinema, no national film style had yet appeared that depended on the long take. The great films that inspired Soviet filmmakers, like *Intolerance* and some French Impressionist efforts, were based largely on editing juxtapositions.

Not all of the young theoreticians agreed on exactly what the Montage approach to editing was to be. Pudovkin, for example, believed that shots were like bricks, to be joined together to build a sequence. Eisenstein disagreed, saying that the maximum effect would be gained if the shots did not fit together perfectly, if they created a jolt for the spectator. He also favored juxtaposing shots in order to create a concept, as we have already seen with his use of conceptual editing in *October* (pp. 339–343). Vertov disagreed with both theorists, favoring a cinema-eye approach to recording and shaping documentary reality.

Pudovkin's *Storm over Asia* makes use of conceptual editing similar to that of Eisenstein's *October.* Shots of a military officer and his wife being dressed in their accessories are intercut with shots of the preparation at the temple (**12.23–12.26**). Pudovkin's parallel montage points up the absurdity of both rituals.

The Montagists' approach to narrative form set them apart from the cinemas of other countries. Soviet narrative films tended to downplay character psychology as a cause; instead, social forces provided the major causes. Characters were interesting for the way these social causes affected their lives. Films of the Soviet Montage movement did not always have a single protagonist. Social groups could form a collective hero, as in Eisenstein's films before *Old and New* (1929). In keeping with this de-emphasis of individual personalities, Soviet filmmakers often avoided well-known actors, preferring to cast parts by searching out nonactors. This practice was called **typage,** since the filmmakers would often choose an individual

12.23 *Storm over Asia:* After a medium close-up of an elaborate piece of jewelry being lowered over the head of a priest, there is a cut . . .

12.24 . . . to a close-up of a servant placing a necklace around the neck of the officer's wife . . .

12.25 . . . then a cut back to a large headdress being positioned on a priest's head . . .

12.26 . . . juxtaposed with a close-up of a tiara being set on the wife's head.

whose appearance seemed at once to convey the type of character he or she was to play. Except for the hero, Pudovkin used nonactors to play all of the Mongols in *Storm over Asia.*

By the end of the 1920s, each of the major directors of this movement had made about four important films. The decline of the movement was not caused primarily, as in Germany and France, by industrial and economic factors. Instead, government political pressures exerted a strong control that discouraged the use of the Montage style. By the late 1920s, Vertov, Eisenstein, and Dovzhenko were being criticized for their excessively formal and esoteric approaches. In 1929 Eisenstein went to Hollywood to study the new technique of sound; by the time he returned in 1932, the attitude of the film industry had changed. While he was away, a few filmmakers carried their Montage experiments into sound cinema in the early 1930s. But the Soviet authorities, under Stalin's direction, encouraged filmmakers to create simple films that would be readily understandable to all audiences. Stylistic experimentation or nonrealistic subject matter was often criticized or censored.

This trend culminated in 1934, when the government instituted a new artistic policy called Socialist Realism. This policy dictated that all artworks must depict revolutionary development while being firmly grounded in realism. The great Soviet directors continued to make films, occasionally masterpieces, but the Montage experiments of the 1920s had to be discarded or modified. Eisenstein managed to continue his work on Montage but occasionally incurred the wrath of the authorities up until his death in 1948. As a movement, the Soviet Montage style can be said to have ended by 1933, with the release of such films as Vertov's *Enthusiasm* (1931) and Pudovkin's *Deserter* (1933).

THE CLASSICAL HOLLYWOOD CINEMA AFTER THE COMING OF SOUND

The introduction of sound technology came about through the efforts of certain Hollywood firms to widen their power. During the mid-1920s Warner Bros. was in the process of investing a great deal of money to expand its facilities and holdings. One of these expansions was the investment in a sound system using records in synchronization with film images **(12.27).**

By releasing *Don Juan* (1926) with orchestral accompaniment and sound effects on disc, along with a series of sound vaudeville shorts with singing and talking, Warner Bros. began to popularize the idea of sound films. In 1927, *The Jazz Singer* (a part-talkie with some scenes accompanied only by music) had a tremendous success, and the Warner Bros. investment began to pay off.

The success of *Don Juan, The Jazz Singer,* and the shorts convinced other studios that sound contributed to profitable filmmaking. Unlike the early period of filmmaking and the Motion Picture Patents Company, there was now no fierce competition within the industry. Instead, firms realized that whatever sound system the studios finally adopted, it would have to be compatible with the projection machinery of any theater. Eventually a sound-on-film rather than a sound-on-disc system became the standard and continues so to the present. (That is, as we saw in Chapter 1, the sound track is printed on the strip of film alongside the image.) By 1930 most theaters in America were wired for sound.

For a few years, sound created a setback for Hollywood film style. The camera had to be put inside a sound booth so that its motor noise would not be picked up

12.27 An early projector with a turntable (lower center) attached.

12.28   A posed publicity still demonstrated the limitations of early sound filming.

"You know, when talkies first came in they were fascinated by sound—they had frying eggs and they had this and that—and then people became infatuated with the movement of the camera; I believe, the big thing right now is to move a hand-held camera. I think the director and his camerawork should not intrude on the story."

— George Cukor, director

by the microphone. The components of a dialogue scene in a 1928 MGM film can be seen in **12.28.** The camera operator can hear only through his earphones, and the camera cannot move except for short pans to reframe. The bulky microphone, on the table at the right, also did not move. The actors had to stay within a limited space if their speech was to register on the track. The result of such restrictions was a brief period of static films resembling stage plays.

Still, from the very beginning of sound filming, solutions were found for these problems. Sometimes several cameras, all in soundproof booths, would record the scene from different angles simultaneously. The resulting footage could be cut together to provide a standard continuity editing pattern in a scene, with all the sound synchronized perfectly. The whole camera booth might be mounted on wheels to create camera movements, or a scene might be shot silent and a sound track added later. Early sound films such as Rouben Mamoulian's *Applause* (1929) demonstrate that the camera soon regained a great flexibility of movement. Later, smaller cases, enclosing only the camera body, replaced the cumbersome booths. These *blimps* **(12.29)** permitted cinematographers to place the camera on movable supports. Similarly, microphones mounted on booms and hanging over the heads of the actors could also follow moving action without a loss of recording quality.

Once camera movement and subject movement were restored to sound films, filmmakers continued to use many of the stylistic characteristics developed in Hollywood during the silent period. Diegetic sound provided a powerful addition to the system of continuity editing. Overlapping dialogue with the cuts, for instance, could create smooth temporal continuity and suggest spaces outside the frame.

Within the overall patterns of continuity style and classical narrative form, each of the large studios developed a distinctive approach of its own. Thus MGM,

12.29   A blimped camera during the early 1930s allowed the camera tripod to be placed on a rolling dolly.

for example, became the prestige studio, with a huge number of stars and technicians under long-term contract. MGM lavished money on settings, costumes, and special effects, as in *The Good Earth* (1937), with its locust attack, or *San Francisco* (1936), in which the great earthquake is spectacularly re-created. Warner Bros., in spite of its success with sound, was still a relatively small studio and specialized in less expensive genre pictures. Its series of gangster films (*Little Caesar, Public Enemy*) and musicals (*42nd Street, Gold Diggers of 1933, Dames*) were among the studio's most successful products. Even lower on the ladder of prestige was Universal, which depended on imaginative filmmaking rather than established stars or expensive sets in its atmospheric horror films such as *Frankenstein* (1931) and *The Old Dark House* (1932, **12.30**).

One major genre, the musical, became possible only with the introduction of sound. Indeed, the original intention of the Warners when they began their investment in sound equipment was to circulate vaudeville acts on film. The form of most musicals involved separate numbers inserted into a linear narrative, although a few revue musicals simply strung together a series of numbers with little or no connecting narrative. One of the major studios, RKO, made a series of musicals starring Fred Astaire and Ginger Rogers: *Swing Time* (George Stevens, 1936) illustrates how a musical can be a classically constructed narrative (see pp. 125–126).

During the 1930s, color film stocks became widely used for the first time. In the 1920s, a small number of films had Technicolor sequences, but the process was crude, using only two colors in combination to create all other hues. The result tended to emphasize greenish-blue and pink tones; it was also too costly to use extensively **(12.31).** By the early 1930s, however, Technicolor had been improved. It

12.30   Heavy shadows, spiky shapes, and eccentric performances mixed a menacing atmosphere with a touch of humor in *The Old Dark House.*

12.31 *Under a Texas Moon* (1930): Typical two-strip Technicolor, with mostly orange and green hues.

now used three primary colors and thus could reproduce a large range of hues. Though still expensive, it was soon proved to add hugely to the appeal of many films. After *Becky Sharp* (1935), the first feature-length film to use the new Technicolor, and *The Trial of the Lonesome Pine* (1936), studios began using Technicolor extensively. The Technicolor process was used until the early 1970s. (For a variety of examples of Technicolor, running from the 1940s to the 1960s, see 6.42–6.44, 6.80, 6.130, 6.131, 7.5, and 7.54.)

Technicolor needed a great deal of light on the set, and the light had to favor certain hues. Thus, brighter lights specifically designed for color filmmaking were introduced. Some cinematographers began to use the new lights for black-and-white filming. These brighter lights, combined with faster film stocks, made it easier to achieve greater depth of field with more light and a smaller aperture. Many cinematographers stuck to the standard soft-focus style of the 1920s and 1930s, but others began to experiment. By the late 1930s, there was a definite trend toward a deep-focus style.

Mervyn Leroy's *Anthony Adverse* (1936), Alfred L. Werker's *The Adventures of Sherlock Holmes* (1939), and the Sam Wood–William Cameron Menzies *Our Town* (1940) also used deep focus to a considerable degree. But it was *Citizen Kane* that in 1941 brought deep focus strongly to the attention of spectators and filmmakers alike. Welles's compositions placed the foreground figures close to the camera and the background figures deep in the space of the shot. In some cases, the apparently deep-focus image was actually achieved through matting and rear projection. Overall, *Citizen Kane* helped make the tendency toward deep focus a major part of classical Hollywood style in the next decade. Many films using the technique soon appeared. *Citizen Kane*'s cinematographer, Gregg Toland, worked on some of them, such as *The Little Foxes* (**12.32**).

The light necessary for deep focus also tended to lend a hard-edge appearance to objects. Gauzy effects were largely eliminated, and much 1940s cinema became visually quite distinct from that of the 1930s. But the insistence on the clear narrative functioning of all these techniques remained strong. The classical Hollywood narrative modified itself over the years but did not change radically.

12.32 William Wyler stages in depth in *The Little Foxes*.

ITALIAN NEOREALISM (1942–1951)

There is no definitive source for the term *Neorealism,* but it first appeared in the early 1940s in the writings of Italian critics. From one perspective, the term represented a younger generation's desire to break free of the conventions of ordinary Italian cinema. Under Mussolini, the motion-picture industry had created colossal historical epics and sentimental upper-class melodramas (nicknamed *white-telephone films*), and many critics felt these to be artificial and decadent. A new realism was needed. Some critics found it in French films of the 1930s, especially works by Jean Renoir. Other critics turned closer to home to praise films like Luchino Visconti's *Ossessione* (1942).

Today most historians believe that Neorealist filmmaking was not a complete break with Italian cinema under Mussolini. Pseudo-documentaries such as Rossellini's *White Ship* (1941), even though propagandistic, prepared the way for more forthright handling of contemporary events. Other current trends, such as regional dialect comedy and urban melodrama, encouraged directors and scriptwriters to turn toward realism. Overall, spurred by both foreign influences and indigenous traditions, the postwar period saw several filmmakers beginning to work with the goal of revealing contemporary social conditions. This trend became known as the Neorealist movement.

Economic, political, and cultural factors helped Neorealism survive. Nearly all the major Neorealists—Roberto Rossellini, Vittorio De Sica, Luchino Visconti, and others—came to the movement as experienced filmmakers. They knew one another, frequently shared scriptwriters and personnel, and gained public attention in the journals *Cinema* and *Bianco e Nero.* Before 1948 the Neorealist movement had enough friends in the government to be relatively free of censorship. There was even a correspondence between Neorealism and an Italian literary movement of the same period modeled on the *verismo* of the previous century. The result was an array of Italian films that gained worldwide recognition: Visconti's *La Terra Trema* (1947); Rossellini's *Rome Open City* (1945), *Paisan* (1946), and *Germany Year Zero* (1947); De Sica's *Shoeshine* (1946) and *Bicycle Thieves* (1948); and works of Lattuada, Blasetti, and De Santis.

Neorealism created a somewhat distinctive approach to film style. By 1945 the fighting had destroyed most of Cinecittà, so studio settings were in short supply and sound equipment was rare. As a result, Neorealist mise-en-scene relied on actual locales, and its photographic work tended toward the raw roughness of documentaries. Rossellini has told of buying bits of negative stock from street photographers, so that much of *Rome Open City* was shot on film with varying photographic qualities.

Shooting on the streets and in private buildings made Italian camera operators adept at cinematography that often avoided the three-point lighting system of Hollywood (6.37). Although Neorealist films often featured famous stage or film actors, they also made use of nonactors, recruited for their realistic looks or behavior. For the adult "star" of *Bicycle Thieves,* De Sica chose a factory worker: "The way he moved, the way he sat down, his gestures with those hands of a working man and not of an actor . . . everything about him was perfect." The Italian cinema had a long tradition of dubbing, and the ability to postsynchronize dialogue permitted the filmmakers to work on location with smaller crews and to move the camera freely. With a degree of improvisational freedom in the acting and setting went a certain flexibility of framing, well displayed in the death of Pina in *Rome Open City,* the final

12.33   One of the magnificent landscapes in depth in *La Terra Trema*.

12.34   The famous scene in *Bicycle Thieves* in which the hero takes shelter along with a group of priests during a rain shower.

"The sentiment of [*Bicycle Thieves*] is expressed overtly. The feelings invoked are a natural consequence of the themes of the story and the point of view it is told from. It is a politically committed film, fuelled by a quiet but burning passion. But it never lectures. It observes rather than explains."

— Sally Potter, director

sequence of *Germany Year Zero,* and *La Terra Trema* **(12.33).** The tracking shots through the open-air bicycle market in *Bicycle Thieves* illustrate the possibilities that the Neorealist director found in returning to location filming.

Perhaps even more influential was the Neorealist sense of narrative form. Reacting against the intricately plotted white-telephone dramas, the Neorealists tended to loosen up narrative relations. The earliest major films of the movement, such as *Ossessione, Rome Open City,* and *Shoeshine,* contain relatively conventionally organized plots (albeit with unhappy endings). But the most formally innovative Neorealist films allow the intrusion of noncausally motivated details **(12.34).** Although the causes of characters' actions are usually seen as concretely economic and political (poverty, unemployment, exploitation), the effects are often fragmentary and inconclusive. Rossellini's *Paisan* is frankly episodic, presenting six anecdotes of life in Italy during the Allied invasion; often we are not told the outcome of an event, the consequence of a cause.

The ambiguity of Neorealist films is also a product of narration that refuses to yield an omniscient knowledge of events, as if acknowledging that the totality of reality is simply unknowable. This is especially evident in the films' endings. *Bicycle Thieves* concludes with the worker and his son wandering down the street, their stolen bicycle still missing, their future uncertain. Although ending with the defeat of the Sicilian fishermen's revolt against the merchants, *La Terra Trema* does not cancel the possibility that a later revolt will succeed. Neorealism's tendency toward a slice-of-life plot construction gave many films of the movement an open-ended quality quite opposed to the narrative closure of the Hollywood cinema.

As economic and cultural forces had sustained the Neorealist movement, so they were prime causes of its cessation. When Italy began to prosper after the war, the government looked askance at films so critical of contemporary society. After 1949, censorship and state pressures began to constrain the movement. Large-scale Italian film production began to reappear, and Neorealism no longer had the freedom of the small production company. In addition, the Neorealist directors, now famous, began to pursue more individualized concerns: Rossellini's investigation of Christian humanism and Western history, De Sica's sentimental romances, Luchino Visconti's examination of upper-class milieus. Most historians date the end of the Neorealist movement with the public attacks on De Sica's *Umberto D* (1951). Nevertheless, Neorealist elements are still quite visible in the early works of Federico Fellini (*I. Vitelloni,* 1954, is a good example) and Michelangelo Antonioni (*Cronaca di un amore,* 1951); both directors had worked on Neorealist films. The movement exercised a strong influence on individual filmmakers such as Ermanno Olmi and Satyajit Ray and on groups such as the French New Wave.

THE FRENCH NEW WAVE (1959–1964)

The late 1950s and early 1960s saw the rise of a new generation of filmmakers around the world. In country after country there emerged directors born before World War II but grown to adulthood in the postwar era of reconstruction and rising prosperity. Japan, Canada, England, Italy, Spain, Brazil, and the United States all had their new waves or young cinema groups—some trained in film schools, many allied with specialized film magazines, most in revolt against their elders in the industry. The most generally influential of these groups appeared in France.

In the mid-1950s a group of young men who wrote for the Paris film journal *Cahiers du cinéma* made a habit of attacking the most artistically respected French filmmakers of the day. "I consider an adaptation of value," wrote François Truffaut, "only when written by a *man of the cinema.* Aurenche and Bost [the leading scriptwriters of the time] are essentially literary men and I reproach them here for being contemptuous of the cinema by underestimating it." Addressing 21 major directors, Jean-Luc Godard asserted, "Your camera movements are ugly because your subjects are bad, your casts act badly because your dialogue is worthless; in a word, you don't know how to create cinema because you no longer even know what it is." Truffaut and Godard, along with Claude Chabrol, Eric Rohmer, and Jacques Rivette, championed certain directors considered somewhat outdated (Jean Renoir, Max Ophuls) or eccentric (Robert Bresson, Jacques Tati).

More important, the young men saw no contradiction in rejecting the French filmmaking establishment while loving blatantly commercial Hollywood. The young rebels of *Cahiers* claimed that in the works of certain directors—certain *auteurs* (authors)—artistry existed in the American cinema. An **auteur** usually did not literally write scripts but managed nonetheless to stamp his or her personality on genre and studio products, transcending the constraints of Hollywood's standardized system. Howard Hawks, Otto Preminger, Samuel Fuller, Vincente Minnelli, Nicholas Ray, Alfred Hitchcock—these were more than craftsmen. Each person's total output constituted a coherent world. Truffaut quoted Giraudoux, "There are no works, there are only *auteurs.*" Godard remarked later, "We won the day in having it acknowledged in principle that a film by Hitchcock, for example, is as important as a book by Aragon. Film *auteurs,* thanks to us, have finally entered the history of art." And indeed, many of the Hollywood directors these critics and filmmakers praised gained reputations that have persisted up to the present.

Writing criticism did not, however, satisfy these young men. They itched to make movies. Borrowing money from friends and filming on location, each started to shoot short films. By 1959 they had become a force to be reckoned with. In that year Rivette filmed *Paris nous appartient* (*Paris Belongs to Us*); Godard made *À Bout de souffle* (*Breathless*); Chabrol made his second feature, *Les Cousins;* and in April Truffaut's *Les Quatre cent coups* (*The 400 Blows*) won the Grand Prize at the Cannes Festival.

The novelty and youthful vigor of these directors led journalists to nickname them *la nouvelle vague*—the *New Wave.* Their output was staggering. All told, the five central directors made 32 feature films between 1959 and 1966; Godard and Chabrol made 11 apiece. So many films must of course be highly disparate, but there are enough similarities for us to identify a broadly distinctive New Wave approach to style and form.

The most obviously revolutionary quality of the New Wave films was their casual look. To proponents of the carefully polished French *cinema of quality,* the young directors must have seemed hopelessly sloppy. The New Wave directors had admired the Neorealists (especially Rossellini) and, in opposition to studio filmmaking, took as their mise-en-scene actual locales in and around Paris. Shooting on location became the norm. Similarly, glossy studio lighting was replaced by available light and simple supplemental sources. Few postwar French films would have shown the dim, grimy apartments and corridors featured in *Paris Belongs to Us.*

Cinematography changed too. The New Wave camera moves a great deal, panning and tracking to follow characters or trace out relations within a locale. Furthermore, shooting cheaply on location demanded flexible, portable equipment. Fortunately, Eclair had recently developed a lightweight camera that could be handheld. (That the Eclair had been used primarily for documentary work accorded perfectly with the realistic mise-en-scene of the New Wave.) New Wave films were

"We were all critics before beginning to make films, and I loved all kinds of cinema—the Russians, the Americans, the neorealists. It was the cinema that made us—or me, at least—want to make films. I knew nothing of life except through the cinema."

— Jean-Luc Godard, director

12.35 *Vivre sa vie:* A clip from Dreyer's *The Passion of Joan of Arc . . .*

12.36 . . . helps dramatize the heroine's feelings as she watches it.

intoxicated with the new freedom offered by the hand-held camera. In *The 400 Blows* the camera explores a cramped apartment and rides a carnival centrifuge. In *Breathless* the cinematographer held the camera while seated in a wheelchair to follow the hero along a complex path in a travel agency's office (11.36).

One of the most salient features of New Wave films is their casual humor. These young men deliberately played with the medium. In Godard's *Band of Outsiders* the three main characters resolve to be silent for a minute, and Godard dutifully shuts off *all* the sound. In Truffaut's *Shoot the Piano Player,* a character swears that he's not lying: "May my mother drop dead if I'm not telling the truth." Cut to a shot of an old lady keeling over. But most often the humor lies in esoteric references to other films, Hollywood or European. There are homages to admired *auteurs:* Godard characters allude to *Johnny Guitar* (Ray), *Some Came Running* (Minnelli), and "Arizona Jim" (from Renoir's *Crime of M. Lange*). In *Les Carabiniers* Godard parodies Lumière, and in *Vivre sa vie* he visually quotes *La Passion de Jeanne d'Arc.* (**12.35, 12.36**). Hitchcock is frequently cited in Chabrol's films, and Truffaut's *Les Mistons* re-creates a shot from a Lumière short. Such homages even became in-jokes, as when New Wave actors Jean-Claude Brialy and Jeanne Moreau walk on in *The 400 Blows* or when a Godard character mentions "Arizona Jules" (combining names from *Crime of M. Lange* and *Jules and Jim*). Such gags, the New Wave directors felt, took some of the solemnity out of filmmaking and film viewing.

New Wave films also pushed further the Neorealist experimentation with plot construction. In general, causal connections became quite loose. Is there actually a political conspiracy going on in *Paris Belongs to Us?* Why is Nana shot at the end of *Vivre sa vie?* In *Shoot the Piano Player* the first sequence consists mainly of a conversation between the hero's brother and a man he accidentally meets on the street; the latter tells of his marital problems at some length, even though he has nothing to do with the film's narrative.

Moreover, the films often lack goal-oriented protagonists. The heroes may drift aimlessly, engage in actions on the spur of the moment, spend their time talking and drinking in a café or going to movies. New Wave narratives often introduce startling shifts in tone, jolting our expectations. When two gangsters kidnap the hero and his girlfriend in *Shoot the Piano Player,* the whole group begins a comic discussion of sex. Discontinuous editing further disturbs narrative continuity; this tendency reaches its limit in Godard's jump cuts (pp. 336–337, 431–432).

Perhaps most important, the New Wave film typically ends ambiguously. We have seen this already in *Breathless* (p. 430). Antoine in *The 400 Blows* reaches the sea in the last shot, but as he moves forward, Truffaut zooms in and freezes the frame, ending the film with the question of where Antoine will go from there (3.8). In Chabrol's *Les Bonnes Femmes* and *Ophelia,* in Rivette's *Paris Belongs to Us,* and in nearly all the work of Godard and Truffaut in this period, the looseness of the causal chain leads to endings that remain defiantly open and uncertain.

Curiously, despite the demands that the films placed on the viewer and despite the critical rampages of the filmmakers, the French film industry was not hostile to the New Wave. The decade 1947–1957 had been good to film production: The government supported the industry through enforced quotas, banks had invested heavily, and there was a flourishing business of international co-productions. But in 1957 cinema attendance fell off drastically, chiefly because television became more widespread. By 1959 the industry was in a crisis. The independent financing of low-budget films seemed to offer a good solution. New Wave directors shot films much more quickly and cheaply than did reigning directors. Moreover, the young directors helped one another out and thus reduced the financial risk by the established companies. Thus the French industry supported the New Wave through distribution, exhibition, and eventually production.

Indeed, it is possible to argue that by 1964, although each New Wave director had his or her own production company, the group had become absorbed into the French film industry. Godard made *Le Mépris* (*Contempt,* 1963) for a major commercial producer, Carlo Ponti; Truffaut made *Fahrenheit 451* (1966) in England for Universal; and Chabrol began turning out parodies of James Bond thrillers.

Dating the exact end of the movement is difficult, but most historians select 1964, when the characteristic New Wave form and style had already become diffused and imitated (by, for instance, Tony Richardson in his 1963 English film *Tom Jones*). Certainly, after 1968 the political upheavals in France drastically altered the personal relations among the directors. Chabrol, Truffaut, and Rohmer became firmly entrenched in the French film industry, whereas Godard set up an experimental film and video studio in Switzerland, and Rivette began to create narratives of staggering complexity and length (such as *Out One,* originally about 12 hours long). By the mid-1980s, Truffaut had died, Chabrol's films were often unseen outside France, and Rivette's output had become esoteric. Rohmer retained international attention with his ironic tales of love and self-deception among the upper-middle class [*Pauline at the Beach* (1982) and *Full Moon over Paris* (1984)]. Godard continued to attract notoriety with such films as *Passion* (1981) and his controversial retelling of the Old and New Testaments, *Hail Mary* (1983). In 1990 he released an elegant, enigmatic film ironically entitled *Nouvelle vague*—that bears little relationship to the original tendency. In retrospect, the New Wave not only offered several original and valuable films but also demonstrated that renewal in the film industry could come from talented, aggressive young people inspired in large part by the sheer love of cinema.

THE NEW HOLLYWOOD AND INDEPENDENT FILMMAKING

Midway through the 1960s, the Hollywood industry seemed very healthy, with blockbusters like *The Sound of Music* (1965) and *Dr. Zhivago* (1965) yielding huge profits. But soon problems arose. Expensive studio pictures failed miserably. Television networks, which had paid high prices for broadcasting films after theatrical release, stopped bidding for pictures. American movie attendance flattened out at around 1 billion tickets per year (a figure that, despite home video, remained fairly constant until the early 1990s). By 1969 Hollywood companies were losing over $200 million annually.

Producers fought back. One strategy was to produce counterculture-flavored films aimed at young people. The most popular and influential were Dennis Hopper's low-budget *Easy Rider* (1969) and Robert Altman's *M*A*S*H* (1970). By and large, however, other *youthpix* about campus revolution and unorthodox lifestyles proved not to be big box-office attractions. What did help lift the industry's fortunes was a series of immense hits made by young directors. The most successful were Francis Ford Coppola's *The Godfather* (1972); William Friedkin's *The Exorcist* (1973); Steven Spielberg's *Jaws* (1975) and *Close Encounters of the Third Kind* (1977); John Carpenter's *Halloween* (1978); and George Lucas's *American Graffiti* (1973), *Star Wars* (1977), and *The Empire Strikes Back* (1980). In addition, films by Brian De Palma (*Obsession,* 1976) and Martin Scorsese (*Taxi Driver,* 1976; *Raging Bull,* 1980) attracted critical praise.

These and other directors came to be known as the movie brats. Instead of coming up through the ranks of the studio system, most had gone to film schools.

At New York University, the University of Southern California, and the University of California at Los Angeles, they had not only mastered the mechanics of production but also learned about film aesthetics and history. Unlike earlier Hollywood directors, the movie brats often had an encyclopedic knowledge of great movies and directors. Even those who did not attend film school were admirers of the classical Hollywood tradition.

As had been the case with the French New Wave, these film-buff directors produced some personal, highly self-conscious films. The movie brats worked in traditional genres, but they also tried to give them an autobiographical coloring. Thus *American Graffiti* was not only a teenage musical but also Lucas's reflection on growing up in California in the 1960s. Coppola imbued both *Godfather* films with a vivacious and melancholy sense of the intense bonds within the Italian American family. Paul Schrader poured his own obsessions with violence and sexuality into his scripts for *Taxi Driver* and *Raging Bull* and his own directed films, such as *Hard Core* (1979).

Since movies had been a major part of the young directors' lives, many films of the New Hollywood were based on the old Hollywood. De Palma's films borrowed heavily from Hitchcock, with *Dressed to Kill* (1980) an overt redoing of *Psycho.* Peter Bogdanovich's *What's Up, Doc?* (1972) was an updating of screwball comedy, with particular reference to Howard Hawks's *Bringing Up Baby.* Carpenter's *Assault on Precinct 13* (1976) derived partly from Hawks's *Rio Bravo;* the editing is credited to "John T. Chance," the character played by John Wayne in Hawks's Western.

At the same time, many directors admired the European tradition, with Scorsese drawn to the visual splendor of Luchino Visconti and British director Michael Powell. Some directors dreamed of making complex art films in the European mold. The best known effort is probably Coppola's *The Conversation* (1974), a mystery-story reworking of Antonioni's *Blow-Up* (1966) that plays ambiguously between reality and hallucination (p. 376–377). Robert Altman and Woody Allen, in quite different ways, displayed creative attitudes fed by European cinema: Altman's *Three Women* (1977) and Allen's *Interiors* (1978), for example, owed a good deal to Ingmar Bergman's work.

Altman and Allen were of a slightly older generation, but many movie brats proved the most continuously successful directors of the era. Lucas and Spielberg became powerful producers, working together on the Indiana Jones series and personifying Hollywood's new generation. Coppola failed to sustain his own studio, but he remained an important director. Scorsese's reputation rose steadily: By the end of the 1980s he was the most critically acclaimed living American filmmaker.

During the 1980s fresh talents won recognition, creating a New New Hollywood. Many of the biggest hits of the decade continued to come from Lucas and Spielberg, but other, somewhat younger directors were successful: James Cameron (*The Terminator,* 1984; *Terminator 2: Judgment Day,* 1991), Tim Burton (*Beetlejuice,* 1988; *Batman,* 1989), and Robert Zemeckis (*Back to the Future,* 1985; *Who Framed Roger Rabbit?,* 1988). Many of the successful films of the 1990s came from directors from both these successive waves of the Hollywood renaissance: Spielberg's *Jurassic Park* (1993), De Palma's *Mission: Impossible* (1996), and Lucas's *The Phantom Empire* (1999), as well as Zemeckis's *Forrest Gump* (1994), Cameron's *Titanic* (1997), and Burton's *Sleepy Hollow* (1999).

The resurgence of mainstream film was also fed by filmmakers from outside Hollywood. Many directors came from abroad—from Britain (Tony and Ridley Scott), Australia (Peter Weir, Fred Schepisi), Germany (Wolfgang Peterson), the Netherlands (Paul Verhoeven), and Finland (Rennie Harlin). During the 1980s and

"I love the idea of not being an independent filmmaker. I've liked working within the system. And I've admired a lot of the older directors who were sort of 'directors for hire.' Like Victor Fleming was in a contract all those years to Metro and Selznick and Mayer . . . he made *Captains Courageous.* And you know, his most famous films: *Wizard of Oz* and *Gone with the Wind.*"

— Steven Spielberg, producer/director

1990s, more women filmmakers also became commercially successful, such as Amy Heckerling (*Fast Times at Ridgemont High,* 1982; *Look Who's Talking,* 1990), Martha Coolidge (*Valley Girl,* 1983; *Rambling Rose,* 1991), and Penelope Spheeris (*Wayne's World,* 1992).

Several directors from independent film managed to shift into the mainstream, making medium-budget pictures with widely known stars. David Lynch moved from the midnight movie *Eraserhead* (1978) to the cult classic *Blue Velvet* (1986), while Canadian David Cronenberg, a specialist in low-budget horror films such as *Shivers* (1975), won wider recognition with *The Dead Zone* (1983) and *The Fly* (1986). The New New Hollywood also absorbed some minority directors from independent film. Wayne Wang was the most successful Asian American filmmaker (*Chan Is Missing,* 1982; *Smoke,* 1995). Spike Lee (*She's Gotta Have It,* 1986; *Malcolm X,* 1992) led the way for young African American directors such as Reginald Hudlin (*House Party,* 1990), John Singleton (*Boyz N the Hood,* 1991), Mario van Peebles (*New Jack City,* 1991), and Allen and Albert Hughes (*Menace II Society,* 1993).

Still other directors remained independent and more or less marginal to the studios. In *Stranger than Paradise* (1984) and *Down by Law* (1986), Jim Jarmusch presented quirky, decentered narratives peopled by drifting losers. Allison Anders treated the contemporary experiences of disaffected young women, either in small towns (*Gas Food Lodging,* 1992) or city centers (*Mi Vida Loca,* 1994). Leslie Harris's *Just Another Girl on the IRT* (1994; 1.39) likewise focused on the problems of urban women of color.

Stylistically, no single coherent film movement emerged during the 1970s and 1980s. The most mainstream of the young directors continued the tradition of classical American cinema. Continuity editing remained the norm, with clear signals for time shifts and new plot developments. Some directors embellished Hollywood's traditional storytelling strategies with new or revived visual techniques. In films from *Jaws* onward, Spielberg used deep-focus techniques reminiscent of *Citizen Kane.* Lucas developed motion-control techniques for filming miniatures for *Star Wars,* and his firm Industrial Light and Magic became the leader in new special-effects technology. With the aid of ILM, Zemeckis astutely exploited digital imaging for *Forrest Gump* (5.6). Spielberg and Lucas also led the move toward digital sound and high-quality theater reproduction technology.

Less well funded Hollywood filmmaking cultivated more flamboyant styles. Scorsese's *Taxi Driver, Raging Bull,* and *The Age of Innocence* (1993) use camera movement and slow motion to extend the emotional impact of a scene. De Palma has been an even more outrageous stylist; his films flaunt long takes, startling overhead compositions, and split-screen devices. Coppola has experimented with fast-motion black-and-white in *Rumble Fish* (1983), phone conversations handled in the foreground and background of a single shot (*Tucker,* 1988), and old-fashioned special effects to lend a period mood to *Bram Stoker's Dracula* (1993).

Several of the newer entrants into Hollywood enriched mainstream conventions of genre, narrative, and style. We have already seen one example of this strategy in our discussion of Spike Lee's *Do the Right Thing* (Chapter 11, pp. 423–428). Another intriguing example is Wayne Wang's *The Joy Luck Club* (1993). Set among Chinese American families, the film concentrates on four emigrant mothers and their four assimilated daughters. In presenting the women's lives the film adheres to narrative principles that recall *Citizen Kane.* At a party, the three surviving mothers recall their lives before coming to America, and a lengthy flashback is devoted to each one. Alongside each mother's flashback, however, the plot sets flashbacks tracing the experiences of each woman's daughter in the United States. The result is a rich set of dramatic and thematic parallels. Sometimes the

12.37 *The Joy Luck Club.*

12.38 Wide-angle tracking shots follow crawling babies along the floor and under furniture in *Raising Arizona*.

12.39 In *Trust*, a melodramatic scene between mother and daughter is intensified through deep-space staging and tight close-up.

mother–daughter juxtapositions create sharp contrasts; at other times, they blend together to emphasize commonalities across generations **(12.37)**. The women's voice-over commentaries always orient the viewer to the shifts in narration while still enabling Wang and his screenwriters to treat the flashback convention in ways that intensify the emotional effect.

An even more experimental attitude pervades the work of other independent directors. The brothers Joel and Ethan Coen treat each film as a pretext for exploring cinema's expressive resources. In *Raising Arizona* (1987), high-speed tracking shots cooperate with distorting wide-angle close-ups to create comic-book exaggerations **(12.38)**. A somewhat similar approach is taken in Gregg Araki's gay road picture *The Living End* (1992). In films such as *Trust* (1991), Hal Hartley mutes a melodramatic plot through slow pacing, brooding close-ups, and dynamic foreground/background compositions **(12.39)**.

Independent directors have also experimented with narrative construction. The Coens' *Barton Fink* (1991) passes unnoticeably from a satiric portrait of 1930s Hollywood into a hallucinatory fantasy. Quentin Tarantino's *Reservoir Dogs* (1993) and *Pulp Fiction* (1994) juggle story and plot time in ways that recall the complex flashbacks of the 1940s. Unlike the flashbacks in *The Joy Luck Club,* moreover, the switches are not motivated as characters' memories; the audience is forced to puzzle out the purposes served by the time shifts. In *Daughters of the Dust* (1991) Julie Dash incorporates the rich Gullah dialect and explores a complex time scheme that seeks to fuse present and future. In one scene, optical effects give the characters a glimpse of a child who is as yet unborn.

So, while in the 1980s and 1990s younger studio directors adapted classical conventions to modern tastes, an energetic independent film tradition began pushing the envelope. By the end of the 1990s, the two trends were merging in surprising ways. As independent films began to win larger audiences, major studios eagerly acquired distribution companies like Miramax and October Films. Much media journalism fostered the impression that Hollywood was becoming subverted by independent filmmaking, but in fact more and more the major studios controlled audiences' access to formerly independent productions. The Sundance Film Festival, founded as a forum for the off-Hollywood scene, came to be treated as a talent market by the studios, which often bought films in order to line up the filmmaker for more mainstream projects. Thus after Kevin Smith found success with *Clerks* (1994), he directed *Mallrats* (1995), a tame twentysomething comedy for Universal. Robert Rodriguez's similarly microbudgeted *El Mariachi* (1992) proved a hit, so he was hired to remake it as an all-out action picture starring Antonio Banderas (*Desperado,* 1995).

Yet sometimes the big-budget films of independent filmmakers conveyed a distinctly experimental attitude. Kevin Smith used the star-filled *Dogma* (1999) to question Catholic doctrine. David O. Russell, who had worked his way into the system with off-kilter comedies (*Spanking the Monkey,* 1994; *Flirting with Disaster,* 1996), made *Three Kings* (1999), an action picture that criticized Gulf War policies and that reveled in a flamboyant, digital-era style. Following in the path of *Pulp Fiction,* studio pictures began to play more boldly with narrative form. A genre thriller like *The Sixth Sense* (1999) encouraged viewers to see it twice in order to detect how the narration had misled them. Stories might be told through complicated flashbacks, as in Steven Soderbergh's *The Limey* **(12.40)**. (See also Box, pp. 77–79.) A film might reveal that one character was the imaginary creation of another (David Fincher's *Fight Club,* 1999) or that a person could crawl into another's brain (Spike Jonze's *Being John Malkovich,* 1999) or that the external world was merely an illusion produced by sophisticated software (the Wachowski brothers' *The Matrix,* 1999). In their willingness to experiment with ambiguous and teasing modes of narration, many American studio films began rivaling their overseas counterparts like *Breaking the Waves* (1996), *Sliding Doors* (1998), and *Run Lola Run* (1998).

At the end of the century, many of the most thrilling Hollywood films were being created by a robust new generation, born in the 1960s and 1970s and brought up on videotape, videogames, and the Internet. Like their predecessors, these directors were reshaping the formal and stylistic conventions of the classical cinema while also making their innovations accessible to a broad audience.

12.40   An ambiguous image that recurs throughout *The Limey:* It may be construed either as a flashback to the protagonist's trip to the United States or as a flashforward to his trip back to Britain, presented in the final scene.

CONTEMPORARY HONG KONG CINEMA

While the New Hollywood directors were revamping American films, a young generation of directors in Hong Kong found footing in their industry and recast its traditional genres and creative methods. The result was not a unified film movement, but a local cinema with a robust identity. Hong Kong's innovations in cinematic style and storytelling vigorously influenced world filmmaking at the end of the 20th Century.

Hong Kong produced films in the silent era and during the 1930s, although World War II halted production. When the industry revived in the 1950s, the most powerful studio was Shaw Brothers. Shaws owned theatres throughout East Asia and used Hong Kong as a production base for films in several languages, chiefly Mandarin Chinese. Shaws made films in many genres, but among its biggest successes were dynamic, gory swordfighting films (*wuxia pian,* or "tales of martial chivalry"). In the 1970s another studio, Golden Harvest, triumphed with kung-fu films starring Bruce Lee. Although Lee completed only four martial-arts films before his early death in 1973, he brought Hong Kong cinema to worldwide attention and forever identified it with films of acrobatic and violent action.

Several major directors worked in this period. Most famous is King Hu, who started as a Shaws director. In films like *Dragon Gate Inn* (1967) and *The Valiant Ones* (1975; 7.75), Hu reinvigorated the *wusia pian* through graceful airborne swordplay and inventive cutting. Zhang Che, another Shaws director, turned the swordplay film toward violent male melodrama (such as *The One-Armed Swordsman,* 1967) before specializing in flamboyant kung-fu films like *Crippled Avengers* (also called *Mortal Combat,* 1978). Neither King Hu nor Zhang Che was a practitioner of martial arts, but Lau Kar-leung was a fight choreographer before becoming a full-fledged director. Lau created a string of inventive films (such as *Shaolin Master Killer,* 1978; *The Eight-Diagram Pole Fighter,* 1983) that showcased a range of dazzling marital-arts techniques.

By the early 1980s, traditional kung-fu was fading in popularity, and Shaws turned from moviemaking to its lucrative television business. At the same time, a new generation of directors came forward. One group had little formal education but had grown up in the film industry, working as stuntmen and martial artists. Among those who became directors were choreographers Yuen Wo-ping and Yuen Kuei (*Yes, Madam!,* 1985). Sammo Hung choreographed, directed, and starred in many lively action films (such as *Eastern Condors,* 1987).

The most famous graduate of the studio system was Jackie Chan, who labored as a copy of Bruce Lee before finding his feet in comic kung-fu. With *Drunken Master* (1978, directed by Yuen Wo-ping), he became a star throughout Asia and gained power to direct his own films. In the early 1980s Chan and his colleagues realized that kung-fu could be incorporated into Hollywoodish action-adventure movies. Chan made the historical adventure *Project A* (1983, also starring Hung) and the contemporary cop drama *Police Story* (1985). These and others were huge hits across Asia, partly because of Chan's lovably goofy star persona, partly because of his ingenious and dangerous action scenes (8.35–8.55).

Another group of directors had more formal training, with many attending film schools in the United States or Britain. When Ann Hui, Allen Fong, and others returned to Hong Kong, they found work in television before moving to feature film-making. For a time they constituted a local art cinema, attracting attention at festivals with such films as Hui's *Boat People* (1982). But most of this group gravitated toward independent companies turning out comedies, dramas, and action films. Tsui Hark was the leader of this trend. As both director and producer Tsui revived and reworked a range of genres: swordplay fantasy (*Zu: Warriors of the Magic Mountain,* 1979), romantic comedy (*Shanghai Blues,* 1984), historical adventure (*Peking Opera Blues,* 1986), supernatural romance (*A Chinese Ghost Story,* 1987, directed by Ching Siu-tung), and classic kung-fu (*Once upon a Time in China,* 1990).

Seeing the success that modern cops-and-crooks films were enjoying, Tsui partnered with John Woo on *A Better Tomorrow* (1986), a remake of a 1960s movie. Woo was something of an in-between figure, having been a successful studio comedy director during the 1970s. With Tsui as producer, *A Better Tomorrow* became Woo's comeback effort, one of the most successful Hong Kong films of the 1980s and a star-making vehicle for the charismatic Chow Yun-fat. Tsui, Woo, and Chow teamed again for a sequel and for the film that made Woo famous in the West, *The Killer* (1989), a lush and baroque story of the unexpected alliance between a hit-man and a detective **(12.41).**

Hong Kong cinema of the 1980s and early 1990s burst with almost reckless energy. The rushed production schedules did not allow much time to prepare scripts, so the plots, borrowing freely from Chinese legend and Hollywood genres, tended to be less tightly unified than those in U.S. films. They avoided tight linkage of cause and effect in favor of a more casual, episodic construction—not, as in Italian Neorealism, to suggest the randomness of everyday life but rather to permit chases and fights to be inserted easily. While action sequences were meticulously choreographed, connecting scenes were often improvised and shot quickly. Similarly, the kung-fu films had often bounced between pathos and almost silly comedy, and this tendency to mix tones continued through the 1980s. In *A Better*

12.41   Cop and hitman as blood brothers in *The Killer.*

12.42 Blocks of unrealistic light for *The Longest Nite* (Patrick Yau, 1998).

Tomorrow, for example, Tsui Hark appears in a slapstick interlude involving a cello. Again, because of rushed shooting, the plots often end abruptly, with a big action set-piece but little in the nature of a mood-setting epilogue. One of Tsui's innovations was to provide more satisfying conclusions, as in the lilting railroad-station finale of *Shanghai Blues.*

At the level of visual style, Hong Kong directors brought the action film to a new pitch of excitement. Gunmen (and gunwomen) leaped and fired in slow motion, hovering in midair like 1970s swordfighters and kung-fu warriors. John Woo, who had been an assistant director for Zhang Che, pushed such shot to extravagant limits. Directors also developed florid color designs, with rich reds, blues, and yellows glowing out of smoky nightclubs or narrow alleyways. Well into the 1990s, unrealistically tinted mood lighting was a trademark of Hong Kong cinema **(12.42).** Above all, everything was sacrificed to constant motion; even in dialogue scenes, the camera or the characters seldom stood still.

Aiming to energize the viewer, the new action directors built on the innovations of King Hu and his contemporaries. They developed a staccato cutting technique based on the tempo of martial-arts routines and Peking Opera displays, alternating rapid movement with sudden pauses. If shot composition was kept simple, an action could be cut to flow across shots very rapidly, while another cut could accentuate a moment of stillness **(12.43–12.44).** Most Hong Kong directors were

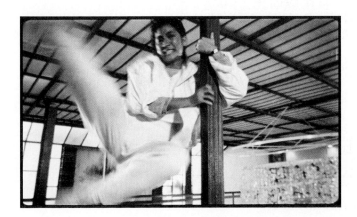

12.43 Crisp editing in *Yes, Madam!* In a shot only 7 frames long, Michele Yeoh swings swiftly . . .

12.44   . . . to knock the villain spinning (15 frames) . . .

12.45   . . . before she drops smoothly into a relaxed posture on the rail (17 frames).

unaware of the Soviet Montage movement, but in their efforts to arouse viewers kinesthetically through expressive movement and editing, they were reviving ideas of concern to 1920s filmmakers.

The 1990s brought the golden age of Hong Kong action cinema to a close. Jackie Chan, John Woo, Chow Yun-fat, Sammo Hung, and action star Jet Li began working in Hollywood, with Yuen Wo-ping designing the action choreography for *The Matrix* (1999) and *Crouching Tiger, Hidden Dragon* (2000). A recession after Hong Kong's 1997 handover to China depressed the local film industry. As Hollywood began imitating Hong Kong movies (as in *Replacement Killers,* 1998), local audiences developed a taste for U.S. films. At the same time, the art-cinema wing became more ambitious, and festivals rewarded the offbeat works of Wong Kar-wai (see the analysis of *Chungking Express,* pp. 437–442). The action tradition was maintained by only a few directors such as Johnnie To, whose laconic *film noir The Mission* (1999) brought a leanness and pictorial abstraction to the gangster genre.

NOTES AND QUERIES

General

Allen, Robert C., and Douglas Gomery. *Film History: Theory and Practice.* New York: Random House, 1985.

Bordwell, David. *On the History of Film Style.* Cambridge, Mass.: Harvard University Press, 1997.

Branigan, Edward. "Color and Cinema: Problems in the Writing of History." *Film Reader* **4,** "Metahistory of Film" (1979): 16–34.

Knight, Arthur. *The Liveliest Art.* New York: New American Library, 1957.

Luhr, William, ed. *World Cinema since 1945.* New York: Ungar, 1987.

MacGowan, Kenneth. *Behind the Screen.* New York: Dell, 1965.

"Metahistory of Film." Issue of *Film History* **4** (1979).

Mitry, Jean. *Histoire du cinéma,* Vols. 1–3. Paris: Êditions Universitaires, 1967, 1969, 1973; Vols. 4–5. Paris: Jean-Pierre Delarge, 1980.

Rotha, Paul. *The Film Till Now.* London: Spring, 1967.

Sadoul, Georges. *Histoire générale du cinéma.* 6 vols. Paris: Denoël, 1973–1977.

Salt, Barry. *Film Style and Technology: History and Analysis,* 2d ed. London: Starword, 1992.

Thompson, Kristin, and David Bordwell. *Film History: An Introduction,* 2d ed. New York: McGraw-Hill, 2003.

Early Cinema

Abel, Richard, *The Ciné Goes to Town: French Cinema 1896–1914.* Berkeley: University of California Press, 1994.

Allen, Robert C. *Vaudeville and Film, 1895–1915: A Study in Media Interaction.* New York: Arno, 1980.

"Archives, Document, Fiction." Issue of *Iris* **2,** 1 (1984).

Brewster, Ben, and Lea Jacobs. *Theatre to Cinema: Stage Pictorialism and the Early Feature Film.* Oxford: Oxford University Press, 1997.

Chanan, Michael. *The Dream That Kicks: The Prehistory and Early Years of Cinema in Britain.* London: Routledge & Kegan Paul, 1980.

Cherchi Usai, Paolo. *Silent Cinema: An Introduction.* London: British Film Institute, 2000.

Cherchi Usai, Paolo, and Lorenzo Codelli, eds. *Before Caligari: German Cinema, 1895–1920.* Pordenone: Edizioni Biblioteca dell' Immagine, 1990.

Dibbets, Karl, and Bert Hogenkamp, eds. *Film and the First World War.* Amsterdam: Amsterdam University Press, 1995.

"Early Cinema Audiences." Issue of *Iris* **11** (Summer 1990).

Elsaesser, Thomas, ed. *Early Cinema: Space, Frame, Narrative.* London: British Film Institute, 1990.

"Essays on D. W. Griffith." Issues of *Quarterly Review of Film Studies* **6,** 1 (Winter 1981).

Fell, John L., ed. *Film before Griffith.* Berkeley: University of California Press, 1983.

Fullerton, John, ed. *Celebrating 1895: The Centenary of Cinema.* Sydney: John Libbey, 1998.

Gunning, Tom. *D. W. Griffith and the Origins of American Narrative Film: The Early Years at Biograph.* Urbana and Chicago: University of Illinois Press, 1991.

Hammond, Paul. *Marvelous Méliès.* New York: St. Martin's, 1975.

Hendricks, Gordon. *The Edison Motion Picture Myth.* Berkeley: University of California Press, 1961.

Leyda, Jay, and Charles Musser, eds. *Before Hollywood: Turn-of-the-Century Film from American Archives.* New York: American Federation of the Arts, 1986.

Mayne, Judith. "Immigrants and Spectators." *Wide Angle* **5,** 2. (1982): 32–41.

Musser, Charles. *Before the Nickelodeon: Edwin S. Porter and the Edison Manufacturing Company.* Berkeley: University of California Press, 1991.

———. *The Emergence of Cinema: The American Screen to 1907.* New York: Scribner's, 1991.

Musser, Charles, with Carol Nelson. *High-Class Moving Pictures: Lyman H. Howe and the Forgotten Era of Traveling Exhibition, 1880–1920.* Princeton, N.J.: Princeton University Press, 1991.

Pratt, George, ed. *Spellbound in Darkness.* Greenwich, Conn.: New York Graphic Society, 1973.

Rossell, Deac. *Living Pictures: The Origins of the Movies.* Albany: State University of New York Press, 1998.

Spehr, Paul C. *The Movies Begin.* Newark, N.J.: Newark Museum, 1977.

Thompson, Kristin, and David Bordwell. "Linearity, Materialism, and the Study of Early American Cinema." *Wide Angle* **5,** 3 (1983): 4–15.

Tsivian, Yuri, ed. *Testimoni silenziosi: Film russi 1908–1919.* Pordenone: Edizioni Biblioteca dell'Immagine, 1989. (Bilingual in Italian and English.)

Youngblood, Denise. *The Magic Mirror: Moviemaking in Russia, 1908–1918.* Madison: University of Wisconsin Press, 1999.

Classical Hollywood Cinema (1908–1927)

Balio, Tino, ed. *The American Film Industry,* rev. ed. Madison: University of Wisconsin Press, 1985.

Bordwell, David, Janet Staiger, and Kristin Thompson. *The Classical Hollywood Cinema: Film Style and Mode of Production to 1960.* New York: Columbia University Press, 1985.

Bowser, Eileen. *The Transformation of Cinema, 1907–1915.* New York: Scribner's, 1990.

Brownlow, Kevin. *The Parade's Gone By.* New York: Knopf, 1968.

Cherchi Usai, Paolo, and Lorenzo Codelli, eds. *Sulla via di Hollywood 1911–1920. (The Path to Hollywood 1911–1920.)* Pordenone: Edizioni Biblioteca dell'Immagine, 1988. (Bilingual in Italian and English.)

DeBauche, Leslie Midkiff. *Reel Patriotism: The Movies and World War I.* Madison: University of Wisconsin Press, 1997.

Gomery, Douglas. *Shared Pleasures: A History of American Moviegoing.* Madison: University of Wisconsin Press, 1992.

Hampton, Benjamin B. *History of the American Film Industry.* 1931. Reprinted. New York: Dover, 1970.

Koszarski, Richard. *An Evening's Entertainment: The Age of the Silent Feature Picture, 1915–1928.* New York: Scribner's, 1990.

Staiger, Janet. *Interpreting Films: Studies in the Historical Reception of American Cinema.* Princeton, N.J.: Princeton University Press, 1992.

Vasey, Ruth. *The World According to Hollywood, 1928–1939.* Madison: University of Wisconsin Press, 1997.

German Expressionism

Barlow, John D. *German Expressionist Film.* Boston: Twayne, 1982.

Bronner, Stephen Eric, and Douglas Kellner, eds. *Passion and Rebellion: The Expressionist Heritage.* South Hadley, Mass.: J. F. Bergin, 1983.

Budd, Mike, ed. *The Cabinet of Dr. Caligari: Texts, Contexts, Histories.* New Brunswick: Rutgers University Press, 1990.

Courtade, Francis. *Cinéma expressioniste.* Paris: Henri Veyrier, 1984.

Eisner, Lotte, *F. W. Murnau.* Berkeley: University of California Press, 1983.

———. *Fritz Lang.* New York: Oxford University Press, 1977.

———. *The Haunted Screen.* Berkeley: University of California Press, 1969.

Kracauer, Siegfried. *From Caligari to Hitler.* Princeton, N.J.: Princeton University Press, 1947.

Kreimeier, Klaus. *The UFA Story: A History of Germany's Greatest Film Company 1918–1945.* Translated by Robert and Rita Kimber. New York: Hill & Wang, 1996.

Myers, Bernard S. *The German Expressionists.* New York: Praeger, 1963.

Robinson, David. *Das Cabinet des Dr. Caligari.* London: British Film Institute, 1997. (In English.)

Selz, Peter. *German Expressionist Painting.* Berkeley: University of California Press, 1957.

Willett, John. *Expressionism.* New York: McGraw-Hill, 1970.

———. *The New Sobriety: Art and Politics in the Weimar Republic, 1917–1933.* London: Thames & Hudson, 1978.

French Impressionism

Abel, Richard. *French Cinema: The First Wave, 1915–1929.* Princeton, N.J.: Princeton University Press, 1984.

———. *French Film Theory and Criticism, 1907–1939,* Vol. 1. Princeton, N.J.: Princeton University Press, 1988.

Bordwell, David. *French Impressionist Cinema: Film Culture, Film Theory, and Film Style.* New York: Arno, 1980.

Brownlow, Kevin. *"Napoleon": Abel Gance's Classic Film.* New York: Knopf, 1983.

Clair, René. *Cinema Yesterday and Today.* New York: Dover, 1972.

King, Norman. *Abel Gance: A Politics of Spectacle.* London: British Film Institute, 1984.

Liebman, Stuart. "French Film Theory, 1910–1921." *Quarterly Review of Film Studies* **8,** 1 (Winter 1983): 1–23.

Sadoul, Georges. *The French Cinema.* London: Falcon Press, 1952.

Soviet Montage

Bordwell, David. *The Cinema of Eisenstein.* Cambridge, Mass.: Harvard University Press, 1993.

Bowlt, John, ed. *Russian Art of the Avant-Garde.* New York: Viking, 1973.

Carynnyk, Marco, ed. *Alexander Dovzhenko: Poet as Filmmaker.* Cambridge, Mass.: MIT Press, 1973.

Christie, Ian. "Soviet Cinema—Making Sense of Sound." *Screen* **23,** 2 (July–August 1982): 34–49.

Eisenstein, S. M. *S. M. Eisenstein: Writings 1922–1934,* Richard Taylor, ed. London: British Film Institute, 1988; *Eisenstein, Volume 2, Towards a Theory of Montage,* Michael Glenny and Richard Taylor, eds. London: British Film Institute, 1991; *Eisenstein Writings 1934–1947.* Richard Taylor, ed. London: British Film Institute, 1996. *Beyond the Stars: The Memoirs of Sergei Eisenstein,* Vol. 4, Richard Taylor, ed., William Powell, trans. London: British Film Institute, 1995.

Fuelop-Miller, René. *The Mind and Face of Bolshevism.* New York: Harper & Row, 1965.

Kepley, Vance. *In the Service of the State: The Cinema of Alexander Dovzhenko.* Madison: University of Wisconsin Press, 1986.

Kuleshov, Lev. *Kuleshov on Film.* Edited and translated by Ronald Levaco. Berkeley: University of California Press, 1974.

Leyda, Jay. *Kino,* 3d ed. Princeton, N.J.: Princeton University Press, 1983.

Lodder, Christina. *Russian Constructivism.* New Haven, Conn.: Yale University Press, 1983.

Michelson, Annette, ed. *Kino-Eye: The Writings of Dziga Vertov.* Berkeley: University of California Press, 1984.

Nilsen, Vladimir. *The Cinema as a Graphic Art.* New York: Hill & Wang, 1959.

Petric, Vlada. *Constructivism in Film: The Man with a Movie Camera—A Cinematic Analysis.* London: Cambridge University Press, 1987.

Pudovkin, V. I. *Film Technique and Film Acting.* New York: Grove, 1960.

Schnitzer, Luda, Jean Schnitzer, and Marcel Martin, eds. *Cinema and Revolution.* New York: Hill & Wang, 1973.

Taylor, Richard. *The Politics of the Soviet Cinema, 1917–1929.* Cambridge: Cambridge University Press, 1979.

Taylor, Richard, and Ian Christie, eds. *The Film Factory: Russian and Soviet Cinema in Documents, 1896–1939.* Cambridge, Mass.: Harvard University Press, 1988.

———. *Inside the Film Factory: New Approaches to Russian and Soviet Cinema.* London: Routledge, 1991.

Thompson, Kristin. "Early Sound Counterpoint." *Yale French Studies* **60** (1980): 115–140.

Youngblood, Denise. *Soviet Cinema in the Silent Era, 1918–1933.* Ann Arbor, Mich.: UMI Research Press, 1985.

The Classical Hollywood Cinema after the Coming of Sound

Balio, Tino. *Grand Design: Hollywood as a Modern Business Enterprise, 1930–1939.* New York: Scribner's, 1993.

Balio, Tino, ed. *The American Film Industry,* rev. ed. Madison: University of Wisconsin Press, 1985.

Balio, Tino, ed. *Hollywood in the Age of Television,* Boston: Unwin Hyman, 1990.

Bordwell, David, Janet Staiger, and Kristin Thompson. *The Classical Hollywood Cinema: Film Style and Mode of Production to 1960.* New York: Columbia University Press, 1985.

Crafton, Donald. *The Talkies: American Cinema's Transition to Sound 1926–1931.* New York: Scribner's, 1997.

Gomery, Douglas. *The Hollywood Studio System.* New York: St. Martin's, 1986.

Koszarski, Richard, ed. *Hollywood Directors, 1914–1940.* New York: Oxford University Press, 1976.

Maltby, Richard. *Harmless Entertainment: Hollywood and the Ideology of Consensus.* Metuchen, N.J.: Scarecrow, 1983.

Schatz, Thomas. *Boom and Bust: American Cinema in the 1940s.* Berkeley: University of California Press, 1997.

Silver, Alain, and Elizabeth Ward. *Film Noir: An Encyclopedic Reference to the American Style.* Woodstock, N.Y.: Overlook Press, 1979.

Staiger, Janet, ed. *The Studio System.* New Brunswick, N.J.: Rutgers University Press, 1995.

Walker, Alexander. *The Shattered Silents: How the Talkies Came to Stay.* New York: Morrow, 1979.

"Widescreen." Issue of *Velvet Light Trap* **21** (Summer 1985).

Italian Neorealism

Armes, Roy. *Patterns of Realism.* New York: A. S. Barnes, 1970.

Bazin, André. "Cinema and Television." *Sight and Sound* **28,** 1 (Winter 1958–59): 26–30.

———. *What Is Cinema?* Vol. 2. Berkeley: University of California Press, 1971.

Bondanella, Peter. *Italian Cinema from Neorealism to the Present.* New York: Ungar, 1983.

Brunette, Peter. *Roberto Rossellini.* New York: Oxford University Press, 1987.

Leprohon, Pierre. *The Italian Cinema.* New York: Praeger, 1984.

Liehm, Mira. *Passion and Defiance: Film in Italy from 1942 to the Present.* Berkeley: University of California Press, 1984.

Marcus, Millicent. *Italian Film in the Light of Neorealism.* Princeton, N.J.: Princeton University Press, 1986.

Overbey, David, ed. *Springtime in Italy: A Reader on Neo-Realism.* London: Talisman, 1978.

Pacifici, Sergio J. "Notes toward a Definition of Neorealism." *Yale French Studies* **17** (Summer 1956): 44–53.

Sitney, P. Adams. *Vital Crises in Italian Cinema: Iconography, Stylistics, Politics.* Austin: University of Texas Press, 1995.

The French New Wave

Armes, Roy. *The French Cinema since 1946,* Vol. 2. New York: A. S. Barnes, 1970.

Brown, Royal S., ed. *Focus on Godard.* Englewood Cliffs, N.J.: Prentice-Hall, 1972.

Burch, Noël. "Qu'est-ce que la Nouvelle Vague?" *Film Quarterly* **13,** 2 (Winter 1959): 16–30.

Crisp, Colin. *The Classic French Cinema, 1930–1960.* Bloomington: Indiana University Press, 1994.

Godard, Jean-Luc. *Godard on Godard.* New York: Viking, 1972.

Graham, Peter, ed. *The New Wave.* Garden City, N.J.: Doubleday, 1968.

Hillier, Jim, ed. *Cahiers du Cinéma: The 1950s: Neo-Realism, Hollywood, New Wave.* Cambridge, Mass.: Harvard University Press, 1985.

———. *Cahiers du Cinéma: The 1960s: New Wave, New Cinema, Reevaluating Hollywood.* Cambridge, Mass.: Harvard University Press, 1986.

Insdorf, Annette. *François Truffaut.* New York: William Morrow, 1979.

Monaco, James. *The New Wave: Truffaut, Godard, Chabrol, Rohmer, Rivette.* New York: Oxford University Press, 1976.

Mussman, Toby, ed. *Jean-Luc Godard.* New York: Dutton, 1968.

Neupert, Richard. *A History of the French New Wave Cinema.* Madison: University of Wisconsin Press, 2002.

Truffaut, François. *The Films in My Life.* Translated by Leonard Mayhew. New York: Simon & Schuster, 1978.

The New Hollywood and Independent Filmmaking

Andrew, Geoff. *Stranger than Paradise: Maverick Film-Makers in Recent American Cinema.* London: Prion, 1998.

Cones, John W. *Film Finance and Distribution: A Dictionary of Terms.* Los Angeles: Silman-James, 1992.

Diawara, Manthia, ed. *Black American Cinema.* New York: Routledge, 1993.

Donahue, Suzanne Mary. *American Film Distribution: The Changing Marketplace.* Ann Arbor, Mich.: UMI Research Press, 1987.

Fuchs, Cynthia, ed. *Spike Lee Interviews.* Jackson: University Press of Mississippi, 2002.

Gomery, Douglas. "The American Film Industry of the 1970s: Stasis in the 'New Hollywood.'" *Wide Angle* **5,** 4 (1983): 52–59.

———. "Corporate Ownership and Control in the Contemporary U.S. Film Industry." *Screen* **25,** 4–5 (July–October 1984): 60–69.

Goodwin, Michael, and Naomi Wise. *On the Edge: The Life and Times of Francis Coppola.* New York: Morrow, 1989.

Hillier, Jim. *The New Hollywood.* New York: Continuum, 1994.

Kaufman, Anthony, ed. *Steven Soderbergh Interviews.* Jackson: University Press of Mississippi, 2002.

Levy, Emmanuel. *Cinema of Outsiders: The Rise of American Independent Film.* New York: New York University Press, 1999.

Lewis, Jon, ed. *The New American Cinema.* Durham: Duke University Press, 1998.

Lindenmuth, Kevin J. *The Independent Film Experience.* Jefferson, : McFarland & Company, 2002.

McBride, Joseph. *Steven Spielberg: A Biography.* New York: Simon & Schuster, 1997.

McGilligan, Patrick. *Robert Altman: Jumping Off the Cliff.* New York: St. Martin's, 1989.

Neale, Steve, and Murray Smith, eds. *Contemporary Hollywood Cinema.* New York: Routledge, 1998.

Noriega, Chon A. *Chicanos and Film: Representation and Resistance.* Minneapolis: University of Minnesota Press, 1992.

Pye, Michael, and Lynda Myles. *The Movie Brats: How the Film Generation Took Over Hollywood.* New York: Holt, Rinehart and Winston, 1979.

Reid, Mark A. *Redefining Black Film.* Berkeley: University of California Press, 1993.

Squires, Jason E. *The Movie Business Book,* 2d ed. New York: Simon & Schuster, 1992.

Thompson, Kristin. *Storytelling in the New Hollywood: Understanding Classical Narrative Technique.* Cambridge, Mass.: Harvard University Press, 1999.

Welbon, Yvonne. "Calling the Shots: Black Women Directors Take the Helm." *Independent* **15,** 2 (March 1992): 18–22.

Contemporary Hong Kong Cinema

Bordwell, David. *Planet Hong Kong: Popular Cinema and the Art of Entertainment.* Cambridge, Mass.: Harvard University Press, 2000.

Charles, John. *The Hong Kong Filmography, 1977–1997.* Jefferson, : McFarland & Company, 2000.

Fu, Poshek, and Desser, David, ed. *The Cinema of Hong Kong: History, Arts, Identity.* Cambridge: Cambridge University Press, 2000.

Hammond, Stefan. *Hollywood East: Hong Kong Movies and the People Who Make Them.* Chicago: Contemporary Books, 2000.

Logan, Bey. *Hong Kong Action Cinema.* London: Titan Books, 1995.

Stokes, Lisa Odham and Hoover, Michael. *City of Fire: Hong Kong Cinema.* London: Verso, 1999.

Teo, Stephen. *Hong Kong Cinema: The Extra Dimensions.* London: British Film Institute, 1997.

Wood, Miles. *Cine East: Hong Kong Cinema through the Looking Glass.* Guildford, England: FAB Press, 1998.

Yau, Esther C. M., ed. *At Full Speed: Hong Kong Cinema in a Borderless World.* Minneapolis: University of Minnesota Press, 2001.

Glossary

abstract form A type of filmic organization in which the parts relate to one another through repetition and variation of such visual qualities as shape, color, rhythm, and direction of movement.

Academy ratio The standardized shape of the film frame established by the Academy of Motion Picture Arts and Sciences. In the original ratio, the frame was $1\frac{1}{3}$ times as wide as it was high (1.33:1); later the width was normalized at 1.85 times the height (1.85:1).

aerial perspective A cue for suggesting represented depth in the image by presenting objects in the distance less distinctly than those in the foreground.

anamorphic lens A lens for making widescreen films using regular *Academy ratio* frame size. The camera lens takes in a wide field of view and squeezes it onto the frame, and a similar projector lens unsqueezes the image onto a wide theater screen.

angle of framing The position of the frame in relation to the subject it shows: above it, looking down (a high angle); horizontal, on the same level (a straight-on angle); looking up (a low angle). Also called camera angle.

animation Any process whereby artificial movement is created by photographing a series of drawings (see also *cel animation*), objects, or computer images one by one. Small changes in position, recorded frame by frame, create the illusion of movement.

aspect ratio The relationship of the frame's width to its height. The standard *Academy ratio* is currently 1.85:1.

associational form A type of organization in which the film's parts are juxtaposed to suggest similarities, contrasts, concepts, emotions, and expressive qualities.

asynchronous sound Sound that is not matched temporally with the movements occurring in the image, as when dialogue is out of synchronization with lip movements.

auteur The presumed or actual author of a film, usually identified as the director. Also sometimes used in an evaluative sense to distinguish good filmmakers (*auteurs*) from bad ones.

axis of action In the *continuity editing* system, the imaginary line that passes from side to side through the main actors, defining the spatial relations of all the elements of the scene as being to the right or left. The camera is not supposed to cross the axis at a cut and thus reverse those spatial relations. Also called the 180° line. (See also *180° system*.)

backlighting Illumination cast onto the figures in the scene from the side opposite the camera, usually creating a thin outline of highlighting on those figures.

boom A pole upon which a microphone can be suspended above the scene being filmed and that is used to change the microphone's position as the action shifts.

camera angle See *angle of framing*.

canted framing A view in which the frame is not level; either the right or left side is lower than the other, causing objects in the scene to appear slanted out of an upright position.

categorical form A type of filmic organization in which the parts treat distinct subsets of a topic. For example, a film about the United States might be organized into 50 parts, each devoted to a state.

cel animation Animation that uses a series of drawings on pieces of celluloid, called *cels* for short. Slight changes between the drawings combine to create an illusion of movement.

CGI Computer-generated imagery: Using digital software systems to create figures, settings, or other material in the frame.

cheat cut In the *continuity editing* system, a cut that presents continuous time from shot to shot but that mismatches the positions of figures or objects.

cinematography A general term for all the manipulations of the film strip by the camera in the shooting phase and by the laboratory in the developing phase.

close-up A framing in which the scale of the object shown is relatively large; most commonly a person's head seen from the neck up, or an object of a comparable size that fills most of the screen.

closure The degree to which the ending of a narrative film reveals the effects of all the causal events and resolves (or "closes off") all lines of action.

continuity editing A system of cutting to maintain continuous and clear narrative action. Continuity editing relies on matching screen direction, position, and temporal relations from shot to shot. For specific techniques of continuity editing, see *axis of action, crosscutting, cut-in, establishing shot, eyeline match, match on action, reestablishing shot, screen direction, shot/reverse shot*.

contrast In cinematography, the difference between the brightest and darkest areas within the frame.

crane shot   A shot with a change in framing accomplished by having the camera above the ground and moving through the air in any direction.

crosscutting   Editing that alternates shots of two or more lines of action occurring in different places, usually simultaneously.

cut   1. In filmmaking, the joining of two strips of film together with a splice. 2. In the finished film, an instantaneous change from one framing to another. See also *jump cut.*

cut-in   An instantaneous shift from a distant framing to a closer view of some portion of the same space.

deep focus   A use of the camera lens and lighting that keeps both the close and distant planes being photographed in sharp focus.

deep space   An arrangement of mise-en-scene elements so that there is a considerable distance between the plane closest to the camera and the one farthest away. Any or all of these planes may be in focus. (See *shallow space.*)

depth of field   The measurements of the closest and farthest planes in front of the camera lens between which everything will be in sharp focus. A depth of field from 5 to 16 feet, for example, would mean everything closer than 5 feet and farther than 16 feet would be out of focus.

dialogue overlap   In editing a scene, arranging the cut so that a bit of dialogue coming from shot A is heard under a shot that shows another character on another element in the scene.

diegesis   In a narrative film, the world of the film's story. The diegesis includes events that are presumed to have occurred and actions and spaces not shown onscreen. See also *diegetic sound, nondiegetic insert, nondiegetic sound.*

diegetic sound   Any voice, musical passage, or sound effect presented as originating from a source within the film's world. See also *nondiegetic sound.*

direct sound   Music, noise, and speech recorded from the event at the moment of filming; opposite of *postsynchronization.*

discontinuity editing   Any alternative system of joining shots together using techniques unacceptable within *continuity editing* principles. Possibilities would include mismatching of temporal and spatial relations, violations of the *axis of action,* and concentration on graphic relationships. See also *elliptical editing, graphic match, intellectual montage, jump cut, nondiegetic insert, overlapping editing.*

dissolve   A transition between two shots during which the first image gradually disappears while the second image gradually appears; for a moment the two images blend in *superimposition.*

distance of framing   The apparent distance of the frame from the mise-en-scene elements. Also called camera distance and shot scale. See also *close-up, extreme close-up, extreme long shot, medium close-up, medium shot, plan américain.*

distribution   One of the three branches of the film industry; the process of supplying the finished film to the places where it will be shown. See also *exhibition, production.*

dolly   A camera support with wheels, used in making *tracking shots.*

dubbing   The process of replacing part or all of the voices on the sound track in order to correct mistakes or rerecord dialogue. See also *postsynchronization.*

duration   In a narrative film, the aspect of temporal manipulation that involves the time span presented in the *plot* and assumed to operate in the *story.* See also *frequency, order.*

editing   1. In filmmaking, the task of selecting and joining camera takes. 2. In the finished film, the set of techniques that governs the relations among shots.

ellipsis   In a narrative film, the shortening of *plot* duration achieved by omitting intervals of *story* duration. See also *elliptical editing, viewing time.*

elliptical editing   Shot transitions that omit parts of an event, causing an *ellipsis* in plot and story duration.

establishing shot   A shot, usually involving a distant framing, that shows the spatial relations among the important figures, objects, and setting in a scene.

exhibition   One of the three branches of the film industry; the process of showing the finished film to audiences. See also *distribution, production.*

exposure   The adjustment of the camera mechanism in order to control how much light strikes each frame of film passing through the aperture.

external diegetic sound   Sound represented as coming from a physical source within the story space that we assume characters in the scene also hear. See also *internal diegetic sound.*

extreme close-up   A framing in which the scale of the object shown is very large; most commonly, a small object or a part of the body.

extreme long shot   A framing in which the scale of the object shown is very small; a building, landscape, or crowd of people will fill the screen.

eyeline match   A cut obeying the *axis of action* principle, in which the first shot shows a person looking off in one direction and the second shows a nearby space containing what he or she sees. If the person looks left, the following shot should imply that the looker is offscreen right.

fade   1. *Fade-in:* A dark screen that gradually brightens as a shot appears. 2. *Fade-out:* A shot gradually disappears as the screen darkens. Occasionally, fade-outs brighten to pure white or to a color.

fill light   Illumination from a source less bright than the *key light,* used to soften deep shadows in a scene. See also *three-point lighting.*

film noir   Dark film, a term applied by French critics to a type of American film, usually in the detective or thriller genres, with low-key lighting and a somber mood.

film stock   The strip of material upon which a series of still photographs is registered; it consists of a clear base coated on one side with a light-sensitive emulsion.

filter   A piece of glass or gelatin placed in front of the camera or printer lens to alter the quality or quantity of light striking the film in the aperture.

flashback   An alteration of story order in which the plot moves back to show events that have taken place earlier than ones already shown.

flashforward   An alteration of story order in which the plot presentation moves forward to future events and then returns to the present.

focal length   The distance from the center of the lens to the point at which the light rays meet in sharp focus. The focal length determines the perspective relations of the space represented on the flat screen. See also *normal lens, telephoto lens, wide-angle lens.*

focus   The degree to which light rays coming from the same part of an object through different parts of the lens reconverge at the same point on the film frame, creating sharp outlines and distinct textures.

following shot   A shot with framing that shifts to keep a moving figure onscreen.

form   The general system of relationships among the parts of a film.

frame   A single image on the strip of film. When a series of frames is projected onto a screen in quick succession, an illusion of movement is created.

framing   The use of the edges of the film frame to select and to compose what will be visible onscreen.

frequency   In a narrative film, the aspect of temporal manipulation that involves the number of times any *story* event is shown in the *plot*. See also *duration, order.*

front projection   Composite process whereby footage meant to appear as the background of a shot is projected from the front onto a screen; figures in the foreground are filmed in front of the screen as well. This is the opposite of *rear projection.*

frontal lighting   Illumination directed into the scene from a position near the camera.

frontality   In staging, the positioning of figures so that they face the viewer.

function   The role or effect of any element within the film's form.

gauge   The width of the film strip, measured in millimeters.

genres   Various types of films that audiences and filmmakers recognize by their familiar narrative conventions. Common genres are musical, gangster, and Western films.

graphic match   Two successive shots joined so as to create a strong similarity of compositional elements (e.g., color, shape).

hand-held camera   The use of the camera operator's body as a camera support, either holding it by hand or using a harness.

hard lighting   Illumination that creates sharp-edged shadows.

height of framing   The distance of the camera above the ground, regardless of the *angle of framing.*

high-key lighting   Illumination that creates comparatively little contrast between the light and dark areas of the shot. Shadows are fairly transparent and brightened by *fill light.*

ideology   A relatively coherent system of values, beliefs, or ideas shared by some social group and often taken for granted as natural or inherently true.

intellectual montage   The juxtaposition of a series of images to create an abstract idea not present in any one image.

internal diegetic sound   Sound represented as coming from the mind of a character within the story space. Although we and the character can hear it, we assume that the other characters cannot. See also *external diegetic sound.*

interpretation   The viewer's activity of analyzing the implicit and symptomatic meanings suggested in a film. See also *meaning.*

iris   A round, moving *mask* that can close down to end a scene (iris-out) or emphasize a detail, or that can open to begin a scene (iris-in) or to reveal more space around a detail.

jump cut   An elliptical cut that appears to be an interruption of a single shot. Either the figures seem to change instantly against a constant background, or the background changes instantly while the figures remain constant. See also *ellipsis.*

key light   In the three-point lighting system, the brightest illumination coming into the scene. See also *backlighting, fill light, three-point lighting.*

lens   A shaped piece of transparent material (usually glass) with either or both sides curved to gather and focus light rays. Most camera and projector lenses place a series of lenses within a metal tube to form a compound lens.

linearity   In a narrative, the clear motivation of a series of causes and effects that progress without significant digressions, delays, or irrelevant actions.

long shot   A framing in which the scale of the object shown is small; a standing human figure would appear nearly the height of the screen.

long take   A shot that continues for an unusually lengthy time before the transition to the next shot.

low-key lighting   Illumination that creates strong contrast between light and dark areas of the shot, with deep shadows and little *fill light.*

mask   An opaque screen placed in the camera or printer that blocks part of the frame off and changes the shape of the photographed image, leaving part of the frame a solid color. As seen on the screen, most masks are black, although they can be white or colored.

masking   In exhibition, stretches of black fabric that frame the theater scene. Masking can be adjusted according to the *aspect ratio* of the film to be projected.

match on action   A continuity cut that splices two different views of the same action together at the same moment in the movement, making it seem to continue uninterrupted.

matte shot   A type of *process shot* in which different areas of the image (usually actors and setting) are photographed separately and combined in laboratory work.

meaning   1. *Referential meaning:* Allusion to particular items of knowledge outside the film that the viewer is expected to recognize. 2. *Explicit meaning:* Significance presented overtly, usually in language and often near the film's beginning or end. 3. *Implicit meaning:* Significance left tacit, for the viewer to discover upon analysis or reflection. 4. *Symptomatic meaning:* Significance that the film divulges, often against its will, by virtue of its historical or social context.

medium close-up   A framing in which the scale of the object shown is fairly large; a human figure seen from the chest up would fill most of the screen.

medium long shot   A framing at a distance that makes an object about four or five feet high appear to fill most of the screen vertically. See also *plan américain,* the special term for a medium long shot de picting human figures.

medium shot   A framing in which the scale of the object shown is of moderate size; a human figure seen from the waist up would fill most of the screen.

mise-en-scene   All of the elements placed in front of the camera to be photographed: the settings and props, lighting, costumes and makeup, and figure behavior.

mixing   Combining two or more sound tracks by recording them onto a single one.

mobile frame   The effect on the screen of the moving camera, a *zoom lens,* or certain *special effects;* the framing shifts in relation to the scene being photographed. See also *crane shot, pan, tilt, tracking shot.*

monochromatic color design   Color design that emphasizes a narrow set of shades of a single color.

montage   1. A synonym for *editing.* 2. An approach to editing developed by the Soviet filmmakers of the 1920s; it emphasizes dynamic, often discontinuous, relationships between shots and the juxtaposition of images to create ideas not present in either shot by itself. See also *discontinuity editing, intellectual montage.*

montage sequence   A segment of a film that summarizes a topic or compresses a passage of time into brief symbolic or typical images. Frequently *dissolves, fades, superimpositions,* and *wipes* are used to link the images in a montage sequence.

motif   An element in a film that is repeated in a significant way.

motion control   A computerized method of planning and repeating camera movements on miniatures, models, and process work.

motivation   The justification given in the film for the presence of an element. This may be an appeal to the viewer's knowledge of the real world, to genre conventions, to narrative causality, or to a stylistic pattern within the film.

narration   The process through which the *plot* conveys or withholds *story* information. The narration can be more or less restricted to character knowledge and more or less deep in presenting characters' mental perceptions and thoughts.

narrative form   A type of filmic organization in which the parts relate to each other through a series of causally related events taking place in time and space.

nondiegetic insert   A shot or series of shots cut into a sequence, showing objects that are represented as being outside the space of the narrative.

nondiegetic sound   Sound, such as mood music or a narrator's commentary, represented as coming from a source outside the space of the narrative.

nonsimultaneous sound   Diegetic sound that comes from a source in time either earlier or later than the images it accompanies.

normal lens   A lens that shows objects without severely exaggerating or reducing the depth of the scene's planes. In 35mm filming, a normal lens is 35 to 50mm. See also *telephoto lens, wide-angle lens.*

offscreen sound   Simultaneous sound from a source assumed to be in the space of the scene but outside what is visible onscreen.

offscreen space   The six areas blocked from being visible on the screen but still part of the space of the scene: to each side and above and below the frame, behind the set, and behind the camera. See also *space.*

180° system   The continuity approach to editing dictates that the camera should stay on one side of the action to ensure consistent left-right spatial relations between objects from shot to shot. The 180° line is the same as the *axis of action.* See also *continuity editing, screen direction.*

order   In a narrative film, the aspect of temporal manipulation that involves the sequence in which the chronological events of the *story* are arranged in the *plot.* See also *duration, frequency.*

overlap   A cue for suggesting represented depth in the film image by placing closer objects partly in front of more distant ones.

overlapping editing   Cuts that repeat part or all of an action, thus expanding its viewing time and plot duration.

pan   A camera movement with the camera body turning to the right or left. On the screen, it produces a mobile framing that scans the space horizontally.

pixillation   A form of single-frame animation in which three-dimensional objects, often people, are made to move in staccato bursts through the use of stop-action cinematography.

plan américain   A framing in which the scale of the object shown is moderately small; the human figure seen from the shins to the head would fill most of the screen. This is sometimes referred to as a *medium long shot,* especially when human figures are not shown.

plan-séquence   French term for a scene handled in a single shot, usually a *long take.*

plot   In a narrative film, all the events that are directly presented to us, including their causal relations, chronological order, duration, frequency, and spatial locations. Opposed to *story,* which is the viewer's imaginary construction of all the events in the narrative. See also *duration, ellipsis, frequency, order, viewing time.*

point-of-view shot (POV shot)   A shot taken with the camera placed approximately where the character's eyes would be, showing what the character would see; usually cut in before or after a shot of the character looking.

postsynchronization   The process of adding sound to images after they have been shot and assembled. This can include *dubbing* of voices, as well as inserting diegetic music or sound effects. It is the opposite of *direct sound.*

process shot   Any shot involving rephotography to combine two or more images into one or to create a special effect; also called composite shot. See also *matte shot, rear projection, special effects.*

production One of the three branches of the film industry; the process of creating the film. See also *distribution, exhibition.*

racking focus Shifting the area of sharp focus from one plane to another during a shot; the effect on the screen is called rack-focus.

rate In shooting, the number of frames exposed per second; in projection, the number of frames thrown on the screen per second. If the two are the same, the speed of the action will appear normal, while a disparity will create slow or fast motion. The standard rate in sound cinema is 24 frames per second for both shooting and projection.

rear projection A technique for combining a foreground action with a background action filmed earlier. The foreground is filmed in a studio, against a screen; the background imagery is projected from behind the screen. The opposite of *front projection.*

reestablishing shot A return to a view of an entire space after a series of closer shots following the *establishing shot.*

reframing Short panning or tilting movements to adjust for the figures' movements, keeping them onscreen or centered.

rhetorical form A type of filmic organization in which the parts create and support an argument.

rhythm The perceived rate and regularity of sounds, series of shots, and movements within the shots. Rhythmic factors include beat (or pulse), accent (or stress), and tempo (or pace).

rotoscope A machine that projects live-action motion picture frames one by one onto a drawing pad so that an animator can trace the figures in each frame. The aim is to achieve more realistic movement in an animated cartoon.

scene A segment in a narrative film that takes place in one time and space or that uses crosscutting to show two or more simultaneous actions.

screen direction The right-left relationships in a scene, set up in an establishing shot and determined by the position of characters and objects in the frame, by the directions of movement, and by the characters' eyelines. *Continuity editing* will attempt to keep screen direction consistent between shots. See also *axis of action, eyeline match, 180° system.*

segmentation The process of dividing a film into parts for analysis.

sequence Term commonly used for a moderately large segment of film, involving one complete stretch of action. In a narrative film, often equivalent to a *scene.*

shallow focus A restricted *depth of field,* which keeps only one plane in sharp focus; the opposite of *deep focus.*

shallow space Staging the action in relatively few planes of depth; the opposite of *deep space.*

shot 1. In shooting, one uninterrupted run of the camera to expose a series of frames. Also called a *take.* 2. In the finished film, one uninterrupted image with a single static or mobile framing.

shot/reverse shot Two or more shots edited together that alternate characters, typically in a conversation situation. In *continuity editing,* characters in one framing usually look left, in the other framing, right. Over-the-shoulder framings are common in shot/reverse-shot editing.

side lighting Lighting coming from one side of a person or object, usually in order to create a sense of volume, to bring out surface tensions, or to fill in areas left shadowed by light from another source.

simultaneous sound Diegetic sound that is represented as occurring at the same time in the story as the image it accompanies.

size diminution A cue for suggesting represented depth in the image by showing objects that are farther away as smaller than foreground objects.

soft lighting Illumination that avoids harsh bright and dark areas, creating a gradual transition from highlights to shadows.

sound bridge 1. At the beginning of one scene, the sound from the previous scene carries over briefly before the sound from the new scene begins. 2. At the end of one scene, the sound from the next scene is heard, leading into that scene.

sound over Any sound that is not represented as coming from the space and time of the images on the screen. This includes both nonsimultaneous diegetic sound and nondiegetic sounds. See also *nondiegetic sound, nonsimultaneous sound.*

sound perspective The sense of a sound's position in space, yielded by volume, timbre, pitch, and, in stereophonic reproduction systems, binaural information.

space Most minimally, any film displays a two-dimensional graphic space, the flat composition of the image. In films that depict recognizable objects, figures, and locales, a three-dimensional space is represented as well. At any moment, three-dimensional space may be directly depicted, as onscreen space, or suggested, as *offscreen space.* In narrative film, we can also distinguish between story space, the locale of the totality of the action (whether shown or not), and plot space, the locales visibly and audibly represented in the scenes.

special effects A general term for various photographic manipulations that create fictitious spatial relations in the shot, such as *superimposition, matte shots,* and *rear projection.*

story In a narrative film, all the events that we see and hear, plus all those that we infer or assume to have occurred, arranged in their presumed causal relations, chronological order, duration, frequency, and spatial locations. Opposed to *plot,* which is the film's actual presentation of events in the story. See also *duration, ellipsis, frequency, order, space, viewing time.*

storyboard A tool used in planning film production, consisting of comic-strip-like drawings of individual shots or phases of shots with descriptions written below each drawing.

style The repeated and salient uses of film techniques characteristic of a single film or a group of films (for example, a filmmaker's work or a national movement).

superimposition The exposure of more than one image on the same film strip.

synchronous sound Sound that is matched temporally with the movements occurring in the images, as when dialogue corresponds to lip movements.

take   In filmmaking, the shot produced by one uninterrupted run of the camera. One shot in the final film may be chosen from among several takes of the same action.

technique   Any aspect of the film medium that can be chosen and manipulated in making a film.

telephoto lens   A lens of long focal length that affects a scene's perspective by enlarging distant planes and making them seem close to the foreground planes. In 35mm filming, a lens of 75mm length or more. See also *normal lens, wide-angle lens.*

three-point lighting   A common arrangement using three directions of light on a scene; from behind the subjects (*backlighting*), from one bright source (*key light*), and from a less bright source balancing the key light (*fill light*).

tilt   A camera movement with the camera body swiveling upward or downward on a stationary support. It produces a mobile framing that scans the space vertically.

top lighting   Lighting coming from above a person or object, usually in order to outline the upper areas of the figure or to separate it more clearly from the background.

tracking shot   A mobile framing that travels through space forward, backward, or laterally. See also *crane shot, pan,* and *tilt.*

typage   A performance technique of Soviet Montage cinema whereby an actor is given features believed to characterize a social class or other group.

underlighting   Illumination from a point below the figures in the scene.

unity   The degree to which a film's parts relate systematically to each other and provide motivations for all the elements used.

variation   In film form, the return of an element with notable changes.

viewing time   The length of time it takes to watch a film when it is projected at the appropriate speed.

whip pan   An extremely fast movement of the camera from side to side, which briefly causes the image to blur into a set of indistinct horizontal streaks. Often an imperceptible cut will join two whip pans to create a trick transition between scenes.

wide-angle lens   A lens of short focal length that affects a scene's perspective by distorting straight lines near the edges of the frame and by exaggerating the distance between foreground and background planes. In 35mm filming, a wide-angle lens is 30mm or less. See also *normal lens, telephoto lens.*

wipe   A transition between shots in which a line passes across the screen, eliminating one shot as it goes and replacing it with the next one.

zoom lens   A lens with a focal length that can be changed during a shot. A shift toward the *telephoto* range enlarges the image and flattens its planes together, giving an impression of magnifying the scene's space, while a shift toward the *wide-angle* range does the opposite.

Credits

Grateful acknowledgement is made for use of the following:

Figure 1.23 Wisconsin Center for Film and Theater Research; **1.32** Museum of Modern Art; **1.36** courtesy Manex Visual Effects; **5.52** Museum of Modern Art; **5.56–5.69** courtesy Bruce Conner; **5.72** courtesy Norman McLaren; **6.128** courtesy Norman McLaren; **7.39** courtesy Ernie Gehr; **7.201–7.203** courtesy Michael Snow; **10.60–10.68** courtesy Bruce Conner; **11.43–11.61** courtesy New Yorker Films; **12.1** George Eastman House; **12.27** Museum of Modern Art; **12.28–12.29** Wisconsin Center for Film and Theater Research.

Index

A, 210
À Bout de Souffle. See Breathless
above-the-line costs, 25
Abraham, Murray, 203
abstract form, 147–150
   in *Ballet mécanique,* 150–154, 155, 333,
     407–409
   and depth cues, 212, 213
   and editing, 333
   and French avant-garde, 474
   and misc-en-scene, 176
   and *Tokyo Story,* 437
   and zoom shots, 241–242
The Abyss, 166, 291
Academy ratio, 254, 255
accents, 217, 360
Accident, 373
ACE (American Cinema Editors), 31
Ace Ventura, Pet Detective, 115
Achbar, Mark, 40
acting, 199–207
   and comedy, 223
   context of, 205–207
   and German Expressionism, 205, 473
   and graphic design, 205
   and Griffith, 470
   and make-up, 189, 190
   and narrative form, 222
   and realism, 199–200, 202, 204, 460, 485
   stylization, 202–205
   tools of, 201–203
action films, 118, 210, 493–495
action scenes, 29
actors. *See* acting; cast
adaptations, 24
additional photography, 31
ADR (automated dialogue replacement), 32
The Adventures of Prince Achmed, 164
The Adventures of Sherlock Holmes, 484
Advise and Consent, 22
aerial perspective, 214, 216
African American coming-of-age films, 116
L'Age d'or, 477

The Age of Innocence, 491
Agnus Dei, 285
airplane shots, 267
Akerman, Chantal, 217
Akira, 173, 174
Alexander Nevsky, 365
"Alice in Cartoonland" series, 166
Alien, 264
   cause and effect in, 73
   emotional effects in, 121
   genre in, 116
   Aliens
   acting in, 207
   color in, 210, 211
   editing in, 298
   emotional effects in, 121
   social ideology in, 117–118
   widescreen ratio in, 254, 255
Allen, Dede, 426
Allen, Woody
   on emotions, 54
   Hannah and Her Sisters, 90, 204
   Manhattan, 21
   Mighty Aphrodite, 116
   and New Hollywood, 490
   production control, 37
   The Purple Rose of Cairo, 195, 196, 197
   and realism, 202, 204
   What's Up, Tiger Lily?, 372
   Zelig, 81
All of Me, 200
All Quiet on the Western Front, 304
All the President's Men, 180
Almendros, Nestor, 193
Altman, Robert
   and improvisation, 177
   Nashville, 90
   and New Hollywood, 489, 490
   The Player, 24
   production control, 41
   and USA Films, 17
Amadeus, 203
Amateur, 16

ambiguity
   in *Citizen Kane,* 92, 99, 100
   and depth of knowledge, 86
   and discontinuity editing, 342
   and documentaries, 132
   in *Do the Right Thing,* 426
   and French New Wave, 488
   and Italian neorealism, 486
   and narrators, 87
   in *Raging Bull,* 460, 461
   and sound, 370, 375–376, 377
   and time, 91
American Cinema Editors (ACE), 31
American Friend, 374
American Graffiti
   music in, 353, 367
   and New Hollywood, 489, 490
   time in, 424
American Movie, 130, 131
American Mutoscope & Biograph, 468
The Americano, 470
American Pie, 115
American Society of Cinematography
   (ASC), 31
Amistad, 392–393
L'Amour Fou, 90
analog image synthesis, 226
analog video, 10
anamorphic widescreen ratios, 254, 255, 256
Anchors Aweigh, 166
An Andalusian Dog (Un Chien andalou),
   477, 478
Anders, Allison, 491
Anderson, Paul Thomas, 22, 370
Angelopoulos, Theo, 272
Angels with Dirty Faces, 61
Anger, Kenneth, 52, 147, 149, 157, 366
Angilirq, Paul Apak, 39
angle of framing. *See* camera angle
Animal House, 115
animated films, 162–171
   acting in, 207
   color in, 210, 213

acting in, *(continued)*
    computer-generated imagery in, 164–166, 169
    deep focus in, 242
    defined, 40
    experimental, 147, 149, 169–171
    framing, 259–260
    mise-en-scene in, 176, 191, 198–199
    mobile framing in, 164, 270, 271
    musicals, 124
    narrative form in, 68, 167–169
    overview, 162–166
    resources on, 173–174
    sound in, 360
    and video, 11
animatics, 249
anime, 166, 173–174
Annaud, Jean-Jacques, 206
The Anniversary Party, 10
À Nous la liberté, 304
answer print, 33
Anthony Adverse, 92, 484
Anticipation of the Night, 333
Antonioni, Michelangelo
    L'Avventura, 90, 219, 257, 258
    Blow-Up, 490
    Cronaca di un amore, 273, 486
    L'Eclisse, 82
    Il Grido, 212
Aparajito, 192
Apocalypse Now, 30, 370, 371
Apollo 13, 131, 291
apparent motion, 3
Applause, 482
appointments, 90
Arachnophobia, 27
Araki, Gregg, 492
Are Parents People?, 470, 471
L'Argent
    color in, 182–183, 213
    costume in, 187
    and French Impressionist movement, 476, 477
Armageddon, 34, 312, 327
Arnheim, Rudolf, 265, 387
Arrabal, 231–232
The Arrival of a Train at La Ciotat, 252, 253, 467
L'Arroseur arrosé (The Waterer Watered), 179, 467
Artaud, Antonin, 477
art directors, 26
ASC (American Society of Cinematography), 31
Ashes and Diamonds, 215, 216
aspect ratio, 253–257, 292
The Asphalt Jungle, 113, 191

Assault on Precinct 13, 334, 490
assembly stage, 25
assistant editors, 30
associate producers, 24, 29
associational form, 154, 156–162, 404
    in *Man with a Movie Camera,* 443–446
    in *A Movie,* 157–162, 409, 451
    in *The Thin Blue Line,* 451
Astaire, Fred, 123, 125, 483
asynchronous sound, 371–372
Atanarjuat: The Fast Runner, 10–11, 39
The Atomic Cafe, 130
attached shadows (shading), 191
Attack of the Clones, 11
Au Hasard Balthasar, 205
Austin Powers: The Spy Who Shagged Me, 19
auteurs, 487, 488
authenticity, 180
authorship, 40–41
automated dialogue replacement (ADR), 32
Autry, Gene, 116
An Autumn Afternoon, 216, 334
avant-garde films. *See* experimental films; French Impressionism
L'Avventura, 90, 219, 257, 258
axis of action. *See* 180° system

Babe, 261, 291
Baby's Meal, 252–253
Back and Forth, 277
backlighting, 192, 194, 459
backstage musicals, 123, 124, 125–126
Back to the Future, 19, 490
Back to the Future films
    lighting in, 195
    marketing, 19
    and New Hollywood, 490
    plot development in, 81
    time in, 78, 79
The Bad and the Beautiful, 219
Badlands, 433
Baillie, Bruce, 146
balance, 210–212, 216
Baldwin, Craig, 132
Ballet mécanique, 146
    form in, 150–154, 155, 333, 407–409
    style in, 407–409
Ballhaus, Michael, 235
Bambi, 213
Bamboozled, 10, 29
Banderas, Antonio, 492
Band of Outsiders, 374–375, 488
The Band Wagon, 71, 124, 125
Bangkok Dangerous, 114
Barnes, Paul, 344
Barravento, 241

Barton Fink, 492
Baruchello, Gianfranco, 148
base, 4
Bashō, 156
Batman, 116, 181, 490
The Battle at Elderbush Gulch, 322, 325
Bay, Michael, 45
Bazin, André
    on depth, 227, 228
    on mobile framing, 280
    on origins of cinema, 41
    on realism, 225
    on setting, 179
    on shot duration, 284, 285, 292–293
    on sound, 387
beat, 217, 359
Beatty, Warren, 181
Becky Sharp, 291, 484
Beetlejuice, 19, 123, 490
beginnings. *See* openings
Begone, Dull Care, 213
Being John Malkovich, 109–110, 492
Belle du jour, 86, 478
La Belle nivernaise, 475
below-the-line costs, 25
Berge, François, 473
Bergman, Ingmar, 230, 490
Berkeley, Busby, 123, 217, 218, 304, 333–334
Berlin, Symphony of a Great City, 444
Berlusconi, Sylvio, 20
Bernhardt, Curtis, 366
Bertolucci, Bernardo, 206, 207
    Last Tango in Paris, 243, 244, 254, 255
best boys, 28
The Best Years of Our Lives, 41, 227
A Better Tomorrow, 494–495
A Better Tomorrow III, 210
Bezhin Meadow, 194, 227
Bianco e Nero, 485
Bicycle Thieves, 212, 485, 486
Big, 115
Big Deal on Madonna Street, 113
Bigger than Life, 256
The Big Heat, 112
The Big Sleep
    depth of knowledge in, 85, 86, 90
    director role in, 41
    range of knowledge in, 83
Bill and Ted's Excellent Adventure, 115
Billy the Kid vs. Dracula, 116
biographies, 92, 131
Biography, 40
The Birds
    continuity editing in, 314
    cuts in, 295–296
    framing in, 264

graphic continuity/discontinuity in, 297, 300–303
rhythm in, 303–304
space in, 304, 305
storyboard for, 26
style in, 393, 396
time in, 306, 308, 309
The Birth of a Nation
content of, 50
costume in, 186
depth of knowledge in, 85
editing in, 294, 469–470
meaning in, 55
unrestricted narration in, 83
black-and-white films, 210, 290–291
Black Maria, 466–467
Blade Runner, 114, 116, 196
The Blair Witch Project
hand-held shots in, 270
popularity of, 122
production, 39
promotion, 18, 132
Blank, Les, 134–135. *See also* Gap-Toothed Women
Blasetti, 485
Blazing Saddles, 369
blimps, 482, 483
blind booking, 9
Blind Chance, 78
Blinkety Blank, 163
Block, Mitchell, 132
block booking, 9
Blood and Sand, 291
Blood Simple, 114
Blow Out, 33
Blow-Up, 490
bluescreen, 29–30
Blue Velvet, 114, 491
Boat People, 494
Bob le Flambeur, 113
The Bodyguard, 112, 193–194
Bogart, Humphrey, 41
Bogdanovich, Peter, 490
The Bonfire of the Vanities, 269
Les Bonnes Femmes, 488
Bonnie and Clyde, 433
boom operators, 28
Boom Town, 245
Boorman, John, 308, 312
Borthwick, Dave, 164
Bound, 113, 114
Bowling for Columbine, 13
Boy Meets Girl, 215, 243
Boyz N the Hood, 116, 242, 491
Brakhage, Stan
on color, 227
Dog Star Man, 38, 146

editing, 333
Mothlight, 163
Reflections on Black, 232, 233
Bram Stoker's Dracula, 181, 235, 491
branding, 14
Brando, Marlon, 177, 199
Breakdown, genre of, 112
Breaking the Waves, 230, 232, 493
Breathless (À Bout de Souffle)
acting in, 205–206
critical analysis, 428–433
editing in, 335–336, 337, 431–432
ending of, 430, 488
and expectations, 52
and French New Wave, 487
genre of, 114
hand-held shots in, 431, 488
Breer, Robert, 146, 147, 163, 169–171, 333
Bresson, Robert
and acting, 205
Four Nights of a Dreamer, 364
and French New Wave, 487
Lancelot du Lac, 216
Pickpocket, 191, 265
on production, 20, 24
on sound, 379
style, 389
See also A Man Escaped
Breton, André, 477, 478
Brialy, Jean-Claude, 488
The Bride Wore Black, 267
Brighton School, 468
Bringing Up Baby, 317, 318, 490
British Society of Cinematography (BSC), 31
Broken Arrow, 119
Brooks, Mel, 369
The Brothers McMullen, 16, 37
Broughton, James, 148
Brownlow, Kevin, 220
BSC (British Society of Cinematography), 31
Bubblegum Crisis, 173
buddy-cop films, 115
The Buena Vista Social Club, 10
Buffy the Vampire Slayer, 19
A Bug's Life, 19, 21
Bugsy Malone, 111
Bullock, Sandra, 190
Buñuel, Luis, 86, 178, 477, 478
Burch, Noël, 228, 258–259
Burke, Kenneth, 66–67
Burns, Edward, 16, 37
Burton, Tim, 164, 181, 189, 190, 291, 490
Burtt, Ben, 351
Bye Bye Birdie, 257

Byrne, David, 109, 297

cabaretera, 108
The Cabinet of Dr. Caligari
acting in, 203, 205
genre of, 122, 472–473
narrative form in, 91
and realism, 177
Cahiers du cinema, 486–487
camera, 3
camera angle, 260–261, 263, 264, 265, 266
camera distance, 262–263
and acting, 201, 206
and filters, 233
functions of, 263, 264, 265–266
Griffith, 470
Ondříček on, 332
and selective focus, 242
and sound, 350
and style, 408
camera height, 261–262
camera lenses, 236–243
and French Impressionism, 476
wide-angle, 237, 238, 492
zoom, 240–241, 271, 272
camera movement, 266–270
and introduction of sound, 482, 483
motion control, 250, 269, 491
zoom shots, 240–241, 271, 272
See also mobile framing
camera negative, 33
camera operators, 27
camera position, 260–266
Cameron, James, 21, 69, 166, 199, 490
Campion, Jane, 37, 393
canted framing, 261, 263, 264, 407
Les Carabiniers, 230–231, 488
Carax, Leos, 196, 215, 243
Carpenter, John, 489, 490
Carrey, Jim, 200
Carrie, 122
Casablanca, 41, 230
Casanova, 187, 188, 210, 213
cast, 27, 485. *See also* acting
Cast Away, 291, 351
casting directors, 31
cast shadows, 191, 214
The Cat and the Canary, 121
categorical form, 132, 133–134
in experimental films, 147
in *Gap-Toothed Women,* 134–140
Cat People, 121, 122, 123
cause and effect, 72–74
in *Citizen Kane,* 73, 94–95
in classical Hollywood cinema, 90
and climax, 82
and crosscutting, 324, 326

cause and effect, *(continued)*
  and definition of narrative, 69
  and French New Wave, 488
  in *His Girl Friday,* 415–416
  and narration, 87, 89
  and sound, 378
  and Surrealism, 477
  and temporal scrambling, 77, 78, 79, 91
Cavalcanti, Alberto, 444
cel animation, 11, 163, 166, 167–169, 199
Cenere, 231, 232
central linear perspective, 215
CGI. *See* computer-generated imagery
Chabrol, Claude, 339, 487, 488, 489
A Chairy Tale, 164
Une Chambre en Ville, 254, 255
Chan, Jackie, 309–310, 493–494, 496
Chaney, Lon, 121
change, 90, 207
change in knowledge, 80
Chan Is Missing, 491
Chaplin, Charlie
  acting, 201
  framing, 265
  and Hollywood studio system, 471, 475
  and parody, 115
  and sound, 352
Character Mapper, 249
character parts, 31
characters
  in *Breathless,* 428–429, 430
  and cause and effect, 72, 94–95
  in classical Hollywood cinema, 89, 90
  and computer-generated imagery, 249, 250
  conflict among, 63
  in crime thrillers, 112, 113–114
  in *Do the Right Thing,* 424, 425
  and emotions, 53
  in French Impressionism, 475
  and French New Wave, 488
  in *His Girl Friday,* 415–416
  in horror films, 121
  in *Meet Me in St. Louis,* 453–454, 456–457
  and mobile framing, 278, 279
  and motivation, 98, 99
  narrators, 86–87, 88–89, 101, 366, 370, 374
  and 180° system, 313
  in *Raging Bull,* 459, 460–461
  vs. setting, 179
  and sound, 348
  and Soviet Montage, 480–481
  in *The Thin Blue Line,* 450
  traits, 72, 94, 98
  and web-of-life plots, 437–438
  in Westerns, 119–120

The Charge of the Light Brigade, 214
Che, Zhang, 493
The Cheat, 191, 470, 475
cheat cuts, 319–320
Chelovek s kinoapparatom. See Man with a Movie Camera
Chen, Joan, 16
Chen Kaige, 237, 238
Cherkasov, Nikolai, 203, 204
chiaroscuro, 196, 470
Chicken Run, 164
Un Chien andalou (An Andalusian Dog), 477, 478
China Express, 240
A Chinese Ghost Story, 494
Ching Siu-tung, 494
La Chinoise, 29, 192, 213, 336, 337
Chirico, Giorgio de, 478
choreographers, 27
Choreography for Camera, 146, 339
Chow Yun-fat, 494, 496
Choy, Christine, 39
The Chronicle of Anna Magdalena Bach
  black and white in, 291
  deep space in, 214, 215
  framing in, 261
  special effects in, 248, 252
Chuck and Buck, 10
Chung Hing sam Iam. See Chungking Express
Chungking Express (Chung Hing sam Iam)
  and contemporary Hong Kong cinema, 496
  critical analysis, 437–442
  and expectations, 52
  genre of, 114, 442
Chunhyang, 257, 258
Chytilová, Ver[v]á, 69–70, 232, 252
Cimino, Michael, 460
Cinderella, , 169
Cinderella (1899), 468
Cinema, 485
CinemaScope, 254, 256, 292
cinematographers (directors of photography), 27
cinematography, 229–293
  and computer-generated imagery, 250
  defined, 229
  and French Impressionism, 476
  and French New Wave, 487–488
  and Italian neorealism, 485
  in *Man with a Movie Camera,* 443–444
  resources on, 290–293
  speed of motion, 234–236
  and style, 402, 410
  tonality, 229–234
  See also framing; perspective relations; shot duration

cinéma-vérité, 130, 132, 176, 270. *See also* documentaries
Cissé, Souleymane, 184
Citizen Kane, 27, 91–102
  alternative memories in, 79
  cause and effect in, 73, 94–95
  deep focus in, 242, 243, 396, 484, 491
  depth in, 227
  editing in, 299, 399
  expectations in, 91–92
  framing in, 263, 264, 277, 396
  motivation in, 98–99
  mystery plot pattern in, 73, 94, 97–98
  narration in, 100–102, 397
  parallelism in, 97, 99, 398–399
  plot development in, 99–100, 491–492
  production of, 27, 41
  props in, 183
  range of knowledge in, 84, 101, 396
  resources on, 105
  search plot pattern in, 94, 97–98, 102, 394
  shot duration in, 285
  sound in, 351, 398, 399–400
  story/plot distinction in, 92–94, 95, 97
  style in, 394–401
  time in, 74, 75, 95–98, 400–401
City Lights, 201, 352
City of Sadness, 218–219
city symphonies, 444
Civilization, 470
Clair, René, 266
  Le Million, 81, 187, 304, 334, 365, 366
  on sound, 387
clapper boys, 31
classical Hollywood cinema, 89–91
  acting in, 200, 202
  and *Breathless,* 428–429
  and *Citizen Kane,* 92, 98, 99, 100
  and French Impressionism, 475
  and French New Wave, 487
  history of, 468–471, 481–484
  lighting in, 194–195, 470, 484
  projection process work in, 244
  resources on, 105, 497, 499
  See also continuity editing; *specific films and directors*
claymation, 164
Clear and Present Danger, 269
Clerks, 38, 492
click track, 32
climax, 82
Close Encounters of the Third Kind, 243, 489
A Close Shave, 164
close-ups
  and acting, 201
  defined, 262, 263

and filters, 233
functions of, 263, 264, 265
Ondříček on, 332
and selective focus, 242
closure, 82
in classical Hollywood cinema, 90–91
lack of, 82, 91, 92, 100, 430
Coen, Ethan, 17, 41, 114, 390, 492
Coen, Joel, 17, 41, 114, 390, 492
Coeur fidèle, 334, 475, 476
coherence, 58
Cohn, Norman, 39
collective production, 38–39
color
and cinematography, 231–232, 290–291
in contemporary Hong Kong cinema, 495
and costume, 187, 188
and depth cues, 213
and editing, 297
and emulsion, 5
grading, 251
introduction of, 483–484
and lighting, 196–197
in *Meet Me in St. Louis,* 231, 291, 454
in musicals, 125, 291
resources on, 227, 290–291
and setting, 182, 184
and space, 209–210, 211, 216
and style, 393
in *The Thin Blue Line,* 451–452
and variation, 63
and video, 10
color timer (grader), 231
color timers, 31
Colossus, 251
Columbia, 9
comedies
and expectations, 51
framing in, 265–266
and genre mixing, 116
make-up in, 189, 190
and mise-en-scene, 223–225
origins of, 115
sound in, 365, 371
comic-book films, 115–116, 174
Comingore, Dorothy, 27
commercials, 140, 345, 426
The Commitments, 123
Communism, 478
compilation films, 40, 130
complexity, 58–59
composers, 32
composite (process) shots, 244–247
composition. *See* space
computer-generated imagery (CGI)
and animation, 164–166, 169, 226
and digital video, 11

in fantasy and science fiction films, 34–35
and fiction films vs. documentaries, 132, 133
in horror films, 121
and lighting, 197–198
in *The Lord of the Rings,* 249–251
matte work, 246
and mise-en-scene, 248, 249, 250
and movement, 199
and New Hollywood, 491
resources on, 226
and setting, 182–183
computer technology
grading, 231, 250–251
motion control, 250, 269, 491
See also computer-generated imagery; digital technology
concession stands, 13
concreteness, 56–57, 66
conflict
in classical Hollywood cinema, 90
and discontinuity editing, 340
in *Do the Right Thing,* 425, 426
and variation, 63
Conner, Bruce, 309. *See also A Movie*
contact printers, 4
Contempt (Le Mépris), 179, 292, 489
continuity, 26. *See also* continuity editing
continuity editing, 310–333
axis shifts, 317–318
cheat cuts, 319–320
crossing the axis, 321–322, 323
development of, 469, 470, 471
in *Do the Right Thing,* 426
in *His Girl Friday,* 417
intensified, 327–331, 345
and Kuleshov effect, 318–319
and New Hollywood, 491
point-of-view editing, 320, 321, 322
resources on, 345
and shot duration, 284–285
and sound, 332, 482
and Soviet Montage, 479
and style, 411
and Surrealism, 478
and time, 326, 331–333
See also crosscutting; 180° system
contrast, 229–230
contrast ratio, 10
conventions. *See* genre conventions
The Conversation, 241, 376–377, 490
Cook, William, 251
Coolidge, Martha, 491
Coppola, Francis Ford
Apocalypse Now, 30, 370, 371
Bram Stoker's Dracula, 181, 235, 491
The Conversation, 241, 376–377, 490

and New Hollywood, 489, 490, 491
Rumble Fish, 196, 247, 491
on sound, 387
Tucker: A Man and His Dream, 233
Copy Cat, 112
Corliss, Richard, 115
corporate ownership, 9, 13, 14–15, 17–18, 20
Cosmic Ray, 333
costume, 184, 186–188
and comedy, 223
costume designer/staff, 26, 28
and narrative form, 221
in Westerns, 119
costume designers, 26
costume staff, 28
Les Cousins, 487
Coutard, Raoul, 431, 432
coverage, 29
Craig, Stuart, 183
The Cranes Are Flying, 238
crane shots, 267, 268
Creature Comforts, 164
The Crime of M. Lange
emotions in, 54
and French New Wave, 488
mobile framing in, 273, 274, 275
props in, 183–184
crime thrillers, 112–114
Crippled Avengers (Mortal Combat), 493
criteria, 58
critical analysis, 413–462
Breathless, 428–433
Chungking Express, 437–442
Do the Right Thing, 423–428
His Girl Friday, 415–418
Man with a Movie Camera, 443–446
Meet Me in St. Louis, 452–457
North by Northwest, 418–423
Raging Bull, 457–462
resources on, 462
The Thin Blue Line, 446–452
Tokyo Story, 433–437
critical flicker fusion, 2–3
Critical Mass, 146
Cronaca di un amore (Story of a Love Affair), 273, 486
Cronenberg, David, 37, 189, 190, 491
crosscutting
defined, 306
and discontinuity editing, 342
functions of, 324, 326
and Griffith, 322, 325, 469–470
in *North by Northwest,* 422–423
crossing the axis, 321–322, 323
crosslighting (sidelighting), 192
cross-promotion, 19

Crouching Tiger, Hidden Dragon, 13, 16–17, 496
The Crow, 334
The Cruise, 39, 130
Crumb, 130
The Crying Game, 13
Cubism, 150
Cukor, George, 482
Cure, 114
curiosity
    and expectations, 52, 69
    and motivation, 98
    and multiple narrators, 101
    and mystery plot pattern, 73
    and restricted narration, 83
Curtis, Edward, 332
Curtis, Tony, 237
Curtiz, Michael, 41, 214
cutaways, 308
cut-out animation, 164
cuts, 295. *See also* editing
cycles, 115–116

Dada, 473, 474
dailies (rushes), 30
Daisies, 232, 233, 252
Dalí, Salvador, 477, 478
Dames, 483
Damned If You Don't, 146
dance, 217
Dancer in the Dark, 11, 16, 29
Dash, Julie, 492
Dassin, Jules, 444
Daughters of the Dust, 492
Dave, 115, 130
Davies, Terence, 75
Dawn of the Dead, 121
Day for Night, 33, 264
day for night, 233, 234
A Day in the Country, 264
Day of Wrath, 130–131, 215–216, 218, 393
Dead Again, 116
Dead End, 424
Deadkins, Roger, 390
deadlines, 90, 439
Dead Man Walking, 390
Dead Men Don't Wear Plaid, 306
The Dead Zone, 491
The Death Ray, 334, 480
Decla, 472–473
deep focus, 242–243, 396, 484, 491
deep space, 214, 215
    and comedy, 223–224
    vs. depth of field, 242
    resources on, 227, 228
    and style, 397
    and suspense, 222

and time, 218–219
The Deer Hunter, 460
Delerue, Georges, 357
Delluc, Louis, 475
De Mille, Cecil B., 191, 470, 475
Demme, Jonathan, 357. *See also* The Silence of the Lambs
De Niro, Robert, 199, 460
De Palma, Brian
    Blow Out, 33
    and camera movement, 269
    and deep focus, 243, 244
    and New Hollywood, 489, 490, 491
    Snake Eyes, 114, 269
    and split-screen imagery, 257–258
depth cues, 208, 212–215. *See also* deep space
depth of field, 242–243. *See also* deep focus
depth of knowledge, 85–86, 87–88, 90. *See also* subjectivity
depth staging. *See* deep space
Deren, Maya, 38, 146, 339, 477
De Santis, 485, 486
Deserter, 481
de Sica, Vittorio, 212, 485
designers, 473
desire, 89–90
Desperado, 492
detective films, 73, 75, 81. *See also* mystery plot pattern
development, 63–65
    and associational form, 162
    and categorical form, 134
    and long takes, 287
    See also plot development
devotionals, 108
Diagonal-symphonie, 473
dialogue
    automated dialogue replacement, 32
    in *Breathless,* 429
    emphasis on, 352
    and multiple cameras, 29
    overlap, 353–355, 482
    rhythm in, 360
    staff, 26, 31
    synchronization, 371
    See also sound
dialogue coaches, 26
dialogue editors, 31
dialogue overlap, 353–355, 482
Dickson, W. K. L., 252, 253, 466
Dick Tracy, 181
diegesis, 70–71
diegetic sound, 366–371
    and continuity editing, 482
    internal vs. external, 368
    vs. nondiegetic sound, 366–367, 369–370

onscreen vs. offscreen, 367–368
    and perspective, 370–371
    and time, 332, 372–375
    See also dialogue
Die Hard, 19, 112, 235
Dietrich, Marlene, 350
digital compositing, 226
digital computer animation, 226. *See also* computer-generated imagery
Digital Domain, 291
digital doubles, 250
digital sound, 6, 8
digital technology, 34–35
    editing, 32, 34
    sound, 6, 8, 32
    video, 10–12, 38, 39
    See also computer-generated imagery; computer technology
digital video (DV), 10–12, 38, 39
Diller, Barry, 17
Dimensions of Dialogue, 198, 199
direct-cinema documentaries, 130
directors, 26, 37
    as auteurs, 487, 488
    and authorship, 40–41
    and crime thrillers, 114
    resources on, 43
director's crew, 26–27
directors of photography (DPs) (cinematographers), 27
disaster films, 72, 115
discontinuity editing, 334–343
    in *Breathless,* 335–336, 337, 431–432
    in *Do the Right Thing,* 426
    and French New Wave, 488
    in *October,* 339–343
    resources on, 345–346
    and space, 335–336
    and Surrealism, 478
    and time, 336–339, 342
    in *Tokyo Story,* 435–436
The Discreet Charm of the Bourgeoisie, 178, 478
Disney/Buena Vista, 9
dissolves, 294, 295, 304, 332, 478
Distant Voices, Still Lives, 75
distribution, 9, 13–15, 18–20, 20, 42
disunity, 65
La Dixième symphonie, 475
Dmytryk, Edward, 87
documentaries, 128–146
    camera movement in, 270
    characters in, 72
    and classical Hollywood cinema, 89
    cross-promotion, 19
    defined, 128–130
    editing in, 305, 344

vs. fiction films, 130–132
framing in, 265
and French New Wave, 487
Gap-Toothed Women, 134–140, 401–404
Man with a Movie Camera, 129, 235, 443–446
mise en scene in, 176
narrative form in, 68, 69–70, 87, 89, 132, 447–449
narrators in, 87
production, 38, 39, 40
resources on, 171–172
rhetorical form in, 140–142
The River, 87, 142–146, 404–407
speed of motion in, 236
style in, 401–407
The Thin Blue Line, 132, 133, 176, 306, 344, 446–452
types of, 130
See also categorical form
Dogma, 492
Dog Star Man, 38, 146
Dolby technology, 355
dolly grips, 31
dolly shots. *See* tracking shots
Donen, Stanley. *See Singin' in the Rain*
Don Juan, 481
Don't Look Now, 237
Do the Right Thing
critical analysis, 423–428
editing in, 309, 331, 426
lack of closure in, 100
and New Hollywood, 491
double-exposure effects, 443
Double Indemnity, 428
Double Jeopardy, 112, 116
Dovzhenko, Alexander, 480, 481
Down by Law, 491
Dracula, 122, 123, 186. *See also* Bram Stoker's Dracula
Dragon Gate Inn, 493
The Draughtsman's Contract, 210, 213
drawn animation, 163
Dreams of Toyland, 164, 165
Dressed to Kill, 490
Dreyer, Carl
on color, 227
Day of Wrath, 130–131, 215–216, 218, 393
and "dead time", 91
and French New Wave, 488
and long takes, 285
Ordet, 267
See also La Passion de Jeanne d'Arc
drivers, 28
Dr. Jekyll and Mr. Hyde, 121
Drums Along the Mohawk, 109

Drunken Master, 493
Dryburgh, Stuart, 393
dry recording, 353
Dr. Zhivago, 489
dubbing (looping), 32, 388, 485
Duck Amuck, 167–169, 170–171, 365
Dude, Where's My Car?, 115
Duel, 112
Dulac, Germaine, 475, 476, 477
Dune, 368
Dupont, E. A., 292
DVDs, 21
dynamics, 350

early cinema, 252–253, 465–468, 496–497.
See also silent films; *specific films and directors*
Early Summer, 275, 335, 336
Earthquake, 115
Eastern Condors, 493
Eastman, George, 465
Easy Rider, 489
Eat, 52, 146
Eat, Sleep, 294
Eat Drink Man Woman, 16
Eclair, 487
L'Eclisse (The Eclipse), 82
edge (rim) lighting, 192, 193, 213
Edison, Thomas, 466, 468
Edison-Lumiere ratio, 253, 292
editing, 294–346
and acting, 206
in *The Birth of a Nation,* 294, 469–470
in *Breathless,* 335–336, 337, 431–432
in contemporary Hong Kong cinema, 495–496
defined, 294–296
digital, 32, 34
and French Impressionism, 304, 334, 476
in *Man with a Movie Camera,* 443, 444, 445–446
and postproduction, 30, 32–33
in *Raging Bull,* 459
resources on, 344–346
and rhythm, 303–304, 333–334, 476
and shot duration, 293, 294, 303–304
and Soviet Montage, 304, 334, 446, 480
and space, 304–306
and style, 399, 408, 411
and Surrealism, 478
in *The Thin Blue Line,* 306, 344, 449–450, 451
and time, 306–310
See also continuity editing; discontinuity editing; graphic continuity/discontinuity
editors (supervising editors), 30

Edward Scissorhands, 74, 189, 190
Eggeling, Viking, 473
Eiga-zuke (Pickled Film), 91
8 1/2
costume in, 186
depth of knowledge in, 86
film production in, 33
sound in, 374
The Eight-Diagram Pole Fighter, 493
Eisenstein, Sergei
Alexander Nevsky, 365
Bezhin Meadow, 194, 227
on color, 227
and deep space, 227
editing, 446, 480
on framing, 254
montage, 91
Potemkin, 90, 187, 232, 294, 339, 480
protagonists, 90
on sound, 348
and Soviet Montage movement, 479, 480, 481
See also Ivan the Terrible; October; Strike
El Dorado, 476
Election, 184, 185
ellipses, 97, 308, 332, 342, 431
in *Tokyo Story,* 433–434
Emak Bakia, 477
emotions
and climax, 82
and form, 53–54, 67
in French Impressionism, 476
and horror films, 120–121
in *North by Northwest,* 419
and rhetorical form, 141
and style, 393, 407, 410
Empire, 294
The Empire Strikes Back, 72, 247, 489
empty frames, 308
emulsion, 4–5
The End, 261
endings
in *Breathless,* 430, 488
in *Citizen Kane,* 92, 98, 100, 395–396
in classical Hollywood cinema, 90–91
in contemporary Hong Kong cinema, 495
in *Do the Right Thing,* 100, 425–426
and expectations, 69
in experimental films, 154, 162
and formal development, 64–65, 82
in *The 400 Blows,* 73–74, 82, 488
in French New Wave, 488
in Italian neorealism, 486
in *Meet Me in St. Louis,* 456
in *Raging Bull,* 461
in Westerns, 120
The English Patient, 355

Enthusiasm, 481
enthymemes, 141, 144, 145
Entr'acte, 266
Epstein, Jean, 334, 475, 476
Eraserhead, 491
Erice, Hector, 196
establishing shots, 313
E.T.: The Extraterrestrial, 121, 254
Eternity and a Day, 240
evaluation, 58–59
Everest, 130
The Evil Dead, 21
executive producers, 24
exhibition, 8–9, 10–12, 42, 370–371
exit polling, 19
Exodus, 80
The Exorcist
   and New Hollywood, 489
   plot development in, 121
   popularity of, 122
   and social ideology, 123
   sound in, 353
expansion editing, 308, 339
expectations
   and balance, 210
   and discontinuity editing, 337
   in experimental films, 151–152, 154
   and form, 50–52, 54
   and mise-en-scene, 208
   and mobile framing, 283
   and narration, 89, 435
   and narrative form, 68–69, 91–92
   and plot development, 81–82
   and sound, 348, 365, 369
   and style, 391, 407
   and subjectivity, 86
   See also genre conventions
experience, 52–53
experimental films, 146–162
   abstract form in, 147–154, 155
   animated, 147, 149, 169–171
   associational form in, 154, 156–162
   focal length in, 241–242
   and independent filmmaking, 492–493
   mobile framing in, 274, 275, 280, 283
   narrative form in, 68, 147
   resources on, 172–173
   sound in, 149–150, 352
explicit meaning, 55–56
   in documentaries, 139–140
   in experimental films, 157
   in *Meet Me in St. Louis,* 456
exploitation films, 37
exposition, 80
exposure, 232–233
external diegetic sound, 368

The Extraordinary Adventures of Mr. West in
   the Land of the Bolsheviks, 479–480
extras, 27
extreme close-ups, 262, 263, 264
extreme long shots, 262
eyeline matches, 312, 314, 318, 342, 470.
   See also continuity editing
Eyes Wide Shut, 33
Eyes without a Face, 317–318, 319, 321

fade-ins, 294, 332
fade-outs, 294, 332
Fahrenheit 451, 489
Fail-Safe, 203
Fairbanks, Douglas, 470, 471, 475, 479
Fallen Angels, 261
Fall of the House of Usher (Epstein), 334
The Fall of the House of Usher (Watson &
   Webber), 147
The Falls, 147
false perspective, 250, 252
The Family Plot, 114
fans, 18, 110, 174
fan sites, 18
"fantasies of displacement", 115
fantasy films
   acting in, 200
   color in, 291
   computer-generated imagery in,
      34–35
   and German Expressionism, 473
   movement in, 198
   sound in, 368, 369
   special effects in, 291
Far From Heaven, 18
Fargo, 113
fast cutting, 327–331
   and digital technology, 34
   and French Impressionism, 476
   and genre conventions, 111
   in *Raging Bull,* 459
   and rhythm, 304
   and style, 408–409
fast-motion effects, 235
Fast Times at Ridgemont High, 491
Faust, 473–474
Fellini, Federico
   Casanova, 187, 188, 210, 213
   8 1/2, 33, 86, 186, 374
   and Italian neorealism, 486
   on lighting, 191
   Nights of Cabiria, 196, 197
The Fellowship of the Ring. See The Lord of
   the Rings: The Fellowship of the Ring
feminism, 117–118
La Femme infidèle, 339

La Femme Nikita, 114
Feuillade, Louis, 181
fictional biographies, 92
fiction films, 40, 130–132. *See also specific*
   genres and films
fidelity, 365–366
Field, Todd, 17
The Fifth Element, 183
Fight Club, 492
fill light, 193, 194
Film about a Woman Who..., 87, 146–147,
   148
film history, 464–500
   classical Hollywood cinema, 468–471,
      481–484, 497, 499
   contemporary Hong Kong cinema,
      493–496, 500
   early cinema, 465–468, 496–497
   French Impressionism, 474–477, 498
   French New Wave, 486–489, 499
   German Expressionism, 472–474,
      497–498
   independent filmmaking, 492–493,
      499–500
   Italian Neorealism, 485–486, 499
   New Hollywood, 489–492, 499–500
   resources on, 496–500
   Soviet Montage, 478–481, 498
   Surrealism, 477–478
film movements, 464–465. *See also specific*
   movements
film noir
   and *Breathless,* 428, 429, 430, 431
   and French Impressionism, 477
   and German Expressionism, 474
   lighting in, 196
   and *The Thin Blue Line,* 450
   tonality in, 232
film stocks, 4–5, 229–231
film technology, 2–8, 41–42
filters, 233, 234
Final Fantasy, 174
final (fine) cut, 30
Finally Got the News, 39
Fincher, David, 45, 492
fine (final) cut, 30
Finye (The Wind), 184, 186, 299
Fire!, 469
Fires Were Started, 129
Fireworks, 114
first assistant directors, 26
Fischinger, Oskar, 163
Fist Fight, 146, 147, 333
Fist of the North Star, 173
Fitzhamon, Lewin, 469
Five Star Final, 92

flashbacks, 74–75, 76, 77
  in *Citizen Kane,* 92, 95–96, 97, 99–100, 396
  in crime thrillers, 114
  and depth of knowledge, 86
  and editing, 306, 326, 331
  in French Impressionism, 475
  and New Hollywood, 491–492
  and plot development, 81, 99–100
  in *Raging Bull,* 459
  in *The Thin Blue Line,* 448
flashforwards, 75, 91, 306–307
flashing, 233
The Flavor of Green Tea over Rice, 275
Flirting with Disaster, 492
The Fly, 189, 190, 491
Flynn, Errol, 167
focal length, 237–242
Focus Features, 17–18
focus in cinematography, 242–243
Foley, Jack, 31
foley artists, 31
following shots, 273
Fonda, Henry, 202, 203
Fong, Allen, 494
Footlight Parade, 304, 334
For a Few Dollars More, 119
For a Fistful of Dollars, 116
Ford, John
  and editing, 41
  How Green Was My Valley, 350, 374
  My Darling Clementine, 118
  The Quiet Man, 87
  The Searchers, 119–120, 234
  She Wore a Yellow Ribbon, 177, 360, 364
  Straight Shooting, 119, 120
  Young Mr. Lincoln, 209
  See also Stagecoach
foreign films
  director's role, 41
  and distribution, 13, 14
  dubbing/subtitles, 388
form, 48–67
  associational, 154, 156–162, 404, 409, 443–446, 451
  and cause and effect, 72–74
  vs. content, 50
  defined, 49
  development, 63–65
  and emotions, 53–54, 67
  and evaluation, 58–59
  and expectations, 50–52, 54
  function, 60–61
  and long takes, 287
  and meaning, 55–58, 67
  and mise-en-scene, 176, 208

and prior experience, 52–53
  repetition, 61
  rhetorical, 133, 140–146
  and sound, 356–359
  and style, 389, 391–392, 404
  as system, 48–49
  unity, 65
  variation, 62–63
  See also abstract form; categorical form; narrative form
Forrest Gump, 34, 132, 133, 166, 490, 491
42nd Street, 123, 217, 218, 304, 483
  editing in, 333, 334
Foster, Jodie, 295
found-footage films, 147, 158–162
The 400 Blows (Les Quatre cent coups), 73–74, 82, 487, 488
Four Nights of a Dreamer, 364
Fox Film Corporation, 469
frame. *See* screen space
frame enlargements, 44–45
frames, 2
frame velocity, 276
framing, 252–283
  animated films, 259–260
  camera angle, 260–261, 263, 264, 265, 266
  camera height, 261–262
  in *Citizen Kane,* 263, 264, 277, 396
  dimensions, 253–257, 292
  early cinema, 252–253
  functions of, 263–266
  and Italian neorealism, 485–486
  level, 261
  split-screen imagery, 257–258
  and style, 402, 407, 408
  in *The Thin Blue Line,* 449
  and video, 21–23
  See also camera distance; mobile framing; offscreen space
Frampton, Hollis, 52, 146, 191
Franju, Georges, 317–318, 319
Frankenstein, 121, 122
Frankenstein (1931), 483
Frank Film, 164
Freak Orlando, 186, 187
Frears, Stephen, 49
freeze-framing, 236
French Impressionism, 474–477, 498
  and editing, 304, 334, 476
  and lighting, 470
  See also specific films and directors
French New Wave, 486–489, 499. *See also specific films and directors*
frequency. *See* repetition
Freudian psychology, 477
Freund, Karl, 474

Friedkin, William, 489
Friedrich, Su, 146
From Dusk to Dawn, 114
From Hell, 112
frontality, 218–219
frontal lighting, 192
front projection, 244–246
The Fugitive
  editing in, 306
  genre of, 112
  sound in, 371
  special effects in, 248
Fuji, 147, 163, 169–171
Fuller, Samuel, 270, 292, 487
full-frame images, 21, 22, 23
Full Moon over Paris, 489
function, 60–61
Fury, 264, 265, 320, 336
futzing, 353

gaffers, 28
Galapogos, 130
Galeta, Ivan, 147
Gallardo, Carlos, 37
Gance, Abel
  and French Impressionist movement, 475, 477
  Napoleon, 253, 292, 476, 477
  rhythmic editing, 304
  La Roue, 257, 258, 294, 334, 476
gangster/outlaw films
  and *Breathless,* 428, 433
  and crime thrillers, 113
  and cycles, 115
  social ideology in, 117
Gap-Toothed Women
  form in, 134–140
  style in, 401–404
Garbo, Greta, 201
Garland, Judy, 123
Garlic Is as Good as Ten Mothers, 134
Garmes, Lee, 292
Gas Food Lodging, 491
Gaudreault, André, 469
gauge, 5–8
gauges, 5
Gehr, Ernie, 241–242
genre conventions, 52–53, 110–111
  in *Citizen Kane,* 92, 400
  and form, 52–53, 59
  in horror films, 121
  in musicals, 126
  in *North by Northwest,* 109, 418–419
  and sound, 368
  in Westerns, 119
  See also genres; iconography

, 108–118
    and *Chungking Express,* 114, 442
    definitions, 108–110
    development of, 111, 115–116
    and *Man with a Movie Camera,* 444
    resources on, 127
    and social ideology, 116–118, 123, 127
    and special effects, 291
    See also genre conventions; *specific genres*
Gentiño, Octavio, 285
Geography of the Body, 146, 148
German Expressionism, 472–474
    and acting, 205, 473
    and horror films, 122, 473, 474
    and mise-en-scene, 177, 473
    resources on, 497–498
    See also specific films and directors
Germany Year Zero, 179, 485, 486
Ghostbusters, 254, 255
Ghost in the Shell, 174
Ghosts before Breakfast, 473
Giraudoux, 487
Gish, Lillian, 201
La Glace à trois faces, 334
Gladiator, 29, 116
Glass, Philip, 449
glass shots, 243
The Gleaners and I, 39
GO, 77
goal-oriented plots, 80–81, 89–90
Godard, Jean-Luc
    Band of Outsiders, 374–375, 488
    Les Carabiniers, 230–231, 488
    La Chinoise, 29, 192, 213, 336, 337
    Contempt, 179, 292, 489
    and "dead time", 91
    and French New Wave movement, 487, 489
    Passion, 192, 489
    Pierrot le fou, 337–338
    Two or Three Things I Know about Her, 370
    and widescreen ratios, 292
    See also Breathless
The Godfather
    editing in, 306–307, 331
    genre of, 110, 115, 130
    and New Hollywood, 489, 490
    sound in, 355
The Godfather Part III, 189
Goldblum, Jeff, 190
Gold Diggers of 1933, 117, 334, 483
Gold Diggers of 1935, 334
The Golden Boat, 16
Goldman, William, 49
Gone with the Wind, 50
The Good, the Bad, and the Ugly, 50

"good bad man", 119
The Good Earth, 483
Good Machine, 16–17
Goodman, Jenniphr, 17
Gosford Park, 17
Goskino, 479
grader (color timer), 231
grading, 231, 250–251
The Graduate, 237
A Grand Day Out, 164
Grand Hotel, 437
Grand Illusion
    genre of, 110
    mobile framing in, 277–283
    style in, 391, 393, 394
Grandma's Reading Glass, 292
graphic continuity/discontinuity, 297–303
    in *The Birds,* 297, 300–303
    in *October,* 341–342
    and rhythm, 333–334
    and style, 406, 408–409, 411
    and time, 332
    in *Tokyo Story,* 437
graphic design, 205
graphic matching, 297, 298, 332, 408, 411, 437
Grease, 19
The Great K & A Train Robbery, 115
The Great Train Robbery, 469
Greed, 180, 268
Greenaway, Peter, 147, 210, 258, 259
greenery men, 31
The Green Room, 197
Il Grido, 212
Griffith, D. W., 469–470
    The Battle at Elderbush Gulch, 322, 325
    and Hollywood studio system, 471
    and MPCC, 468
    Musketeers of Pig Alley, 259, 260
    and Soviet Montage, 479
    See also The Birth of a Nation; Intolerance
grips, 28
Grooms, Red, 147, 149
grosses, 13
gross-out comedies, 115
Groundhog Day, 77–78, 109, 115, 184
grouping. *See* associational form
group styles, 390
Grunt, 249
La Guerre est finie, 271, 337
guide tracks, 32
Gun Crazy, 428
Gundam, 173
Güney, Yilmaz, 209–210, 214

haiku, 156
Hail Mary, 489

hairdressers, 28
Halloween, 489
Hamlet, 368
Hammid, Alexander, 38
hand coloring, 232, 233
hand-held shots, 269–270
    in *Breathless,* 431, 488
    in documentaries, 402
    and French New Wave, 487–488
Hannah and Her Sisters, 90, 204
Hans Christian Andersen, 124
Hanson, Curtis. *See L.A. Confidential*
Hard Core, 490
A Hard Day's Night, 275
hard mattes, 254
Harlan County, U.S.A., 38, 39, 130
Harlin, Rennie, 490
Harris, Leslie, 38, 491
Hart, William S., 119, 177, 470, 475
Hartley, Hal, 16, 492
The Haunting, 121
Hawks, Howard
    The Big Sleep, 41, 83, 85, 86, 90
    Bringing Up Baby, 317, 318, 490
    on close-ups, 263
    continuity editing, 311
    on dialogue, 416
    and French New Wave, 487
    See also His Girl Friday
Haynes, Todd, 16, 18, 350–351
Head, Edith, 40
head-on shots, 322
Heart Like a Wheel, 131
Heat, 113, 189
Heckerling, Amy, 491
height of framing, 261–262
Heimatfilm, 108
Heist, 113
heist/caper films, 112–113
helicopter shots, 267
Hell's Hinges, 119
Help!, 275
Henry: Portrait of a Serial Killer, 113
Hepworth, Cecil, 468, 469
Herzog, Werner, 265
hierarchy of knowledge, 84, 419
high-definition (HD) video, 10
high-definition television (HDTV), 21
high-key lighting, 195
High Noon, 230
high-speed cinematography, 236
Hindle, Will, 276
Hiroshima mon amour, 86, 306
Hirsch, Paul, 306
His Girl Friday
    and *Citizen Kane,* 92
    closure in, 100

conflict in, 90
costume in, 186–187
critical analysis, 415–418
focal length in, 238
reframing in, 273
sound in, 367
His New Job, 115
historical films
color in, 291
form in, 50
genre of, 131
and German Expressionism, 473
make-up in, 189
special effects in, 291
Hitchcock, Alfred
and depth of knowledge, 85
The Family Plot, 114
and French Impressionism, 477
and French New Wave, 487, 488
and mobile framing, 273
Notorious, 25, 418
on range of knowledge, 84–85
Rear Window, 112, 320, 321, 322, 396
rhythmic editing, 334
Saboteur, 264
and shot duration, 285–286
and UFA, 472
Vertigo, 244, 245, 273
*See also The Birds; The Man Who Knew
Too Much; North by Northwest; Psycho*
hit-man films, 112
Hollywood, 291, 468. *See also* classical
Hollywood cinema; *specific films and
directors*
Homer, 53
Hong Kong cinema, contemporary, 116,
493–496, 500. *See also specific films
and directors*
Hong Kong movies, 116
Hoop Dreams
genre of, 130
narrator in, 87
parallelism in, 70
plot development in, 81
publicity, 19
Hope, Ted, 16, 17–18
Hopkins, Anthony, 202
Hopper, Dennis, 489
horror films, 120–123
cause and effect in, 73
and crime thrillers, 113, 114
and French Impressionism, 477
and genre mixing, 116
and German Expressionism, 122, 473,
474
lighting in, 193, 196
make-up in, 121–122, 189, 190

resources on, 127
sound in, 348
violence in, 123, 457
Horse Feathers, 190, 242
Hot Shots, 371
Hou Hsiao-hsien, 218–219
Hour of the Furnaces, 285
house nut, 13
House of Games, 74, 114
House Party, 491
Howard, Ron, 271, 390
How Green Was My Valley, 350, 374
Howitt, Peter, 77
Hu, King, 254, 493, 495
Hudlin, Reginald, 491
Hughes, Albert, 491
Hughes, Allen, 491
Hui, Ann, 494
Huillet, Danièle, 91
The Chronicle of Anna Magdalena Bach,
214, 215, 248, 252, 261, 291
Hulce, Tom, 203
The Hulk, 17
humor, 488. *See also* comedies
Hung, Sammo, 493, 494, 496
Hunter, Tim, 373–374
The Hunt for Red October
genre of, 112
sound in, 7, 32, 354–355, 360
Huston, John, 191. *See also* The Maltese
Falcon

The Ice Storm, 16
iconography
and genre, 111, 122–123
in horror films, 121, 122–123
in musicals, 125
in Westerns, 119
ideology. *See* social ideology
Igloolik Isuma Productions, 39
Imagine, 40
Imax system, 5, 7, 130
Im Kwon-Taek, 257, 258
implicit meaning, 56–57
in documentaries, 140, 446
in experimental films, 157, 162
Impressionism. *See* French Impressionism
improvisation, 177
Ince, Thomas H., 470, 475
independent filmmaking, 16–18
and classical Hollywood cinema, 471
crime thrillers, 114
and distribution, 13
and narrative form, 492–493
production, 37–38
resources on, 499–500
time manipulation in, 77

See also specific films and directors
Indiana Jones films, 490
individualization, 200, 202
Industrial Light & Magic, 166, 291, 491
inference, 73
in medias res openings, 80
Innocence Unprotected, 232, 233
L'Inondation, 475
inserts, 30, 32, 449–450
nondiegetic, 336–337
The Insider, 199, 236
intensifed continuity editing, 327–331, 345
intensity of effect, 58
Interiors, 490
internal diegetic sound, 368
international distribution, 20, 33, 114
internegative, 33
Internet, 18, 19
interpositive, 33
interpretation, 56–57
and discontinuity editing, 343
in experimental films, 157
intertitles, 208
interview documentaries, 130
In the Bedroom, 17, 199
In the Line of Fire, 112
In the Year of the Pig, 130
Intolerance
editing in, 304, 306, 470, 480
framing in, 257, 258, 275
setting in, 180
and Soviet Montage, 479
Invaders from Mars, 132
investigation plot pattern, 81, 112. *See also*
mystery plot pattern
iris masking, 257, 258, 271, 476
The Italian, 470
Italian Neorealism, 199, 485–486, 487, 499.
See also specific films and directors
Itami, Juzo, 181–182, 299
Ivan the Terrible
acting in, 203, 204
compositional balance in, 210–211
costume in, 186
deep space in, 227
editing in, 308
lighting in, 193, 197, 198
make-up in, 189
mobile framing in, 267, 268
setting in, 180–181
sound in, 350
Ivens, Joris, 129
I. Vitelloni, 486

J'accuse, 292
Jackie Brown, 113, 114
Jackson, Peter, 249

, Ken, 146, 236
Jacquot, Benoit, 243
Jannings, Emil, 474
Janowitz, Hans, 472–473
Janscó, Miklós, 274, 285
Japanese anime, 166, 173–174
Jarman, Derek, 8, 147, 366
Jarmusch, Jim, 38, 491
Jaws
    cause and effect in, 73
    characters in, 72
    climax of, 82
    deep focus in, 243, 491
    genre of, 122
    mobile framing in, 273–274
    montage sequence in, 332
    and New Hollywood, 489
    sound in, 348
The Jazz Singer, 123, 481
*Jeanne Dielman, 23 quai du Commerce,
    1808 Bruxelles,* 217
Jennings, Humphrey, 129
Jerry Maguire, 201, 202, 324, 326
La Jetée, 364
Jet Lag, 13
Jezebel
    continuity editing in, 319, 320
    framing in, 259, 272, 275
    lighting in, 194–195
JFK, 132
Jobs, Steve, 166
Johnny Guitar, 488
Jones, Charles M. (Chuck), 167–169, 213,
    243
Jonze, Spike, 45, 492
journey plot pattern, 53, 63
The Joy Luck Club, 491–492
Jules and Jim
    editing in, 339
    and French New Wave, 488
    music in, 357–359, 360
    narrator in, 87
julien donkey-boy, 11, 270
jump cuts, 335–336, 337
    in *Breathless,* 431
    and French New Wave, 488
Jurassic Park
    computer-generated imagery in, 30, 166,
        226
    and New Hollywood, 490
    production, 25
    sound in, 6, 353, 355
    special effects in, 28
Just Another Girl on the IRT, 38, 491
Just Imagine, 115
juxtaposition
    and abstract form, 150

and associational form, 154, 156
    and discontinuity editing, 340, 342
    in documentaries, 444, 445
    and Soviet Montage, 480

Kael, Pauline, 105
Kalatazov, Mikhail, 238
Kaminski, Janusz, 392
Kanal, 196
Karloff, Boris, 121, 122
Kasbah, 233, 234
Kawin, Bruce F., 104
Kazan, Elia, 390
Kean, 334
Keaton, Buster
    framing, 265–266
    and MGM, 471
    style, 389
    See also Our Hospitality
Keep on Rocking, 270
Kelley, William, 24
Kelly, Gene, 40, 123. *See also* Singin' in the
    Rain
key grips, 28
key light, 193, 194
Kiarostami, Abbas, 259, 260
Kieslowski, Krzysztof, 78, 390
Kiki's Delivery Service, 173
The Killer, 74, 113, 114, 494
Killifer, Jack, 332
The Killing, 87, 114, 431
Kinetoscope, 466
King, Stephen, 322
King Kong, 121, 164
Kino, 13
Kino-Glaz, 443
Kino-Pravda, 479
Kiss Me Deadly, 65
Kitano, Takeshi, 275
The Kleptomaniac, 469
Koppel, Barbara, 38, 39
Korine, Harmony, 11, 270
Koyaanisqatsi
    associational form in, 154, 156, 157
    and city symphony genre, 444
    focal length in, 237, 238
    meaning in, 162
    speed of motion in, 235
Kracauer, Siegfried, 225, 387
Kramer, Robert, 39
Kubelka, Peter, 333
Kubrick, Stanley, 33, 431
Kuleshov, Lev, 305, 334, 479–480
Kuleshov effect, 305–306, 318–319, 478
Kunuk, Zacharias, 39
Kuras, Ellen, 10
Kurosawa, Akira

and focal length, 237, 238, 239–240
    and genre mixing, 116
    Sanjuro, 254, 256
    on sound, 348
    and widescreen ratios, 292
    See also Rashomon; Seven Samurai

L.A. Confidential
    cause and effect in, 73
    costume in, 187
    editing in, 327–331
    plot development in, 112
Lady in the Lake, 292
Lancelot du Lac, 216, 294
Lane, Anthony, 353
Lang, Fritz, 264, 265, 292, 324, 473–474
Lapis, 165
Larks on a String, 209
Lasky, Jesse L., 469
The Last Laugh, 292
The Last of the Mohicans, 119, 361–364
The Last Seduction, 113
Last Tango in Paris, 243, 244, 254, 255
Last Year at Marienbad
    alternative memories in, 78–79
    editing in, 339
    mobile framing in, 273
    subjectivity in, 86, 91
Lattuada, 485
Lau Kar-leung, 493
Laura, 273
Lawrence of Arabia, 371
leading roles, 31
lead men, 31
Lean, David, 371
Lee, Ang, 16–17
Lee, Bruce, 493
Lee, Spike
    Bamboozled, 10, 29
    and New Hollywood, 491
    She's Gotta Have It, 318, 320, 491
    and video, 45
    See also Do the Right Thing
The Left-Handed Gun, 119
The Legend of Fong Sai-Yuk, 305
Léger, Fernand. *See Ballet mécanique*
Lemon, 191
Lenica, Jan, 210
Lenin, V. I., 479
Leone, Sergio, 33, 116, 119
Léon Gaumont, 475
Leon the Professional, 112
Leroy, Mervyn, 484
Lessons of Darkness, 265
Lester, Richard, 275
Lethal Weapon, 14, 115
letterboxing, 21

Letter from Siberia, 348, 349
A Letter to Three Wives, 199
level of framing, 261
Lévi-Strauss, Claude, 127
Lewton, Val, 122
L'Herbier, Marcel, 475, 476, 477
Li, Jet, 495
The Life of an American Fireman, 469
Life on a String, 211, 237, 238
lighting, 191–198
    in animated films, 164
    in *Breathless,* 428, 430–431
    in classical Hollywood cinema, 194–195,
        470, 484
    color, 196–197
    and computer-generated imagery,
        197–198
    in contemporary Hong Kong cinema, 495
    and De Mille, 470
    and depth cues, 213
    direction, 192–193, 194
    and editing, 297
    and French Impressionism, 470
    and French New Wave, 487
    and genre conventions, 111
    and Italian neorealism, 485
    in *Meet Me in St. Louis,* 455–456
    in musicals, 125
    and narrative form, 221–222
    quality, 191–192
    in *Raging Bull,* 459
    source, 193–196
Lilo and Stitch, 124
Liman, Doug, 77
The Limey, 492, 493
limited palette, 210, 216
Linde, David, 16, 17
linear perspective, 214–215
line producers, 24
The Lion King, 19, 124
lip-synching, 125
literary theory, 103, 104
Little Big Man, 119
Little Caesar, 483
The Little Foxes, 227, 238, 484
Little Shop of Horrors, 369
Little Stabs at Happiness, 146
live-action films, 162, 166, 167
The Living End, 492
loaders, 31
Local Hero, 356–357
location shooting, 179, 430–431
Lock, Stock, and Two Smoking Barrels, 114
Lola Montés, 277
Long Day's Journey into Night, 81
The Longest Nite, 495
long shots, 262

long takes, 284–289
    in animated films, 168
    in *Do the Right Thing,* 426, 427
    and editing, 293, 294
    and mobile framing, 286–289
Look Who's Talking, 491
looping (dubbing), 32, 388, 485
Lord, Peter, 164
The Lord of the Rings (Tolkien), 53
*The Lord of the Rings: The Fellowship
    of the Ring*
    DVD release, 21
    music in, 357
    special effects in, 246, 248, 249–251, 252,
        291
    tonality in, 232, 233
The Lord of the Rings films, 357. *See also
    The Lord of the Rings: The Fellowship
    of the Ring*
Lorentz, Pare, 142–146
Losey, Joseph, 373
Lost Highway, 114
loudness, 350
*Love Affair, or the Case of the Missing
    Switchboard Operator,* 91
Love Me Tonight, 235, 304, 334, 351
low-budget filmmaking, 122
low-key illumination, 196
Lubitsch, Ernst, 472
Lucas, George
    and digital cinema, 11
    Industrial Light & Magic, 166, 291, 491
    and New Hollywood, 489, 490, 491
    THS theater-certification program, 347
    THX 1138, 187, 188, 210
Lumet, Sidney, 81, 202
Lumière, Auguste, 177, 466, 467
Lumière, Louis
    and framing, 252–253
    and French New Wave, 488
    and Méliès, 177
    and projection, 466
    and setting, 179, 467
La Lune á une mètre, 178
Lye, Len, 231
Lynch, David
    and crime thriller genre, 114
    on crossing the axis, 322
    Dune, 368
    and New Hollywood, 491
    on sound, 355
    The Straight Story, 37, 131, 265
    and video, 45

M, 183, 324, 474
Maas, Willard, 146
Mackendrick, Alexander, 218

Maclaine, Christopher, 261
Maclean, Alison, 200
Macross, 173
Madame Dubarry (Passion), 472
Mad Max beyond Thunder Dome, 27
*Mad Max II. See The Road Warrior (Mad
    Max II)*
"magical comedies", 115
Magnani, Anna, 199
magnetic sound tracks, 7, 8
The Magnificent Ambersons
    depth in, 227
    sound in, 366, 369–370, 375
    widescreen ratio in, 257, 258
The Magnificent Seven, 116
Magnolia, 22, 23, 370, 424, 437
Les Maîtres fous, 38
Makavejev, Dušan, 91, 232
make-up, 189–191
    and German Expressionism, 473
    in horror films, 121–122, 189, 190
    in *Raging Bull,* 459
    staff, 28
    and style, 408
Malcolm X, 131, 491
Maldoror, Sarah, 213
Malick, Terence, 267
Mallrats, 492
The Maltese Falcon
    continuity editing in, 313–317, 319–320,
        332
    director role in, 41
    as *film noir,* 428
    framing in, 264, 265
    style in, 392, 394
Mamet, David, 114, 208
Mamoulian, Rouben, 227, 235, 304, 334,
    351, 482
A Man Escaped, 377–385
    motifs in, 380
    music in, 380–381
    narration in, 377–378
    scene analysis, 381–385
    sound in, 352, 378–379
    style in, 391, 392, 393
manga, 174
Manhattan, 21
Mann, Anthony, 81, 243
Mann, Michael, 113, 236, 361–364
*Manufacturing Consent: Noam Chomsky
    and the Media,* 40
The Man Who Knew Too Much, 72, 73
The Man Who Shot Liberty Valance, 183, 351
The Man Who Wasn't There, 17, 114
*Man with a Movie Camera (Chelovek s
    kinoapparatom),* 129, 235
    critical analysis, 443–446

The Man with the Rubber Head, 244, 245
Marey, Étienne-Jules, 465
El Mariachi, 37, 492
Marker, Chris, 348, 349, 364
marketing. *See* promotion
Mars Attacks!, 211
martial arts films, 493–495
Martin, Steve, 200
Marx, Groucho, 190
Mary Jane's Mishap, 469
The Mascot, 165, 207
M*A*S*H, 489
masking, 254, 257, 258, 271, 476
Mass for the Dakota Sioux, 146
Massive, 249, 250
master shot, 29
matches on action
    and continuity editing, 315, 332
    development of, 470
    and discontinuity editing, 335, 336, 339
    in *Tokyo Story,* 435–436
The Matrix
    computer-generated imagery in, 34–35,
        166, 226
    and contemporary Hong Kong cinema,
        496
    genre mixing in, 116
    and independent filmmaking, 114,
        492–493
matte artists, 31
matte lines, 247
matte work, 246–247, 249, 484
Mauvais sang, 196
Mayer, Carl, 472–473
Mayer, Louis B., 36
Maysles, Albert, 134
Maytime, 92
Mazursky, Paul, 394
McLaren, Norman, 163, 164, 213
McTiernan, John. *See The Hunt for Red
    October*
meaning
    in documentaries, 139–140, 445, 446
    in experimental films, 157, 162
    and form, 55–58, 67
    and framing, 263
    in *Meet Me in St. Louis,* 456–457
    and style, 394
Mean Streets, 460
medium close-ups, 262
medium long shots, 262
medium shots, 262
Meet Me in St. Louis
    color in, 231, 291, 454
    critical analysis, 452–457
    genre of, 124
    social ideology in, 57, 117

Melbourne–Cooper, Arthur, 164
Méliès, Georges
    and mise-en-scene, 177–179, 467–468
    and special effects, 291
    and superimposition, 243–244, 245
melodramas, 115, 116
Melville, Jean-Pierre, 112
Memento, 77, 114
Memphis Belle, 132
Menace II Society, 116, 491
Menichelli, Pina, 202, 203
Men in Black, 123
Men in Black II, 123
mental subjectivity, 85, 88, 101
Menzel, Jir[v]í, 209
Menzies, William Cameron, 484
Le Mépris (Contempt), 179, 292, 489
merchandising, 18–19
The Mermaid, 178
Meshes of the Afternoon, 38
Metropolis, 473–474
Metz, Christian, 67
MGM, 469, 482–483
Mickey Mousing, 360
Microcosmos, 130
Mighty Aphrodite, 116
Milestone, 13
Milestone, Lewis, 304
Miller, Bennett, 130
Miller, George, 269. *See also* The Road
        Warrior (Mad Max II)
Le Million
    costume in, 187
    editing in, 304, 334
    plot development in, 81
    sound in, 365, 366
miniatures, 182–183, 198, 199, 249
Minnelli, Vincente, 487, 488. *See also Meet
        Me in St. Louis*
Minority Report, 109, 114
minor players, 27
The Minus Man, 113
The Miracle Worker, 194
Miramax, 13, 16, 492
mise-en-scene, 176–228
    in *Breathless,* 430–431
    and change, 207
    and computer-generated imagery, 248,
        249, 250
    costume, 26, 28, 119, 184, 186–188, 221,
        223
    defined, 176–177
    Do the Right Thing, 423–424
    and expectations, 208
    and French New Wave, 487
    and German Expressionism, 177, 473
    in *His Girl Friday,* 417–418

    and Italian neorealism, 485
    and long takes, 286
    in *Man with a Movie Camera,* 445
    in *Meet Me in St. Louis,* 454–455
    Méliès, 177–179, 467–468
    and mobile framing, 278–279
    movement, 198–199
    and narrative form, 220–225
    and realism, 177, 225–226
    resources on, 225–227
    setting, 179–184
    and special effects, 248
    and style, 397–398, 402–403, 407–408,
        409–410
    and Surrealism, 478
    and time, 217–219
    See also acting; lighting; makeup;
        space
Mission: Impossible, 490
The Mission, 496
Les Mistons, 488
Mitra, Subrata, 196
Mi Vida Loca, 491
Mix, Tom, 118
mixing sound, 353–355
Miyazaki, Hayao, 14, 166, 173
Mizoguchi, Kenji
    and long takes, 285, 286–287, 288
    and mobile framing, 275
    Naniwa Elegy, 219
    Sansho the Bailiff, 86
    Sisters of Gion, 227, 286–287, 288
mobile framing, 266–283
    in animated films, 164, 270, 271
    in *Do the Right Thing,* 426–427
    and French Impressionism, 476
    and French New Wave, 487
    in *Grand Illusion,* 277–283
    and introduction of sound, 482, 483
    and long takes, 286–289
    motion control, 250, 269, 491
    in musicals, 125
    and omniscient narration, 102
    patterns of, 276–277
    in *Raging Bull,* 269, 459
    and space, 269, 272–274
    and style, 408
    and temporal duration, 284
    and time, 275–276
    types of, 266–272
mockumentaries, 132, 147, 270
model-makers, 31
model (puppet) animation, 164, 165
Modern Times, 352
monochromatic color design, 210, 211
Mon Oncle d'Amérique, 335
monophonic sound, 6, 8

Monsoon Wedding, 17
Monsters, Inc., 166
montage, 91, 402. *See also* montage
    sequences
montage sequences
    in *Citizen Kane,* 92, 97
    and continuity editing, 332–333
    and dissolves, 304
    and French Impressionism, 477
Montage style. *See* Soviet Montage
Montgomery, Robert, 292
Moore, Julianne, 350–351
Moore, Michael, 13, 72, 87, 172
moral criteria, 58
Moreau, Jeanne, 488
Morgan!, 268
Morris, Errol. *See The Thin Blue Line*
Morrison, Toni, 69
Mortal Combat (Crippled Avengers), 493
Mosjoukin, Ivan, 334
Mother, 211
Mother's Day, 148
Mothlight, 163
motifs, 61, 62
    and cause and effect, 72–73
    in *The Cheat,* 470
    in *Chungking Express,* 440–441
    in experimental films, 151, 152, 154, 162
    and lighting, 196
    in *Man with a Movie Camera,* 443, 444
    in *Meet Me in St. Louis,* 454–455
    and mobile framing, 278–279
    in *North by Northwest,* 419
    in *Our Hospitality,* 222–223
    and props, 183–184
    in *Raging Bull,* 459, 461
    and sound, 351, 357–358, 380
    and style, 404–405, 410
    in *The Thin Blue Line,* 449–450, 451–452
    See also repetition
motion control, 250, 269, 491
Motion Picture Patents Company (MPCC),
    468
motivation, 60–61
    and cause and effect, 72–73
    in *Citizen Kane,* 98–99
    in classical Hollywood cinema, 90
    lack of, 91
Moulin Rouge, 345
Mouris, Frank, 164
movement
    and editing, 303
    and mise-en-scene, 198–199
    and mobile framing, 273
    and space, 209, 213–214, 216
    and style, 408
    and time, 217

    See also camera movement; mobile
      framing
A Movie
    editing in, 306, 333
    form in, 157–162, 409, 451
    found footage in, 147, 157
    sound in, 356, 366, 411
    style in, 409–412
"movie brats", 489–490
Mozhukin, Ivan, 478
Mr. Arkadin, 261
Mr. Hulot's Holiday
    editing in, 335
    sound in, 353, 365, 366
    space in, 81
Mr. Smith Goes to Washington, 332
Mulholland Drive, 114
multiple-frame (split-screen) imagery,
    257–258, 476
multiplexes, 9
Multiplicity, 34
The Mummy (1932), 122
The Mummy (1999), 122
Murch, Walter, 345, 370
Murder, My Sweet, 87
Murdoch, Rupert, 19
Murnau, F. W., 227, 235, 292, 473–474
Murphy, Dudley. *See Ballet mécanique*
Murphy, J. J., 63, 149–150
music
    in animated films, 163, 174
    and dialogue, 352
    in documentaries, 143–144, 405–406, 449
    in experimental films, 157, 160
    and form, 356–359
    and genre conventions, 111
    in *A Man Escaped,* 380–381
    and montage sequences, 332
    resources on, 387–388
    and rhythm, 360, 361–364, 476
    and silent films, 348
    and style, 399–400, 405–406
    video alteration, 21
    See also sound
musicals, 123–126, 483
    and *Citizen Kane,* 92
    color in, 125, 291
    editing in, 333–334
    and genre mixing, 116
    motivation in, 90
    origins of, 115
    resources on, 127
    rhythm in, 360
    social ideology in, 117, 124–125,
      452–457
music videos, 334, 426
Musketeers of Pig Alley, 259, 260

Mutoscope, 3
Muybridge, Eadweard, 465
My Big Fat Greek Wedding, 18, 19
My Darling Clementine, 118
My Hustler, 285, 286
My Left Foot, 13
My Man Godfrey, 61, 72–73
My Neighbor Totoro, 14, 173
Myrick, Daniel, 18
mystery plot pattern, 63
    in *Citizen Kane,* 73, 94, 97–98
    and restricted narration, 83, 90
    and sound, 348
    vs. suspense, 418
    temporal order in, 75
mythologicals, 108

Nair, Mira, 17
The Naked City, 87, 444
The Naked Gun, 371
The Naked Kiss, 270, 292
Naniwa Elegy, 219
Napoleon, 253, 292, 476, 477
narration, 82–89
    in *Chungking Express,* 438–439
    in *Citizen Kane,* 100–102, 397
    and depth of knowledge, 85–86, 87–88
    and Italian neorealism, 486
    in *Raging Bull,* 460
    and range of knowledge, 83–85, 87, 88,
      101
    resources on, 104
    in *The Road Warrior,* 87–89
    and setting, 181–182
    and sound, 356, 366, 367, 374, 377–379
    in *Tokyo Story,* 433–434, 435, 437
    See also narrators
narrative form, 49, 68–105
    in animated films, 68, 167–169
    in classical Hollywood cinema, 89–91,
      469, 470, 471, 484
    in contemporary Hong Kong cinema,
      494–495
    in crime thrillers, 114
    and crosscutting, 324
    and curiosity, 52
    defined, 69–70
    in documentaries, 68, 69–70, 87, 89, 132,
      447–449
    in early cinema, 468
    and expectations, 68–69, 91–92
    in experimental films, 68, 147
    and framing, 264
    and independent filmmaking, 492–493
    and Italian neorealism, 486
    and mise-en-scene, 220–225
    and mobile framing, 275–276, 277–278

narrative form, *(continued)*
  plot development, 80–82, 99–100
  resources on, 103–104
  and Soviet Montage, 480–481
  and space, 76, 80
  and story/plot distinction, 70–72, 73, 74, 80
  and style, 397–398
  and time, 74–76, 77–79, 95–98, 104
  See also cause and effect; narration; plot development
narrators, 86–87, 88–89
  multiple, 101
  nondiegetic, 366, 370
  nonsimultaneous, 374
The Narrow Trail, 470
Nashville, 90, 424, 437
nature documentaries, 130
negative cost, 25
Neighbors, 164
Neorealism. *See* Italian Neorealism
The Net, 112
New Hollywood, 489–492, 499–500. *See also specific films and directors*
New Jack City, 491
newspaper-reporter genre, 92
Newsreel, 39
New Wave. *See* French New Wave
New York, New York, 241
New York Actors Studio, 199
The Nibelungen, 473
Niblo, Fred, 470
Nick of Time, 112
Night and Fog, 299
The Nightmare before Christmas, 164, 165
Night of the Living Dead, 122
The Night of the Shooting Stars, 187, 188
Nights of Cabiria, 196, 197
Nixon, 131
Noailles, Vicomte de, 478
Nolan, Christopher, 77
No Lies, 132
noncharacter narrators, 87
nondiegetic elements, 71
  in *Do the Right Thing,* 426
  inserts, 336–337
  sound, 366–367, 369–370
  nondiegetic inserts, 336–337
nonlinear systems, 32
nonsimultaneous sound, 372
nontheatrical exhibition, 8, 9. *See also* video
normal lenses, 237, 238
norms, 53
North by Northwest
  characters in, 72
  closure in, 100
  critical analysis, 418–423
  depth of knowledge in, 86

framing in, 263, 264
genre of, 109, 418–419
plot development in, 53, 81, 82, 112, 418–419
range of knowledge in, 84, 85, 90, 419–420, 421, 422–423
sound in, 366
space in, 80
story/plot in, 70–71
time in, 75, 419
North to Alaska, genre of, 109
Nosferatu
  depth in, 227
  and German Expressionism, 473
  make-up in, 122
  speed of motion in, 235
  and Surrealism, 477
Notorious, 25, 418
Not Reconciled, 91
Notting Hill, 284
Nouvelle vague, 489
Nowhere to Hide, 114
Nuñez, Victor, 37

objective narration, 85, 86
  in *Citizen Kane,* 101, 102
  in classical Hollywood cinema, 90
  See also subjectivity
Obsession, 489
Ocean's 11, 113
October
  editing in, 308, 334, 339–343, 480
  and expectations, 52.
  framing in, 263, 264
  lack of protagonist in, 90
  style in, 391, 392, 393
  temporal duration in, 76
October Films, 17, 492
Odyssey (Homer), 53
off-center linear perspective, 214–215
offscreen space
  and comedy, 266
  and mobile framing, 272
  and sound, 259, 352, 360, 364, 367, 427
  zones of, 258–259, 260
O'Gara, Sean Morijiro Sunada, 146
Ohayu, 334, 335, 393
Old and New, 227, 339
The Old Dark House, 483
Olmi, Ermanno, 486
Olympia, Part 2, 133–134, 294
omniscient narration, 83, 102, 366, 397
Once upon a Time in America, 33
Once Upon a Time in China, 494
Ondr[v]íc[v]ek, Miorslav, 332
The One-Armed Swordsman, 493
One Froggy Evening, 213, 243
180° system

defined, 310–313
development of, 470
and discontinuity editing, 335, 432, 435
in *The Maltese Falcon,* 313–317
See also continuity editing; discontinuity editing
The Only Son, 284
On the Waterfront, 177, 199
openings
  in *Citizen Kane,* 96, 395
  in experimental films, 149, 151, 158
  and formal development, 64–65, 80
  in *Man with a Movie Camera,* 444
  in *Meet Me in St. Louis,* 453
  in *Raging Bull,* 458–459
  in *Tokyo Story,* 434
Ophelia, 488
Ophuls, Max, 277, 487
optical effects. *See* special effects
optical effects, 31
optical point-of-view shots. *See* point-of-view (POV) shots
optical printing, 4, 236, 250, 270–271, 272
optical sound tracks, 6, 8
Ordet, 267
originality, 59
Osaka Elegy, 227
Ossessione, 485, 486
Othello, 189
The Others, 121
Ottinger, Ulrike, 186, 187
Our Hitler: A Film from Germany, 75
Our Hospitality, 220–225, 242, 265–266, 391, 394, 471
Our Town, 484
outlaw films. *See* gangster/outlaw films
Out of Sight, 77, 114
Out One, 489
outtakes, 30
overlap (depth), 213, 216
overlapping editing, 308
Ozu, Yasujiro
  An Autumn Afternoon, 216, 334
  editing, 334, 335, 336
  and framing, 262, 275
  and narrative form, 90, 91
  Ohayu, 334, 335, 393
  The Only Son, 284
  Record of a Tenement Gentleman, 209
  Tokyo Story, 433–437

Pacino, Al, 189
Paisan, 485, 486
The Pajama Game, 125
pan and scan method, 21
Panavision, 254
Panic, 112
Panic Room, genre of, 112

pan shots, 267
The Paper, 271, 272, 390
parallelism
    in *Chungking Express,* 439, 440–441
    in *Citizen Kane,* 97, 99, 398–399
    in crime thrillers, 113
    and narrative form, 69–70
    and style, 405
    in *The Wizard of Oz,* 61, 62, 69
    See also motifs; repetition
Paramount, 9, 469
Parenthood, 317
Paris, Texas, 299, 301
Paris nous appartient (Paris Belongs to Us), 487, 488
Park, Nick, 164
parody, 115, 123
Parsifal, 246
Passion (Godard), 192, 489
La Passion de Jeanne d'Arc
    depth cues in, 212
    editing in, 306
    framing in, 263, 264, 265, 266
    and French New Wave, 488
    lack of make-up in, 189
    setting in, 181
Passion (Madame Dubarry), 472
Pastorale d'éte[ ], 276
Pathé Frères, 468, 475
Patriot Games, 34
Paul, Robert William, 467
Pauline at the Beach, 489
Payne, Alexander, 184, 185
Peggy Sue Got Married, 115
Peking Opera Blues, 494
Pennebaker, Don, 270
Pennies from Heaven, 124
perceptual subjectivity, 85, 88, 264
Pereira dos Santos, Nelson, 232, 233
Perfect Blue, 174
performance. *See* acting
Perkins, V. F., 225
Perry, Hart, 38
persistence of vision, 2
perspective relations, 236–252
    in *Citizen Kane,* 242, 243, 396, 484, 491
    and depth cues, 214–215, 216
    and depth of field, 242–243
    false perspective, 250, 252
    and focal length, 237–242
    and New Hollywood, 491
    and sound, 85, 370–371
    and special effects, 243–248, 252
    See also deep focus
Peter Pan, 271
Peterson, Wolfgang, 490
The Phantom Empire, 490
The Phantom of the Opera, 121

photography, 465
photography unit, 27
The Pianist, 18
Pickford, Mary, 471, 479
Pickpocket, 191, 265
Picture Snatcher, 92
Pierrot le fou, 337–338
pitch, 350–351
pitch sessions, 24
Pixar Animation, 166
pixillation, 164, 165, 443, 444
planes, 212–213
plans-séquence (sequence shots), 285
plausibility, 58
The Player, 24
Play Time
    color in, 182
    costume in, 187
    editing in, 335
    framing in, 266, 267
    music in, 364
    time in, 217–218
Pleasantville, 115, 116
plot. *See* cause and effect; narration;
    narrative form; plot development;
    story/plot distinction
plot development, 63–65
    in *Breathless,* 429
    in *Chungking Express,* 437–438
    in *Citizen Kane,* 99–100, 491–492
    in crime thrillers, 112–113
    investigation plot pattern, 81, 112
    journey plot pattern, 53, 63
    in *Man with a Movie Camera,* 444
    in musicals, 123–124
    and narrative form, 80–82
    and New Hollywood, 491–492
    in *North by Northwest,* 53, 81, 82, 112, 418–419
    in *Raging Bull,* 459
    and restricted narration, 83, 90
    search plot pattern, 63, 81, 94, 97–98, 102, 394
    and setting, 221
    and sound, 348
    and style, 392–393
    web-of-life plots, 437–438
    "what if" plots, 77–78, 79
    See also mystery plot pattern; plot
        segmentations
plot points, 44
plot segmentations, 63–64
    Citizen Kane, 93–94
    Do the Right Thing, 423
    His Girl Friday, 415
    Raging Bull, 458
    resources on, 67
    The Thin Blue Line, 447–448

The Wizard of Oz, 64
poetry, 156
point of view, 85–86, 104
point-of-view cutting
    and continuity editing, 320, 321, 322
    and depth of knowledge, 86
    and French Impressionism, 476
    See also point-of-view (POV) shots
point-of-view (POV) shots, 85
    and camera movement, 269
    defined, 264
    in *North by Northwest,* 419–420, 421, 422, 423
    in *Raging Bull,* 460
    resources on, 292
    in *The Road Warrior,* 87–88
    and sound perspective, 371
    See also point-of-view cutting
Poison, 16
Pokémon: The First Movie, 174
Polanski, Roman, 18
Police Story, 309–310, 494
Poltergeist, 123
Polyvision, 476
Pommer, Erich, 472–473, 474
Ponti, Carlo, 489
Porky's, 115
Porter, Edwin S., 469
portrait documentaries, 130
Portrait of a Lady, 393
The Poseidon Adventure, 115
Possessed, 366
postclassical cinema, 105
postproduction phase, 30, 32–33
    and computer-generated imagery, 250, 251
Potemkin
    color in, 232
    costume in, 187
    editing in, 294, 339
    lack of protagonist in, 90
    and Soviet Montage movement, 480
Potter, Sally, 486
Powell, Michael, 490
The Power and the Glory, 92
Preminger, Otto, 22, 80, 273, 487
preproduction phase, 24–26
previsualization, 35, 249
Primal Fear, 113
Primary, 129
    camera movement in, 270
    climax of, 82
    genre of, 128, 130
    narrative form in, 68
    narrator in, 87
Princess Mononoke, 166
principal photography, 26–30, 31
printers, 4

Print Generation, 63, 149–150
prior experience, 52–53
process (composite) shots, 244–247
producers, 24
producer's crew, 29
production, 20, 24–41
    and authorship, 40–41
    exploitation, 37
    and independent filmmaking, 37–38
    large-scale, 33, 36–37, 40
    postproduction phase, 30, 32–33
    preproduction phase, 24–26
    production (shooting) phase, 26–30
    resources, 42–43
    small-scale, 38–40, 44
    terms/roles, 31
production accountant (production auditor),
    29
production assistants (PAs), 29
production auditor (production accountant),
    29
production coordinators, 29
production designers, 26
production design (set) unit, 26
production managers, 29
production recordists (sound mixers), 28
production secretaries, 29
production (shooting) phase, 26–30
production stills, 44–45
product placement, 14, 19
profit participants, 13
Project A, 494
Project A-Ko, 173
projection process work, 244–246, 248, 252
projectors, 3, 234–235, 465–466
promotion, 14, 15, 18–19, 110
property masters, 31
props, 183–186, 187, 221
Prospero's Books, 258, 259
protagonists, 89–90, 113–114, 119–120. *See
    also* characters
Protazanov, Yakov, 479
Providence, 375–376
Psycho
    editing in, 294
    genre of, 109, 110
    mobile framing in, 276–277
    mystery in, 418
    narrative form in, 114
    props in, 183
    range of knowledge in, 85
    setting in, 121
    sound in, 350, 352
Public Enemy, 255, 483
publicists, 31
publicity. *See* promotion
Pudovkin, V. I., 211, 295, 479, 480, 481
pulling (racking) focus, 243, 244

Pulp Fiction
    box-office receipts, 13
    disunity in, 65
    editing in, 299, 300
    marketing, 16
    and New Hollywood, 492
    plot in, 437–438
    time in, 75, 76, 77
Pummell, Simon, 162
punctuation, 308
puppet (model) animation, 164, 165
The Purple Rose of Cairo, 195, 196, 197
Pushing Hands, 16

Les Quatre cent coups (The 400 Blows),
    73–74, 82, 487, 488
Queenan, Joe, 37
The Quiet Man, 87
Qulitalik, Paul, 39

racism, 119
racking (pulling) focus, 243, 244
Raging Bull, 256
    critical analysis, 457–462
    mobile framing in, 269, 459
    and New Hollywood, 489, 490, 491
    production, 25–26
Raiders of the Lost Ark, 27, 81, 303
Railroad Turnbridge, 148–149, 150
Raimi, Sam, 21, 274
Rainbow Dance, 231
Rainer, Yvonne, 146, 148
Raising Arizona, 357, 492
Rambling Rose, 491
Ramis, Harold, 77–78
ramping, 235–236
range of knowledge, 83–85, 87, 88
    in *Citizen Kane,* 84, 101, 396
    in classical Hollywood cinema, 90
    and crosscutting, 324
    in *North by Northwest,* 84, 85, 90,
        419–420, 421, 422–423
    and sound, 379
Ranma 1/2, 173
Ransom, 112
Rashomon, 78, 196, 197
rate, 234
rating, 21
Ray, Man, 477
Ray, Nicholas, 256, 292, 487, 488
Ray, Satyajit, 192, 298, 486
realism
    and acting, 199–200, 202, 204, 460, 485
    in *Citizen Kane,* 400, 401
    and color, 291
    and make-up, 189
    and mise-en-scene, 177, 225–226
    and narrators, 87

    in *Raging Bull,* 459–460
    and setting, 180
    See also Italian neorealism
realistic criteria, 58
rear projection, 244, 245, 248, 252, 484
Rear Window
    continuity editing in, 320, 321, 322
    plot development in, 112
    style in, 396
Record of a Tenement Gentleman, 209
The Red and the White, 274
Red Beard, 239, 240
Red Imps, 479
Red Psalm, 285
Red Rock West, 112, 113
Reed, Carol, 261
reestablishing shots, 314
Reeves, Keanu, 190
referential meaning, 55, 456
reflectionism, 118
Reflections on Black, 232, 233
reframing, 273
Reggio, Godfrey. *See Koyaanisqatsi*
La Région centrale, 274, 275, 294
Reimann, Walter, 472
Reiner, Carl, 306
Reiner, Rob, 132
Reiniger, Lotte, 164
Reisz, Karel, 268
release prints, 33
"Rembrandt" lighting, 470
Renoir, Jean
    The Crime of M. Lange, 54, 183–184,
        273, 274, 275, 488
    and French New Wave, 487, 488
    Grand Illusion, 110, 277–283, 391, 393,
        394
    and improvisation, 177
    and Italian neorealism movement, 485
    and long takes, 285, 293
    Rules of the Game, 44–45, 63, 255, 294
rentals, 13
repetition, 61
    in *Citizen Kane,* 97
    in crime thrillers, 114
    and editing, 309
    in experimental films, 153, 161–162
    and style, 404–405
    and time, 74, 76
    See also motifs
Replacement Killers, 496
Report, 309, 333
rerecording mixers, 33
Rescued by Rover, 469
Reservoir Dogs, 16, 84, 492
Resnais, Alain
    editing, 335
    La Guerre est finie, 271, 337

Hiroshima mon amour, 86, 306
Last Year at Marienbad, 78–79, 86, 91, 273, 339
Mon Oncle d'Amérique, 335
Night and Fog, 299
Providence, 375–376
restricted narration, 83, 90, 379, 419–420.
    See also range of knowledge
Return of the Jedi, 365
reversal images, 5
reverse motion, 236
rhetorical form, 133, 140–142
    in *The River,* 142–146
rhythm
    and editing, 303–304, 333–334, 476
    and mise-en-scene, 217
    and sound, 359–365
Rhythm & Hues, 291
Richardson, Tony, 489
Richter, Hans, 473
The Riddle of Lumen, 38
Riefenstahl, Leni, 133–134
Rien que les heures, 444
Rififi, 113
rim (edge) lighting, 192, 193, 213
Rimmer, David, 209
Rio Bravo, 490
The River, 87
    form in, 142–146
    style in, 404–407
The River's Edge, 373–374
Rivette, Jacques, 90, 487, 488, 489
RKO, 483
The Road Warrior (Mad Max II)
    and documentaries, 132
    editing in, 303, 322, 323
    narration in, 87–89
    subjectivity in, 88, 90
    unity in, 102
The Roaring Twenties, 332
Robbins, Tim, 390
Robinson, Bill "Bojangles", 126
Robocop, 198, 199
The Rocky Horror Picture Show, 116
Rodriguez, Robert, 11, 37
Roeg, Nicholas, 237
Roger and Me
    characters in, 72
    genre of, 130
    narrator in, 87
    resources on, 172
    space in, 80
    time in, 129
Rogers, Ginger, 123, 483
Rogers, Roy, 116
Rohmer, Eric, 487, 489
Röhrig, Walter, 472
Rolf, Tom, 353

A Romance of Happy Valley, 470
romantic comedies, 124
romantic thrillers, 116
Romeo + Juliet, 334
Rome Open City, 444, 485, 486
Romero, George, 121, 122
Ronin, 113
Rooney, Mickey, 123
Rope, 285–286
Rosemary's Baby, 122
Rossellini, Roberto
    Bazin on, 293
    and French New Wave, 487
    Germany Year Zero, 179, 485, 486
    Rome Open City, 444, 485, 486
rotoscoping, 169–170
Rouch, Jean, 38
La Roue
    editing in, 294, 334, 476
    framing in, 257, 258
rough cut, 30
The Royal Tigress (Tigre Reale), 202, 203
Rubin, Bruse Joel, 90
Rudolph, Alan, 37
Ruiz, Raoul, 16
Rules of the Game, 44–45, 63, 255, 294
Rumble Fish, 196, 247, 491
Run Lola Run, 76, 78, 79, 493
rushes (dailies), 30
Rush Hour, 114
Russell, David O., 12, 492
Russell, Ken, 187
Russian Ark, 286
Russian Revolution, 472
Ruttmann, Walter, 444
Rydstrom, Gary, 367
Rygiel, Jim, 251

Saboteur, 264
Sadoul, Georges, 474
Safe, 16, 350–351
Sambizanga, 213, 214
Le Samourai, 112
samurai genre, 116
Sanchez, Eduardo, 18
San Francisco, 483
Sanjuro, 254, 256
Sansho the Bailiff, 86
Sans toi ni loi (Vagabonde), 243, 256
Saturday Night Fever, 124, 125
Saving Private Ryan, 34, 117
scanning, 218
Scarface, 332
The Scarlet Pumpernickel, 167
"Scary Movie" series, 123
scenes, 63–64, 92–93. *See also* plot segmentations
Scenes from under Childhood, 333

scenic artists, 31
Schamus, James, 16, 17
Schepisi, Fred, 490
Schindler's List, 131
Schlesinger, Leon, 167
Schrader, Paul, 490
Schreck, Max, 122
Schwartzbaum, Lisa, 115
Schwechater, 333
science fiction films
    animated, 173
    cause and effect in, 73
    computer-generated imagery in, 34–35
    and fans, 110
    and genre mixing, 116
    genre of, 116
    make-up in, 189
    movement in, 198
    social ideology in, 117–118
    special effects in, 291
    violence in, 457
The Score, 113
Scorpio Rising, 52, 147, 149, 157, 366
Scorsese, Martin
    on character, 461
    and New Hollywood, 489, 491
    New York, New York, 241
    production control, 41
    and video, 45
    See also Raging Bull
Scott, Ridley, 116, 264, 490
Scott, Tony, 490
Scream, 13
"Scream" series, 123
screen direction, 312
screen duration, 75–76, 284. *See also* story/plot distinction; temporal duration
screenplays, 24–25
screen space, 80, 168–169, 208
screenwriters, 24, 43–44
Screen Writers' Guild, 25
scripts, 24, 43–44
script supervisors, 26
Se7en, 112, 196, 261
The Searchers, 119–120, 234
search plot pattern, 63, 81
    in *Citizen Kane,* 94, 97–98, 102, 394
The Seashell and the Clergyman, 477, 478
Seberg, Jean, 205–206
second assistant directors, 26
second unit, 30, 32
second unit directors, 27
The Secret Adventures of Tom Thumb, 164
segmentations. *See* plot segmentations
Seldes, Gilbert, 146
selective focus, 242, 243
September 11, 2001 terrorist attacks, 118

sequences, 92
sequence shot (plan-séquence), 285
Serene Velocity, 241–242
serial-killer films, 113
Series 7: The Contenders, 11
Serra, Richard, 148–149
set decorators, 26
set dressers, 26
set (production design) unit, 26
setting, 179–186
    in *Chungking Express,* 438–439
    and comedy, 223
    and costume, 187
    Do the Right Thing, 423–424
    in horror films, 121
    and Italian neorealism, 485
    and narrative form, 220–221
    props, 183–186, 187, 221
    and special effects, 182–183, 249
    and style, 398, 402–403
    in *Tokyo Story,* 436
    See also mise-en-scene; space
Seven Samurai
    editing in, 295, 296, 297, 298
    genre of, 116
    lighting in, 198
    sound in, 356, 370
70mm film, 5, 7
sex, lies, and videotape, 16
Sexy Beast, 114
shading (attached shadows), 191
Shadow of a Doubt, 112
shadows, 191, 212
Shahani, Kumar, 233, 234
Shakespeare in Love, 13
shallow-space composition, 215, 216
Shall We Dance, 124
Shanghai Blues, 494, 495
Shanghai Express, 194
Shaolin Master Killer, 493
Shaw Brothers, 493
She's Gotta Have It, 318, 320, 491
She's the One, 16
She Wore a Yellow Ribbon, 177, 360, 364
Shivers, 491
shock cuts, 400, 401
Shoeshine, 485, 486
shooting (production) phase, 26–30
shooting schedules, 25–26
shooting scripts, 24–25
Shoot the Piano Player, 488
Shore, Howard, 357
Short Cuts, 437
shot duration, 284–289
    in animated films, 168
    and continuity editing, 284–285
    in *Do the Right Thing,* 426, 427
    and editing, 293, 294, 303–304

and mobile framing, 286–289
    resources on, 292–293
shot/reverse shot editing
    in *Breathless,* 431
    development of, 470
    and dialogue overlap, 353–355
    and discontinuity editing, 335
    in *The Maltese Falcon,* 314–316
    See also continuity editing
sidelighting (crosslighting), 192
Signs, 19, 109, 284
Sijan, Slobodan, 311
silence, 348, 380, 381
The Silence of the Lambs
    acting in, 202
    broadcast version, 21
    cause and effect in, 73
    editing in, 294
    genre of, 109
    montage sequence in, 332–333
    plot development in, 112
    sound in, 373
    style in, 393
silent films
    acting in, 201
    color in, 231–232
    glass shots in, 243
    horror films, 122
    and music, 348
    and sound, 386–387
    speed of motion in, 234–235
Silent Möbius, 163
Simple Men, 16
A Simple Plan, 113, 114
simultaneous sound, 372
Singer, Bryan, 114
Singin' in the Rain, 33
    editing in, 297
    genre of, 109, 110, 123
    mobile framing in, 276
    sound in, 372
Singleton, John, 242, 491
Sirk, Douglas, 197, 198
Sisters, 258
Sisters of Gion, 227, 286–287, 288
16mm film, 5, 6, 38
The Sixth Sense
    depth of knowledge in, 86
    genre of, 112, 122
    lighting in, 193
    narrative form in, 69, 492
size, 212, 214
size diminution, 214, 216
Skladanowsky, Max, 466
slapstick comedies, 115
slasher films, 121, 123
slates, 29
Sleepy Hollow, 490

Sliding Doors, 77, 79, 115, 493
slow motion, 111, 235, 236, 460
Smalley, Philips, 258
small-scale production, 38–40, 44
The Smiling Mme. Beudet, 476
Smith, Chris, 130, 131
Smith, G. Albert, 468, 469
Smith, Kevin, 38, 492
Smoke, 491
Snake Eyes, 114, 269
Snatch, 114
Snow, Michael
    Back and Forth, 277
    La Région centrale, 274, 275, 294
    Wavelength, 241, 280, 283, 392
Snow White and the Seven Dwarfs, 124,
    163, 169
Sobocinski, Piotr, 390
social ideology
    and documentaries, 140, 445
    and form, 57
    and genre, 116–118, 123, 127
    in musicals, 117, 124–125, 452–457
    in *Raging Bull,* 457–462
    and rhetorical form, 140–141, 142, 143
Socialist Realism, 481
social problem films, 423–428
Soderbergh, Steven, 12, 17, 77, 492
Sokurov, Aleksander, 286
Solanas, Humberto, 285
Soldier Blue, 119
Some Came Running, 488
Something Different, 69–70
Son of Frankenstein, 474
Sony, 10, 13
Sony Pictures Imageworks, 291
sound, 347–388
    and continuity editing, 332, 482
    in *Do the Right Thing,* 427
    editing, 32–33
    in experimental films, 149–150, 352
    fidelity, 365–366
    and form, 356–359
    in *His Girl Friday,* 367, 417–418
    introduction of, 386–387, 481–482
    and mise-en-scene, 208
    mixing, 353–355
    and motifs, 351, 357–358, 380
    and narration, 356, 366, 367, 374, 377–379
    nondiegetic, 366–367, 369–370
    and offscreen space, 259, 352, 360, 364,
        367, 427
    perceptual properties of, 350–351
    and perspective, 85, 370–371
    power of, 348–350
    resources on, 385–388
    and rhythm, 359–365
    selection/manipulation, 352–353

sound effects, 31, 352, 360, 366, 378–379
sound tracks, 6, 7
  and space, 366–371
  and speed of motion, 234
  and style, 398, 403–404, 411
  and time, 332, 371–377
  See also music; sound effects
sound bridges, 373–374, 424
sound designers, 28
sound editors, 32
sound effects, 352
  foley artists, 31
  in *A Man Escaped,* 378–379
  nondiegetic, 366
  and rhythm, 360
sound localization, 370–371
sound mixers (production recordists), 28
The Sound of Music, 489
sound over, 368
sound perspective, 85, 370–371
sound unit, 28
South Park: Bigger, Longer & Uncut, 164
Soviet Montage, 478–481
  editing, 304, 334, 446, 480
  and Griffith, 470
  resources on, 498
  See also specific films and directors
space, 208–216
  and balance, 210–212
  and color, 209–210, 211, 216
  depth cues, 208, 212–215, 218–219
  and discontinuity editing, 335–336
  and editing, 304–306
  in *His Girl Friday,* 417
  and mobile framing, 269, 272–274
  and movement, 209, 213–214, 216
  and plot development, 81
  resources on, 227–228
  and size, 212
  and sound, 366–371
  and story/plot distinction, 76, 80
  in *Tokyo Story,* 434, 436–437
  See also continuity editing; deep space;
    offscreen space
spaced-out teenager films, 115
The Spanish Prisoner, 114
Spanking the Monkey, 492
special effects
  in *Man with a Movie Camera,* 443–444
  and mobile framing, 270–271
  and New Hollywood, 491
  and perspective relations, 243–248, 252
  and production phase, 29–30
  resources on, 291
  and setting, 182–183, 249
  and style, 394–395, 410–411
  See also computer-generated imagery
special-effects unit, 28

spectators, 104, 391. *See also* expectations
speech. *See* dialogue
Speed, 187, 190, 248
speed of motion, 234–236
Spheeris, Penelope, 491
Spiderman, 116, 291
The Spider's Stratagem, 206, 207
Spielberg, Steven
  Amistad, 392–393
  and deep focus, 243, 491
  and New Hollywood, 489, 490
  production control, 41
  Raiders of the Lost Ark, 27, 81, 303
  and shot duration, 286
  and video, 45
  See also Jaws
Spirited Away, 14
Splash, 115
split-screen (multiple-frame) imagery,
  257–258
spotting, 32
Spy Kids 2, 11
Stagecoach
  continuity editing in, 322, 325
  plot development in, 53
  sound in, 367, 368, 369, 370
Stage Fright, 418
staging, in documentaries, 128–129, 132
Stalin, Joseph, 481
Stalker, 231
Stalling, Carl, 352
Starevich, Ladislav, 164, 207
A Star Is Born, 116
stars, 27, 111. *See also* acting
Startup.com, 39
Star Wars: Episode II—Attack of the Clones,
  11, 19
Star Wars: The Phantom Menace, 34, 183
Star Wars films
  characters in, 72
  computer-generated imagery in, 34
  digital production, 11
  and genre cycles, 116
  merchandising, 19
  and New Hollywood, 489
  settings in, 183
  sound in, 347, 365, 371
  special effects in, 291, 491
  video piracy, 19
Steadicam, 269, 286, 459
stereophonic sound, 6, 8
stereophonic sound tracks, 6, 7
Stewart, James, 203, 204, 351
still photographers, 31
still shots, 270–271
Stone, Oliver, 132, 304
stop-action, 198, 199
Storm over Asia, 480, 481

storyboards, 26
*Story of a Love Affair (Cronaca di un
    amore),* 273, 486
story/plot distinction, 70–72, 80
  and cause and effect, 73
  in *Citizen Kane,* 92–94, 95, 97
  in crime thrillers, 114
  and shot duration, 284
  and sound, 372
  and space, 76, 80
  and time, 74–75, 76, 77–79
  See also narration; time
Straight Shooting, 119, 120
The Straight Story, 37, 131, 265
Strangers on a Train, 187
Stranger than Paradise, 38, 491
Straub, Jean-Marie, 91, 352
  The Chronicle of Anna Magdalena Bach,
    214, 215, 248, 252, 261, 291
A Streetcar Named Desire, 199
Street Scene, 424
stretch printing, 236
Strike
  acting in, 204
  editing in, 308, 336, 339, 342
  lack of protagonist in, 90
  and Soviet Montage movement, 480
Stroheim, Erich von, 184, 186
  Greed, 180, 268
studio filmmaking
  and classical Hollywood cinema, 469
  early, 466–467
  Méliès, 178–179, 291
  and production, 33, 36, 40
  and setting, 179–180
  and special effects, 291
stunt coordinators, 27
stunt doubles, 250
stunt persons, 27
stunts, and multiple cameras, 29
style, 389–412
  analysis method, 391–394
  in *Ballet mécanique,* 407–409
  in *Chungking Express,* 438, 442
  in *Citizen Kane,* 394–401
  in *Do the Right Thing,* 427
  and French Impressionism, 476
  in *Gap-Toothed Women,* 401–404
  and Italian neorealism, 485
  in *Meet Me in St. Louis,* 454
  in *A Movie,* 409–412
  resources on, 412
  as system, 49
  in *The Thin Blue Line,* 451
  in *Tokyo Story,* 433
stylistic elements, 49
stylization
  in acting, 202–205

stylization, *(continued)*
   and German Expressionism, 472, 473
   and violence, 457
subjectivity, 85–86, 91
   and camera movement, 269, 270
   in *Citizen Kane,* 101
   and continuity editing, 320, 321
   and French Impressionism, 475, 476
   and German Expressionism, 473
   in *Raging Bull,* 460
   resources on, 292
   in *The Road Warrior,* 88, 90
   See also point-of-view (POV) shots
subtitles, 388
Sundance, 16
Sundance Film Festival, 492
Sunrise, 227
Super 8mm film, 5, 6
Super 16mm film, 8, 292
Super 35mm film, 21, 292
superimposition, 243–244, 476, 478
supervising editors, 30
supporting players, 27
El Sur, 196
surprise
   and comedy, 51, 223–224
   in crime thrillers, 113, 114
   and narrative form, 69
   and plot development, 82
   and restricted narration, 83
   and temporal order, 75
Surrealism, 477–478. *See also specific films and directors*
suspense
   in *Citizen Kane,* 96
   in crime thrillers, 113, 114
   and crosscutting, 324
   and expectations, 51, 54, 69
   and mise-en-scene, 222
   and mobile framing, 283
   and multiple narrators, 101
   in *North by Northwest,* 420–421
   and plot development, 82, 418
   and range of knowledge, 84–85, 88
   and sound, 348
   and split-screen imagery, 257–258
Suspense, 258
Švankmajer, Jan, 198, 199
Svilova, Elizaveta, 445
Swing Time, 125–126, 360, 483
"sword and sandal" epics, 116
Syberberg, Hans Jürgen, 75, 245–246
symbolism. *See* iconography
symmetry, 210–211
symptomatic meaning, 57–58
   in documentaries, 140, 446
   in *Meet Me in St. Louis,* 456–457
synchronization, 371–372

synergy, 14
synthetic documentaries, 130

tableaux, 467–468
tail-on shots, 322
The Tailor of Panama, 112
takes, 29, 30
The Talented Mr. Ripley, 113
The Tall Target, 81, 243
Tampopo, 181–182, 299
The Tao of Steve, 17
Tape, 39
Tappy Toes, 147, 149
Tarantino, Quentin, 84, 492. *See also Pulp Fiction*
Tarkovsky, Andrei, 231
Tarzan, 21
Tati, Jacques
   editing, 335
   framing, 265
   and French New Wave, 487
   Mr. Hulot's Holiday, 81, 335, 353, 365, 366
   sound, 352
   See also Play Time
Tavernier, Bernard, 352
Taxi Driver, 199, 460, 489, 490, 491
Taylor, Richard, 249
Technicolor, 231, 483–484
telephoto lenses, 237, 238, 239–240
television, 327–328, 345
Tell Me Something, 114
temb dub, 32
tempo, 217, 360
temporal duration
   in *Citizen Kane,* 75, 97
   in classical Hollywood cinema, 90
   and editing, 307–308, 331–333, 339, 342
   in *His Girl Friday,* 417
   and mobile framing, 284
   and narrative form, 75–76
   and shot duration, 284
   and sound, 372
   See also time
temporal order, 74–75
   in *Citizen Kane,* 74, 95–96
   in classical Hollywood cinema, 90
   in documentaries, 129
   and editing, 306–307, 326, 331
   See also time
temporal scrambling, 77–79, 91
The Terminator, 334, 490
Terminator 2: Judgment Day, 32, 183, 199, 226, 490
La Terra Trema, 218, 485, 486
Testament of Dr. Mabuse, 474
That Obscure Object of Desire, 86
That Thing You Do!, 123
theatrical exhibition, 8, 11–12, 370–371

Them!, 121
theme-and-variations
   and comedy, 224
   in experimental films, 149–150, 151, 152
themes
   in *Chungking Express,* 440–442
   in crime thrillers, 112
   in experimental films, 146
   and form, 56
   and genre, 110
   in horror films, 121
   in musicals, 124–125
   and sound, 352
   in Westerns, 118–119
There's Something about Mary, 115
They Live By Night, 428
They Shoot Horses, Don't They?, 307
The Thin Blue Line
   critical analysis, 446–452
   editing in, 306, 344, 449–450, 451
   mise-en-scene in, 176
   reenactments in, 132, 133
The Thin Red Line, 267, 351
third assistant directors, 26
The Third Man, 261, 262, 263
third men, 28
35mm film, 5, 6
The 39 Steps, 112, 365
This Is Spinal Tap, 132
Thoms, Randy, 351
Thomson, Virgil, 143
360° space, 335, 436
"three-act" structure, 43
Three Colors: Red, 390
three-dimensional space, 208, 212–215, 269.
      See also deep space
Three Kings, 12, 492
The Three Musketeers, 470
three-point lighting, 194–195, 213
Three Women, 490
thrillers, 112–114
THX, 347
THX 1138, 187, 188, 210
Tigre Reale (The Royal Tigress), 202, 203
tilt shots, 267
timbre, 351, 370, 380, 398
time, 69, 74–76
   in animated films, 168
   in *Chungking Express,* 439–440
   in *Citizen Kane,* 74, 75, 95–98, 400–401
   in classical Hollywood cinema, 90
   and continuity editing, 326, 331–333
   and discontinuity editing, 336–339, 342
   and editing, 306–310
   in French Impressionism, 475
   in *His Girl Friday,* 416–417
   in *Man with a Movie Camera,* 444, 446
   in *Meet Me in St. Louis,* 452

and mise-en-scene, 217–219
and mobile framing, 275–276
and New Hollywood, 492
in *North by Northwest,* 75, 419
and plot development, 81
in *Raging Bull,* 459
resources on, 104
and shot duration, 284–289, 292–293
and sound, 332, 371–377
and story/plot distinction, 74–75, 76, 77–79
in *Tokyo Story,* 437
Time Code, 437
time compression, 21
time-lapse cinematography, 236
timers, 31
A Time to Live, a Time to Die, 243
tinting, 231–232
Titanic
    costume in, 187
    and New Hollywood, 490
    production, 36
    special effects in, 291
    video release, 21, 23
To, Johnnie, 496
Together, 13
Tohoscope, 254, 256
Tokyo Story (Tokyo Monogatari), 433–437
Toland, Gregg, 27, 40, 41, 484
Tolkien, J. R. R., 53, 249
Tomb of the Fireflies, 173
Tom Jones, 489
Tomorrow Never Dies, 19
Tom Tom the Piper's Son, 236
tonality, 229–234
toning, 231, 232, 233
Tootsie
    focal length in, 237, 239
    mise-en-scene in, 208
    montage sequence in, 332
    narration in, 84
top lighting, 193, 194
Touch of Evil
    editing in, 299, 300
    lighting in, 192
    long takes in, 287, 288–289
    mobile framing in, 275
    style in, 393, 396
Towne, Robert, 61
The Toxic Avenger, 37
Toy Story, 11, 166
Toy Story 2, 21
tracking shots
    defined, 267
    in *Greed,* 268
    and Italian neorealism, 486
    and New Hollywood, 492
    and Steadicam, 269, 286, 459
    and temporal duration, 284

See also mobile framing
Traffic (Soderbergh), 12, 17, 437
Traffic (Tati), 335
trailers, 15
traits, 72, 94, 98
Trauberg, Ilya, 240
traveling mattes, 247
Travis, Neil, 34
treatments, 24
The Trial of the Lonesome Pine, 484
Tribulation 99: Alien Anomalies under America, 132
trick perspective, 250, 252
Trier, Lars von, 11, 16, 29, 232
A Trip to the Moon, 178
triptychs, 253, 476
Troma Films, 37
TRON, 165–166
Trouble in Paradise, 202–203, 204
trucking shots. *See* tracking shots
True Romance, 433
True Stories, 109, 297
Truffaut, François
    The Bride Wore Black, 267
    Day for Night, 33, 264
    and "dead time, ", 91
    and French New Wave movement, 487, 488, 489
    The Green Room, 197
    Jules and Jim, 87, 339, 357–359, 360, 488
    Shoot the Piano Player, 488
    and widescreen ratios, 292
    See also The 400 Blows
The Truman Show, 34, 115, 200
Trust, 16, 492
Tsui Hark, 494, 495
Tucker: A Man and His Dream, 233
Tucker, 491
TV versions, 21
Twelve Angry Men, 75–76
Twentieth Century Fox, 9
23rd Psalm Branch, 38
Two or Three Things I Know about Her, 370
2001: A Space Odyssey
    editing in, 332
    front projection in, 245
    and genre conventions, 111
    matte work in, 247
Two Times in One Space, 147
Tykwer, Tom, 78
typage, 202, 204, 480–481
types, 200, 202–203

UFA, 291, 472, 473, 474
Ulee's Gold, 37
Ulysses' Gaze, 272
Umberto D, 486
Uncle Tom's Cabin (Stowe), 115

Under a Texas Moon, 484
underlighting, 193
Under the Olive Trees, 259, 260
United Artists, 471
unit publicists, 31
unit system, 470
unity, 65, 102, 419
Universal, 9, 469, 483
unrestricted narration, 83–84, 88, 90. *See also* range of knowledge
The Untouchables, 244
Urotsu-kidoji: Legend of the Overfiend, 173
Urusei Yatsura, 173
USA Films, 17
U.S. Film Service, 146
The Usual Suspects
    lighting in, 196
    opening of, 80
    time in, 76, 81, 114

Vachon, Christine, 26
Vagabonde (Sans toi ni loi), 243, 256
The Valiant Ones, 254, 255, 493
Valley Girl, 491
values. *See* social ideology
The Vampires, 181
van Peebles, Mario, 491
Van Sant, Gus, 8
Varda, Agnès, 243, 256
variable-area, 8
variation, 62–63, 152, 161–162
Variety, 292
Veidt, Conrad, 474
Verhoeven, Paul, 490
La Verifica inserta, 148
Vertigo, 244, 245, 273
Vertov, Dziga
    on editing, 304
    Man with a Movie Camera, 129, 235, 443–446
    and Soviet Montage movement, 479, 480, 481
Vidas Secasr, 232, 233
video
    digital, 10–12, 38, 39
    distribution, 19
    vs. film, 10–12, 45
    and framing, 21–23
    music videos, 334, 426
    popularity of, 9
    video piracy, 14, 19
video assists, 31
video games, 174
video piracy, 14, 19
Vidor, King, 471
viewers. *See* spectators
Vigo, Jean, 478

violence
    in horror films, 123, 457
    in *Raging Bull,* 457–462
    and slow motion, 235
    and social ideology, 118
virtual reality, 250
Visconti, Luchino, 218, 485, 486, 490
visual perception, 2–3, 228
Viva la Muerte!, 231–232
Viva Zapata!, 390
Vivendi Universal, 17
Vivre sa vie, 488
volume (sound), 350, 370
volume (space), 212. *See also* depth cues
von Sternberg, Josef, 191, 192, 193, 194
Vorkapich, Slavko, 332

Wachowski, Andy, 35, 114, 116, 492–493
Wachowski, Larry, 35, 114, 116, 492–493
Waddell, Hugh, 352
Waiting to Exhale, 18
Wajda, Andrzej, 45, 196, 215
The Wall, 214
walla, 32
Wallace, Earl, 24
Walt Disney, 167
Wang, Wayne, 491–492
war films, 118
Warhol, Andy
    and "dead time", 91
    Eat, 52, 146
    and shot duration, 285, 286, 294
Warm, Hermann, 40, 472, 473
Warner Bros., 9, 167–168, 469, 483
War Requiem, 366
The War Room, 39
Watching for the Queen, 209
The Waterer Watered (L'Arroseur arrosé),
    179, 467
Watson, James Sibley, Jr., 147
Wavelength, 241, 280, 283, 392
Waxworks, 473
Wayne, John, 351, 490
Wayne's World, 115, 491
Webber, Melville, 147
web-of-life plots, 437–438
The Wedding Banquet, 16
Weir, Peter, 24, 351, 490
Welles, Orson
    on *Citizen Kane,* 100
    and depth, 227
    and long takes, 285, 293
    Mr. Arkadin, 261
    photo of, 27
    production roles, 41
    See also Citizen Kane; The Magnificent
        Ambersons; Touch of Evil

Wenders, Wim, 10, 181, 368, 369, 374
Werker, Alfred L., 484
Western History, 333
Westerns, 118–120
    and genre mixing, 116
    origins of, 115
    resources on, 127
West Side Story, 124, 125
Weta Digital, 249, 251, 291
"what if" plots, 77–78, 79
What's Love Got to Do with It, 123
What's Up, Doc?, 490
What's Up, Tiger Lily?, 372
whip pans, 401
White, Pearl, 475
White Heat, 198
White Ship, 485
Whitney, James, 165
Who Framed Roger Rabbit?
    animation in, 166, 167
    lighting in, 191
    matte work in, 247
    and New Hollywood, 490
Whoopee!, 115
Whoopie, 125
wide-angle lenses, 237, 238, 492
widescreen ratios
    and French Impressionism, 476
    methods for creating, 254, 255, 256
    resources on, 292
    and video, 21, 22, 23
    visual effects of, 254, 257, 258
Wild and Woolly, 470
The Wild Bunch, 119
Wild Strawberries, 230
Williamson, James, 468, 469
Winchester 73, 119, 202, 204
The Wind (Finye), 184, 186, 299
Window Water Baby Moving, 38
Wings, 193
Wings of Desire, 181, 368, 369
Winterwind, 285
Wintonick, Peter, 40
wipes, 295, 296, 332
Witness, 24, 80, 351
The Wizard of Oz
    acting in, 200
    color in, 63, 125, 291
    conventions in, 52, 53
    costume in, 187
    desire in, 89
    emotions in, 54
    function in, 60
    genre of, 124
    meaning in, 55–57
    narrative form in, 49, 51, 52
    parallelism in, 61, 62, 69

plot development in, 63, 64–65, 81–82
    sound in, 351
    variation in, 62–63
Wölfflin, Heinrich, 464
Wolper, David, 40
The Woman's Film, 39
Women in Love, 187, 188, 392
Wong Kar-wai, 52, 261, 437–442, 496
Woo, John
    A Better Tomorrow, 494–495
    The Killer, 74, 113, 114, 494
    on lenses, 236
    and video, 45
Wood, Sam, 484
Word is Out, 130
work prints, 32
The World at War, 40
World of Apu, 298
World War I, 472, 475
wranglers, 27
The Wrath of the Gods, 231, 232
Written on the Wind, 197, 198
The Wrong Trousers, 164
wuxia pian, 493
Wyler, William, 41, 132, 227, 293. *See also*
    Jezebel

The X-Files, 14
Xiu Xiu the Sent-Down Girl, 16
X-Men, 114
XXX, 29

The Year of the Horse, 6
Yentl, 116
Yes, Madam!, 493, 494–495
Yojimbo, 116
Yol, 209–210
Young and Innocent, 273
Young Frankenstein, 123
The Young Girls of Rochefort, 124
Young Mr. Lincoln, 209
You Ought to Be in Pictures, 167
You've Got Mail, 117
Yuen, Corey, 305
Yuen Kuei, 493
Yuen Wo-ping, 16, 493, 496

Zelig, 81
Zellwegger, Renee, 201
Zemeckis, Robert, 78, 490, 491
Zéro de Conduite, 478
Zinnemann, Fred, 230
Zoetrope, 3
zoom lenses, 240–241, 271, 272
Zorns Lemma, 52
Zu: Warriors of the Magic Mountain, 494
Zwigoff, Terry, 130